A Short History of the American Nation

Volume Two ▪ Since 1865

Sixth Edition

JOHN A. GARRATY
Gouverneur Morris Professor of History
Columbia University

HarperCollins*CollegePublishers*

For Kathy, Jack, and Sarah

Executive Editor: *Bruce Borland*
Developmental Editor: *Alice Solomon*
Project Editor: *Ellen MacELree*
Design Supervisor: *Lucy Krikorian*
Cover Design: *Lucy Krikorian*
Cover Illustration: John Sloan: *Hill, Main Street, Gloucester.* c. 1916. Oil on canvas. The Parrish Art Museum, Southampton, New York, Littlejohn Collection. Photographed by Noel Rowe.
Photo Researcher: *Leslie Coopersmith*
Production Manager/Assistant: *Willie Lane/Sunaina Sehwani*
Compositor: *ComCom Division of Haddon Craftsmen, Inc.*
Printer and Binder: *R. R. Donnelley & Sons Company*
Cover Printer: The Lehigh Press, Inc.

A Short History of the American Nation, Sixth Edition

Library of Congress Cataloging-in-Publication Data

Garraty, John Arthur, 1920–
[American nation]
A short history of the American nation / John A. Garraty — 6th ed.
p. cm.
An Abridgment of the author's The American nation, 7th ed.
Includes index.
Single Volume Edition
ISBN 0-06-500741-7
Contents: v. 1. To 1877 — v. 2. Since 1865.
ISBN 0-06-500742-5 (v. 1). — ISBN 0-06-500743-3 (v. 2)
1. United States—History. I. Title.
E178.1.G24 1992
973–dc20 92-19979
CIP

92 93 94 95 9 8 7 6 5 4 3 2 1

CONTENTS

CHAPTER 27

The New Era, 1921–1933 427

CHAPTER 28

The New Deal, 1933–1941 443

CHAPTER 29

War and Peace 462

CHAPTER 30

The American Century 477

MAPS AND GRAPHS

PREFACE

This is the sixth edition of *A Short History of the American Nation,* the fifth time that I have revised the book, and the process remains for me both challenging and endlessly fascinating. What is important to point out about the past changes constantly as more information comes to light and as current events raise new questions about the events and people of earlier times. Keeping up with the hundreds of books and articles dealing with American history keeps authors like me who write textbooks very busy. As a result, this new edition contains much new material; I believe it is the widest-ranging restructuring and rethinking of the work that I have made.

Organizational Changes

To improve the flow of topics, I have shifted many sections to different chapters, for example, moving the discussion of the Great Awakening and the colonial Enlightenment to the chapter on the events leading to the Revolution, where these topics seem more properly to belong. I have also placed the material on the Federalist era and on the Jefferson administrations into separate chapters, and I have divided the previously combined account of the political and economic events of the Monroe and J. Q. Adams period.

Similarly, the chapters covering the period 1877–1896 have been reorganized, and the chapter on World War I has been expanded to include an account of the Red Scare and other events of the immediate postwar period. The chapters dealing with the 1920s and 1930s have been drastically restructured, and I have made changes only slightly less extensive in the post–World War II chapters. In addition, I have brought the last chapter up to date, carrying the story through the presidential election of 1992.

New Coverage

Readers will notice that there is much more information in this edition about society in the colonial period and about southern political and religious institutions; on the activities of women during the American Revolution and other social changes of the period; on the Whiskey Rebellion and the opening of the Ohio country after the Revolution; on changes in early 19th-century family life; on the westward movement, the Second Great Awakening, and the Know-Nothing movement; and on plantation life, particularly the lives of southern women, slave and free.

In Chapter 20, "American Society in the Industrial Age," there is new material about middle-class life, about the daily activities of farmers, about the family lives and social attitudes of wage earners of both sexes, about social and economic mobility in the 1870s and 1880s, and about spectator sports and other leisure activities. There is also expanded coverage of radical movements before and immediately after World War I, of the effects of the Great Depression, of the treatment of minorities during World War II and the contributions of women in that conflict, of the "baby boom" generation that followed the war, of the counterculture of the 1960s, of the modern women's movement, and many other topics.

Approach

In making these changes and other less important ones, I have not, I trust, altered my basic approach to American history, which is to deal with the subject in narrative fashion and to use the political history of the nation as the frame within which social, economic, and cultural developments are portrayed. The American nation (the United States) is, after all, a political institution.

The people of the United States, in their infinite variety, also remain central to my account. The theory that a few great individuals have shaped the course of past events oversimplifies history. But the past becomes more comprehensible when attention is paid to how the major figures on the historical stage have reacted to events and to one another. Since generalizations require concrete illustration if they are to be grasped fully, readers will find many anecdotes and quotations on the following pages, along with the facts and dates and statistics every good history must contain. This illustrative material is interesting, and much of it is entertaining, but I believe it is also instructive.

I also believe that one need not be an uncritical admirer of the American nation and its people to recognize that the history of the United States deserves to be treated with dignity and respect. Individually and as a society, we have rarely lived up to the principles enunciated in the Declaration of Independence and the Constitution, but recent events in Eastern Europe demonstrate how cherished these "American" values are by people who have been deprived of them. American values are not well served either by patriotic hoopla or by slighting or excusing dark and discreditable aspects of the American past. The English radical Oliver Cromwell is said to have told an artist who was painting his picture to portray him "warts and all." Cromwell wanted to be remembered as he was, confident that, on balance, history would judge him fairly. That is what I have tried to do in this portrayal of America's history. In shortening *The American Nation* I have eliminated only details and some illustrative material; no important topic covered in the larger book has been omitted.

Acknowledgments

To the following reviewers who gave generously of their time and knowledge to read the manuscript and provide thoughtful evaluations and suggestions for revision of the text, I express my gratitude: Sidney R. Bland, James Madison University; George Davis, Wabash College; Donald Higginbotham, University of North Carolina; Michael S. Mayer, University of Montana; and James Ward, Angelo State University.

JOHN A. GARRATY

ABOUT THE AUTHOR

John A. Garraty is Gouverneur Morris Professor of History Emeritus at Columbia University. He received his B.A. from Brooklyn College, an M.A. and a Ph.D. from Columbia, and an L.H.D. from Michigan State University, where he taught before joining the Columbia faculty. Professor Garraty is the author and editor of scores of books and articles, among them biographies of Silas Wright, Henry Cabot Lodge, Woodrow Wilson, and George W. Perkins. He contributed a volume, *The New Commonwealth,* to the New American Nation series. He edited *Quarrels That Have Shaped the Constitution,* Supplements 4 through 7 of the *Dictionary of American Biography,* and *The Reader's Companion to American History.* He is also the author of *1001 Things Everyone Should Know About American History.* Professor Garraty has served as vice-president and head of the teaching division of the American Historical Association. His areas of special research interest include the Gilded Age, unemployment (in a historical sense), and the Great Depression of the 1930s.

A Short History of the American Nation

CHAPTER 17

■ ■ ■ ■ ■ ■ ■

Reconstruction and the South

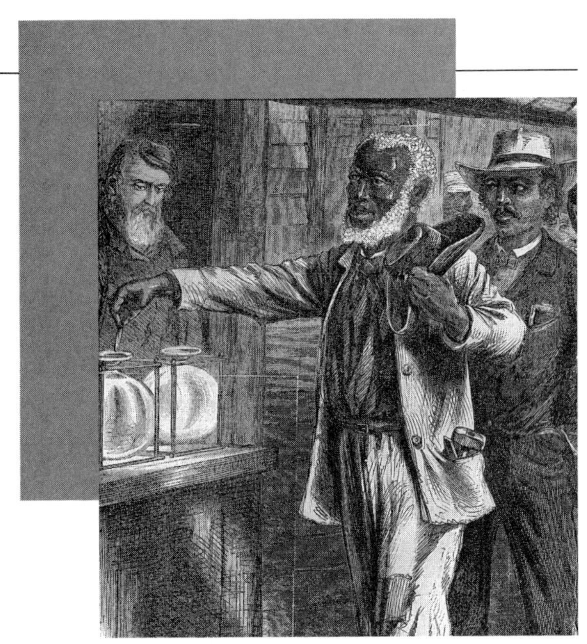

■ ■ ■ ■ ■ ON APRIL 5, 1865, ABRAHAM LINCOLN visited Richmond. The fallen capital lay in ruins, sections blackened by fire, but the president was able to walk the streets unmolested and almost unattended. Black people crowded around him, hailing him as a messiah. Even the whites seemed to have accepted defeat without resentment. A few days later, in Washington, Lincoln delivered an important speech on reconstruction, urging compassion and open-mindedness. Then, on April 14, while he was watching a performance of the play *Our American Cousin* at Ford's Theater, a half-mad actor, John Wilkes Booth, slipped into his box and shot him in the head with a small pistol. The next morning, without having regained consciousness, Lincoln died. With him perished the South's best hope for a mild peace. The awesome drama was still unfolding; retribution and a final humbling of the South were inevitable.

Presidential Reconstruction

Despite its bloodiness, the Civil War had caused less intersectional hatred than might have been expected. Although civilian property was often seized or destroyed, the invading armies treated the southern population with remarkable forbearance, both during the war and after Appomattox. Jefferson Davis and a few other Confederate officials spent short periods behind bars, but the only southerner executed for war crimes was Major Henry Wirz, the commandant of Andersonville military prison.

The legal questions related to bringing the defeated states back into the Union were extremely complex. Since southerners believed that secession was legal, logic should have compelled them to argue that they were out of the Union and would thus have to be formally readmitted. Northerners should have taken the contrary position, for they had fought to prove that secession was illegal. Yet the people of both sections did just the opposite. Senator Charles Sumner and Congressman Thaddeus Stevens, in 1861 uncompromising expounders of the theory that the Union was indissoluble, now insisted that the

Chapter-opening illustration:
"The First Vote," the cover illustration from the November 16, 1867, issue of *Harper's Weekly*, shows blacks exercising their right to vote, guaranteed to them by the Fifteenth Amendment to the Constitution.

Confederate states had "committed suicide" and should be treated like "conquered provinces." Lincoln believed the issue a "pernicious abstraction" and tried to ignore it.

The process of readmission began in 1862, when Lincoln appointed provisional governors for the parts of the South that had been occupied by federal troops. On December 8, 1863, he issued a proclamation setting forth a general policy. With the exception of high Confederate officials and a few other special groups, all southerners could reinstate themselves as United States citizens by taking a simple loyalty oath. When, in any state, a number equal to 10 percent of those voting in the 1860 election had taken this oath, they could set up a state government. Such governments had to be republican in form, recognize the "permanent freedom" of the slaves, and provide for their education. The plan, however, did not require that blacks be given the right to vote.

The "10 Percent Plan" reflected Lincoln's lack of vindictiveness and his political wisdom. The regimes established under this plan in Tennessee, Louisiana, and Arkansas bore, in the president's mind, the same relation to finally reconstructed states that an egg bears to a chicken. "We shall sooner have the fowl by hatching it than by smashing it," he remarked. He knew that eventually representatives of the southern states would again be sitting in Congress, and he wished to lay the groundwork for a strong Republican party in the section. Yet he realized that Congress had no intention of seating representatives from the "10 percent" states at once.

The Radicals in Congress disliked the 10 Percent Plan, partly because of its moderation and partly because it enabled Lincoln to determine Union policy toward the recaptured regions. In July 1864 they passed the Wade-Davis bill, which provided for constitutional conventions only after a *majority* of the voters in a southern state had taken a loyalty oath. Besides prohibiting slavery, the new state constitutions would have to repudiate Confederate debts. Lincoln disposed of the Wade-Davis bill with a pocket veto, and there matters stood when Andrew Johnson became president following the assassination.

From origins even more lowly than Lincoln's, Johnson had risen to be congressman, governor of Tennessee, and United States senator. He was able but fundamentally unsure of himself, as could be seen in his boastfulness and stubbornness. His political strength came from the poor whites and yeomen farmers of eastern Tennessee, and he was fond of extolling the common man and attacking "stuck-up aristocrats." Free homesteads, public education, absolute social equality—such were his objectives. The father of communism, Karl Marx, wrote approvingly of Johnson's "deadly hatred of the oligarchy."

Andrew Johnson, as recorded by Mathew Brady's camera in 1865. Johnson, Charles Dickens reported, radiated purposefulness but no "genial sunlight."

Johnson was a Democrat, selected as the Republican Lincoln's running mate because of his record and his reassuring penchant for excoriating southern aristocrats. The Republicans in Congress were prepared to cooperate with him, but the president proved temperamentally incapable of working with them. Like Randolph of Roanoke, his antithesis intellectually and socially, opposition was his specialty; he soon alienated every powerful Republican in Washington.

Radical Republicans listened to Johnson's diatribes against secessionists and the great planters and assumed that he was antisouthern. Nothing could have been further from the truth. He believed in states' rights and shared most of his poor white Tennessee constituents' contempt for blacks. "Damn the negroes, I am fighting these traitorous aristocrats, their masters," he told a friend during the war. "I wish to God," he said on another occasion, "every head of a family in the United States had one slave to take the drudgery and menial service off his family."

The new president did not want to injure or humiliate all southerners. He issued an amnesty proclamation only slightly more rigorous than Lincoln's. By the time Congress convened in December, all the southern states had organized governments, ratified the Thirteenth Amendment abolishing slavery, and elected senators and representatives. Johnson promptly recommended these new governments to Congress.

Republican Radicals

Peace found the Republicans in Congress no more united than they had been during the war. A small group of "ultra" Radicals were demanding immediate civil and political equality for blacks as well as a plot of land and access to a decent education. Senator Sumner led this faction. A second group of Radicals agreed with the ultras' objectives but were prepared to accept half a loaf if necessary to win the support of less radical colleagues. Nearly all Radicals, however, drew the line at social equality.

The moderate Republicans wanted to protect ex-slaves from exploitation and guarantee their basic rights but were unprepared to push for full political equality. A handful of Republicans sided with the Democrats in support of Johnson's approach, but all the rest insisted at least on the minimum demands of the moderates. Thus Johnsonian Reconstruction was doomed.

Johnson's proposal had no chance in Congress for reasons having little to do with black rights. The Thirteenth Amendment had the effect of increasing the representation of the southern states in Congress because it made the Three-fifths Compromise meaningless. Henceforth, ex-slaves would be counted as whole persons in apportioning seats in the House of Representatives. If Congress seated the southerners, the balance of power might swing to the Democrats.

Southern voters had provoked further northern resentment by their choice of congressmen. Georgia elected Alexander H. Stephens, vice-president of the Confederacy, to the Senate, although he was still in a federal prison awaiting trial for treason! Several dozen men who had served in the Confederate Congress had been elected to either the House or the Senate, together with four generals and many other high officials. Understandably, these choices would sit poorly with northerners.

Finally, the so-called Black Codes enacted by the new southern governments to control former slaves alarmed the North. Although the codes were a considerable improvement over slavery, they placed formidable limitations on freedom. Blacks could not bear arms, be employed in occupations other than farming and domestic service, or leave their jobs without forfeiting back pay. The Louisiana code required them to sign labor contracts for the year during the first ten days of January. In Mississippi drunkards, vagrants, beggars, "common night-walkers," and even persons who "misspend what they earn" and who could not pay the stiff fines assessed were to be "hired out . . . at public outcry" to the white person who would take them for the shortest period in return for paying their fines. Such laws, apparently designed to get around the Thirteenth Amendment, outraged northerners.

For all these reasons the Republicans in Congress rejected Johnsonian Reconstruction. Quickly they created a joint committee on Reconstruction, headed by Senator William P. Fessenden of Maine, a moderate, to study the question of readmitting the southern states. The committee held hearings that produced much evidence of the mistreatment of blacks. The hearings strengthened the Radicals, who had been claiming all along that the South was perpetuating slavery under another name.

President Johnson's attitude speeded the swing toward the Radical position. While the hearings were in progress, Congress passed a bill expanding and extending the Freedmen's Bureau, which had been established in March 1865 to care for refugees. The bureau, a branch of the War Department, was already exercising considerable coercive and supervisory power in the South. Now Congress sought to add to its authority in order to protect the black population. Although the bill had wide support, Johnson vetoed it. Congress then passed a civil rights act that not only declared that blacks were citizens of the United States but also denied the states the power to restrict their rights to testify in court, make contracts, and hold property. In other words, it put teeth in the Thirteenth Amendment.

Once again the president refused to go along, although his veto was sure to drive more moderates into the arms of the Radicals. On April 9, 1866, Congress repassed the Civil Rights Act by a two-thirds majority, the first time in American history that a major piece of legislation became law over the veto of a president. This event marked a revolution in the history of Reconstruction. Thereafter, Congress, not President Johnson, had the upper hand.

But the Radicals encountered grave problems in fighting for their program. Northerners might object to the Black Codes and to seating "rebels" in Congress, but few believed in racial equality. Between 1865 and 1868, Wisconsin, Minnesota, Connecticut, Nebraska, New Jersey, Ohio, Michigan, and Pennsylvania all rejected bills granting blacks the vote.

The Radicals were in effect demanding not merely equal rights for freedmen but extra rights, not merely the vote but special protection of that right against the pressure that southern whites would surely apply to undermine it. This idea flew in the face of conventional American beliefs in equality before the law and individual self-reliance. Events were to show that the Radicals were correct—that what amounted to a political revolution in state-federal relations was essential if blacks were to achieve real equality. But in the climate of that day their proposals encountered bitter resistance, and not only from southerners.

Thus, while the Radicals sought partisan advantage in their battle with Johnson and sometimes played on war-bred passions, they were taking large political risks in defense of genuinely held principles. One historian has aptly called them the "moral trustees" of the Civil War.

The Fourteenth Amendment

In June 1866, Congress submitted to the states a new amendment to the Constitution. The Fourteenth Amendment was a truly radical measure. Never before had newly freed slaves been granted significant political rights. It was also a milestone along the road to the centralization of political power in the United States, for it significantly reduced the power of all the states. In this sense it confirmed the great change wrought by the Civil War: the growth of a more complex, more integrated social and economic structure requiring closer national supervision. Few persons understood this aspect of the amendment at the time.

First the amendment supplied a broad definition of American citizenship: "All persons born or naturalized in the United States, and subject to the jurisdiction thereof, are citizens of the United States and of the State wherein they reside." Obviously this included blacks. Then it struck at discriminatory legislation like the Black Codes: "No State shall make or enforce any law which shall abridge the privileges or immunities of citizens of the United States; nor shall any State deprive any person of life, liberty, or property, without due process of law." The next section attempted to force the southern states to permit blacks to vote. If a state denied the vote to any class of its adult male citizens, its representation was to be reduced proportionately. Under another clause, former federal officials who had served the Confederacy were barred from holding either state or federal office unless specifically pardoned by a two-thirds vote of Congress. Finally, the Confederate debt was repudiated.

Although the amendment did not specifically outlaw segregation or prevent a state from disfranchising blacks, the southern states would have none of it, and without them the necessary three-fourths majority of the states could not be obtained. President Johnson vowed to make the choice between the Fourteenth Amendment and his own policy the main issue of the 1866 congressional elections. He embarked on "a swing around the circle" to rally the public to his cause. He failed dismally. Northern women objected to the implication that black men were more fitted to vote than white women, but most northern voters were determined that blacks must have at least formal legal equality. The Republicans won better than two-thirds of the seats in both houses, together with control of all the northern state governments. Johnson emerged from the campaign discredited, the Radicals stronger and determined to have their way.

The Reconstruction Acts

Had the southern states been willing to accept the Fourteenth Amendment, coercive measures might have been avoided. Their recalcitrance and continuing indications that local authorities were persecuting blacks finally led to the passage, on March 2, 1867, of the First Reconstruction Act. This law divided the former Confederacy—exclusive of Tennessee, which had ratified the Fourteenth Amendment—into five military districts, each controlled by a major general. It gave these officers almost dictatorial power to protect the civil rights of "all persons," maintain order, and supervise the administration of justice. To rid themselves of military rule, the former states were required to adopt constitutions guaranteeing blacks the right to vote and disfranchising broad classes of ex-Confederates. If these new constitutions proved satisfactory to Congress, and if the new governments ratified the Fourteenth Amendment, their representatives would be admitted to Congress and military rule ended. Johnson's veto of the act was easily overridden.

Although drastic, the Reconstruction Act was so vague that it proved unworkable. In deference to moderate Republican views, it did not spell out the process by which the new constitutions were to be drawn up. Southern whites preferred the status quo, even under army control, to enfranchising blacks and retiring their own respected leaders. They made no effort to follow the steps laid down in the law. Congress therefore passed a second act, requiring the military authorities to register voters and supervise the election of delegates to constitutional conventions. A third act further clarified procedures.

Still white southerners resisted. The laws required that the constitutions be approved by a majority of the registered voters. Simply by staying away from the polls, whites prevented ratification in state after state. At last, in March 1868, a full year after the First Reconstruction Act was passed, Congress changed the rules again. The constitutions were to be ratified by a majority of the *voters.* In June 1868, Arkansas, having fulfilled the requirements, was readmitted to the Union, and by July a sufficient number of states had ratified the Fourteenth Amendment to make it part of the Constitution. But it was not until July 1870 that the last southern state, Georgia, qualified to the satisfaction of Congress.

Congress Takes Charge

To carry out this program in the face of determined southern resistance required single-mindedness over a long period to an extent seldom demonstrated by an American legislature. The persistence resulted in part from the suffering and frustrations of the war years and the refusal of the South to accept the spirit of even the mild reconstruction designed by Johnson. President Johnson's stubbornness also influenced the Republicans. They became obsessed with the need to defeat him. The unsettled times and the large Republican majorities, always threatened by the possibility of a Democratic resurgence if "unreconstructed" southern congressmen were readmitted, sustained their determination.

These considerations led Republicans to attempt a kind of grand revision of the federal government, one that almost destroyed the balance between judicial, executive, and legislative power established in 1789. A series of measures passed between 1866 and 1868 increased the authority of Congress over the army, over the process of amending the Constitution, and over Cabinet members and lesser appointive officers. Finally, in a showdown caused by emotion more than by practical considerations, the Republicans attempted to remove President Johnson from office.

Johnson was a poor president and out of touch with public opinion, but he had done nothing to merit ejection from office. Though he had a low opinion of blacks, his opinion was so widely shared by whites that it is inappropriate to condemn him as a reactionary on this ground. Johnson believed that he was fighting to preserve constitutional government. He was honest and devoted to duty, and his record easily withstood the most searching examination. When Congress passed laws taking away powers granted him by the Constitution, he refused to submit.

The chief issue was the Tenure of Office Act of 1867, which prohibited the president from removing officials who had been appointed with the consent of the Senate without first obtaining Senate approval. In February 1868, Johnson "violated" this act by dismissing Secretary of War Edwin M. Stanton, who had been openly in sympathy with the Radicals for some time. The House, acting under the procedure set up in the Constitution for removing the president, promptly impeached him before the bar of the Senate, Chief Justice Salmon P. Chase presiding.

The trial was conducted in a partisan and vindictive manner. Johnson's lawyers easily established that he had removed Stanton only in an effort to prove the Tenure of Office Act unconstitutional. Nevertheless, the Radicals pressed the charges (11 separate articles) relentlessly. Tremendous pressure was applied to the handful of Republican senators who were unwilling to disregard the evidence.

Seven of them resisted to the end, and the Senate failed by a single vote to convict Johnson. This was probably fortunate. Had he been forced from office on such flimsy grounds, the independence of the executive might have been permanently weakened. Then the legislative branch would have become supreme.

The Fifteenth Amendment

The failure of the impeachment did not affect the course of Reconstruction. The president was acquitted on May 16, 1868. A few days later, the Republican National Convention nominated General Ulysses S. Grant for the presidency. At the Democratic convention Johnson had considerable support, but the delegates nominated Horatio Seymour, a former governor of New York. In November, Grant won an easy victory in the electoral college, 214 to 80, but the popular vote total was close: 3 million to 2.7 million. Grant's margin was supplied by southern blacks enfranchised under the Reconstruction Acts, about 450,000 of whom supported him. A majority of white voters probably preferred Seymour. Since many citizens undoubtedly voted Republican because of personal admiration for General Grant, the election statistics suggest that a substantial white majority opposed the policies of the Radicals.

The Reconstruction Acts and the ratification of the Fourteenth Amendment achieved the purpose of enabling black southerners to vote. The Radicals, however, were not satisfied; they wished to guarantee the right of blacks to vote in every state. Another amendment seemed the only way to accomplish this objective. The 1868 presidential election, which demonstrated how important the black vote could be, strengthened their determination. After considerable bickering over details, the Fifteenth Amendment was sent to the states for ratification in February 1869. It forbade all the states to deny the vote to anyone "on account of race, color, or previous condition of servitude." Once again nothing was said about denial of the vote on the basis of sex.

Most southern states, still under federal pressure, ratified the amendment swiftly. The same was true in most of New England and in some western states. Bitter battles were waged in Connecticut, New York, Pennsylvania, and the states immediately north of the Ohio River, but by March 1870 most of them had ratified the amendment, and it became part of the Constitution.

"Black Republican" Reconstruction: Scalawags and Carpetbaggers

The Radicals had at last succeeded in imposing their will on the South. Throughout the region, former slaves voted, held office, and exercised the "privileges" and enjoyed the "immunities" guaranteed them by the Fourteenth Amendment. Almost to a man they voted Republican.

The spectacle of blacks not five years removed from slavery in positions of power and responsibility attracted much attention at the time and has since been examined exhaustively by historians. The subject is controversial, but certain facts are beyond argument. Black officeholders were neither numerous nor inordinately influential. None was ever elected governor of a state; during the entire period, fewer than 20 served in Congress. Blacks held many minor offices and were influential in southern legislatures, though they made up the majority only in South Carolina.

The real rulers of the "black Republican" governments were white: the "scalawags"—southerners willing to cooperate with the Republicans because they accepted the results of the war and to advance their own interests—and the "carpetbaggers"—northerners who went to the South as idealists eager to help the freed slaves, as employees of the federal government, or more commonly as settlers hoping to improve themselves.

A few scalawags were prewar politicians or well-to-do planters, but most were ordinary people who had supported the Whig party before secession.

The Freedmen's Bureau established 4,329 schools, attended by some 250,000 ex-slaves, in the postwar South. *Harper's Weekly* artist Alfred Waud sketched a Freedmen's Bureau school in Vicksburg, Mississippi, in 1866. Many of the teachers were white women from the North.

The carpetbaggers were a particularly varied lot. Most had mixed motives, and personal gain was among them. But so were opposition to slavery and the belief that blacks deserved to be treated decently. Many northern blacks became carpetbaggers: ex-soldiers, ministers, teachers, and lawyers. Some of these blacks became southern officeholders, but their influence was limited.

That blacks should fail to dominate southern governments is certainly understandable. They lacked experience in politics and were mostly poor and uneducated. They were nearly everywhere a minority. Those blacks who held office during Reconstruction tended to be better educated and more prosperous. In an interesting analysis of South Carolina black politicians, Thomas Holt reveals that a disproportionate number of them had been free before the war. Of the rest, a large percentage had been house servants or artisans, not field hands. Mulatto politicians were also disproportionately numerous and (as a group) more conservative and economically better off than other black leaders.

In South Carolina and elsewhere, blacks proved in the main able and conscientious public servants: able because the best tended to rise to the top in such a fluid situation and conscientious because most of those who achieved importance sought eagerly to demonstrate the capacity of their race for self-government.

Not all black legislators and administrators were paragons of virtue. In *The Prostrate South* (1874), James S. Pike, a northern journalist, called the government of South Carolina "a huge system of brigandage." This was a gross exaggeration, but waste and corruption were common enough. Some legislators paid themselves large salaries and surrounded themselves with armies of useless, incompetent clerks. One Arkansas black took $9,000 from the state for repairing a bridge that had cost only $500 to build. A South Carolina legislator was voted an additional $1,000 in salary after he lost that sum on a horse race.

However, the corruption must be seen in perspective. The big thieves were nearly always white;

blacks got mostly crumbs. Furthermore, graft and callous disregard of the public interest characterized government in every section and at every level during the decade after Appomattox. Big-city bosses in the North embezzled sums that dwarfed the most brazen southern frauds. The New York City Tweed Ring probably made off with more money than all the southern thieves, black and white, combined. The evidence does not justify the southern corruption, but it suggests that the unique features of Reconstruction politics—black suffrage, military supervision, carpetbagger and scalawag influence—do not explain it.

Southerners who complained about the ignorance and irresponsibility of blacks conveniently forgot that the tendency of 19th-century American democracy was away from educational, financial, or any other restrictions on the franchise. Thousands of white southerners were as illiterate and uncultured as the freedmen, yet no one suggested depriving them of the ballot.

In fact, the Radical southern governments accomplished a great deal. They spent money freely but not entirely wastefully. Tax rates zoomed, but the money financed the repair and expansion of the South's dilapidated railroad network, rebuilt crumbling levees, and expanded social services. Before the Civil War, as Eric Foner points out in *Reconstruction: America's Unfinished Revolution,* planters possessed a disproportionate share of political as well as economic power, and they spent relatively little public money on education and other public services. During Reconstruction an enormous gap had to be filled, and it took money to fill it. The Freedmen's Bureau made a start, and northern religious and philanthropic organizations did important work. Eventually, however, the state governments established and supported hospitals, asylums, and school systems that, though segregated, greatly benefited whites as well as blacks.

The former slaves eagerly grasped the opportunities to learn. Nearly all appreciated the immense importance of knowing how to read and write; the sight of elderly men and women poring laboriously over elementary texts beside their grandchildren was common everywhere. Schools and other institutions were supported chiefly by property taxes, and these, of course, hit well-to-do planters hard. Hence much of the complaining about the "extravagance" of Reconstruction governments concealed traditional selfish objections to paying for necessary public projects.

The Ravaged Land

The South's grave economic problems complicated the rebuilding of its political system. The section had never been as prosperous as the North, and wartime destruction left it desperately poor by any standard. In the long run the abolition of slavery released immeasurable quantities of human energy previously stifled, but the immediate effect was to create confusion. Freedom to travel without a pass, to "see the world," was one of the ex-slaves' most cherished rights. Understandably, many at first equated legal freedom with freedom from having to earn a living, a tendency reinforced for a time by the willingness of the Freedmen's Bureau to provide rations and other forms of relief in war-devastated areas. Most, however, soon realized they would have to earn a living; a small plot of land, they hoped, would complete their independence.

This objective was forcefully supported by the relentless Congressman Thaddeus Stevens, whose hatred of the planter class was pathological. "The property of the chief rebels should be seized," he stated. If the lands of the richest "70,000 proud, bloated and defiant rebels" were confiscated, the federal government would obtain 394 million acres. Every adult male ex-slave could easily be supplied with 40 acres. The beauty of his scheme, Stevens insisted, was that "nine-tenths of the [southern] people would remain untouched." Dispossessing the great planters would make the South "a safe republic," its lands cultivated by "the free labor of intelligent citizens." If the plan drove the planters into exile, "all the better."

Although Stevens's figures were faulty, many Radicals agreed with him. "We must see that the freedmen are established on the soil," Senator Sumner declared. "The great plantations, which have been so many nurseries of the rebellion, must be broken up, and the freedmen must have the pieces." But the extremists' view was simplistic. Land without tools, seed, and other necessities would have done the freedmen little good. Congress did throw open 46 million acres of poor-quality federal land in the South to blacks under the Homestead Act, but few settled on it. Establishing former slaves on small farms with adequate financial aid would have been of incalculable benefit to them and to the nation. This would have been practicable, but it was not done.

The former slaves therefore had to work out their destiny within the established framework of southern agriculture. White planters expected the ex-slaves to be incapable of self-directed effort. If allowed to become independent farmers, they would either starve to death or descend into barbarism. Of course, the blacks did neither. True, southern agriculture output declined precipitously after slavery was abolished. On the average, free blacks produced much less than slaves had produced. However, the decline in productivity was not caused by the inability of free blacks to work independently. It was simply that being free, they chose no longer to work like slaves. They let their children play instead of forcing them into the fields. Mothers devoted more time to child care and housework, less to farm labor. Elderly blacks worked less. In any case, emancipated blacks were far better off materially than under slavery, when all they got from their masters was mere subsistence.

White southerners misunderstood the reasonable desire of blacks to devote more time to leisure and family activities; they took it as evidence that blacks were lazy. A leading southern magazine complained in 1866 that black women now expected their husbands "to support them in idleness." It would never have made such a comment about white wives who devoted themselves to housework and child care.

The family life of ex-slaves was changed in other ways. Male authority increased when husbands became true heads of families. When blacks became citizens, the men acquired rights and powers denied to all women, such as the right to hold public office and serve on juries. Similarly, black women became more like white women, devoting themselves to separate "spheres" where their lives revolved around housekeeping and child rearing.

Sharecropping and the Crop Lien System

Immediately after the war, blacks usually labored for wages, but the wage system did not work well for two reasons. Money was scarce, and banking capital, never adequate even before the collapse of the Confederacy, accumulated slowly. This situation made it

After the Civil War, most blacks worked as sharecroppers on land owned by whites. In this photograph, black sharecroppers pick cotton, a major cash crop of the South. Because the price for cotton remained low, sharecroppers often fell into debt and were tied to the land almost as tightly as under slavery.

difficult for landowners to pay workers in cash. More important, blacks did not like working for wages because it kept them under the direction of whites and thus reminded them of slavery.

Since the voluntary withdrawal of so much black labor from the work force had produced a shortage, the blacks had their way. Quite swiftly, a new agricultural system known as sharecropping emerged. Instead of cultivating the land by gang labor as in antebellum times, planters broke up their estates into small units and established on each a black family. The planter provided housing, agricultural implements, draft animals, seed, and other supplies, and the family provided labor. The crop was divided between them, usually on a fifty-fifty basis. If the landlord supplied only land and housing, the laborer got a larger share. This was called share tenancy.

Sharecropping gave blacks the day-to-day independence they craved and the hope of earning enough to buy a small farm. But few achieved this ambition because whites resisted their efforts adamantly. As late as 1880, blacks owned less than 10 percent of the agricultural land in the South, though they made up more than half of the region's farm population.

Many white farmers were also trapped by the sharecropping system. New fencing laws kept them from grazing livestock on undeveloped land, a practice common before the Civil War. But the main cause of southern rural poverty for whites as well as blacks was the lack of sufficient capital to finance the sharecropping system. Like their colonial ancestors, the landowners had to borrow against October's harvest to pay for April's seed. Thus the crop lien system developed, and to protect their investments, lenders insisted that growers concentrate on readily marketable cash crops: tobacco, sugar, and especially cotton.

The system injured everyone. Diversified farming would have reduced the farmers' need for cash, preserved the fertility of the soil, and, by placing a premium on imagination and shrewdness, aided the best of them to rise in the world. Under the crop lien system, both landowner and sharecropper depended on credit supplied by local bankers, merchants, and storekeepers for everything from seed, tools, and fertilizer to overalls, coffee, and salt. Small southern merchants were almost equally victimized by the system, for they also lacked capital, bought goods on credit, and had to pay high interest rates.

Seen in broad perspective, the situation is not difficult to understand. The South, drained of every resource by the war, was competing for funds with the North and the West, both vigorous and expanding and therefore voracious consumers of capital. Reconstruction, in the literal sense of the word, was accomplished chiefly at the expense of the standard of living of the producing classes. The crop lien system and the small storekeeper were merely the agents of an economic process dictated by national, perhaps even worldwide, conditions.

This does not mean that recovery and growth did not take place. But compared with the rest of the country, progress was slow. Just before the Civil War, cotton harvests averaged about 4 million bales. During the conflict, output fell to about half a million, and the former Confederate states did not enjoy a 4 million–bale year again until 1870. Only after 1874 did the crop begin to top that figure consistently.

In manufacturing, the South made important gains after the war. The tobacco industry, stimulated by the sudden popularity of cigarettes, expanded rapidly. The exploitation of the coal and iron deposits of northeastern Alabama in the early 1870s made a boomtown of Birmingham. The manufacture of cotton cloth also increased, productive capacity nearly doubling between 1865 and 1880. Yet the mills of Massachusetts alone had eight times the capacity of the entire South in 1880. Despite the increases, the South's share of the national output of manufactured goods declined sharply during the Reconstruction era.

The White Counterrevolution

Radical southern governments could sustain themselves only so long as they had the support of a significant proportion of the white population, for except in South Carolina and Louisiana, the blacks were not numerous enough to win elections alone. The key to Radical survival lay in the hands of the wealthy merchants and planters, mostly former Whigs. People of this sort did not fear black economic competition. Taking a broad view, they could see that improving the lot of former slaves would benefit all classes.

Southern white Republicans used the Union League of America, a patriotic club founded during the war, to control the black vote. Powerless to check the league by open methods, dissident southerners established a number of secret terrorist societies, bearing such names as the Ku Klux Klan, the Knights of the White Camelia, and the Pale Faces.

The most notorious of these organizations was the Klan, which originated in Tennessee in 1866. At first it was purely a social club, but by 1868 it had been taken over by vigilante types dedicated to driving blacks out of politics, and it was spreading rapidly across the South. Sheet-clad night riders roamed the countryside, frightening the impressionable and chastising the defiant:

Niggers and Leaguers, get out of the way,
We're born of the night and we vanish by day.
No rations have we, but the flesh of man—
And love niggers best—the Ku Klux Klan;
We catch 'em alive and roast 'em whole,
Then hand 'em around with a sharpened pole.
Whole Leagues have been eaten, not leaving a man,
And went away hungry—the Ku Klux Klan.

When intimidation failed, the Klansmen resorted to force, in hundreds of cases murdering their victims, often in the most gruesome manner.

Congress struck at the Klan with three Force Acts (1870–1871), which placed elections under federal jurisdiction and imposed fines and prison sentences on persons convicted of interfering with any citizen's exercise of the franchise. Troops were dispatched, and by 1872 the federal authorities had arrested enough Klansmen to break up the organization.

Nevertheless, the Klan contributed substantially to the destruction of Radical regimes in the South. Even respectable white southerners came to the conclusion that terrorism was the most effective way of controlling the black population and escaping northern domination.

Gradually it became respectable to intimidate black voters. Beginning in Mississippi in 1874, terrorism spread through the South. Instead of hiding behind masks and operating in the dark, these terrorists donned red shirts, organized into military companies, and paraded openly. The Mississippi redshirts seized militant blacks and whipped them publicly. When blacks dared to fight back, heavily armed whites easily put them to rout. In other states similar results followed.

Terrorism fed on fear, fear on terrorism. White violence led to fear of black retaliation and thus to even more brutal attacks. The slightest sign of resistance came to be seen as the beginning of race war, and when the blacks suffered indignities and persecutions in silence, the awareness of how much they must resent the mistreatment made them appear more dangerous still. Thus self-hatred was displaced, guilt suppressed, aggression justified as self-defense, individual conscience submerged in the animality of the mob. Before long the blacks learned to stay home on election day. "Conservative" parties—Democratic in national affairs—took over southern state governments.

The North had subjected the South to control from Washington while preserving state sovereignty in the North itself. In the long run this discrimination proved unworkable. The war was fading into the past and with it the anger it had generated. Northern voters could still be stirred by references to the sacrifices Republicans had made to save the Union and by reminders that the Democratic party was the organization of rebels, Copperheads, and the Ku Klux Klan. Yet emotional appeals could not convince northerners that it was still necessary to maintain a large army in the South. In 1869 the occupying force was down to 11,000 men.

Nationalism was reasserting itself. Had not Washington and Jefferson been Virginians? Was not Andrew Jackson Carolina-born? Since most northerners had little real love or respect for blacks, their interest in racial equality flagged once they felt reasonably certain that blacks would not be reenslaved if left to their own devices in the South.

Another, subtler force was also at work. Prewar Republicans had stressed the common interest of workers, manufacturers, and farmers in a free and mobile society, a land of opportunity where self-reliant citizens worked together in harmony. Southern whites had insisted that laborers must be disciplined if large enterprises were to be run efficiently. By the 1870s, as large industrial enterprises developed in the northern states, the thinking of business leaders became more sympathetic to southern demands for more control over "their" labor force.

Grant as President

Other matters occupied the attention of northern voters. The expansion of industry and the rapid development of the West, stimulated by a new wave of railroad building, loomed more important to many than the fortunes of ex-slaves. Heated controversies arose over tariff policy, with western agricultural interests seeking to force reductions from the high levels established during the war, and over the handling of the wartime greenback paper money. Debtor groups and many manufacturers favored further expansion of the supply of dollars, and conservative merchants and bankers argued for retiring the greenbacks in order to return to a "sound" currency.

More damaging to the Republicans was the failure of Ulysses S. Grant to live up to expectations as president. Qualities that had made Grant a fine military leader for a democracy—his dislike of political maneuvering and his simple belief that the popular will could best be observed in the actions of Congress—made him a poor chief executive. When Congress failed to act on his suggestion that the quality of the civil service needed improvement, he announced meekly that if Congress did nothing, he would assume that the country did not want anything done. Grant was honest, but in a naive way that made him the dupe of unscrupulous friends and schemers.

Grant did nothing to prevent the scandals that disgraced his administration and, out of a misplaced belief in the sanctity of friendship, he protected some of the worst culprits and allowed calculating tricksters to use his good name and the prestige of his office to advance their own interests at the country's expense.

The worst of the scandals—such as the Whiskey Ring affair, which implicated Grant's private secretary, Orville E. Babcock, and cost the government millions in tax revenue, and the defalcations of Secretary of War William W. Belknap in the management of Indian affairs—did not become public knowledge during Grant's first term. However, in 1872, Republican reformers, alarmed by rumors of corruption and disappointed by Grant's failure to press for civil service reform, organized the Liberal Republican party and nominated Horace Greeley, the able but eccentric editor of the *New York Tribune,* for president.

The Liberal Republicans were well-educated, socially prominent types—editors, college presidents, and economists, along with a sprinkling of businessmen and politicians. Their liberalism was of the laissez-faire variety; they were for low tariffs and sound money and against measures benefiting particular groups, whether labor unions or railroad companies or farm organizations. They disparaged universal suffrage, which, one of them said, "can only mean in plain English the government of ignorance and vice."

The Democrats also nominated Greeley, though he had devoted his political life to flailing the Democratic party in the *Tribune.* That surrender to expediency, together with Greeley's temperamental unsuitability for the presidency, made the campaign a fiasco for the reformers. Grant triumphed easily, with a popular majority of nearly 800,000 votes.

Nevertheless, the defection of the Liberal Republicans hurt the Republican party in Congress. In the 1874 elections, no longer hampered as in the presidential contest by Greeley's notoriety and Grant's fame, the Democrats carried the House of Representatives. It was clear that the days of military rule in the South were ending. By the end of 1875 only three southern states—South Carolina, Florida, and Louisiana—were still under Republican control.

The Disputed Election of 1876

Against this background the presidential election of 1876 took place. Since corruption in government was the most widely discussed issue, the Republicans nominated Governor Rutherford B. Hayes of Ohio, a former general with an unsmirched reputation. The Democrats picked Governor Samuel J. Tilden of New York, a wealthy lawyer who had attracted national attention for his part in breaking up the Tweed Ring in New York City.

In November early returns indicated that Tilden had carried New York, New Jersey, Connecticut, Indiana, and the entire South, including Louisiana, Florida, and South Carolina, where the Republican party was still in control. This seemed to give him 203 electoral votes to Hayes's 165.

However, Republican leaders had anticipated the possible loss of Florida, South Carolina, and Louisiana and were prepared to use their control of the election machinery in those states to throw out sufficient Democratic ballots to alter the results if doing so would change the national outcome. Realizing that the electoral votes of those states were exactly enough to elect their man, they telegraphed their henchmen on the scene and ordered them to go into action. The local Republicans then invalidated Democratic ballots in wholesale lots and filed returns showing Hayes the winner. Naturally, the local Democrats protested vigorously and filed their own returns.

Congress created an electoral commission to decide the disputed cases. The commission consisted of five senators (three Republicans and two Democrats), five representatives (three Democrats and two Republicans), and fivè justices of the Supreme Court (two Democrats, two Republicans, and one independent, David Davis). Since it was a foregone conclusion that the others would vote for their party no matter what the evidence, Davis would presumably swing the balance in the interest of fairness.

However, before the commission met, the Illinois legislature elected Davis senator! He had to resign from the Court and the commission. Since independents were rare even on the Supreme Court, no neutral was available to replace him. The vacancy went to Associate Justice Joseph P. Bradley of New Jersey, a Republican.

Evidence presented before the commission revealed a disgraceful picture of election shenanigans. On the one hand, in all three disputed states Democrats had clearly cast a majority of the votes; on the other, it was unquestionable that many blacks had been forcibly prevented from voting.

In truth, both sides were shamefully corrupt. Lew Wallace, a northern politician later famous as the author of the novel *Ben Hur,* visited Louisiana and Florida shortly after the election. "It is terrible to see the extent to which all classes go in their determination to win," he wrote his wife from Florida. "Money and intimidation can obtain the oath of white men as well as black to any required statement. . . . If we win, our methods are subject to impeachment for possible fraud. If the enemy win, it is the same thing."

Most modern authorities take the view that in a fair election the Republicans would have carried South Carolina and Louisiana but that Florida would have gone to Tilden, giving him the election, 188 electoral votes to 181. In the last analysis, this opin-

THE COMPROMISE OF 1877

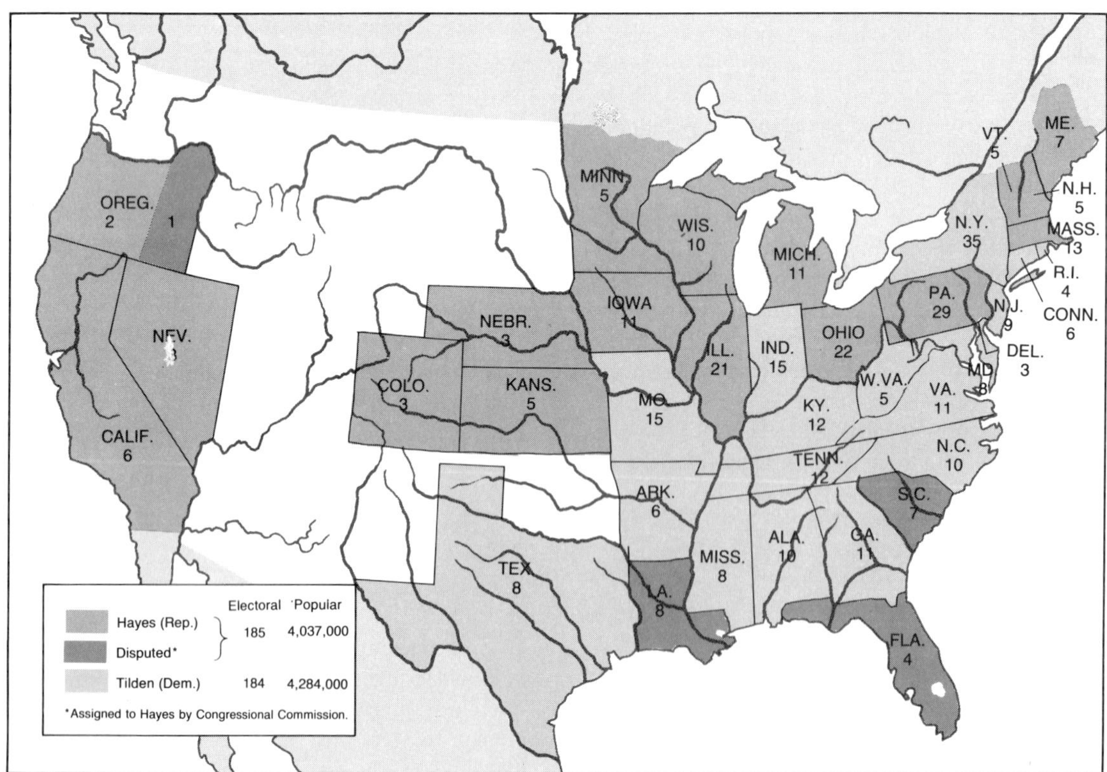

ion has been arrived at simply by counting white and black noses: blacks were in the majority in South Carolina and Louisiana. Amid the tension and confusion of early 1877, however, even a Solomon would have been hard pressed to judge rightly amid the rumors, lies, and contradictory statements. The Democrats had some hopes that Justice Bradley would be sympathetic to their case, for he was known to be opposed to harsh Reconstruction policies. On the eve of the commission's decision in the Florida controversy, he was apparently ready to vote in favor of Tilden. But the Republicans subjected him to tremendous political pressure. When he read his opinion on February 8, it was for Hayes. Thus by a vote of 8 to 7 the commission awarded Florida's electoral votes to the Republicans.

Vote after vote, both on details and in the final decisions in the other cases, followed party lines exactly. The atmosphere of judicial inquiry and deliberation was a façade. The commission assigned all the disputed electoral votes to Hayes.

To such a level had the republic of Jefferson and John Adams descended. Democratic institutions, shaken by the South's refusal to go along with the majority in 1860 and by the suppression of civil rights during the rebellion, and further weakened by military intervention and the intimidation of blacks in the South during Reconstruction, seemed now a farce. Democrats talked of not being bound by so obviously partisan a judgment. Tempers flared in Congress, where some spoke ominously of a filibuster that would prevent the recording of the electoral vote and leave the country, on March 4, with no president at all.

The Compromise of 1877

Fortunately, forces for compromise had been at work behind the scenes in Washington for some time. Although northern Democrats threatened to fight to the last ditch, many southern Democrats were willing to accept Hayes if he would promise to remove the troops and allow the southern states to manage their internal affairs by themselves. Ex-Whig planters and merchants who had reluctantly abandoned the carpetbag governments and who sympathized with Republican economic policies hoped that by supporting Hayes they might contribute to the restoration of the two-party system. With the tacit support of many Democrats, the electoral vote was counted by the president of the Senate on March 2, and Hayes was declared elected, 185 votes to 184.

Like all compromises, this agreement was not entirely satisfactory; like most, it was not honored in every detail. Hayes recalled the last troops from South Carolina and Louisiana in April. He appointed a former Confederate general, David M. Key of Tennessee, postmaster general and delegated to him the congenial task of finding southerners willing to serve their country as officials in a Republican administration. The new alliance of ex-Whigs and northern Republicans did not flourish, however, and the South remained solidly Democratic. The major significance of the compromise, one of the great intersectional political accommodations of American history, has been well summarized by C. Vann Woodward:

> *The Compromise of 1877 marked the abandonment of principles and force and a return to the traditional ways of expediency and concession. . . . It wrote an end to Reconstruction and recognized a new regime in the South. More profoundly than Constitutional amendments and wordy statutes it shaped the future of four million freedmen and their progeny for generations to come.*

For most of the former slaves, this future was to be bleak. Forgotten in the North, manipulated and then callously rejected by the South, rebuffed by the Supreme Court, voiceless in national affairs, they and their descendants were condemned in the interests of sectional harmony to lives of poverty, indignity, and little hope. Meanwhile, the rest of the United States continued its golden march toward wealth and power.

Milestones

1863 Lincoln announces "10 Percent Plan" for Reconstruction
1865 Freedmen's Bureau established
Abraham Lincoln assassinated; Andrew Johnson becomes president
Johnson's amnesty plan
Thirteenth Amendment ratified
1865–1866 Southern states enact Black Codes
1866 Civil Rights Act passed over Johnson's veto
Johnson campaigns for his Reconstruction policy
1867 First Reconstruction Act
1868 House of Representatives impeaches Johnson
Fourth Reconstruction Act
Senate acquits Johnson
Fourteenth Amendment ratified
Ulysses S. Grant elected president
1868–1872 Ku Klux Klan in action
1870 Fifteenth Amendment ratified
1870–1871 Force Acts destroy Klan
1872 Liberal Republican party nominates Horace Greeley for president; Grant reelected
1876 Disputed presidential election
1877 Electoral commission awards disputed votes to Rutherford B. Hayes
Hayes agrees to Compromise of 1877

Supplementary Reading

Eric Foner, **Reconstruction: America's Unfinished Revolution** (1988) is an excellent survey or the period. See also Foner, **Nothing but Freedom** (1984). W. E. B. Du Bois, **Black Reconstruction in America** (1935), is militantly pro-black and a classic.

On Andrew Johnson, J. E. Sefton, **Andrew Johnson and the Uses of Constitutional Power** (1980), is a good brief biography. See also E. L. McKitrick, **Andrew Johnson and Reconstruction** (1960), H. L. Trefousse, **The Radical Republicans** (1969), and M. L. Benedict, **The Impeachment and Trial of Andrew Johnson** (1973). J. M. McPherson, **The Struggle for Equality: Abolitionists and the Negro in the Civil War and Reconstruction** (1964), is also important. On the Fourteenth Amendment, see Joseph James, **The Framing of the Fourteenth Amendment** (1956); on the Fifteenth, William Gillette, **The Right to Vote: Politics and the Passage of the Fifteenth Amendment** (1965).

Conditions in the South during Reconstruction are discussed in R. H. Abbott, **The Republican Party and the South** (1986), Joel Williamson, **The Crucible of Race: Black-White Relations in the American South** (1984), Michael Perman, **Reunion Without Compromise** (1973), H. N. Rabinowitz, **Race Relations in the Urban South** (1978), and J. L. Roark, **Masters Without Slaves** (1977).

Useful state studies include Thomas Holt, **Black over White: Negro Political Leadership in South Carolina** (1977), and Joel Wiliamson, **After Slavery: The Negro in South Carolina during Reconstruction** (1965).

On the Ku Klux Klan, see G. C. Rable, **But There Was No Peace** (1984), and A. W. Trelease, **White Terror: the Ku Klux Klan Conspiracy** (1971). On southern agriculture during Reconstruction, see R. L. Ransom and Richard Sutch, **One Kind of Freedom** (1977), and G. D. Jaynes, **Branches Without Roots** (1986).

The best treatment of Grant's presidency is W. S. McFeely, **Grant** (1981). See also J. G. Sproat, **"The Best Men": Liberal Reformers in the Gilded Age** (1968). For the disputed election of 1876 and the compromise following it, consult C. V. Woodward, **Reunion and Reaction** (1951). William Gillette, **Retreat from Reconstruction** (1980), is also useful.

CHAPTER 18

In the Wake of War

WHEN AMERICANS TURNED FROM fighting and making weapons to more constructive occupations, they transformed their agriculture, trade, manufacturing, mining, and means of communication. Immigration increased rapidly. Cities grew in size and number, exerting on every aspect of life an influence at least as pervasive as that exercised on earlier generations by the frontier. Farm production rose to new heights, invigorated by new marketing methods and the increased use of machinery. Railroad construction stimulated and unified the economy, helping to make possible still larger and more efficient industrial and agricultural enterprises. The flow of gold and silver from western mines excited people's imaginations and their avarice. More than a mere change of scale, these developments altered the structure of the economy and the society.

The American Commonwealth

Most students of the subject have concluded that the political history of the United States in the last quarter of the 19th century was singularly divorced from the meaningful issues of that day. When controversial measures were debated, they excited far less argument than they merited. A graduated income tax was enacted during the Civil War, repealed after that conflict, reenacted in 1894, and then declared unconstitutional in 1895 without causing much more than a ripple in the world of partisan politics. This was typical; as the English observer James Bryce noted in *The American Commonwealth* (1888), the politicians were "neglecting to discover and work out new principles capable of solving the problems which now perplex the country."

"Root, Hog, or Die"

After Appomattox, the immense resources of the United States, combined with the high value most Americans assigned to work and achievement, made the people strongly materialistic.

The failures of Reconstruction seemed to make Americans even more enamored of material values. They were tired of sacrifice, eager to act for themselves, committed more strongly to a government

Chapter-opening illustration:
The meeting of the rails at Promontory Point, Utah, on May 10, 1869.

policy of noninterference, or laissez faire. People now tolerated the grossest kind of waste and appeared to care little about corruption in high places, so long as no one interfered with their personal pursuit of profit. Mark Twain, raised in an earlier era, called this the Gilded Age, dazzling on the surface, base metal beneath.

Certain intellectual currents encouraged the exploitative drives of the people. By the 1870s Charles Darwin's theory of evolution was beginning to influence opinion in the United States. That nature had ordained a kind of inevitable progress, governed by the natural selection of the individual organisms best adapted to survive in a particular environment, seemed reasonable to most Americans, for it fitted well with their own experiences. All-out competition, unhampered by government regulations or other restrictions, would mean that only the most efficient would survive in every field of human endeavor.

Yale professor William Graham Sumner sometimes used the survival-of-the-fittest analogy in teaching undergraduates. "Professor," one student asked Sumner, "don't you believe in any government aid to industries?" "No!" Sumner replied, "it's root, hog, or die." The student persisted: "Suppose some professor of political science came along and took your job away from you. Wouldn't you be sore?" "Any other professor is welcome to try," Sumner answered promptly. "If he gets my job, it is my fault. My business is to teach the subject so well that no one can take the job away from me." Sumner's philosophy came to be known as social Darwinism, the idea that economic and social relations were governed by the Darwinian principle that unrestricted, the fittest will always survive.

Few businessmen were directly influenced by Darwin's ideas. Most accepted any aid they could get from the government. Nevertheless, most were sincere individualists. They believed in competition, being convinced that the nation would prosper most if all people were free to seek their personal fortunes by their own methods.

The Shape of Politics

A succession of weak presidents occupied the White House, and Congress dominated the government, the Senate generally overshadowing the House of Representatives. Critics called the Senate a "rich man's club," and it did contain many millionaires. However, the true sources of the Senate's influence lay in the long tenure of many of its members and in its reputation for wisdom, intelligence, and statesmanship.

The House of Representatives, by contrast, was one of the most disorderly and ineffectual legislative bodies in the world. An infernal din rose from the crowded chamber. Desks slammed; members held private conversations, hailed pages, shuffled from place to place, clamored for the attention of the Speaker—all while some poor orator tried to discuss the question of the moment. Speaking in the House, one writer said, was like trying to address the crowd on a passing bus from a curb in front of the Astor House in New York City.

The major political parties seldom took clearly opposing positions on the questions of the day. Democrats were separated from Republicans more by accidents of geography, religious affiliation, and ethnic background than by economic issues.

The fundamental division between Democrats and Republicans was sectional, a result of the Civil War. The South, after the political rights of blacks had been drastically circumscribed, became heavily Democratic. Most of New England was solidly Republican. Elsewhere the two parties stood in fair balance, although the Republicans tended to have the advantage.

The personalities of political leaders often dictated the voting patterns of individuals and groups. In 1892, when Grover Cleveland defeated Benjamin Harrison for president, a prominent steel manufacturer wrote to his even more prominent competitor, Andrew Carnegie, "I am very sorry for President Harrison, but I cannot see that our interests are going to be affected one way or the other." Carnegie replied, "We have nothing to fear. . . . Cleveland is [a] pretty good fellow. Off for Venice tomorrow."

The balance of political power after 1876 was almost perfect. Majorities in the Senate and the House fluctuated continually. Between 1876 and 1896 the "dominant" Republican party controlled both houses of Congress and the presidency at the same time for only one two-year period.

Issues of the Gilded Age

Four questions obsessed politicians in these years. One was the "bloody shirt." The term, which became part of the language after a Massachusetts congressman dramatically displayed the blood-stained shirt of an Ohio carpetbagger who had been flogged by terrorists in Mississippi, referred to the tactic of reminding northern voters that the men who had taken the South out of the Union had been Democrats and that they and their descendants were still Democrats. "Every man that endeavored to tear down the old flag," a Republican orator proclaimed in 1876, "was a Democrat. . . . The man that assassinated Abraham Lincoln was a Democrat. . . . Soldiers, every scar you have on your heroic bodies was given you by a Democrat." Republicans waved the bloody shirt to divert the attention of voters from their party's shortcomings, effectively obscuring the real issues of the day.

Waving the bloody shirt was related intimately to the issue of the rights of blacks. Throughout this period Republicans vacillated between trying to build up their organization in the South by appealing to black voters—which required them to make sure that blacks in the South could vote—and trying to win conservative white support by stressing economic issues such as the tariff. When the former strategy seemed wise, they waved the bloody shirt with vigor; in the latter case, they piously announced that the blacks' future was "as safe in the hands of one party as it is in the other."

The tariff was a perennial issue in post–Civil War politics. Manufacturers desired protective tariffs to keep out competing products, and a majority of their workers were convinced that wage levels would fall if goods produced by cheap foreign labor entered the United States untaxed. Many farmers supported protection, though few competing agricultural products were being imported. Congressman William McKinley of Ohio, who reputedly could make reciting a tariff schedule sound like poetry, stated the majority opinion in the clearest terms: High tariffs foster the growth of industry and thus create jobs. "Reduce the tariff and labor is the first to suffer," he declared.

The Democrats professed to believe in moderation, yet whenever party leaders tried to revise the tariff downward, Democratic congressmen from industrial states like Pennsylvania and New York sided with the Republicans. Every new tariff bill became an occasion for logrolling, lobbying, and outrageous politicking rather than for sane discussion and careful evaluation of the public interest.

Another political question in this period was currency reform. During the Civil War, it will be recalled, the government, faced with obligations it could not meet by taxing or borrowing, suspended specie payments and issued nearly $450 million in paper money. The greenbacks did not command the full confidence of people accustomed to money readily convertible into gold or silver. Greenbacks seemed to threaten inflation, for how could one trust the government not to issue them in wholesale lots to avoid passing unpopular tax laws? Thus when the war ended, strong sentiment developed for withdrawing the greenbacks from circulation and returning to a bullion standard.

Beginning during Reconstruction prices declined sharply. The deflation increased the real income of bondholders and other creditors but injured debtors. Farmers were hit particularly hard, for many of them had borrowed heavily during the wartime boom to finance expansion.

Here was a question of real significance, yet the major parties refused to confront it. Though the Republicans professed to be the party of sound money, most western Republicans favored expansion of the currency. And while one wing of the Democrats flirted with the Greenbackers, the conservative, or "Bourbon," Democrats favored deflation as much as Republicans did.

In 1874 a bill to increase the supply of greenbacks was defeated in a Republican-dominated Congress only by the veto of President Grant. The next year Congress voted to resume specie payments, but in order to avoid a party split on the question, the Republicans agreed to allow $300 million in greenbacks to remain in circulation and to postpone actual resumption of specie payments until 1879.

Yet another major political issue of these years was civil service reform. That the federal bureaucracy needed overhauling nearly everyone agreed. As American society grew larger and more complex, the government necessarily took on more functions. The need for professional administration increased. The number of federal employees rose from 53,000 in 1871 to 256,000 at the end of the century. Corruption flourished; waste and inefficiency were the normal state of affairs.

Every honest observer could see the need for reform, but the politicians argued that patronage was the lifeblood of politics, that parties could not function without armies of loyal political workers, and that the workers expected and deserved the rewards of office when their efforts were crowned with vic-

tory at the polls. Typical was the attitude of the New York assemblyman who, according to Theodore Roosevelt, had "the same idea about Public Life and the Civil Service that a vulture has of a dead sheep."

Blacks After Reconstruction

Minorities were treated with callousness and contempt in the postwar decades. That the South would deal harshly with the former slaves once federal control was relaxed probably should have been expected. President Hayes had urged blacks to trust southern whites. A new Era of Good Feelings had dawned, he announced after making a goodwill tour of the South shortly after his March 1877 inauguration. By December he was disillusioned. However, he did nothing to remedy the situation. Frederick Douglass called Hayes's policy "sickly conciliation."

Hayes's successors in the 1880s did no better. "Time is the only cure," President Garfield said, thereby confessing that he had no policy at all. President Arthur gave federal patronage to antiblack groups in an effort to split the Democratic South. In President Cleveland's day, blacks had scarcely a friend in high places, North or South. Hayes, Garfield, and Arthur were Republicans, Cleveland a Democrat; party made little difference. Both parties subscribed to hypocritical statements about equality and constitutional rights. Neither did anything to implement them.

For a time blacks were not totally disfranchised in the South, but in the 1890s the southern states, led by Mississippi, began to deprive blacks of the vote despite the Fifteenth Amendment. Poll taxes raised a formidable economic barrier, one that also disfranchised many poor whites. Literacy tests completed the work; a number of states provided a loophole for illiterate whites by including an "understanding" clause whereby an illiterate person could qualify by demonstrating an ability to explain the meaning of a section of the state constitution when an election official read it to him. Blacks who attempted to take the test were invariably declared to have failed it.

In Louisiana 130,000 blacks voted in the election of 1896. Then the law was changed. In 1900 only 5,000 votes were cast by blacks. With unctuous hypocrisy, white southerners insisted that they loved "their" blacks dearly and wished only to protect them from "the machinations of those who would use them only to further their own base ends." "We take away the Negroes' votes," a Louisiana politician explained, "to protect them just as we would protect a little child and prevent it from injuring itself with sharp-edged tools."

Practically every Supreme Court decision after 1877 that affected blacks somehow "nullified or curtailed" their rights. The *Civil Rights Cases* (1883) declared the Civil Rights Act of 1875 unconstitutional. Blacks who were refused equal accommodations or privileges by hotels, theaters, and other privately owned facilities had no recourse at law, the Court announced. The Fourteenth Amendment guaranteed their civil rights against invasion by the states, not by individuals.

In *Plessy* v. *Ferguson* (1896) the Court ruled that even in places of public accommodation, such as railroads and, by implication, schools, segregation was legal so long as facilities of equal quality were provided. "If one race be inferior to the other socially, the Constitution of the United States cannot put them upon the same plane." In a noble dissent in the Plessy case, Justice John Marshall Harlan protested this line of argument. "Our Constitution is color-blind," he said. "The arbitrary separation of citizens, on the basis of race . . ., is a badge of servitude wholly inconsistent with civil freedom and the equality before the law established by the Constitution." Alas, more than half a century was to pass before the Court came around to Harlan's reasoning and reversed the Plessy decision. Meanwhile, total segregation was imposed throughout the South. Separate schools, prisons, hospitals, recreational facilities, and even cemeteries were provided for blacks, and these were almost never equal to those available to whites.

Most northerners supported the government and the Court. Newspapers presented a stereotyped, derogatory picture of blacks, no matter what the circumstances. "The Negro's day is over," the tough-minded William Graham Sumner explained.

Booker T. Washington and the Atlanta Compromise

Since nearly all biologists, physicians, and other supposed experts on race were convinced that blacks were inferior beings, educated northerners generally accepted black inferiority as fact. James Bryce

Frances Benjamin Johnston, the first black woman photographer of note, documented Tuskegee Institute's activities in the early years of the century. Here students help with building construction about 1900.

encountered many Americans of this type and absorbed their point of view. Negroes, Bryce wrote, were docile, pliable, submissive, lustful, childish, impressionable, emotional, heedless, and "unthrifty." They had "no capacity for abstract thinking, for scientific inquiry, or for any kind of invention."

Like Bryce, most Americans did not especially wish blacks ill; they simply refused to consider them quite human and consigned them complacently to oblivion, along with the Indians. A vicious circle was established: By denying blacks decent educational opportunities and good jobs, the dominant race could use the blacks' resultant ignorance and poverty to justify the inferior facilities offered them.

Southern blacks reacted to this deplorable situation in a variety of ways. Some sought redress in racial pride and what would later be called black nationalism. A few became so disaffected that they tried to revive the African colonization movement. "Africa is our home," insisted Bishop Henry M. Turner, who had served as an army chaplain during the war and as a member of the Georgia legislature during Reconstruction; "there is no future in this country for the Negro." T. Thomas Fortune, editor of the *New York Age* and founder of the Afro-American League (1887), called on blacks to demand full civil rights, better schools, and fair wages and to fight against discrimination of every sort. "Let us stand up like men in our own organization," he urged. "If others use . . . violence to combat our peaceful arguments, it is not for us to run away from violence."

Militancy and black separatism won few adherents in the Southern. Life was better than it had been under slavery. But the forces of repression were extremely powerful. The late 19th century saw more lynchings in the South than any other period of American history. This helps explain the tactics of Booker T. Washington, one of the most extraordinary Americans of that generation.

Washington had been born a slave in Virginia in 1856. Laboriously, he obtained an education, supporting himself while a student by working as a janitor. In 1881, with the financial help of northern philanthropists, he founded Tuskegee Institute in Alabama. Washington's experiences convinced him that blacks must lift themselves by their own bootstraps but must also accommodate themselves to white prejudices.

In 1895 Washington made a now-famous speech

to a mixed audience in Atlanta. To the blacks he said: "Cast down your bucket where you are," by which he meant stop fighting segregation and second-class citizenship and concentrate on learning useful skills. Progress up the social and economic ladder would come not from "artificial forcing" but from self-improvement. He asked the whites of what he called "our beloved South" to lend blacks a hand in their efforts to advance themselves. If you will do so, he promised, you will be "surrounded by the most patient, faithful, law-abiding, and unresentful people that the world has seen."

This so-called Atlanta Compromise delighted white southerners, but blacks responded with mixed feelings. Accepting Washington's approach might relieve them of many burdens and dangers and bring them considerable material assistance. Obsequiousness might, like discretion, be the better part of valor. But the cost was high in surrendered personal dignity and lost hopes of obtaining real justice.

Washington's career illustrates the terrible dilemma that American blacks have always faced: the choice between confrontation and accommodation. This choice was particularly difficult in the late 19th century.

Washington chose accommodation. It is easy to condemn him as a toady but difficult to see how, at that time, a more aggressive policy could have succeeded. One can even interpret the Atlanta Compromise as a subtle form of black nationalism; in a way, Washington was not urging blacks to accept inferiority and racial slurs but to ignore them. His own behavior lends force to this view, for his method of operating was indeed subtle, even devious. In public he minimized the importance of civil and political rights and accepted separate but equal facilities—if they were truly equal. Behind the scenes he lobbied against restrictive measures, marshaled large sums of money to fight test cases in the courts, and worked hard in northern states to organize the black vote and make sure that black political leaders got a share of the spoils of office.

The West After the Civil War

The West displayed these aspects of the age, and a number of others, in heightened form. Nearly a third of all Californians were foreign-born, as were more than 40 percent of Nevadans and over half the residents of Idaho and Arizona. There were, of course, large populations of Spanish-speaking Americans of Mexican origin all over the Southwest. Chinese and Irish laborers were pouring into California by the thousands, and there were substantial numbers of Germans, Scandinavians, and other Europeans on the high plains east of the Rockies.

Although the image of the West as the land of great open spaces is accurate enough, the region contained several bustling cities. San Francisco, with a population approaching 250,000 in the late 1870s, had long outgrown its role as a rickety boomtown. Denver, San Antonio, and Salt Lake City were smaller but growing rapidly and equally "urban."

There was, in short, no one West, no typical westerner. If the economy was predominantly agricultural and extractive, it was also commercial and entering the early stages of industrial development. The seeds of such large enterprises as Wells Fargo, Levi Strauss, and half a dozen important department store empires were sown in the immediate postwar decades.

Above all, however, the West epitomized the "every man for himself" psychology of post-Reconstruction American society. In 1879 several thousand southern blacks suddenly migrated to western Kansas. When asked why, one leader replied: "The white people [in the South] treat our people so bad . . . that it is impossible for them to stand it." But their treatment in Kansas was not much better. California had been a free state from the moment of its entry in the Union, but it treated its black citizens poorly, even refusing to ratify the Fifteenth Amendment.

Beginning in the mid-1850s a steady flow of Chinese immigrated to the West Coast region. About 4,000 or 5,000 a year came until the negotiation of the Burlingame Treaty of 1868, the purpose of which was to provide cheap labor for railroad construction crews. Thereafter, the annual influx more than doubled. When the railroads were completed and the Chinese began to compete with native workers, riots broke out in San Francisco. Chinese workers were called "groveling worms," "more slavish and brutish than the beasts that roam the fields." When the migration suddenly increased in 1882 to nearly 40,000, Congress passed a law prohibiting all Chinese immigration for ten years. Later legislation extended the ban indefinitely.

Chinese immigrants caused genuine social problems. Most did not intend to remain in the United States and therefore made little effort to accommodate themselves to American ways. But the westerners' attitude toward the Chinese differed only in degree from their attitude toward the Mexicans who flocked into the Southwest to work as farm laborers and to help build railroads.

The Plains Indians

"Whites," the historian Rodman Paul wrote, "did not shed their old attitudes when they crossed into a new country." Paul's generalization applies with special force to the way western whites dealt with the Indians. For 250 years the Indians had been driven back steadily, yet on the eve of the Civil War they still inhabited roughly half the United States. By the time of Hayes's inauguration, however, the Indians had been shattered as an independent people, and in another decade the survivors were penned up on reservations.

In 1860 in the deserts of the Great Basin between the Sierra and the Rockies, in the mountains themselves, and on the semiarid, grass-covered plains between the Rockies and the edge of white civilization in eastern Kansas and Nebraska, nearly a quarter of a million Indians dominated the land. By far the most important lived on the High Plains. These tribes possessed a generally uniform culture. Although they seemed the epitome of freedom, pride, and self-reliance, they had already begun to fall under the sway of white power. They eagerly adopted the products of the more technically advanced culture—cloth, metal tools, weapons, cheap decorations. However, the most important thing the whites gave them had nothing to do with technology: It was the horse.

Cortés brought the first modern horses to America in the 16th century. Multiplying rapidly thereafter, the animals soon roamed wild from Texas to the Argentine. By the 18th century the Indians of the plains had made them a vital part of their culture. Mounted Indians could run down buffalo instead of stalking them on foot. Indians on horseback could move more easily over the country and fight more effectively too. The Indians also adopted modern weapons: the cavalry sword and the rifle. Both added to their effectiveness as hunters and fighters. However, like the whites' liquor and diseases, horses and guns caused problems too. The buffalo herds began to diminish, and warfare became bloodier and more frequent.

In a familiar tragic pattern, the majority of the western tribes greeted the first whites to enter their domains in a friendly fashion. As late as the 1830s, white hunters and trappers ranged freely over most of the West, trading with the Indians and often marrying Indian women. But after the start of the gold rush, the whites began to undermine the Indian empire in the West. Deliberately, the government in Washington prepared the way. In 1851 Thomas Fitzpatrick, an Indian agent, summoned a great "council" of the tribes at Horse Creek, 37 miles east of Fort Laramie, in what is now Wyoming. The Indians respected Fitzpatrick, who had recently married a woman who was half Indian. At Horse Creek he persuaded each tribe to accept definite limits to its hunting grounds. In return the Indians were promised gifts and annual payments. This policy, known as "concentration," was designed to cut down on intertribal warfare and—far more important—to enable the government to negotiate separately with each tribe. It was the classic strategy of divide and conquer.

Although it made a mockery of diplomacy to treat Indian tribes as though they were European powers, the United States maintained that each tribe was a sovereign nation, to be dealt with as an equal in solemn treaties. Both sides knew that this was not the case. When Indians agreed to meet in council, they were tacitly admitting defeat. They seldom drove hard bargains or broke off negotiations. Moreover, tribal chiefs had only limited power; young braves frequently refused to respect agreements made by their elders.

Indian Wars

No sooner had the Kansas-Nebraska bill become law than the Kansas, Omaha, Pawnee, and Yankton Sioux tribes began to feel pressure for further concessions of territory. Thus it happened that in 1862, after federal troops had been pulled out of the West for service against the Confederacy, most of the plains Indians rose up against the whites. For five years intermittent but bloody clashes kept the entire area in a state of alarm.

This was guerrilla warfare, with all its horror and treachery. In 1864 a party of Colorado militia fell upon an unsuspecting Cheyenne community at Sand Creek and killed an estimated 450. "Kill and scalp all, big and little," Colonel J. M. Chivington, a minister in private life, told his men. "Nits make lice." General Nelson A. Miles called this Chivington Massacre the "foulest and most unjustifiable crime in the annals of America," but it was no worse than many incidents in earlier conflicts with Indians and not very different from what was later to occur in guerrilla wars involving American troops in the Philippines and, more recently, in Vietnam. In turn the Indians slaughtered dozens of isolated white families, ambushed small parties, and fought many successful skirmishes against troops and militia. They achieved their most notable triumph in December 1866, when the Oglala Sioux, under their great chief Red Cloud, wiped out a party of 82 soldiers under Captain W. J. Fetterman.

In 1867 the government tried a new strategy. All the plains Indians would be confined to two small reservations, one in the Black Hills of Dakota Territory, the other in Oklahoma, and be forced to become farmers. At two great conclaves held in 1867 and 1868 at Medicine Lodge Creek and Fort Laramie, the principal chiefs yielded to the government's demands. Many Indians refused to abide by these agreements. With their way of life at stake, they swept across the plains, as destructive as a prairie fire.

That a relative handful of "savages," without central leadership or plan, could hold off the cream of the army, battle-hardened in the Civil War, can be explained by the character of the vast, trackless country and the ineptness of many American commanders. Few Indian chiefs were capable of organizing a campaign. But Indians made superb guerrillas. Every observer called them the best cavalry soldiers in the world. Armed with stubby, powerful bows capable of driving an arrow clear through a bull buffalo, they were a fair match for troops equipped with

Preparing to surrender to General Crook, Geronimo (mounted, left) and Natiche stand with their respective sons and Geronimo's grandson; the sons wear ceremonial paint. This photograph was taken in the Sierra Madre mountains of Mexico in 1886, just before the surrender.

carbines and Colt revolvers. Trouble flared here one week, next week somewhere else, perhaps 500 miles away. No less an authority than General William Tecumseh Sherman testified that a mere 50 Indians could often "checkmate" 3,000 soldiers.

If one concedes that no one could reverse the direction of history or stop the invasion of Indian lands, some version of the small reservation policy would probably have been best for the Indians. Had they been guaranteed a reasonable amount of land and adequate subsidies and allowed to maintain their way of life, they might have accepted the situation and ceased to harry the whites.

Whatever chance that policy had was weakened by the government's maladministration of Indian affairs. An "Indian Ring" in the Department of the Interior systematically stole funds and supplies intended for the reservation Indians. General Sherman, in overall command of the Indian country, claimed in 1875: "We could settle Indian troubles in an hour, but Congress wants the patronage of the Indian bureau, and the bureau wants the appropriations without any of the trouble of the Indians themselves." General Sheridan, no lover of Indians, said: "We took away their country and their means of support . . . and it was for this and against this that they made war. Could anyone expect less?"

President Grant wished to place the reservations under army control, but the Indians opposed this. They fared no better around army camps than on the reservations. In 1869 Congress created the nonpolitical Board of Indian Commissioners to oversee Indian affairs, but the bureaucrats in Washington stymied the commissioners at every turn.

In 1874 gold was discovered in the Black Hills Indian reservation. By the next winter thousands of miners had invaded the reserved area. Already alarmed by the approach of crews building the Northern Pacific Railroad, the Sioux once again went on the warpath. Joining with nontreaty tribes to the west, they concentrated in the region of the Bighorn River, in southern Montana Territory.

The summer of 1876 saw three columns of troops in the field against them. The commander of one column, General Alfred H. Terry, sent ahead a small detachment of the 7th Cavalry under Colonel George A. Custer with orders to locate the Indians' camp and then block their escape route into the inaccessible Bighorn Mountains. Custer was both vain and rash, grave handicaps when fighting Indians. Grossly underestimating the number of the Indians, he decided to attack directly with his tiny force of 264 men. At the Little Bighorn late in June he found himself surrounded by 2,500 Sioux under Rain-in-the-Face and Crazy Horse. He and all his men died on the field.

Because it was so one-sided, "Custer's Last Stand" was not a typical battle, though it may be taken as symbolic of the Indian warfare of the period in the sense that it was characterized by bravery, foolhardiness, and a tragic waste of life. The battle greatly heartened the Indians, but it did not gain them their cause. That autumn, short of rations and hard-pressed by overwhelming numbers of soldiers, they surrendered and returned to the reservation.

The Destruction of Tribal Life

Thereafter, the fighting slackened, chiefly due to the building of the transcontinental railroads and the destruction of the buffalo. An estimated 13 to 15 million head had roamed the plains in the mid-1860s. Then the slaughter began. Thousands were butchered to feed the gangs of laborers engaged in building the Union Pacific Railroad. Thousands more fell before the guns of sportsmen. Railroads made it possible to move supplies and troops swiftly to trouble spots during conflicts with the Indians. The roads also ran excursion trains for hunters. The discovery in 1871 of a way to make commercial use of buffalo hides completed the tragedy. In the next three years about 9 million head were killed; after another decade the animals were almost extinct.

By the 1880s the advance of whites into the plains had become irresistible, and large numbers of disinterested whites believed that the only way to solve the "Indian problem" was to persuade the Indians to abandon their tribal cultures and live on family farms. The "wild" Indian must become a "civilized" member of "American" society.

To accomplish this goal, Congress passed the Dawes Severalty Act of 1887. Tribal lands were to be split up into individual allotments. To keep speculators from wresting the allotments from the Indians while they were adjusting to their new way of life, the land could not be disposed of for 25 years. Funds were to be appropriated for educating and training the Indians, and those who accepted allotments and "adopted the habits of civilized life" were to be granted United States citizenship.

The sponsors of the Severalty Act thought they were effecting a fine humanitarian reform. "We must throw some protection" over the Indian, Senator Henry L. Dawes declared. "We must hold up his hand." But the law had disastrous results in the long run. It assumed that Indians could be transformed into small agricultural capitalists by an act of Congress. It shattered what was left of the Indians' culture without enabling them to adapt to white ways. Moreover, unscrupulous white men tricked many Indians into leasing their allotments for a pittance, and local authorities often taxed Indian lands at excessive rates. In 1934, after about 86 million of the 138 million acres assigned under the Dawes Act had passed into white hands, the government returned to a policy of encouraging tribal ownership of Indian lands.

Exploiting Mineral Wealth in the West

Americans had long regarded the West as a limitless treasure to be grasped as rapidly as possible, and after 1865 they engrossed its riches still faster and in a wider variety of ways. From the mid-1850s to the mid-1870s thousands of prospectors fanned out through the Rockies, panning every stream and hacking furiously at every outcropping from the Fraser River country of British Columbia to Tucson in southern Arizona, from the eastern slopes of the Sierra to the Great Plains.

Gold and silver were scattered throughout the area, though usually too thinly to make mining profitable. Whenever anyone made a strike, prospectors, driven by what a critic called an "unhealthy desire" for sudden wealth, flocked to the site, drawn by rumors of streambeds gleaming with gold-rich gravel and of nuggets the size of men's fists. For a few months the area teemed with activity. Towns of 5,000 or more sprang up overnight; improvised roads were crowded with men and supply wagons. Claims were staked out along every stream and gully. Then, usually, expectations faded in the light of reality: high prices, low yields, hardships, violence, and deception. The boom collapsed, and the towns died as quickly as they had risen. A few would have found wealth, the rest only backbreaking labor and disappointment—until tales of another strike sent them dashing feverishly across the land on another golden chase.

In a sense the Denvers, Aurarias, Virginia Cities, Orofinos, and Gold Creeks of the West during the war years were harbingers of the attitudes that flourished in the East in the age of President Grant and his immediate successors. The miners enthusiastically adopted the get-rich-quick philosophy, willingly enduring privations and laboring hard, always with the objective of striking it rich. The idea of reserving any part of the West for future generations never entered their heads.

The sudden prosperity of the mining towns attracted every kind of shady character—according to one forty-niner, "rascals from Oregon, pickpockets from New York, accomplished gentlemen from Europe, interlopers from Lima and Chile, Mexican thieves, gamblers from no particular spot, and assassins manufactured in Hell." Gambling dens, dance halls, saloons, and brothels mushroomed wherever precious metal was found.

Law enforcement was a constant problem. Gold and silver dominated people's thoughts and dreams. Ostentation characterized the successful, braggadocio those who failed. During the administration of President Grant, Virginia City, Nevada, was at the peak of its vulgar prosperity. It had 25 saloons before it had 4,000 people. By the 1870s its mountainside site was disfigured by ugly, ornate mansions where successful mine operators ate from fine china and swilled champagne as though it were water.

In 1873, after the discovery of the Big Bonanza, a seam of ore more than 50 feet thick, the future of Virginia City seemed boundless. Other discoveries shortly thereafter indicated to optimists that the mining boom in the West would continue indefinitely. The finds in the Black Hills in 1875 and 1876, heralding deposits yielding eventually $100 million, led to the mushroom growth of Deadwood, home of Wild Bill Hickok, Deadwood Dick, Calamity Jane, and such lesser-known characters as California Jack and Poker Alice. New strikes in Colorado in 1876 and 1877 caused the town of Leadville to boom; in 1880 there were 30,000 people in the area. However, this was the last important flurry to ruffle the mining frontier. The West continued to yield much gold and, especially, silver, but big corporations produced

Nat Love was a cowboy who earned the nickname "Deadwood Dick" in the Dakotas in the 1880s for his prowess with a lariat. His autobiography, published in 1907, attests to the role blacks played in settling the Wild West.

nearly all of it. The mines around Deadwood were soon controlled by one large company, Homestake Mining.

This is the culminating irony of the mining frontier: Shoestring prospectors, independent and enterprising, made the key discoveries, established local institutions, and supplied the West with much of its color and folklore, but the stockholders of large corporations, many of whom had never seen a mine, made off with the lion's share of the wealth. To operate profitably, large capital investments, heavy machinery, railroads, and hundreds of hired hands were required. A typical successful mine owner was George Hearst, senator from California and father of the newspaper tycoon William Randolph Hearst, who, by shrewd speculations, obtained large blocks of stock in mining properties scattered from Montana to Mexico.

Though marked by violence, fraud, greed, and shattered hopes, the gold rushes caused a great increase of interest in the West. A valuable literature appeared, part imaginative, part reportorial, describing the mining camps and the life of the prospectors. These works fascinated contemporaries (as they have continued to fascinate succeeding generations when adapted to the motion picture and to television). Mark Twain's *Roughing It* (1872), based in part on his experiences in the Nevada mining country, is the most famous example of this literature.

Each new strike and rush, no matter how ephemeral, brought permanent settlers along with the prospectors: farmers, cattlemen, storekeepers, teamsters, lawyers, and ministers. In every mining town—along with the saloons and brothels—schools, churches, and newspaper offices sprang up.

The mines also speeded the political organization of the West. Colorado and Nevada became territories in 1861, Arizona and Idaho in 1863, Montana in 1864. Although Nevada was admitted before it had 60,000 residents in 1864 to ratify the Thirteenth Amendment and help reelect Lincoln, most of these territories did not become states for decades. But thanks to the miners, the framework for future development was early established.

The Land Bonanza

While the miners were engrossing the mineral wealth of the West, other interests were snapping up the region's choice farmland. The Homestead Act of 1862 had presumably ended the reign of the speculator and the large landholder. The West, land reformers had assumed, would soon be dotted with 160-acre family farms.

They were doomed to disappointment. Most landless Americans were too poor to become farmers, even when they could obtain land free of charge. The expense of moving a family to the ever-receding frontier exceeded the means of many, and the costs of hoes and scythes, harvesting machines, fencing, and housing presented a formidable barrier. As for the industrial workers for whom the free land was supposed to provide a "safety valve," they had neither the skills nor the inclination to become farmers.

And despite the intent of the law, speculators often managed to obtain large tracts. They hired men to stake out claims, falsely swear that they had fulfilled the conditions laid down in the law for obtaining legal title, and then deed the land over to their employers.

Furthermore, 160 acres was not enough for raising livestock or for the kind of commercial agriculture that was developing west of the Mississippi. Congress made a feeble attempt to make larger holdings available to homesteaders by passing the Timber Culture Act of 1873, which permitted individuals to claim an additional 160 acres if they would agree to plant a quarter of it in trees within ten years. This law proved helpful to some farmers in Kansas, Nebraska, and the Dakotas. Nevertheless, fewer than 25 percent of the 245,000 who took up land under it obtained final title to the property. Raising large numbers of seedling trees on the plains was a difficult task.

While futilely attempting to make a forest of parts of the treeless plains, the government permitted private interests to gobble up and destroy many of the great forests that clothed the slopes of the Rockies and the Sierra. The Timber and Stone Act of 1878 allowed anyone to acquire a quarter section of forest land for $2.50 an acre if it was "unfit for civilization." This laxly drawn measure enabled lumber companies to obtain thousands of acres by hiring dummy entrymen, whom they marched in gangs to the land offices, paying them a few dollars for their time after they had signed over their claims.

Had the land laws been better drafted and more honestly enforced, it is still unlikely that the policy of granting free land to small homesteaders would have succeeded. Aside from the built-in difficulties faced by small-scale agriculturalists, frontier farmers of the 1870s and 1880s had to grapple with novel problems. The soil was rich, but the climate, especially in the semiarid regions beyond the 98th meridian of longitude, made agriculture frequently difficult and often impossible. Blizzards, floods, grasshopper plagues, and prairie fires caused repeated heartaches, but periodic drought and searing summer heat were the worst hazards.

At the same time, the flat immensity of the land, combined with newly available farm machinery and the development of rail connections with the East, encouraged the growth of enormous corporation-controlled "bonanza" farms. Bonanza farmers could buy supplies wholesale and obtain concessions from railroads and processors; even the biggest organizations could not cope with prolonged drought, however, and most of the bonanza outfits failed in the dry years of the late 1880s. Wise farmers who diversified their crops and cultivated their land intensively fared better in the long run, though even they could not hope to earn a profit in really dry years.

Despite the hazards of plains agriculture, the region became the breadbasket of America in the decades following the Civil War. By 1889 Minnesota topped the nation in wheat production, and ten years later four of the five leading wheat states lay west of the Mississippi. The plains also accounted for heavy percentages of the nation's other cereal crops, together with immense quantities of beef, pork, and mutton.

Like other exploiters of the nation's resources, farmers took whatever they could from the soil with little heed for preserving its fertility or preventing erosion. The consequent national loss was less apparent because it was diffuse and slow to assume drastic proportions, but it was nonetheless real.

Western Railroad Building

Further exploitation of land resources by private interests resulted from the government's policy of subsidizing western railroads. Here was a clear illustration of the conflict between the idea of the West as a national heritage to be disposed of to deserving citizens and the concept of the region as a cornucopia pouring forth riches to be carted off by anyone powerful and determined enough to take them. To serve the valuable national purpose, the linking of the sections by rail, the land of the West was dispensed wholesale as a substitute for cash subsidies.

Federal land grants to railroads began in 1850 with those allotted the Illinois Central, but the most lavish gifts of the public domain were those made directly to builders of intersectional trunk lines. These roads received more than 155 million acres, although about 25 million acres reverted to the government because some companies failed to lay the required miles of track. Unless the government had been willing to build the transcontinental lines itself—and this was unthinkable in an age dominated by belief in individual exploitation and wary of any activity that entrusted the spending of large sums by politicians—some system of subsidy was essential. Private investors would not hazard the huge sums needed to lay tracks across hundreds of miles of rugged, empty country when traffic over the road could not possibly produce profits for many years.

Grants of land seemed a sensible way of financing construction. The method avoided direct outlays of public funds, for the companies could pledge the land as security for bond issues or sell it directly for cash. Moreover, land and railroad values were intimately linked in contemporary thinking. In many cases the value of the land granted might be recovered by the government when it sold other lands in the vicinity, for such properties would certainly be worth more after transportation facilities to eastern markets had been constructed.

The Pacific Railway Act of 1862 established the pattern for these grants. It gave the builders of the Union Pacific and Central Pacific railroads 5 square miles of public land on each side of their right-of-way for each mile of track laid. The land was allotted in alternate sections, forming a pattern like a checkerboard, the squares of one color representing railroad property, the other government property. Presumably this arrangement benefited the entire nation, since half the land close to the railroad remained in public hands. However, whenever grants were made to railroads, the adjacent government lands were not opened to homesteaders, on the theory that free land in the immediate vicinity of a line would prevent the road from disposing of its properties at good prices.

Historians have argued at length about the fairness of the land-grant system. No railroad corporation got rich directly from its land holdings, which sold for $2 to $5 an acre. But land-lines encouraged the growth of the West by advertising their property widely and by providing cheap transportation for settlers and shipping services for farmers. They were required by law to carry troops and handle government business free or at reduced rates, which saved the government many millions over the years. At the same time, the system imposed no effective restraints on how the railroads used the funds raised with federal aid. Being able to lay track with money obtained from land grants, the operators tended to be extravagant and often downright corrupt.

The Union Pacific [illegible] built by a construction company, the Crédit Mobilier, which was owned by the promoters. These men awarded themselves contracts at prices that assured the Crédit Mobilier of fat profits. When Congress threatened to investigate the Union Pacific in 1868, Oakes Ames, a stockholder in both companies who was also a member of Congress, sold key congressmen and government officials over 300 shares of Crédit Mobilier stock at a price far below its real value. When these transactions were exposed, the House of Representatives censured Ames, but such was the temper of the times that neither he nor most of his associates believed he had done anything wrong.

The construction of the Central Pacific in the 1860s illustrates how the system encouraged extravagance. In addition to land grants, the Central Pacific and the Union Pacific were given loans in the form of government bonds—from $16,000 to $48,000 for each mile of track laid, depending on the difficulty of the terrain. The two lines competed for the subsidies, the Central Pacific building eastward from Sacramento, the Union Pacific westward from Nebraska. Each put huge crews to work grading and laying track, bringing up supplies over the already completed road. The Union Pacific employed Civil War veterans and Irish immigrants; the Central, Chinese immigrants.

This plan favored the Union Pacific. While the Central Pacific was inching upward through the gorges and granite of the mighty Sierra, the Union Pacific was racing across the level plains. To prevent the Union Pacific from making off with most of the government aid, the Central Pacific wasted huge sums by working through the winter in the High Sierra. Often the men labored in tunnels dug through 40-foot snowdrifts to get at the frozen ground. In 1866, over the most difficult terrain, they laid 28 miles of track—at a cost of more than $280,000 a mile. Experts later estimated that 70 percent of this sum could have been saved had speed not been a factor.

But these herculean efforts paid off. The mountains were conquered, and then the crews raced across the Great Basin to Salt Lake City and beyond. The meeting of the rails—the occasion of a national celebration—took place at Promontory, north of Ogden, Utah, on May 10, 1869. The Union Pacific had built 1,086 miles of track; the Central, 689 miles.

In the long run the wasteful way in which the Central Pacific was built hurt the road severely. It was ill-constructed, over grades too steep and around curves too sharp, and burdened with debts

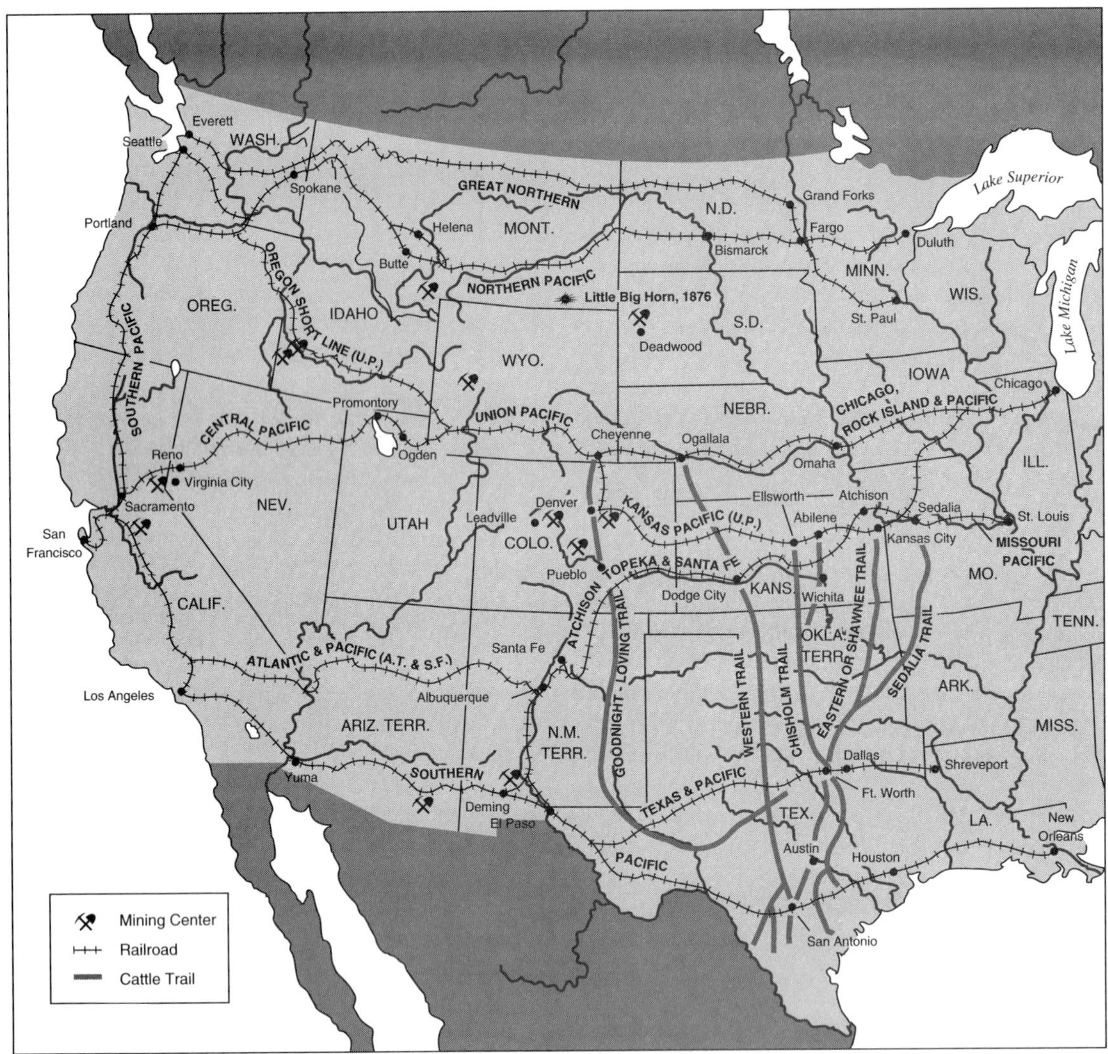

THE WEST: CATTLE, RAILROADS, AND MINING, 1850–1893

that were too heavy. Such was the fate of nearly all the railroads constructed with the help of government subsidies. The only transcontinental built without land grants was the Great Northern, running from St. Paul, Minnesota, to the Pacific. Spending private capital, its guiding genius, James J. Hill, was compelled to build economically and to plan carefully. As a result, his was the only transcontinental line to weather the depression of the 1890s without going into bankruptcy.

The Cattle Kingdom

While miners were digging out the mineral wealth of the West and railroaders were taking possession of much of its land, another group was exploiting endless acres of its grass.

Columbus brought the first cattle to the New World in 1493, on his second voyage, and later conquistadores took them to every corner of Spain's

American empire. Mexico proved to be so well suited to cattle raising that herds were allowed to roam free. They multiplied rapidly, and by the late 18th century what is now southern Texas harbored enormous numbers. The beasts interbred with nondescript "English" cattle, brought into the area by settlers from the United States, to produce the Texas longhorn. Hardy, wiry, ill-tempered, and fleet, with horns often attaining a spread of 6 feet, these animals were far from ideal as beef cattle and almost as hard to capture as wild horses. But they existed in southern Texas by the million, most of them unowned.

The lack of markets and transportation explains why Texas cattle were regarded so lightly. But conditions were changing. Industrial growth in the East was causing an increase in the urban population and a consequent rise in the demand for food. At the same time, the expansion of the railroad network made it possible to move cattle cheaply over long distances. As the iron rails inched across the plains, astute cattlemen began to do some elementary figuring. Longhorns could be had locally for $3 or $4 a head. In the northern cities they would bring ten times that much, perhaps even more. Why not round them up and herd them northward to the railroads, allowing them to feed along the way on the abundant grasses of the plains?

In 1866 a number of Texans drove large herds northward toward Sedalia, Missouri, railhead of the Missouri Pacific. This route took the herds through wooded and settled country and across Indian reservations, provoking many difficulties. At the same time, Charles Goodnight and Oliver Loving drove 2,000 head through New Mexico Territory to Colorado.

The next year the drovers, inspired by an Illinois cattle dealer named Joseph G. McCoy and other entrepreneurs, led their herds north across unsettled grasslands to the Kansas Pacific line at Abilene, Kansas, which McCoy described as "a very small, dead place." They earned excellent profits, and during the next five years about 1.5 million head made the "long drive" over the Chisholm Trail to Abilene, where they were sold to ranchers, feedlot operators, and eastern meat packers. Other shipping points sprang up as the railroads pushed westward.

The technique of the long drive, which involved guiding herds of 2,000 to 3,000 cattle slowly across as much as a thousand miles of country, produced the American cowboy, hero of song, story, and film. Half a dozen of these men could control several thousand steers. Mounted on wiry ponies, they would range alongside the herd, keeping the animals on the move but preventing stampedes, allowing them time to rest yet steadily pressing them toward the yards of Abilene.

Cattle towns such as Abilene had their full share of saloons, gambling dens, and "dance houses" patronized by cowboys and by other transients bent on having a good time. Most were young, male, and single. Violence punctuated their activities, but tales of individual desperadoes and gangs of outlaws "shooting up" cattle towns and terrorizing honest citizens are fictitious. Police forces were well organized. Indeed, "respectable" town residents tended to urge leniency for lawbreakers because of the money they and their fellows brought to the towns.

Open-Range Ranching

Soon cattlemen discovered that the hardy Texas stock could survive the winters of the northern plains. Attracted by the apparently limitless forage, they began to bring up herds to stock the vast regions where the buffalo had so recently roamed. By 1880 some 4.5 million head had spread across the sea of grass that ran from Kansas to Montana and west to the Rockies.

The prairie grasses offered cattlemen a bonanza almost as valuable as the gold mines. Open-range ranching required actual ownership of no more than a few acres along some watercourse. In this semiarid region, control of water enabled a rancher to dominate all the surrounding area back to the divide separating his range from the next stream without investing a cent in the purchase of land. His cattle, wandering freely on the public domain, fattened on grass owned by all the people, to be turned into beefsteak and leather for the profit of the rancher.

Ordinarily, a group of ranchers acted together, obtaining legal title to the lands along the bank of a stream and grazing their cattle over the area drained by it. The herds became thoroughly intermixed, each owner's being identified by a brand mark. Every spring and fall the ranchers staged a great roundup, driving in all the cattle to a central place, separating them by brand marks, culling steers for shipment to market, and branding new calves.

With the demand for meat rising and transportation cheap, princely fortunes could be made in a few years. Capitalists from the East and from Europe began to pour funds into the business. Eastern "dudes" like Theodore Roosevelt, a young New York assemblyman who sank over $50,000 in his Elkhorn Ranch in Dakota Territory in 1883, bought up cattle as a sort of profitable hobby. (Roosevelt, clad in buckskin and bearing a small arsenal of rifles and six-shooters, made quite a splash in Dakota Territory, but not as a rancher.) Soon large outfits such as the Nebraska Land and Cattle Company dominated the business, just as large companies had taken over most of the important gold and silver mines.

In 1885 masked Nebraskans seeking access to water posed for photographer S. D. Butcher, who captioned the picture "Settlers taking the law in their own hands: cutting 15 miles of the Brighton Ranch fence."

Barbed-Wire Warfare

The leading ranchers banded together in cattlemen's associations to deal with overcrowding and with such problems as quarantine regulations, water rights, and thievery, functions that would better have been performed by the government.

To keep other ranchers' cattle from the sections of the public domain they considered their own, the associations and many individuals began to fence huge areas. This was possible only because of the invention in 1874 of barbed wire by Joseph F. Glidden. By the 1880s thousands of miles of the new fencing had been strung across the plains, often across roads and in a few cases around entire communities. "Barbed-wire wars" resulted, fought by rancher against rancher, cattleman against sheepman, herder against farmer.

By stringing so much wire, the cattlemen were unwittingly destroying their own way of doing business. On a truly open range, cattle could fend for themselves, instinctively finding water during droughts, drifting safely downwind before blizzards. Barbed wire prevented their free movement. During winter storms these slender strands became as lethal as high-tension wires; the drifting cattle piled up against them and died by the thousands. "The advent of barbed wire," Walter Prescott Webb wrote in his classic study *The Great Plains* (1931), "brought about the disappearance of the open, free range and converted the range country into the big-pasture country."

The boom times were ending. Overproduction was driving down the price of beef; expenses were on the rise; many sections of the range were overgrazed. The dry summer of 1886 left the stock in poor condition. Winter that year arrived early and with unparalleled fury. Blizzards raged, and temperatures plummeted far below zero. Cattle crowded into low places only to be engulfed in giant snowdrifts; barbed wire took a fearful toll. When spring finally came, between 80 and 90 percent of all cattle on the range were dead.

That cruel winter finished open-range cattle raising. The large companies were bankrupt; many independent operators, Roosevelt among them, became discouraged and sold out. When the industry revived, it was on a smaller, more efficiently organized scale. Cattle raising, like mining before it, ceased to be an adventure in rollicking individualism and became a business.

By the late 1880s the bonanza days of the West were over. No previous frontier had caught the imagination of Americans so completely as the Great West, with its heroic size, its awesome emptiness, its massive, sculptured beauty. Now the frontier was no more. Big companies were taking over all the West's resources. The nation was becoming more powerful, richer, larger, its economic structure more complex and diversified as the West yielded its treasures. But the East, especially eastern industrialists and financiers, increasingly dominated the economy of the nation.

Milestones

1859 Charles Darwin's *Origin of Species*
Comstock Lode discovered
1864 Chivington Massacre
1869 Union Pacific Railroad completed
Board of Indian Commissioners established
1873 Timber Culture Act
1875 Civil Rights Act
1876 Battle of Little Bighorn
1878 Timber and Stone Act
1879 Specie payments resumed
1881 Tuskegee Institute founded
1883 *Civil Rights Cases*
1886–1887 Blizzards put an end to open-range ranching
1887 Dawes Severalty Act
1888 James Bryce, *The American Commonwealth*
1890–1900 Blacks deprived of the vote in the South
1895 Booker T. Washington's Atlanta Compromise speech
1896 *Plessy* v. *Ferguson* sanctions segregation

Supplementary Reading

James Bryce, **The American Commonwealth** (1888), is a fascinating contemporary analysis of the American political system. The economic and political ideas current in this period are covered in Sidney Fine, **Laissez-Faire and the General Welfare State** (1956). Morton Keller, **Affairs of State** (1977), describes the public life of the era. For the views of businessmen, see E. C. Kirkland, **Dream and Thought in the Business Community** (1956), and T. C. Cochran, **Railroad Leaders** (1953).

National political issues are covered in P. S. Hirshson, **Farewell to the Bloody Shirt** (1962), Allen Weinstein, **Prelude to Populism** (1970), Irwin Unger, **The Greenback Era** (1964), and W. T. K. Nugent, **Money and American Society** (1968).

R. A. Billington and Martin Ridge, **Westward Expansion** (1982), is an excellent survey. R. W. Paul, **The Far West and the Great Plains** (1988), and P. N. Limerick, **The Legacy of Conquest** (1987) put more emphasis on social developments. J. R. Jeffrey, **Frontier Women** (1979), covers the immediate post Civil War era.

On western Indians see R. W. Mardock, **The Reformers and the American Indian** (1971), Robert Wooster, **The Military and U. S. Indian Policy** (1988), and F. P. Prucha, **The Great Father: The U. S. Government and the Indians** (1984). On other minority groups consult R. W. Logan, **The Negro in American Life and Thought** (1954), Joel Williamson, **The Crucible of Race** (1984), L. R. Harlan, **Booker T. Washington** (1972), and Gunther Barth, **Bitter Strength: A History of the Chinese in the United States** (1964).

The mining frontier is described in R. W. Paul, **Mining Frontiers of the Far West** (1963), D. A. Smith **Rocky Mountain Mining Camps** (1967), and Paula Petric, **No Step Backward: Women and Family on the Rocky Mountain Frontier** (1987). F. A. Shannon describes **The Farmer's Last Frontier** (1945), H. M. Drache, **The Day of the Bonanza** (1964).

For western railroad development see O. O. Winther, **The Transportation Frontier** (1964), Albro Martin, **James J. Hill** (1976), and R. G. Athearn, **Union Pacific Country** (1971). The cattle kingdom is described in Lewis Atherton, **The Cattle Kings** (1961), R. R. Dykstra, **The Cattle Towns** (1968), and Don Worcester, **The Chisholm Trail** (1980).

CHAPTER 19

■ ■ ■ ■ ■ ■ ■

An Industrial Giant

■ ■ ■ ■ ■ WHEN THE CIVIL WAR BEGAN, THE country's industrial output, though increasing, did not approach that of major European powers. By the end of the century the United States had become far and away the colossus among world manufacturers, dwarfing the production of Great Britain and Germany. The world had never seen such rapid economic growth. The output of goods and services in the country (the gross national product, or GNP) increased by 44 percent between 1874 and 1883 and continued to expand in succeeding years.

Industrial Growth: An Overview

American manufacturing flourished for many reasons. New natural resources were discovered and exploited steadily, thereby increasing opportunities. These opportunities in turn attracted the brightest and most energetic of a vigorous and expanding population. The growth of the country added constantly to the size of the national market, and high tariffs shielded that market from foreign competition. The dominant spirit of the time encouraged businessmen to maximum effort by emphasizing progress, glorifying material wealth, and justifying aggressiveness. European immigrants provided the additional labor needed by expanding industry; 2.5 million arrived in the 1870s, twice that number in the 1880s.

It was a period of rapid advances in basic science, and technicians created a bountiful harvest of new machines, processes, and power sources that increased productivity and created new industries. In agriculture there were better harvesters, binding machines, and combines that could thresh and bag 450 pounds of grain a minute. An 1886 report of the Illinois Bureau of Labor Statistics claimed that "new machinery has displaced fully 50 percent of the muscular labor formerly required to do a given amount of work in the manufacture of agricultural implements." As a result of improvements in the milling of grain, packaged cereals appeared on the American breakfast table. The commercial canning of food ex-

Chapter-opening illustration:
The billowing smokestacks of the Paterson Iron Company of Paterson, New Jersey, and the locomotive on the tracks alongside the iron foundry are two symbols of the industrial growth of the United States during the last quarter of the nineteenth century.

panded rapidly. The perfection of the typewriter by the Remington Company in the 1880s revolutionized the way office work was performed.

Railroads: The First Big Business

The railroads were probably the most significant element in American economic development, railroad executives the most powerful people in the country. Railroads were important first as an industry in themselves. Less than 35,000 miles of track existed when Lee laid down his sword at Appomattox. In 1875 railroad mileage exceeded 74,000, and the skeleton of the network was complete. By 1900 the nation had 193,000 miles of track.

The emphasis in railroad construction after 1865 was on organizing integrated systems. The lines had high fixed costs: taxes, interest on their bonds, maintenance of track and rolling stock, salaries of office personnel. A short train with half-empty cars required almost as many workers and as much fuel to operate as a long one jammed with freight or passengers. To earn profits, the railroads had to carry as much traffic as possible. They therefore spread out feeder lines to draw business to their main lines the way the root network of a tree draws water into its trunk.

Before the Civil War, as we have seen, passengers and freight could travel by rail from beyond Chicago and St. Louis to the Atlantic Coast, but only after the war did true interregional trunk lines appear. In 1861, for example, the New York Central ran from Albany to Buffalo. One could proceed from Buffalo to Chicago, but on a different company's trains. In 1867 the Central passed into the hands of "Commodore" Cornelius Vanderbilt, who had made a large fortune in the shipping business. In 1873 he integrated the Lake Shore and Michigan Southern into his empire, two years later the Michigan Central. At his death in 1877 the Central operated a network of more than 4,500 miles of track between New York City and most of the principal cities of the Middle West.

While Vanderbilt was putting together the New York Central complex, Thomas A. Scott was fusing roads to Cincinnati, Indianapolis, St. Louis, and Chicago to his Pennsylvania Railroad, which linked Pittsburgh and Philadelphia. In 1871 the Pennsylvania obtained access to New York; it soon reached Baltimore and Washington. By 1869 another important system, the Erie, extended from New York to Cleveland, Cincinnati, and St. Louis. Soon thereafter it too tapped the markets of Chicago and other principal cities. In 1874 the Baltimore and Ohio also obtained access to Chicago.

The transcontinentals were trunk lines from the start; the emptiness of the western country would have made short lines unprofitable, and builders quickly grasped the need for direct connections to eastern markets and thorough integration of feeder lines.

The dominant system builder of the Southwest was Jay Gould. With millions acquired in shady railroad and stock market ventures, Gould invaded the West in the 1870s, buying 370,000 shares of Union Pacific stock. He took over the Kansas Pacific, running from Denver to Kansas City, which he consolidated with the Union Pacific, and the Missouri Pacific, a line from Kansas City to St. Louis, which he expanded through mergers and purchases into a 5,300-mile system. Often Gould put together such properties merely to unload them on other railroads at a profit, but his grasp of the importance of integration was sound.

In the Northwest, Henry Villard, a German-born ex-newspaperman, constructed another great complex based on his control of the Northern Pacific. James J. Hill controlled the Great Northern system, still another western network.

The trunk lines interconnected and thus had to standardize many of their activities. The present system of time zones was developed in 1883 by the roads. The standard track gauge (4 feet 8½ inches) was established in 1886. Standardized signal systems and even standard methods of accounting were essential to the effective functioning of the network.

The lines sought to work out fixed rates for carrying different types of freight, charging more for valuable manufactured goods than for bulky products like coal or wheat, and they agreed to permit rate concessions to shippers when necessary to avoid hauling empty cars. To enforce cooperation, they founded regional organizations such as the Eastern Trunk Line Association and the Western Traffic Association.

The railroads stimulated the economy indirectly. Like foreign commerce and the textile in-

Minnesota's Mesabi range (shown in 1899) was developed largely with Rockefeller money. It shipped 4,000 tons of iron ore in 1892 and within a decade tripled that amount.

dustry in earlier times, they served as a "multiplier," speeding development. In 1869 they bought $41.6 million worth of cars and locomotives; in 1889, $90.8 million. Their purchases created thousands of jobs and led to countless technological advances.

Because of their voracious appetite for traffic, railroads in sparsely settled regions and in areas with undeveloped resources devoted much money and effort to stimulating local economic growth. The Louisville and Nashville, for instance, was a prime mover in the expansion of the iron industry in Alabama in the 1880s.

To speed the settlement of new regions, the land-grant railroads sold land cheaply and on easy terms, for sales meant future business as well as current income. They offered reduced rates to travelers interested in buying farms and set up "bureaus of immigration" that distributed elaborate brochures describing the wonders of the new country. Their agents greeted immigrants at the great eastern ports and tried to steer them to railroad property. Overseas branches advertised the virtues of American farmland.

Technological advances in railroading accelerated economic development in complex ways. In 1869 George Westinghouse invented the air brake. By enabling an engineer to apply the brakes to all cars simultaneously (formerly each car had to be braked separately by its own conductor or brakeman), this invention made possible revolutionary increases in the size of trains and the speed at which they could safely operate. The sleeping car, invented in 1864 by George Pullman, now came into its own.

To pull the heavier trains, more powerful locomotives were needed. They in turn produced a call for stronger and more durable rails to bear the additional weight. Steel, itself reduced in cost because of technological developments, supplied the answer, for steel rails outlasted iron many times despite the use of much heavier equipment.

Iron, Oil, and Electricity

The transformation of iron manufacturing affected the nation almost as much as railroad development. Output rose from 920,000 tons in 1860 to 10.3 million tons in 1900, but the big change came in the development of ways to mass-produce steel. Steel was expensive to manufacture until the invention in the 1850s of the Bessemer process, perfected independently by Henry Bessemer, an Englishman, and

William Kelly of Kentucky. The Bessemer process and the open-hearth method, a slower but more precise technique that enabled producers to sample the molten mass and thus control quality closely, were introduced commercially in the United States in the 1860s. In 1870 some 77,000 tons of steel were manufactured; by 1900, nearly 11.4 million tons.

Such growth would have been impossible but for the huge supplies of iron ore in the United States and the coal necessary to fire the furnaces that refined it. In the 1870s the great iron fields rimming Lake Superior began to yield their treasures. The enormous iron concentrations of the Mesabi region made a compass needle spin like a top. Mesabi ores could be mined with steam shovels, almost like gravel. Pittsburgh, surrounded by vast coal deposits, became the iron and steel capital of the country, the Minnesota ores reaching it by way of steamers on the Great Lakes and rail lines from Cleveland.

The petroleum industry expanded even more swiftly than iron and steel. Edwin L. Drake drilled the first successful well in Pennsylvania in 1859. During the Civil War, production ranged between 2 and 3 million barrels a year. By 1890 the figure had leaped to about 50 million barrels.

Before the invention of the gasoline engine and the automobile, the most important petroleum product was kerosene, which was burned in lamps. By the early 1870s, refiners had learned how to "crack" petroleum by applying high temperatures to the crude oil in order to rearrange its molecular structure, thereby increasing the percentage of kerosene yielded. By-products such as naphtha, gasoline (used in vaporized form as an illuminating gas), rhigolene (a local anesthetic), cymogene (a coolant for refrigerating machines), and many lubricants and waxes began to appear on the market. At the same time, a great increase in the supply of crude oil—especially after the German-born chemist Herman Frasch perfected a method for removing sulfur from low-quality petroleum—drove prices down. These circumstances put a premium on refining efficiency. Larger plants using expensive machinery and employing skilled technicians became more important.

Two other important new industries were the telephone and electric light businesses. Both were typical of the period, being products of technical advances and intimately related to the growth of a high-speed, urban civilization that put great stress on communication. The telephone was invented in 1876 by Alexander Graham Bell, who had been led to the study of acoustics through his interest in the education of the deaf. The invention soon proved its practical value. By 1900 there were almost 800,000 phones in the country, twice the total for all of Europe. The American Telephone and Telegraph Company, a consolidation of over 100 local systems, dominated the business.

When Western Union, the telegraph company, realized the importance of the telephone, it tried for a time to compete with Bell by developing a machine of its own. The man it commissioned to devise this machine was Thomas A. Edison, but Bell's patents proved unassailable. Edison had already made a number of contributions toward solving what he called the "mysteries of electrical force," including a multiplex telegraph capable of sending four messages over a single wire at the same time. At Menlo Park, New Jersey, he built the prototype of the modern research laboratory, where specific problems could be attacked on a mass scale by a team of trained specialists.

Edison's most significant achievement was unquestionably his perfection of the incandescent lamp, or electric light bulb. Others before Edison had experimented with the idea of producing light by passing electricity through a filament in a vacuum. Always, however, the filaments quickly burned out. Edison tried hundreds of fibers before producing, in 1879, a carbonized filament that would glow brightly in a vacuum tube for as long as 170 hours without crumbling.

In 1882 his Edison Illuminating Company opened a power station in New York and began to supply current for lighting to 85 consumers. Soon central stations were springing up everywhere until, by 1898, there were about 3,000 in the country.

Electricity was soon used to produce power as well as light. The substitution of electricity for steam power in factories was as liberating as that of steam for waterpower before the Civil War. Small, safe electric motors replaced dangerous and cumbersome mazes of belts and wheels.

Competition and Monopoly: The Railroads

During the post–Civil War era, expansion in industry went hand in hand with concentration. The principal cause of this trend, aside from the obvious economies resulting from large-scale production and the growing importance of expensive machinery, was the downward trend of prices after 1873. The deflation, caused mainly by the failure of the money supply to keep pace with the rapid increase in the volume of goods produced, lasted until 1896 or 1897.

Falling prices kept a steady pressure on profit margins, and this led to increased production and thus to intense competition for markets. According to contemporary economists, competition advanced the public interest by keeping prices low and assuring the most efficient producer the largest profit. Up to a point, it accomplished these purposes in the years after 1865, but it had side effects that injured both the economy and society as a whole. Railroad managers, for instance, found it impossible to enforce "official" rate schedules and maintain their regional associations once competitive pressures mounted. In 1865 it had cost from 96 cents to $2.15 per 100 pounds, depending on the class of freight, to ship goods from New York to Chicago. In 1888 rates ranged from 35 cents to 75 cents.

Competition cut deeply into railroad profits, causing the lines to seek desperately to increase volume. They did so chiefly by reducing rates still more, on a selective basis. They gave rebates (secret reductions below the published rates) to large shippers in order to capture their business. In the 1870s the New York Central regularly reduced the rates important shippers were charged by 50 to 80 percent. One large Utica dry goods merchant received a rate of 9 cents while others paid 33 cents.

Railroad officials disliked rebating but found no way to avoid the practice. In extreme cases the railroads even gave large shippers drawbacks, which were rebates on the business of the shippers' competitors!

Besides rebating, railroads battled directly with one another in ways damaging both to themselves and to the public. To make up for losses forced on them by competitive pressures, railroads charged higher rates at way points along their tracks where no competition existed. Frequently it cost more to ship a product a short distance than a longer one. Rochester, New York, was served only by the New York Central. In the 1870s it cost 30 cents to transport a barrel of flour from Rochester to New York City, a distance of 350 miles. At the same time, flour could be shipped from Minneapolis to New York, a distance of well over 1,000 miles, for only 20 cents a barrel.

Although cheap transportation stimulated the economy, few persons benefited from cutthroat competition. Small shippers—and all businessmen in cities and towns with limited rail outlets—suffered; railroad discrimination speeded the concentration of industry in large corporations located in major centers. The instability of rates even troubled interests like the middle western flour millers who benefited from the competitive situation, for it hampered planning. Nor could manufacturers who received rebates be entirely happy, since few could be sure that some other producer was not getting a larger reduction.

Probably the worst sufferers were the roads themselves. The loss of revenue resulting from rate cutting, combined with inflated debts, put most of them in grave difficulty when faced with a downturn in the business cycle. In 1876 two-fifths of all railroad bonds were in default; three years later 65 lines were bankrupt. Wits called Samuel J. Tilden, the 1876 Democratic presidential candidate, the "Great Forecloser" because of his work reorganizing bankrupt railroads at this time.

Since the public would not countenance bankrupt railroads going out of business, these companies were placed in the hands of court-appointed receivers. The receivers, however, seldom provided efficient management and had no funds at their disposal for new equipment.

During the 1880s the major roads responded to these pressures by building or buying lines in order to create interregional systems. These were the first giant corporations, capitalized in the hundreds of millions of dollars. Their enormous cost led to another wave of bankruptcies when a depression struck in the 1890s. The consequent reorganizations brought most of the big systems under the control of financiers, notably J. Pierpont Morgan, and such other private bankers as Kuhn, Loeb of New York and Lee, Higginson of Boston. The economic historian A. D. Noyes described in 1904 what the bankers did: "Bondholders were requested to scale down interest charges, receiving new stock in compensation. . . . [The bankers] combined to guarantee that the requisite money should be raised. . . . Fixed charges were diminished and a sufficient fund for road improvement and new equipment was provided."

Critics called the reorganizations "Morganizations." Representatives of the bankers sat on the board of every line they saved, and their influence was predominant. They consistently opposed rate wars, rebating, and other competitive practices. In effect, control of the railroad network became centralized, even though the companies maintained their separate existences and operated in a seemingly independent manner. When Morgan died in 1913, "Morgan men" dominated the boards of the New York Central, the Erie, the Atchison, Topeka and Santa Fe; and many other lines.

Competition and Monopoly: Steel

The iron and steel industry was also intensely competitive. Despite the trend toward higher production, demand varied erratically from year to year, even from month to month. In good times producers built new facilities, only to suffer heavy losses when demand declined. The forward rush of technology put a tremendous emphasis on efficiency; expensive plants quickly became obsolete. Improved transportation facilities allowed manufacturers in widely separated places to compete with one another.

The kingpin of the industry was Andrew Carnegie. Carnegie was born in Scotland and came to the United States in 1848 at the age of 12. His first job, as a bobbin boy in a cotton mill, brought him $1.20 a week, but his talents fitted the times perfectly, and he rose rapidly: to Western Union messenger boy, to telegrapher, to private secretary, to railroad manager. He saved his money, made some shrewd investments, and by 1868 had an income of $50,000 a year.

At about this time he decided to specialize in the iron business. Carnegie possessed great talent as a salesman, boundless faith in the future of the country, an uncanny knack of choosing topflight subordinates, and enough ruthlessness to survive in the iron and steel jungle. Where other steelmen built new plants in good times, he preferred to expand in bad times, when it cost far less to do so. During the 1870s, he later recalled, "many of my friends needed money. . . . [I] bought out five or six of them. That is what gave me my leading interest in this steel business."

Carnegie grasped the importance of technological improvements. He was also a driver of men and a merciless competitor. When a plant manager announced, "We broke all records for making steel last week," Carnegie replied, "Congratulations! *Why not do it every week?*" By 1890 the Carnegie Steel Company dominated the industry, and its output increased nearly tenfold during the next decade. Profits soared. Alarmed by Carnegie's increasing control of the industry, the makers of finished steel products such as barbed wire and tubing began to combine and to consider entering the primary field. Carnegie, his competitive temper aroused, threatened to turn to finished products himself. A colossal steel war seemed imminent.

However, Carnegie longed to retire to devote himself to philanthropic work. He believed that wealth entailed social responsibilities and that it was a disgrace to die rich. When J. P. Morgan approached him through an intermediary with an offer to buy him out, he assented readily. In 1901 Morgan put together United States Steel, the "world's first billion-dollar corporation." This combination included all the Carnegie properties, the Federal Steel Company (Carnegie's largest competitor), and such important fabricators of finished products as the American Steel and Wire Company, the American Tin Plate Company, and the National Tube Company. Vast reserves of Minnesota iron ore and a fleet of Great Lakes ore steamers were also included. U.S. Steel was capitalized at $1.4 billion, about twice the value of its component properties but not necessarily an overestimation of its profit-earning capacity. The owners of Carnegie Steel received $492 million, of which $250 million went to Carnegie himself.

Competition and Monopoly: Oil

The pattern of fierce competition leading to combination and monopoly is well illustrated by the history of the petroleum industry. Irresistible pressures pushed the refiners into a brutal struggle to dominate the business. Production of crude oil, subject to the uncertainties of prospecting and drilling, fluctuated constantly and without regard for need. In general, output surged far ahead of demand.

By the 1870s the largest oil-refining center was

John D. Rockefeller as monarch of the railroads and the Standard Oil monopoly; a cartoon from *Puck*.

Cleveland, chiefly because the New York Central and Erie railroads competed fiercely for its oil trade and the Erie Canal offered an alternative route. The Standard Oil Company of Cleveland, founded in 1870 by a 31-year-old merchant named John D. Rockefeller, emerged as the giant among the refiners. Rockefeller exploited every possible technical advance and employed fair means and foul to persuade competitors either to sell out or to join forces. By 1879 he controlled 90 percent of the nation's oil-refining capacity, along with a network of oil pipelines and large reserves of petroleum in the ground.

Standard Oil emerged victorious in the competitive wars because Rockefeller and his associates were the toughest and most imaginative fighters as well as the most efficient refiners in the business. In addition to obtaining from the railroads a 10 percent rebate and drawbacks on its competitors' shipments, Standard Oil cut prices locally to force small independents to sell out or face ruin. The company employed spies to track down the customers of independents and offer them oil at bargain prices. Bribery was also a Standard practice; the reformer Henry Demarest Lloyd quipped that the company had done everything to the Pennsylvania legislature except refine it.

Although a bold planner and a daring taker of necessary risks, Rockefeller was far too orderly and astute to enjoy the free-swinging battles that plagued his industry. He sought efficiency, order, and stability. His forte was meticulous attention to detail: Stories are told of his ordering the number of drops of solder used to seal oil cans reduced from 40 to 39 and of his insisting that the manager of one of his refineries account for 750 missing barrel bungs. Not miserliness but a profound grasp of the economies of large-scale production explains this behavior. He competed ruthlessly, not primarily to crush other refiners but to persuade them to join with him, to share the business peaceably and rationally so that all could profit.

Having achieved his monopoly, Rockefeller stabilized and structured it by creating a new type of business organization, the trust. Standard Oil was an Ohio corporation, prohibited by local law from owning plants in other states or holding stock in out-of-state corporations. As Rockefeller and his associates took over dozens of companies with facilities scattered across the country, serious legal and managerial difficulties arose. How could these many organizations be integrated with Standard Oil of Ohio?

A rotund, genial little Pennsylvania lawyer named Samuel C. T. Dodd came up with an answer to this question in 1879. The stock of Standard of Ohio and of all the other companies that the Rockefeller interests had swallowed up was turned over to nine trustees, who were empowered to "exercise general supervision" over all the properties. Stockholders received in exchange trust certificates, on which dividends were paid. This seemingly simple device brought order to the petroleum business. Competition almost disappeared; prices steadied; profits skyrocketed.

From the company's point of view, monopoly was not the purpose of the trust—that had been achieved before the device was invented. Centralization of the management of diverse and far-flung operations in the interest of efficiency was its chief function. Standard Oil headquarters in New York became the brain of a complex network where information from salaried managers in the field was collected and digested, where top managerial decisions were made, and whence orders went out to armies of drillers, refiners, scientists, and salesmen.

Competition and Monopoly: Retailing and Utilities

The pattern of competition leading to dominance by a few great companies was repeated in many other businesses. The period saw the growth of huge department stores by merchants such as Alexander T. Stewart in New York, John Wanamaker in Philadelphia, and Marshall Field in Chicago. In life insurance, an immense expansion took place. High-pressure salesmanship prevailed; agents gave rebates to customers by shaving their own commissions; companies stole crack agents from their rivals and raided new territories. By 1900, three giants dominated the industry—Equitable, New York Life, and Mutual Life, each with approximately $1 billion of insurance in force.

The telephone and electric lighting industries were also plagued by competition. Bell and Edison had to fight mighty court battles to protect their patents. Western Union hired Edison himself in a futile effort to get around Bell's telephone patents. In 1892 Edison merged with his most powerful competitor to form General Electric. It and the Westinghouse Company thereafter dominated in business.

Americans' Reactions to Big Business

The expansion of industry and its concentration in fewer and fewer hands changed the way many people felt about the role of government in economic and social affairs. The fact that Americans disliked powerful governments in general and strict regulation of the economy in particular had never meant that they objected to all government activity in the economic sphere. Banking laws, tariffs, internal-improvement legislation, and the granting of public land to railroads are only the most obvious of the economic regulations enforced in the 19th century by both the federal government and the states. Americans saw no contradiction between government activities of this type and the free enterprise philosophy, for such laws were intended to release human energy and thus increase the area in which freedom could operate. Tariffs stimulated industry and created new jobs, railroad grants opened up new regions for development, and so on.

The growth of huge industrial and financial organizations and the increasing complexity of economic relations frightened people yet made them at the same time greedy for more of the goods and services the new society was turning out. To many, the great new corporations and trusts resembled Frankenstein's monster—marvelous and powerful but a grave threat to society. The astute James Bryce described the changes in *The American Commonwealth* (1888):

> *Modern civilization . . . has become more exacting. It discerns more benefits which the organized power of government can secure, and grows more anxious to attain them. Men live fast, and are impatient of the slow working of natural laws. . . . Unlimited competition seems to press too hard on the weak. The power of groups of men organized by incorporation as joint-stock companies, or of small knots of rich men acting in combination, has developed with unexpected strength in unexpected ways, overshadowing individuals and even communities, and showing that the very freedom of association which men sought to secure by law . . . may, under the shelter of the law, ripen into a new form of tyranny.*

To some extent public fear of the industrial giants reflected concern about monopoly. If Standard Oil dominated oil refining, it might raise prices inordinately at vast cost to consumers. Although in isolated cases monopolists did raise prices unreasonably, generally they did not. On the contrary, prices tended to fall until by the 1890s a veritable "consumer's millennium" had arrived.

Far more important in causing resentment was the fear that the monopolists were destroying economic opportunity and threatening democratic institutions. It was not the wealth of tycoons like Carnegie and Rockefeller and Morgan so much as their influence that worried people. In the face of the growing disparity between rich and poor, could republican institutions survive?

Some observers believed either autocracy or a form of revolutionary socialism to be almost inevitable. In 1890 former president Hayes pondered "the wrong and evils of the money-piling tendency of our country, which is changing laws, government, and morals and giving all power to the rich" and decided that he was going to become a "nihilist." John Boyle O'Reilly, a liberal Catholic journalist, wrote in 1886: "There is something worse than Anarchy, bad as that is; and it is irresponsible power in the hands of mere wealth." William Cook, a New York lawyer, warned in *The Corporation Problem* (1891) that "colossal aggregations of capital" were "dangerous to the republic."

As criticism mounted, business leaders rose to their own defense. Rockefeller described in graphic terms the chaotic conditions that plagued the oil industry before the rise of Standard Oil:

> *It seemed absolutely necessary to extend the market for oil . . . and also greatly improve the process of refining so that oil could be made and sold cheaply, yet with a profit. We proceeded to buy the largest and best refining concerns and centralized the administration of them with a view to securing greater economy and efficiency.*

Carnegie, in an essay published in 1889, insisted that the concentration of wealth was necessary if humanity was to progress, softening this "Gospel of Wealth" by insisting that the rich must use their money in the manner "best calculated to produce the most beneficial results for the community."

Reformers: George, Bellamy, Lloyd

The voices of the critics were louder, if not necessarily more influential. In 1879 Henry George published *Progress and Poverty,* a forthright attack on the maldistribution of wealth in the United States. George argued that labor was the true and only source of capital. Observing the speculative fever of the West, which enabled landowners to reap profits merely by holding property while population increased, George proposed a property tax that would confiscate this "unearned increment." The value of land depended on society and should belong to society. This "single tax," as others called it, would bring in so much money that no other taxes would be necessary, and the government would have plenty of funds to establish new schools, museums, theaters, and other badly needed social and cultural services. Though the single tax was never adopted, George's ideas attracted enthusiastic attention. Single tax clubs sprang up throughout the nation, and *Progress and Poverty* became a best-seller.

Even more spectacular was the reception afforded *Looking Backward, 2000–1887,* a utopian novel written in 1888 by Edward Bellamy. This book, which sold over a million copies in its first few years, described a future America that was completely socialized, all economic activity carefully planned. Bellamy suggested that the ideal socialist state, in which all citizens shared equally, would arrive without revolution or violence. The trend toward consolidation would continue, he predicted, until one monster trust controlled all economic activity. At this point everyone would realize that nationalization was essential.

A third influential attack on monopoly was that of Henry Demarest Lloyd, whose *Wealth Against Commonwealth* (1894) denounced the Standard Oil Company. Lloyd's forceful, uncomplicated arguments and his copious references to official documents made *Wealth Against Commonwealth* utterly convincing to thousands.

The popularity of these publications indicates that the trend toward monopoly in the United States worried many people. But despite the drastic changes suggested in their pages, none of these writers questioned the underlying values of the middle-class majority. They insisted that reform could be accomplished without serious inconvenience to any individual or class.

Nor did most of their millions of readers seriously consider trying to apply the reformers' ideas. The national discontent was apparently not as profound as the popularity of these works might suggest. If John D. Rockefeller became the bogeyman of American industry because of Lloyd's attack, no one prevented him from also becoming the richest man in the United States.

Reformers: The Marxists

By the 1870s the ideas of Marxian socialists were beginning to penetrate the United States, and in 1877 a Marxist Socialist Labor party was founded. Laurence Gronlund in *The Cooperative Commonwealth* (1884) made the first serious attempt to explain Marx's ideas to Americans.

Capitalism, Gronlund claimed, contained the seeds of its own destruction. The state ought to own all the means of production, middlemen were "parasites," speculators "vampires." "Capital and Labor," he wrote in one of the rare humorous lines in his book, "are just as harmonious as roast beef and a hungry stomach." Gronlund expected the millennium to arrive in an orderly manner.

The leading voice of the Socialist Labor party, Daniel De Leon, was a different type. He was born in the West Indies and in the 1870s emigrated to the United States, where he was progressively attracted by the ideas of Henry George, then Edward Bellamy, and finally Marx. Ordinarily mild-mannered and kindly, when he put pen to paper, he became a doctrinaire revolutionary. He insisted that industrial workers could improve their lot only by adopting socialism and joining the Socialist Labor party. He paid scant attention, however, to the practical needs or even to the opinions of rank-and-file working people. The labor historian Philip Taft aptly characterized him as a "verbal revolutionary."

Government Reactions to Big Business: Railroad Regulation

Political action to check big business came first on the state level and dealt chiefly with the regulation of railroads. Although a number of New England states established railroad commissions before the Civil War, strict regulation was largely the result of agitation by western farm groups, principally the

National Grange of the Patrons of Husbandry. The Grange, founded in 1867 by Oliver H. Kelley, was created to provide social and cultural benefits for isolated rural communities. As it spread and grew in influence, the movement became political too. "Granger" candidates won control of a number of state legislatures in the West and the South. Railroad regulation invariably followed.

The Illinois Granger laws were typical. They established "reasonable maximum rates" and outlawed "unjust discrimination." The legislature also and set up a commission to enforce the laws and punish violators. The railroads protested, insisting that they were being deprived of property without due process of law. In *Munn* v. *Illinois* (1877), a case that involved the owner of a grain elevator who refused to comply with a state warehouse act, the Supreme Court upheld the constitutionality of this kind of law. Any business that served a public interest, such as a railroad or a grain warehouse, was subject to state control, the justices ruled. Legislatures might fix maximum charges; if the charges seemed unreasonable, the parties concerned should direct their complaints to the legislatures or to the voters, not to the courts.

Regulation of the railroad network by the individual states was inefficient, and in some cases the commissions were incompetent and even corrupt. When the Supreme Court, in the Wabash case (1886), declared unconstitutional an Illinois regulation outlawing long and short-haul inequalities, federal action became necessary. The Wabash, St. Louis and Pacific Railroad had charged 25 cents per 100 pounds for shipping goods from Gilman, Illinois, to New York City but only 15 cents from Peoria, which was 86 miles farther from New York. Illinois judges had held this to be illegal, but the Supreme Court decided that Illinois could not regulate interstate shipments.

Congress in 1887 filled the gap by passing the Interstate Commerce Act. All charges made by railroads "shall be reasonable and just," the act stated. Rebates, drawbacks, inconsistent rates, and other competitive practices were declared unlawful, and so were their monopolistic counterparts, pools and traffic-sharing agreements. Railroads were required to publish schedules of rates and were forbidden to change them without due public notice. Most important, the law established the Interstate Commerce Commission (ICC), the first federal regulatory board, to supervise the affairs of railroads, investigate complaints, and issue cease and desist orders when the roads acted illegally.

The Interstate Commerce Act broke new ground, yet it was neither radical nor particularly effective. Its terms were contradictory some having been designed to stimulate competition, others to penalize it. The chairman of the commission soon characterized the law as an "anomaly." It sought, he said, to "enforce competition" at the same time that it outlawed "the acts and inducements by which competition is ordinarily effected." The new commission had less power than the law seemed to give it. It could not fix rates, only take the roads to court when it considered rates unreasonably high. Such cases could be extremely complicated; applying the law was "like cutting a path through a jungle." With the truth so hard to determine and the burden of proof on the commission, the courts in nearly every instance decided in favor of the railroads.

Nevertheless, by describing so clearly the right of Congress to regulate private corporations engaged in interstate commerce, the Interstate Commerce Act challenged the philosophy of laissez-faire. Later legislation made the commission more effective. The commission also served as the prototype for a host of similar federal administrative authorities, such as the Federal Communications Commission (1934).

Government Reactions to Big Business: The Sherman Antitrust Act

As with railroad legislation, the first antitrust laws originated in the states, but they were southern and western states with relatively little industry, and most of the statutes were vaguely worded and ill-enforced. Federal action came in 1890 with the passage of the Sherman Antitrust Act. Any combination "in the form of trust or otherwise" that was "in restraint of trade or commerce among the several states, or with foreign nations" was declared illegal. Persons forming such combinations were subject to fines of $5,000 and a year in jail. Individuals and businesses suffering losses because of actions that violated the law were authorized to sue in the federal courts for triple damages.

Whereas the Interstate Commerce Act sought to outlaw the excesses of competition, the Sherman Act was supposed to restore competition. If businessmen joined together to "restrain" (monopolize) trade in a particular field, they should be punished, and their deeds undone. But the Sherman Act was rather loosely worded—Thurman Arnold, a modern authority, once said that it made it "a crime to violate a vaguely stated economic policy." Critics have argued that the congressmen were more interested in quieting the public clamor for action against the trusts than in actually breaking up any of the new combinations. This was certainly one of their objectives. However, they were trying to solve a new problem and were not sure how to proceed. A law with teeth too sharp might do more harm than good. Most Americans assumed that the courts would deal with the details, as they always had in common-law matters.

In fact the Supreme Court quickly emasculated the Sherman Act. In *United States* v. *E. C. Knight Company* (1895) it held that the American Sugar Refining Company had not violated the law by taking over a number of important competitors. Although the Sugar Trust now controlled about 98 percent of all sugar refining in the United States, it was not restraining trade. "Doubtless the power to control the manufacture of a given thing involves in a certain sense the control of its disposition," the Court said in one of the great judicial understatements of all time. "Although the exercise of that power may result in bringing the operation of commerce into play, it does not control it, and affects it only incidentally and indirectly."

If the creation of the Sugar Trust did not violate the Sherman Act, it seemed unlikely that any other combination of manufacturers could be convicted under the law. But in several cases in 1898 and 1899 the Supreme Court ruled that agreements to fix prices or divide markets did violate the act. These decisions precipitated a wave of outright mergers in which a handful of large corporations swallowed up hundreds of smaller ones. Presumably mergers were not illegal. When, Andrew Carnegie was asked by a committee of the House of Representatives some years after his retirement to explain how he had dared participate in the formation of the U.S. Steel Corporation, he replied: "Nobody ever mentioned the Sherman Act to me, that I remember."

The Union Movement

At the time of the Civil War, most union members were cigarmakers, printers, carpenters, and other skilled artisans. Aside from ironworkers, railroad workers, and miners, few industrial laborers were organized. Nevertheless, the union was the workers' response to the big corporation: a combination designed to eliminate competition for jobs and to provide efficient organization for labor.

After 1865 the growth of national craft unions, which had been stimulated by labor dissatisfaction during the Civil War, quickened perceptibly. In 1866 a federation of these organizations, the National Labor Union, was founded, but most of its leaders were out of touch with the practical needs and aspirations of workers. They opposed the wage system, strikes, and anything that increased the laborers' sense of being members of the working class.

Far more remarkable was the Knights of Labor, founded in 1869 by Philadelphia garment workers. Its head, Uriah S. Stephens, was a reformer of wide interests. He and his successor, Terence V. Powderly, supported political objectives that had no direct connection with working conditions, such as currency reform and the curbing of land speculation. They rejected the idea that workers must resign themselves to remaining wage earners. "There is no good reason," Powderly wrote in his autobiography, "why labor cannot, through cooperation, own and operate mines, factories, and railroads." The leading Knights saw no contradiction between their denunciation of "soulless" monopolies and "drones" like bankers and lawyers and their talk of "combining all branches of trade in one common brotherhood." Such muddled thinking led the Knights to attack the wage system and to frown on strikes as "acts of private warfare."

If the Knights had one foot in the past, they also had one foot in the future. They rejected the traditional grouping of workers by crafts and developed a concept closely resembling modern industrial unionism. They welcomed blacks (though mostly in segregated locals), women, and immigrants, and they accepted unskilled workers as well as artisans. The eight-hour day was one of their basic demands.

The growth of the union, however, had little to do with ideology. As late as 1879 it had fewer than 10,000 members. But between 1882 and 1886 suc-

cessful strikes by local "assemblies," including one against the hated Jay Gould's Missouri Pacific Railroad, brought recruits by the thousands. The membership passed 110,000 in 1885 and the next year soared beyond the 700,000 mark. Alas, sudden prosperity was too much for the Knights. Its national leadership was unable to control local groups. A number of poorly planned strikes failed dismally, and the public was alienated by sporadic acts of violence and intimidation. Disillusioned recruits began to drift away.

Circumstances largely fortuitous caused the collapse of the organization. By 1886 the movement for the eight-hour day had gained wide support among workers. In Chicago, a center of the eight-hour movement, about 80,000 workers were involved, and a small group of anarchists was trying to take advantage of the excitement to win support. When a striker was killed in a fracas at the McCormick Harvesting Machine Company, the anarchists called a protest meeting on May 4, at Haymarket Square. Police intervened to break up the meeting, and someone—whose identity has never been established—hurled a bomb into their ranks. Seven policemen were killed and many others injured.

The American Federation of Labor

Organized labor, especially the Knights, suffered heavily as a result of the Haymarket bombing. No tie with the Knights could be established, but the union had been closely connected with the eight-hour agitation, and the public tended to associate that with violence and radicalism. Its membership declined dramatically until soon the union ceased to exist.

Its place was taken by the American Federation of Labor, a combination of national craft unions established in 1886. Its principal leaders, Adolph Strasser and Samuel Gompers of the Cigarmakers Union, concentrated on organizing skilled workers and fighting for "bread and butter" issues such as higher wages and shorter hours. "Our organization does not consist of idealists," Strasser explained to a congressional committee. "We do not control the production of the world. That is controlled by the employers. . . . I look first to cigars."

The AFL accepted the fact that most workers would remain wage earners all their lives and tried to develop in them a sense of common purpose and pride in their skills and station. Rank-and-file AFL members were naturally eager to win wage increases and other benefits, but most also valued their unions for the companionship they provided, the sense of belonging to a group. In other words, despite statements such as Strasser's, unions, in and out of the AFL, were a kind of club as well as a means of defending and advancing their members' material interests.

The chief weapon of the federation was the strike. "I have my own philosophy and my own dreams," Gompers once told a left-wing French politician, "but first and foremost I want to increase the workingman's welfare year by year. . . . The French workers waste their economic force by their political divisions."

Gompers's approach to labor problems produced solid, if unspectacular, growth for the AFL. Unions with a total of about 150,000 members formed the federation in 1886. By 1892 the membership had reached 250,000, and in 1901 it passed the million mark.

Labor Militancy Rebuffed

The stress of the AFL on the strike weapon reflected the increasing militancy of labor. Workers felt themselves threatened by the growing size and power of their corporate employers, the substitution of machines for human skills, and the invasion of foreign workers willing to accept substandard wages. The average employer behaved like a tyrant when dealing with workers. He discharged any who tried to organize unions; he hired scabs to replace strikers; he frequently failed to provide the most rudimentary protections against injury on the job. Most employers would not bargain with labor collectively.

The industrialists of the period were not all ogres; they were as alarmed by the rapid changes of the times as their workers, and since they had more at stake materially, they were probably more frightened by the uncertainties. Deflation, technological change, and intense competition kept even the most successful under constant pressure. Their thinking was remarkably confused. They considered workers who joined unions "disloyal," yet at the same time they treated labor as a commodity to be purchased as cheaply as possible. When labor was scarce, employers resisted demands for higher wages by arguing that the price of labor was controlled by its productivity; when it was plentiful, they justified reducing wages by referring to the law of supply and demand.

Thus capital and labor were often spoiling for a fight. In 1877 a great railroad strike convulsed much of the nation. It began on the Baltimore and Ohio system in response to a wage cut and spread until about two-thirds of the railroad mileage of the country had been shut down. Violence broke out; rail yards were put to the torch. Frightened businessmen formed militia companies to patrol the streets of Chicago and other cities. Eventually, President Hayes sent federal troops to restore order, and the strike collapsed.

The disturbances of 1877 were a response to a business slump, those of the next decade a response to good times. Twice as many strikes occurred in 1886 as in any previous year. The situation was so disturbing that President Grover Cleveland, in the first presidential message devoted to labor problems, urged Congress to create a voluntary arbitration board to aid in settling labor disputes—a remarkable suggestion for a man of Cleveland's conservative, laissez-faire approach to economic issues.

In 1892 a violent strike broke out among silver miners at Coeur d'Alene, Idaho, and a far more important clash shook Andrew Carnegie's Homestead steel plant near Pittsburgh when strikers attacked 300 private guards brought in to protect strikebreakers. The Homestead affair was part of a struggle between capital and labor in the steel industry. The steelmen insisted that the workers were holding back progress by resisting technological advances, while the workers believed that the company was refusing to share the fruits of more efficient operation fairly. The defeat of the 24,000-member Amalgamated Association of Iron and Steel Workers destroyed unionism as an effective force in the steel industry and set back the progress of organized labor all over the country.

As in the case of the Haymarket bombing, the activities of radicals on the fringe of the dispute turned the public against the steelworkers. The boss of Homestead was Henry Clay Frick, a tough-minded foe of unions. Frick made the decision to bring in strikebreakers and to employ Pinkerton detectives to protect them. During the course of the strike, Alexander Berkman, an anarchist unconnected with the union, burst into Frick's office and shot him. Frick was only slightly wounded, but the attack brought him much sympathy and unjustly discredited the strikers.

The most important strike of the period took place in 1894. It began when the workers at George Pullman's Palace Car factory outside Chicago walked out in protest against wage cuts. Some Pullman workers belonged to the American Railway Union, headed by Eugene V. Debs, and the union voted to refuse to handle trains with Pullman cars. The resulting strike tied up trunk lines running in and out of Chicago. The railroad owners appealed to President Cleveland to send troops to preserve order. On the pretext that the soldiers were needed to ensure the movement of the mails, Cleveland agreed. When Debs defied a federal injunction to end the walkout, he was jailed for contempt, and the strike was broken.

Whither America, Whither Democracy?

Each year more of the nation's wealth and power seemed to fall into fewer hands. As with the railroads, other industries were coming to be influenced, if not completely dominated, by bankers. The firm of J. P. Morgan and Company controlled many railroads; the largest steel, electrical, agricultural machinery, rubber, and shipping companies; two life insurance companies; and a number of banks. By 1913 Morgan and the Rockefeller National City Bank group between them could name 341 directors to 112 corporations worth over $22.2 billion. The "Money Trust," a loose but potent fraternity of financiers, seemed fated to become the ultimate monopoly.

Centralization increased efficiency in industries that used expensive machinery to turn out goods for the masses and for markets where close coordination of output, distribution, and sales was important. The public benefited immensely from the productive efficiency of the new empires. Living standards rose. But the trend toward giantism raised doubts. With ownership falling into fewer hands, what would be the ultimate effect of big business on American democracy? What did it mean for ordinary people when a few tycoons possessed huge fortunes and commanded such influence even on Congress and the courts?

The crushing of the Pullman strike demonstrated the power of the courts to break strikes by issuing injunctions. And the courts seemed concerned only with protecting the interests of the rich and powerful. Particularly ominous for organized labor was the fact that the federal government based its request for the injunction that broke the strike on the Sherman Antitrust Act, arguing that the American Railway Union was a combination in restraint of trade.

While serving his sentence for contempt, Eugene Debs was visited by a number of prominent socialists who sought to convert him to their cause. One gave him a copy of Karl Marx's *Capital,* which he found too dull to finish, but he did read *Looking Backward* and *Wealth Against Commonwealth.* In 1897 he became a socialist.

Milestones

1859 First oil well drilled in Pennsylvania
1868 Carnegie Steel Company formed
1869 George Westinghouse invents the air brake
Knights of Labor founded
1870 Standard Oil Company formed
1870–1890 Railroad trunk lines completed
1876 Alexander Graham Bell invents the telephone
1877 Great Railroad Strike
Munn v. *Illinois* upholds state regulatory laws
1879 Thomas Edison invents the electric light
Henry George, *Progress and Poverty*
1884 Laurence Gronlund, *The Cooperative Commonwealth*
1886 Haymarket bombing
American Federation of Labor founded
1887 Interstate Commerce Act
1888 Edward Bellamy, *Looking Backward, 2000–1887*
1889 Andrew Carnegie, "Gospel of Wealth"
1890 Sherman Antitrust Act
1892 Homestead strike
General Electric Company formed
1894 Pullman strike
Henry Demarest Lloyd, *Wealth Against Commonwealth*
1895 *United States* v. *E. C. Knight Company* weakens Sherman Act
1901 U.S. Steel Corporation formed

Supplementary Reading

Of works dealing with industrial growth, E. C. Kirkland, **Industry Comes of Age** (1961), is the best general introduction. Matthew Josephson, **The Robber Barons** (1934), is highly critical but provocative. A. D. Chandler, Jr., **The Visible Hand** (1977), covers the way businesses were organized and managed.

For the railroad industry, consult A. D. Chandler, Jr., **Railroads: The Nation's First Big Business** (1965), J. F. Stover, **American Railroads** (1961), and Julius Grodinsky, **Transcontinental Railway Strategy** (1962). The iron and steel business is discussed in detail in J. F. Wall, **Andrew Carnegie** (1970), and Peter Temin, **Iron and Steel in Nineteenth-Century America** (1964), an economic analysis. For the oil industry, see Carl Solberg, **Oil Power** (1976), a good survey, and for more detail, H. F. Williamson and A. R. Daum, **The American Petroleum Industry: Age of Illumination** (1959). The electrical industry is discussed in Matthew Josephson, **Edison** (1959). On the telephone, see John Brooks, *Telephone* (1976), and R. V. Bruce, **Alexander Graham Bell** (1973).

Many of these volumes deal with the problems of competition and monopoly. See also Gabriel Kolko, **Railroads and Regulation** (1965), which is critical of both railroad leaders and government policy. H. D. Lloyd, **Wealth Against Commonwealth** (1894), attacks the oil trust mercilessly.

For the radical critics see J. L. Thomas, **Alternative Americas: Henry George, Edward Bellamy, Henry Demarest Lloyd** (1983), and also the radicals' own writings. On the growth of unions see David Montgomery, **Beyond Equality** (1967), Harold Livesay, **Samuel Gompers and Organized Labor in America** (1978), and Nick Salvatore, **Eugene V. Debs** (1982). The important strikes and labor violence of the period are covered in R. V. Bruce, **1877: Year of Violence** (1959), Paul Arvich, **The Haymarket Tragedy** (1984), Leon Wolff, **Lockout** (1965), and Almont Lindsey, **The Pullman Strike** (1942).

The background of government regulation of industry is treated in Sidney Fine, **Laissez-Faire and the General-Welfare State** (1956) and J. A. Garraty, **The New Commonwealth** (1968). Other useful volumes include Ari and Olive Hoogenboom, **A History of the ICC** (1976), and G. W. Miller, **Railroads and the Granger Laws** (1971).

CHAPTER 20

American Society in the Industrial Age

■ ■ ■ ■ ■ THE INDUSTRIALIZATION THAT FOLlowed the Civil War profoundly affected every aspect of American life. New machines, improvements in transportation and communication, the appearance of the great corporation with its uncertain implications for the future—all made deep impressions on the economy and on the social and cultural development of the nation. The growth of cities and the influx of tens of thousands of non-English-speaking immigrants who knew little about urban life had large effects on the lives of all Americans.

Middle-Class Life

In so large and diverse a country as the United States, it is hard to generalize about how people lived and worked. Some, as we have just seen, became fabulously wealthy in the new industrial society, in no small part because neither the federal government nor the states taxed their incomes.

Members of the professions and the shopkeepers, small manufacturers, skilled craftsmen, and established farmers that made up the middle class lived in varying degrees of comfort. A family with an annual income of $1,000 in the 1880s would have no need to skimp on food, clothing, or shelter.

In such families, husbands and wives continued to maintain their separate spheres, the men going off to their shops and offices, the women devoting their main energies to supervising or caring for children and household. Middle-class women maintained the trend toward having fewer children. Much stress was placed on their being "little ladies and gentlemen," meaning having good manners and doing what their elders told them to do. This was the height of Victorian prudery, so in most families "young people" (today we call them teenagers) were closely chaperoned when in the company of "members of the opposite sex."

Wage Earners

Wage earners felt the full force of the industrial tide, being affected in countless ways, some beneficial,

Chapter-opening illustration:
"The Anarchist Riot in Chicago," from *Harper's Weekly* magazine, 1886.

others not. As manufacturing and mining became more important, the number of workers in these fields multiplied rapidly: from 885,000 in 1860 to more than 3.2 million in 1890. More efficient methods of production enabled them to increase their output, making possible a rise in their standard of living. The working day was shortening perceptibly. In 1860 the average had been 11 hours, but by 1880 only one worker in four labored more than ten hours, and radicals were beginning to talk about eight hours as a fair day's work.

Skilled industrial workers—such as railroad engineers and conductors, machinists, and iron molders—were quite well off. But unskilled laborers could still not earn enough to maintain a family decently by their own efforts alone.

James H. Ducker's *Men of the Steel Rails* throws much light on working conditions and workers' attitudes. Laborers were paid from $1.00 to $1.25 a day, whereas engineers received three times that amount or more. In addition, many of the better-paid workers picked up additional sums by renting spare rooms to other workers.

Railroad management tried to discipline the labor force by establishing rules, but it had difficulty enforcing them. Drunkenness on the job was a constant problem. Many conductors were said to be "color blind," referring to their inability to tell the difference between the road's money and their own. Transient workers, called "boomers," had "a deserved reputation as rowdies," Ducker reports. Many other workers, of course, were law-abiding, hardworking family men.

Industrialization created other problems. By and large, skilled workers, always better off than the unskilled, improved their positions relatively, despite the increased use of machinery. Furthermore, when machines took the place of skilled humans, jobs became monotonous. Mechanization undermined both the artisans' pride and their bargaining power vis-à-vis their employers. Machines more than workers controlled the speed of work and its duration. The time clock regulated the labor force more rigidly than the most exacting foreman. The pace of work increased; so did the danger involved in working around heavy, high-speed machinery.

As businesses grew larger, personal contact between employer and hired hand tended to disappear. Relations between them became more businesslike, even ruthless. But large enterprises usually employed a higher percentage of managerial and clerical workers than smaller companies, thus providing opportunities for blue-collar workers to rise in the industrial hierarchy.

Another problem for workers was that industrialization tended to accentuate swings of the business cycle. On the upswing, something approaching full employment existed, but in periods of depression, unemployment affected workers without regard for their individual abilities.

Working Women

Women continued to make up a significant part of the industrial working force, but now many more of them were working outside their homes. At least half of all working women were domestic servants; textile mills and the "sewing trades" accounted for a large percentage of the rest. In all fields women were paid substantially lower wages than men.

Women found many new types of work in these years, a fact commented on by the *New York Times* as early as 1869. They made up the overwhelming majority of salespersons and cashiers in the big new department stores. Managers considered women more polite, easier to control, and more honest than male workers, all qualities of value in the huge emporiums. Over half of the more than 1,700 employees in A. T. Stewart's New York store were women.

Educated, middle-class women also dominated the new field of nursing. Nursing seemed the perfect female profession, since it required the same characteristics that women were thought to have by nature: selflessness, cleanliness, kindliness, tact, sensitivity, and submissiveness to male control. "Since God could not care for all the sick, he made women to nurse," one purported authority pontificated. Why it had not occurred to the Lord to make more women physicians, or for that matter members of other prestigious professions like law and the clergy, this man did not explain, probably because it had not occurred to him either.

Middle-class women did replace men as teachers in most of the nation's grade schools, as clerks and secretaries, and as operators of the new typewriters in government departments and business

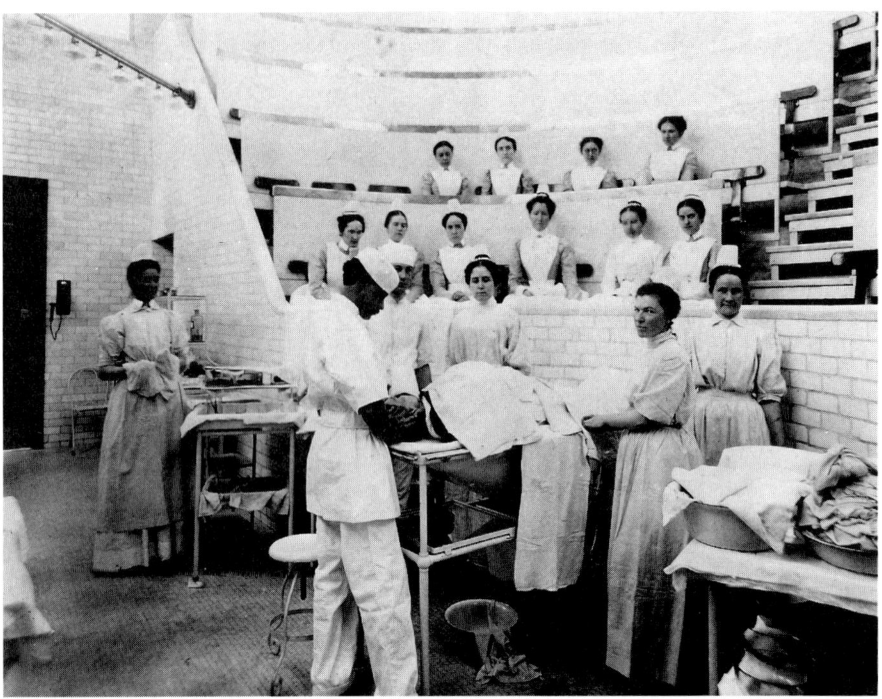

In a society that still believed that the sexes should maintain "separate spheres," the new profession of nursing was viewed as particularly suited to women. Doctoring was reserved for men.

offices. Most men with the knowledge of spelling and grammar that these positions required had better opportunities and were uninterested in office work, so women high school graduates, of whom there was an increasing number, filled the gap.

Both department store clerks and "typewriters" (as they were called) earned more money than unskilled factory workers. According to one advertisement of the period, "No invention has opened for women so broad and easy an avenue to profitable and suitable employment." However, managerial posts in these fields remained almost exclusively in the hands of men.

Farmers

Long the backbone of American society, independent farmers and their agricultural way of life were rapidly being left behind in the race for wealth and status. The number of farmers and the volume of agricultural production continued to rise, but agriculture's relative place in the national economy was declining. Industry was expanding far faster, and the urban population, quadrupling in the period, would soon overtake and pass that of the countryside.

Along with declining income, farmers suffered a decline in status. Compared to middle-class city dwellers, they seemed provincial and behind the times. People in the cities began to refer to farmers as "rubes," "hicks," and "hayseeds" and to view them with bemused tolerance or even contempt.

This combination of circumstances angered and frustrated farmers. Waves of radicalism swept the agricultural regions, giving rise to demands for social and economic experiments that played a major role in breaking down rural laissez-faire prejudices.

Not all farmers were affected by economic developments in the same way. Because of the steady decline of the price level, those in newly settled regions were usually worse off than those in older areas, since they had to borrow money to get started and were therefore burdened with fixed interest charges that became harder to meet each year. In the 1870s farmers in Illinois and Iowa suffered most—which accounts for the strength of the Granger movement in that region.

By the late 1880s farmers in the old Middle West had also become better established. Even when prices dipped and a general depression gripped the country, they were able to weather the bad times by taking advantage of lower transportation costs, better farm machinery, and new fertilizers and insecticides to increase output and by shifting from wheat to corn, oats, hogs, and cattle, which had not declined so drastically in price.

On the agricultural frontier from Texas to the Dakotas and through the states of the old Confederacy, farmers were less fortunate. The burdens of the crop lien system kept thousands of southern farmers in penury, while on the plains life was a succession of hardships. The first settlers in western Kansas, Nebraska, and the Dakotas took up land along the rivers and creeks where they found enough timber for home building, fuel, and fencing. Later arrivals had to build houses of the tough prairie sod and depend on hay, sunflower stalks, and buffalo dung for fuel.

Frontier farm families had always had to work hard and endure the hazards of storm, drought, and insect plagues, along with isolation and loneliness. But all these burdens were magnified on the prairies and the High Plains. Life was particularly hard for farm women, who in addition to child care and housework performed endless farm chores—milking cows, feeding livestock, raising vegetables, and so on. "I . . . am set and running every morning at half-past four o'clock, and run all day, often until half-past eleven P.M.," one farm woman explained. "Is it any wonder I have become slightly demoralized?"

On the plains, women also had to endure drab, cheerless surroundings without the companionship of neighbors or the respites and stimulations of social life. After the writer Hamlin Garland's mother read the grim discussions of women's lot in his book, *Main-Travelled Roads,* she wrote him: "You might have said more, but I'm glad you didn't. Farmers' wives have enough to bear as it is."

Working-Class Family Life

Social workers who visited the homes of industrial laborers in this period reported enormous differences in the standard of living of people engaged in the same line of work, differences related to such variables as health, intelligence, the wife's ability as a homemaker, and pure luck. Some families spent most of their income on food; others saved substantial sums even when earning no more than $400 or $500 a year.

Consider the cases of two Illinois coal miners, hardworking union men with large families, each earning $1.50 a day in 1883. One was out of work nearly half the year; his income in 1883 was only $250. He, his wife, and their five children existed almost exclusively on a diet of bread and salt meat. Nevertheless, as an investigator reported, their two-room tenement home was neat and clean, and three of the children were attending school.

The other miner, father of four children, worked full time and brought home $420 in 1883. He owned a six-room house and an acre of land, where the family raised vegetables. Their food bill for the year was more than ten times that of the family just described. These two admirable families were probably similar in social attitudes and perhaps in political loyalties but were possessed of very different standards of living.

The cases of two families headed by railroad brakemen provide a different kind of contrast. One man brought home only $360 to house and feed a wife and eight children. Here is the report of a state official who interviewed the family: "Clothes ragged, children half-dressed and dirty. They all sleep in one room. . . . The entire concern is as wretched as could be imagined. Father is shiftless. . . . Wife is without ambition or industry."

The other brakeman and his wife had only two children, and he earned $484 in 1883. They owned a well-furnished house, kept a cow, and raised vegetables for home consumption. Though far from rich, they managed to put aside enough for insurance, reading matter, and a few small luxuries.

Working-Class Attitudes

Social workers and government officials made many efforts in the 1880s and 1890s to find out how working people felt about all sorts of matters connected with their jobs. Their reports reveal a wide spectrum of opinion. To the question asked of two Wisconsin carpenters, "What new laws, in your opinion, ought to be enacted?" one replied, "Keep down strikes and rioters. Let every man attend to his own business." But the other answered, "Complete nationalization of land and all ways of transportation. Burn all government bonds. A graduated income tax. . . . Abolish child labor and [pass] any other act that capitalists say is wrong."

Every variation of opinion between these extremes was expressed by working people. In 1881 a woman textile worker in Lawrence, Massachusetts, said to an interviewer: "If you will stand by the mill, and see the people coming out, you will be surprised to see the happy, contented look they all have."

Despite such remarks and the general improvement in living standards, it is clear from the many bitter strikes of the period that there was a great deal of dissatisfaction among industrial workers. Writing in 1885, the labor leader Terence V. Powderly reported that "a deep-rooted feeling of discontent pervades the masses." A few years later a Connecticut official conducted an informal survey of labor opinion in the state and found a "feeling of bitterness" and "distrust of employers" to be endemic.

The discontent had many causes. For some workers, poverty was still the chief problem, but for others, rising aspirations triggered discontent. Workers were confused. They wanted to believe their bosses and the politicians when those worthies voiced the old slogans about a classless society and the community of interest of capital and labor. "Our men," William Vanderbilt of the New York Central said in 1877, "feel that, although I . . . may have my millions and they the rewards of their daily toil, still we are about equal in the end. If they suffer, I suffer, and if I suffer, they cannot escape." "The poor," another conservative spokesman said a decade later, "are not poor because the rich are rich." Instead "the service of capital" softened their lot and gave them many benefits.

Statements such as these, though self-serving, were essentially correct. The rich were growing richer, more people were growing rich, and ordinary workers were better off too. However, the gap between the very rich and the ordinary citizen was widening.

Mobility: Social, Economic, and Educational

To study mobility in a large industrial country is extraordinarily difficult. Census records show that there was considerable geographic mobility in urban areas throughout the last half of the 19th century and into the 20th. In most cities this mobility was accompanied by some economic and social improvement. On the average, about a quarter of the manual laborers traced rose to middle-class status during their lifetimes, and the sons of manual laborers were still more likely to improve their place in society.

Progress was primarily the result of the economic growth the nation was experiencing and of the energy and ambition of the people, native-born and immigrant alike, who were pouring into the cities in such numbers.

The public education system gave an additional boost to the upwardly mobile. The history of American education after about 1870 reflects the impact of social and economic change. Horace Mann, Henry Barnard, and others had laid the foundations for state-supported school systems, but most of these systems became compulsory only after the Civil War, when the growth of cities provided the concentration of population and financial resources necessary for economical mass education. In the 1860s about half the children in the country were getting some formal education, but this did not mean that half the children were attending school at any one time. Sessions were short, especially in rural areas. President Calvin Coolidge noted in his autobiography that the one-room school he attended in rural Vermont in the 1880s was open only when the twenty-odd students were not needed in the fields.

Attendance in the public schools increased from 6.8 million in 1870 to 15.5 million in 1900. A typical elementary school graduate, at least in the cities, could count on having studied, besides the traditional "three Rs," history, geography, a bit of science, drawing, and physical training. But fewer than half a million of these graduates went on to high school; secondary education was still assumed to be only for students with special abilities or whose families were well off.

Industrialization created demands for vocational and technical training; both employers and unskilled workers quickly grasped the possibilities. In 1880 Calvin M. Woodward opened the Manual Training School in St. Louis, and soon a number of similar schools were offering courses in carpentry, metalwork, sewing, and other crafts. By 1890 fully 36 cities had established vocational public high schools.

Because manual training attracted the backing of industrialists, organized labor was at first suspicious of the new trend. One union leader called trade schools "breeding schools for scabs and rats." Fortunately, the usefulness of such training soon became evident to the unions; by 1910 the AFL was lobbying side by side with the National Association of Manufacturers for more trade schools.

More than the absence of real opportunity, the unrealistic expectations inspired by the rags-to-riches myth probably explain why so many workers, even when expressing dissatisfaction with life as it was, continued to subscribe to such middle-class values as hard work and thrift. They simply continued to hope.

The "New" Immigration

Industrial expansion increased the need for labor, and this in turn stimulated immigration. Between 1866 and 1915 about 25 million foreigners entered the United States. Industrial growth alone does not explain the influx. The launching of the 19,000-ton English steamship *Great Eastern* in 1858 opened a new era in transatlantic travel, and competition soon made the crossing cheap as well as safe and rapid. Improved transportation produced unexpected and disruptive changes in the economies of many European countries. Cheap wheat from the United States, Russia, and other parts of the world poured into Europe, bringing disaster to farmers from England and the Scandinavian countries to Italy and Greece. The spreading industrial revolution and the increased use of farm machinery led to the collapse of the peasant economy of central and southern Europe. Political and religious persecutions pushed still others into the migrating stream. But the main reason for emigrating remained the desire for economic betterment.

While immigrants continued to people the farms of America, industry absorbed an ever-increasing number of them. In 1870 one industrial worker in three was foreign-born. When congressional investigators examined 21 major industries early in the new century, they discovered that well over half of the labor force had been born outside the United States.

Before 1882, when—in addition to the Chinese—criminals, idiots, lunatics, and persons liable to become public charges were excluded, entry into the United States was almost unrestricted. Indeed, until 1891 the Atlantic Coast states, not the federal government, exercised whatever controls were imposed on newcomers. On average only 1 immigrant in 50 was rejected.

Private agencies, philanthropic and commercial, served as a link between the new arrivals and employers looking for labor. Numerous nationality groups assisted (and sometimes exploited) their compatriots by organizing "immigrant banks" that recruited labor in the old country, arranged transportation, and then housed the newcomers in boardinghouses in the United States while finding them jobs. The *padrone* system of the Italians and Greeks was typical. The *padrone,* a sort of contractor who agreed to supply gangs of unskilled workers to companies for a lump sum, usually signed on immigrants unfamiliar with American wage levels at rates that assured him a healthy profit.

Beginning in the 1880s, the spreading effects of industrialization in Europe caused a shift in the sources of immigration from northern and western to southern and eastern sections of the Continent. In 1882, when 789,000 immigrants entered the United States, more than 350,000 came from Great Britain and Germany, only 32,000 from Italy, and fewer than 17,000 from Russia. In 1907—the all-time peak year, with 1,285,000 immigrants—Great Britain and Germany supplied fewer than half as many as they had 25 years earlier, while Russia and Italy were supplying 11 times as many as before.

The Old Immigrants and the New

The new immigrants, like the "old" Irish of the 1840s and 1850s, were mostly peasants. They seemed more than ordinarily clannish; southern Italians typically called all people outside their families *forestieri,* "foreigners." Old-stock Americans thought them harder to assimilate, and in fact many were. Some Italian immigrants, for example, had come to the United States only to earn enough money to buy a farm back home. Such people made hard and willing workers but were not much concerned with being part of an American community.

The "birds of passage" formed a substantial minority, but the immigrants who saved in order to bring wives and children or younger brothers and sisters to America were more typical. They were almost desperately eager to become Americans, though of course they retained and nurtured much of their traditional culture.

Cultural differences among immigrants were often large and had important effects on their relations with native-born Americans and with other immigrant groups. Italians who settled in the city of Buffalo, the historian Virginia Yans-McLaughlin has shown, adjusted relatively smoothly to urban industrial life because of their close family and kinship ties. Polish immigrants in Buffalo, having different traditions, found adjustment more difficult.

German-American and Irish-American Catholics had different attitudes that caused them to clash over such matters as the policies of the Catholic University in Washington. Controversies erupted between Catholic and Protestant German-Americans, between Greek-Americans supporting different political factions in their homeland, and many other immigrant groups.

Confused by such differences and conflicts, many Americans of longer standing concluded, wrongly but understandably, that the new immigrants were incapable of becoming good citizens and hence should be kept out. Reformers were worried by the social problems that arose when so many poor immigrants flocked into cities already bursting at the seams. The directors of charitable organizations that bore the burden of aiding the most unfortunate of the immigrants were soon complaining that their resources were being exhausted by the needs of the flood.

Social Darwinists and people obsessed with pseudoscientific ideas about "racial purity" also found the new immigration alarming. Misunderstanding the findings of the new science of genetics, they attributed the social problems associated with mass immigration to supposed physiological characteristics of the newcomers. Forgetting that earlier Americans had accused pre–Civil War Irish and German immigrants of similar deficiencies, they decided that the peoples of southern and eastern Europe were racially (and therefore permanently) inferior to "Nordic" and "Anglo-Saxon" types and ought to be kept out.

Workers, fearing the competition of people with low living standards and no bargaining power, spoke out against the "enticing of penniless and unapprised immigrants . . . to undermine our wages and social welfare." Some corporations, especially in fields like mining, which employed large numbers of unskilled workers, made use of immigrants as strikebreakers, and this particularly angered union members.

Employers were not disturbed by the influx of people with strong backs willing to work hard for low wages. Nevertheless, by the late 1880s many of them were alarmed about the supposed radicalism of the immigrants. The Haymarket bombing focused attention on the handful of foreign-born extremists in the country and loosed a flood of unjustified charges that "anarchists and communists" were dominating the labor movement. Nativism, which had waxed in the 1850s under the Know-Nothing banner and waned during the Civil War, now flared up again. Denunciations of "long-haired, wild-eyed, bad-smelling, atheistic, reckless foreign wretches," of "Europe's human and inhuman rubbish," of the "cutthroats of Beelzebub from the Rhine, the Danube, the Vistula and the Elbe" crowded the pages of the nation's press.

The nativists denounced Catholics and other minority groups for more than their immigrant status. The largest nativist organization of the period, the American Protective Association, founded in 1887, existed primarily to resist what its members called the "Catholic menace." The Protestant majority treated new immigrants as underlings, tried to keep them out of the best jobs, and discouraged their efforts to climb the social ladder. This prejudice functioned only at the social and economic levels. But nowhere in America did prejudice lead to interference with religious freedom in the narrow sense. And neither labor leaders nor important industrialists, despite their misgivings about immigration, took a broadly antiforeign position.

After the Exclusion Act of 1882 and an almost meaningless 1885 ban on importing contract labor, no further restrictions were imposed on immigration until the 20th century. Strong support for a literacy test for admission developed in the 1890s, pushed by a new organization, the Immigration Restriction League. Since there was much more illiteracy in the southeastern quarter of Europe than in the northwestern, such a test would discriminate without seeming to do so on national or racial grounds. A literacy test bill passed both houses of Congress in 1897, but President Cleveland vetoed it.

The Expanding City and Its Problems

Americans who favored restricting immigration made much of the fact that so many of the newcomers crowded into the cities, aggravating problems of housing, public health, crime, and immorality. Immigrants concentrated in the cities because the jobs created by expanding industry were located there. So, of course, did native-born Americans; the proportion of urban dwellers had been steadily increasing since about 1820.

After 1890 the immigrant concentration became even denser. The new migrants from eastern and southern Europe lacked the resources to travel to the agriculturally developing regions (to say nothing of the sums necessary to acquire land and farm

An alley known as "Bandit's Roost," on New York's Lower East Side, photographed for the *New York Sun* in 1887 by police reporter Jacob Riis, himself an immigrant. "What sort of an answer, think you, would come from these tenements to the question 'Is life worth living?' " Riis asked in his book *How the Other Half Lives.*

equipment). As the concentration progressed, it fed on itself, for all the eastern cities developed many ethnic neighborhoods, in each of which immigrants of one particular nationality congregated. Lonely, confused, often unable to speak English, the Italians, the Greeks, the Polish and Russian Jews, and other immigrants tended to settle where their predecessors had settled.

Most newcomers intended to become "good Americans," to be absorbed in the famous American "melting pot." But they also wanted to maintain their traditional culture. They supported "national" churches, schools, newspapers, and clubs. Each great American city became a Europe in microcosm where it sometimes seemed that every language in the world but English could be heard. New York, the great entrepôt, had Italian, Polish, Greek, Jewish, Bohemian quarters—and even a Chinatown.

Although ethnic neighborhoods were crowded, unhealthy, and crime-ridden and many of the residents were desperately poor, they were also places where hopes and ambitions were fulfilled, where people worked hard and endured hardships to improve their own lot and that of their children.

Observing the immigrants' attachment to "foreign" values and institutions, numbers of native-born citizens accused the newcomers of resisting Americanization and blamed them for urban problems. The immigrants were involved in these problems, but the rapidity of urban expansion explains the troubles associated with city life far better than the high percentage of foreigners.

The Urban Infrastructure

The cities were suffering from growing pains. Sewer and water facilities frequently could not keep pace with skyrocketing needs, fire protection became increasingly inadequate, garbage piled up in the streets faster than it could be carted away, and the streets themselves crumbled beneath the pounding of heavy traffic. Urban growth proceeded with such speed that new streets were laid out more rapidly than they could be paved. Chicago, for example, had more than 1,400 miles of dirt streets in 1890.

People poured into the great cities faster than housing could be built to accommodate them. The influx into areas already densely packed in the 1840s became unbearable as rising property values and the absence of zoning laws conspired to make builders use every possible foot of space, squeezing out light and air ruthlessly in order to wedge in a few additional family units.

Substandard living quarters aggravated other evils such as disease and the disintegration of family life, with its attendant mental anguish, crime, and juvenile delinquency. The bloody New York City riots of 1863, though sparked by dislike of the Civil War draft and of blacks, reflected the bitterness and frustration of thousands jammed together amid filth and threatened by disease. A citizens' committee seeking to discover the causes of the riots expressed its amazement after visiting the slums "that so much misery, disease, and wretchedness can be huddled together and hidden . . . unvisited and unthought of, so near our own abodes." New York City created the Metropolitan Health Board in 1866, and a state tenement house law the following year made a feeble beginning at regulating city housing. Another law in 1879 placed a limit on the percentage of lot space that could be covered by new construction and established minimum standards of plumbing and ventilation.

Despite these efforts at reform, in 1890 more than 1.4 million persons were living on Manhattan Island, and in some sections the population density exceeded 900 persons per acre. Jacob Riis, a reporter, captured the horror of these crowded warrens in his classic study of life in the slums, *How the Other Half Lives* (1890):

> *Be a little careful, please! The hall is dark and you might stumble. . . . Here where the hall turns and dives into utter darkness is . . . a flight of stairs. You can feel your way, if you cannot see it. Close? Yes! What would you have? All the fresh air that enters these stairs comes from the hall-door that is forever slamming. . . . The sinks are in the hallway, that all the tenants may have access—and all be poisoned alike by their summer stenches. . . . Here is a door. Listen! That short, hacking cough, that tiny, helpless wail—what do they mean? . . . The child is dying of measles. With half a chance it might have lived; but it had none. That dark bedroom killed it.*

The unhealthiness of the tenements was notorious; in 1900 three out of five babies born in one poor district of Chicago died before their first birthday.

Equally frightening was the impact of overcrowding on the morals of the tenement dweller. The number of prison inmates in the United States increased by 50 percent in the 1880s, and the homicide rate nearly tripled, most of the rise occurring in cities. Driven into the streets by the squalor of their homes, slum youths formed gangs. From petty thievery and shoplifting they graduated to housebreaking, bank robbery, and murder.

Slums bred criminals—the wonder was that they bred so few. They also drove well-to-do residents into exclusive neighborhoods and to the suburbs. From Boston's Beacon Hill and Back Bay to San Francisco's Nob Hill, the rich retired into great cluttered mansions and ignored conditions in the poorer parts of town.

Modernizing the Cities

As American cities grew larger and more crowded, thereby aggravating a host of social problems, practical forces operated to bring about improvements. Once the relationship between polluted water and disease was fully understood, everyone saw the need for decent water and sewage systems. Though some businessmen profited from corrupt dealings with the city machines, more of them wanted efficient and honest government in order to reduce their tax bills. City dwellers of all classes resented dirt, noise, and ugliness, and in many communities public-spirited groups formed societies to plant trees, clean up littered areas, and develop recreational facilities. When one city undertook improvements, others tended to follow suit, spurred on by local pride and the booster spirit.

Gradually, the basic facilities of urban living were improved. Streets were paved, first with cobblestones and wood blocks and then with smoother, quieter asphalt. Gaslight, then electric arc lights, and finally Edison's incandescent lamps brightened the cities after dark, making law enforcement easier, stimulating nightlife, and permitting factories and shops to operate after sunset.

Urban transportation underwent tremendous changes. Until the 1880s, horse-drawn cars were the main means of urban transportation. But horsecars had drawbacks. Enormous numbers of horses were needed, and feeding and stabling the animals was costly. Their droppings (10 pounds per day per horse) became a major source of urban pollution. That is why the invention of the electric trolley car in the 1880s put an end to horsecar transportation. Trolleys were cheaper and less unsightly than horsecars and quieter than steam-powered trains. By 1895 some 850 lines were busily hauling city dwellers over 10,000 miles of track, and mileage more than tripled in the following decade. As with other new enterprises, control of street railways quickly became centralized until a few big operators controlled the trolleys of more than 100 eastern cities and towns.

Streetcars changed the character of big-city life. Before their introduction, urban communities were limited by the distances people could conveniently walk to work. The "walking city" could not easily extend more than 2½ miles from its center. Streetcars increased this radius to 6 miles or more, which meant that the area of the city expanded enormously. Dramatic population shifts resulted as the better-off moved from the center in search of air and space, abandoning the crumbling, jam-packed older neighborhoods to the poor. Thus economic segregation speeded the growth of ghettos. Older peripheral towns that had maintained some of the self-contained qualities of village life were swallowed up,

However noisy and unsightly their overhead rails, the electric trolleys represented a tremendous improvement in the urban environment over their waste-discharging horsecar predecessors when introduced in the 1880s.

becoming metropolitan centers. The village of Medford, Massachusetts, had 11,000 residents in 1890 when the first trolley line from Boston reached it. By 1905 its population was 23,000.

As time passed, each new area, originally peopled by rising economic groups, tended to become crowded and then to deteriorate. By extending their tracks beyond the developed areas, the streetcar companies further speeded suburban growth because they assured developers and home buyers of efficient transportation to the center of town. By keeping fares low the lines also enabled poor people to "escape" to the countryside on holidays. As Kenneth T. Jackson explains in *Crabgrass Frontier,* "First, streetcar lines were built out to existing villages. . . . These areas subsequently developed into large communities. Second the tracks actually created residential neighborhoods where none existed before." In Los Angeles, Henry E. Huntington built his Pacific Electric Railway primarily to aid in selling homesites on land he had bought for a song before the tracks were laid. "For the first time in the history of the world," Jackson writes, the combined activities of builders, trolley operators, and real estate developers made it possible for middle-class families "to buy a detached home on an accessible lot in a safe and sanitary environment."

Advances in bridge design, notably John A. Roebling's perfection of the steel-cable suspension bridge, aided the ebb and flow of metropolitan populations. The Brooklyn Bridge, described by a poet as "a weird metallic Apparition . . . the cables, like divine messages from above . . . cutting and dividing into innumerable musical spaces the nude immensity of the sky," was Roebling's triumph. Completed in 1883 at a cost of $15 million, it was soon carrying more than 33 million passengers a year over the East River between Manhattan and Brooklyn.

Even the high cost of urban real estate, which spawned the tenement, produced some beneficial results in the long run. Instead of crowding squat structures cheek by jowl on 25-foot lots, architects began to build upward. The introduction of iron-skeleton construction, which freed the walls from bearing the immense weight of a tall building, was the work of a group of Chicago architects including William Le Baron Jenney, John A. Holabird, Martin Roche, John W. Root, and Louis H. Sullivan. Jenney's Home Insurance Building, completed in 1885, was the first metal-frame edifice. Height alone, however, did not satisfy these innovators; they sought a form that would reflect the structure and purpose of their buildings.

Their leader was Louis Sullivan. Architects must discard "books, rules, precedents, or any such educational impedimenta" and design functional buildings, he argued. Sullivan's Wainwright Building in St. Louis and his Prudential Building in Buffalo, both completed in the early 1890s, combined beauty, modest construction costs, and efficient use of space in pioneering ways. Soon a "race to the skies" was on in the cities, and the words *skyscraper* and *skyline* entered the language.

The remarkable White City built for the Chicago World's Fair of 1893 by Daniel H. Burnham, with its broad vistas and acres of open space, led to a City Beautiful movement, the most lasting result of which was the development of many public parks. But efforts to relieve congestion in slum districts made little headway.

Leisure Activities: More Fun and Games

By bringing together large numbers of people, cities permitted many kinds of social activity that were difficult or impossible in rural areas. Cities remained unsurpassed as centers of artistic and intellectual life. New York saw the founding of the American Museum of Natural History and the Metropolitan Museum of Art in 1870, the Metropolitan Opera in 1883. Boston's Museum of Fine Arts was founded in 1870 and the Boston Symphony in 1881. Other cities were equally hospitable to such endeavors.

Less sophisticated forms of recreation also flourished in urban environments. Saloons—seemingly on every street corner—were strictly male working-class institutions, usually decorated with pictures and other mementos of sports heroes, the bar perhaps under the charge of a retired pugilist. For workingmen, the saloon was a kind of club, a place to meet friends, exchange news and gossip, gamble, and eat as well as drink. The gradual reduction of the workday left men with more free time, which may explain the proliferation of saloons and the popularity of vaudeville and burlesques (these last described by one straight-laced critic as a "disgraceful spectacle of padded legs juggling and tight-laced wriggling").

Opposition to sports as a frivolous waste of valuable time was steadily evaporating, replaced among the upper and middle classes by the realization that games like golf and tennis were "healthy occupations for mind and body." Bicycling became a fad, both as a means of getting from place to place and as a form of exercise and recreation.

Many of the new streetcar companies built picnic grounds and amusement parks at the ends of their lines. Thousands seeking to relax flocked to these "trolley parks" to enjoy a fresh-air meal or patronize the shooting galleries, merry-go-rounds, and "freak shows."

The postwar era also saw the development of spectator sports, again because cities provided the concentrations of population necessary to support them. Curious relationships developed between upper- and working-class interests and between competitive sports as pure enjoyment for players and spectators and sports as something to bet on. Horse racing had strictly upper-class origins, but racetracks attracted huge crowds of ordinary people more intent on picking a winner than on improving the breed.

Professional boxing was in a sense a hobby of the rich, who sponsored favorite gladiators, offered prizes, and often wagered large sums on the matches. But the audiences were made up overwhelmingly of young working-class males. The gambling and also the brutality of the bloody, bare-knuckle character of the fights led many communities to outlaw boxing.

The first widely popular pugilist was the legendary "Boston Strong Boy," John L. Sullivan, who became heavyweight champion in 1882. Sullivan's idea of fighting, according to his biographer, "was simply to hammer his opponent into unconsciousness." He became an international celebrity and made and lost large sums of money. Yet boxing remained a raffish, clandestine occupation. One of Sullivan's important fights took place in France, on the estate of Baron Rothschild, yet when it ended both he and his opponent were arrested.

Three major team games—baseball, football, and basketball—took their modern form during the last quarter of the century. Organized baseball teams, in most cases made up of upper-class amateurs, had emerged in the 1840s, and gained widespread popularity during the Civil War, as a major form of camp recreation for the troops.

The first professional team, the Cincinnati Red Stockings, paid players between $800 and $1,400 for the season. In 1876, teams in eight cities formed the National League. The American League was founded in 1901. After a brief rivalry, the two leagues made peace in 1903, the year of the first World Series.

Organized play led to codification of the rules and improvements in technique and strategy, for example, the development of "minor" leagues, impartial umpires calling balls and strikes and ruling on close plays, the use of catcher's masks and padded gloves, and the invention of various kinds of curves and other erratic pitches. As early as the 1870s, baseball was being called "the national game." Despite its urban origins, its broad green fields and dusty basepaths gave the game a rural character that has only recently begun to fade.

Nobody "invented" baseball, but both football and basketball owe their present form to individuals. In 1891, while a student at a YMCA school, James Naismith attached peach baskets to the edge of an elevated running track in the gymnasium and drew up what are still the basic rules of basketball. The game was popular from the start, but since it was played indoors, it was not an important spectator sport until much later.

Football evolved out of English rugby. For many decades it remained almost entirely a college sport, played by upper- and middle-class types. The first intercollege football game was held in 1869 (Princeton defeated Rutgers), and by the 1880s college football had become extremely popular.

Much of the game's modern form was the work of Walter Camp, the athletic director and football coach at Yale. Camp cut the size of teams from 15 to 11 players, and he invented the scrimmage line, the four-down system, and the key position of quarterback. Camp's prestige was such that when he named his first All America team after the 1889 season, no one challenged his judgment. Camp claimed that amateur sports like football taught the value of hard work, cooperation, and fair play, but he was no angel, recruiting players who could not meet Yale's academic standards and finding ways of lining his players' pockets. All the problems that emphasis on athletic achievement poses for modern institutions of higher education existed in microcosm well before 1900.

Spectator sports had little appeal to women for many decades, and few women participated in organized athletics. Sports were "manly" activities; a women might ride a bicycle or play croquet and perhaps a little tennis, but to express interest in excelling in a sport was considered unfeminine.

Religious Responses to Industrial Society

The modernization of the great cities was not solving most of the social problems of the slums. As this fact became clear, a number of urban religious leaders began to take a hard look at the situation. Traditionally, American churchmen had insisted that where sin was concerned, there were no extenuating circumstances. To the well-to-do they preached the virtues of thrift and hard work; to the poor they extended the possibility of a better existence in the next world; to all they stressed taking responsibility for one's own behavior—and thus for one's own salvation. Such a point of view brought meager comfort to residents of slums. Consequently, the churches lost influence in the poorer sections. Furthermore, as better-off citizens followed the streetcar lines out from the city centers, their church leaders followed them.

An increasing proportion of the residents of the blighted districts were Catholics, and the Roman church devoted much effort to distributing alms, maintaining homes for orphans and old people, and other forms of social welfare. But church leaders seemed unconcerned with the social causes of the blight; they were deeply committed to the idea that sin and vice were personal, that poverty was an act of God. They deplored the rising tide of crime, disease, and destitution among their coreligionists, yet they failed to see the connection between these evils and the squalor of the slums.

The Catholic hierarchy tended to be at best neutral toward organized labor. Cardinal James Gibbons spoke favorably of the Knights of Labor in 1886 after the Haymarket bombing, but he took a dim view of strikes. The clergy's attitude changed somewhat after Pope Leo XIII issued his encyclical *Rerum novarum* (1891), which criticized the excesses of capitalism, defended the right of labor to form unions, and stressed the duty of government to care for the poor. Workers were entitled to wages that would guarantee their families a reasonable and frugal comfort, Leo declared. Concrete action by American Catholic leaders, however, was slow in coming.

The conservatism of most Protestant and Catholic clergymen did not prevent some earnest preachers from working directly to improve the lot of the city poor. Some followed the path blazed by Dwight L. Moody, a lay evangelist who conducted a vigorous campaign in the 1870s to persuade the denizens of the slums to cast aside their sinful ways. He went among them full of enthusiasm and God's love and made an impact no less powerful than that of George Whitefield during the Great Awakening of the 18th century or Charles Grandison Finney in the first part of the 19th. The evangelists founded mission schools in the slums and were prominent in the establishment of the Young Men's Christian Association (1851) and the Salvation Army (1880).

The evangelists paid little heed to the causes of urban poverty and vice, but a number of Protestant clergymen who had become familiar with the terrible problems of the slums began to preach the so-called Social Gospel, which focused on improving living conditions rather than on saving souls. If people were to lead pure lives, they must have food, decent homes, and opportunities to develop their talents. Social Gospelers advocated child labor legislation, the regulation of big corporations, and heavy taxes on incomes and inheritances.

The most influential preacher of the Social Gospel was probably Washington Gladden. At first Gladden, who was raised on a farm, had opposed all government interference in social and economic affairs, but his experiences as a minister in Springfield, Massachusetts, and Columbus, Ohio, exposed him to the realities of life in industrial cities, and his views changed. In *Applied Christianity* (1886) he defended labor's right to organize and strike and denounced the idea that supply and demand should control wage rates. He favored factory inspection laws, strict regulation of public utilities, and other reforms.

Gladden never questioned the basic values of capitalism. By the 1890s a number of ministers had gone all the way to socialism. The Reverend William D. P. Bliss of Boston, for example, believed in the kind of welfare state envisioned by Edward Bellamy in *Looking Backward*. In addition to nationalizing industry, Bliss and other Christian Socialists advocated government unemployment relief programs, public housing and slum clearance projects, and other measures designed to aid the city poor.

The Settlement Houses

A number of earnest souls began to grapple with slum problems by organizing what were known as settlement houses. These were community centers located in poor districts that provided guidance and services to all who would use them. The settlement workers, most of them idealistic, well-to-do young people, lived in the houses and were active in neighborhood affairs.

The prototype of the settlement house was London's Toynbee Hall, founded in the early 1880s; by the turn of the 20th century, 100 such houses had been established in America, the most famous being Jane Addams's Hull House in Chicago (1889), Robert A. Woods's South End House in Boston (1892), and Lillian Wald's Henry Street Settlement in New York (1893).

Though some men were active in the movement, the most important settlement house workers were women fresh from college—the first generation of young women to experience the trauma of having developed their abilities only to find that society offered few opportunities to use them. The settlements provided an outlet for their hopes and energies. A reformer who visited Hull House around the turn of the century described the residents as "strong-minded energetic women, bustling about their various enterprises" and "mild-mannered men who slide from room to room apologetically."

Settlement workers explained American ways to the immigrants. Unlike most charity workers, who acted out of a sense of upper-class responsibility toward the unfortunate, they expected to benefit themselves by experiencing a way of life different from their own. Lillian Wald, a nurse by training, explained the concept succinctly in *The House on Henry Street* (1915): "We were to live in the neighborhood, . . . identify ourselves with it socially, and, in brief, contribute to it our citizenship."

Settlement workers soon discovered that practical problems absorbed most of their energies. They agitated for tenement house laws, regulation of the labor of women and children, and better schools. They established playgrounds in the slums, along with libraries, classes in arts and crafts, social clubs, and day nurseries. In Chicago, Jane Addams provided classes in music and art and maintained an excellent "little theater" group. Hull House soon boasted a gymnasium, a day nursery, and several social clubs. Addams also campaigned tirelessly for improved public services and for social legislation of all kinds.

A few critics considered the settlement houses mere devices to socialize the unruly poor, but almost everyone appreciated their virtues. By the end of the century even the Catholics, slow to take up practical social reform, were joining the movement, partly because they were losing communicants to socially minded Protestant churches.

With all their accomplishments, the settlement houses seemed to be fighting a losing battle. "Private beneficence," Jane Addams wrote, "is totally inadequate to deal with the vast numbers of the city's disinherited." The slums, fed by an annual influx of hundreds of thousands, blighted new areas faster than settlement house workers could clean up old ones. It became increasingly apparent that the wealth and authority of the state must be brought to bear to keep abreast of the problem.

Civilization and Its Discontents

As the 19th century died, a majority of Americans—especially the comfortably well-off, the residents of small towns, the shopkeepers, many farmers, and some skilled workers—remained uncritical admirers of their civilization. However, blacks, immigrants, and others who failed to share equitably in the good things of life, along with a growing number of humanitarian reformers, found much to lament in their increasingly industrialized society. Giant monopolies flourished despite federal restrictions. The gap between rich and poor appeared to be widening, while the slum spread its poison and the materially successful made a god of their success. Human values seemed in grave danger of being crushed by impersonal forces typified by the great corporations.

In 1871 Walt Whitman, usually so full of extravagant praise for everything American, had called his fellow countrymen the "most materialistic and money-making people ever known. . . . I say we had best look our times and lands searchingly in the face, like a physician diagnosing some deep disease. Never was there, perhaps, more hollowness of heart than at present."

By the late 1880s a well-known journalist could write to a friend: "The wheel of progress is to be run over the whole human race and smash us all." Others noted an alarming jump in the national divorce rate and an increasing taste for all kinds of luxury. "People are made slaves by a desperate struggle to keep up appearances," a Massachusetts commentator declared, and the economist David A. Wells expressed concern over statistics showing that heart disease and mental illness were on the rise. These "diseases of civilization," Wells explained, were "one result of the continuous mental and nervous activity which modern high-tension methods of business have necessitated."

Of course, intellectuals tend to be critical of the world they live in; Thoreau denounced materialism and the worship of progress in the 1840s as vigorously as any late-19th-century prophet of gloom. But the voices of the dissatisfied were rising. Despite the many benefits that industrialization had made possible, it was by no means clear around 1900 that the American people were really better off under the new dispensation.

Milestones

1851 Young Men's Christian Association founded

1858 English liner *Great Eastern* launched

1876 National Baseball League founded

1880 Salvation Army founded

1880s "New immigration" begins

1882 John L. Sullivan wins heavyweight boxing championship

1883 Brooklyn Bridge completed

1887 American Protective Association founded

1888 First urban electric streetcar system

1889 Jane Addams founds Hull House

Walter Camp's first All America football team

1890 Jacob Riis, *How the Other Half Lives*

Calvin Woodward opens his Manual Training School

1891 Pope Leo XIII issues *Rerum novarum* encyclical

1901 American Baseball League founded

Supplementary Reading

J. A. Garraty, **The New Commonwealth** (1968), treats many of the subjects covered in this chapter and A. M. Schlesinger's classic study, **The Rise of the City** (1933), provides a wealth of information about social trends. See also the appropriate sections of Steven Mintz and Susan Kellogg, **Domestic Revolutions: A Social History of the American Family** (1988), and C. N. Degler, **At Odds: Women and the Family in America** (1980).

On industrial workers, see David Montgomery, **Beyond Equality** (1967), Walter Licht, **Working on the Railroad** (1984), and H. G. Gutman, **Work, Culture, and Society in Industrializing America** (1977). David Brody, **Steelworkers in America** (1960), and Stephan Thernstrom, **Poverty and Progress: Social Mobility in a Nineteenth-Century City** (1964), throw much light on the lives of workingmen. S. M. Rothman, **Woman's Proper Place** (1978), discusses the new job opportunities for women. Thernstrom's **The Other Bostonians** (1973), is a brilliant analysis of social and geographical mobility. Businessmen's attitudes are covered in E. C. Kirkland, **Dream and Thought in the Business Community** (1956).

On immigration, see John Higham, **Send These to Me** (1975). Oscar Handlin, **The Uprooted** (1951), describes the life of the new immigrants somewhat romantically, while John Higham, **Strangers in the Land** (1955), stresses the reactions of native-born Americans to successive waves of immigration. Moses Rischin, **The Promised City: New York's Jews** (1962), Thomas Kessner, **The Golden Door: Italian and Jewish Immigrant Mobility** (1977), Virginia Yans-McLaughlin, **Family and Community: Italian Immigrants in Buffalo** (1977), and T. N. Brown, **Irish-American Nationalism** (1966), are important monographs.

K. T. Jackson, **Crabgrass Frontier** (1985), is a pioneering history of suburban development and J. C. Teaford, **The Unheralded Triumph** (1984), gives weight to the accomplishments of the cities as well as their inadequacies. For the growing pains of American cities, consult R. H. Bremner, **From the Depths** (1956), and Roy Lubove, **The Progressives and the Slums** (1962). S. B. Warner, Jr. **Streetcar Suburbs** (1962), a study of Boston's development, is full of suggestive ideas about late-19th-century growth.

On the development of sports, see R. A. Smith, **Sports and Freedom: The Rise of Big-Time College Athletics** (1988), and Gunther Barth, **City People** (1980). The response of religion to industrialism is discussed in H. F. May, **Protestant Churches and Industrial America** (1949), and A. I. Abell, **American Catholicism and Social Action** (1960). For the settlement house movement, see A. F. Davis, **Spearheads for Reform** (1967) and **American Heroine** (1973), a life of Jane Addams.

CHAPTER 21

Intellectual and Cultural Trends

■ ■ ■ ■ ■ INDUSTRIALIZATION ALTERED THE way Americans thought at the same time that it transformed their ways of making a living. Technological advances revolutionized the communication of ideas more drastically than they did the transportation of goods or the manufacture of steel. The materialism that permeated American attitudes toward business affected contemporary education and literature. Charles Darwin's theory of evolution influenced American philosophers, lawyers, and historians. New ideas about how children should be educated and what they should be taught emerged along with new methods of communicating information to adults. As society became more complex, higher education became more important, and Americans began to make significant contributions both in the so-called hard sciences, such as chemistry and physics, and in relatively new soft social sciences, such as psychology, political science, and sociology. A new literary flowering comparable to the renaissance of the 1840s and 1850s occurred in the 1870s and 1880s. By the end of the 19th century, America had finally emerged intellectually from the shadow of Europe.

Chapter-opening illustration:
Mark Twain is caricatured riding his "Celebrated Jumping Frog of Calaveras County" in this 1872 cartoon by English artist Frederick Waddy.

The Pursuit of Knowledge

Improvements in public education and the needs of an increasingly complex society for every type of intellectual skill caused a veritable revolution in how knowledge was discovered, disseminated, and put to use. Observing the effects of formal education on their children, many older people were eager to experience some of its benefits. Nothing illustrates the desire for new information so well as the rise of the Chautauqua movement, founded by John H. Vincent, a Methodist minister, and Lewis Miller, an Ohio manufacturer of farm machinery. In 1874 they organized a two-week summer course for Sunday school teachers on the shores of Lake Chautauqua in New York. Besides instruction, they offered good meals, evening songfests around the campfire, and a relaxing atmosphere—all for $6 for the two weeks. The idea caught on, and soon the leafy shore of Lake Chautauqua became a city of tents each summer as thousands poured into the region from all over the country. The founders expanded their offerings to include instruction in literature, science, government, and economics. Eventually Chautauqua even offered correspondence courses leading over a four-year period to a diploma.

By 1900 there were about 200 Chautauqua-type organizations. Intellectual standards in these programs varied; in general they were low, for they reflected the prevailing tastes of the American people—diverse, enthusiastic, uncritical, and shallow. Nevertheless, the movement provided opportunities for thousands seeking stimulation and intellectual improvement.

Newspapers were an even more important means for disseminating information and educating the masses. Here new technology supplied the major incentive for change. The development by Richard Hoe and Stephen Tucker of the web press (1871), which printed simultaneously on both sides of paper fed into it from large rolls, and Ottmar Mergenthaler's linotype machine (1886), which cast rows of type as needed directly from molten metal, cut printing costs dramatically. By 1895 machines were printing, cutting, and folding 32-page newspapers at the rate of 24,000 an hour.

The telegraph and transoceanic cables wrought a similar transformation in the gathering of news. Press associations, led by the New York Associated Press, flourished; the syndicated article appeared; and a few publishers—Edward W. Scripps was the first—began to assemble chains of newspapers.

Population growth and better education created an ever-larger demand for printed matter. At the same time, the integration of the economy enabled manufacturers to sell their goods all over the country. Advertising became important, and sellers soon learned that newspapers and magazines were excellent means of placing their products before millions of eyes. Rich men such as the railroad magnate Jay Gould and the mining tycoon George Hearst invested heavily in newspapers in the post–Civil War decades.

Publishers tended to be conservative, but reaching the masses meant lowering intellectual and cultural standards, appealing to emotions, and adopting popular, sometimes radical causes. The first to reach a truly massive audience was Joseph Pulitzer, a Hungarian-born immigrant who made a first-rate paper of the *St. Louis Post-Dispatch.* In 1883 Pulitzer bought

John Singer Sargent's 1905 portrait of Joseph Pulitzer. On his death six years later, Pulitzer's will provided for the endowment of the Columbia School of Journalism and the establishment of Pulitzer Prizes in journalism, letters, and other categories.

the *New York World,* a sheet with a circulation of perhaps 20,000. Within a year he was selling 100,000 copies daily, and by the late 1890s the *World*'s circulation regularly exceeded 1 million.

Pulitzer achieved this brilliant success by casting a wide net. To the masses he offered bold black headlines devoted to crime (ANOTHER MURDERER TO HANG), scandal (VICE ADMIRAL'S SON IN JAIL), catastrophe (TWENTY-FOUR MINERS KILLED), society and the theater (LILY LANGTRY'S NEW ADMIRER), together with feature stories, political cartoons, sports pages, comics, and pictures. For the educated and affluent he provided better political and financial coverage than the most respectable New York journals. Pulitzer made the *World* a crusader for civic improvement by attacking political corruption, monopoly, and slum problems. "The *World* is the people's newspaper," he boasted, and in the sense that it interested men and women of every sort, he was correct.

Pulitzer's methods were quickly copied by competitors, especially George Hearst's son, William Randolph Hearst, who purchased the *New York Journal* in 1895 and soon outdid the *World* in sensationalism. But no other newspaperman of the era approached Pulitzer in originality, boldness, and the knack of reaching the masses without abandoning seriousness of purpose and basic integrity.

Magazine Journalism

Growth and ferment also characterized the magazine world. In 1865 there were about 700 magazines in the country; by the turn of the century, more than 5,000. Until the mid-1880s, few of the new magazines were in any way unusual. A handful of serious periodicals, such as the *The Nation,* the *Atlantic Monthly, Harper's,* and *The Century,* dominated the field. They were staid in tone and conservative in political caste. Articles on current affairs, a good deal of fiction and poetry, and historical and biographical studies, filled their pages. None approached a mass circulation because of the limited size of the upper-middle-class audience they aimed at.

After about 1885, changes began to take place. New magazines such as *The Forum* (1886) and *The Arena* (1889) emphasized hard-hitting articles on controversial subjects by leading experts. In 1889 Edward W. Bok became editor of the *Ladies' Home Journal.* Besides advice columns ("Ruth Ashmore's Side Talks with Girls"), he offered articles on child care, gardening, and interior decorating, published work by fine contemporary novelists, and commissioned public figures to discuss important questions. He printed colored reproductions of art masterpieces—the invention of cheap photoengraving was of enormous significance in the success of mass-circulation magazines—and crusaded for women's suffrage, conservation, and other reforms. Bok did more than cater to public tastes; he created new tastes.

Colleges and Universities

The same forces that were affecting the dissemination of information were also altering higher education and professional training. Less than 2 percent of the college-age population attended college, but the aspirations of young people were rising, and more and more parents had the financial means necessary for fulfilling them.

More significant than the expansion of the colleges were the alterations in their curricula and in the atmosphere on the average campus. State universities proliferated; the federal government's land-grant program in support of training in "agriculture and the mechanic arts," established under the Morrill Act of 1862, came into its own; wealthy philanthropists poured fortunes into old institutions and founded new ones; educators introduced new courses and adopted new teaching methods; professional schools of law, medicine, education, business, journalism, and other specialties increased in number.

In the forefront of reform was Harvard, the oldest and most prestigious college in the country. In the 1860s it possessed an excellent faculty, but teaching methods were antiquated, and the curriculum had remained almost unchanged since the colonial period. In 1869, however, a dynamic president, the chemist Charles W. Eliot, introduced the elective system, gradually eliminating required courses and expanding offerings in such areas as modern languages, economics, and the laboratory sciences. He encouraged the faculty to experiment with new teaching methods. The standards of the medical school were raised, and the case method was introduced in the law school. In some respects Eliot went too far—the elective system encouraged superficiality and laxness in many students—but on balance he transformed Harvard from a college, "a place to which a young man is sent," to a university, a place "to which he goes."

An even more important development in higher education was the founding of Johns Hopkins in 1876. This university was one of many established in the period by wealthy industrialists; its benefactor, the Baltimore merchant Johns Hopkins, had made his fortune in the Baltimore and Ohio Railroad. Its distinctiveness, however, was due to the vision of Daniel Coit Gilman, its first president. Gilman modeled Johns Hopkins on the German universities, where meticulous research and freedom of inquiry were the guiding principles. In staffing the institution, he sought scholars of the highest reputation, scouring Europe as well as America in his search for talent. Gilman promised his teachers good students and ample opportunity to pursue their own research (which explains why Hopkins professors repeatedly turned down attractive offers from other universities).

Johns Hopkins specialized in graduate education. In the generation after its founding, it turned out a remarkable percentage of the most important scholars in the nation, including Woodrow Wilson in political science, John Dewey in philosophy, Frederick Jackson Turner in history, and John R. Commons in economics. The seminar conducted by Herbert Baxter Adams was particularly productive; the Adams-edited *Johns Hopkins Studies in Historical and Political Science,* consisting of the doctoral dissertations of his students, was "the mother of similar studies in every part of the United States."

The example of Johns Hopkins encouraged other wealthy individuals to endow universities offering advanced work. Of these, the most important was John D. Rockefeller's creation, the University of Chicago (1892). Its president, William Rainey Harper, was a brilliant biblical scholar—he received his Ph.D. from Yale at the age of 18—and an imaginative administrator.

Like Daniel Coit Gilman, Harper sought top-flight scholars for his faculty. He offered such high salaries that he was besieged with more than a thousand applications. Chicago offered first-class graduate and undergraduate education. During its first year there were 120 instructors for fewer than 600 students, and despite fears that the mighty tycoon Rockefeller would force his social and economic views on the institution, academic freedom was the rule.

State and federal aid to higher education expanded rapidly. The Morrill Act, granting land to each state at the rate of 30,000 acres for each senator and representative, provided the endowments that gave many important modern universities, such as Illinois, Michigan State, and Ohio State, their start. Although the federal assistance was earmarked for specific subjects, the land-grant institutions offered a full range of courses, and all received additional state funds.

Important advances were made in women's higher education, beginning with Vassar College, which opened its doors to 300 women students in 1865. Wellesley and Smith, both founded in 1875, completed the so-called Big Three women's colleges. These three, the already established Mount Holyoke, and Bryn Mawr (1885), Barnard (1889), and Radcliffe (1893) became known as the Seven Sisters.

The only professional careers easily available to women graduates were teaching, nursing, and the new area called social work. Nevertheless, the women that these institutions trained were conscious of their uniqueness and determined to demonstrate their capabilities.

Not all the changes in higher education were beneficial. Under the elective system, some students gained a smattering of knowledge of many subjects but mastery of none. Intensive graduate work often produced a narrow outlook and research monographs on trivial subjects. The gifts of rich industrialists sometimes came with strings, and college boards of trustees tended to be dominated by businessmen who sometimes attempted to impose their own social and economic beliefs on faculty members. Few professors lost their positions because their views offended trustees, but at many institutions trustees exerted constant nagging pressures that limited academic freedom and scholarly objectivity. At state colleges, politicians often interfered in academic affairs, treating professorships as part of the patronage system.

As universities grew, administration became more complicated, and the prestige of administrators rose inordinately. At many institutions, professors came to be regarded as mere hired hands. And as the number of college graduates increased, the influence of alumni on educational policies began to make itself felt, not always happily. Campus social activities became more important. Fraternities proliferated. Interest in organized sports first appeared as a laudable outgrowth of the general expansion of the curriculum, but soon athletic contests were playing a role all out of proportion to their significance. Football became a source of revenue that many colleges dared not neglect. Since students, alumni, and the public demanded winning teams, college administrators stooped to subsidizing student athletes, in extreme cases employing players who were not students at all. In short, higher education reflected American values, with all their strengths and weaknesses.

Scientific Advances

Much has been made of the crassness of late-19th-century American life, yet the period boasted intellectual achievements of the highest quality. If the business mentality dominated society, and if the great barons of industry, exalting practicality over theory, tended to look down on the life of the mind, intellectuals, quietly pondering the problems of their generation, nonetheless created works that affected the country as profoundly as the achievements of industrial organizers like Rockefeller and Carnegie and technicians like Edison and Bell.

In pure science America produced a number of outstanding figures in these years. The giant among them, whose contributions some experts rank with those of Newton, Darwin, and Einstein, was Josiah Willard Gibbs, professor of mathematical physics at Yale from 1871 to 1903. Gibbs created an entirely new science, physical chemistry, and made possible the study of how complex substances respond to changes in temperature and pressure. Purely theoretical at the time, Gibbs's ideas led to vital advances in metallurgy and in the manufacture of plastics, drugs, and other products.

Of lesser but still major significance was the work of Albert A. Michelson of the University of Chicago, who made the first accurate measurements of the speed of light. Michelson's research helped pave the way for Einstein's theory of relativity; in 1907 Michelson became the first American scientist to win a Nobel Prize.

The New Social Sciences

In the social sciences, the achievements of the leading thinkers were closely connected with the practical issues of the age. The application of the theory of evolution to every aspect of human relations, the impact of industrialization on society, the development of institutions and their interactions—such topics were of intense concern to American social scientists. Controversies over trusts, slum conditions, and other problems drew scholars into practical affairs.

Among economists something approaching a revolution took place in the 1880s. The classical school, which maintained that immutable natural laws governed all human behavior and used the insights of Darwin only to justify unrestrained competition and laissez-faire, was challenged by a group of young economists who argued that as times changed, economic theories and laws must be modified in order to remain relevant. Richard T. Ely, another of the scholars who made Johns Hopkins a font of new ideas in the 1880s, summarized the thinking of this group in 1885. The state, Ely proclaimed, is "an educational and ethical agency whose positive aid is an indispensable condition of human progress." Laissez-faire was outmoded and dangerous. Economic problems were basically moral problems; their solution required "the united efforts of Church, state and science." The proper way to study these problems was by analyzing actual conditions, not by applying abstract laws or principles. This approach produced the so-called institutionalist school of economics, whose members made detailed, on-the-spot investigations of labor unions, sweatshops, factories, and mines.

A similar revolution struck sociology in the mid-1880s. Prevailing opinion up to that time rejected the idea of government interference with the organization of society. The influence of the English social Darwinist Herbert Spencer, who objected even to public schools and the postal system, was immense. Spencer twisted the ideas of Darwin to mean that society could be changed only by the force of evolution, which moved with cosmic slowness.

Such a point of view made little sense in America, where society was changing rapidly and the range of government social and economic activity was expanding. It was first challenged by an obscure scholar employed by the U.S. Geological Survey, Lester Frank Ward, whose *Dynamic Sociology* was published in 1883. Ward assailed the Spencerians for ignoring the possibility of "the improvement of society by cold calculation." In *The Psychic Factors of Civilization* (1893) he blasted the "law of competition." Human progress, he argued, consisted of "triumphing little by little over this law," for example, by interfering with biological processes through the use of medicines to kill harmful bacteria. Society must indeed evolve, but through careful social planning. Ward had little direct influence, but his arguments laid the theoretical basis for the modern welfare state.

The new political scientists were also evolutionists and institutionalists. The Founding Fathers had conceived of the political system as an impersonal set of institutions and principles, a government of laws rather than of men. Nineteenth-century thinkers (John C. Calhoun is the best example) concerned themselves with abstractions, such as states' rights, and ignored the extralegal aspects of politics, such as parties and pressure groups. In the 1880s political scientists began to employ a different approach. In his doctoral dissertation at Johns Hopkins, *Congressional Government* (1885), Woodrow Wilson analyzed the American political system. He concluded that the real locus of authority lay in the committees of Congress, which had no constitutional basis at all. Wilson viewed politics as a dynamic process and offered no theoretical objection to the expansion of state power. In *The State* (1889) he distinguished between essential functions of government, such as the punishment of crime, and "ministrant" functions, such as education, the regulation of corporations, and social welfare legislation. The desirability of any particular state action of the latter type was simply a matter of expediency.

Progressive Education

Traditionally, American teachers had emphasized the three Rs and relied on strict discipline and rote learning. But the ideas of early-19th-century German educators, notably Johann Friedrich Herbart, were attracting attention in the United States. According to Herbart, teachers could best arouse the interest of their students by relating new information to what they already knew; good teaching called for professional training, psychological insight, enthusiasm, and imagination, not merely facts and a birch rod. At the same time, evolutionists were pressing for a kind of education that would help children to "survive" by adapting to the demands of their environment.

Forward-looking educators seized on these ideas because social changes were making the old system increasingly inadequate. Settlement house workers discovered that slum children needed training in handicrafts, good citizenship, and personal hygiene as much as in reading and writing. Gradually they came to regard educational reform as central to the problem of improving society. "We are impatient with the schools which lay all stress on reading and writing," Jane Addams declared. This type of education "fails to give the child any clew to the life about him."

The philosopher who summarized and gave direction to these forces was John Dewey, a professor at the University of Chicago. Essentially, Dewey's approach was ethical. Was the nation's youth being properly prepared for the tasks it faced in the modern world? Education, Dewey insisted, was "the fundamental method of social progress and reform." Moreover, in an industrial society the family no longer performed many of the educational functions it had carried out in an agrarian society. Farm children learn about nature, about work, about human character in countless ways denied to children in cities. The schools can fill the gap. At the same time, education should center on the child, and new information should be related to what the child already knows. Children's imaginations, energies, and curiosity are tools for broadening their outlook and increasing their store of information. Finally, the school should become an instrument for social reform, "saturating" children with the "spirit of service" and helping to produce a society that is "worthy, lovely, and harmonious."

Although the gains made in public education before 1900 were more quantitative than qualitative and the philosophy dominant in most schools was not very different at the end of the century from that prevailing in Horace Mann's day, change was in the air.

Law and History

Even jurisprudence, by its nature conservative and rooted in tradition, felt the pressure of evolutionary thought and the new emphasis on studying institutions as they actually are. In 1881 Oliver Wendell Holmes, Jr., published *The Common Law.* Rejecting the ideas that judges should limit themselves to the mechanical explication of statutes and that law consisted only of what was written in law books, Holmes argued that "the felt necessities of the time" rather than precedent should determine the rules by which people are governed. "The life of the law has not been logic; it has been experience," he wrote. "It is revolting," he added on another occasion, "to have no better reason for a rule of law than that it was laid down in the time of Henry IV."

Holmes went on to a long and brilliant judicial career during which he repeatedly stressed the right of the people, through their elected representatives, to deal with contemporary problems in any reasonable way, unfettered by outmoded conceptions of the proper limits of government authority.

The new approach to knowledge did not always advance the cause of liberal reform. Historians in the graduate schools became intensely interested in studying the origins and evolution of political institutions. They concluded, after much "scientific" study of old charters and law codes, that the roots of democracy were to be found in the customs of the ancient tribes of northern Europe. This theory of the "Teutonic origins" of democracy, which has since been thoroughly discredited, fitted well with the prejudices of people of British stock, and it provided ammunition for those who favored restricting immigration and for those who argued that blacks were inferior beings.

Out of this work, however, came an essentially democratic concept, the frontier thesis of Frederick Jackson Turner, still another scholar trained at Johns Hopkins. Turner's essay "The Significance of the Frontier in American History" (1893) argued that the frontier experience, through which every section of the country had passed, had affected the thinking of the people and the shape of American institutions. The isolation of the frontier and the need during each successive westward advance to create civilization anew account, Turner wrote, for the individualism of Americans and the democratic character of their society. Nearly everything unique in our culture, he claimed, could be traced to the existence of the frontier.

Life on the frontier was not as democratic as Turner believed, and it certainly does not explain American development as completely as he said it did. Nevertheless, his work showed how important it was to investigate the evolution of institutions, and it encouraged historians to study social and economic, as well as purely political, subjects.

Realism in Literature

When the Gilded Age began, American literature was dominated by the romantic mood. Romanticism, however, had lost its creative force; most writing in the decade after 1865 was sentimental trash pandering to the preconceptions of middle-class readers. The unreality, even dishonesty, of contemporary fiction eventually caused a reaction, but the most important forces giving rise to the Age of Realism were those that were transforming every other aspect of American life: industrialism, with its associated complexities and social problems; the theory of evolution, which made people more aware of the force of the environment and the basic conflicts of existence; and the new science, which taught dispassionate, empirical observation.

Novelists examined social problems such as slum life, the conflict between capital and labor, and political corruption. They created multidimensional characters, depicted persons of every social class, used dialect and slang to capture the flavor of particular types, and fashioned painstaking descriptions of the surroundings into which they placed their subjects.

Mark Twain

Easy as it was to romanticize the West, that region lent itself to the realistic approach. Almost of necessity, novelists writing about the West described coarse characters from the lower levels of society and dealt with crime and violence. It would have been difficult indeed to write a genteel romance about a mining camp. The outstanding figure of western literature, the first great American realist, was Mark Twain.

Twain was born Samuel L. Clemens in 1835. He grew up in Hannibal, Missouri, on the banks of the Mississippi. After mastering the printer's trade and working as a riverboat pilot, he went west to Nevada in 1861, supporting himself as a prospector and then a reporter. Soon he was publishing humorous stories about the local life under the nom de plume Mark Twain. In 1865, living in California, he wrote "The Celebrated Jumping Frog of Calaveras County," a story that brought him national recognition. A tour of Europe and the Holy Land in 1867–1868 led to *The Innocents Abroad* (1869), which made him famous.

Twain's greatness stemmed from his keen reportorial eye and ear, his eagerness to live life to the fullest, his marvelous sense of humor, and his ability to be at once in society and outside it, to love humanity yet be repelled by human vanity and perversity. He wrote tirelessly about America and Europe, about his own times and the feudal past,

Mark Twain was both a satirist of American optimism in his writings and its victim in misguided business ventures that brought him to the brink of bankruptcy. This photograph was taken five years before his death in 1910.

about tourists, slaves, tycoons, cracker-barrel philosophers—and human destiny.

Twain surpassed every contemporary in the portrayal of character. In his biting satire *The Gilded Age* (1873) he created that magnificent mountebank Colonel Beriah Sellers, purveyor of eyewash ("the Infallible Imperial Oriental Optic Liniment") and false hopes, ridiculous, unscrupulous, but lovable. In *Huckleberry Finn* (1884), Twain's masterwork, his portrait of the slave Jim, loyal, patient, naive, yet withal a man, is unforgettable. When Huck takes advantage of Jim's credulity merely for his own amusement, the slave turns from him coldly and says: "Dat truck dah is *trash;* en trash is what people is dat puts dirt on de head er dey fren's en makes 'em ashamed." And there is Huck Finn himself, devilish, romantic, amoral, and at bottom the complete realist.

Twain always put much of his own experience and feeling into his work. He could not rise above the sentimentality and prudery of his generation entirely, for these qualities were part of his nature. Often, even in *Huckleberry Finn,* he contrived to end his tales on absurdly optimistic notes that ring false after so many brilliant pages portraying life as it is. Rough and uneven like the man himself, Twain's works catch more of the spirit of the age he named than those of any other writer.

William Dean Howells

Mark Twain's realism was far less self-conscious than that of his longtime friend William Dean Howells. Like Twain, Howells had little formal education. He learned the printer's trade from his father and became a reporter. After the Civil War he worked briefly for *The Nation* in New York and then moved to Boston, where he became editor of the *Atlantic Monthly.* In 1886 he returned to New York as editor of *Harper's.*

A long series of novels and much literary criticism poured from Howells's pen over the next 34 years. He was not at first a critic of society, being content to write about what he called the "smiling aspects" of life. But he had a real social conscience. Gradually he became aware of the problems that industrialization had created. In *The Rise of Silas Lapham* (1885), he dealt with some of the ethical conflicts faced by businessmen in a competitive society. The harsh public reaction to the Haymarket bombing in 1886 stirred him, and he threw himself into a futile campaign to prevent the execution of the anarchist suspects. Thereafter he moved rapidly toward the left; soon he was calling himself a socialist.

But Howells was more than a reformer. In *A Hazard of New Fortunes* (1890) he attempted to portray the full range of metropolitan life, weaving the destinies of a dozen interesting personalities from diverse sections and social classes. The book represents a triumph of realism in its careful descriptions of various neighborhoods of New York and the ways of life of rich and poor, in the intricacy of its characters, and in its rejection of sentimentality and romantic love. "A man knows that he can love and wholly cease to love, not once merely, but several times," the narrator says, "but in regard to women he cherishes the superstition of the romances that love is once for all, and forever."

Howells was also the most influential critic of his time. He helped bring the best contemporary foreign writers, including Tolstoy, Dostoyevski, Ibsen, and Zola, to the attention of readers in the United States, and he encouraged many important young American novelists, among them Stephen Crane, Theodore Dreiser, Frank Norris, and Hamlin Garland.

Some of these writers went far beyond Howells's realism to what they called naturalism. They believed that the human being was essentially an animal, a helpless creature whose fate was determined by environment. Their world was Darwin's—mindless, without mercy or justice. They wrote chiefly about the most primitive emotions—lust, hate, greed. In *Maggie, A Girl of the Streets* (1893) Stephen Crane described the seduction, degradation, and eventual suicide of a young woman, all set against the background of a sordid slum; in *The Red Badge of Courage* (1895) he captured the pain and humor of war. In *McTeague* (1899) Frank Norris told the story of a brutal, dull-witted dentist who murdered his greed-crazed wife with his bare fists.

Such stuff was too strong for Howells, yet he recognized its importance and befriended the younger writers in many ways. Even Theodore Dreiser, who was contemptuous of Howells's writings and considered him hopelessly middle-class in point of view, appreciated his aid and praised his influence on American literature. Dreiser's first novel, *Sister Carrie* (1900), treated sex so forthrightly that it was withdrawn after publication.

Henry James

Henry James was very different in spirit and background from the tempestuous naturalists. Born to wealth, he spent most of his mature life in Europe, writing novels, short stories, plays, and volumes of criticism. Although far removed from the world of practical affairs, he was preeminently a realist, determined, as he once said, "to leave a multitude of pictures of my time" for the future to contemplate. "All life belongs to you," he told his fellow novelists. "There is no impression of life, no manner of seeing it and feeling it, to which the plan of the novelist may not offer a place."

James's major theme was the clash of American and European cultures, his primary interest the close-up examination of wealthy, sensitive, yet often corrupt persons in a cultivated but far from polite society. He dealt with social issues such as feminism and the difficulties faced by artists in the modern world, but he subordinated them to his interest in his subjects as individuals. *The American* (1877) told of the love of a wealthy American in Paris for a French noblewoman who rejected him because her family disapproved of his background. *The Portrait of a Lady* (1881) described the disillusionment of an intelligent woman married to a charming but morally bankrupt man and her eventual decision to remain with him nonetheless.

Realism in Art

American painters responded to the times as writers did, but with one difference: Despite the new concern for realism, the romantic tradition retained its vitality. Preeminent among the realists was Thomas Eakins. The scientific spirit of the age suited Eakins perfectly. He mastered human anatomy; some of his finest paintings, such as *The Gross Clinic* (1875), are graphic illustrations of surgical operations. He was an early experimenter with motion pictures, using the camera to capture exactly the attitudes of human beings and animals in action. Like his friend Walt Whitman, whose portrait is one of the artist's greatest achievements, Eakins gloried in the ordinary. But he had none of Whitman's weakness for sham and self-delusion.

Winslow Homer, a master of the watercolor medium, was also influenced by realist ideas. Aesthetics seemed not to concern him at all; he liked to shock people by referring to his profession as "the picture line," prided himself on painting each object "exactly as it appears." There are romantic elements in his work. *Gulf Stream* (1899), depicting a sailor on a small, broken boat menaced by a waterspout and a school of sharks, and *Fox Hunt* (1893), in which huge, ominous crows hover over a fox at bay, reflect his interest in the violence and drama of raw nature, a distinctly romantic theme. However, his approach, even in these works, was utterly prosaic. When some women complained about the fate of the black sailor in *Gulf Stream,* Homer wrote his dealer sarcastically: "Tell these ladies that the unfortunate Negro . . . will be rescued and returned to his friends and home, and live happily ever after."

The careers of Eakins and Homer show that the late-19th-century American environment was not uncongenial to first-rate artists. Nevertheless, at least two major American painters abandoned their native shores for Europe. One was James A. McNeill Whistler, whose portrait of his mother, which he called *Arrangement in Grey and Black,* may well be the most famous canvas ever painted by an American. Whistler made a profession of eccentricity, but he was a remarkably talented and versatile artist. Some of his portraits are triumphs of realism, while his misty studies of the London waterfront, which he described as visual expressions of poetry, are thoroughly romantic in conception. Paintings such as his portrait of his mother represent still another expression of his talent. Spare and muted in tone, they are more interesting as precise arrangements of color and space than as images of particular objects; they had a tremendous influence on the course of modern art.

The second important expatriate artist was Mary Cassatt, daughter of a wealthy Pittsburgh banker and sister of Alexander J. Cassatt, president of the Pennsylvania Railroad around the turn of the century. She went to Paris as a tourist and dabbled in art like many conventional young socialites, then was caught up in the impressionist movement and decided to become a serious painter. Her work is more French than American and was little appreciated in the United States before the First World War. When once she returned to America for a visit, the *Philadelphia Public Ledger* reported: "Mary Cassatt, sister of Mr. Cassatt, president of the Pennsylvania Railroad, returned from Europe yesterday. She has been studying painting in Paris, and owns the smallest Pekinese dog in the world."

Interest in art in America was considerable. Museums and art schools increased in number, and settlement house workers staged exhibitions that attracted enthusiastic crowds. Wealthy patrons gave commissions to portrait painters and poured fortunes into collecting. Martin A. Ryerson, with money made in lumber, bought the works of the French impressionists when few Americans recognized their importance. Charles L. Freer of the American Car and Foundry Company was a specialist in oriental art; John G. Johnson, a corporation lawyer, in Italian primitive.

The Pragmatic Approach

It would have been remarkable indeed if the intellectual ferment of the late 19th century had not affected contemporary ideas about the meaning of life, the truth of revealed religion, moral values, and similar fundamental issues. In particular, the theory of evo-

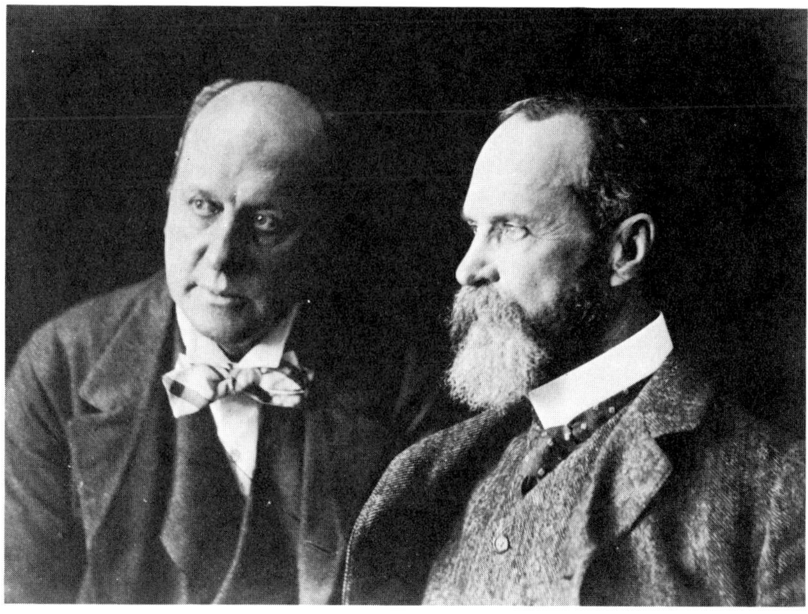

William James (with the beard) and his novelist brother Henry in a photographic portrait taken around 1900.

lution—so important in altering contemporary views of science, history, and social relations—produced significant changes in American thinking about religious and philosophical questions.

Evolution posed an immediate challenge to religion: If Darwin was correct, the biblical account of the creation was obviously untrue, and the idea that man had been formed in God's image was highly unlikely. A bitter controversy erupted. While millions continued to believe in the literal truth of the Bible, among intellectuals victory went to the evolutionists because, in addition to the arguments of the geologists and the biologists, scholars were throwing light on the historical development of the Bible, showing it to be of human rather than divine origin.

Evolution did not undermine the faith of any large percentage of the population. If the account of the creation in Genesis could not be taken literally, the Bible remained a repository of wisdom and inspiration. As the liberal preacher Washington Gladden put it, evolution was "a most impressive demonstration of the presence of God in the world."

The effects of Darwinism on philosophy were less dramatic but in the end far more significant. Fixed systems and eternal verities were difficult to justify in a world that was constantly evolving. By the early 1870s a few philosophers had begun to reason that ideas and theories mattered little except when applied to specifics. In "How to Make Our Ideas Clear" (1878), Charles S. Peirce argued that concepts could be fairly understood only in terms of their practical effects. Once the mind accepted the truth of evolution, Peirce believed, logic required that it accept the impermanence even of scientific laws. There was, he wrote, "an element of indeterminacy, spontaneity, or absolute chance in nature."

This startling philosophy, which Peirce called pragmatism, was expressed in less technical language by William James, brother of the novelist. James, one of the most remarkable Americans of his generation, was professor at Harvard successively of comparative anatomy, psychology, and philosophy. His *Principles of Psychology* (1890) established that discipline as a modern science. His *Varieties of Religious Experience* (1902), which treated the subject from both psychological and philosophical points of view, helped thousands of readers reconcile their religious faith with their increasing knowledge of psychology and the physical universe.

Although less rigorous a logician than Peirce, James's wide range and his verve and imagination as a writer made him by far the most influential philosopher of his time. He rejected the deterministic interpretation of Darwinism and all other one-idea explanations of existence. Belief in free will was one of his axioms; environment might influence survival, but so did the *desire* to survive, which existed independently of surrounding circumstances. Even truth was relative; it did not exist in the abstract but rather *happened* under particular circumstances. What a person thought helped make that thought occur, or come true. The mind, James wrote in a typically vivid phrase, has "a vote" in determining truth. Religion was true, for example, because people were religious.

The pragmatic approach inspired much of the reform spirit of the late 19th century and even more of that of the early 20th. James's hammer blows shattered the laissez-faire extremism of Herbert Spencer. In "Great Men and Their Environment" (1880) James argued that social changes were brought about by the actions of geniuses whom society had selected and raised to positions of power, rather than by the impersonal force of the environment. Such reasoning fitted the preconceptions of rugged individualists yet encouraged those dissatisfied with society to work for change. Educational experts like John Dewey, the institutionalist school of economists, settlement house workers, and other reformers adopted pragmatism eagerly.

Yet pragmatism brought Americans face to face with somber problems. Though relativism made them optimistic, it bred insecurity, for there could be no certainty, no comforting reliance on any eternal value in the absence of absolute truth. Pragmatism also seemed to suggest that the end justified the means, that what worked was more important than what ought to be. By emphasizing practice at the expense of theory, the new philosophy encouraged materialism, anti-intellectualism, and other unlovely aspects of the American character. And what place had conventional morality in such a system? Perhaps pragmatism placed too much reliance on the free will of human beings, ignoring their capacity for selfishness and self-delusion.

The people of the new century found pragmatism a heady wine. They would quaff it freely and enthusiastically—down to the bitter dregs.

Milestones

1865 Vassar College founded
1869 Charles W. Eliot becomes president of Harvard
1874 Chautauqua movement beings
1876 Johns Hopkins University founded
1881 Oliver Wendell Holmes, Jr., *The Common Law*
1883 Joseph Pulitzer purchases the *New York World*
1886 Ottmar Merganthaler invents the linotype machine
William Dean Howells becomes editor of *Harper's*
1889 Edward W. Bok becomes editor of the *Ladies' Home Journal*
1890 William James, *Principles of Psychology*
1893 Frederick Jackson Turner, "The Significance of the Frontier in American History"
1899 John Dewey, *The School and Society*

Supplementary Reading

H. S. Commager, **The American Mind** (1950), and P. A. Carter, **The Spiritual Crisis of the Gilded Age** (1971), discuss the intellectual history of this period. On education, see L. A. Cremin, **The Transformation of the School: Progressivism in American Education** (1961). The best treatment of the Chautauqua movement is Victoria and R. O. Case, **We Called It Culture** (1948). Trends in the history of journalism are discussed in B. A. Weisberger, **The American Newspaperman** (1961). Also useful are George Juergens, **Joseph Pulitzer** (1966), and W. A. Swanberg, **Citizen Hearst** (1961).

On higher education, see L. R. Veysey, **The Emergence of the American University** (1965), two books by Hugh Hawkins, **Pioneer** (1960) on Johns Hopkins University, and **Between Harvard and America** (1972), on Charles W. Eliot. E. A. Green, **Mary Lyon and Mount Holyoke** (1979), is also useful. For developments in American science, see the essay by P. F. Boller, Jr., in H. W. Morgan (ed.), **The Gilded Age** (1970). A good introduction to the work of the social scientists is Sidney Fine, **Laissez-Faire and the General-Welfare State** (1957).

The literary figures of the age are discussed in Everett Carter, **Howells and the Age of Realism** (1954), E. H. Cady, **The Realist at War** (1958), Justin Kaplan, **Mr. Clemens and Mark Twain** (1966), and Leon Edel, **Henry James** (1953–1962). Art is discussed in Barbara Novak, **American Painting of the Nineteenth Century** (1969), and Russell Lynes, **The Lively Audience** (1985). On pragmatism, see Bruce Kuklick, **The Rise of American Philosophy** (1977).

CHAPTER 22

Politics: Local, State, and National

THE MAJOR AMERICAN POLITICAL PARties have nearly always avoided clear-cut stands on controversial questions in order to appeal to as wide a segment of the electorate as possible, but in the last quarter of the 19th century, their equivocations assumed abnormal proportions. This was due in part to the precarious balance of power between them: Neither dared declare itself too clearly on any question lest it drive away more voters than it attracted.

The rapid pace of social and economic change also militated against political decisiveness. No one in or out of politics had as yet devised effective solutions for many current problems. When party leaders tried to deal with the financial matters, they discovered that the bankers and the professional economists were as confused as the public at large. How could mere politicians act rationally or consistently in such circumstances?

On tariff questions the parties stumbled badly because in a complex industrial economy tariffs should not be determined by counting noses. Reformers could thunder self-righteously against the spoils system, but how could political parties exist without it? Young economists like Richard T. Ely were insisting that laissez faire was outmoded, but no one had yet devised the techniques and instruments needed if the economy was to be measured and managed effectively by a central authority. If the politicians steered clear of the real issues, they did so as much out of a healthy respect for their own ignorance as out of any desire to avoid controversy.

Political Decision Making: Ethnic and Religious Issues

The major parties met in national conventions every four years to select their presidential candidates and draft platforms, but they remained essentially separate state organizations. Professionals spent far more time dealing with local people and local issues than they did thinking about matters of broad national concern. That meant entering a veritable maze of diverse and often conflicting interests. People's ethnic backgrounds, their religious affiliations, whether they lived in cities or on farms, and how they felt about the Civil War had no apparent relationship to national political issues but affected whether they voted Republican or Democratic.

The politicians were not shy about explaining

Chapter-opening illustration:
Detail from an engraving by Compton & Dry, "1888 Democratic National Convention, St. Louis."

why people voted the way they did. Senator George Frisbie Hoar of Massachusetts, for example, offered such an analysis in an 1889 magazine article. The Republicans, he wrote, were

> *the men who do the work of piety and charity in our churches . . . who administer our school systems . . . who own and till their own farms . . . who perform skilled labor . . . who went to the war . . . who paid the debt, and kept the currency sound, and saved the nation's honor.*

The Democrats, he went on, were "the old slave-owner and slave-driver, the saloon-keeper, the ballot-box-stuffer, the Kuklux, the criminal class of the great cities, and men who cannot read or write."

Despite the partisan nature of Hoar's analysis, it contained an element of truth; at least in the North, most of the "best people" were Republicans. But if Hoar had been correct, the Republicans would have swept the northern states at every election, which they assuredly did not. In any case, it was even more difficult to discover *why* people voted one way or the other. People of Irish descent tended to vote Democratic, but whether they did so because they lived in cities or because they were Roman Catholics or because they believed that most Americans of British descent voted Republican was not always clear.

Plausible generalizations break down when examined closely. Northerners were Republicans, southerners Democrats; Catholics were Democrats, Protestants Republicans; German-Americans voted Democratic; Americans of Scandinavian descent, Republican. All these statements are subject to a multitude of exceptions. They offer little guidance for predicting how, for example, a German Lutheran living in Tennessee would vote.

Local and state issues also interacted with religious and ethnic background to affect political attitudes. On prohibition, public education, and other sectarian matters subject to state and local control, voters split, surprisingly, along religious and ethnic lines. These tangles influenced political leaders' strategies and choice of candidates for office. And how voters felt about local issues almost invariably affected how they voted in national elections.

City Government

City governments were influenced by the religious and ethnic character of the inhabitants and were further complicated by the special problems of late-19th-century urban life, including helter-skelter growth, the influx of European immigrants, crime and corruption, and the need to develop costly transportation and public utility systems. The movement to the suburbs of middle-class city people who might have been expected to supply the political leadership needed to deal with these problems created a vacuum that was filled by political bosses, with their informal but powerful "machines."

The immigrants who flocked into American cities in the 1880s and early 1890s had come from societies unacquainted with the blessings of democracy and thus had no experience with representative government. The tendency of urban workers to move frequently in search of better jobs further lessened the likelihood that they would develop political influence independently. Furthermore, the difficulties of life in the slums bewildered newcomers, both native and foreign-born. They could hardly be expected to take a broad view of social problems when so beset by personal ones. This enabled shrewd urban politicians, most of them in this period of Irish origin, to take command of the city masses and march them in obedient phalanxes to the polls.

Most city machines were not bureaucracies ruled by a single leader but rather loose-knit neighborhood organizations headed by ward bosses. "Big Tim" Sullivan of New York's Lower East Side was typical of the breed. People like Sullivan performed many useful services for what they liked to think of as their constituents. They found jobs for new arrivals and distributed food and other help to all in bad times. Sullivan provided turkey dinners for 5,000 or more homeless people each Christmas, distributed new shoes to the poor children of his district on his birthday, and arranged summer boat rides and picnics for young and old alike. Informally, probably without consciously intending to do so, the bosses educated the immigrants in the complexities of American civilization.

The price of such aid—the bosses were not altruists—was unquestioning political support, which the bosses converted into cash. In New York, Sullivan levied tribute on gambling, had a hand in the liquor business, and controlled the issuance of peddlers' licenses. When he died in 1913, he was reputedly worth $1 million. Yet 25,000 grieving constituents followed Big Tim's coffin on its way to the grave.

The more visible and better-known city bosses

played less socially justifiable roles than the ward bosses. Their principal technique for extracting money from the public till was the kickback. To get city contracts, suppliers were made to pad their bills and turn over the excess to the politicians. Similarly, operators of streetcar lines, gas and electricity companies, and other public utilities were compelled to pay huge bribes to obtain favorable franchises.

The most notorious of the 19th-century city bosses was William Marcy Tweed, whose "Tweed Ring" extracted tens of millions of dollars from New York City during the brief period from 1869 to 1871. Tweed was swiftly jailed. More typical was Richard Croker, who ruled New York's Tammany Hall organization from the mid-1880s to the end of the century. Croker's power rested on his position as chairman of the Tammany Hall finance committee. He accumulated a large fortune and owned a $200,000 mansion and a stable of racehorses, one of which was good enough to win the English Derby.

Despite their welfare work and their popularity, most bosses were essentially thieves. Efforts to romanticize them as the Robin Hoods of industrial society grossly distort the facts. However, the system developed and survived because too many middle-class city dwellers were indifferent to the fate of the poor.

Honest citizens who had no selfish stake in the system and who were repelled by the sordidness of city government were seldom sufficiently concerned to do anything about it. When the young Theodore Roosevelt decided to seek a political career in 1880, his New York socialite friends laughed in his face. They told him, Roosevelt wrote in his autobiography, "that politics were 'low'; that the organizations were not controlled by 'gentlemen'; that I would find them run by saloon-keepers, horse-car conductors, and the like." A British visitor in Chicago struck at the root of the urban problem of the era. "Everybody is fighting to be rich," he said, "and nobody can attend to making the city fit to live in."

Republicans and Democrats

As for national politics, with the Democrats invincible in the South and the Republicans predominant in New England and beyond the Mississippi, the outcome of presidential elections was usually determined in a handful of populous states: New York (together with its satellites, New Jersey and Connecticut), Ohio, Indiana, and Illinois. That opinion in these states on important questions such the tariffs and monetary policy was divided and that every imaginable religious and ethnic interest was represented in the electorate go far to explain why the parties hesitated to commit themselves on issues. In every presidential election, Democrats and Republicans concentrated their heaviest guns on these states. Between 1868 and 1900, only three presidential candidates were not from New York, Ohio, Indiana, or Illinois, and all three lost.

Partisanship was intense in these states; politics was a form of popular entertainment, elections a kind of holiday for hardworking factory workers and farmers. Campaigns were conducted in a carnival atmosphere, amusement being substituted for serious debate. Large sums were spent on brass bands, barbecues, uniforms, and banners. Speakers of national reputation were imported to attract crowds, and spellbinders noted for their leather lungs—this was before the day of the loudspeaker—and their ability to arouse popular emotions were brought in to address mass meetings.

With success depending on so few swing voters, political morality plummeted. Mudslinging, character assassination, and plain lying were standard practice; bribery was routine. Drifters and other dissolute citizens were paid in cash—or more often in free drinks—to vote the party ticket. The names of persons long dead were solemnly inscribed in voting registers, their votes cast by impostors. During the 1880 campaign the Democratic national chairman, hearing that the Republicans were planning to transport Kentuckians into Indiana to vote illegally in that crucial state, urged Indiana Democrats to "check this outrageous fraud." Then, perhaps seeking an easier solution to the problem, he added: "If necessary . . . keep even with them." Presidents were sometimes made and unmade in this sordid fashion.

The Men in the White House

The leading statesmen of the period showed as little interest in important contemporary questions as the party hacks who made up the rank and file of their organizations. Consider the presidents.

Rutherford B. Hayes, president from 1877 to 1881, came to office with a distinguished record. Although he had a family to support, he volunteered for military service within weeks after the first shell fell on Fort Sumter. He was wounded at South Mountain, on the eve of Antietam, and later served under Sheridan in the Shenandoah Valley campaign of 1864. Entering the army as a major, he emerged a major general. In 1864 he was elected to Congress; four years later he became governor of Ohio, serving three terms altogether. The Republicans nominated him for president in 1876 because of his reputation for honesty and moderation, and his election, made possible by the Compromise of 1877, seemed to presage an era of sectional harmony and political probity.

Hayes saw himself more as a caretaker than a leader and believed that Congress should assume the main responsibility for solving national problems. One historian writes that he showed "no capacity for such large-minded leadership as might have tamed the political hordes and aroused the enthusiasm, or at least the interest, of the public."

Hayes complained about the South's failure to treat blacks decently after the withdrawal of federal troops, but he took no action. He worked for civil service reform yet failed to achieve the "thorough, rapid and complete" change he had promised. In most matters, he was content to "let the record show that he had made the requests."

Hayes's successor, James A. Garfield, was assassinated four months after his inauguration, but even in that short time, his ineffectiveness had been demonstrated. His great weakness was indecisiveness, and political patronage proved to be his undoing: The Republican party in 1880 was split into two factions, the "Stalwarts" and the "Half-Breeds." The Stalwarts, led by New York Senator Roscoe Conkling, believed in the blatant pursuit of the spoils of office. The Half-Breeds did not disagree but behaved more circumspectly, hoping to attract the support of independents. Competition for office was the main reason for their rivalry.

Garfield had been a compromise choice at the 1880 Republican convention. His election precipitated a great battle over patronage, the new president standing in a sort of no-man's-land between the factions. He did stand up to the most grasping politicians, resisting in particular the demands of Senator Conkling. By backing the investigation of a post office scandal and by appointing a Half-Breed collector of the Port of New York, he infuriated the Stalwarts. In July 1881 an unbalanced Stalwart lawyer named Charles J. Guiteau shot Garfield in the Washington railroad station. After lingering for weeks, the president died on September 19.

The assassination of Garfield elevated Chester A. Arthur to the presidency. Arthur was an early convert to the Republican party and rose rapidly in its local councils. In 1871 Grant gave him the juiciest political plum in the country, the collectorship of the Port of New York, which he held until removed by Hayes in 1878 for refusing to keep his hands out of party politics. The only elective position he ever held was the vice-presidency.

The tragic circumstances of his elevation to the presidency sobered Arthur considerably. He handled patronage matters with restraint, and he gave at least nominal support to the movement for civil service reform, which had been strengthened by the public indignation following the assassination of Garfield. In 1883 Congress passed the Pendleton Act, "classifying" about 10 percent of all government jobs and creating the bipartisan Civil Service Commission to administer competitive examinations for these positions. The law made it illegal to force officeholders to make political contributions and empowered the president to expand the list of classified positions at his discretion.

Many politicians resented the new system—one senator denounced it as "un-American"—but the Pendleton Act opened a new era in government administration. The results have been summed up by the historian Ari Hoogenboom:

> *"An unprofessional civil service became more professionalized. Better educated civil servants were recruited and society accorded them a higher place. . . . Local political considerations gave way in civil servants' minds to the national concerns of a federal office. Business influence and ideals replaced those of the politician.*

Arthur urged the appointment of a nonpartisan commission to study tariff rates and to suggest rational reductions. When the commission was created, he urged Congress to adopt its recommendations. He came out for federal regulation of railroads several years before the passage of the Interstate Commerce Act. As an administrator he was systematic, thoughtful, businesslike, and at the same time cheerful and considerate; nevertheless, he was a political failure. He made no real attempt to push his program through Congress, instead devoting most of his energies to a futile effort to build up his personal following in the Republican party by distributing favors. But the Stalwarts would not forgive his "desertion," and the reform element could not forget his past. At the 1884 convention the politicos shunted him aside.

The election of 1884 brought the Democrat Grover Cleveland to the White House. Elected governor of New York in 1882, his no-nonsense attitude toward public administration endeared him to civil service reformers at the same time that his basic conservatism pleased businessmen. When he vetoed a popular bill to force a reduction in the fares charged by the New York City elevated railway on the grounds that it was an unconstitutional violation of the company's franchise, his stock soared, and the Democrats nominated him for president in 1884.

The election revolved around personal issues, for the platforms of the parties were almost identical. On the one hand, the Republican candidate, the dynamic James G. Blaine, had an immense following, but his reputation had been soiled by the publication of the "Mulligan letters," which connected him with the corrupt granting of congressional favors to the Little Rock and Fort Smith Railroad. On the other hand, it came out during the campaign that Cleveland, a bachelor, had fathered an illegitimate child.

Blaine lost more heavily in the mudslinging than Cleveland, whose quiet courage telling the truth when his past was brought to light contrasted favorably with Blaine's unconvincing denials. A significant group of eastern Republicans, known as Mugwumps, campaigned for the Democrats.* However, Blaine ran a strong race against a general pro-Democratic trend; Cleveland won the election by fewer than 25,000 votes. The change of 600 ballots in New York would have given that state, and the presidency, to his opponent.

Civil service reformers overestimated Cleveland's commitment to their cause, for he believed in rotation in office, being as convinced as Andrew Jackson that anyone of "reasonable intelligence" could handle most government jobs. He did, however, insist on honesty and efficiency; as a result, he made few poor appointments. However, Cleveland had little imagination and too narrow a conception of his powers and duties to be a successful president. He could defend a position against heavy odds, yet he lacked flexibility. He took a fairly broad view of the powers of the federal government, but he thought it unseemly to put pressure on Congress, believing in "the entire independence of the executive and legislative branches."

Toward the end of his term Cleveland bestirred himself and tried to provide constructive leadership on the tariff question. The government was embarrassed by a large surplus revenue, which Cleveland hoped to reduce by cutting the duties on necessities and on raw materials used in manufacturing. He devoted his entire annual message of December 1887 to the tariff, thereby focusing public attention on the subject.

The House of Representatives, dominated by southern Democrats, passed a bill reducing many duties, but the measure, known as the Mills bill, was flagrantly partisan: It slashed rates on iron products, glass, wool, and other items made in the North but left those on southern goods almost untouched. The Republican-controlled Senate rejected the Mills bill, and the issue was left to be settled by the voters at the 1888 election.

In that contest, Cleveland obtained a plurality of the popular vote, but his opponent, Benjamin Harrison, grandson of President William Henry Harrison, carried most of the key northeastern industrial states by narrow margins, thereby obtaining a comfortable majority in the electoral college, 233 to 168.

Although intelligent and able, Harrison was too reserved to make a good politician. He did not suffer fools gladly and kept even his most important advisers at arm's length. One observer called him a "human iceberg." He believed ardently in protective tariffs, stating firmly, if illogically, that he was against "cheaper coats" because cheaper coats seemed "necessarily to involve a cheaper man and woman under the coat."

Harrison professed to favor civil service reform. He appointed the vigorous young reformer Theodore Roosevelt to the Civil Service Commission and then proceeded to undercut him systemati-

*The Mugwumps considered themselves reformers, but on social and economic questions nearly all of them were very conservative. They were sound-money proponents and advocates of laissez-faire. Reform to them consisted almost entirely of doing away with corruption and making the government more efficient.

cally. Before long the frustrated Roosevelt was calling the president a "cold blooded, narrow minded, prejudiced, obstinate, timid old psalm singing Indianapolis politician."

Under Harrison, Congress distinguished itself by expending, for the first time in a period of peace, more than $1 billion in a single session. It raised tariffs to an all-time high. The Sherman Antitrust Act was passed; so was the Silver Purchase Act, authorizing the government to coin large amounts of that metal, a measure much desired by mining interests and advocates of inflation. A "force" bill providing for federal control of elections as a means of protecting the right of southern blacks to vote—a right increasingly under attack—passed the House only to be filibustered to death in the Senate.

Harrison had little to do with these measures. By and large he failed, as one historian has said, to give the people "magnetic and responsive leadership." The Republicans lost control of Congress in 1890, and two years later Grover Cleveland swept back into power, defeating Harrison by more than 350,000 votes.

Congressional Leaders

Among the lesser politicians of the period, the most outstanding was unquestionably James G. Blaine of Maine, who served in Congress from 1863 to 1881, first in the House and then in the Senate. Blaine had many of the qualities that mark a great leader: personal dynamism, imagination, political intuition, oratorical ability, and a broad view of the national interest. He was basically a reasonable man. He favored sound money without inflexibly opposing every suggestion for increasing the volume of the currency. He supported the protective tariff system yet advocated reciprocity agreements to increase foreign trade. He adopted a tolerant attitude toward the South. Almost alone among the politicians of his generation, he was deeply interested in foreign affairs. His personal warmth captivated thousands.

That Blaine, though perennially an aspirant, never became president was in part a reflection of his abilities and his participation in so many controversial affairs. Naturally, he aroused jealousies and made many enemies. But some inexplicable flaw marred his character. He had a streak of recklessness entirely out of keeping with his reasonable position on most issues. The scandal of the Mulligan letters made a dark blot on his record. Blaine moved through history amid cheers and won a host of spectacular if petty triumphs, yet his career was barren, essentially tragic.

Roscoe Conkling's was another remarkable but empty career. Conkling served in Congress almost continually from 1859 to 1881 and was a great power, yet no measure of importance was attached to his name. He squandered his energies in acrimonious personal quarrels, caring only for partisan advantage.

Dozens of other figures might be mentioned. Congressman William McKinley of Ohio was the most personally attractive. A man of simple honesty, nobility of character, and quiet warmth, he was a politician to the core. The tariff was McKinley's special competence, the principle of protection his guiding star. In the early 1890s, the pinnacle of his career still lay in the future.

Another Ohioan, John Sherman, brother of the famous Civil War general, accomplished the remarkable feat of holding national office continuously for nearly half a century, from 1855 to 1898. However, he was colorless and stiff and altogether too willing to compromise his beliefs for political advantage. Sherman gave his name (and not much else) to the Antitrust Act of 1890 and to other important legislation, but in retrospect he left little mark on the history of the country despite his long service.

Thomas B. Reed, Republican congressman from Maine, was elected Speaker of the House in 1890 and quickly won the nickname "Czar" because of his autocratic way of expediting business. His control became so absolute that Washington jokesters said that representatives dared not breathe without his permission. Reed had large ambitions and the courage of his convictions, but his vindictiveness kept him from exercising a constructive influence on his times.

Agricultural Discontent

The vacuity of American politics may well have stemmed from the complacency of the middle-class majority. The country was growing, no foreign enemy threatened it, and the poor were mostly recent immigrants, blacks, and others with little influence, easily ignored by those in comfortable circumstances. However, one important group in society suffered increasingly as the years rolled by: the farmers. Out of their travail came the force that finally, in the 1890s, brought American politics face to face with the problems of the age.

Immediately after the Civil War, wheat sold for nearly $1.50 a bushel, and in the early 1870s it was still worth well over a dollar. By the mid-1890s the average price stood in the neighborhood of 60 cents. Cotton, the great southern staple, which sold for more than 30 cents a pound in 1866 and 15 cents in the early 1870s, at times in the 1890s fell below 6 cents.

The tariff on manufactured goods appeared to aggravate the farmers' predicament, and so did the domestic marketing system, which enabled a multitude of middlemen to gobble up a large share of the profits of agriculture. The shortage of credit, particularly in the South, was an additional burden. Furthermore, the improvements in transportation that made it practicable for farmers in Australia, Canada, Russia, and Argentina to sell their produce in western European markets increased the competition faced by Americans seeking to dispose of surplus produce abroad.

Throughout the mid-1880s farmers on the plains had experienced boom conditions. Adequate rainfall produced bountiful harvests, credit was available, and property values rose rapidly. In the 1880s the population of Kansas increased by 43 percent, that of Nebraska by 134 percent, that of the Dakotas by 278 percent. This agricultural expansion contributed to the destruction of open-range cattle raising and changed the economy of cattle towns like Dodge City, which came to depend more on farmers than on cowboys and ranchers for business.

Speculative booms occur periodically in every frontier district; like all others, this one collapsed when settlers and investors took a more realistic look at the prospects of the region. In this case special circumstances turned the slump into a catastrophe. A succession of dry years shattered the hopes of the farmers. The downward swing of the business cycle in the early 1890s completed the devastation. Settlers who had paid more for their lands than they were worth and borrowed money at high interest rates to do so found themselves squeezed relentlessly. Thousands lost their farms and returned eastward, penniless and dispirited. The population of Nebraska increased by fewer than 4,000 persons in the entire decade of the 1890s.

The Populist Movement

The agricultural depression triggered a new outburst of farm radicalism, the alliance movement. Alliances were organizations of farmers' clubs, most of which had sprung up during the bad times of the late 1870s. The first Knights of Reliance group was founded in 1877 in Lampasas County, Texas. As the Farmers Alliance, this organization expanded in northeastern Texas, and after 1885 it spread rapidly throughout the cotton states. Alliance leaders stressed cooperation. Their co-ops bought fertilizer and other supplies in bulk and sold them at fair prices to members. They sought to market their crops cooperatively but could not raise the necessary capital from banks—with the result that some of them began to question the workings of the American financial and monetary system. They became economic and social radicals in the process. In the northern regions a similar though less influential alliance movement developed.

The alliances adopted somewhat differing policies, but all agreed that agricultural prices were too low, that transportation costs were too high, and that something was radically wrong with the nation's financial system. All agreed, too, on the need for political action if the lot of the agriculturalist was to be improved.

Although the state alliances of the Dakotas and Kansas joined the Southern Alliance in 1889, for a time local prejudices and conflicting interests prevented the formation of a single national organization. Northern farmers mostly voted Republican, southerners Democratic, and resentments dating back to the Civil War lingered in all sections. Cotton-producing southerners opposed the protective tariff; most northerners, fearing the competition of foreign grain producers, favored it. Railroad regulation and federal land policy seemed vital questions to northerners; financial reform loomed largest in southern eyes. Northerners were receptive to the idea of forming a third party, while southerners, wedded to the one-party system, preferred working to capture local Democratic machines.

The farm groups entered local politics in the 1890 elections. Convinced of the righteousness of their cause, they campaigned with tremendous fervor. The results were encouraging. In the South, Alliance-sponsored gubernatorial candidates won in Georgia, Tennessee, South Carolina, and Texas; 8 southern legislatures fell under Alliance control, 44 congressmen and 3 senators committed to Alliance objectives were sent to Washington. In the West, Alliance candidates swept Kansas and captured a majority in the Nebraska legislature. In Minnesota and South Dakota they won enough offices to hold the balance of power between the major parties.

Such success, coupled with the reluctance of the Republicans and Democrats to make concessions to their demands, encouraged Alliance leaders to create a new national party. By uniting southern and western farmers, they broke the sectional barrier erected by the Civil War. If they could recruit industrial workers, perhaps a real political revolution could be accomplished. In February 1892 farm leaders, representatives of the Knights of Labor, and various professional reformers organized the People's, or Populist, party and issued a call for a national convention to meet at Omaha in July.

That convention nominated General James B. Weaver of Iowa for president and drafted a platform that called for a graduated income tax and national ownership of the railroads and the telegraph and telephone systems. It also proposed "subtreasury" plan that would permit farmers to hold nonperishable crops off the market when prices were low. To combat deflation further, the platform demanded the unlimited coinage of silver and an increase in the money supply "to no less than $50 per capita."

To make the government more responsive to

Jeremiah "Sockless Jerry" Simpson speaking at a political debate in Kansas in 1892. Like many Populists a flamboyant campaigner, Simpson earned his nickname by using the claim that he wore no socks against his well-dressed opponent for a congressional seat.

public opinion, the Populists urged the adoption of the initiative and referendum procedures and the election of United States senators by popular vote. To win the support of industrial workers, the platform denounced the use of Pinkerton detectives in labor disputes and backed the eight-hour day and the restriction of "undesirable" immigration.

The Populists created what the historian Lawrence Goodwyn has called "a multi-sectional institution of reform." They were not, however, revolutionaries. They saw themselves not as a persecuted minority but as a victimized majority betrayed by what would now be called the establishment. They were ambivalent about the free enterprise system, and they tended to attribute social and economic injustices not to built-in inequities in the system but to nefarious conspiracies organized by selfish interests in order to subvert the system.

The appearance of the new party was the most exciting and significant aspect of the presidential campaign of 1892, which saw Harrison and Cleveland refighting the election of 1888. The Populists put forth a host of colorful spellbinders: Tom Watson, a hot-tempered Georgia congressman; William A. Peffer, a senator from Kansas whose long beard and grave demeanor gave him the look of a Hebrew prophet; "Sockless Jerry" Simpson of Kansas, unlettered but full of grass-roots shrewdness and wit; Ignatius Donnelly, who claimed to be an authority on science, Shakespeare, and economics and whose widely read novel, *Caesar's Column* (1891), pictured an America of the future wherein a handful of plutocrats tyrannized masses of downtrodden workers and serfs.

In the one-party South, Populist strategists sought to wean black farmers away from the ruling Democratic organization. Their competition forced the "subsidies" paid for black votes up to as much as a dollar—two days' wages. Southern black farmers had their own Colored Alliance, and even before 1892 their leaders had worked closely with the white alliances. Of course, the blacks would be useless if they could not vote; therefore, white Populist leaders opposed the southern trend toward disfranchising blacks and called for full civil rights for all. In the Northwest the Populists assailed the "bankers' conspiracy" in unbridled terms. Ignatius Donnelly, running for governor of Minnesota, made 150 speeches, vowing to make the campaign "the liveliest ever seen" in the state.

The results proved disappointing. Tom Watson lost his seat in Congress, and Donnelly ran a poor third in the Minnesota gubernatorial race. The Populists did sweep Kansas. They elected local officials in other western states and cast over a million votes for General Weaver. But the effort to unite white and black farmers in the South failed miserably. Conservative Democrats, while continuing with considerable success to attract black voters, played on racial fears cruelly, insisting that the Populists sought to undermine white supremacy. Since most white Populists saw the alliance with blacks as at best a marriage of convenience, this argument had a deadly effect. Elsewhere, the party made no significant impression. Urban workers remained aloof.

By standing firmly for conservative financial policies, Cleveland attracted considerable Republican support and won a solid victory over Harrison in the electoral college, 277 to 145. Weaver's electoral vote was 22.

Showdown on Silver

One conclusion that politicians reached after analyzing the 1892 returns was that the money question was of paramount interest to the voters. By the early 1890s, discussion of federal monetary policy revolved around the coinage of silver. Traditionally, the United States had been on a bimetallic standard: Both gold and silver were coined, the number of grains of each in the dollar being adjusted periodically to reflect the commercial value of the two metals. An act of 1792 established a 15-to-1 ratio—371.25 grains of silver and 24.75 grains of gold were each worth one dollar at the Mint. In 1834 the ratio was changed to 16 to 1, and in 1853 to 14.8 to 1 to reflect the new discoveries of gold in California. This ratio slightly undervalued silver; in 1861, for example, the amount of silver bullion in a dollar was worth $1.03 on the open market, so no one took silver to the Mint for coinage. However, an avalanche of silver from the mines of Nevada and Colorado gradually depressed the price until, around 1874, it again became profitable for miners to coin their bullion. Alas, when they tried to do so, they discovered that the Coinage Act of 1873, taking account of the fact that no silver had been presented to the Mint in years, had demonetized the metal.

The silver miners denounced this "Crime of '73," and inflationists, who wanted more money put into circulation regardless of its base, joined them in demanding a return to bimetallism. Conservatives, still fighting the battle against greenback paper money, resisted strongly. The result was a series of compromises. In 1878 the Bland-Allison Act authorized the purchase of $2 to $4 million of silver a month at the market price, but this had little inflationary effect because the government consistently purchased the minimum amount. In 1890 the Sherman Silver Purchase Act required the government to buy 4.5 million *ounces* of silver monthly, but in the face of increasing supplies, the price of silver fell still further. The ratio reached 26 to 1 in 1893 and 32 to 1 in 1894 a year later.

The compromises satisfied no one. Silver miners grumbled because their bullion brought in only half what it had in the early 1870s. Debtors noted angrily that because of the general decline in prices, the dollars they used to meet their obligations were worth more than twice as much as in 1865. Advocates of the gold standard feared that unlimited silver coinage would be authorized, "destroying the value of the dollar." When a financial panic brought on by the collapse of the London banking house of Baring Brothers ushered in a severe industrial depression, the confidence of both silverites and "gold bugs" was further eroded.

President Cleveland believed that the controversy over silver had caused the depression by shaking the confidence of the business community. He summoned a special session of Congress, and by exerting immense political pressure, he obtained the repeal of the Sherman Silver Purchase Act in October 1893. All that this accomplished was to split the Democratic party, its southern and western wings deserting him almost to a man.

During 1894 and 1895, while the nation floundered in the worst depression it had ever experienced, a series of events further undermined public confidence. In the spring of 1894 several "armies" of the unemployed, the most imposing led by Jacob S. Coxey, an eccentric Ohio businessman, marched on Washington to demand relief. Coxey wanted the government to undertake a program of federal public works and to authorize local communities to exchange non-interest-bearing bonds with the Treasury for $500 million in paper money, the funds to be used to hire unemployed workers to build roads. The scheme, Coxey claimed, would pump money into the economy, provide work for the jobless, and benefit the entire nation by improving transportation facilities.

When Coxey's group of demonstrators, perhaps 500 in all, reached Washington, he and two other leaders were arrested for trespassing on the grounds of the Capitol. Their followers were dispersed by club-wielding policemen. This callous treatment convinced many Americans that the government had little interest in the suffering of the people, an opinion strengthened when Cleveland, in July 1894, used federal troops to crush the Pullman strike.

The next year the Supreme Court handed down several reactionary decisions. In *United States* v. *E. C. Knight Company* it refused to employ the Sherman Antitrust Act to break up the Sugar Trust. In *Pollock* v. *Farmers' Loan and Trust Company* it invalidated a federal income tax law. Finally, the Court denied a writ of habeas corpus to Eugene V. Debs of the American Railway Union, who was languishing in prison for disobeying a federal injunction during the Pullman strike.

On top of these indications of official conservatism came a desperate financial crisis. Throughout 1894 the Treasury's supply of gold dwindled as worried citizens exchanged greenbacks (now convertible into gold) for hard money and foreign investors cashed in large amounts of American securities. Early in 1895 the gold reserve touched a low point of $41 million.

At this juncture a syndicate of bankers headed by J. P. Morgan turned the tide by underwriting a $62 million bond issue, guaranteeing that half the gold would come from Europe. This caused a great public outcry; the spectacle of the nation being saved from bankruptcy by a private banker infuriated millions.

As the presidential election of 1896 approached, with the Populists demanding unlimited coinage of silver at a ratio of 16 to 1, the major parties found it impossible to continue straddling the money question. The Populist vote had increased by 42 percent in the 1894 congressional elections. After a generation of political equivocation, the major parties had to face an important issue squarely.

The Republicans, meeting to choose a candidate at St. Louis in June 1896, came out in favor of the gold standard and nominated Ohio's William McKinley for president. The Democratic convention met in July at Chicago. The pro-gold Cleveland element made a hard fight, but the silverites swept them aside. The high point came when a youthful Nebraskan named William Jennings Bryan spoke for silver against gold, for western farmers against the industrial East. His every sentence provoked ear-shattering applause. "Burn down your cities and leave our farms," he said, "and your cities will spring up again as if by magic; but destroy our farms and the grass will grow in the streets of every city in the country." He ended with a marvelous figure of speech that set the tone for the coming campaign. "You shall not press down upon the brow of labor this crown of thorns," he warned, bringing his hands down suggestively to his temples. "You shall not crucify mankind upon a cross of gold!" Dramatically, he extended his arms to the side, the very figure of the crucified Christ. The convention promptly adopted a platform calling for "the free and unlimited coinage of both silver and gold at the present legal ratio of 16 to 1" and went on to nominate Bryan, who was barely 36, for president.

This action put tremendous pressure on the Populists. If they supported Bryan, they risked losing their party identity; if they nominated another candidate, they would ensure McKinley's election. Those more concerned with immediate political advantage, especially incumbent and potential officeholders, took the former position. Others (mostly old Alliance members raised in the cooperative movement) who considered free silver a minor issue and a poor substitute for the subtreasury plan as an approach to the deflation problem, rejected "fusion" with the Democrats. In part because the delegates could not find a person of stature willing to become a candidate against him, the Populist convention nominated Bryan, seeking to preserve the party identity by substituting Tom Watson for the Democratic vice-presidential nominee, Arthur Sewall of Maine.

Portraits of William Jennings Bryan with his wife and children, along with the text of the "Cross of Gold" speech, appeared on this typically colorful campaign poster for the 1896 campaign.

The Election of 1896

Never did a presidential campaign arouse such intense emotions. The Republicans from the silver-mining states swung solidly behind Bryan. The gold Democrats refused to accept the decision of the Chicago convention and nominated a candidate of their own, 79-year-old Senator John M. Palmer of Illinois. Palmer ran only to injure Bryan. "Fellow Democrats," he announced, "I will not consider it any great fault if you decide to cast your vote for William McKinley."

At the start the Republicans seemed to have everything in their favor. Bryan's youth and relative lack of political experience—two terms in the House—contrasted unfavorably with McKinley's long service in Congress and as governor of Ohio and with his reputation for honesty and good judgment. The severe depression operated in favor of the party out of power. Furthermore, the newspapers came out almost unanimously for the Republicans. The Democrats had very little money and few well-known speakers to fight the campaign.

But Bryan proved to be a formidable opponent. Casting aside tradition, he took to the stump personally, traveling 18,000 miles and making over 600 speeches. He was one of the great orators, projecting an image of absolute sincerity without appearing fanatical or argumentative. At every major stop on his tour, huge crowds assembled. Everywhere he hammered away at the money question. Yet he did not neglect other issues. He was defending, he said, "all the people who suffer from the operations of trusts, syndicates, and combines."

McKinley's campaign was managed by a new type of politician, Marcus Alonzo Hanna, an Ohio businessman. In a sense Hanna was a product of the Pendleton Civil Service Act. When deprived of the contributions of officeholders, the parties turned to business for funds, and Hanna had one foot in each camp. He spent about $100,000 of his own money on the preconvention campaign. Before most Republicans realized how effective Bryan was on the stump, Hanna perceived the danger and sprang into action. Since the late 1880s the character of political organization had been changing. The Civil Service Act was also cutting down on the number of jobs available to reward campaign workers. At the same time, the new mass-circulation newspapers and the nationwide press associations were increasing the pressure on candidates to speak openly and often on national issues. This trend put a premium on party organization and consistency—the political trick of speaking out of one side of the mouth to one audience and out of the other to another no longer worked very well. The old military metaphors of political discourse, the terms *campaign* and *spoils* and *standard bearer,* remained, but others more businesslike became popular: *boss, machine, lobbyist.*

As the federal government became more involved in economic issues, business interests found more reason to be concerned about national elections and were more willing to spend money on behalf of candidates whose views they approved. In the campaign of 1888 the Republicans had set up a businessmen's "advisory board" to raise money and stir up enthusiasm for Benjamin Harrison.

Hanna understood what was happening to politics. Certain that money was the key to political power, he raised an enormous campaign fund. When businessmen hesitated to contribute, he pried open their purses by a combination of persuasion and intimidation. Banks and insurance companies were "assessed" a percentage of their assets, big corporations a share of their receipts, until some $3.5 million had been collected.

Hanna disbursed these funds with efficiency and imagination. He sent 1,500 speakers into the doubtful districts and blanketed the land with 250 million pieces of campaign literature, printed in a dozen languages. "He has advertised McKinley as if he were a patent medicine," Theodore Roosevelt exclaimed.

McKinley conducted a "front-porch campaign," making the proceedings seem delightfully informal. From every corner of the land, groups representing various regions, occupations, and interests descended on McKinley's unpretentious frame house in Canton, Ohio. Gathering on the lawn—the grass was soon reduced to mud, the fence stripped of pickets by souvenir hunters—the visitors paid their compliments to the candidate and heard him deliver a brief speech, while beside him on the porch his aged mother and adoring invalid wife listened with rapt attention. Then there was a small reception, during which the delegates were given an opportunity to shake their host's hand.

Despite the air of informality, these performances were carefully staged. The delegations arrived on a tightly coordinated schedule worked out by McKinley's staff and the railroads, which operated cut-rate excursion trains to Canton from all over the nation. McKinley was fully briefed on the special interests and attitudes of each group and on occasion even wrote the visitors' speeches himself. His own talks were carefully prepared, each calculated to make a particular point. All were reported fully in the newspapers. Thus without moving from his doorstep, McKinley met thousands of people from every section of the country.

These tactics worked admirably. On election day McKinley carried the East; the Middle West, including even Iowa, Minnesota, and North Dakota; and the Pacific Coast states of Oregon and California. Bryan won in the South, the plains states, and the Rocky Mountain region. McKinley collected 271 electoral votes to Bryan's 176, the popular vote being 7,036,000 to 6,468,000.

The Meaning of the Election

The sharp sectional division marked the failure of the Populist effort to unite northern and southern

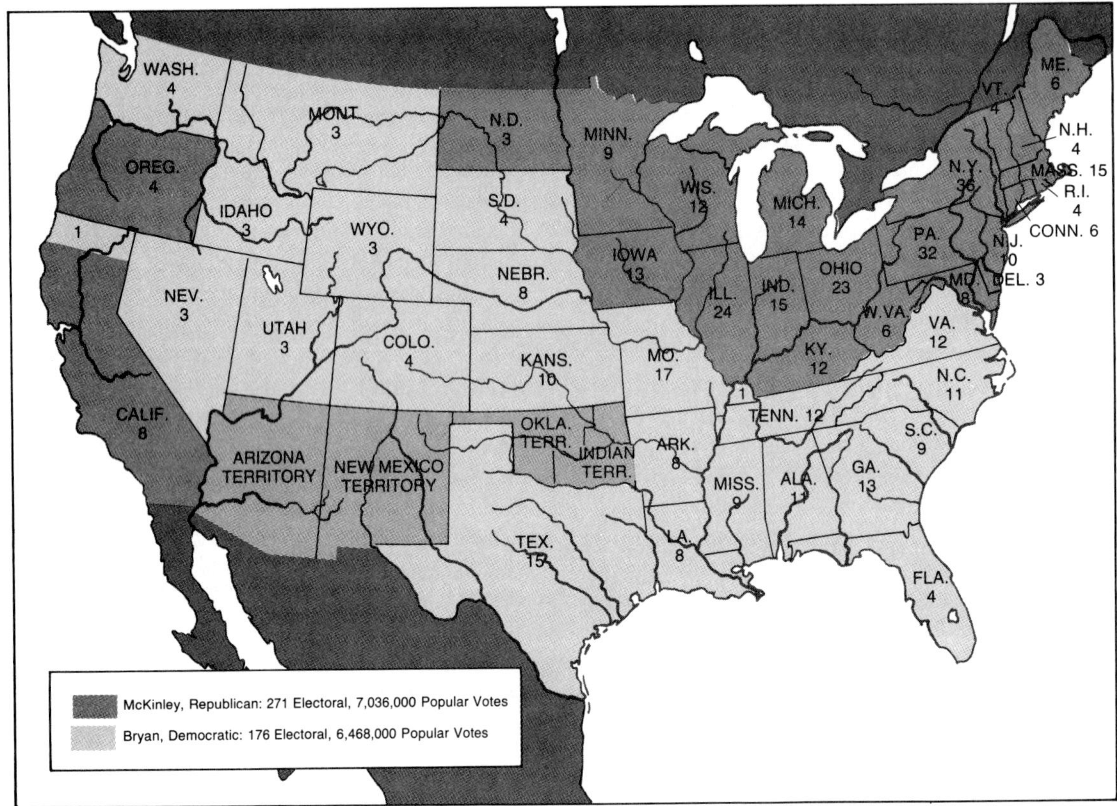

THE ELECTION OF 1896

farmers and also the triumph of the industrial part of the country over the agricultural. Business and financial interests voted solidly for the Republicans, but other groups were far from united. Many thousands of farmers voted for McKinley, and a preponderance of the labor vote went to him as well. The Republicans carried nearly all the large cities, and in closely contested states like Illinois and Ohio this made the difference between victory and defeat.

During the campaign some frightened Republicans had laid plans for fleeing the country if Bryan were elected, and belligerent ones, such as Theodore Roosevelt, at the time police commissioner of New York City, readied themselves to meet the "social revolutionaries" on the battlefield. Victory sent such people into transports of joy. Most conservatives concluded happily that the way of life they so fervently admired had been saved for all time.

However heartfelt, such sentiments were not founded on fact. With workers standing beside capitalists and with the farm vote split, it cannot be said that the election divided the nation class against class or that McKinley's victory saved the country from revolution.

Far from representing a triumph for the status quo, the election marked the coming of age of modern America. The battle between gold and silver, which everyone had considered so vital, had little real significance. The inflationists seemed to have been beaten, but new gold discoveries in Alaska and South Africa and improved methods of extracting gold from low-grade ores soon led to a great expansion of the money supply. Within two decades the system of basing the volume of currency on bullion had been abandoned.

Bryan and the "political" Populists who supported him, supposedly the advance agents of revolution, were oriented more toward the past than the future. Their ideal was the rural America of Jefferson and Jackson. McKinley, for all his innate conservatism, was capable of looking ahead toward the new century. His approach was national where Bryan's was basically parochial. Though never daring and seldom imaginative, McKinley was able to deal pragmatically with current problems. Before long, as the United States became increasingly an exporter of manufactures, he would even modify his position on the tariff. And no one better reflected the spirit of the age than Mark Hanna, the outstanding political realist of his generation. Far from preventing change, the outcome of the election of 1896 made possible still greater changes when the United States moved into the 20th century.

Milestones

1873 Congress suspends the coining of silver ("Crime of '73")
1877 Farmers Alliance movement begins
1878 Bland-Allison Act
1879 Greenback paper money made convertible into gold
1881 President Garfield assassinated
1883 Pendleton Civil Service Act
1887 Interstate Commerce Act
Cleveland's "tariff message"
1890 Sherman Silver Purchase Act
1892 Founding of the People's (Populist) party
1893 Panic of 1893
1894 Coxey's Army marches to Washington to demand relief
1895 Supreme Court declares federal income tax unconstitutional (*Pollock* v. *Farmers' Loan and Trust Company*)
J. P. Morgan raises $62 million in gold for the U.S. Treasury
1896 William Jennings Bryan, "Cross of Gold" speech
McKinley elected president

Supplementary Reading

The political history of this period is covered in H. W. Morgan, **From Hayes to McKinley** (1969). H. U. Faulkner, **Politics, Reform, and Expansion** (1959), treats the politics of the 1890s in some detail, while J. A. Garraty, **The New Commonwealth** (1968), attempts to trace the changing character of the political system after 1877 and D. J. Rothman, **Politics and Power: The United States Senate** (1966), analyzes the shifting structure of the upper house.

J. C. Teaford, **The Unheralded Triumph: City Government** (1984), B. C. Campbell, **Representative Democracy** (1980), R. J. Jensen, **The Winning of the Midwest** (1971), and Paul Kleppner, **The Cross of Culture** (1977) are important studies of the character of state and local politics.

Among biographies of political leaders, the following are especially worth consulting: Ari Hoogenboom, **The Presidency of Rutherford B. Hayes** (1988), Allan Peskin, **Garfield** (1978), F. C. Reeves, **Gentleman President: Chester A. Arthur** (1978), J. D. Doenecke, **The Presidency of James A. Garfield and Chester A. Arthur** (1981), Allan Nevins, **Grover Cleveland** (1932), H. E. Socolovsky and A. B. Spetter, **The Presidency of Benjamin Harrison** (1987), and H. W. Morgan, **William McKinley and His America** (1963).

For the farmers' problems, see F. A. Shannon, **The Farmer's Last Frontier** (1945), J. D. Hicks, **The Populist Revolt** (1931), and Theodore Saloutos, **Farmer Movements in the South** (1960). Populism has been the subject of intensive study. Richard Hofstadter, **The Age of Reform** (1955), takes a dim view of Populism as a reform movement, while Lawrence Goodwyn, **Democratic Promise: The Populist Movement in America** (1976), calls it "a people's movement of mass democratic aspiration." R. W. Cherny, **Populism, Progressivism, and the Transformation of Nebraska Politics** (1981), and Sheldon Hackney, **Populism to Progressivism in Alabama** (1969), are more than local studies. See also Steven Hahn, **The Roots of Southern Populism** (1983).

On the depression of the 1890s, consult Charles Hoffman, **The Depression of the Nineties** (1970), Carlos Schwantes, **Coxey's Army** (1985), Stanley Buder, **Pullman** (1967), and Nick Salvatore, **Eugene V. Debs** (1982). On Bryan and the election of 1896 see P. E. Glad, **The Trumpet Soundeth** (1960), R. W. Cherny, **William Jennings Bryan** (1985), and S. L. Jones, **The Presidential Election of 1896** (1964).

CHAPTER 23

From Isolation to Empire

AMERICANS HAVE ALWAYS BEEN somewhat ambivalent in their attitudes toward other nations. At no time was this more clearly the case than in the decades following the Civil War. Occupied with the task of exploiting the West and building their great industrial machine, they gave little thought to foreign affairs.

America's Divided View of the World

Late-19th-century Americans never ignored world affairs entirely. They had little direct concern for what went on in Europe, but their interest in Latin America was great and growing, in the Far East only somewhat less so. Economic developments, especially certain shifts in foreign commerce resulting from industrialization, were strengthening this interest with every passing year.

The disdain of the people of the United States for Europe was based on faith in the unique character of American civilization—and the opposite of that belief, suspicion of Europe's aristocratic and supposedly decadent society. When occasional conflicts with one or another of the great powers erupted, the United States pressed its claims hard. It insisted, for example, that Great Britain pay for the loss of some 100,000 tons of American shipping sunk by Confederate cruisers that had been built in British yards during the Civil War. In 1871 the two nations signed the Treaty of Washington, agreeing to arbitrate these so-called *Alabama* claims. The next year the judges awarded the United States $15.5 million for the ships and cargoes that had been destroyed.

In the 1880s a squabble developed with Germany, France, and a number of other countries over their banning of American pork products, ostensibly because some uninspected American pork was discovered to be diseased. The affair produced a great deal of windy oratory denouncing European autocracy and led to threats of economic retaliation. Congress eventually provided for the inspection of meat destined for export, and in 1891 the European nations lifted the ban. Similarly, there were repeated alarms and outbursts of anti-British feeling in the

Chapter-opening illustration:
Joseph Keppler's 1904 drawing, "The Eagle of American Imperialism." The caption reads, "Gee, but this is an awful stretch!"

United States in connection with Great Britain's treatment of Ireland, motivated chiefly by the desire of politicians to appeal to Irish-American voters.

Origins of the Large Policy

The nation's interests elsewhere in the world gradually increased. During the Civil War, France had established a protectorate over Mexico, installing Archduke Maximilian of Austria as emperor. In 1866 Secretary of State William H. Seward demanded that the French withdraw, and the government moved 50,000 soldiers to the Rio Grande. Fearing American intervention, among other reasons, the French did pull their troops out of Mexico during the winter of 1866–1867. Shortly thereafter, at Seward's instigation, the United States purchased Alaska from Russia for $7.2 million, thereby ridding the continent of another foreign power.

That same year, 1867, the aggressive Seward acquired the Midway Islands in the western Pacific, which had been discovered in 1859 by an American naval officer, N. C. Brooks. Seward also made overtures toward annexing the Hawaiian Islands, and he looked longingly at Cuba. But the nation was unready for such grandiose schemes; Seward had to admit that there was no significant support in the country for his expansionist plans.

Americans' preoccupation with internal growth eventually led them to look outward. In the late 1880s the country was exporting a steadily increasing share of its agricultural and industrial output. The character of foreign trade was also changing: Manufactures loomed ever more important among exports. When American industrialists became conscious of their ability to compete with Europeans in far-off markets, they took more interest in world affairs, particularly during periods of depression, when domestic consumption fell.

Shifting intellectual currents further altered attitudes. Darwin's theories, applicable by analogy to international relations, gave the concept of manifest destiny a new plausibility. Darwinists like the historian John Fiske argued that the American democratic system of government was so clearly the world's "fittest" that it was destined to spread peacefully over "every land on the earth's surface." In *Our Country* (1885), Josiah Strong found racist and religious justifications for American expansionism, again based on the theory of evolution.

The completion of the conquest of the West encouraged Americans to consider expansion beyond the seas. "For nearly 300 years the dominant fact in American life has been expansion," declared Frederick Jackson Turner, propounder of the frontier thesis. "That these energies of expansion will no longer operate would be a rash prediction."

Military and strategic arguments were advanced to justify adopting a "large" policy. Although no foreign power menaced the country, the army commanders were much concerned with developing and maintaining a professional officer corps. The decrepit state of the navy vexed many of its officers and led one of them, Captain Alfred Thayer Mahan, to develop a startling theory about the importance of sea power, which he explained to the public in two important books, *The Influence of Sea Power upon History* (1890) and *The Influence of Sea Power upon the French Revolution and Empire* (1892). According to Mahan, history proved, that a nation with a powerful navy and the overseas bases necessary to maintain it would be invulnerable in war and prosperous in time of peace. Applied to the current American situation, this meant that in addition to building a modern fleet, the United States should obtain a string of coaling stations and bases in the Caribbean, annex the Hawaiian Islands, and cut a canal across Central America. Writing at a time when the imperialist-minded European nations were showing signs of extending their influence in South America and the Pacific, Mahan attracted many influential disciples who helped persuade Congress to increase naval appropriations.

The Course of Empire in the Pacific

The interest of the United States in the Pacific and the Far East began in the late 18th century, when the first American merchant ship dropped anchor in Canton harbor. The Hawaiian Islands were an important way station on the route to China, and by 1820 merchants and missionaries were making contacts there. As early as 1854 a movement to annex the islands existed, though this foundered because Hawaii insisted on being admitted to the Union as a state. Commodore Perry's expedition to Japan led to the signing of a commercial treaty (1858) that opened several Japanese ports to American traders.

The United States pursued a policy of cooperating with the European powers in expanding commercial opportunities in the Far East. This policy did not change radically after the Civil War. Despite Chinese protests over the exclusion of their nationals from the United States after 1882, American commercial privileges in China were not disturbed. American influence in Hawaii increased; the descendants of missionary families, most of them engaged in raising sugar, dominated the Hawaiian monarchy. In 1875 a reciprocity treaty admitted Hawaiian sugar to the United States free of duty in return for a promise to yield no territory to a foreign power. When this treaty was renewed in 1887, the United States obtained the right to establish a naval base at Pearl Harbor. In addition to occupying Midway Island, America obtained a foothold in the Samoan Islands in the South Pacific.

During the 1890s American interest in the Pacific area steadily intensified. Conditions in Hawaii had much to do with this. The McKinley Tariff Act of 1890, discontinuing the duty on raw sugar and compensating American producers of cane and beet sugar by granting them a bounty of 2 cents a pound, struck Hawaiian sugar growers hard, for it destroyed the advantage they had gained in the reciprocity treaty. The following year the death of the complaisant King Kalakaua brought Queen Liliuokalani, a determined nationalist, to the throne. Placing herself at the head of a "Hawaii for the Hawaiians" movement, she abolished the existing constitution under which the white minority had pretty much controlled the islands and attempted to rule as an absolute monarch.

The resident Americans then staged a coup. In January 1893, with the connivance of the United States minister, John L. Stevens, who ordered 150 marines from the cruiser *Boston* into Honolulu, they deposed Queen Liliuokalani and set up a provisional government. Stevens recognized the regime at once, and the new government promptly sent a delegation to Washington to seek a treaty of annexation.

In the closing days of the Harrison administration such a treaty was negotiated and sent to the Senate, but when Cleveland took office in March, he withdrew it, dismissed Stevens, and attempted to restore Queen Liliuokalani. Since the provisional government was by that time firmly entrenched, this could not be accomplished peacefully, and Cleveland was unwilling to use force against the Americans in the islands, however much he objected to their actions. The revolutionary government of Hawaii remained in power, independent yet eager to be annexed.

The Hawaiian debate continued sporadically over the next four years. It provided a thorough airing of the question of overseas expansion. Fears that another power—Great Britain or perhaps Japan—might step into the void created by Cleveland's refusal to act alarmed advocates of annexation. When the Republicans returned to power in 1897, a new annexation treaty was negotiated, but domestic sugar producers now threw their weight against it, and the McKinley administration could not obtain the necessary two-thirds majority in the Senate. Finally, in July 1898, after the outbreak of the Spanish-American War, Congress annexed the islands by joint resolution, a procedure requiring only a simple majority vote.

The Course of Empire in Latin America

Most of the arguments for extending American influence in the Pacific applied more strongly to Central and South America, where the United States had much larger economic interests and where the strategic importance of the region was clear. Furthermore, the Monroe Doctrine had long conditioned the American people to the idea of acting to protect national interests in the Western Hemisphere.

As early as 1869 President Grant had come out for an American-owned canal across the isthmus of Panama, in spite of the fact that the United States had agreed in the Clayton-Bulwer Treaty with Great Britain (1850) that neither nation would "obtain or maintain for itself any exclusive control" over an interoceanic canal. In 1880, when the French engineer Ferdinand de Lesseps organized a company to build a canal across the isthmus, President Hayes announced that the United States would not permit a European power to control such a waterway. "The policy of the country is a canal under American control," he announced, again blithely disregarding of the Clayton-Bulwer agreement.

Aside from minor incidents, no trouble developed in Latin America until 1895. Then, quite suddenly, the United States found itself on the verge of war as a result of a crisis in Venezuela. Before this issue was settled Cleveland had proclaimed the most powerful statement of American hegemony in the hemisphere ever uttered.

The tangled borderland between Venezuela and British Guiana had long been in dispute, Venezuela demanding more of the region than it was entitled to and Great Britain submitting exaggerated claims and imperiously refusing to submit the question to arbitration. What made a crisis of the controversy was the political situation in the United States. With his party rapidly deserting him because of his stand on the silver question, and with the election of 1896 approaching, President Cleveland desperately needed a popular issue.

There was considerable latent anti-British feeling in the United States. By taking the Venezuelan side in the boundary dispute, Cleveland would be defending a weak neighbor against a great power, a position certain to evoke a popular response.

Cleveland did not resist the temptation to intervene. In July 1895 he ordered Secretary of State Richard Olney to send a near-ultimatum to the British. By occupying the disputed territory, Olney insisted, Great Britain was invading Venezuela and violating the Monroe Doctrine. Quite gratuitously, he went on to boast: "To-day the United States is practically sovereign on this continent, and its fiat is law upon the subjects to which it confines its interposition." Unless Great Britain responded promptly by agreeing to arbitration, the president would call the question to the attention of Congress.

The note threatened war, but the British ignored it for months. They did not take the United States seriously as a world power. When Lord Salisbury, the prime minister and foreign secretary, finally replied, he rejected outright the argument that the Monroe Doctrine had any status under international law and refused to arbitrate what he called the "exaggerated pretensions" of the Venezuelans.

If Olney's note had been belligerent, this reply was supercilious and sharp to the point of asperity. Cleveland was furious. On December 17, 1895, he asked Congress for authority to appoint an American commission to determine the correct line between British Guiana and Venezuela. When that had been done, he added, the United States should "resist by every means in its power" the appropriation by Great Britain of any territory "we have determined of right belongs to Venezuela." Congress responded at once, unanimously appropriating $100,000 for the boundary commission. Popular approval was almost universal.

In Great Britain, government and people suddenly awoke to the seriousness of the situation. No one wanted a war with the United States over a remote patch of tropical real estate. Canada would be terribly vulnerable to American attack. The immense potential strength of the United States could no longer be ignored. Why make an enemy of a nation of 70 million, already the richest industrial power in the world? To fight with the United States, the British now realized, "would be an absurdity as well as a crime."

Great Britain agreed to arbitrate the boundary. The war scare subsided. When the arbitrators awarded nearly all the disputed region to Great Britain, whatever ill feeling the surrender may have occasioned in that country faded away. Instead of leading to war, the affair marked the beginning of an era of Anglo-American friendship. It had the unfortunate effect, however, of adding to the long-held American conviction that the nation could get what it wanted in international affairs by threat and bluster—a dangerous illusion.

The Cuban Revolution

On February 10, 1896, scarcely a week after Venezuela and Great Britain signed the treaty ending their dispute, General Valeriano Weyler arrived in Havana from Spain to take up his duties as governor of Cuba. His assignment to this post was occasioned by the guerrilla war that Cuban nationalist rebels had been waging for almost a year. Weyler began herding the rural population into wretched "reconcentration" camps in order to deprive the rebels of food and recruits. Resistance in Cuba hardened.

Public sympathy went to the Cubans, who seemed to be fighting for liberty and democracy against an autocratic Old World power. Most American newspapers supported the rebels; labor unions, veterans' organizations, many Protestant clergymen, and important politicians in both major parties demanded that the United States aid their cause. Rapidly increasing American investments in Cuban sugar plantations, now approaching $50 million, were endangered by the fighting and by the social

Instability in Latin America led to speculation that the United States would play an increasingly dominant role in the region. In Louis Dalrymple's 1895 cartoon, Uncle Sam wins the affections of the damsel Cuba as Spanish misrule and native insurgency lay waste to each other.

chaos sweeping the island. Cuban propagandists in the United States played on American sentiments cleverly. When reports, often exaggerated, of the cruelty of "Butcher" Weyler and the horrors of his reconcentration camps began to filter into America, the cries for action intensified.

In April 1896, Congress adopted a resolution suggesting that the revolutionaries be granted the rights of belligerents. Since it would have been akin to formal recognition, Cleveland would not go that far, but he did exert diplomatic pressure on Spain to remove the causes of the rebels' complaints, and he offered the services of his government as mediator. The Spanish rejected the suggestion.

For a time the issue subsided. The election of 1896 deflected American attention from Cuba, and then McKinley refused to take any action that might disturb Spanish-American relations. Business interests—except those with holdings in Cuba—backed McKinley because they feared that a crisis would upset the economy, which was just beginning to pick up after the depression. In Cuba, General Weyler made some progress toward stifling rebel resistance.

American expansionists, however, continued to demand intervention, and the press, especially Joseph Pulitzer's *New York World* and William Randolph Hearst's *New York Journal,* competing fiercely to increase circulation, kept resentment alive with tales of Spanish atrocities. McKinley remained adamant. In a message to Congress in December 1897, he urged that Spain be given "a reasonable chance to realize her expectations" in the island.

Spain, however, failed to "realize her expectations." The fighting in Cuba continued. When riots broke out in Havana in January 1898, McKinley ordered the battleship *Maine* to Havana harbor to protect American citizens. Shortly thereafter, Hearst's *Journal* printed a letter written to a friend in Cuba by the Spanish minister in Washington, Depuy de Lôme. The letter had been stolen by a spy. De Lôme, an experienced but arrogant diplomat, failed to appreciate McKinley's efforts to avoid intervening in Cuba. In the letter he characterized the president as a *politicastro,* or "small-time politician," which was a gross error, and a "bidder for the admiration of the crowd," which was equally insulting, though somewhat closer to the truth. Americans were outraged, and de Lôme's hasty resignation did little to soothe their feelings.

Then, on February 15, the *Maine* exploded and sank in Havana harbor, 260 of its crew perishing in the disaster. Interventionists in the United States accused Spain of having destroyed the ship and clamored for war. The willingness of Americans to blame Spain indicates the extent of anti-Spanish opinion in the United States by 1898. No one has ever discovered what actually happened. A naval court of inquiry decided that the vessel had indeed been sunk by a submarine mine, but it now seems more likely that an internal explosion destroyed the *Maine.* The Spanish government could hardly have been so foolish as to commit an act so likely to bring American troops into Cuba.

With admirable courage, McKinley refused to panic, but he could not resist the urging of millions of citizens that something be done to stop the fighting and allow the Cubans to determine their own fate. The president faced a dilemma. Most of the business interests of the country, to which he was particularly sensitive, opposed intervention. His personal feelings were equally firm. "I have been through one war," he told a friend. "I have seen the dead piled up, and I do not want to see another." Congress, however, seemed determined to act, and should Congress declare war on its own, the administration would be discredited. In April the president drafted a message asking for authority to use the armed forces "to secure a full and final termination of hostilities" in Cuba.

The "Splendid Little" Spanish-American War

On April 20 Congress, by joint resolution, recognized the independence of Cuba and authorized the use of the armed forces to drive the Spanish out. An amendment proposed by Senator Henry M. Teller disclaiming any intention of adding Cuban territory to the United States passed without opposition. Four days later Spain declared war on the United States.

The Spanish-American War was fought to free Cuba, but the first action took place on the other side of the globe, in the Philippine Islands. Weeks earlier, Assistant Secretary of the Navy Theodore Roosevelt had alerted Commodore George Dewey, who was in command of the United States Asiatic Squadron located at Hong Kong, to move against the Spanish base at Manila if war came. When word of the declaration of war reached Dewey, he steamed from Hong Kong across the South China Sea with four cruisers and two gunboats. On the night of April 30 he entered Manila Bay, and at daybreak his warships opened fire on the Spanish fleet at 5,000 yards. All ten of Admiral Montojo's ships were destroyed. Not a single American was killed in the engagement.

McKinley took the fateful step of dispatching some 11,000 soldiers and additional naval support. On August 13 these forces, assisted by Filipino irregulars under the nationalist leader Emilio Aguinaldo, captured Manila.

Meanwhile, in the main theater of operations, the United States had won a swift and total victory. Since a Spanish fleet under Admiral Pascual Cervera was known to be in Caribbean waters, no invading army could safely embark until the fleet could be located. On May 29, American ships found Cervera at Santiago harbor, on the eastern end of Cuba, and established a blockade. In June a 17,000-man expeditionary force commanded by General William Shafter landed at Daiquiri, east of Santiago, and pressed quickly toward the city, handicapped more by its own poor staff work than by the enemy, though the Spanish troops resisted bravely. On July 1 the Americans broke through undermanned Spanish defenses and stormed San Juan Hill, the intrepid Theodore Roosevelt, now a lieutenant colonel in the regiment of "Rough Riders," in the vanguard.

With Santiago harbor in range of American artillery, Admiral Cervera had to run the blockade. On July 3 his black-hulled ships, flags proudly flying, steamed forth from the harbor and fled westward along the coast. Like hounds after rabbits, five American battleships and two cruisers, commanded by Rear Admiral William T. Sampson and Commodore Winfield Scott Schley, ran them down. In four hours the entire Spanish force was destroyed by a hail of

8-inch and 13-inch projectiles. Damage to the American ships was superficial; only one seaman lost his life in the engagement.

The end came abruptly. Santiago surrendered on July 17. A few days later, other United States troops completed the occupation of Puerto Rico. On August 12, one day before the fall of Manila, Spain agreed to get out of Cuba and to cede Puerto Rico and the island of Guam in the Marianas to the United States. The future of the Philippines was to be settled at a formal peace conference, convening in Paris on October 1.

Developing a Colonial Policy

Although the Spanish resisted surrendering the Philippines at Paris, they had been so thoroughly defeated that they had no choice. The decision hung rather on the outcome of a conflict over policy within the United States. The war, won at so little cost militarily, produced problems far larger than those it solved. The nation had become a great power in the world's eyes. European leaders had been impressed by the forcefulness of Cleveland's diplomacy in the Venezuela boundary dispute and by the efficiency displayed by the navy in the war. The annexation of Hawaii and other overseas bases intensified their conviction that the United States was determined to become a major force in international affairs.

But were the American people willing to exercise that force? The debate over taking the Philippine Islands throws much light on their attitudes. The imagination of Americans had been captured by the trappings of empire, not by its essence. It was titillating to think of a world map liberally sprinkled with American flags and of the economic benefits that colonies might bring, but most citizens were not prepared to join in a worldwide struggle for power and influence. They entered blithely upon adventures in far-off regions without facing the implications.

Since the United States (in the Teller Amendment) had foresworn any claim to Cuba, logic dictated that a similar policy be applied to the Philippines. But now expansionists were eager to annex the entire archipelago. President McKinley adopted a cautious stance, but he too favored "the general principle of holding on to what we can get." A speaking tour of the Middle West in October 1898, during which he experimented with varying degrees of commitment to expansionism, convinced him that the public wanted the islands. Business opinion had shifted dramatically during the war. Business leaders were now calling the Philippines the gateway to the markets of the Far East.

The Anti-imperialists

An important minority objected strongly to the United States' acquiring overseas possessions. These anti-imperialists insisted that since no one would consider statehood for the Philippines, it would be unconstitutional to annex them. It was a violation of the spirit of the Declaration of Independence to govern a foreign territory without the consent of its inhabitants, Senator George Frisbie Hoar of Massachusetts argued. By taking over "vassal states" in "barbarous archipelagoes," the United States was "trampling . . . on our own great Charter, which recognizes alike the liberty and the dignity of individual manhood."

McKinley was sensitive to this appeal to idealism and tradition, which was the heart of the anti-imperialist argument, but he rejected it for several reasons. Many people who opposed Philippine annexation were neither idealists nor constitutional purists. Partisanship led numbers of Democrats to object. Other anti-imperialists were governed by racial and ethnic prejudices, as Senator Hoar's statement indicates. They opposed not expansion as such but expansion that brought under the American flag people whom they believed unfit for American citizenship. Labor leaders particularly feared the competition of "the Chinese, the Negritos, and the Malays" who would presumably flood into the United States if the Philippines were taken.

More compelling to McKinley was the absence of any practical alternative to annexation. Public opinion would not sanction restoring Spanish authority in the Philippines or allowing some other power to have them. That the Filipinos were sufficiently advanced and united socially to form a stable government if granted independence seemed unlikely. Senator Hoar believed that "for years and for generations, and perhaps for centuries, there would have been turbulence, disorder and revolution" in the islands if left to their own devices.

Strangely—for he was a kind and gentle man—Hoar faced this possibility with equanimity. McKinley was unable to do so. The president searched the depths of his soul and could find no solution but annexation. Of course, the state of public feeling made the decision easier. And he probably found the idea of presiding over an empire appealing. Certainly the commercial possibilities did not escape him. In the end it was with a heavy sense of responsibility that he ordered the American peace commissioners to insist on acquiring the Philippines. To salve the feelings of the Spanish, the United States agreed to pay $20 million for the archipelago, but it was a forced sale, accepted by Spain under duress.

The peace treaty faced a hard battle in the U.S. Senate, where a combination of partisan politics and anticolonialism made it difficult to amass the two-thirds majority necessary for ratification. McKinley had shrewdly appointed three senators, including one Democrat, to the peace commission. This predisposed many members of the upper house to approve the treaty, but the vote was close. William Jennings Bryan, titular head of the Democratic party, could probably have prevented ratification. Although he was personally opposed to taking the Philippines, he did not do so. To reject the treaty would leave the United States technically at war with Spain and the fate of the Philippines undetermined; better to accept the islands and then grant them independence. The question should be decided, Bryan said, in the forthcoming presidential election. Perplexed by Bryan's stand, a number of Democrats allowed themselves to be persuaded by the expansionists' arguments and by McKinley's judicious use of patronage; the treaty was ratified in February 1899 by a vote of 57 to 27.

The Philippine Rebellion

The national referendum that Bryan had hoped for never materialized. Bryan himself confused the issue in 1900 by making free silver a major plank in his platform, thereby driving conservative anti-imperialists into McKinley's arms. Moreover, early in 1899, the Filipino nationalists under Aguinaldo, furious because the United States would not withdraw, rose in rebellion. A savage guerrilla war resulted, one that cost far more in lives and money than the Spanish-American conflict.

Typical of combat waged in tangled country chiefly by small, isolated units surrounded by a hostile civilian population, neither side displayed much regard for the "rules" of war. Horrible tales of rape, arson, and murder by American troops began to filter back home, providing ammunition for the anti-imperialists. A commission that McKinley had sent to the Philippines in 1899 attributed the revolt to the ambitions of the nationalist leaders and recommended that the Philippines be granted independence at some indefinite future date. In 1900 McKinley sent a federal judge, William Howard Taft, to establish a government. Taft's policy of encouraging Filipinos to participate in a territorial government attracted many converts, but the rebellion went on.

Actually, McKinley's reelection in 1900 settled the Philippine question so far as most Americans were concerned. Anti-imperialists still claimed that it was unconstitutional to take over territories without the consent of the local population. Their reasoning, no matter how genuine, was naive: No American government had seriously considered the wishes of the American Indians, the French and Spanish settlers in Louisiana, the Eskimos of Alaska, or the people of Hawaii when it had seemed in the national interest to annex their lands.

Cuba and the United States

Grave constitutional questions arose as a result of the acquisitions that followed the Spanish-American War. McKinley had acted with remarkable independence in handling the problems involved in expansion. He set up military governments, for example, in Cuba, Puerto Rico, and the Philippines without specific congressional authority. But eventually both Congress and the Supreme Court took a hand in shaping colonial policy. In 1900 Congress passed the Foraker Act, establishing a civil government for Puerto Rico. It did not give the Puerto Ricans either American citizenship or full local self-government, and it placed tariffs on Puerto Rican products imported into the United States.

The tariff provision was promptly challenged in the courts on the grounds that Puerto Rico was part of the United States, but in *Downes* v. *Bidwell* (1901) the Supreme Court upheld the legality of the duties. In this and other "insular cases" the reasoning of the judges was more than ordinarily difficult to follow. The effect, however, was clear: The Constitution did not follow the flag; Congress could act toward the colonies almost as it pleased. A colony, one dissenting justice said, could be kept "like a disembodied shade, in an indeterminate state of ambiguous existence for an indefinite period."

The most heated arguments raged over Philippine policy, but the most difficult colonial problems concerned the relationship between the United States and Cuba, for there idealism and self-interest clashed painfully. Despite the desire of most Americans to free Cuba, an independent government could not easily be created. The insurgent government was feeble, corrupt, and oligarchic, the Cuban economy in a state of collapse, life chaotic. The first Americans entering Havana found the streets littered with garbage and the corpses of horses and dogs. All public services were at a standstill; it seemed essential for the United States, as McKinley said, to give "aid and direction" until "tranquillity" could be restored.

As soon as American troops landed in Cuba, trouble broke out between them and the populace. Most American soldiers viewed the ragged, half-starved insurgents as "thieving dagoes" and displayed an unfortunate race prejudice against their dark-skinned allies. General Shafter did not help matters. He believed the Cubans "no more fit for self-government than gun-powder is for hell," and he used the insurgents chiefly as labor troops. After the fall of Santiago, he refused to let rebel leaders participate in the formal surrender of the city. This infuriated the proud and idealistic Cuban commander, General Calixto Garcia.

When McKinley established a military government for Cuba late in 1898, it was soon embroiled with local leaders. Then an eager horde of American promoters descended on Cuba in search of profitable franchises and concessions.

The problems were indeed knotty, for no strong local leader capable of uniting Cuba appeared. European observers expected that the United States would eventually annex Cuba, and many Americans, including General Leonard Wood, who became military governor in December 1899, considered this the best solution. The desperate state of the people, the heavy economic stake of Americans in the region, and its strategic importance militated against withdrawal.

In the end the United States did withdraw, after doing a great deal to modernize sugar production, improve sanitary conditions, establish schools, and restore orderly administration. In November 1900 a Cuban constitutional convention met at Havana and proceeded without substantial American interference or direction to draft a frame of government. The chief restrictions imposed on Cuba's freedom concerned foreign relations; it authorized American intervention whenever necessary "for the preservation of Cuban independence" and "the maintenance of a government adequate for the protection of life, property, and individual liberty." Cuba had to grant naval bases on its soil to the United States.

This arrangement, known as the Platt Amendment, was accepted, after some grumbling, by the Cubans. It also had the support of most American opponents of imperialism. In May 1902 the United States turned over the reins of government to the new republic. The next year the two countries signed a reciprocity treaty tightening the economic bonds between them.

True friendship did not result. Although American troops occupied Cuba only once more, in 1906, at the specific request of Cuban authorities, the United States repeatedly used the threat of intervention to coerce the Cuban government. American economic penetration proceeded rapidly and without regard for the well-being of the Cuban peasants, many of whom lived in a state of peonage on great sugar plantations. Nor did their good intentions make up for the tendency of Americans to consider themselves innately superior to the Cubans and to overlook the fact that Cubans did not always wish to adopt American customs and culture.

The United States in the Caribbean

If the purpose of the Spanish-American War had been to bring peace and order to Cuba, the Platt Amendment was a logical step. The same purpose soon necessitated a further extension of the principle, for once the United States accepted the role of protector and stabilizer in part of the Caribbean, it seemed desirable, for the same economic, strategic, and humanitarian reasons, to supervise the entire region.

The Caribbean countries were economically underdeveloped, socially backward, politically unstable, and desperately poor. Everywhere a few families owned most of the land and dominated social and political life. The mass of the people were uneducated peasants, many of them little better off than slaves. Rival cliques of wealthy families struggled for power, force being the usual method of effecting a change in government. Most of the meager income of the average Caribbean state was swallowed up by the military or diverted into the pockets of the current rulers.

Cynicism and fraud poisoned the relations of most of these nations with the great powers. European merchants and bankers systematically cheated their Latin American customers, who in turn frequently refused to honor their obligations. Foreign bankers floated Caribbean bond issues on outrageous terms, while revolutionary Caribbean governments annulled concessions and repudiated debts with equal disdain for honest business dealing. Because these countries were weak, the powers tended to intervene whenever their nationals were cheated or when chaotic conditions endangered the lives and property of foreigners.

In 1902, shortly after the United States had pulled out of Cuba, trouble erupted in Venezuela, where a dictator, Cipriano Castro, was refusing to honor debts owed the citizens of European nations. To force him to pay up, Germany and Great Britain established a blockade of Venezuelan ports and destroyed a number of Venezuelan gunboats and harbor defenses. Under American pressure the Europeans agreed to arbitrate the dispute. For the first time, European powers had accepted the broad implications of the Monroe Doctrine.

By this time Theodore Roosevelt had become president of the United States, and he quickly capitalized on the new European attitude. In 1903 the Dominican Republic defaulted on bonds totaling some $40 million. When European investors urged their governments to intervene, Roosevelt announced that under the Monroe Doctrine the United States could not permit foreign nations to intervene in Latin America. But, he added, Latin American nations should not be allowed to escape their obligations. The president therefore arranged for the United States to take charge of the Dominican customs service—the one reliable source of revenue in that poverty-stricken country. Fifty-five percent of the customs duties would be devoted to debt payment, the remainder turned over to the Dominican government for its internal needs. Roosevelt defined his policy, known as the Roosevelt Corollary to the Monroe Doctrine, in a message to Congress in December 1904. "Chronic wrongdoing" in Latin America, he stated with his typical disregard for the subtleties of complex affairs, might require outside intervention. Since, under the Monroe Doctrine, no other nation could step in, the United States must "exercise . . . an international police power."

In the short run this policy worked admirably. Dominican customs duties were collected honestly for the first time, and the country's finances were put in order. The presence of American warships in the area provided a needed measure of political stability. In the long run, however, the Roosevelt Corollary caused resentment in Latin America, for it added to nationalist fears that the United States sought to exploit the region for its own benefit.

The Open Door Policy

The insular cases, the Platt Amendment, and the Roosevelt Corollary established the framework for American policy both in Latin America and east Asia. Coincidental with the Cuban rebellion of the 1890s, a far greater upheaval had convulsed the ancient empire of China. In 1894 and 1895 Japan had easily defeated China in a war over Korea. Alarmed by Japan's aggressiveness, the European powers hastened to carve out for themselves new spheres of influence along China's coast. After the annexation of the Philippines, McKinley's secretary of state, John Hay, urged on by businessmen fearful of losing out in the scramble to exploit the Chinese market, tried to prevent the further absorption of China by the great powers. For the United States to join in the dismemberment of China was politically impossible because of anti-imperialist feeling, so Hay sought to protect American interests by clever diplomacy. In a series of "Open Door" notes in 1899, he asked the powers to agree to respect the trading rights of all countries and to impose no discriminatory duties within their spheres of influence.

The replies to the Open Door notes were at best noncommittal, yet Hay blandly announced in March 1900 that the powers had "accepted" his suggestions! Thus he could claim to have prevented

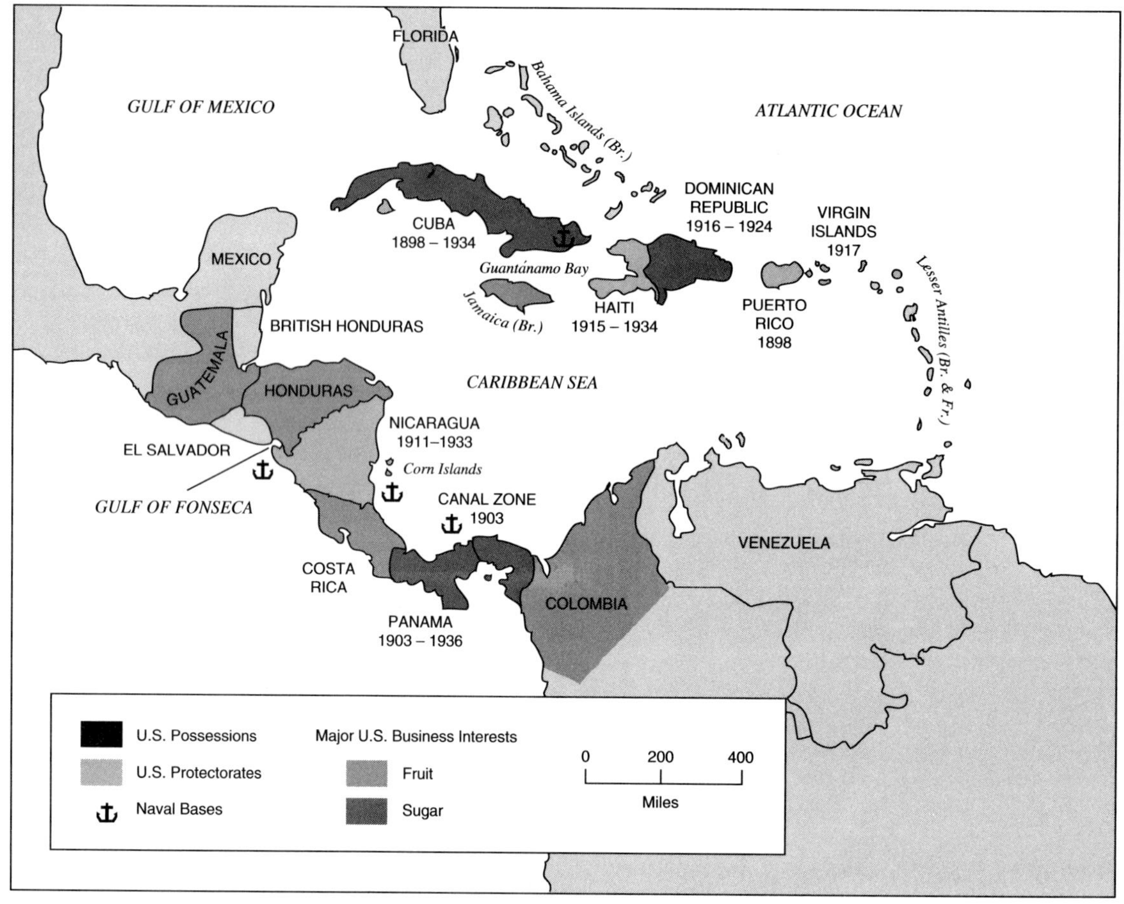

THE UNITED STATES IN THE CARIBBEAN

Puerto Rico was ceded by Spain after the Spanish-American War; the Virgin Islands were bought from Denmark; and the Canal Zone was leased from Panama. The ranges of dates indicate years during which the United States either had troops in occupation or had some other protectorate relationship with that country.

the breakup of the empire and protected the right of Americans to do business freely in its territories. In reality nothing had been accomplished; the imperialist nations did not extend their political control of China only because they feared that by doing so they might precipitate a major war among themselves. Nevertheless, Hay's action marked a bold advance into the complicated and dangerous world of international power politics.

Within a few months of Hay's announcement, the Open Door policy was put to the test. Chinese nationalists launched the so-called Boxer Rebellion. They swarmed into Peking and drove foreigners within the walls of their legations, which were placed under siege. For weeks, until an international rescue expedition broke through to free them, the fate of the foreigners was unknown. Fearing that the Europeans would use the rebellion as a pretext for further expropriations, Hay sent off another round of Open Door notes announcing that the United States believed in the preservation of "Chinese territorial and administrative entity" and in "the principle of equal and impartial trade with all parts of the Chinese Empire." This broadened the Open Door policy to include all China, not merely the European spheres of influence.

Hay's diplomacy was superficially successful. Though the United States maintained no important military force in the Far East, American business and commercial interests there were free to develop and to compete with Europeans. But once again European jealousies and fears rather than American cleverness were responsible. The United States was being caught up in the power struggle in the Far East without having faced the implications of its actions.

Eventually the country would pay a heavy price for this unrealistic attitude, but in the decade following 1900 its policy of diplomatic meddling unbacked by bayonets worked fairly well. Japan attacked Russia in a quarrel over Manchuria, smashing the Russian fleet in 1905 and winning a series of battles on the mainland. Eager to preserve the balance in the Far East, which enabled the United States to exert influence without any significant commitment of force, Roosevelt invited the belligerents to a conference at Portsmouth, New Hampshire. At the conference the Japanese won title to Russia's sphere around Port Arthur, a free hand in Korea, and part of Sakhalin Island. But the Japanese people had expected more and blamed Roosevelt for forcing a compromise. Ill feeling against Americans increased in 1906 when the San Francisco school board, responding to local opposition to the influx of cheap labor from Japan, instituted a policy of segregating Asian children in a special school. Japan protested, and President Roosevelt persuaded the San Franciscans to abandon segregation in exchange for his pledge to cut off further Japanese immigration. He accomplished this through a "Gentlemen's Agreement" (1907) in which the Japanese promised not to issue passports to laborers seeking to come to America. Discriminatory legislation based specifically on race was thus avoided. However, the atmosphere between the two countries remained charged. Japanese resentment at American race prejudice was great; many Americans talked fearfully of the "yellow peril."

Theodore Roosevelt was preeminently a realist in foreign relations. "Don't bluster," he once said. "Don't flourish a revolver, and never draw unless you intend to shoot." In the Far East, however, he failed to follow his own advice. He considered the situation in that part of the world fraught with peril. The Philippines, he eventually concluded, were "our heel of Achilles," indefensible in case of a Japanese attack. But even though he did not appreciably increase American naval and military strength in the Orient, neither did he stop trying to influence the course of events in the area. "The 'Open Door' policy," he advised his successor, "completely disappears as soon as a powerful nation determines to disregard it." Nevertheless, he allowed the belief to persist in the United States that the nation could influence the course of Far Eastern history without risk or real involvement.

The Isthmian Canal

In the Caribbean region, American policy centered on building an interoceanic canal across Central America. The first step was to get rid of the old Clayton-Bulwer Treaty with Great Britain, which barred the United States from building a canal on its own. In 1901 Lord Pauncefote, the British ambassador, and Secretary of State John Hay negotiated an agreement abrogating the Clayton-Bulwer pact and giving America the right to build, and by implication fortify, a transisthmian waterway. The United States agreed in turn to maintain any such canal "free and open to the vessels of commerce and of war of all nations."

One possible canal route lay across the Colombian province of Panama, where the French-controlled New Panama Canal Company had taken over the franchise of the old De Lesseps company. Only 50 miles separated the oceans in Panama, but the terrain was rugged and unhealthy. Though the French company had sunk much money into the project, it had little to show for its efforts aside from some rough excavations. A second possible route ran across Nicaragua. This route was about 200 miles long but was relatively easy since much of it traversed Lake Nicaragua and other natural waterways.

President McKinley appointed a commission to study the alternatives. It reported that the Panamanian route was technically superior but recommended building in Nicaragua because the New Panama Canal Company was asking $109 million for its assets, which the commission valued at only $40 million. Lacking another purchaser, the French company quickly lowered its price to $40 million, and President Roosevelt settled on the Panamanian route.

In January 1903, Secretary of State Hay negotiated a treaty with Colombia. In return for a 99-year lease on a zone across Panama 6 miles wide, the United States agreed to pay Colombia $10 million and an annual rent of $250,000. The Colombian senate, however, unanimously rejected this treaty, demanding $15 million directly from the United States, plus $10 million of the New Panama Canal Company's share.

A little more patience might have produced a mutually satisfactory settlement, but Roosevelt regarded the Colombians as highwaymen who were "mad to get hold of the $40,000,000 of the Frenchmen." When Panamanians, egged on by the French company, staged a revolution in November 1903, Roosevelt ordered the cruiser *Nashville* to Panama. Colombian government forces found themselves looking down the barrels of the guns of the *Nashville* and, shortly thereafter, eight other American warships. The revolution succeeded. Roosevelt instantly recognized the new Republic of Panama and negotiated a treaty granting the United States a zone 10 miles wide in perpetuity, on the same terms as those rejected by Colombia.*

Historians have condemned Roosevelt for his actions in this shabby affair, and with good reason. It was not that he fomented the revolution, for he did not. Nor was it that he prevented Colombia from suppressing the revolution. He sinned, rather, in his disregard of Latin American sensibilities. He referred to the Colombians as "dagoes" and insisted smugly that he was defending "the interests of collective civilization" when he overrode their opposition to his plans. "Have I defended myself?" Roosevelt asked Secretary of War Elihu Root. "You certainly have, Mr. President," Root retorted. "You were accused of seduction and you have conclusively proved that you were guilty of rape." Throughout Latin America, especially as nationalist sentiments grew stronger, Roosevelt's intolerance and aggressiveness in the canal incident bred resentment and fear.

The canal was built—the first vessels passed through its locks in 1914—and American hegemony in the Caribbean expanded. Yet even in that strategically vital area there was more show than substance to American strength. The navy ruled Caribbean waters largely by default.

*Panama was independent in name only because of American control of the canal. In 1978 the United States and Panama agreed to a treaty turning the entire Canal Zone over to Panama in the year 2000.

The tendency was to try to influence outlying areas without actually controlling them. Roosevelt's successor, William Howard Taft, called this policy "dollar diplomacy," his reasoning being that economic penetration would bring stability to underdeveloped areas and power and profit to the United States without having to commit American troops or spend public funds.

Under Taft the State Department won a place for American bankers in an international syndicate engaged in financing railroads in Manchuria. When Nicaragua defaulted on its foreign debt in 1911, the department arranged for American bankers to reorganize Nicaraguan finances and manage the customs service. Although the government truthfully insisted that it did not "covet an inch of territory south of the Rio Grande," dollar diplomacy provoked further apprehension in Latin America.

Economic penetration proceeded briskly. American investments in Cuba reached $500 million by 1920, and smaller but significant investments were made in the Dominican Republic and in Haiti. In Central America the United Fruit Company accumulated large holdings in banana plantations, railroads, and other ventures, and some U.S. firms plunged heavily into Mexico's rich mineral resources.

Noncolonial Imperial Expansion

The United States deserves fair marks for effort in its foreign relations following the Spanish-American War, barely passable marks for performance, and failing marks for results. If one defines imperialism narrowly as a policy of occupying and governing foreign lands, American imperialism lasted for an extremely short time. With trivial exceptions, all the American colonies—Hawaii, the Philippines, Guam, Puerto Rico, the Guantánamo base in Cuba, and the Canal Zone—were obtained between 1898 and 1903. In retrospect it seems clear that the urge to own colonies was only fleeting; the questions raised by anti-imperialists and the headaches connected with the management of overseas possessions soon produced a change of policy.

Hay's Open Door notes (which anti-imperialists praised) marked the beginning of the retreat from imperialism as thus defined, and the Roosevelt Corollary and dollar diplomacy signaled the consolidation of a new policy. Elihu Root summarized this policy toward underdeveloped countries in 1905: "We do not want to take them for ourselves. We do not want any foreign nations to take them for themselves. We want to help them."

Yet imperialism can be given a broader definition. The historian William Appleman Williams, a sharp critic, described 20th-century American foreign policy as one of "noncolonial imperial expansion." Its object was to obtain profitable American economic penetration of underdeveloped areas without the trouble of owning and controlling them. Its subsidiary aim was to encourage these countries to "modernize," that is, to remake themselves in the image of the United States.

Williams criticizes American policy *not* because it failed to work or because it led to trouble with the powers but because of its harmful effects on underdeveloped countries. Its creators were not evil; they merely lacked vision. They did not recognize the contradictions in their ideas and values. They saw American expansion as beneficial to all concerned—and not exclusively in materialistic terms. They genuinely believed that they were exporting democracy along with capitalism and industrialization.

Williams probably goes too far in arguing that American statesmen consciously planned their foreign policy in these terms. Yet he is correct in pointing out that western economic penetration has had many unfortunate results for the nonindustrial nations. It is also true that Americans were unimpressed by the different social and cultural patterns of people in far-off lands and insensitive to the wishes of these people to develop in their own ways.

The primary objectives of dollar diplomacy were the avoidance of violence and the economic development of Latin America; small heed was paid to the maintenance of peace or the distribution of the fruits of development. The policy, was therefore self-defeating, for long-run stability depended on the support of the people, and this was seldom forthcoming.

By the eve of World War I, the United States had become a world power and had assumed what it saw as a duty to guide the development of many countries with traditions far different from its own. The American people, however, did not really understand what this involved. They stood ready to extend their influence into distant lands with little awareness of the implications of their behavior for themselves or for other peoples. The national psychology remained fundamentally isolationist. Americans understood that their wealth and numbers made their nation strong and that geography made it practically invulnerable. They proceeded, then, to do as they pleased in foreign affairs, limited more by conscience than by rational analysis of probable consequences. This policy seemed safe enough—in 1914.

Milestones

1850 Clayton-Bulwer Canal Treaty
1858 Commercial treaty with Japan
1867 Alaska purchased from Russia
1871 Treaty of Washington, settling the *Alabama* claims
1875 Hawaiian reciprocity treaty
1885 Josiah Strong, *Our Country*
1890 A. T. Mahan, *The Influence of Sea Power upon History*
1893 Queen Liliuokalani of Hawaii overthrown
1895 Venezuela boundary dispute
1898 *Maine* explodes in Havana harbor
Spanish-American War breaks out
Battle of Manila Bay
Battle of San Juan Hill
Annexation of Hawaii
1899 Open Door notes
1900 Platt Amendment to the Cuban constitution
1901 Hay-Pauncefote Canal Treaty
Supreme Court decides insular cases on control of colonies
1902 Venezuela bond dispute
1904 Roosevelt Corollary to the Monroe Doctrine
1907 Gentlemen's Agreement" with Japan

Supplementary Reading

For the foreign relations of the era, Walter LaFeber, **The New Empire** (1963), presents a forceful but somewhat overstated argument on the extent of expansionist sentiment, especially on the part of American businessmen. See also Milton Plesur, **America's Outward Thrust** (1971), and C. S. Campbell, Jr., **Transformation of American Foreign Relations** (1976).

On the Spanish-American War, consult D. F. Trask, **The War with Spain in 1898** (1981), Frank Freidel, **The Splendid Little War** (1958), H. W. Morgan, **America's Road to Empire** (1965), and E. R. May, **Imperial Democracy** (1961). American imperialism is discussed in D. F. Healy, **U.S. Expansionism** (1970), Healy, **Drive to Hegemony** (1988), and W. A. Williams, **The Tragedy of American Diplomacy** (1962), the last critical of what the author calls "noncolonial imperial expansion."

R. L. Beisner, **Twelve Against Empire: The Anti-imperialists** (1968), contains lively and thoughtful sketches of leading foes of expansion. See also E. B. Thompkins, **Anti-imperialism in the United States** (1970). For colonial problems, see D. F. Healy, **The United States in Cuba: 1898–1902** (1963), R. E. Welch, **Response to Imperialism: The United States and the Philippine-American War** (1979), D. G. Munro, **Intervention and Dollar Diplomacy in the Caribbean: 1900–1921** (1964), and David McCullough, **The Path Between the Seas** (1977). R. E. Osgood, **Ideals and Self-Interest in America's Foreign Relations** (1953), and G. F. Kennan, **American Diplomacy: 1900–1950** (1951), are important interpretations of early 20th-century U.S. policy.

CHAPTER 24

Progressivism: The Age of Reform

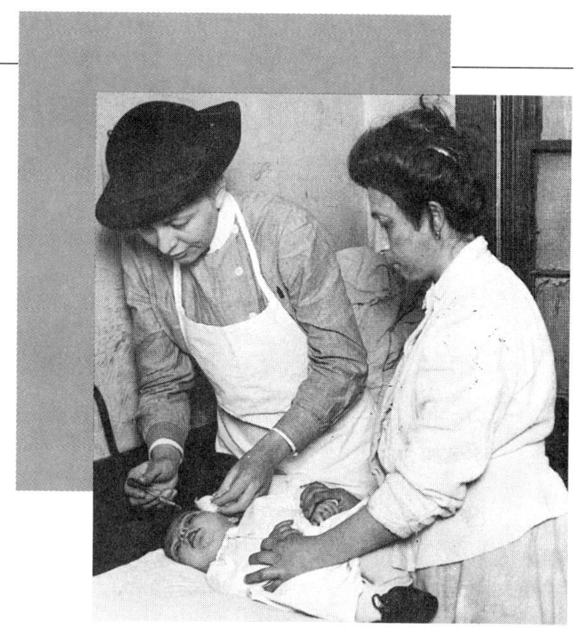

THE PERIOD BOUNDED ROUGHLY BY the end of the Spanish-American War and American entry into World War I is usually called the Progressive Era, though that is a great simplification. Whether *progressive* is taken to mean "tending toward change or improvement or is merely used to suggest an attitude of mind, it was neither a unique nor a universal characteristic of the early years of the 20th century. Progressive elements had existed in earlier periods and did not disappear when the first American soldiers shipped out for France. In important ways the progressivism of the time was a continuation of the response to industrialism that began after the Civil War.

Roots of Progressivism

The progressives were never a single group seeking a single objective. The movement sprang from many sources. One of them was the fight against corruption and inefficiency in government, which began with the Liberal Republicans of the Grant era and was continued by the Mugwumps of the 1880s. The continuing power of corrupt big-city political machines and the growing influence of large corporations outraged thousands of citizens and led them to seek ways of purifying politics and making the machinery of government at all levels responsive to the majority rather than to special-interest groups.

Progressivism also had roots in the effort to regulate and control big business, which characterized the Granger and Populist agitation of the late 19th century. The failure of the Interstate Commerce Act to end railroad abuses and of the Sherman Antitrust Act to check the growth of monopolies became increasingly apparent after 1900. Between 1897 and 1904 the trend toward concentration in industry accelerated. Such new giants as U.S. Steel (1901) and International Harvester (1902) attracted most of the attention, but in a single year, 1899, more than 1,200 firms were absorbed in mergers, the resulting combinations being capitalized at $2.2 billion. By 1904 there were 318 industrial combinations in the country, with an aggregate capital of $7.5 billion. People who considered bigness inherently

Chapter-opening illustration:
A visiting nurse from the Infant Welfare Society tends to the infant of an immigrant family living in the slums of Chicago.

evil demanded that the huge new "trusts" be broken up or at least strictly controlled.

Settlement house workers and other reformers concerned about the welfare of the urban poor made up a third battalion in the progressive army. This was the area in which women made the most important contributions. The working and living conditions of slum dwellers remained abominable, and the child labor problem was particularly acute; in 1900 about 1.7 million children under the age of 16 were working full-time—more than the membership of the American Federation of Labor. In addition, laws regulating the hours and working conditions of women in industry were far from adequate, and almost nothing had been done to enforce safety rules or to provide compensation or insurance for workers injured on the job. As the number of professionally competent social workers grew, the movement for social welfare legislation gained momentum.

All these tendencies may be summed up in Robert H. Wiebe's phrase "the search for order." America was becoming more urban, more industrial, more mechanized, more centralized—in short, more complex. This trend put a premium on efficiency and cooperation. It seemed obvious to the progressives that people must become more socially minded, the economy more carefully organized.

By attracting additional thousands of sympathizers to the general cause of reform, the return of prosperity after 1896 fueled the progressive movement. Good times made the average person more tolerant and more generous. Middle-class Americans became conscience-stricken when they compared their own comfortable circumstances with those of the "huddled masses" of immigrants and native poor.

Giant corporations threatened not so much the economic well-being as the ambitions and sense of importance of the middle class. What owner of a small mill or shop could now hope to rise to the heights attained by Carnegie or by merchants like John Wanamaker and Marshall Field? The growth of large labor organizations worried such types. In general, character and moral values seemed less influential; organizations—cold, impersonal, heartless—were coming to control business, politics, and too many other aspects of life.

The historian Richard Hofstadter suggested still another explanation of the progressive movement: the status revolution. Moderately prosperous businessmen, members of the professions, and other educated persons felt threatened by the increasing power and status of the new tycoons, many of them coarse, domineering, and fond of vulgar display. The antics of machine politicians, who made a mockery of the traditions of duty, service, and patriotism associated with statesmanship, also troubled them.

Protestant pastors accustomed to the respect and deference of their flocks found their moral leadership challenged by materialistic vestrymen who did not even pay them decent salaries. College professors worried about their institutions falling under the sway of wealthy trustees who had little interest in or respect for learning. Lawyers, once "the aristocracy of the United States," had become the servants of industrial and financial capitalists.

All these vaguely alienated people could support reform measures without feeling radical because they were resisting change and because the intellectual currents of the time harmonized with their ideas of social improvement and the welfare state. The new doctrines of the social scientists, the Social Gospel religious leaders, and the philosophers of pragmatism provided a favorable climate for progressivism. Many of the thinkers who formulated these doctrines in the 1880s and 1890s turned to the task of putting them into practice in the new century.

The Muckrakers

As the diffuse progressive army gradually formed its battalions, a new journalistic fad suddenly brought the movement into focus. For many years magazines had been publishing articles on current political, social, and economic problems. The tempo and forcefulness of this type of literature increased steadily. Then, in the fall of 1902, *McClure's* began publishing two particularly hard-hitting series of articles, one on Standard Oil by Ida Tarbell, the other on big-city political machines by Lincoln Steffens. These articles provoked much comment. When the editor, S. S. McClure, decided to include in the January 1903 issue an attack on labor gangsterism in the coal fields along with installments of the Tarbell and Steffens series, he called attention to the circumstance in a striking editorial.

Something was radically wrong with the "American character," McClure wrote. These articles showed that large numbers of American employers, workers, and politicians were fundamentally immoral. Lawyers were becoming tools of big business, judges were permitting evildoers to escape justice, the churches were materialistic, educators were incapable of understanding what was happening. "There is no one left; none but all of us," McClure concluded. "We have to pay in the end." This editorial loosed a chain reaction. Thousands of readers found their own vague apprehensions brought into focus, some becoming active in progressive movements, more lending passive support.

Other editors jumped to adopt the McClure formula. A small army of professional writers was soon flooding the periodical press with denunciations of the insurance business, the drug business, college athletics, prostitution, sweatshop labor, political corruption, and dozens of other subjects.

Theodore Roosevelt, with his gift for vivid language, compared these journalists to "the Man with the Muck-Rake" in John Bunyan's *Pilgrim's Progress,* whose attention was so fixed on the filth at his feet that he could not notice the "celestial crown" that was offered him in exchange. Roosevelt's characterization misrepresented the literature of exposure, but the label *muckraking* was thereafter affixed to the type. Despite the connotations, *muckraker* became a term of honor.

The Progressive Mind

Progressives sought to arouse the conscience of "the people" in order to "purify" American life. They were convinced that human beings were by nature decent, well intentioned, and kind. More deeply than earlier reformers they believed that the source of society's evils lay in the structure of its institutions, not in the weaknesses or sinfulness of individuals.

Therefore, local, state, and national government must be made more responsive to the will of decent citizens who stood for the traditional virtues. Then the government must act; laissez-faire was obsolete. Businessmen, especially big businessmen, must be compelled to behave fairly, their acquisitive drives curbed in the interests of justice and equal opportunity for all. The weaker elements in society—women, children, the poor, the infirm—must be protected against unscrupulous power.

Despite its fervid and democratic rhetoric, progressivism was paternalistic, moderate, and often softheaded. Typical reformers of the period oversimplified complicated issues and treated their personal values as absolute standards of truth and morality. Many progressives who genuinely wanted to improve the living standards of industrial workers rejected the proposition that workers could help themselves best by organizing powerful national unions. Union leaders favored government action to outlaw child labor and restrict immigration but adopted a laissez-faire attitude toward wages-and-hours legislation; they preferred to win these objectives through collective bargaining, thereby justifying their own existence. Progressives stressed individual freedom yet gave strong backing to the drive to deprive the public of its right to drink alcoholic beverages.

The progressives never challenged the fundamental principles of capitalism, nor did they attempt a basic reorganization of society. They would have little to do with the socialist brand of reform, they were anti-immigrant, and only a handful had anything to offer blacks, surely the most exploited group in American society.

A good example of the limited radicalism of most progressives is offered by the experiences of progressive artists. Early in the century a number of painters turned to city streets and the people of the slums for their models. These "ashcan school" artists supported political and social reform and were caught up in the progressive movement. Most saw themselves as rebels. But artistically, the ashcan painters were not very advanced. They were uninfluenced by the outburst of postimpressionist activity then taking place in Europe. To their dismay, when they included canvases by such European painters as Matisse and Picasso in a show of their own works at the 69th Regiment Armory in New York City in 1913, the "advanced" Europeans got all the attention.

"Radical" Progressives: The Wave of the Future

There were, of course, some Americans whose views were more fundamentally radical. In 1900 the labor leader Eugene V. Debs ran for president on the

Socialist ticket. He polled fewer than 100,000 votes. When he ran again four years later he got more than 400,000. Labor leaders hoping to organize unskilled workers in heavy industry were frustrated by the craft orientation of the American Federation of Labor, and some saw in socialism a way to win rank-and-file backing.

In 1905 Debs, William "Big Bill" Haywood, of the Western Federation of Miners, Mary Harris "Mother" Jones, a former organizer for the United Mine Workers; and a few others organized a new union, the Industrial Workers of the World. The IWW was openly anticapitalist. The preamble to its constitution began: "The working class and the employing class have nothing in common."

Other "advanced" European ideas affected the thinking and behavior of progressive intellectuals. Sigmund Freud's psychoanalytical theories attracted numbers of Americans, especially after Freud lectured at Clark University in 1909. Not many progressives actually read any of Freud's works, none of which was translated into English before 1909, but many picked up enough of the vocabulary of psychoanalysis to discourse impressively about the significance of slips of the tongue, sublimation, and infant sexuality.

Some saw in Freud's ideas reason to effect a "revolution of manners and morals" that would have shocked (or at least embarrassed) Freud, who was personally quite conventional. They advocated easy divorce, trial marriage, the legalization of contraception, and an end to the double standard in all matters relating to sex.

Most large cities boasted groups of these "bohemian" thinkers, the most famous centered in New York City's Greenwich Village. The dancer Isadora Duncan, the photographer Alfred Stieglitz, several of the ashcan artists, and the playwright Eugene O'Neill rubbed shoulders with Big Bill Haywood of the IWW, the anarchist Emma Goldman, and the militant feminist advocate of birth control, Margaret Sanger. Most Greenwich Village intellectuals displayed what their historian Leslie Fishbein calls "a highly personalistic concern" for their own interests, but Goldman, Haywood, Sanger, and a few others were genuine radicals who sought basic changes in bourgeois society.

The creative writers of the era, applying the spirit of progressivism to the realism they had inherited from Howells and the naturalists, tended to adopt an optimistic tone. Ezra Pound talked grandly of an American Renaissance and fashioned a new kind of poetry called imagism, which, while not appearing to be realistic, abjured all abstract generalizations and concentrated on concrete word pictures to convey meaning. The poet Carl Sandburg, the best-known representative of the "Chicago school," denounced the local plutocrats but sang the praises of the city they had made: "Hog Butcher for the World," "City of the Big Shoulders."

Most progressive writers took Freud's teachings to mean that they should cast off the restrictions of Victorian prudery; they ignored his essentially dark view of human nature. Theirs was an "innocent rebellion," exuberant and rather muddle-headed.

The impact of *The Silent War,* a 1906 novel by J. Ames Mitchell that dealt with the growing class struggle in America, was enhanced by William Balfour Ker's graphic illustration, "From the Depths."

Political Reform: Cities First

To ordinary progressives, political corruption and inefficiency lay at the root of the evils plaguing American cities. Despite the efforts of the 19th-century urban reformers, corruption and inefficiency persisted into the Progressive Era. As the cities grew, their boss-ridden administrations became more and more disgraceful. In San Francisco, for example, Abe Ruef ruled one of the most powerful and dissolute political machines in the nation. When the gas company sought a rate increase, Ruef, who was already collecting a $1,000-a-month "retainer" from the company, demanded and got a bribe of $20,000. Prostitution flourished, with the Ruef machine sharing in the profits. There was a brisk illegal trade in liquor licenses and other favors.

Similar conditions existed in dozens of communities. For his famous muckraking series for *McClure's,* Lincoln Steffens visited St. Louis, Minneapolis, Pittsburgh, New York, Chicago, and Philadelphia and found them all riddled with corruption.

Beginning in the late 1890s, progressives mounted a massive assault on dishonest and inefficient urban governments. In San Francisco a group headed by the newspaperman Fremont Older and Rudolph Spreckels, a wealthy sugar manufacturer, broke the machine and lodged Ruef in jail. In Toledo, Ohio, Samuel M. "Golden Rule" Jones won election as mayor in 1897 and succeeded in arousing the local citizenry against the corruptionists. Other important progressive mayors were Tom L. Johnson of Cleveland, whose administration Lincoln Steffens called the best in the United States; Seth Low and later John P. Mitchell of New York; and Hazen S. Pingree of Detroit.

City reformers could seldom destroy the machines without changing urban political institutions. Some cities obtained "home rule" charters that gave them greater freedom from state control in dealing with local matters. Many created research bureaus that investigated government problems in a scientific and nonpartisan manner. A number of middle-sized communities (Galveston, Texas, was the prototype) experimented with a system that integrated executive and legislative powers in the hands of a small elected commission, thereby concentrating responsibility and making it easier to coordinate complex activities. Out of this experiment came the city manager system, under which the commissioners appointed a professional manager to administer city affairs on a nonpartisan basis.

Political Reform: The States

To carry out this kind of change required the support of state legislatures, since all municipal government depends on the authority of a sovereign state. Such approval was often difficult to obtain—local bosses were usually entrenched in powerful state machines, and most legislatures were controlled by rural majorities insensitive to urban needs. Therefore, the progressives had to strike at inefficiency and corruption at the state level too.

During the first decade of the new century, Wisconsin, the progressive state par excellence, was transformed by Robert M. La Follette, one of the most remarkable figures of the age. La Follette had served three terms as a Republican congressman (1885–1891) and developed a reputation as an uncompromising foe of corruption before being elected governor in 1900. That the people would always do the right thing if properly informed and inspired was the fundamental article of his political faith.

Despite the opposition of railroad and lumbering interests, Governor La Follette implemented a direct primary system for nominating candidates, a corrupt practices act, and laws limiting campaign expenditures and lobbying activities. In power he became something of a boss himself. He made ruthless use of patronage, demanded absolute loyalty of his subordinates, and often stretched, or at least oversimplified, the truth when presenting complex issues to the voters.

La Follette was a consummate showman, and he never rose entirely above rural prejudices, being prone to scent a nefarious "conspiracy" organized by "the interests" behind even the mildest opposition to his proposals. But he was devoted to the cause of honest government. Realizing that some state functions called for specialized technical knowledge, he used commissions and agencies to handle such matters as railroad regulation, tax assessment, conservation, and highway construction.

The success of what became known as the Wisconsin idea led other states to adopt similar programs. Reform administrations swept into office in Iowa and Arkansas (1901), Oregon (1902), Minnesota, Kansas, and Mississippi (1904), New York and Georgia (1906), Nebraska (1909), and New Jersey and Colorado (1910). In some cases the reformers were Republicans, in others Democrats, but in all these states and in many others, the example of Wisconsin was influential.

State Social Legislation

The first state laws aimed at social problems long antedated the Progressive Era. In 1874 Massachusetts restricted the working hours of women to ten per day, and by the 1890s, many other states, mostly in the East and the Middle West, had followed suit. Illinois passed an eight-hour law for women workers in 1893. A New York law of 1882 struck at the sweatshops of the slums by prohibiting the manufacture of cigars in premises "occupied as a house or residence."

As part of this trend, some states established special rules for workers in hazardous industries. In the 1890s several states limited the hours of railroad workers on the grounds that fatigue sometimes caused railroad accidents. Utah restricted miners to eight hours in 1896. Before 1900 the impact of these laws was not impressive. Powerful manufacturers and landlords often succeeded in defeating the bills or rendering them innocuous. The federal system further complicated the task of obtaining effective legislation.

The Fourteenth Amendment to the Constitution, although enacted to protect the civil rights of blacks, imposed a revolutionary restriction on the states by forbidding them to "deprive any person of life, liberty, or property without due process of law." Since much state social legislation represented new uses of police power that conservative judges considered dangerous and unwise, the Fourteenth Amendment gave them an excuse to overturn the laws on the grounds that they deprived someone of liberty or property.

As stricter and more far-reaching laws were enacted, many judges, sensing what they took to be a trend toward socialism and regimentation, adopted an increasingly narrow interpretation of state police power. The United States Supreme Court upheld the Utah mining law of 1896 (*Holden* v. *Hardy,* 1898), but in 1905 it declared in the case of *Lochner* v. *New York* that New York's ten-hour limit for bakers deprived those workers of the liberty of working as long as they wished and thus violated the Fourteenth Amendment.

Nevertheless, the progressives continued to battle for legislation based on police power. Women played a particularly important part in these struggles. Sparked by the National Child Labor Committee, organized in 1904, reformers over the next ten years obtained laws in nearly every state banning the employment of young children and limiting the hours of older ones. Many of these laws were poorly enforced, yet when Congress passed a federal child labor law in 1916, the Supreme Court, in *Hammer* v. *Dagenhart* (1918), declared it unconstitutional.*

By 1917 nearly all the states had placed limitations on the hours of women industrial workers, and about ten had set minimum wage standards for women. But once again federal action that would have extended such regulation to the entire country did not materialize.

Laws protecting workers against on-the-job accidents were also enacted by many states. Disasters like the 1911 fire in New York City, in which nearly 150 women perished because the Triangle shirtwaist factory had no fire escapes, led to the passage of stricter municipal building codes and factory inspection acts. By 1910 most states had modified the common-law principle that a worker accepted the risk of accident as a condition of employment and was not entitled to compensation if injured unless it could be proved that the employer had been negligent. Gradually, the states adopted accident insurance plans, and some began to grant pensions to widows with small children. Most manufacturers favored these measures, if for no other reason than that they regularized procedures and avoided costly lawsuits.

The passage of so much state social legislation sent conservatives scurrying to the Supreme Court for redress. Such persons believed that no government had the power to deprive either workers or

*A second child labor law, passed in 1919, was also thrown out by the Court, and a child labor amendment, submitted in 1924, failed to achieve ratification by the necessary three-fourths of the states.

employers of the right to negotiate any kind of labor contract they wished. When an Oregon law limiting women laundry workers to ten hours a day was challenged in *Muller* v. *Oregon* (1908), Florence Kelley and Josephine Goldmark of the Consumers' League persuaded Louis D. Brandeis to defend the statute before the Court.

The Consumers' League, whose slogan was "investigate, agitate, legislate," was probably the most effective of the many women's reform organizations of the period. With the aid of League researchers, Brandeis prepared a remarkable brief stuffed with economic and sociological evidence indicating that long hours damaged both the health of individual women and the health of society. This nonlegal evidence greatly impressed the justices. After 1908 the right of states to protect the weaker members of society by special legislation was widely accepted. The use of the "Brandeis brief" technique to demonstrate the need for legislation became standard practice.

Progressives also launched a massive if, ill-coordinated, attack on problems related to monopoly. The variety of regulatory legislation passed by the states between 1900 and 1917 was almost infinite. Wisconsin set up a powerful railroad commission staffed with nonpartisan experts; it enacted a graduated income tax and strengthened the state tax commission, which then proceeded to force corporations to bear a larger share of the cost of government; it overhauled the laws regulating insurance companies and established a small state-owned life insurance company to serve as a yardstick for evaluating the rates of private companies. In 1911, besides creating an industrial commission to enforce the state's labor and factory legislation, Wisconsin progressives appointed a conservation commission, headed by Charles R. Van Hise, president of the University of Wisconsin.

A similar spate of legislation characterized the brief reign of Woodrow Wilson as governor of New Jersey (1911–1913). Economic reforms in other states were less spectacular but impressive in the mass. In New York an investigation of the big life insurance companies led to comprehensive changes in the insurance laws. In Iowa stiff laws regulating railroads were passed in 1906. In Nebraska the legislature created a system of bank deposit insurance in 1909. Minnesota levied an inheritance tax and built a harvesting machine factory to compete with the harvester trust. Georgia raised the taxes on corporations.

Political Reform in Washington

On the national level the Progressive Era saw the culmination of the struggle for women's suffrage. The shock occasioned by the failure of the Fourteenth and Fifteenth amendments to give women the vote resulted in a split among feminists. One group, the American Women's Suffrage Association, focused on the vote question alone. The more radical National Women's Suffrage Association (NWSA), led by Elizabeth Cady Stanton and Susan B. Anthony, concerned itself with many issues of importance to women as well as the suffrage. The NWSA put the immediate interests of women ahead of everything else. It was deeply involved in efforts to unionize women workers, yet it urged women to be strikebreakers if they could get better jobs by doing so.

Aside from their lack of unity, the feminists were handicapped by Victorian sexual inhibitions, which most of their leaders shared. Even under the best of circumstances, dislike of male-dominated society is hard enough to separate from dislike of men. At a time when sexual feelings were often deeply repressed, some of the advocates of women's rights probably did not understand themselves. Most feminists, for example, opposed contraception, insisting that birth control by any means other than continence would encourage what they called masculine lust. The Victorian idealization of female "purity" and the popular image of women as the revered guardians of home and family further confused many reformers.

These ideas and prejudices enticed feminists into a logical trap. If women were morally superior to men—a tempting conclusion—giving women the vote would improve the electorate. Politics would become less corrupt, and war would be a thing of the past. "City housekeeping has failed," said Jane Addams of Hull House in arguing for the reform of municipal government, "partly because women, the traditional housekeepers, have not been consulted."

The trouble with this argument (aside from the fact that opponents could easily demonstrate that in states where women did vote, governments were no

better or worse than elsewhere) was that it surrendered the principle of equality. In the long run this was to have serious consequences for the women's movement, though the immediate effect of the "purity" argument probably was to advance the suffragists' cause.

In 1890 the two major women's groups combined as the National American Women's Suffrage Association (NAWSA). New leaders were emerging, the most notable being Carrie Chapman Catt, a woman who combined superb organizing abilities and political skills with commitment to broad social reform. The NAWSA made winning the right to vote its main objective and concentrated on a state-by-state approach. By 1896 Wyoming, Utah, Colorado, and Idaho had been won over to women's suffrage. The burgeoning of the progressive movement helped as middle-class recruits of both sexes adopted the cause. California voted for women's suffrage in 1911, and then several other states fell into line. Large numbers of working-class women began to agitate for the vote.

The suffragists then shifted the campaign back to the national level, the lead taken by a militant new organization, the Congressional Union, headed by Alice Paul. After some hesitation the NAWSA began to campaign for a constitutional amendment. By 1920 the necessary three-fourths of the states had ratified the Nineteenth Amendment; the long fight was over.

The progressive drive for political democracy also found expression in the Seventeenth Amend-

A banner in a 1911 women's suffrage parade carries one of the longest-standing arguments in favor of women getting the vote.

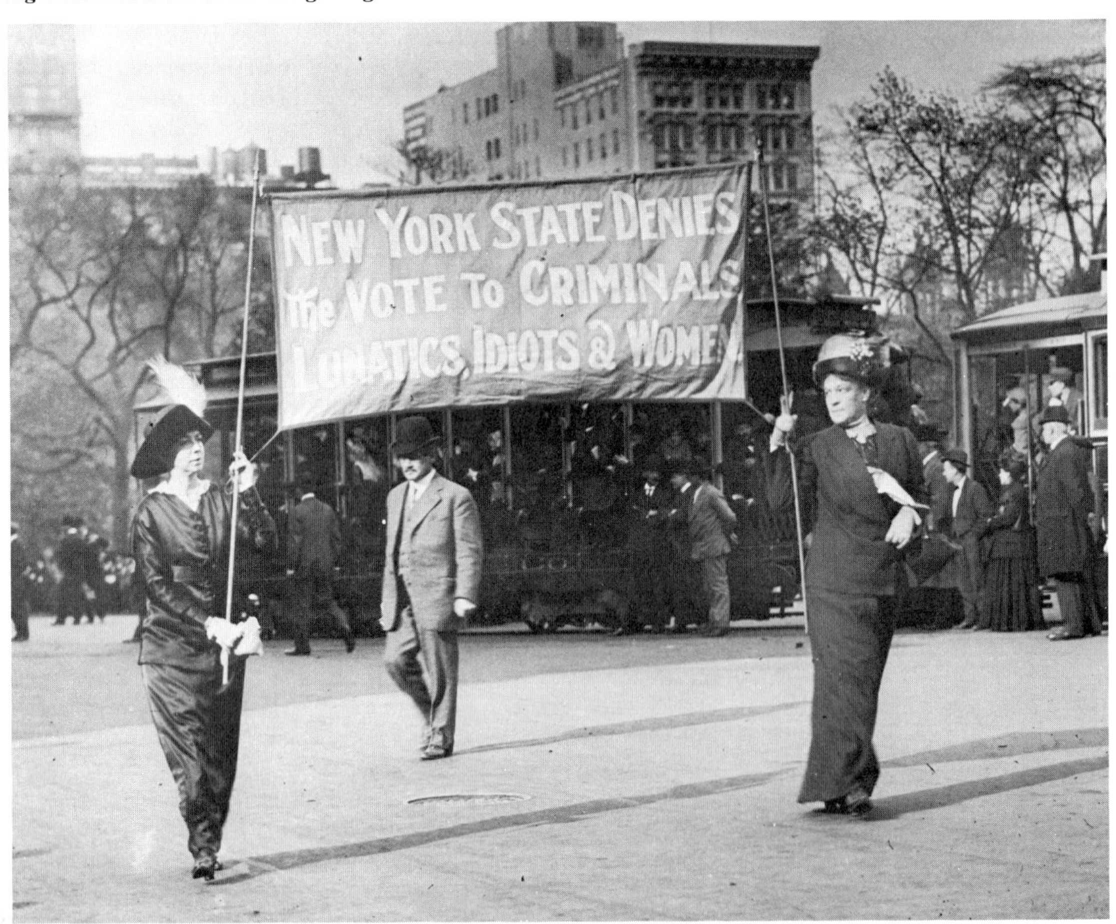

ment to the Constitution, ratified in 1913, which required the popular election of senators. And a group of "insurgent" congressmen managed to reform the House of Representatives by limiting the power of the Speaker. Thereafter, appointments to committees were determined by the whole membership, acting through party caucuses. This change was thoroughly progressive. "We want the House to be representative of the people and each individual member to have his ideas presented and passed on," explained George W. Norris, who had led the insurgents.

Theodore Roosevelt: Cowboy in the White House

In September 1901 an anarchist named Leon Czolgosz assassinated President McKinley, and Theodore Roosevelt became president of the United States. His ascension to the presidency marked the beginning of a new era in national politics.

Although only 42, by far the youngest president in the nation's history up to that time, Roosevelt brought solid qualifications to the office. In addition to political experience gained during three terms in the New York Assembly, six years on the United States Civil Service Commission, two years as police commissioner of New York City, another as assistant secretary of the navy, and a term as governor of New York, he had been a rancher in Dakota Territory and a soldier in the Spanish-American War. Politically, he had always been a loyal Republican. He rejected the Mugwump heresy in 1884, despite his distaste for Blaine, and during the tempestuous 1890s he vigorously denounced populism, Bryanism, and "labor agitators."

Nevertheless, Roosevelt's elevation to the presidency alarmed many conservatives, and not without reason. He did not fit their conception, based on a composite image of the chief executives from Hayes to McKinley, of what a president should be like. He seemed too undignified, too energetic, too outspoken, too unconventional. It was one thing to have operated a cattle ranch, another to have captured a gang of rustlers at gunpoint; one thing to have run a metropolitan police force, another to have roamed New York slums in the small hours to catch patrolmen fraternizing with thieves and prostitutes; one thing to have commanded a regiment, another to have killed a Spaniard personally.

Roosevelt had been a sickly child, plagued by asthma and poor eyesight, and he seems to have spent much of his adult life compensating for the sense of inadequacy that these troubles bred in him. He worshiped aggressiveness and was extremely sensitive to any threat to his honor as a gentleman. When another young man showed some slight interest in Roosevelt's fiancée, he sent for a set of French dueling pistols. His teachers found him an interesting student, intelligent and imaginative if rather annoyingly argumentative. "Now look here, Roosevelt," one Harvard professor finally said to him, "let me talk. I'm running this course."

Few individuals have rationalized or sublimated their feelings of inferiority as effectively as Roosevelt or to such good purpose. And few have been more genuinely warmhearted, more full of spontaneity, more committed to the ideals of public service and national greatness. As a political leader he was energetic and hard-driving. Conservatives and timid souls, sensing his aggressiveness even when he held it in check, distrusted Roosevelt's judgment, fearing he might go off half-cocked in some crisis. In fact, his judgment was nearly always sound; responsibility usually tempered his aggressiveness.

Above all Roosevelt believed in action. It would have been unthinkable for him to preside over a mere caretaker administration devoted to maintaining the status quo. However, the reigning Republican politicos, basking in the sunshine of the prosperity that had contributed so much to their victory in 1900, distrusted anything suggestive of change.

Had Roosevelt been the impetuous hothead that conservatives feared, he would have plunged ahead without regard for their feelings and influence. Instead he moved slowly and often got what he wanted by using his executive power rather than by persuading Congress to pass new laws. His domestic program included some measure of control of big corporations, more power for the Interstate Commerce Commission, and the conservation of natural resources. By consulting congressional leaders and following their advice not to bring up controversial matters like the tariff and currency reform, he obtained a modest budget of new laws.

The Newlands Act (1902) funneled the proceeds from land sales in the West into federal irrigation projects. A 1903 law created the Department of

Theodore Roosevelt in full oratorical flight. Journalists were captivated by him; even when proceeding cautiously, which was most of the time as president, he brought verve to national politics.

Commerce and Labor, which was to include a Bureau of Corporations with authority to investigate industrial combines and issue reports. The Elkins Railroad Act of 1903 strengthened the Interstate Commerce Commission's hand against the railroads by making receiving or granting of rebates illegal and by forbidding the roads to deviate in any way from their published rates.

Roosevelt and Big Business

Roosevelt soon became known as a trustbuster, and in the sense that he considered the monopoly problem the most pressing issue of the times, this was accurate to an extent. But he did not believe in breaking up big corporations indiscriminately. Regulation seemed the best way to deal with them.

With Congress unwilling to pass a stiff regulatory law, Roosevelt resorted to the Sherman Act to get at the problem. Although the Supreme Court decision in the Sugar Trust case seemed to have emasculated that law, in 1902 the president ordered the Justice Department to bring suit against the Northern Securities Company.

The Northern Securities Company controlled the Great Northern, the Northern Pacific, and the Chicago, Burlington and Quincy railroads. It had been created in 1901 after a titanic battle on the New York Stock Exchange between the forces of J. P. Morgan and James J. Hill and those of E. H. Harriman, who was associated with the Rockefeller interests. Neither side could win a clear-cut victory, so they decided to put the stock of all three railroads into a holding company owned by the two groups. Since Harriman already controlled the Union Pacific and the Southern Pacific, a virtual monopoly of western railroads was effected.

The announcement of the suit caused consternation in the business world. Attorney General Philander C. Knox pressed the case vigorously, and in 1904 the Supreme Court ordered the dissolution of the Northern Securities Company. Roosevelt then ordered suits against the meat packers, the Standard Oil Trust, and the American Tobacco Company. His stock among progressives rose, yet he had not embarrassed the conservatives in Congress by demanding new antitrust legislation.

The president went out of his way to assure cooperative corporation magnates that he was not against size per se. At a White House conference in 1905, he and Elbert H. Gary, chairman of the board of U.S. Steel, reached a "gentlemen's agreement" whereby Gary promised to cooperate with the government "in every possible way." The Bureau of Corporations would conduct an investigation of U.S. Steel, Gary allowing it full access to company records. Roosevelt in turn promised that if the investigation revealed any corporate malpractices, he would allow Gary to set matters right voluntarily, thereby avoiding an antitrust suit. A similar agreement was struck with the International Harvester Company two years later.

There were limits to the effectiveness of such arrangements; Standard Oil, for example, agreed to a similar détente and then reneged, refusing to turn over vital records to the bureau. The Justice Department brought suit against the company under the Sherman Act, and eventually it was broken up at the order of the Supreme Court. Roosevelt would have preferred a more binding kind of regulation, but when he asked for laws giving the government supervisory authority over big combinations, Congress refused to act.

Square Dealing

Roosevelt made remarkable use of his executive power during the anthracite coal strike of 1902. In June the United Mine Workers, led by John Mitchell, laid down their picks and demanded higher wages, an eight-hour day, and recognition of the union. The coal companies were dead set against concessions; when the men walked out, they shut down their properties and prepared to starve the strikers into submission.

The strike dragged on through summer and early fall. The miners conducted themselves with great restraint, avoiding violence and offering to submit their claims to arbitration. As the price of anthracite soared with the approach of winter, sentiment in their behalf mounted.

Roosevelt shared the public's sympathy for the miners, and the threat of a coal shortage alarmed him. Early in October he summoned both sides to a conference in Washington and urged them to sacrifice any "personal consideration" for the "general good." His action enraged the coal operators, for they believed he was trying to force them to recognize the union. Mitchell, aware of the immense prestige that Roosevelt had conferred on the union by calling the conference, cooperated fully with the president.

Encouraged by this state of affairs, Roosevelt took a bold step: He announced that unless a settlement was reached promptly, he would order federal troops into the anthracite regions, not to break the strike but to seize and operate the mines. The threat of government intervention brought the owners to terms. The miners went back to the pits, and all issues between them and the coal companies were submitted for settlement to a commission appointed by Roosevelt. In March 1903 the commission granted the miners a 10 percent wage increase and a nine-hour day.

To the public the incident seemed a perfect illustration of the progressive spirit—in Roosevelt's words, everyone had received a "square deal." In fact the results were by no means so clear-cut. The miners gained relatively little, and the companies lost still less, for they were not required to recognize the union and the commission recommended a 10 percent increase in the price of coal, ample compensation for the increased wage costs. The president was the main winner. The public acclaimed him as a fearless, imaginative, public-spirited leader. Without calling on Congress for support, he had expanded his own authority and hence that of the federal government. His action marked a major step forward in the evolution of the modern presidency.

T.R.: President in His Own Right

By reviving the Sherman Act, settling the coal strike, and pushing moderate reforms through Congress, Roosevelt ensured that he would be reelected president in 1904. Progressives, if not yet captivated, were at least pleased by his performance. Conservative Republicans offered no serious objection. Sensing that Roosevelt had won over the liberals, the Democrats nominated a conservative, Judge Alton B. Parker of New York, and bid for the support of eastern industrialists. This strategy failed, for businessmen continued to eye the party of Bryan with intense suspicion. Roosevelt swept the country, piling up a majority of more than 2.5 million votes.

Encouraged by this landslide and by the increasing militancy of progressives, Roosevelt pressed for more reform legislation. The Elkins Railroad Act had proved a disappointment, for the courts continued to favor the railroads in most cases. Rebating remained a serious problem. With progressive state governors demanding federal action and with farmers and manufacturers, especially in the Middle West, clamoring for relief against discriminatory rates, Roosevelt was ready by 1905 to make railroad legislation his major objective. The Interstate Commerce Commission should be empowered to fix rates, not merely to challenge unreasonable ones. It should have the right to inspect the private records of the railroads, since fair rates could not be determined unless the true financial condition of the roads was known.

Because these proposals struck at rights that businessmen considered sacrosanct, many congressmen balked. But Roosevelt applied presidential pressure, and in June 1906 the Hepburn bill became law. It gave the commission the power to inspect the books of railroad companies, to set maximum rates (once a complaint had been filed by a shipper), and to control sleeping car companies, owners of oil pipelines, and other firms engaged in transportation. Railroads could no longer issue passes freely—an important check on their political influence. The Hepburn Act made the ICC a more powerful and more active body. Though it did not outlaw judicial review of ICC decisions, thereafter those decisions were seldom overturned by the courts.

Congress also passed meat inspection and pure food and drug legislation. In 1906 Upton Sinclair published *The Jungle,* a devastating exposé of the filthy conditions in the Chicago slaughterhouses. Sinclair was more interested in writing a socialist tract than in meat inspection, but his book, a best-seller, raised a storm against the packers. After Roosevelt read *The Jungle,* he sent two officials to Chicago to investigate. Their report was so shocking, he said, that its publication would "be well-nigh ruinous to our export trade in meat." He threatened to release the report, however, unless Congress acted. After a hot fight, the meat inspection bill passed. The Pure Food and Drug Act, forbidding the manufacture and sale of adulterated or fraudulently labeled products, rode through Congress on the coattails of this measure.

To liberals Roosevelt's achievements seemed limited when placed beside his professed objectives and his smug evaluations of what he had done. How could he be a reformer and a defender of established interests at the same time? Roosevelt found no difficulty in holding such a position. As one historian has said, "He stood close to the center and bared his teeth at the conservatives of the right and the liberals of the extreme left."

Tilting Left

As the progressive movement advanced, Roosevelt advanced with it. He never accepted all the ideas of what he called its "lunatic fringe," but he took steadily more liberal positions. He always insisted that he was not hostile to business interests, but when these interests sought to exploit the national domain, they had no more implacable foe.

Conservation of natural resources was probably Roosevelt's most significant achievement as president. He placed some 150 million acres of forest lands in federal reserves, and he strictly enforced the laws governing grazing, mining, and lumbering. In 1908 he organized the National Conservation Conference, attended by 44 governors and 500 other persons, to discuss conservation matters. As a result of this meeting, most of the states created conservation commissions.

As Roosevelt became more liberal, conservative Republicans began to balk at following his lead. The sudden panic that struck the financial world in October 1907 speeded the trend. Government policies had no direct bearing on the panic, which began with a run on several important New York trust companies and spread to the Stock Exchange when speculators found themselves unable to borrow money to meet their obligations. In this emergency, Roosevelt authorized the deposit of large amounts of government cash in New York banks. He informally agreed to the acquisition of the Tennessee Coal and Iron Company by U.S. Steel when the bankers told him that the purchase was necessary to end the panic. In spite of his efforts, conservatives referred to the financial collapse as "Roosevelt's panic" and blamed the president for the depression that followed.

Roosevelt, however, turned left rather than right. In 1908 he came out for federal income and inheritance taxes, stricter regulation of interstate corporations, and reforms designed to help industrial workers. He denounced "the speculative folly and the flagrant dishonesty" of "malefactors of great wealth," further alienating conservative, or Old Guard, Republicans, who resented the attacks on their integrity implicit in many of Roosevelt's statements. When the president began criticizing the courts, the last bastion of conservatism, he lost all chance of obtaining further reform legislation.

William Howard Taft: The Listless Progressive

Roosevelt remained popular and politically powerful; before his term ended, he chose William Howard Taft, his secretary of war, to succeed him and easily obtained Taft's nomination. William Jennings Bryan was again the Democratic candidate. Campaigning on Roosevelt's record, Taft carried the country by well over a million votes, defeating Bryan 321 to 162 in the electoral college.

Taft was intelligent, experienced, and public-spirited; he seemed ideally suited to carry out Roosevelt's policies. He supported the Square Deal loyally. This, together with his mentor's ardent endorsement, won him the backing of most progressive Republicans. Yet the Old Guard liked him too; although outgoing, he had none of Roosevelt's impetuosity and aggressiveness. His genial personality and his obvious desire to avoid conflict appealed to moderates.

However, Taft lacked the physical and mental stamina required of a modern chief executive. Though not lazy, he weighed over 300 pounds and needed to rest this vast bulk more than the job allowed. Campaigning bored him, speech making seemed a useless chore. He was too reasonable to control a coalition and not ambitious enough to impose his will on others. Extremists he found irritating and persistent people (including his wife) difficult to resist. He supported many progressive measures, but he never absorbed the progressive spirit.

Taft honestly desired to carry out most of Roosevelt's policies. He enforced the Sherman Act vigorously and continued to expand the national forest reserves. He signed the Mann-Elkins Act of 1910, which empowered the Interstate Commerce Commission to suspend rate increases without waiting for a shipper to complain and established the Commerce Court to speed the settlement of railroad rate cases. An eight-hour day for all persons engaged in work on government contracts, mine safety legislation, and several other reform measures received his approval. He even summoned Congress into special session specifically to reduce tariff duties—something that Roosevelt had not dared to attempt.

But Taft had been disturbed by Roosevelt's sweeping use of executive power. Whereas Roosevelt had excelled at finding ways to accomplish his objectives without waiting for Congress to act, Taft adamantly refused to use such tactics. His restraint was in many ways admirable, but it reduced his effectiveness.

In case after case, Taft's lack of vigor and political ineptness led to trouble. In the matter of the tariff, he favored downward revision. When the special session met in 1909, the House promptly passed a bill that was roughly in line with his desires. But Senate protectionists restored the high rates of the 1897 act on most items. A group of insurgent senators opposed these changes. They were fighting the president's battle, yet Taft did little to help them. He signed the final Payne-Aldrich measure and called it "the best [tariff] bill that the Republican party ever passed." His attitude dumbfounded the progressives.

In 1910 Taft got into difficulty with the conservationists. The issue concerned the integrity of his secretary of the interior, Richard A. Ballinger. A less than ardent conservationist, Ballinger returned to the public domain certain waterpower sites that the Roosevelt administration had withdrawn. Ballinger's action alarmed Chief Forester Gifford Pinchot, the darling of the conservationists. When Pinchot learned that Ballinger intended to validate the shaky claim of powerful mining interests to a large tract of coal-rich land in Alaska, he launched an intemperate attack on the secretary. In the controversy, Taft felt obliged to support his own man. When Pinchot persisted in criticizing Ballinger, Taft dismissed him, bringing down upon himself the wrath of the conservationists.

Breakup of the Republican Party

One ominous aspect of the Ballinger-Pinchot affair was that Pinchot was a close friend of Theodore Roosevelt. After Taft's inauguration, Roosevelt had gone off to hunt big game in Africa. When he emerged from the wilderness in March 1910, bearing more than 3,000 trophies, including 9 lions, 5 elephants, and 13 rhinos, he was caught up in the squabble between the progressive members of his party and its titular head. Roosevelt hoped to steer a middle course, but the progressives' complaints impressed him. No immediate break took place, but Taft sensed the former president's coolness and was offended by it.

Perhaps the resulting rupture was inevitable. The Republican party was dividing into two factions, the progressives and the Old Guard. Forced to choose between them, Taft threw in his lot with the Old Guard. Roosevelt backed the progressives. Speaking at Osawatomie, Kansas, in August 1911, he came out for a comprehensive program of social legislation, which he called the New Nationalism. Besides attacking "special privilege" and the "unfair money-getting" practices of "lawbreakers of great wealth," he called for a broad expansion of federal power.

The final break came in October 1911, when President Taft ordered an antitrust suit against U.S. Steel. Roosevelt, of course, opposed breaking up large corporations. "The effort at prohibiting all combinations has substantially failed," he said in his New Nationalism speech. What angered Roosevelt, however, was Taft's emphasis in the suit on U.S. Steel's absorption of the Tennessee Coal and Iron Company, which Roosevelt had unofficially authorized during the panic of 1907. He began to criticize Taft publicly, and early in 1912 he declared himself a candidate for the Republican presidential nomination.

Roosevelt plunged into the preconvention campaign with typical energy. He was almost uniformly victorious in the states that held presidential primaries, carrying even Ohio, Taft's home state. However, the president controlled the party machinery and at the national convention won easily on the first ballot.

Had Roosevelt had swallowed his resentment and bided his time, Taft would almost certainly have been defeated in the election, and the 1916 Republican nomination would have been Roosevelt's for the asking. But when his leading supporters urged him to organize a third party, he agreed to make the race. In August, amid scenes of hysterical enthusiasm, the first convention of the Progressive party met at Chicago and nominated him for president. Announcing that he felt "as strong as a bull moose," Roosevelt delivered a stirring "confession of faith," calling for strict regulation of corporations, a tariff commission, national presidential primaries, minimum wage and workers' compensation laws, the elimination of child labor, and many other reforms.

The Election of 1912

The Democrats made the most of the Republican schism. They nominated Woodrow Wilson, who had achieved a remarkable liberal record as governor of New Jersey. Wilson called his program the New Freedom. The federal government could best advance the cause of social justice, he reasoned, by eradicating the special privileges that had enabled the "interests" to flourish. Where Roosevelt had lost faith in competition as a way of protecting the public against monopolies, Wilson insisted that competition could be restored. "If America is not to have free enterprise, then she can have freedom of no sort whatever," he said. This vague argument appealed to thousands of voters who found the growing power of corporations disturbing but hesitated to make the thoroughgoing commitment to government control of business that Roosevelt was advocating.

Roosevelt's reasoning was perhaps theoretically sound. Laissez-faire made less sense than it had in earlier times. The complexities of the modern world called for a positive approach, a plan, the close application of human intelligence to current social and economic problems. As Herbert Croly pointed out in *The Promise of American Life* (1909), the time had come to employ Hamiltonian means to achieve Jeffersonian ends.

Roosevelt dismissed Wilson's New Freedom as "rural toryism," but being less drastic and more in line with American experience than the New Nationalism, it had much to recommend it. The danger that selfish individuals would use the power of the state for their own ends had certainly not disappeared, despite the efforts of progressives to make government more responsive to popular opinion. Any considerable expansion of national power would increase the danger and probably create new difficulties. Managing so complicated an enterprise as an industrialized nation was sure to be a formidable task. Furthermore, individual freedom of opportunity merited the toleration of a certain amount of inefficiency.

To choose between the New Nationalism and the New Freedom, between the dynamic Roosevelt and the idealistic Wilson, was indeed difficult. Thousands grappled with this problem before going to the polls, but partisan politics determined the outcome of the election. Taft got the hard-core Republican vote and lost the progressive wing of the GOP to Roosevelt. Wilson had the solid support of both conservative and liberal Democrats. As a result, Wilson won an easy victory in the electoral college, receiving 435 votes to Roosevelt's 88 and Taft's 8. The popular vote was Wilson, 6,286,000; Roosevelt, 4,126,000; and Taft, 3,484,000. But if partisan politics had determined the winner, the election was nonetheless an overwhelming endorsement of progressivism. Wilson was a minority president, but he took office with a clear mandate to press forward with further reforms.

Wilson: The New Freedom

No man ever rose more suddenly or spectacularly in American politics than Woodrow Wilson. In the spring of 1910 he was president of Princeton University; in the fall of 1912 he was president-elect of the United States. Yet if his rise was meteoric, in a sense he had devoted his life to preparing for it. While still in college he dreamed of representing his state in the Senate. He studied law solely because he thought it the best avenue to public office, and when he discovered that he did not like legal work, he took a doctorate at Johns Hopkins in political science. He wrote several influential books, among them *Congressional Government* and *The State,* and achieved an outstanding reputation as a teacher and lecturer. In 1902 he was chosen president of Princeton and soon won a place among the nation's leading educators.

Wilson was an immediate success as president. Since Roosevelt's last year in office, Congress had been almost continually at war with the executive branch and with itself. Legislative achievements had been few. Now a small avalanche of important measures received the approval of the lawmakers. In October 1913 the Underwood Tariff brought the first significant reduction of duties since before the Civil War. To compensate for the expected loss of revenue, the act provided for a graduated tax on personal incomes.*

Two months later the Federal Reserve Act gave the country a central banking system for the first time since Jackson destroyed the Bank of the United States. The measure divided the nation into 12 banking districts, each under the supervision of a Federal Reserve bank, a sort of bank for bankers. All national banks in each district and any state banks that wished to participate had to invest 6 percent of their capital and surplus in the reserve bank, which was empowered to exchange (the technical term is *rediscount*) paper money, called Federal Reserve notes, for the commercial and agricultural paper that member banks took in as security from borrowers. The volume of currency was no longer at the mercy of the supply of gold or any other particular commodity.

The nerve center of the system was the Federal Reserve Board in Washington, which appointed a majority of the directors of the Federal Reserve banks and had some control over rediscount rates (the commission charged by the reserve banks for performing the rediscounting function). The board exercised some public control over the banks, but the great New York banks remained strong. Nevertheless, a true central banking system was created.

When inflation threatened, the reserve banks could raise the rediscount rate, discouraging borrowing and thus reducing the amount of money in circulation. In bad times it could lower the rate, making it easier to borrow and injecting new dollars into the economy. The nation finally had a flexible yet safe currency.

*The Sixteenth Amendment, ratified in February 1913, had authorized the imposition of a federal income tax.

In 1914 Congress passed two important laws affecting corporations. One created the Federal Trade Commission (FTC) to replace Roosevelt's Bureau of Corporations. In addition to investigating corporations and publishing reports, this nonpartisan board could issue cease and desist orders against "unfair" trade practices brought to light through its research. The law did not define *unfair,* and the commission's rulings could be appealed in the federal courts, but the FTC was nonetheless a powerful instrument for protecting the public against the trusts.

The second measure, the Clayton Antitrust Act, made certain specific business practices illegal, including price discrimination that tended to foster monopoly; "tying" agreements, which forbade retailers from handling the products of a firm's competitors; and the creation of interlocking directorates as a means of controlling competing companies. The act exempted labor unions and agricultural organizations from the antitrust laws and curtailed the use of injunctions in labor disputes. The officers of corporations could be held individually responsible if their companies violated the antitrust laws.

Although Wilson was not in sympathy with all the terms of these laws, they reflected his desires, and his imaginative and aggressive use of presidential power was decisive. He called the legislators into special session in April 1913 to lay out his program. He followed the course of administration bills closely. When lobbyists tried to frustrate his plans for tariff reform by bringing pressure to bear on key senators, Wilson made a dramatic appeal to the people. "The public ought to know the extraordinary exertions being made by the lobby in Washington," he told reporters. "Only public opinion can check and destroy it." The voters responded so strongly that the Senate passed the tariff bill substantially as Wilson desired it.

Wilson explained his success by saying, only half humorously, that running the government was child's play for anyone who had managed the faculty of a university. Despite his career as a political theorist, he was not doctrinaire. In practice the differences between his New Freedom and Roosevelt's New Nationalism tended to disappear. The Underwood Tariff and the Clayton Antitrust Act fitted the philosophy Wilson had expounded during the campaign, but the Federal Trade Commission and the Federal Reserve system represented steps toward the kind of regulated economy that Roosevelt advocated.

There were limits to Wilson's progressivism, imposed partly by his temperament and partly by his philosophy. He objected as strenuously to laws granting special favors to farmers and workers as to those benefiting the tycoons. When a bill was introduced in 1914 making low-interest loans available to farmers, he refused to support it. He considered the provision exempting unions from the antitrust laws equally unsound. Nor would he push for a federal law prohibiting child labor. He also refused to back the constitutional amendment giving the vote to women.

By the end of 1914 the Wilsonian record, on balance, was positive but distinctly limited. The president believed that the major progressive goals had been achieved; he had no plans for further reform. Many other progressives thought that a great deal remained to be done.

The Progressives and Minority Rights

On the issue of race relations, Wilson was distinctly reactionary. With a handful of exceptions the progressives exhibited strong prejudices against nonwhite people and against certain categories of whites as well. Many were as unsympathetic to immigrants from Asia and eastern and southern Europe as any of the "conservative" opponents of immigration in the 1880s and 1890s. American Indians were also affected by the progressives' racial attitudes. Where sponsors of the Dawes Act had assumed that Indians were capable of adopting the ways of "civilized" people, progressives tended to write Indians off as fundamentally inferior, second-class citizens at best. Theodore Roosevelt knew from personal experience that some Indians were as energetic and capable as whites, but he considered these "exceptional." It would be many generations before most Indians could "move forward" enough to become "ordinary citizens," Roosevelt believed.

Blacks did not fare well at the hands of progressives either. In the South, segregation became more rigid, white opposition to black voting more monolithic. Elsewhere, many progressive women, eager to attract southern support for their campaign for the vote, adopted racist arguments. They contrasted the supposed corruption and incompetence of black voters with their own "purity" and intelligence. Southern progressives of both sexes argued that disfranchising blacks would reduce corruption by removing from unscrupulous white politicians the temptation to purchase black votes!

The typical southern attitude toward the education of blacks was summed up in a folk proverb: "When you educate a Negro, you spoil a good field hand." In 1910, only about 8,000 black children in the entire South were attending high schools. Despite the almost total suppression of black rights, lynchings continued to occur.

Booker T. Washington was shaken by this trend, but he could find no way to combat it. The times were passing him by. He appealed to his white southern "friends" for help but got nowhere. By the turn of the century a number of young, well-educated blacks, most of them northerners, were breaking away from his accommodationist leadership.

Black Militancy

William E. B. Du Bois was the most prominent of the militants. Du Bois was born in Great Barrington, Massachusetts, in 1868. He showed such brilliance in school that his future education was assured by scholarships: to Fisk University, then to Harvard, then to the University of Berlin. In 1895 he became the first American black to earn a Ph.D. from Harvard; his dissertation, *The Suppression of the African Slave Trade* (1896), remains a standard reference.

Personal success and "acceptance" by whites did not make Du Bois complacent. Outraged by white racism and by the willingness of many blacks to settle for second-class citizenship, he set out to make American blacks proud of their color—"Beauty is black," he said—and of their African origins and culture. American blacks must organize themselves. They must establish their own businesses, run their own newspapers and colleges, write their own literature; they must preserve their identity rather than seek to amalgamate themselves into a society that offered them only contempt.

Du Bois rejected Washington's limited goals and his accommodating approach to white prejudices. Washington "apologizes for injustice," Du Bois charged. "He belittles the emasculating effects of caste distinctions, and opposes the higher training and ambitions of our brightest minds." Du Bois deemed this was totally wrong. "The way for a people to gain their reasonable rights is not by voluntarily throwing them away."

Du Bois was not an uncritical admirer of the ordinary American black. He believed that "immorality, crime, and laziness" were common vices. Quite properly, he blamed the weaknesses of blacks on the treatment afforded them by whites, but his approach to the solution of racial problems was frankly elitist. "The Negro race," he wrote, "is going to be saved by its exceptional men," what he called the "talented tenth" of the black population.

Du Bois exposed both the weaknesses of Washington's strategy and the callousness of white American attitudes. Accommodation was not working. Washington was praised, even lionized by prominent southern whites, yet when Theodore Roosevelt invited him to a meal at the White House they exploded with indignation, and Roosevelt, though not personally prejudiced, meekly backtracked, never repeating his "mistake." He defended his record by saying, "I have stood as valiantly for the rights of the negro as any president since Lincoln," which, alas, was true.

Not mere impatience but despair led Du Bois and a few like-minded blacks to meet at Niagara Falls in July 1905 and issue a list of demands: the unrestricted right to vote; an end to every kind of segregation; equality of economic opportunity; higher education for the talented; equal justice in the courts; and an end to trade-union discrimination. This Niagara Movement did not attract mass support, but it did stir the consciences of some whites, many of them the descendants of abolitionists, who were also becoming disenchanted by the failure of accommodation to provide blacks with real opportunity.

In 1909, the centennial of the birth of Abraham Lincoln, a group of these liberals founded the National Association for the Advancement of Colored People (NAACP). The organization was dedicated to the eradication of racial discrimination. Its leadership was predominantly white in the early years, but Du Bois became a national officer and the editor of its journal, *The Crisis*.

A turning point had been reached. After 1909 virtually every important leader, white and black alike, rejected the Washington approach. More and more, blacks turned to the study of their past in an effort to stimulate pride in their heritage. In 1915 Carter G. Woodson founded the Association for the Study of Negro Life and History; the following year he began editing the *Journal of Negro History,* which became the major organ for the publishing of scholarly studies of the subject.

This militancy produced few results in the Progressive Era. Theodore Roosevelt behaved no differently from earlier Republican presidents; he courted blacks when he thought it advantageous, turned his back when he did not. Wilson, southern-born, was actively antipathetic toward blacks. During the 1912 campaign he appealed to them for support and promised to "assist in advancing the interest of their race." Once elected, he refused even to appoint a privately financed commission to study the race problem. Southerners dominated his administration and Congress; as a result, blacks were further degraded. In Washington employees in many government offices were rigidly segregated, and those who objected were summarily discharged. These actions stirred such a storm that Wilson backtracked a little, but he never abandoned his belief that segregation was in the best interests of both races.

Du Bois, who had supported Wilson in 1912, attacked administration policy in *The Crisis.* In November 1914 the militant editor of the *Boston Guardian,* William Monroe Trotter, led a delegation to the White House to protest the segregation policy of the government. When Wilson accused him of blackmail, Trotter lost his temper and an ugly confrontation resulted. The mood of black leaders had changed completely.

By this time the Great War had broken out in Europe. Soon its effects would be felt by every American, by blacks perhaps more than by any other group. In November 1915, a year almost to the day after Trotter's clash with Wilson, Booker T. Washington died. One era had ended; a new one was beginning.

Milestones

1890 National American Women's Suffrage Association formed

1990 Robert La Follette elected governor of Wisconsin

1901 President McKinley assassinated

1902 National coal strike

1904 *Northern Securities* case revives the Sherman Antitrust Act
National Child Labor Committee established

1905 Industrial Workers of the World founded

1906 Hepburn Act strengthens Interstate Commerce Commission
Upton Sinclair, *The Jungle*

1907 U.S. Steel absorbs the Tennessee Coal and Iron Company

1908 Theodore Roosevelt convenes the National Conservation Conference
Muller v. *Oregon* upholds the law limiting the working hours of women

1909 Herbert Croly, *The Promise of American Life*
National Association for the Advancement of Colored People founded

1910 Ballinger-Pinchot affair

1911 Roosevelt's New Nationalism speech

1912 Roosevelt runs for president on the Progressive party ticket

1913 Sixteenth Amendment authorizes federal income taxes
Seventeenth Amendment provides for direct election of U.S. senators
Underwood Tariff
Federal Reserve Act

1914 Federal Trade Commission Act
Clayton Antitrust Act

1920 Nineteenth Amendment guarantees women the right to vote

Supplementary Reading

The political history of the Progressive Era is surveyed in G. E. Mowry, **The Era of Theodore Roosevelt** (1958). Other influential interpretations of progressivism include Richard Hofstadter, **The Age of Reform** (1955), which stresses the idea of the status revolution, and Gabriel Kolko, **The Triumph of Conservatism** (1963), which sees the period as dominated by the efforts of big business to attain its objectives with the aid of the government. See also J. M. Cooper, Jr., **The Warrior and the Priest: Theodore Roosevelt and Woodrow Wilson** (1983), and D. W. Grantham, **Southern Progressivism** (1983).

On muckraking, consult D. M. Chalmers, **The Social and Political Ideas of the Muckrakers** (1964). The radicals of the period are discussed in Leslie Fishbein, **Rebels in Bohemia** (1982), Thomas Bender, **New York Intellectuals** (1987), and N. G. Hale, **Freud and the Americans** (1971).

State and local progressivism are considered in R. S. Maxwell, **La Follette and the Rise of Progressivism in Wisconsin** (1956), Sheldon Hackney, **Populism to Progressivism in Alabama** (1969), G. B. Tindall, **The Emergence of the New South** (1967), and J. D. Buenker, **Urban Liberalism and Progressive Reform** (1973).

The movement for women's suffrage is described in A. S. Kraditor, **The Ideas of the Woman Suffrage Movement** (1981). Books treating other progressive reforms include A. F. Davis, **Spearheads for Reform: The Social Settlements and the Progressive Movement** (1967), Melvin Dubofsky, **When Workers Organize** (1868), J. H. Timberlake, **Prohibition and the Progressive Movement** (1963), James Weinstein, **The Corporate Ideal and the Liberal State** (1981), Ruth Rosen, **The Lost Sisterhood** (1982), and Albro Martin, **Enterprise Denied: Origins and Decline of American Railroads** (1971). On blacks in this period, see E. M. Rudwick, **W. E. B. Du Bois** (1960), J. R. Kirby, **Darkness at the Dawning** (1972), and August Meier, **Negro Thought in America: 1880–1915** (1963). F. E. Hoxie, **A Final Promise** (1984), deals with the treatment of Indians.

W. H. Harbaugh, **Power and Responsibility: The Life and Times of Theodore Roosevelt** (1961), is the soundest scholarly treatment of Roosevelt's career. On Taft, see D. F. Anderson, **William Howard Taft** (1973). The standard biography of Wilson, **A. S. Link's Wilson** (1947–), is still incomplete; a good one-volume biography is August Heckscher, **Woodrow Wilson** (1991).

CHAPTER 25

Woodrow Wilson and the Great War

PRESIDENT WILSON'S APPROACH TO foreign relations was well intentioned and idealistic but somewhat confused. He wanted to help other countries, especially the republics of Latin America. At the same time, he felt obliged to sustain and protect American interests abroad. The maintenance of the Open Door in China and the completion of the Panama Canal were as important to him as they had been to Theodore Roosevelt. His attitude resembled that of 19th-century Christian missionaries: He wanted to spread the gospel of American democracy, to lift and enlighten the unfortunate and the ignorant—but in his own way.

Missionary Diplomacy

Wilson set out to raise the moral tone of American foreign policy by denouncing dollar diplomacy. Encouraging bankers to lend money to countries like China, he said, implied the possibility of "forcible interference" if the loans were not repaid, and that would be "obnoxious to the principles upon which the government of our people rests." To seek special economic concessions in Latin America was "unfair" and "degrading." The United States would deal with Latin American nations "upon terms of equality and honor."

In certain small matters Wilson succeeded in conducting American diplomacy on this idealistic basis. He withdrew the government's support of the international consortium that was arranging a loan to develop Chinese railroads, and the American bankers pulled out. When the Japanese attempted, in the notorious Twenty-one Demands (1915), to reduce China almost to the status of a Japanese protectorate, he persuaded them to modify their conditions slightly. He also permitted Secretary of State William Jennings Bryan to negotiate conciliation treaties with 21 nations. The distinctive feature of these agreements was the provision for a "cooling-off" period of one year, during which signatories agreed, in the event of a dispute, not to engage in hostilities.

Where more vital U.S. interests were concerned, Wilson sometimes failed to live up to his

Chapter-opening illustration:
The face of a battle-weary corporal in the Argonne Forest reflects the disillusionment of many who found the trench warfare of the Great War a far grimmer reality than the "glorious" war they expected to fight.

promises. Because of the strategic importance of the Panama Canal, he was unwilling to tolerate "unrest" anywhere in the Caribbean. Soon after his inauguration he was pursuing the same tactics that circumstances had forced on Roosevelt and Taft. The Bryan-Chamorro Treaty of 1914, which gave the United States an option to build a canal across Nicaragua, made that country virtually an American protectorate and served to maintain in power an unpopular dictator, Adolfo Díaz.

A much more serious example of missionary diplomacy occurred in Mexico. In 1911 a liberal coalition overthrew the dictator Porfirio Díaz, who had been exploiting the resources and people of Mexico for the benefit of a small class of wealthy landowners, clerics, and military men since the 1870s. Francisco Madero became president.

Madero, though a wealthy landowner, was committed to economic reform and to the drafting of a democratic constitution, but he was weak-willed and a terrible administrator. Conditions in Mexico deteriorated rapidly, and less than a month before Wilson's inauguration, one of Madero's generals, Victoriano Huerta, seized power and had Madero murdered. Since he seemed capable of maintaining the stability that foreign investors desired, most of the European powers promptly recognized Huerta's government.

The American ambassador, together with important American financial and business interests, urged Wilson to do so too, but he refused. "I will not recognize a government of butchers," he said. This was unconventional, since nations do not ordinarily consider the means by which a foreign regime has come to power before deciding to establish diplomatic relations.

Wilson brought enormous pressure to bear against Huerta. He dragooned the British into withdrawing recognition. He dickered with other Mexican factions. He demanded that Huerta hold free elections. Huerta would not yield an inch. Wilson then subordinated his wish to let the Mexicans solve their own problems to his desire to destroy Huerta. The situation exploded in April 1914, when a small party of American sailors was arrested in the port of Tampico, Mexico. Wilson fastened on the affair as an excuse for sending troops into Mexico. When he learned that a German merchantman laden with munitions was expected at Veracruz, Wilson ordered the city occupied to prevent the weapons from reaching the Huertistas. The Mexicans resisted tenaciously, suffering 400 casualties before falling back. This bloodshed caused dismay throughout Latin America and failed to unseat Huerta.

At this point, Argentina, Brazil, and Chile offered to mediate the dispute. Wilson accepted, Huerta also agreed, and the conferees met at Niagara Falls, Ontario, in May. Although no settlement was reached, Huerta, hard pressed by Mexican opponents, abdicated. On August 20, 1914, General Venustiano Carranza entered Mexico City in triumph.

Carranza favored representative government, but he proved scarcely more successful than the tyrant Huerta in controlling the country. One of his own generals, Francisco "Pancho" Villa, rose against him and seized control of Mexico City.

Wilson now made a monumental blunder. Villa professed to be willing to cooperate with the United States, and Wilson took him at his word. However, Villa was little more than an ambitious bandit. Carranza, though no radical, was committed to social reform. Fighting back, he drove the Villistas into the northern provinces.

Wilson finally realized the extent of Carranza's influence in Mexico, and in October 1915 he recognized the Carranza government. Still his Mexican troubles were not over. Early in 1916, Villa, seeking to undermine Carranza by forcing the United States to intervene, stopped a train in northern Mexico and killed 16 American passengers in cold blood. Then he crossed into New Mexico and burned the town of Columbus, killing 19. Having learned his lesson, Wilson would have preferred to bear even this assault in silence, but public opinion forced him to send American troops under General John J. Pershing across the border in pursuit of Villa.

Villa proved impossible to catch. Cleverly, he drew Pershing deeper and deeper into Mexico, which caused Carranza to insist that the Americans withdraw. Several clashes occurred between Pershing's men and Mexican regulars, and for a brief period in June 1916 war seemed imminent. Wilson now acted bravely and wisely. Early in 1917 he recalled Pershing's force, leaving the Mexicans to work out their own destiny.

Missionary diplomacy in Mexico had produced mixed but ultimately beneficial results. By opposing Huerta, Wilson had surrendered to his prejudices, yet he had also helped the real revolutionaries even though they opposed his acts. His bungling bred anti-Americanism in Mexico, but by his later restraint in the face of stinging provocations, he permitted the constitutionalists to consolidate their power.

Outbreak of the Great War

On June 28, 1914, in the Austro-Hungarian provincial capital of Sarajevo, Gavrilo Princip, a young student, assassinated Archduke Franz Ferdinand, heir to the imperial throne. This rash act precipitated a general European war. Within little more than a month, following a complex series of diplomatic challenges and responses, the Central Powers (chiefly Germany and Austria-Hungary) and the Allied Powers (chiefly Great Britain, France, and Russia) were locked in an unexpected and brutal struggle.

The outbreak of the Great War caught Americans psychologically unprepared; few understood the significance of what had happened. President Wilson promptly issued a proclamation of neutrality, and the almost unanimous reaction of Americans, aside from dismay, was that the conflict did not concern them. They were wrong, for this was a world war, and Americans were sure to be affected by its outcome.

There were good reasons why the United States sought to remain neutral. Over a third of its 92 million inhabitants were either European-born or the children of European immigrants. Sentimental ties bound them to the lands of their ancestors. American involvement would create new internal stresses in a society already strained by the task of assimilating so many diverse groups. War was also an affront to the prevailing progressive spirit, which assumed that human beings were reasonable, high-minded, and capable of settling disputes peaceably. Along with the traditional American fear of entanglement in European affairs, these were ample reasons for remaining aloof.

Though most Americans hoped to keep out of the war, nearly everyone was partial to one side or the other. People of German or Austrian descent, about 8 million in number, and the nation's 4.5 million Irish-Americans, motivated chiefly by hatred of the British, sympathized with the Central Powers. The majority of Americans, however, influenced by bonds of language and culture, wanted an Allied victory, and when the Germans launched a mighty assault across neutral Belgium in an effort to outflank the French armies, this unprovoked attack on a tiny nation whose neutrality the Germans had previously agreed to respect caused a great deal of anti-German feeling.

As the war progressed, the Allies cleverly exploited American prejudices, and the Germans also conducted an extensive propaganda campaign. But propaganda did not alter American attitudes; far more important were questions rising out of trade and commerce.

Freedom of the Seas

All the warring nations wanted to draw on American resources. Under international law, neutrals could trade freely with any belligerent. Americans were prepared to do so, but because the British fleet dominated the North Atlantic, they could not. The British declared nearly all commodities, even foodstuffs, to be contraband of war. They set limits on exports to neutral nations such as Denmark and the Netherlands so that these countries could not transship supplies to Germany. They forced neutral merchantmen into Allied ports in order to search them for goods headed for the enemy. Many cargoes were confiscated, often without payment.

Had the United States insisted that Great Britain abandon these "illegal" practices, as the Germans demanded, no doubt it could have prevailed. It is ironic that an embargo, a policy that failed so ignominiously in Jefferson's day, would have been almost instantly effective if applied at any time after 1914, for American supplies were vital to the Allies.

Though British tactics did not involve the loss of innocent lives, they nevertheless exasperated Wilson. He faced a dilemma. To allow the British to make the rules meant siding against the Central Powers. Yet to insist on the old rules meant siding against the Allies because that would have deprived them of much of the value of their naval superiority. Nothing the United States might do would be truly impartial.

In any event, the immense expansion of American trade with the Allies made an embargo unthinkable. While commerce with the Central Powers fell to a trickle, that with the Allies soared from $825 million in 1914 to over $3.2 billion in 1916. An attempt to limit this commerce would have raised a storm; to have eliminated it would have caused a catastrophe.

The Allies soon exhausted their ready cash and by early 1917 had borrowed well over $2 billion. Although these loans violated no principle of international law, they fastened the United States still more closely to the Allies' cause.

During the first months of the Great War, the Germans were not especially concerned about neutral trade or American goods because they expected to crush the Allied armies quickly. When their first swift thrust into France was blunted along the Marne River and the war became a bloody stalemate, they began to challenge the Allies' control of the seas. Unwilling to risk their battleships and cruisers against the much larger British fleet, they resorted to a new weapon, the submarine, commonly known as the U-boat (for *Unterseeboot*).

German submarines played a role in World War I not unlike that of American privateers in the Revolution and the War of 1812: They ranged the seas stealthily in search of merchantmen. However, submarines could not operate under the ordinary rules of war, which required that a raider stop its prey, examine its papers and cargo, and give the crew and passengers time to get off in lifeboats before sending it to the bottom. When surfaced, U-boats were vulnerable to the deck guns that many merchant ships carried; therefore they commonly launched their torpedoes from below the surface without warning. The result was often a heavy loss of life on the torpedoed ships.

In February 1915 the Germans declared the waters surrounding the British Isles a zone of war and announced that they would sink, without warning, all enemy merchant ships encountered in the area. Since Allied vessels sometimes flew neutral flags to disguise their identity, neutral ships entering the zone would do so at their own risk. Wilson—perhaps too hurriedly, considering the importance of the question—warned the Germans that he would hold them to "strict accountability" for any loss of American life or property resulting from violations of "acknowledged [neutral] rights on the high seas." "Strict accountability" ultimately meant war unless the Germans backed down. Yet Wilson was not prepared to fight; he refused even to ask Congress for increased military appropriations, saying that he did not want to "turn America into a military camp."

Wise or unwise, Wilson's position accurately reflected the attitude of most Americans. It seemed barbaric to them that defenseless civilians should be killed without warning, and they refused to surrender their rights as neutrals to cross the North Atlantic on any ship they wished. The depth of their feeling was demonstrated when, on May 7, 1915, the submarine *U-20* sank the British liner *Lusitania* off the Irish coast. Nearly 1,200 persons, including 128 Americans, lost their lives in this catastrophe.

The torpedoing of the *Lusitania* caused as profound and emotional a reaction in the United States as that following the destruction of the *Maine* in Havana harbor. Wilson, like McKinley in 1898, was shocked, but he kept his head. He demanded that Germany disavow the sinking, indemnify the victims, and promise to stop attacking passenger vessels. When the Germans quibbled about these points, he responded with further diplomatic correspondence rather than with an ultimatum.

It would have been difficult politically for the German government to have backed down before an American ultimatum; however, after dragging the controversy out for nearly a year, it did apologize and agree to pay an indemnity. Finally, after the torpedoing of the French channel steamer *Sussex* in March 1916 had produced another stiff American protest, the Germans at last promised, in the *Sussex* pledge, to stop sinking merchant ships without warning.

The Election of 1916

Wilson faced serious political difficulties in his fight for reelection. He had won the presidency in 1912 only because the Republican party had split in two. Now Theodore Roosevelt, the chief defector, had become so incensed by Wilson's refusal to commit the United States to the Allied cause that he was ready to support almost any Republican in order to guarantee the president's defeat. At the same time, many progressives were complaining about Wilson's unwillingness to work for further domestic reforms. Unless he could find additional support, he seemed likely to be defeated.

He attacked the problem by wooing the progressives. In January 1916 he appointed Louis D.

Brandeis to the Supreme Court. In addition to being an advanced progressive, Brandeis was Jewish, the first American of that religion ever appointed to the Court. Wilson's action won him many friends among people who favored fair treatment of minority groups. In July he bid for the farm vote by signing the Farm Loan Act to provide low-cost loans based on agricultural credit. Shortly thereafter, he approved the Keating-Owen Child Labor Act, barring goods manufactured by the labor of children under 16 from interstate commerce, and a worker's compensation act for federal employees. He persuaded Congress to pass the Adamson Act, establishing an eight-hour day for railroad workers, and he modified his position on the tariff by approving the creation of a tariff commission.

Each of these actions represented a sharp reversal. They paid spectacular political dividends when Roosevelt refused to run as a Progressive and came out for the Republican nominee, Associate Justice Charles Evans Hughes. The Progressive convention then endorsed Hughes, who had compiled a fine liberal record as governor of New York, but many of Roosevelt's 1912 supporters felt he had betrayed them and voted for Wilson in 1916.

The key issue in the campaign was American policy toward the warring powers. Wilson intended to stress preparedness, which he was now wholeheartedly supporting. However, during the Democratic convention, the delegates shook the hall with cheers whenever orators referred to the president's success in keeping the country out of the war. One spellbinder, referring to the *Sussex* pledge, announced that the president had "wrung from the most militant spirit that ever brooded above a battlefield an acknowledgement of American rights and an agreement to American demands," and the convention erupted in a demonstration that lasted more than 20 minutes. Thus "He Kept Us Out of War" became the Democratic slogan.

A Wilson campaign truck offered New York City voters a convenient summary of the 1916 Democratic platform. The eight-hour-day plank refers to the president's support of a federal law for railroad workers.

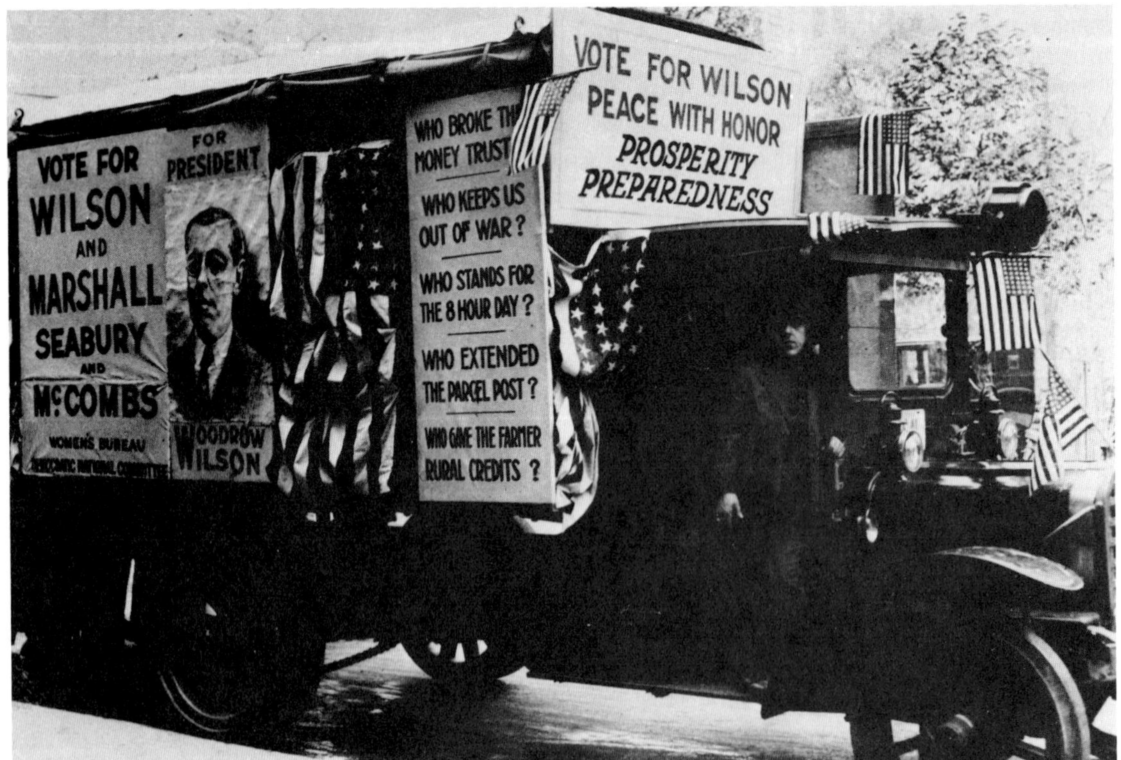

The combination of progressivism and the peace issue placed the Democrats on substantially equal terms with the Republicans; thereafter, personal factors probably tipped the balance. Hughes was very stiff and an ineffective speaker; he offended a number of important politicians, especially in crucial California, where he inadvertently snubbed the popular progressive governor, Hiram Johnson; and he equivocated on a number of issues. Nevertheless, on election night he appeared to have won, having carried nearly all the East and Middle West. Late returns gave Wilson California, however, and with it victory by the narrow margin of 277 to 254 in the electoral college. He led Hughes in the popular vote, 9.1 million to 8.5 million.

The Road to War

Encouraged by his triumph, appalled by the continuing slaughter on the battlefields, fearful that the United States would be dragged into the holocaust, Wilson made one last effort to end the war by negotiation. In 1915 and again in 1916 he had sent his friend Colonel Edward M. House on a secret mission to London, Paris, and Berlin to try to mediate among the belligerents. Each had proved fruitless, but perhaps now, after another long season of bloodshed, the powers were ready to listen to reason.

Wilson's own feelings were more genuinely neutral than at any other time during the war, for the Germans had stopped sinking merchantmen without warning and the British had irritated him repeatedly by their arbitrary restrictions on neutral trade. He drafted a note to the belligerents asking them to state the terms on which they would agree to lay down their arms. When neither side responded encouragingly, Wilson, on January 22, 1917, delivered a moving, prophetic speech aimed, as he admitted, at "the people of the countries now at war" more than at their governments. Any settlement imposed by a victor, he declared, would breed hatred and more wars. There must be a "peace without victory" based on the principles that all nations were equal and that every nationality group should determine its own form of government. He suggested the creation of some kind of international organization to preserve world peace.

This noble appeal met a tragic fate. The Germans had already decided to renounce the *Sussex* pledge and unleash their submarines against all vessels headed for Allied ports. After February 1, any ship in the war zone would be attacked without warning. Possessing more than 100 U-boats, the German military leaders had convinced themselves that they could starve the British people into submission and reduce the Allied armies to impotence by cutting off American supplies. The United States would probably declare war, but the Germans believed that they could overwhelm the Allies before the Americans could get to the battlefields in force.

After the Germans had made their decision, events moved relentlessly, almost uninfluenced by the actors who presumably controlled the fate of the world:

> *February 3: S.S. Housatonic torpedoed. Wilson announces to Congress that he has severed diplomatic relations with Germany. Secretary of State Lansing hands the German ambassador, Count von Bernstorff, his passport. February 24: Walter Hines Page, U.S. ambassador to Great Britain, transmits to the State Department an intercepted German dispatch (the "Zimmermann telegram") revealing that Germany has proposed a secret alliance with Mexico, Mexico to receive, in the event of war with the United States, "the lost territory in Texas, New Mexico, and Arizona." February 25: Cunard liner Laconia torpedoed, two American women perish. February 26: Wilson asks Congress for authority to arm American merchant ships. March 1: Zimmermann telegram released to the press. March 4: President Wilson takes oath of office, beginning his second term. Congress adjourns without passing the armed ship bill, the measure having been filibustered to death by antiwar senators. Wilson characterizes the filibusterers, led by Senator Robert M. La Follette, as "a little group of willful men, representing no opinion but their own." March 9: Wilson, acting under his executive powers, orders the arming of American merchantmen. March 12: Revolutionary provisional government established in Russia. Algonquin torpedoed. March 15: Czar Nicholas II of Russia abdicates. March 16: City of Memphis, Illinois, Vigilancia torpedoed. March 21: New York World, a leading Democratic newspaper, calls for*

declaration of war on Germany. Wilson summons Congress to convene in special session on April 2. March 25: Wilson calls up the National Guard. April 2: Wilson asks Congress to declare war. Germany is guilty of "throwing to the winds all scruples of humanity," he says. America must fight, not to conquer, but for "peace and justice. . . . The world must be made safe for democracy." April 4, 6: Congress declares war—the vote, 82–6 in the Senate, 373–50 in the House.

The bare record conceals Wilson's agonizing search for an honorable alternative to war. To admit that Germany posed a threat to the United States meant confessing that interventionists had been right all along. To go to war meant, besides sending innocent Americans to their death, letting "the spirit of ruthless brutality enter into the very fibre of our national life."

The president's Presbyterian conscience tortured him relentlessly. He lost sleep, appeared gray and drawn. When someone asked him which side he hoped would win, he answered petulantly, "Neither." In the end he could satisfy himself only by giving intervention an idealistic purpose. The war had become a threat to humanity. Unless the United States threw its weight into the balance, western civilization itself might be destroyed. Out of the long bloodbath must come a new and better world. The war must be fought to end, for all time, war itself. Thus in the name not of vengeance and victory but of justice and humanity he sent his people into battle.

Mobilizing the Economy

America's entry into the Great War determined its outcome. The Allies were rapidly running out of money and supplies; their troops, decimated by nearly three years in the trenches, were disheartened and rebellious. After the outbreak of the Russian Revolution in March 1917, the Russian armies collapsed. By December 1917, Russia was out of the war and the Germans were moving masses of men and equipment from the eastern front to France. Without the aid of the United States, it is likely that the war would have ended in 1918 on terms dictated from Berlin. Instead, American men and supplies helped contain the Germans' last drives and then push them back to final defeat.

It was a close thing, for the United States entered the war little better prepared to fight than it had been in 1898. The conversion of American industry to war production had to be organized and carried out without prearrangement. What the historian Harvey A. De Weerd has called "absurdly large" goals were set, far beyond what the army could use. Confusion and waste resulted. The hurriedly designed shipbuilding program was a fiasco. Airplane, tank, and artillery construction programs, all too large to begin with, developed too slowly to affect the war. "The American doughboy," writes David M. Kennedy in *Over Here*, was "transported in a British ship, wore a steel helmet modeled on the British Tommy's, and fought with French ordnance." American pilots such as the great "ace" Captain Eddie Rickenbacker flew British Sopwiths and De Havillands or French Spads and Nieuports.

The problem of mobilization was complicated. It took Congress six weeks of hot debate merely to decide on conscription. Only in September 1917, nearly six months after the declaration of war, did the first draftees reach the training camps, and it is hard to see how Wilson could have speeded this process appreciably.

Wilson was a forceful and inspiring war leader once he grasped what needed to be done. Raising an army was only a small part of the job. The Allies had to be supplied with food and munitions, and immense sums of money had to be collected.

After several false starts, Wilson in July 1917 set up the War Industries Board (WIB) to oversee all aspects of industrial production and distribution. The WIB was given almost dictatorial power to allocate scarce materials, standardize production, fix prices, and coordinate American and Allied purchasing.

Evaluating the mobilization effort raises interesting historical questions. The antitrust laws were suspended, and producers were encouraged, even compelled, to cooperate with one another. Wilson accepted the kind of government-industry agreements developed under Theodore Roosevelt that he had denounced in 1912. Prices were set by the WIB at levels that allowed large profits—U.S. Steel, for example, despite high taxes, cleared over half a billion dollars in two years. It is at least arguable that producers would have turned out just as much even if compelled to charge lower prices.

At the start of the war, army procurement was decentralized and inefficient. One official bought 1,200 typewriters, stacked them in the basement of a government building, and announced proudly: "There is going to be the greatest competition for typewriters around here, and I have them all."

Mobilization required close cooperation between business and the military. However, the army resisted cooperating with civilian agencies. Wilson finally compelled the War Department to place officers on WIB committees, and when the army discovered that its interests were not injured by the system, the foundation was in place for what was later to be known as the "industrial-military complex," the alliance between business and military leaders that was to cause so much controversy after World War II.

The problem of mobilizing agricultural resources was solved more quickly, and this was fortunate because in April 1917 the British had on hand only a six-week supply of food. As food administrator Wilson appointed Herbert Hoover, a mining engineer who had headed the Belgian Relief Commission earlier in the war. Acting under powers granted by the Lever Act of August 1917, Hoover set the price of wheat at $2.20 a bushel in order to encourage production. He established a government corporation to purchase the entire American and Cuban sugar crop, which he then doled out to American and British refiners.

To avoid rationing, Hoover organized a campaign to persuade consumers to conserve food voluntarily. One slogan ran "If U fast U beat U boats," another "Serve beans by all means." "Wheatless Mondays" and "meatless Tuesdays" were the rule, and although no law compelled observance, the public responded patriotically. Boy Scouts dug up backyards and vacant lots to plant vegetable gardens; chefs devised new recipes to save on scarce items; restaurants added horsemeat, rabbit, and whale steak to their menus and doled out butter and sugar to customers in minuscule portions. Mothers pressured their children to "Hooverize" their plates. Without subjecting its own citizens to serious inconvenience, the United States increased food exports from 12.3 million tons to 18.6 million tons. Farmers, of course, profited: Their real income went up nearly 30 percent between 1915 and 1918.

Workers in Wartime

With the army siphoning so many men from the labor market and with immigration reduced to a trickle, unemployment disappeared and wages rose. Although the cost of living soared, the boom produced unprecedented opportunities. Americans, always a mobile people, pulled up stakes in record numbers. Disadvantaged groups, especially blacks, were particularly attracted by jobs in big-city factories.

Early in the conflict, the government began regulating the wages and hours of workers building army camps and manufacturing uniforms. In April 1918, Wilson created the National War Labor Board to settle labor disputes. The board considered more than 1,200 cases and prevented many strikes. A War Labor Policies Board set wages-and-hours standards for each major war industry. Since these were determined in consultation with employers and representatives of labor, they speeded the unionization of workers by compelling management, even in anti-union industries like steel, to deal with labor leaders. Union membership rose by 2.3 million during the war.

Paying for the War

Wilson managed the task of financing the war effectively. The struggle cost the United States about $33.5 billion, not counting pensions and other postwar expenses. About $7 billion of this was lent to the Allies, but since this money was largely spent in America, it contributed to the national prosperity. Over two-thirds of the cost of the war was met by borrowing. Five Liberty and Victory Loan drives, spurred by advertising, parades, and other appeals to patriotism, persuaded the people to open their purses.

In addition to borrowing, the government collected about $10.5 billion in taxes during the war. A steeply graduated income tax took more than 75 percent of the incomes of the wealthiest citizens. A

65 percent excess-profits tax and a 25 percent inheritance tax were also enacted. Thus while many individuals made fortunes out of the war, its cost was distributed far more equitably than that of the Civil War.

Propaganda and Civil Liberties

Wilson was preeminently a teacher and preacher, a specialist in the transmission of ideas. He excelled at mobilizing public opinion and inspiring Americans to work for the better world he hoped would emerge from the war. In April 1917 he created the Committee on Public Information, headed by a journalist, George Creel. Soon 75,000 speakers and writers were deluging the country with propaganda picturing the war as a crusade for freedom and democracy, the Germans as a bestial people bent on world domination.

Most Americans supported the war enthusiastically, but thousands of persons—those of German and Irish ancestry, for example; people of pacifist leanings such as Jane Addams of Hull House; and some who thought both sides in the war wrong—still opposed American involvement. Creel's committee and a number of unofficial "patriotic" groups allowed their enthusiasm for the conversion of the hesitant to become suppression of dissent. Persons who refused to buy war bonds were often exposed to public ridicule and even to assault. People with German names were persecuted without regard for their views; some school boards outlawed the teaching of the German language; sauerkraut was renamed "liberty cabbage." Opponents of the war of unquestionable patriotism were subjected to coarse abuse.

Wilson, "a friend of free speech in theory," David M. Kennedy has written, "was its foe in fact." He signed the Espionage Act of 1917, which imposed fines of up to $10,000 and jail sentences ranging to 20 years on persons convicted of aiding the enemy or obstructing recruiting, and he authorized the postmaster general to ban from the mails any material that seemed treasonable or seditious.

In May 1918, again with Wilson's approval, Congress passed the Sedition Act, which made "saying anything" to discourage the purchase of war bonds a crime. The law also made it illegal to "utter, print,

In 1917 the Germania Life Insurance Building in St. Paul was renamed the Guardian Building; since Germania herself could not be disguised, down she came.

write, or publish any disloyal, profane, scurrilous, or abusive language" about the government, the Constitution, or the uniform of the army or navy. Socialist periodicals were suppressed, and Eugene V. Debs was sentenced to ten years in prison for making an antiwar speech. Ricardo Flores Magón, an anarchist, was sentenced to 20 years in jail for publishing a statement criticizing Wilson's Mexican policy, an issue that had nothing to do with the war.

These laws went far beyond what was necessary to protect the national interest. Citizens were jailed for suggesting that the draft law was unconstitutional and for criticizing private organizations like the Red Cross and the YMCA. One woman was sent to prison for writing: "I am for the people, and the government is for the profiteers."

The wartime hysteria far exceeded anything that happened in Great Britain and France. In 1916 the French novelist Henri Barbusse published *Le Feu (Under Fire),* a graphic account of the horrors and purposelessness of trench warfare. In one chapter Barbusse described a pilot flying over the trenches on a Sunday, observing French and German soldiers at Mass in the open fields, each worshiping the same God. Yet *Le Feu* circulated freely in France and even won the coveted Prix Goncourt.

Wartime Reforms

The American mobilization experience was part and product of the Progressive Era. The work of the progressives at the national and state levels in expanding government functions in order to deal with social and economic problems provided precedents and conditioned the people for the all-out effort of 1917 and 1918. Social and economic planning and the management of huge business operations by public boards and committees got their first practical tests. College professors, technicians, and others with complex skills entered government service en masse. The federal government for the first time entered actively such fields as housing and labor relations.

Many progressives believed that the war was creating a sense of common purpose that would stimulate the people to act unselfishly to benefit the poor and to eradicate social evils. Patriotism and public service seemed at last united. Men and women worked for a dozen causes only remotely related to the war effort. The women's suffrage movement was brought to fruition, as was the campaign against alcohol. Reformers began to talk about health insurance, and a national campaign against prostitution and venereal disease gained strength.

Women and Blacks in Wartime

Although a number of prominent feminists were pacifists, most supported the war. Opposition would lessen their chances of gaining the vote, and they expected that the war would open up many high-paying jobs to women. To some extent it did; about a million women filled in for men in uniform, but the number actually engaged in war industries was small, and the gains were fleeting. When the war ended, most women industrial workers either left their jobs voluntarily of were fired to make room for returning veterans. Some women went overseas as nurses, and a few served as ambulance drivers and YMCA workers.

Most unions were unsympathetic to the idea of enrolling women, and the government did little to encourage women to do more for the war effort than prepare bandages, knit warm clothing for soldiers, participate in food conservation programs, and encourage people to buy war bonds. The Women in Industry Service and the Woman's Committee of the Council of National Defense served primarily as window dressing. The final report of another wartime agency admitted that few women war workers had been paid as much as men and that women had been promoted more slowly than men, were not accepted by unions, and were discharged promptly when the war ended.

The wartime "great migration" of southern blacks to northern cities where jobs were available brought them important economic benefits. Between 1870 and 1890 only about 80,000 blacks had moved to northern cities. Compared with the influx from Europe and from northern farms, this was a trivial number. The black proportion of the population of New York City, for example, fell from over 10 percent in 1800 to under 2 percent in 1900.

Around the turn of the century, as southern repression increased, the northward movement quickened—about 200,000 blacks migrated between 1890 and 1910. Then, after 1914, the war boom drew blacks north in a flood. "Leave the benighted land," the *Chicago Defender*, a newspaper with a considerable circulation in southern states, urged. "Get out of the South." Half a million made the move between 1914 and 1919.

Life for the newcomers was difficult; workers feared them as potential strikebreakers yet refused to admit them into their unions. In East St. Louis, Illinois, a bloody riot erupted during the summer of 1917 in which nine whites and an undetermined number of blacks were killed. As in peacetime, the Wilson administration was at worst antagonistic and at best indifferent to blacks' needs and aspirations.

Nevertheless, the blacks who moved north during the war were infinitely better off, materially and psychologically, than those they left behind. They earned good wages and were accorded at least some human rights. They could vote, send their children to decent schools, and within reasonable limits do and say what they pleased without fear of humiliation or physical attack.

There were two black regiments in the regular army and a number of black national guard units when the war began. At first no blacks were conscripted; southerners in particular were disturbed by the thought of giving large numbers of blacks guns and teaching them how to use them. Blacks were, however, soon drafted, and a larger proportion of them than whites were taken. After a riot in Texas in which black soldiers killed 17 white civilians, black recruits were dispersed among many camps for training to lessen the possibility of trouble.

In the service, all blacks were placed in segregated units. Only a handful were commissioned officers. Most, even those sent overseas, were assigned to labor battalions, working as stevedores and common laborers. But many fought and died for the country. Altogether about 200,000 served overseas. There were black Red Cross nurses in France, and some blacks held relatively high posts in government agencies in Washington, the most important being Emmett J. Scott, who was special assistant for Negro affairs in the War Department.

W. E. B. Du Bois supported the war wholeheartedly. He praised Wilson for making, at last, a strong statement against lynching, which had increased to a shocking extent during the previous decade. He even went along with the fact that black officer candidates were trained in a segregated camp. "Let us," he wrote in *The Crisis,* "while the war lasts, forget our special grievances and close ranks shoulder to shoulder with our fellow citizens and the allied nations that are fighting for democracy."

Many blacks condemned Du Bois's accommodationism (which he promptly abandoned when the war ended), but most saw the war as an opportunity to demonstrate their patriotism and prove their worth. For the moment the prevailing mood was one of optimism. If winning the war would make the world safe for democracy, surely blacks in the United States would be better off when it was won.

"Over There"

All activity on the home front had one ultimate objective: defeating the Central Powers on the battlefield. This was accomplished. The navy performed with special distinction. In April 1917, German submarines sank more than 870,000 tons of Allied shipping; after April 1918, monthly losses never reached 300,000 tons. The decision to send merchantmen across the Atlantic in convoys screened by warships made the reduction possible. Checking the U-boats was essential because of the need to transport American troops to Europe. More than 2 million made the voyage safely.

The first units of the American Expeditionary Force (AEF), elements of the regular army commanded by General John J. Pershing, reached Paris on Independence Day 1917. They took up positions on the front near Verdun in October. Not until the spring of 1918, however, did the "doughboys" play a significant role in the fighting, though their presence boosted French and British morale.

In March 1918 the Germans launched a great spring offensive, their armies strengthened by thousands of veterans from the Russian front. By late May they had reached a point on the Marne River near the town of Châciateau-Thierry, only 50 miles from Paris. Early in June the AEF fought its first major engagements, driving the Germans back from Châciateau-Thierry and Belleau Wood.

In this fighting only about 27,500 Americans saw action, and they suffered appalling losses. By mid-July 85,000 Americans were in the lines, and by late August the American First Army, 500,000 strong, was poised before the Saint-Mihiel salient, a deep extension of the German lines southeast of Verdun. On September 12 this army, buttressed by French troops, struck and in two days wiped out the salient.

Late in September began the greatest American engagement of the war. No fewer than 1.2 million doughboys drove forward west of Verdun into the Argonne Forest. For over a month of indescribable horror they inched ahead through the tangle of the Argonne and the formidable defenses of the Hindenburg line, while to the west French and British armies staged similar drives. In this one offensive the AEF suffered 120,000 casualties. Finally, on November 1, they broke the German center and raced toward the vital Sedan-Mézières railroad. On November 11, with Allied armies advancing on all fronts, the Germans signed the Armistice, ending the fighting.*

Preparing for Peace

On November 11, 1918, the fighting ended, but the shape of the postwar world remained to be determined. Confusion reigned. People wanted peace yet burned for revenge. Millions faced starvation. Other millions were disillusioned by the seemingly purposeless sacrifices of four years of horrible war. Communism—to some an idealistic promise of human betterment, to others a commitment to rational economic and social planning, to still others a danger to individual freedom, toleration, and democracy—having conquered Russia, threatened to envelop Germany and much of the defunct Austro-Hungarian Empire, perhaps even the victorious Allies. How could stability be restored? How could victory be made worth its enormous cost?

Woodrow Wilson had grasped the significance of the war while most statesmen still thought that triumph on the battlefield would settle everything automatically. As early as January 1917 he had realized that victory would be wasted if the winners permitted themselves the luxury of vengeance. Such a policy would disrupt the balance of power and lead to economic and social chaos. American participation in the struggle had not blurred his vision. The victors must build a better society, not punish those they believed had destroyed the old.

In a speech to Congress on January 8, 1918, Wilson outlined a plan, known as the Fourteen Points, designed to make the world "fit and safe to live in." The peace treaty should be negotiated in full view of world opinion, not in secret. It should guarantee the freedom of the seas to all nations, in war as in peacetime. It should tear down barriers to international trade, provide for a drastic reduction of armaments, and establish a colonial system that would take proper account of the interests of the native peoples concerned. European boundaries should be redrawn so that no substantial group would have to live under a government not of its own choosing. More specifically, captured Russian territory should be restored, Belgium evacuated, Alsace-Lorraine returned to France, the heterogeneous nationalities of Austria-Hungary accorded autonomy. Italy's frontiers should be adjusted "along clearly recognizable lines of nationality," the Balkans made free, Turkey divested of its subject peoples, an independent Polish state (with access to the Baltic Sea) created. To oversee the new system, Wilson insisted, "a general association of nations must be formed under specific covenants for the purpose of affording mutual guarantees of political independence and territorial integrity to great and small states alike."

Wilson's Fourteen Points for a fair peace lifted the hopes of people everywhere. After the guns fell silent, however, the vagueness and inconsistencies in his list became apparent. Complete national self-determination was impossible in Europe; there were too many regions of mixed population for every group to be satisfied. Furthermore, the Allies had made territorial commitments to one another in secret treaties that ran counter to the principle of self-determination, and they were not ready to give up all claim to Germany's colonies. In every Allied country millions rejected the idea of a peace without indemnities. They expected to make the enemy pay for the war, hoping, as Sir Eric Geddes, first lord of the Admiralty, said, to squeeze Germany "as a lemon is squeezed—until the pips squeak."

*American losses in the war amounted to 112,432 dead and 230,074 wounded. More than half of the deaths, however, resulted from disease. Though severe, these casualties were trivial compared with those of the other belligerents. British Commonwealth deaths amounted to 947,000; French, 1.38 million; Russian, 1.7 million; Italian, to 460,000. Among the Central Powers, Germany lost 1.8 million men, Austria-Hungary 1.2 million, Turkey 325,000. About 20 million more were wounded.

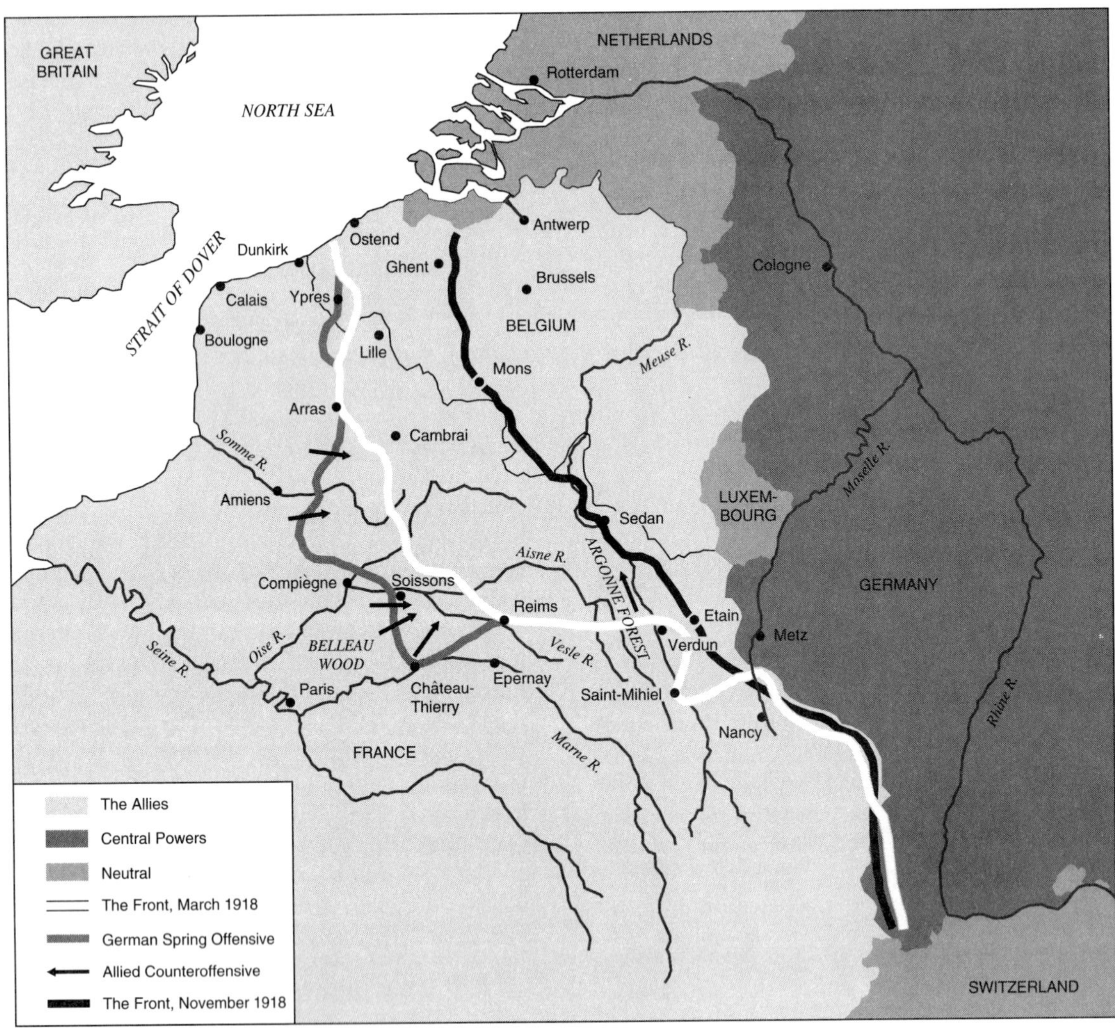

THE WESTERN FRONT, 1918

Wilson assumed that the practical advantages of his program would compel opponents to fall in line. He had the immense advantage of seeking nothing for his own country and the additional strength of being the leader of the only major nation to emerge from the war richer and more powerful than it had been in 1914. Yet this combination of altruism, idealism, and power was his undoing; it intensified his tendency to be overbearing and undermined his judgment. Believing that the fate of humanity hung on his actions, he became in his own mind a prophet, almost, one fears, a kind of god.

In the last weeks of the war Wilson proved to be a brilliant diplomat, first dangling the Fourteen Points before the German people to encourage them to overthrow Kaiser Wilhelm II and sue for an armistice, then sending Colonel House to Paris to persuade Allied leaders to accept the Fourteen Points as the basis for the peace. When the Allies raised objections, House made certain small concessions, but by hinting that the United States might make a separate peace with Germany, he forced them to agree. Under the armistice, Germany had to withdraw behind the Rhine River and surrender its submarines, together with quantities of munitions and other materials. In return it received the assurance of the Allies that the Wilsonian principles would prevail at the peace conference.

Wilson then came to a daring decision: He would personally attend the conference, which convened on January 12, 1919, at Paris, as a member of the United States Peace Commission. This was a precedent-shattering step, for no president had ever left American territory while in office.

Wilson probably erred in going to Paris, but not because of the novelty or possible illegality of the act. In leaving the country he was turning his back on certain obvious domestic problems. Western farmers believed that they had been discriminated against during the war, since wheat prices had been controlled while the price of southern cotton had been allowed to rise from 7 cents a pound in 1914 to 35 cents in 1919. The administration's drastic tax program had angered businessmen. Labor, despite its gains, was restive in the face of reconversion to peacetime conditions. Most important, Wilson intended to break with the isolationist tradition and take the United States into a league of nations. Such a revolutionary change required explanation; he should have undertaken a major campaign to convince the people of the wisdom of this step.

Wilson also erred in his choice of the other commissioners. He selected Colonel House, Secretary of State Lansing, General Tasker H. Bliss, and Henry White, a career diplomat. These men were all thoroughly competent, but only White was a Republican, and he had no stature as a politician. Since the peace treaty would have to be ratified by the Senate, Wilson should have given that body some representation on the commission, and since the Republicans would have a majority in the new Senate, a Republican senator or someone who had the full confidence of the Republican leadership should have been appointed. (The wily McKinley named three senators to the American delegation to the peace conference after the Spanish-American War.)

The Paris Peace Conference

Wilson arrived in Europe a world hero. He toured England, France, and Italy briefly and was greeted ecstatically almost everywhere. The reception tended to increase his sense of mission and to convince him, in the fashion of a typical progressive, that whatever the European politicians might say about it, "the people" were behind his program.

When the conference settled down to its work, control quickly fell into the hands of the so-called Big Four: Wilson, Prime Minister David Lloyd George of Great Britain, Premier Georges Clemenceau of France, and Prime Minister Vittorio Orlando of Italy. Wilson stood out in this group but did not dominate it.

The 78-year-old Clemenceau cared for only one thing: French security. He viewed Wilson cynically, saying that since mankind had been unable to keep God's Ten Commandments, it was unlikely to do better with Wilson's Fourteen Points. Lloyd George's approach was pragmatic and almost cavalier. He sympathized with much that Wilson was trying to accomplish but was baffled by the president's frequent sermonettes about "right being more important than might, and justice being more eternal than force." Orlando was far less influential than his three colleagues. When they failed to meet all his demands, he left the conference in a huff.

The conference labored from January to May 1919 and finally brought forth the Versailles Treaty. American liberals, whose hopes had soared at the thought of a peace based on the Fourteen Points, found the treaty abysmally disappointing. The peace settlement failed to carry out the principle of self-determination properly. It gave Italy a large section of the Austrian Tyrol that contained 200,000 persons who considered themselves Austrians. Other German-speaking groups were incorporated into the new states of Poland and Czechoslovakia. Japan was allowed to take over the Chinese province of Shantung, and the Allies swallowed up all the German colonies in Africa and the Far East.

The victors forced Germany to accept responsibility for having caused the war—an act of senseless vindictiveness as well as a gross oversimplification—and to agree to pay for all damage to civilian properties and even future pensions and other indirect war costs. Instead of attacking imperialism, the treaty attacked German imperialism; instead of seeking a new international social order based on liberty and democracy, it created a great-power entente designed to crush Germany and to exclude Bolshevist Russia from the family of nations. It said nothing about freedom of the seas, the reduction of tariffs, or disarmament.

A skeptical view of the League of Nations: In London's *Punch,* the dove of peace looks askance at Wilson's hefty olive branch, asking, "Isn't this a bit thick?"

The complaints of the critics were individually reasonable, yet their conclusions were not entirely fair. The new map of Europe left fewer people on "foreign" soil than in any earlier period of history. Though the Allies seized the German colonies, they were required, under the mandate system, to submit to the League of Nations annual accounts of their stewardship and to prepare the inhabitants for eventual independence. Above all, Wilson had persuaded the powers to incorporate the League of Nations in the treaty.

Wilson expected the League of Nations to make up for all the inadequacies of the Versailles Treaty. Once the League had begun to function, problems like freedom of the seas and disarmament would solve themselves, he argued, and the relaxation of trade barriers would surely follow. The League would arbitrate international disputes, act as a central body for registering treaties, and employ military and economic sanctions against aggressor nations.

By any standard, Wilson had achieved a remarkably moderate peace, one full of hope for the future. Except for the war guilt clause and the heavy reparations imposed on Germany, he could be justly proud of his work.

The Senate and the League of Nations

When Wilson returned from France, he at long last directed his attention to the task of winning public approval of his handiwork. A large majority of the people probably favored the League of Nations in principle, though few understood all its implications or were entirely happy with every detail. Wilson had persuaded the Allies to accept certain changes in the original draft to mollify American opposition. One provided that no nation could be forced to accept a colonial mandate, another that "domestic questions" such as tariffs and the control of immigration did not fall within the competence of the League.

Many senators found these modifications insufficient. Even before the peace conference ended, 37 Republican senators signed a manifesto devised by Henry Cabot Lodge of Massachusetts opposing Wilson's League and demanding that the question of an international organization be put off until "the urgent business of negotiating peace terms with Germany" had been completed. Wilson rejected this suggestion icily. Thus the stage was set for a monumental test of strength between the president and the Republican majority in the Senate.

Partisanship, principle, and prejudice clashed mightily in this contest. A presidential election loomed. Should the League prove a success, the Republicans wanted to be able to claim a share of the credit, but Wilson had refused to allow them to participate in drafting the document. This predisposed all of them to favor changes. Politics aside, genuine alarm at the possible sacrifice of American sovereignty to an international authority led many Republicans to urge modification of the League covenant (constitution). Personal dislike of Wilson and his high-handed methods motivated others. Yet the noble purpose of the League made many reluctant to reject it entirely.

Wilson could count on the Democratic senators almost to a man, but he had to win over many Republicans to obtain the two-thirds majority necessary for ratification. Republican opinion divided roughly into three segments. At one extreme were some dozen "irreconcilables" led by William E. Borah of Idaho. At the other extreme stood another dozen "mild" reservationists who were in favor of the League but who hoped to alter it in minor ways, chiefly for political purposes. In the middle were the "strong" reservationists, senators willing to go along with the League only if American sovereignty were fully protected and it were made clear that their party had played a major role in fashioning the final document.

Senator Lodge, the leader of the Republican opposition, was chairman of the Senate Foreign Relations Committee. Though not an isolationist, he had little faith in the League. He also had a profound distrust of Democrats, especially Wilson, whom he considered a hypocrite and a coward. The president's pious idealism left him cold. While perfectly ready to see the country participate actively in world affairs, Lodge insisted that its right to determine its own best interests in every situation be preserved. He had been a senator since 1893 and an admirer of senatorial independence since early manhood; when a Democratic president tried to ram the Versailles Treaty through the upper house, he fought him with every weapon he could muster.

Lodge belonged to the strong reservationist faction. His own proposals, known as the Lodge Reservations, limited the United States' obligations to the League and stated in unmistakable terms the right of Congress to decide when to honor these obligations. Some of the reservations were mere quibbles. Others, such as the provision that the United States would not endorse Japan's seizure of Chinese territory, were included mainly to embarrass Wilson by pointing up compromises he had made at Versailles. The most important reservation applied to Article 10 of the League covenant, which committed signatories to protect the political independence and territorial integrity of all member nations. Wilson had rightly called Article 10 the "heart" of the covenant. Lodge's reservation made it inoperable so far as the United States was concerned "unless in any particular case the Congress . . . shall by act or joint resolution so provide."

Lodge performed brilliantly, if somewhat unscrupulously, in uniting the three Republican factions behind his reservations. He got the irreconcilables to agree to them by conceding their right to vote against the final version in any event, and he held the mild reservationists in line by modifying some of his demands and stressing the importance of party unity. Since Lodge's proposals dealt forthrightly with the problem of reconciling traditional concepts of national sovereignty with the new idea of world cooperation, supporters of the League could accept them without sacrifice of principle. Wilson, however, refused to budge.

This foolish intransigence is incomprehensible in a man of Wilson's intelligence and political experience. In part his hatred of Lodge accounts for it, in part his faith in his League. But his physical condition in 1919 also played a role. At Paris he had suffered a violent attack of indigestion that was probably a symptom of a minor stroke. Thereafter, many observers noted small changes in his personality, particularly increased stubbornness and a loss of judgment.

Instead of making concessions, the president set out early in September on a nationwide speaking tour to rally support for the League. His speeches, some of them quite brilliant, had little effect on senatorial opinion, and the effort drained his physical reserves. On September 25, after an address in Pueblo, Colorado, he collapsed. The rest of the trip had to be canceled. A few days later, in Washington, he suffered a stroke that partially paralyzed his left side.

For nearly two months the president was almost totally cut off from affairs of state, leaving supporters of the League leaderless while Lodge maneuvered the reservations through the Senate. Gradually, popular attitudes toward the League shifted. Organized groups of Americans of Italian, Irish, and German extraction, angered by what they considered unfair treatment of their native lands in the Versailles Treaty, clamored for outright rejection. The arguments of the irreconcilables persuaded many citizens that Wilson had made too sharp a break with America's isolationist past and that the Lodge Reservations were therefore necessary. Other issues connected with the reconversion of society to a peacetime basis increasingly occupied the public mind.

A coalition of Democratic and moderate Republican senators could easily have carried the treaty. However, Wilson, bitter and emotionally distraught, urged the Democrats to vote for rejection. Thus the amended treaty failed, 35 to 55, the irreconcilables and the Democrats voting against it. Lodge then allowed the original draft without his reservations to come to a vote. Again the result was defeat, 38 to 53. Only one Republican cast a ballot for ratification.

Dismayed but not yet crushed, friends of the League in both parties forced reconsideration of the treaty early in 1920. Neither Lodge nor Wilson would yield an inch. Lodge, who had little confidence in the effectiveness of any league of nations, was under no compulsion to compromise. That Wilson, whose entire being was tied up in the covenant, would not do so is further evidence of his physical and mental decline. He was probably incompetent to perform the duties of his office. When the Senate balloted again in March, half the Democrats voted for the treaty with the Lodge Reservations. The others, mostly southern party regulars, joined the irreconcilables. Together they mustered 35 votes, 7 more than the one-third that meant defeat.

Demobilization

To win the war, the nation had accepted drastic regulation of the economy. When the war ended, the Wilson administration blithely assumed that the economy could readjust itself without direction. The army was demobilized, pouring millions of veterans into the job market without plan. Nearly all controls established by the War Industries Board and other agencies were dropped overnight. Billions of dollars' worth of war contracts were canceled.

Business boomed in 1919 as consumers spent wartime savings on automobiles, homes, and other goods that had been in short supply during the conflict. But temporary shortages caused inflation; by 1920 the cost of living stood at more than twice the level of 1913.

Inflation in turn produced labor trouble. The unions, grown strong during the war, struck for wage increases. Over 4 million workers, one out of five in the labor force, were on strike at some time during 1919. Then came one of the most precipitous economic declines in American history. Between July 1920 and March 1922, prices, especially agricultural prices, plummeted, and unemployment soared.

The Red Scare

Far more serious than the economic losses were the social effects of these difficulties. Most Americans found strikes frustrating and drew invidious comparisons between the lot of the unemployed soldier who had risked his life for a dollar a day and that of the striker who had drawn fat wages during the war in perfect safety.

The activities of radicals in the labor movement led millions of citizens to associate unionism and strikes with the new threat of communist world revolution. Although there were only a relative handful of communists in the United States, the experience of Russia persuaded many people that a tiny minority of ruthless revolutionaries could take over a nation of millions if conditions were right. When strikes broke out, some accompanied by violence, many people interpreted them as communist-inspired preludes to revolution.

Organized labor in America had seldom been truly radical, but some labor leaders had been attracted to socialism, and many Americans failed to distinguish between the similar ends sought by communists and socialists and the entirely different methods by which they proposed to achieve those ends. A general strike paralyzed Seattle in February 1919. In September 1919 a total of 343,000 steelworkers walked off their jobs, and in the same month the Boston police struck. Violence marked the steel strike, and the suspension of police protection in Boston led to looting and fighting that ended only when Governor Calvin Coolidge called out the National Guard.

During the same period a handful of terrorists attempted to murder various prominent persons, including John D. Rockefeller, Justice Oliver Wendell Holmes, Jr., and Attorney General A. Mitchell Palmer. What particularly aroused the public was the fact that most radicals were not American citizens. Wartime fear of alien saboteurs easily transformed itself into peacetime terror of foreign radicals. In this muddled way, radicalism, unionism, and questions of racial and national origins combined to make many Americans believe that their way of life was in imminent danger. Thus the "Red Scare" was born.

Attorney General Palmer was the key figure in the resulting purge. Pressure from Congress and his growing conviction that the communists really were a menace led him to join the "red hunt." Soon he was saying of the radicals: "Out of the sly and crafty eyes of many of them leap cupidity, cruelty, insanity, and crime; from their lopsided faces, sloping brows, and misshapen features may be recognized the unmistakable criminal type."

In August 1919, Palmer established within the Department of Justice the General Intelligence Division, headed by J. Edgar Hoover, to collect information about clandestine radical activities. In November, Justice Department agents in a dozen cities swooped down on the meeting places of an anarchist organization known as the Union of Russian Workers. More than 650 persons were arrested, but in only 43 cases could evidence be found to justify deportation.

Nevertheless, the public reacted so favorably that Palmer planned an immense roundup of communists. On January 2, 1920, his agents, reinforced by local police and self-appointed vigilantes, struck simultaneously in 33 cities. About 6,000 persons were taken into custody, many of them citizens and therefore not subject to the deportation laws, many others unconnected with any radical cause. In a number of cases, individuals who went to visit prisoners were themselves thrown behind bars on the theory that they too must be communists. Hundreds of suspects were jammed into filthy "bullpens," beaten, and forced to sign "confessions."

The public tolerated these wholesale violations of civil liberties because of the supposed menace of communism. Gradually, however, protests began to be heard. No revolutionary outbreak had taken place. Of the 6,000 seized in the Palmer raids, only 556 proved liable to deportation.

Palmer, attempting to maintain the crusade, announced that the radicals planned a gigantic terrorist demonstration for May Day 1920. In New York and other cities, thousands of police were placed on round-the-clock duty; federal troops stood by anxiously. But the day passed without even a rowdy meeting. Suddenly Palmer appeared ridiculous. The Red Scare swiftly subsided.

The Election of 1920

Wilson still hoped for vindication at the polls in the presidential election, which he sought to make a "great and solemn referendum" on the League. He would have liked to run again himself, but in his enfeebled condition, he attracted no support. The Democrats nominated James M. Cox of Ohio. Cox favored joining the League, but the election did not produce the referendum on the organization that Wilson desired. The Republicans, whose candidate was another Ohioan, Senator Warren G. Harding, equivocated shamelessly on the issue. The election turned on other matters, largely emotional.

Disillusioned by the results of the war, many Americans had had their fill of idealism. They wanted, apparently, to end the long period of moral uplift and reform agitation that had begun under Theodore Roosevelt and return to what Harding called "normalcy." To the extent that the voters were expressing opinions on Wilson's League, they responded overwhelmingly in the negative. Harding had been a strong reservationist, yet he swept the country, winning over 16.1 million votes to Cox's 9.1 million. In July 1921, Congress formally ended the war with the Central Powers by passing a joint resolution.

Milestones

1914 United States invades Veracruz, Mexico
War breaks out in Europe

1915 U-boat torpedoes the *Lusitania*
United States recognizes the Carranza government in Mexico

1916 Louis D. Brandeis named to the Supreme Court
Adamson Act gives railroad workers the eight-hour day
"Pancho" Villa burns Columbus, New Mexico

1917 Wilson's "Peace Without Victory" speech
Germany resumes unrestricted submarine warfare
United States declares war on the Central Powers
Herbert Hoover named Food Administrator
Bernard Baruch named head of the War Industries Board

1918 Sedition Act
Armistice ends the Great War

1919 Steel strike
Red Scare, climaxing in Palmer raids
Paris peace conference
Senate rejects Versailles Treaty

1920 Senate rejects Versailles Treaty

Supplementary Reading

R. H. Ferrell, **Woodrow Wilson and World War I** (1985), surveys the war years. Wilson's handling of foreign relations is discussed in two books by A. S. Link, volumes two and three of **Wilson** and in **Wilson the Diplomatist** (1957). See also F. S. Calhoun, **Power and Principle: Armed Intervention in Wilsonian Foreign Policy** (1986), N. G. Levin, Jr., **Woodrow Wilson and World Politics** (1968), and E. H. Buehrig, **Woodrow Wilson and World Power** (1955).

The war on the home front is covered in D. M. Kennedy, **Over Here: The First World War and American Society** (1980), N. A. Wynn, **From Progressivism to Prosperity** (1986), R. D. Cuff, **The War Industries Board** (1973), M. W. Greewald, **Women, War, and Work** (1980), S. L. Vaughn, **Holding Fast the Inner Lines** (1980), and E. M. Coffman, **The War to End All Wars** (1968). Laurence Stallings, **The Doughboys** (1963), is a good popular account of the American army in France. A. E. Barbeau and F. H. Florette describe the role of blacks in the army in **The Unknown Soldiers** (1974).

On the peace settlement, in addition to the biographies of Wilson, consult A. J. Mayer, **Politics and Diplomacy of Peacemaking** (1967), Ralph Stone, **The Irreconcilables** (1970), W. C. Widenor, **Henry Cabot Lodge and the Search for an American Foreign Policy** (1980), and J. A. Garraty, **Henry Cabot Lodge** (1953). On the election of 1920, see Wesley Bagby, **The Road to Normalcy** (1962), and R. K. Murray, **The Harding Era** (1969).

CHAPTER 26

Postwar Society and Culture: Change and Adjustment

TO MANY PEOPLE WHO LIVED through it, the Great War marked a turning point in history, the real division separating the 20th century from the 19th. Actually most of what seemed new in the 1920s had begun to appear before well before 1917, and the changes were still going on. Americans were adjusting to new social, cultural, and economic forces that were to shape their lives and those of their children and grandchildren.

Closing the Gates

The end of the Red Scare did not signal the disappearance of xenophobia. It was perhaps inevitable and possibly wise that some limitation be placed on the entry of immigrants into the United States after the war. An immense backlog of prospective migrants had accumulated during the conflict, and the desperate postwar economic condition of Europe led hundreds of thousands to seek better circumstances in the United States.

Congress, reflecting widespread prejudice against eastern and southern Europeans, passed an emergency act establishing a quota system. Each year 3 percent of the number of foreign-born residents of the United States in 1910 (about 350,000 persons) might enter the country. Each country's quota was based on the number of its nationals in the United States in 1910. This meant that only a relative handful of the total would be from southern and eastern Europe. In 1924 the quota was reduced to 2 percent and the base year shifted to 1890, thereby lowering further the proportion of southern and eastern Europeans admitted.

In 1929 Congress established a system that allowed only 150,000 immigrants a year to enter the country. Each national quota was based on the supposed origins of the entire white population of the United States in 1920, not merely on the foreign-born. In fact, far fewer than 150,000 people entered because the favored European nations failed to fulfill their quotas. Dislike of the "new" immigrants, many of whom were Jewish, was related to a general growth of anti-Semitism. Prestigious colleges, for example, which had previously admitted Jews on the basis of their academic records, now imposed unofficial quotas. So did medical schools.

Chapter-opening illustration: Ma Rainey and Her Georgia Band.

The United States had closed the gates. Instead of an open, cosmopolitan society eager to accept, in Emma Lazarus's stirring line, the "huddled masses yearning to breathe free," America now became committed to preserving a homogeneous, "Anglo-Saxon" population. Anglo-Saxon and homogeneous it did not become, but the foreign-born percentage of the population fell from about 13 percent in 1920 to 4.7 percent in 1970.

New Urban Social Patterns

The census of 1920 revealed that for the first time a majority of Americans lived in urban rather than rural places. This statement is somewhat misleading because the census classified anyone in a community of 2,500 or more as urban. Of the 54 million urban residents in 1920, over 16 million lived in villages and small towns. A large majority of them held ideas and values like those of rural citizens. But the one person in four who lived in a city of 100,000 or more—and particularly the nearly 16.4 million who lived in metropolises of at least half a million—were increasing steadily in number and influence.

Being a city dweller affected family structure, educational opportunities, and dozens of other aspects of human existence. Indeed, since most of the changes in the relations of husbands, wives, and children that had occurred in the 19th century were related to the fact that people were leaving farms to work in towns and cities, these trends intensified in the early 20th century. In addition, couples continued to marry more out of love and physical attraction than for social or economic reasons, and each decade people married slightly later in life and had fewer children.

Earlier differences between working-class and middle-class family structures persisted. In 1920 about a quarter of the American women who were working were married, but middle-class married women who worked were nearly all either childless or highly paid professionals who were able to employ servants. Most male skilled workers now earned enough to support a family in modest comfort so long as they could work steadily, but an unskilled laborer still could not. Wives in most such families had to work.

However, there were important variations in the roles of wives of different ethnic backgrounds. Those who could not speak English well had difficulty obtaining work. Italian immigrant women rarely worked outside the home. Irish-American wives often found jobs as domestics or, if better educated, as nurses, telephone operators, or clerks. Out of necessity, a far larger proportion of black women, married or single, worked than white women.

By the 1920s the concept of the "companionate" family had emerged. In such families, husbands and wives would deal with each other as equals, which downplayed male authority and stressed mutual satisfaction in sexual and other matters. Procreation did not have to be the main purpose of matrimony, but if there were children, they should be left as free as possible; rigid discipline was limiting and therefore wrong. Divorce should be made easier for couples that did not get along, provided they did not have children.

Much attention was given to "scientific" child raising. One school stressed rigid training: Children could be "spoiled" by indulgence; toilet training should begin early; too much kissing could turn male youngsters into "mama's boys." "Children are made not born," John B. Watson, a highly regarded psychologist, regarded psychologist, explained in *The Psychological Care of Infant and Child* (1928). "Never hug and kiss them, never let them sit in your lap. If you must, kiss them once on the forehead when they say good night."

The other school favored a more permissive approach. Toilet training could wait; parents should pay attention to their children's expressed needs, not impose a generalized set of rules on them. In *The Companionate Marriage* (1927), Benjamin B. Lindsey, a juvenile court judge, suggested a kind of trial marriage, a period during which a young couple could get used to each other before undertaking to raise a family.

Lindsey was one among many self-appointed experts who advocated more freedom for young people and open discussion of all questions related to sex. He was most concerned about the welfare of children, whose natural sexuality, he insisted, was being stupidly repressed by Victorian prudes. Others put more emphasis on married women's rights and the injustice of the double standard. Still others were interested in breaking down 19th-century sexual taboos for all people, married or single.

The Younger Generation

All of these matters were of particular concern to the young adults in the generation that had grown up before and during the Great War. That war had raised their hopes for the future, but its outcome dashed them. Now the narrowness and prudery of so many of their elders and the stuffy conservatism of nearly all politicians seemed not merely old-fashioned but ludicrous. Their models and indeed some of their leaders were the prewar Greenwich Village bohemians.

The 1920s has been dubbed the Jazz Age, the era of "flaming youth," when young people danced to syncopated "African" rhythms, careened about the countryside in automobiles in search of pleasure and forgetfulness, and made gods of movie stars and professional athletes. This view of the period bears only a superficial resemblance to reality: Young people liked having a good time and, like all adolescents moving toward maturity, they were eager to understand the world and make their way in it. They were unconventional because they were adjusting to more rapid changes in their world than their grandparents could have imagined.

Trends that were barely perceptible during the Progressive Era now reached avalanche proportions. This was particularly noticeable in relationships between the sexes. In the late 19th century a typical young man "paid a call" on a female friend. The couple remained at home, the parents nearby if not actually participating in what was essentially a social, almost public event held in a private place.

By the 1920s paying calls was being replaced by dating; the young man called only to "pick up" his date, the two to go off, free of parental supervision, for whatever diversion they wished. A date, the historian Beth L. Bailey has pointed out, was "a private act in the public world."

There is no question that for the young people of the 1920s, relations between the sexes were becoming more relaxed and uninhibited. Respectable young women smoked cigarettes, something previously done in public only by prostitutes and bohemian types. They cast off their heavy corsets, wore lipstick, and shortened their hair and their skirts.

Freudian psychology and the more accessible ideas of the British "sexologist" Havelock Ellis reached steadily deeper into the popular psyche. Since sex was "the central function of life," Ellis argued, it must be "simple and natural and pure and good." Bombarded by these exciting ideas, and by erotic books and movies, to say nothing of their own inclinations, young people found themselves ever more tempted to cast off their inhibitions.

Conservatives bemoaned what they described as the breakdown of moral standards, the fragmentation of the family, and the decline of parental authority—all with some reason. Nevertheless, society was not collapsing. Much of the rebelliousness of the young was faddish, a kind of youthful conformity. This was particularly true of college students, every aspect of whose extracurricular life was governed by elaborate rituals. In *The Damned and the Beautiful,* Paula S. Fass has shown how such matters as fraternity and sorority initiations, styles of dress, and college slang, seemingly aspects of independence and free choice, were nearly everywhere shaped and controlled by peer pressure.

But young people's new ways of relating to one another were not mere fads and were not confined to people under 30. This can be seen most clearly in the birth control movement, the drive to legalize the use of contraceptives.

The "New Woman"

The young people of the 1920s were more open about sex, but this does not mean that most of them engaged in sexual intercourse before marriage. Single young people might "believe in" birth control, but relatively few (at least by modern standards) had occasion to practice it. Contraception was a concern of married people, particularly married women.

The leading American proponent of birth control in the 1920s was Margaret Sanger, one of the less self-centered Greenwich Village bohemians. Before the war she was a political radical. Gradually, however, her attention focused on the plight of the poor women she encountered while working as a nurse; many of these women were burdened by large numbers of children yet knew nothing about contraception. Sanger began to write articles and pamphlets designed to enlighten them, frequently running afoul of narrowly interpreted antiobscenity laws. But she was persistent to the edge of fanaticism. In 1921 she founded the American Birth Control League and two years later a research center.

The medical profession gave some support to the birth control movement, as did the eugenicists, who claimed that unless the fecundity of "unfit" types (people others might describe simply as poor) was curbed, "race suicide" would result. By the end of the decade Sanger was no longer on the cutting edge of the movement or even a very radical feminist. But by that time resistance to the use of contraception was crumbling.

Other sex-based restrictions of particular importance to women also seemed to be breaking down. The divorce laws had been modified in most states. More women were taking jobs; over 10.6 million women were working by the end of the decade in contrast with 8.4 million in 1920. The Department of Labor's Women's Bureau was founded in 1920 and was soon conducting investigations of the working conditions women faced in different industries and how various laws affected them.

But most of these gains were illusory. Relaxation of the strict standards of sexual morality did not eliminate the double standard. More women worked, but most of the jobs they held were still ones that few men wanted: domestic service, elementary school teaching, clerical work, selling behind a counter.

Where they competed for jobs with men, women usually received much lower wages. Yet when the head of the Women's Bureau, Mary Anderson, tried to get employers to raise women's wages, most of them claimed that the men had families to support. When she reminded them that many female employees also had family responsibilities, they told her that there was a "tacit understanding" that women were to make less than men. Efforts to get the American Federation of Labor to take up the issue met with failure; few of the unions in the federation admitted women.

The number of women college graduates continued to climb, but the colleges placed more emphasis on subjects like home economics that seemed designed to make them better housewives rather than professionals or business executives. As one Vassar College administrator (a woman!) said, colleges should provide "education for women along the lines of their chief interests and responsibilities, motherhood and the home."

The 1920s proved disillusioning to feminists, who now paid a price for their single-minded pursuit of the right to vote in the Progressive Era. After the ratification of the Nineteenth Amendment, Carrie Chapman Catt was exultant. "We are no longer petitioners," she announced, "but free and equal citizens." Many activists, assuming the battle won, lost interest in agitating for change. They believed that the suffrage amendment had given them the one weapon needed to achieve whatever women still lacked. In fact, it soon became apparent that women did not vote as a bloc. Many, perhaps most, married women voted for the candidates their husbands supported.

When radical feminists discovered that voting did not automatically bring true equality, they founded the Women's party and began campaigning for an equal rights amendment. Their leader, Alice Paul, dynamic if somewhat fanatical, disdained specific goals such as disarmament, an end to child labor, and liberalized birth control. Total equality for women was the one objective. The party held that protective legislation governing the hours and working conditions of women was discriminatory. This caused the so-called social feminists, who believed that children and working women needed the protection provided by such laws, to break away.

The Women's party never attracted a wide following, but only partly because of the split with the social feminists. Many of the younger radical women, like the bohemians of the Progressive Era, were primarily concerned with their personal freedom to behave as they wished; politics did not interest them. But a more important reason was that nearly all the radicals failed to see that questions of gender—the attitudes that men and women *were taught* to take toward each other, not immutable physical or psychological differences—stood in the way of true sexual equality. Many more women joined the more moderate League of Women Voters, which attempted to mobilize support for a broad spectrum of reforms, some of which had no specific connection with the interests of women as such. The entire women's movement lost momentum. The battle for the equal rights amendment persisted, but by the end of the 1930s the movement was moribund.

Popular Culture: Movies and Radio

The postwar decade saw immense changes in popular culture, changes that seemed in tune with the times, not a reaction against them. This was true in part because they were products as much of technology as of human imagination.

The first motion pictures were made around 1900, but the medium only came into its own after the Great War. The early films, such as the eight-minute epic *The Great Train Robbery* (1903), were brief, action-packed, and unpretentious. Professional actors and most educated people viewed them with contempt. But their success was instantaneous. By 1912 there were more than 13,000 movie houses in the United States. Many were mere storefronts, called nickelodeons because the admission charge was 5 cents.

Success led to rapid technical and artistic improvements. David W. Griffith's 12-reel *Birth of a Nation* (1915) was a particularly important breakthrough in both areas, though Griffith's sympathetic treatment of the Ku Klux Klan of Reconstruction days angered blacks and white liberals.

By the mid-1920s the industry, centered in Hollywood, California, was the fourth largest in the nation in capital investment. Movie "palaces" seating several thousand people sprang up in the major cities, and they counted their yearly audiences in the tens of millions. With the introduction of talking movies, beginning with *The Jazz Singer* (1927), and color films a few years later, the motion picture reached technological maturity. Costs and profits mounted; by the 1930s, million-dollar productions were common.

Many movies were tasteless trash catering to the prejudices of the multitude. Popular actors and actresses tended to be either handsome, talentless sticks or so-called character actors who were typecast over and over again as heroes, villains, or comedians. The stars were paid thousands of dollars a week. Critics charged that the movies were destroying the legitimate stage, corrupting the morals of youth, and glorifying the materialistic aspects of life.

Nevertheless, the motion picture made positive contributions to American culture. Beginning with the work of Griffith, filmmakers created an entirely new theatrical art, using close-ups to portray character and heighten tension, broad panoramic shots to transcend the limits of the stage. They employed with remarkable results special lighting effects, the fade-out, and other techniques impossible in the live theater. Movies enabled dozens of established actors to reach wider audiences and developed many first-rate new ones. In Charlie Chaplin, whose characterization of the sad little tramp with toothbrush moustache and cane, tight frock coat, and baggy trousers became famous throughout the world, the new form found perhaps the supreme comic artist of all time. The animated cartoon, perfected by Walt Disney in the 1930s, was a significant achievement that gave endless delight to millions of children. And as the medium matured, it produced many dramatic works of high quality. At its best the motion picture offered a breadth and power of impact superior to anything on the traditional stage.

Even more pervasive than movies in its effects on the American people was radio. Wireless transmission of sound was developed in the late 19th century by many scientists in Europe and the United States. In 1920 the first commercial station (KDKA in Pittsburgh) began broadcasting, and by the end of 1922 over 500 stations were in operation.

The immediacy of radio explained its tremendous impact. As a means of communicating the latest news, it had no peer; beginning with the broadcast of the 1924 presidential nominating conventions, all major public events were covered "live." Advertisers seized on radio too; it proved to be as useful for selling soap as for transmitting news.

Advertising had mixed effects on broadcasting. The sums paid by business for airtime made possible elaborate entertainments performed by the finest actors and musicians, all without cost to listeners. However, advertisers hungered for mass markets. They preferred to sponsor programs of little intellectual content, aimed at the lowest tastes and utterly uncontroversial. And good and bad alike, programs were continually interrupted by irritating pronouncements extolling the supposed virtues of one commercial product or another.

In 1927 Congress limited the number of stations and parceled out wavelengths to prevent interference. Further legislation in 1934 established the Federal Communications Commission with power to revoke the licenses of stations that failed to operate in the public interest. But the FCC placed no effective controls on programming or on advertising practices.

The Golden Age of Sports

The extraordinary popularity of sports in the postwar period can be explained in a number of ways.

People had more money to spend and more free time to fill. Radio was bringing suspenseful, play-by-play accounts of sports contests into millions of homes, thus encouraging tens of thousands to want to see similar events with their own eyes.

There had been great athletes before, such as Jim Thorpe, a Sac and Fox Indian who won both the pentathlon and the decathlon at the 1912 Olympic Games, made Walter Camp's All America football team in 1912 and 1913, then played major league baseball for several years before becoming a pioneer founder and player in the National Football League. But what truly made the 1920s a golden age was the emergence of a remarkable collection of what today would be called superstars.

In football there was the University of Illinois's Harold "Red" Grange, who averaged over 10 yards a carry during his college career and who in one incredible quarter during the 1924 game between Illinois and Michigan carried the ball four times and scored a touchdown each time, gaining 263 yards in the process. In prize fighting, heavyweight champion Jack Dempsey, the "Manassas Mauler," knocked out a succession of challengers in bloody battles.

During the same years William "Big Bill" Tilden dominated tennis, winning the national singles title every year from 1920 to 1925 along with nearly every other tournament he entered. Beginning in 1923, Robert T. "Bobby" Jones ruled over the world of golf with equal authority, his climactic achievement being his capturing of the amateur and open championships of both the United States and Great Britain in 1930.

A few women athletes dominated their sports during this Golden Age in similar fashion. In tennis Helen Wills was three times U.S. singles champion and the winner of the women's singles at Wimbledon eight times in the late 1920s and early 1930s. The swimmer Gertrude Ederle, holder of 18 world's records by the time she was 17, swam the English Channel on her second attempt in 1926. She was not only the first woman to do so, but she did it faster than any of the four men who had previously made it across.

However, the sports star among stars was "the Sultan of Swat," baseball's George Herman ("Babe") Ruth. Ruth changed baseball from a game ruled by pitchers and low scores to one where hitting was more greatly admired. Originally himself a brilliant pitcher, his incredible hitting ability made him more valuable in the outfield. Ruth hit 54 home runs in 1920, his first year with the New York Yankees, and 60 in 1927. By 1923 he was so feared that he was given a base on balls more than half the times he appeared at the plate.

Football was the preeminent school sport. At many colleges football afternoons came to resemble religious rites—a national magazine titled a 1928 article "The Great God Football," and the editor of a college newspaper denounced "disloyal" students who took seats in the grandstand where they could see what was happening rather than doing their bit in the student cheering section in the end zone.

Tens of thousands of men and women took up tennis, golf, swimming, and calisthenics. Socal dancing became more energetic. The turkey trot, a popular prewar dance, led in the next decade to the Charleston and what one historian called "an imitative swarm of hops, wriggles, squirms, glides and gallops named after all the animals in the menagerie."

Urban-Rural Conflicts: Fundamentalism

These were buoyant times for "modern" people, most of whom lived in big cities. However, the tensions and hostilities of the 1920s exaggerated an older rift in American society—the conflict between the urban and the rural way of life. To many among the scattered millions who tilled the soil and among the millions more who lived in towns and small cities, the new city-oriented culture seemed sinful, overly materialistic, and unhealthy.

Yet there was no denying the appeal of the city, introduced to farmers and townspeople through radio and the movies. These people coveted the excitement of city life even as they condemned its vices. Rural society proclaimed the superiority of its ways at least in part to protect itself from temptation. Change, omnipresent in the postwar world, must be resisted even at the cost of individualism and freedom.

One expression of this intolerance was a resurgence of religious fundamentalism. Rather than a religious idea, fundamentalism was a conservative attitude of mind. Fundamentalists rejected the theory of evolution and all other knowledge about the origins of the universe and the human race that had been discovered during the 19th century.

Urban sophisticates tended to dismiss fundamentalists as boors and hayseed fanatics, yet the persistence of old-fashioned ideas was understandable. In rural areas, where educational standards were low and culture relatively static, old ideas remained unchallenged. The power of reason, so obvious in a technologically advanced society, seemed much less obvious to rural people. Farmers, living in close contact with the capricious, elemental power of nature, tended to have more respect for the force of divine providence than city folk. Beyond this, the majesty and beauty of the King James translation of the Bible, the only book in countless rural homes, made it extraordinarily difficult for many persons to abandon their belief in its literal truth.

What made crusaders of the fundamentalists, however, was their resentment of modern urban culture. The teaching of evolution must be prohibited, they insisted. Throughout the early 1920s they campaigned vigorously for laws banning discussion of Darwin's theory in textbooks and classrooms.

Their greatest asset in this unfortunate crusade was William Jennings Bryan. Age had not improved the "Peerless Leader." After leaving Wilson's Cabinet in 1915, he devoted much time to religious and moral issues, but without applying himself conscientiously to the study of these difficult questions. He went about the country charging that "they"—meaning the mass of educated Americans—had "taken the Lord away from the schools." He denounced the use of public money to undermine Christian principles, and he offered $100 to anyone who would admit to being descended from an ape. His immense popularity in rural areas assured him a wide audience, and no one came forward to take his money.

The fundamentalists won a minor victory in 1925 when Tennessee passed a law forbidding instructors in the state's schools and colleges to teach "any theory that denies the story of the Divine Creation of man as taught in the Bible." Upon learning of the passage of this act, the American Civil Liberties Union announced that it would finance a test case challenging its constitutionality if a Tennessee teacher would deliberately violate the statute. Urged on by friends, John T. Scopes, a young biology teacher in Dayton, stated in class that man was descended from other primates. He was arrested. A battery of nationally known lawyers came forward to defend him; the state obtained the services of Bryan himself. The so-called Monkey Trial became an overnight sensation.

Clarence Darrow, chief counsel for the defendant, stated the issue clearly. "Scopes isn't on trial," he said; "civilization is on trial." The comic aspects of the trial obscured this issue. Big-city reporters like H. L. Mencken of the *Baltimore Evening Sun* flocked to Dayton to make sport of the fundamentalists. Scopes's conviction was a foregone conclusion; after the jury rendered its verdict, the judge fined him $100.

Nevertheless, the trial exposed both the stupidity and the danger of the fundamentalist position. The high point came when Bryan agreed to testify as an expert witness on the Bible. In a sweltering courtroom, both men in shirtsleeves, the lanky, rough-hewn Darrow cross-examined the aging champion of fundamentalism, mercilessly exposing his childlike faith and his abysmal ignorance. Bryan admitted to believing that Eve had been created from Adam's rib and that a whale had swallowed Jonah.

The Monkey Trial ended in frustration for nearly everyone concerned. Scopes moved away from Dayton; the judge, John Raulston, was defeated when he sought reelection; Bryan died in his sleep a few days after the trial. But fundamentalism continued to flourish. In retrospect, the heroes of the Scopes trial—science and freedom of thought—seem somewhat less stainless than they did to liberals at the time. The account of evolution in the textbook used by Scopes was far from satisfactory, and it contained statements that to the modern mind seem at least as bigoted as anything that Bryan said at Dayton. A section on the "races of man," for example, described Caucasians as "the highest type of all . . . represented by the civilized white inhabitants of Europe and America."

Urban-Rural Conflicts: Prohibition

The conflict between the countryside and the city was fought on many fronts, and in one sector the rural forces achieved a quick victory. This was the prohibition of the manufacture, transportation, and sale of alcoholic beverages by the Eighteenth

Amendment, ratified in 1919. Although there were some big-city advocates of prohibition, the Eighteenth Amendment, in the words of the historian Andrew Sinclair, marked a triumph of the "Corn Belt over the conveyor belt."

The temperance movement had been important since the age of Jackson; it was an issue in many states during the Gilded Age, and by the Progressive Era many reformers were eager to prohibit drinking entirely. Indeed, prohibition was a typical progressive reform, moralistic, backed by the middle class, and aimed at frustrating "the interests"—in this case, the distillers.

World War I aided the prohibitionists by increasing the need for food. The Lever Act of 1917 outlawed the use of grain in the manufacture of alcoholic beverages, primarily as a conservation measure. The prevailing dislike of foreigners helped the dry cause still more, as beer drinking was associated with Germans. State and local laws had made a large part of the country dry by 1917. National prohibition became official in January 1920.

This "experiment noble in purpose," as Herbert Hoover called it, achieved a number of socially desirable results. It reduced the national consumption of alcohol. Arrests for drunkenness fell off sharply, as did deaths from alcoholism. Fewer workers squandered their wages on drink. If the drys had been willing to legalize beer and wine, the experiment might have worked. Instead, by insisting on total abstinence, they drove moderates to violate the law. Strict enforcement became impossible, especially in the cities.

In areas where popular opinion favored prohibition strongly, liquor was difficult to find. Elsewhere, smuggling became a major business, *bootlegger* a household word. Private individuals busied themselves learning how to manufacture "bathtub gin." Fraudulent druggists' prescriptions for alcohol were issued freely. The saloon disappeared, replaced by the speakeasy, a supposedly secret bar or club operating usually under the benevolent eye of the local police.

That the law was often violated does not mean that it was ineffective any more than violations of laws against theft and murder mean that those laws are ineffective. Although gangsters such as Alphonse "Scarface Al" Capone of Chicago were engaged in the liquor traffic, their "organizations" had existed before the ratification of the Eighteenth Amendment.

Prohibition almost destroyed the Democratic party as a national organization; Democratic immigrants in the cities hated it, but southern Democrats sang its praises, often while continuing to drink.

The hypocrisy of prohibition had a deleterious effect on politicians, a class seldom famous for candor. Congressmen catered to the demands of the Anti-Saloon League yet failed to grant adequate funds to the Prohibition Bureau. Democratic and Republican leaders, from Wilson and La Follette to Hoover and Franklin D. Roosevelt, equivocated shamelessly on the liquor question. By the end of the decade almost every competent observer recognized that prohibition needed to be overhauled, but the well-organized and powerful dry forces rejected all proposals for modifying it.

The Ku Klux Klan

The most horrible manifestation of the social malaise of the 1920s was the revival of the Ku Klux Klan. This new Klan, founded in 1915 by William J. Simmons, a preacher, admitted only native-born white Protestants. The distrust of foreigners, blacks, Catholics, and Jews implicit in this regulation explains why it flourished in the social climate that spawned religious fundamentalism, immigration restriction, and prohibition. By 1923 it claimed the astonishing total of 5 million members.

The Klan had relatively little appeal in the Northeast or in metropolitan centers in other parts of the country, but it found many members in middle-sized cities and in the small towns and villages of middlewestern and western states like Indiana, Ohio, and Oregon. The scapegoats in such regions were immigrants, Jews, and especially Catholics. The rationale was an urge to return to an older, supposedly finer America and to stamp out all varieties of nonconformity. Klansmen persecuted gamblers, "loose" women, violators of the prohibition laws, and anyone who happened to differ from them on religious questions or who belonged to a "foreign race."

The very success of the Klan led to its undoing. Factionalism sprang up, and rival leaders squabbled over the large sums that had been collected from the membership. The cruel and outrageous behavior of the organization aroused the ire of both liberals and conservatives in every part of the country. When the powerful leader of the Indiana Klan, a middle-aged reprobate named David C. Stephenson, was convicted of assaulting and causing the death of a young woman, the rank and file abandoned the organization in droves. It remained influential for a number of years, contributing to the defeat of the Catholic Alfred E. Smith in the 1928 presidential election, but it ceased to be a dynamic force after 1924. By 1930 it had only some 9,000 members.

Sacco and Vanzetti

The excesses of the fundamentalists, the xenophobes, the Klan, the red-baiters, and the prohibitionists disturbed American intellectuals profoundly. More and more they became alienated, yet their alienation came at a time when society was growing more dependent on brains and sophistication. This compounded the confusion and disillusionment characteristic of the period.

Nothing demonstrates this fact so clearly as the Sacco-Vanzetti case. In April 1920 two men in South Braintree, Massachusetts, killed a paymaster and a guard in a daring daylight robbery of a shoe factory. Shortly thereafter, Nicola Sacco and Bartolomeo Vanzetti were charged with the crime, and in 1921 they were convicted of murder and sentenced to death. Sacco and Vanzetti were anarchists and Italian immigrants. Their trial was a travesty of justice. The presiding judge, Webster Thayer, conducted the proceedings like a prosecuting attorney; privately he referred to the defendants as "those anarchist bastards."

The case became a cause célèbre. Prominent persons throughout the world protested. Vanzetti's quiet dignity and courage in the face of death wrung the hearts of millions. When the two were at last electrocuted, the disillusionment of American intellectuals with current values was profound.

Literary Trends

The literature of the 1920s reflects the disillusionment of the intellectuals. The prewar period had been a time of hopeful experimentation in the world of letters. But writers, along with most other intellectuals, were beginning to abandon this view by about 1912. The wasteful horrors of the World War and then the antics of the fundamentalists and the cruelty of the red-baiters turned them into critics of society. Soon hundreds of young men and women were referring to themselves with almost maudlin self-pity as the "lost generation." The poet Ezra Pound gave up anticipating an American Renaissance and wrote instead of a "botched civilization."

The symbol of the lost generation, in his own mind as well as to his contemporaries and to later critics, was F. Scott Fitzgerald, who rose to sudden fame in 1920 when he published *This Side of Paradise,* a somewhat sophomoric novel that appealed powerfully to college students and captured the fears and confusions of the lost generation. In *The Great Gatsby* (1925), a more mature work, Fitzgerald dissected a modern millionaire—coarse, unscrupulous, jaded, in love with another man's wife. Gatsby's tragedy lay in his dedication to a woman who, Fitzgerald made clear, did not merit his passion.

The tragedy of *The Great Gatsby* was related to Fitzgerald's own. Pleasure-loving and extravagant, he squandered the money earned by *This Side of Paradise.* When *The Great Gatsby* failed to sell as well, he turned to writing potboilers. Despite some first-class later work, Fitzgerald descended into the despair of alcoholism and ended his days as a Hollywood scriptwriter.

Many young American writers and artists became expatriates in the 1920s. They flocked to Rome, Berlin, and especially Paris, where they could live cheaply and escape what seemed to them the "conspiracy against the individual" prevalent in their own country. Ernest Hemingway, the most talented of this group, settled in Paris in 1922 to write. His first novel, *The Sun Also Rises* (1926), portrayed the café world of the expatriate and the rootless desperation, amorality, and sense of outrage at life's meaninglessness that obsessed so many in those years. In *A Farewell to Arms* (1929) he described the confusion and horror of war.

Hemingway's books were best-sellers, and he became a legend in his own time, but his style rather than his ideas explains his towering reputation. Few novelists have been such self-conscious craftsmen or as capable of suggesting powerful emotions and action in so few words. This taut, spare passage is from *A Farewell to Arms:*

> *I went out the door and down the hall to the room where Catherine was to be after the baby came. I*

Contrasting images of two literary stars of the "lost generation": F. Scott Fitzgerald *(top)* as the thoughtful, introspective artist, and Ernest Hemingway *(bottom)*, sportsman and man of action.

> *sat in a chair there and looked at the room. I had the paper in my coat that I had bought when I went out for lunch and I read it. . . . After a while I stopped reading and turned off the light and watched it get dark outside.*

This kind of writing, evoking rather than describing emotion, fascinated readers and inspired hundreds of imitators; it has made a permanent mark on world literature. What Hemingway had to say was of less universal interest—he was an unabashed, rather muddled romantic, an adolescent emotionally. He wrote masterfully about bullfights, hunting and fishing, violence—themes that limited his scope. The critic Alfred Kazin summed Hemingway up in a sentence: "He brought a major art to a minor vision of life."

Two other writers of the 1920s deserve mention: H. L. Mencken and Sinclair Lewis. Mencken, a Baltimore newspaperman and founder of one of the great magazines of the era, the *American Mercury,* was a thoroughgoing cynic. He coined the word *booboisie* to define the complacent, middle-class majority, and he fired superbly witty broadsides at fundamentalists, prohibitionists, and "Puritans." "Puritanism," Mencken once said, "is the haunting fear that someone, somewhere, may be happy."

But Mencken was never indifferent to the many aspects of American life that engendered his contempt. Politics at once fascinated and repelled him, and he assailed the statesmen of his generation with magnificent impartiality:

BRYAN: "If the fellow was sincere, then so was P. T. Barnum. . . . He was, in fact, a charlatan, a mountebank, a zany without sense or dignity."

WILSON: "The bogus Liberal. . . . A pedagogue thrown up to 1000 diameters by a magic lantern."

HARDING: "The numskull, Gamaliel, . . . the Marion stonehead. . . . The operations of his medulla oblongata . . . resemble the rattlings of a colossal linotype charged with rubber stamps."

COOLIDGE: "A cheap and trashy fellow, deficient in sense and almost devoid of any notion of honor—in brief, a dreadful little cad."

HOOVER: "Lord Hoover is no more than a pious old woman, a fat Coolidge. . . . He would have made a good bishop."

Mencken's diatribes, though amusing, were not profound. In retrospect he seems more a professional iconoclast than a constructive critic; like both Fitzgerald and Hemingway, he was something of a perennial adolescent. However, he was a consistent champion of freedom of expression of every sort.

Sinclair Lewis was probably the most popular American novelist of the 1920s. Like Fitzgerald, his first major work brought him instant fame and notoriety—and for the same reason. *Main Street* (1920) portrayed the smug ignorance and bigotry of the American small town so accurately that even Lewis's victims recognized themselves; his title became a symbol for provinciality and middle-class meanness of spirit. In *Babbitt* (1922), he created a businessman of the 1920s, a "booster," blindly orthodox in his political and social opinions, a slave to every cliché, and full of loud self-confidence, but under the surface a bumbling, rather timid fellow.

Lewis went on to dissect the medical profession in *Arrowsmith* (1925), religion in *Elmer Gantry* (1927), fascism in *It Can't Happen Here* (1935). He was preeminently a product of the 1920s. When times changed, he could no longer portray society with such striking verisimilitude; none of his later novels approached the level of his first two. When critics noticed this, Lewis became bewildered, almost disoriented. He died in 1951 a desperately unhappy man.

The "New Negro"

Even more than for white liberals, the postwar reaction had brought despair for blacks. Aside from the barbarities of the Klan, they suffered from the postwar middle-class hostility to labor (and from the persistent reluctance of organized labor to admit black workers to its ranks). The increasing presence of southern blacks in northern cities also caused conflict. Some 393,000 settled in New York, Pennsylvania, and Illinois in the 1920s, most of them in New York City, Philadelphia, and Chicago.

This influx speeded the development of urban ghettos. Harlem, a white, middle-class residential section of New York City as late as 1910, had 50,000 blacks in 1914 and nearly 165,000 in 1930. The restrictions of ghetto life produced a vicious circle of degradation. Population growth and segregation caused a desperate housing shortage; rents in Harlem doubled between 1919 and 1927. Since the average black worker was unskilled and ill-paid, tenants were forced to take in boarders. Landlords converted private homes into rooming houses and allowed their properties to fall into disrepair. These conditions allowed disease and crime rates to rise sharply.

Even in small northern cities where they made up only a tiny proportion of the population, blacks were treated badly. When Robert S. Lynd and Helen M. Lynd made their classic sociological analysis of "Middletown" (Muncie, Indiana), they discovered that despite attending the same schools, blacks and whites were segregated in the churches, the larger movie houses, and other places of public accommodation.

Coming after the hopes inspired by wartime gains, the disappointments of the 1920s produced a new militancy among many blacks. In 1919 W. E. B. Du Bois wrote in *The Crisis*: "We are cowards and jackasses if . . . we do not marshal every ounce of our brain and brawn to fight . . . against the forces of hell in our own land." He increased his commitment to black nationalism, organizing a series of pan-African conferences in an effort—futile, as it turned out—to create an international black movement.

Du Bois never made up his mind whether to work for integration or black separatism. Marcus Garvey, a West Indian whose Universal Negro Improvement Association attracted hundreds of thousands of followers in the early 1920s, had nothing but contempt for whites, for light-skinned Negroes like Du Bois, and for organizations such as the NAACP that sought to bring whites and blacks together to fight segregation and other forms of prejudice. "Back to Africa" was his slogan; the black man must "work out his salvation in his motherland."

Garvey's message was naive, but it served to build racial pride among the masses of poor and unschooled blacks. Both God and Christ were black, he insisted. He organized black businesses of many sorts, including a company that manufactured black dolls. He established a corps of Black Cross nurses and a Black Star Line Steamship Company to transport blacks to Africa.

More sophisticated blacks, including Du Bois, considered Garvey a charlatan. The man's motives are unclear, and he was a terrible businessman. In 1923 his steamship line went into bankruptcy. He was convicted of defrauding the thousands of his supporters who had invested in its stock and was sent to prison. Nevertheless, his message helped to create the "New Negro," proud of being black and prepared to resist both white mistreatment and white ideas: "Up, you mighty race, you can accomplish what you will!"

The ghettos produced compensating advantages for blacks. One effect, not fully used until later, was to increase their political power by enabling them to elect representatives to state legislatures and to Congress and to exert great influence on the parties in closely contested elections. More immediately, city life stimulated self-confidence; despite their horrors, the ghettos offered economic opportunity, political rights, and freedom from the everyday debasements of life in the South.

Black writers, musicians, and artists found in the ghettos both an audience and the "spiritual emancipation" that unleashed their capacities. Jazz, the great popular music of the age, was largely the creation of black musicians working in New Orleans before the turn of the century. By the 1920s it had spread throughout the country and to most of the rest of the world. White musicians and white audiences took it up—in a way, it became a force for racial tolerance and understanding. It was preeminently the music of the 1920s in part because it expressed the desire of so many people to break with tradition and throw off conventional restraints.

Harlem, the largest black community in the world, became in the 1920s a cultural capital, center of the "Harlem Renaissance." Black newspapers and magazines flourished along with theatrical companies and libraries. Du Bois opened *The Crisis* to young writers and artists, and a dozen "little magazines" sprang up. Langston Hughes, one of the fine poets of the era, described the exhilaration of his first arrival in this city within a city, a "magnet" for every black intellectual and artist. "Harlem! I . . . dropped my bags, took a deep breath, and felt happy again."

With some exceptions, black writers like Hughes did not share in the disillusionment that afflicted so many white intellectuals. The persistence of prejudice angered them and made them militant. But to be militant, one must be at some level hopeful, and this they were. Sociologists and psychologists (for whom the ghettos were rich social laboratories) were demonstrating that environment rather than heredity was preventing black economic progress. Together with the achievements of creative blacks, which for the first time were being appreciated by large numbers of white intellectuals, these discoveries seemed to herald the eventual disappearance of race prejudice. The black, Alain Locke wrote in *The New Negro* (1925), "lays aside the status of beneficiary and ward for that of a collaborator and participant in American civilization." Alas, as Locke and other black intellectuals were soon to discover, this prediction, like so many made in the 1920s, did not come to pass.

The "New Era"

Despite the turmoil of the times and the dissatisfactions expressed by some of the nation's best minds, the 1920s was an exceptionally prosperous decade. Business boomed, real wages rose, and unemployment declined. The United States was as rich as all Europe; perhaps 40 percent of the world's total wealth lay in American hands. Little wonder that business leaders and other conservatives described the period as a "new era."

The prosperity rested on many bases, one of which was the friendly, hands-off attitude of the federal government, which bolstered the confidence of the business community. The Federal Reserve Board kept interest rates low, a further stimulus to economic growth. Pent-up wartime demand helped power the boom; the construction business in particular profited from a series of extremely busy years. The continuing mechanization and rationalization of industry provided a more fundamental stimulus to the economy. Greater use of power, especially of electricity, also encouraged expansion—by 1929 the United States was producing more electricity than the rest of the world combined.

Most important, American manufacturing was experiencing a remarkable improvement in efficiency. The method of breaking down the complex processes of production into many simple operations and the use of interchangeable parts were 19th-century innovations; in the 1920s they were adopted on an almost universal scale. The moving assembly line, which carried the product to the worker, perfected by Henry Ford in his automobile plant in the decade before World War I, speeded production and reduced costs. In ten years the hourly output of Ford workers quadrupled.

The Age of the Consumer

The increasing ability of manufacturers to produce goods meant that great efforts had to be made to create new consumer demands. Advertising and salesmanship were raised almost to the status of fine arts. Bruce Barton, one of the advertising "geniuses" of the era, wrote a best-selling book, *The Man Nobody Knows* (1925), in which he described Jesus as the "founder of modern business," the man who "picked up twelve men from the bottom ranks . . . and forged them into an organization that conquered the world." In 1930 Eleanor Roosevelt, wife of the governor of New York, gave a testimonial for a breakfast cereal. It had, she said, "undoubtedly played its part" in building the "robust physique" of her teenage son John.

Producers concentrated on making their goods more attractive and on changing models frequently to entice buyers into the market. The practice of selling goods on the installment plan helped bring expensive items within the reach of the masses. Inventions and technological advances created new or improved products: radios, automobiles, electric appliances such as vacuum cleaners and refrigerators, gadgets like cigarette lighters, new forms of entertainment like motion pictures.

Undeniably, the single most important impact on the nation's economy in the 1920s was made by the automobile. Although well over a million cars a year were being regularly produced by 1916, the real expansion of the industry came after 1921. Output reached 3.6 million in 1923 and fell below that figure only twice during the remainder of the decade. By 1929, 23 million private cars clogged the highways, an average of nearly one per family.

The auto industry created industries that manufactured tires, spark plugs, and other products. It consumed immense quantities of rubber, paint, glass, nickel, and petroleum products. It triggered a gigantic road-building program. Thousands found employment in filling stations, roadside stands, and other businesses catering to the motoring public. The tourist industry profited, and the shift of population from the cities to the suburbs was accelerated.

Henry Ford in his first car, the Quadricycle, built in 1896.

The automobile made life more mobile yet also more encapsulated. It created a generation of amateur mechanics and explorers. It gave Americans a freedom never before imagined. The owner of the most rickety jalopy could travel farther, faster, and far more comfortably than a monarch of old with his blooded steeds and gilded coaches. These benefits were real and priceless. But cars came to have an equally important symbolic significance; they gave their owners a feeling of power and status.

In time there were undesirable, even dangerous results of the automotive revolution: roadside scenery disfigured by billboards and gas stations; traffic jams; soaring accident rates; air pollution; the neglect of public transportation, which was an impor-

A boyish-looking Charles A. Lindbergh during his flying apprenticeship as a stunt pilot in 1925, two years before his solo flight across the Atlantic.

tant cause of the deterioration of inner cities. All these disadvantages were noticed during the 1920s, but they were discounted. The automobile seemed an unalloyed blessing—part toy, part tool, part symbol of American freedom, prosperity, and individualism.

Henry Ford

The person most responsible for the growth of the automobile industry was Henry Ford, a self-taught mechanic from Greenfield, Michigan. In 1908 he designed the Model T Ford, a simple, tough box on wheels. In a year he sold 11,000 of them. Thereafter, relentlessly cutting costs and increasing efficiency by installing the assembly line system, he expanded production at an unbelievable rate. By 1925 he was turning out more than 9,000 cars a day, one approximately every ten seconds, and the price of the Model T had been reduced to below $300.

Ford's profits soared along with sales; since he owned the entire company, he became a billionaire. He also became an authentic folk hero: His homespun style, his dislike of bankers and sophisticated society, and his intense individualism endeared him to millions. He stood as a symbol of the wonders of the American system—he had given the nation a marvelous convenience at a low price, at the same time enriching himself and raising the living standards of his thousands of employees.

Unfortunately, Ford had the defects of his virtues in full measure. He paid high wages but tyrannized his workers. He refused to deal with any union. When he discovered a worker driving any car but a Ford, he had him dismissed.

Success made Ford stubborn. The Model T remained essentially unchanged for nearly 20 years. Other companies, notably General Motors, were soon turning out better vehicles for very little more money. Customers, increasingly affluent and style-conscious, began to shift to Chevrolets and Chryslers. Although his company continued to make a great deal of money, Ford never regained the dominant position he had held for so long.

Henry Ford was enormously uninformed, yet—because of his success and the praise the world heaped on him—he did not hesitate to speak out on subjects far outside his area of competence, from the evils of drink and tobacco to medicine and international affairs. He developed political ambitions and published virulent anti-Semitic propaganda. He said he would not give 5 cents for all the art in the world.

While praising his talents as a manufacturer, historians have not dealt kindly with Ford the man, in part no doubt because he once said, "History is more or less . . . bunk."

The Airplane

Henry Ford also manufactured airplanes, and though the airplane industry was not economically important in the 1920s, its development led to changes in life-styles and attitudes at least as important as those produced by automobiles. The internal combustion gasoline engine with its high ratio of power to weight made the airplane possible, which explains why the first "flying machines" and "gas buggies" were built at about the same time. Wilbur and Orville Wright made their famous flight at Kitty Hawk, North Carolina, in 1903, five years before Ford produced his Model T. Another pair of brothers, Malcolm and Haimes Lockheed, built one of the earliest commercial planes (they used it to take passengers up at $5 a ride) in 1913.

The World War speeded the advance of airplane technology, but practical commercial flight was long delayed. Aerial acrobats, parachute jumpers, wing walkers, and other "daredevils" who put on shows at country fairs and similar places where crowds gathered were the principal aviators of the 1920s. They "barnstormed" from town to town, living the same kind of inbred, encapsulated lives that circus people did.

The great event of the decade for aviation, still awesome achievement, was Charles A. Lindbergh's nonstop flight from New York to Paris in May 1927. It took more than 33 hours for Lindbergh's single-engine *Spirit of St. Louis* to cross the Atlantic, a formidable physical accomplishment for the pilot as well as a feat of skill and courage. When the public learned that the intrepid "Lucky Lindy" was handsome, modest, uninterested in converting his new fame into cash, and a model of propriety (he neither drank nor smoked), his role as an American hero was assured. It was a role Lindbergh detested—one biographer has described him as "by nature solitary"—but could not avoid.

Lindbergh's flight enormously increased public interest in flying, but it was a landmark in aviation technology as well. The day of routine passenger flights was at last about to dawn. Two months after the *Spirit of St. Louis* touched down in France, William E. Boeing of Boeing Air Transport began flying passengers and mail between San Francisco and Chicago, using a plane of his own design and manufacture. Early in 1928 he changed the company name to United Aircraft and Transport, ancestor of the modern giant, United Air Lines. Two years later Boeing produced the first all-metal low-wing plane, and in 1933 the twin-engine 247, called by historian John B. Rae "the first genuinely modern transport plane."

The postwar era seems today more clearly a period of transition than it appeared at the time. Rarely had the old become the new so swiftly, and rarely had the two coexisted in such profusion. Creativity and reaction, hope and despair, freedom and repression—the modern world in all its unfathomable complexity was emerging.

Milestones

1908 Henry Ford begins production of Model T automobile
1919 Eighteenth Amendment outlaws alcoholic beverages
Nineteenth Amendment grants women the vote
1920 Sinclair Lewis, *Main Street*
F. Scott Fitzgerald, *This Side of Paradise*
First commercial radio station, KDKA, begins broadcasting
1921 Margaret Sanger founds the American Birth Control League
1925 Scopes trial in Dayton, Tennessee
1926 Gertrude Ederle swims the English Channel
Ernest Hemingway, *The Sun Also Rises*
1927 Babe Ruth hits 60 home runs
Charles A. Lindbergh flies solo from New York to Paris
Sacco and Vanzetti executed
The Jazz Singer, first motion picture with sound

Supplementary Reading

A comprehensive survey of the twenties is J. D. Hicks, **Republican Ascendancy** (1960), but see also Geoffrey Perrett, **America in the Twenties** (1982), and P. A. Carter, **Another Part of the Twenties** (1977). F. L. Allen, **Only Yesterday** (1931), is still useful.

For nativism and immigration restriction, see John Higham, **Strangers in the Land** (1955). On changes in the family see Steven Mintz and Susan Kellogg, **Domestic Revolutions** (1988). Other social trends are discussed in N. G. Hale, **Freud and the Americans,** Paula Fass, **The Damned and the Beautiful** (1977), and John D'Emilio and Estelle Freedman, **Intimate Matters** (1988). Women's issues are treated in D. M. Brown, **Setting a Course: American Women in the 1920s** (1987), William Chafe, **The American Woman** (1972), and W. D. Wandersee, **Women's Work and Family Values** (1981).

On popular culture, see Russell Lynes, **The Lively Audience** (1985), Robert Sklar, **Movie-made America** (1976), and S. J. Douglas, **Inventing American Broadcasting** (1987).

Fundamentalism is treated in N. F. Furniss, **The Fundamentalist Controversy** (1954), and Lawrence Levine, **Defender of the Faith** (1965). On prohibition see Andrew Sincair, **Prohibition: The Era of Excess** (1962), and N. H. Clark, **Deliver Us from Evil** (1976). For the Ku Klux Klan, see D. M. Chalmers, **Hooded Americanism** (1965), and K. T. Jackson, **The Ku Klux Klan in the City** (1967).

The history of blacks in covered in Gilbert Osofsky, **Harlem: The Making of a Ghetto** (1965), E. D. Cronon, **Black Moses: The Story of Marcus Garvey** (1955), and N. I. Huggins, **Harlem Renaissance** (1971).

Literature during the period is discussed in Alfred Kazin, **On Native Grounds** (1942), and F. J. Hoffman, **The Twenties** (1955). Biographies of novelists include Arthur Mizener, **The Far Side of Paradise** (1951), on Fitzgerald; Mark Shorer, **Sinclair Lewis** (1961); and C. H. Baker, **Hemingway** (1956).

On the New Era, see E. W. Hawley, **The Great War and the Search for a Modern Order** (1979); on consumerism in the 1920s, see Daniel Horowitz, **The Morality of Spending** (1985) and Roland Marchand, **Advertising the American Dream** (1985). On the influence of Henry Ford and the automobile, see Keith Sward, **The Legend of Henry Ford** (1948), J. B. Rae, **The American Automobile Industry** (1984), and J. J. Flink, **The Car Culture** (1975).

CHAPTER 27

The New Era, 1921–1933

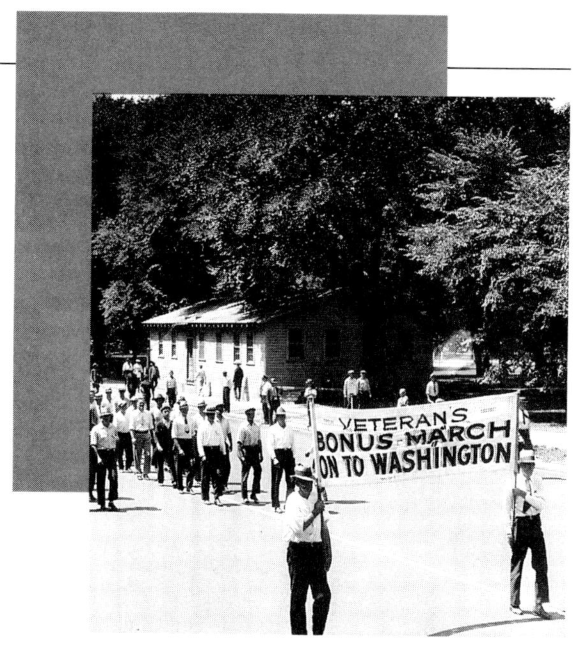

THE MEN WHO PRESIDED OVER THE government of the United States from 1921 to 1929 were Warren G. Harding, of Ohio and Calvin Coolidge, of Massachusetts. Harding was a newspaperman by trade, publisher of the *Marion* (Ohio) *Star,* with previous political experience as a legislator and lieutenant governor in his home state and as a United States senator. No president, before or since, looked more like a statesman; few were less suited for running the country. Coolidge was a taciturn, conservative New Englander with a long record in Massachusetts politics climaxed by his inept but much-admired suppression of the Boston police strike while governor. Harding referred to him as "that little fellow from Massachusetts." Coolidge preferred to follow public opinion and hope for the best.

"Normalcy"

Harding won the 1920 Republican nomination because his genial nature and lack of strong convictions made him attractive to many of the politicos after eight years of the headstrong Wilson. During the campaign he exasperated sophisticates by his ignorance and imprecision. (His most enduring gaffe was unwittingly coining the word *normalcy* when groping for the term *normality.*) "Why does he not get a private secretary who can clothe . . . his 'ideas' in the language customarily used by educated men?" one Boston gentleman demanded of Senator Lodge, who was strongly supporting Harding. Lodge, ordinarily a stickler for linguistic exactitude, replied acidly that he found Harding a paragon by comparison with Wilson, "a man who wrote English very well without ever saying anything." A large majority of the voters, untroubled by the candidate's lack of erudition, shared Lodge's confidence that he would be a vast improvement over Wilson.

Harding has often been characterized as lazy and incompetent. In fact, he was hardworking and politically shrewd; his major weaknesses were indecisiveness and an unwillingness to offend. He turned the most important government departments

Chapter-opening illustration: The "Bonus Army" of World War I veterans marched on Washington, D.C., in 1932 to press for early payment of their veteran's bonuses, due to be paid in 1945, to help them combat the economic woes of the Great Depression.

over to efficient administrators of impeccable reputation: Charles Evans Hughes as secretary of state, Herbert Hoover in the Commerce Department, Andrew Mellon in the Treasury, and Henry C. Wallace in Agriculture. He kept track of what these men did but seldom initiated policy in their areas. However, Harding gave many lesser offices, and a few of major importance, to the unsavory "Ohio Gang" headed by Harry M. Daugherty, whom he made attorney general.

The president was too unambitious to be dishonest. He appointed corruptionists like Daugherty out of a sense of personal obligation or because they were old friends who shared his taste for poker and liquor. Before 1921 he had enjoyed officeholding; he was adept at mouthing platitudes, a loyal party man who seldom questioned the decisions of his superiors. In the lonely eminence of the White House, whence, as President Harry Truman later pointed out, the buck cannot be passed, he found only misery.

"Regulating" Business

In domestic affairs Treasury Secretary Mellon, multimillionaire banker and master of the aluminum industry, dominated administration domestic policy. Mellon set out to lower the taxes of the rich, reverse the low-tariff policies of the Wilson period, return to the laissez-faire philosophy of McKinley, and reduce the national debt by cutting expenses and managing the government more efficiently.

In principle his program had considerable merit, but he carried his policies to unreasonable extremes. He proposed eliminating inheritance taxes and reducing the tax on high incomes by two-thirds in order to stimulate investment, but he opposed lower rates for taxpayers earning less than $66,000 a year, apparently not realizing that economic expansion required greater mass consumption as well. Freeing the rich from "oppressive" taxation, he argued, would enable them to invest more in potentially productive enterprises, the success of which would create jobs for ordinary people.

Although the Republicans had large majorities in both houses of Congress, Mellon's proposals were too reactionary to win unqualified approval. His tax and tariff program ran into stiff opposition from middle western Republicans and southern Democrats, who combined to form the so-called farm bloc. The revival of European agriculture after the World War cut the demand for American farm produce just when the increased use of fertilizers and machinery was boosting output. As in the era after the Civil War, farmers found themselves burdened with heavy debts while their income dwindled. In the decade after 1919 their share of the national income fell by nearly 50 percent.

Mellon epitomized everything the farm bloc disliked. Rejecting his more extreme suggestions, it pushed through the Revenue Act of 1921, which abolished the excess-profits tax and cut the top income tax rate from 73 to 50 percent but raised the tax on corporate profits slightly and left inheritance taxes untouched. Three years later Congress cut the maximum income tax to 40 percent, reduced taxes on lower incomes significantly, and raised inheritance levies.

Congress also overhauled Mellon's tariff proposals. It placed heavy duties on agricultural products in 1921. The Fordney-McCumber Tariff of 1922 granted more than adequate protection to the "infant industries" (rayon, china, toys, and chemicals) yet held to the Wilsonian principle of moderate protection for most industrial products. Agricultural machinery and other items used by farmers remained on the free list.

Mellon nevertheless succeeded in balancing the budget and reducing the national debt by an average of over $500 million a year. So committed were the Republican leaders to retrenchment that they even resisted the demands of veterans, organized in the politically potent American Legion, for an "adjusted compensation" bonus. Arguing, not entirely without reason, that they had served for a pittance while war workers had been drawing down high wages, the veterans sought grants equal to a dollar a day for their period in uniform ($1.25 for time overseas). Congress responded sympathetically, but Harding and Coolidge both vetoed bonus bills in the name of economy. Finally, in 1924 a compromise bill granting the veterans paid-up life insurance policies was passed over Coolidge's veto.

That the business community heartily approved the policies of Harding and Coolidge is not surprising. Both presidents were uncritical advocates of the business point of view. "We want less government in business and more business in government,"

Harding pontificated, to which Coolidge added: "The business of the United States is business." Harding and Coolidge used the power of appointment to convert regulatory bodies like the Interstate Commerce Commission and the Federal Reserve Board into pro-business agencies that ceased almost entirely to restrict the activities of the industries they were supposed to be controlling.

The Harding Scandals

At least Mellon was honest. The Ohio Gang used its power in the most corrupt way imaginable. Jesse Smith, a crony of Attorney General Daugherty, was what today would be called an influence peddler. When he was exposed in 1923, he committed suicide. Charles R. Forbes of the Veterans Bureau siphoned millions of dollars appropriated for the construction of hospitals into his own pocket. When he was found out, he was sentenced to two years in prison. His assistant, Charles F. Cramer, committed suicide. Daugherty himself was implicated in the fraudulent return of German assets seized by the alien property custodian to their original owners. He escaped imprisonment only by refusing to testify on the ground that he might incriminate himself.

The worst scandal involved Secretary of the Interior Albert B. Fall, a former senator. In 1921 Fall arranged with the complaisant secretary of the navy, Edwin Denby, for the transfer to the Interior Department of government oil reserves being held for the future use of the navy. Fall then leased these properties to private oil companies. Edward L. Doheny's Pan-American Petroleum Company got the Elk Hills reserve in California; the Teapot Dome reserve in Wyoming was turned over to Harry F. Sinclair's Mammoth Oil Company. In 1923 the Senate ordered a full-scale investigation, conducted by Senator Thomas J. Walsh of Montana. It soon came out that Doheny had "lent" Fall $100,000 in hard cash, handed over secretly in a "little black bag." Sinclair had given Fall over $300,000 in cash and negotiable securities.

Although the three culprits escaped conviction on the charge of conspiring to defraud the government, Sinclair was sentenced to nine months in jail for contempt of the Senate and for tampering with a jury, and Fall was fined $100,000 and given a year in prison for accepting a bribe. In 1927 the Supreme Court revoked the leases, and the two reserves were returned to the government.

The public still knew little of the scandals when, in June 1923, Harding, on a western speaking tour, came down with what his incompetent physician diagnosed as ptomaine poisoning from having eaten a tainted Japanese crab. In fact the president had suffered a heart attack. He died in San Francisco on August 2.

Few presidents have been more deeply mourned by the people at the moment of their passing. Soon, however, as the scandals came to light, sadness turned to scorn and contempt. The poet e. e. cummings came closer to catching the final judgment of Harding's contemporaries than any historian has:

the first president to be loved by his
"bitterest enemies" is dead
the only man woman or child who wrote
a simple declarative sentence with seven
grammatical
errors "is dead"
beautiful Warren Gamaliel Harding
"is" dead
he's
"dead"
if he wouldn't have eaten them Yapanese
Craps
somebody might hardly never not have been
unsorry, perhaps

Coolidge Prosperity

Had he lived, Harding might well have been defeated in 1924 because of the scandals. Vice-President Coolidge, unconnected with the troubles and not the type to surround himself with cronies of any kind, seemed the ideal person to clean out the corruptionists. He soon became the darling of the conservatives. His admiration for businessmen and his devotion to laissez-faire knew no limit. "The man who builds a factory builds a temple," he said in all seriousness. Andrew Mellon, whom he kept on as secretary of the treasury, became his mentor in economic affairs.

Coolidge won the 1924 Republican nomination

easily. The Democrats, badly split, required 103 ballots to choose a candidate. The southern wing, dry, anti-immigrant, pro-Klan, had fixed on William G. McAdoo, Wilson's secretary of the treasury. The eastern, urban, wet element supported Governor Alfred E. Smith of New York, child of the slums, a Catholic who had compiled a distinguished record in the field of social welfare legislation. After days of futile politicking, the party compromised on John W. Davis, a conservative corporation lawyer closely allied with the Morgan banking interests.

Dismayed by the conservatism of Coolidge and Davis, the aging Robert M. La Follette, backed by the farm bloc, the Socialist party, the American Federation of Labor, and numbers of intellectuals, entered the race as the candidate of a new Progressive party. The Progressives adopted a neopopulist platform calling for the nationalization of railroads, the direct election of the president, the protection of labor's right to bargain collectively, and other reforms.

The situation was almost exactly the opposite of 1912, when one conservative had run against two liberals and had been swamped. Coolidge received 15.7 million votes, Davis 8.4 million, La Follette 4.8 million. In the electoral college La Follette won only his native Wisconsin; Coolidge defeated Davis, 382 to 136. Conservatism was clearly the dominant mood of the country.

Peace Without a Sword

Presidents Harding and Coolidge handled foreign relations in much the same way they managed domestic affairs. Harding deferred to senatorial prejudice against executive domination in the area and let his secretary of state, Charles Evans Hughes, make policy. Coolidge adopted a similar course.

In directing foreign relations, they faced the obstacle of resurgent isolationism. The same forces of war-bred hatred, postwar disillusion, and fear of communist subversion that produced the Red Scare at home led Americans to back away from close involvement in world affairs. The bloodiness and apparent senselessness of the Great War convinced millions that the only way to be sure it would not happen again was to "steer clear" of "entanglements." That these famous words had been used by Washington and Jefferson in vastly different contexts did not deter the isolationists of the 1920s from attributing to them the same authority they gave to Scripture. But the need for both raw materials for industry and foreign markets for America's agricultural and manufactured goods made involvement in developments all over the world unavoidable.

The Open Door concept remained predominant; the State Department worked to uncover opportunities in underdeveloped countries for exporters and investors, hoping both to stimulate the American economy and to bring stability to "backward" nations. This policy sometimes aroused local resentment because it often benefited entrenched elites while the masses of peasants and city workers lived in poverty.

The first important diplomatic event of the period revealed a great deal about American foreign policy after the World War. During the war Japan had greatly increased its influence in the Far East. To maintain the Open Door in China, it would be necessary to check Japanese expansion. In addition, Japan, the United States, and Great Britain were engaged in expensive naval building programs, a competition none wanted.

In November 1921, hoping to reach a general agreement that would keep China open to commerce and slow the armaments race, Secretary of State Hughes convened a conference in Washington. By the following February the Washington conference had drafted three major treaties and a number of lesser agreements.

In the Five-Power Treaty, the United States, Great Britain, France, Japan, and Italy agreed to stop building battleships for ten years and to reduce their fleets of capital ships to a fixed ratio, with Great Britain and the United States limited to 525,000 tons, Japan to 315,000 tons, and France and Italy to 175,000 tons. The new ratio was expected to produce a balance of forces in the Pacific.

The Four-Power Treaty, signed by the United States, Great Britain, Japan, and France, committed these nations to respect one another's interests in the islands of the Pacific and to confer in the event that any other country launched an attack in the area.

All the conferees signed the Nine-Power Treaty, agreeing to respect China's independence and to maintain the Open Door. On the surface, this seemed to mean that Japan had given up its territorial ambitions on the Asian mainland and that both the Japanese and the Europeans had formally endorsed the Open Door concept.

By taking the lead in drafting these agreements, the United States regained some of the moral influence it had lost by not joining the League of Nations. The treaties, however, were uniformly toothless. The signers of the Four-Power pact agreed only to consult in case of aggression in the Pacific; they made no promise to restrict their own freedom of action.

The naval disarmament treaty said nothing about the number of other warships that the powers might build, about the far more important question of land and air forces, or about the underlying industrial and financial structures that controlled the ability of the nations to make war. In addition, the 5:5:3 battleship ratio actually enabled the Japanese to dominate the western Pacific. It made the Philippine Islands undefendable and exposed Hawaii to possible attack. In a sense these American bases became hostages of Japan. Yet Congress was so unconcerned about Japanese sensibilities that it refused to grant any immigration quota to Japan under the National Origins Act of 1924, even though the formula as applied to other nations would have allowed only 100 Japanese a year to enter the country. The law, Secretary Hughes warned, produced in Japan "a sense of injury and antagonism instead of friendship and cooperation."

Resentment of "white imperialism" played into the hands of the military party in Japan, where many army and navy officers considered war with the United States inevitable. "The emotional resentment against America," Akira Iriye writes in *Across the Pacific,* "was reinforced by a more sophisticated view of future Japanese-American conflict that was advocated by some army strategists."

As for the key Nine-Power Treaty, Japan did not abandon its territorial ambitions in China, and China remained so riven by conflict among the warlords and so resentful of the "imperialists" that the economic advantages of the Open Door turned out to be small indeed.

The United States entered into all these agreements without realizing their full implications and not really prepared to play an active part in Far Eastern affairs. The Japanese soon realized that the United States would not do much to defend its interests in China. The result, in Akira Iriye's words, was "a new image of America, as a country that delighted in moralism . . . but that was not likely to challenge Japan with force."

The Peace Movement

The Americans of the 1920s wanted peace but would neither surrender their prejudices and dislikes nor build the defenses necessary to make it safe to indulge these passions. "The people have had all the war, all the taxation, and all the military service that they want," President Coolidge announced in 1925.

Peace societies flourished, among them the Carnegie Endowment for International Peace, designed "to hasten the abolition of war, the foulest blot upon our civilization," and the Woodrow Wilson Foundation, aimed at helping "the liberal forces of mankind throughout the world . . . who intend to promote peace by the means of justice." In 1923 Edward W. Bok, retired editor of the *Ladies' Home Journal,* offered a prize of $100,000 for the best workable plan for preserving international peace. He was flooded with suggestions. Former Assistant Secretary of the Navy Franklin D. Roosevelt drafted one while recovering from an attack of infantile paralysis. Such was the temper of the times that he felt constrained to include in the preamble this statement:

> *We seek not to become involved as a nation in the purely regional affairs of groups of other nations, nor to give to the representatives of other peoples the right to compel us to enter upon undertakings calling for a leading up to the use of armed force without our full and free consent, given through our constitutional procedure.*

So great was the opposition to international cooperation that the United States refused to accept membership on the World Court, although this tribunal could settle disputes only when the nations involved agreed. Probably a majority of the American people favored joining the court, but its advocates were never able to persuade two-thirds of the Senate to ratify the necessary treaty. Too many peace lovers believed that their goal could be attained simply by pointing out the moral and practical disadvantages of war.

The culmination of this illusory faith in preventing war by criticizing it came with the signing of the Kellogg-Briand Pact in 1928. The treaty was born in the fertile brain of French Foreign Minister Aristide Briand, who was eager to collect allies against possible attack by a resurgent Germany. In 1927 Briand proposed to Secretary of State Frank B. Kellogg that their countries agree never to go to war with each other. Kellogg found the idea as repugnant as any conventional alliance, but American isolationists and pacifists found the suggestion fascinating. They plagued Kellogg with demands that he negotiate such a treaty.

To extricate himself from this situation, Kellogg suggested that the pact be broadened to include all nations. Now Briand was angry. Like Kellogg, he saw how meaningless such a treaty would be, especially when Kellogg insisted that it be hedged with a proviso that "every nation is free at all times . . . to defend its territory from attack and it alone is competent to decide when circumstances require war in self-defense." Nevertheless, Briand too found public pressures irresistible. In August 1928, at Paris, diplomats from 15 nations bestowed upon one another an "international kiss," condemning "recourse to war for the solution of international controversies" and renouncing war "as an instrument of national policy." Seldom has so unrealistic a promise been made by so many intelligent people. Yet most Americans considered the Kellogg-Briand Pact a milestone in the history of civilization: The Senate, habitually so suspicious of international commitments, ratified it 85 to 1.

The Good Neighbor Policy

The conflict between the desire to avoid foreign entanglements and the desire to advance American economic interests is well illustrated by events in Latin America. "Yankeephobia" had long been a chronic condition south of the Rio Grande. The continued presence of marines in Central America fed this ill will. Basic was the objection to being controlled by foreigners. The immense wealth and power of the "Colossus of the North" and the feeling of most Latin Americans that the wielders of this strength had little respect for the needs and values of their southern neighbors were further causes of distrust. However, the evident desire of the United States to limit its international involvements had a gradually mollifying effect on Latin American opinion.

In dealing with this part of the world, Harding and Coolidge performed neither better nor worse than Wilson had. In the face of continued radicalism and instability in Mexico, which caused Americans with interests in land and oil rights to suffer heavy losses, President Coolidge acted with forbearance. His appointment of Dwight W. Morrow, a patient, sympathetic ambassador, resulted in an improvement in Mexican-American relations. The Mexicans were able to complete their social and economic revolution in the 1920s without significant interference by the United States.

Under Coolidge's successor, Herbert Hoover, the United States began at last to treat Latin American nations as equals. Hoover reversed Wilson's policy of trying to teach them "to elect good men." The Clark Memorandum (1930), written by Undersecretary of State J. Reuben Clark, disassociated the right of intervention in Latin America from the Roosevelt Corollary. The corollary had been an improper extension of the Monroe Doctrine, Clark declared. The right of the United States to intervene depended rather on "the doctrine of self-preservation."

The distinction seemed slight to Latin Americans, but since it seemed unlikely that the existence of the United States could be threatened in the area, it was important. By 1934 the marines who had been occupying Nicaragua, Haiti, and the Dominican Republic had all been withdrawn, and the United States had renounced the right to intervene in Cuban affairs. Unfortunately, the United States did little to try to improve social and economic conditions in the Caribbean region, so the underlying envy and resentment of "rich Uncle Sam" did not disappear.

The Totalitarian Challenge

The futility and danger of isolationism were exposed in September 1931 when the Japanese, long dominant in Chinese Manchuria, marched in an army and converted it into a puppet state they named Manchukuo. This violated both the Kellogg-Briand and Nine-Power pacts. China, now controlled by General Chiang Kai-shek, appealed to the League of Nations and to the United States for help. Neither would intervene. When League officials asked about the possibility of American cooperation in some kind of police action, President Hoover refused to consider either economic or military reprisals. The United States was not a world policeman, he said. The Nine-Power and Kellogg-Briand treaties were "solely moral instruments."

The League sent a commission to Manchuria to investigate. Henry L. Stimson, Hoover's secretary of state, announced that the United States would never recognize the legality of seizures made in violation of American treaty rights. This so-called Stimson Doctrine served only to irritate the Japanese.

In January 1932, Japan attacked Shanghai, the bloody battle marked by the indiscriminate bombing of residential districts. When the League at last officially condemned their aggressions, the Japanese withdrew from the organization and extended their control of northern China. The lesson of Manchuria was not lost on Adolf Hitler, who became chancellor of Germany on January 30, 1933.

It is easy, in surveying the diplomatic events of 1920–1933, to condemn the United States and the European democracies for their unwillingness to stand up for principles, their refusal to resist when Japan and later Germany and Italy embarked on the aggressions that led to World War II. It is also proper to place some of the blame for the troubles of the era on the same powers: They controlled much of the world's resources and were primarily interested in holding on to what they had.

War Debts and Reparations

The democracies did not take a strong stand against Japan in part because they were quarreling about other matters. Particularly divisive was the controversy over war debts—those of Germany to the Allies and those of the Allies to the United States. The United States had lent more than $10 billion to its comrades in arms. Since most of this money had been spent on weapons and other supplies in the United States, it might well have been considered part of America's contribution to the war effort. The public, however, demanded full repayment—with interest. "These were loans, not contributions," Secretary of the Treasury Mellon firmly declared. Even when the Foreign Debt Commission scaled down the interest rate from 5 percent to about 2 percent, the total, to be repaid over a period of 62 years, amounted to more than $22 billion.

The Allies tried to load their obligations to the United States, along with the other costs of the war, on the backs of the Germans. They demanded reparations amounting to $33 billion. If this sum were collected, they declared, they could rebuild their economies and obtain the international exchange needed to pay their debts to the United States. But Germany was reluctant even to try to pay such huge reparations, and when Germany defaulted, so did the Allies.

Everyone was bitterly resentful: the Germans because they felt they were being bled white; the Americans, as Senator Hiram Johnson of California would have it, because the wily Europeans were treating the United States as "an international sucker"; the Allies because, as the French said, *"l'oncle Shylock"* (a play on the names Uncle Sam and Shylock, the moneylender in Shakespeare's *Merchant of Venice*) was demanding his pound of flesh with interest.

Everyone shared the blame: the Germans be-

A merciless France demands war reparations from Germany in this *Los Angeles Times* cartoon from 1922. American aid to the German economy had little effect in the face of Germany's enormous reparations costs.

cause they resorted to a runaway inflation that reduced the mark to less than one trillionth of its prewar value, at least in part in hopes of avoiding their international obligations; the Americans because they refused to recognize the connection between the tariff and the debt question; the Allies because they made little effort to pay even a reasonable proportion of their obligations.

In 1924 an international agreement, the Dawes Plan, provided Germany with a $200 million loan designed to stabilize its currency. Germany agreed to pay about $250 million a year in reparations. In 1929 the Young Plan further scaled down the reparations bill. In practice, the Allies paid the United States about what they collected from Germany. Since Germany got the money largely from private American loans, the United States would have served itself and the rest of the world far better had it written off the war debts at the start. In any case, in the late 1920s Americans stopped lending money to Germany, the Great Depression struck, Germany defaulted on its reparations payments, and the Allies then gave up all pretense of meeting their obligations to the United States. The last token payments were made in 1933. All that remained was a heritage of mistrust and hostility.

The Election of 1928

Meanwhile, dramatic changes had occurred in the United States. The climax of Coolidge prosperity came in 1928. The president decided not to run again, and Secretary of Commerce Hoover, whom he detested, easily won the Republican nomination. Hoover was the intellectual leader, almost the philosopher, of the New Era. He spoke and wrote of "progressive individualism." American capitalists, he believed, had learned to curb their selfish instincts.

The Democrats, having had their fill of factionalism in 1924, could no longer deny the nomination to Governor Al Smith. Superficially, Smith was Hoover's antithesis. Smith was a street-wise New Yorker; Hoover was an Iowan raised on the West Coast; Smith was a Catholic, Hoover a Quaker; Smith was a wet whereas Hoover supported prohibition; Smith dealt easily with people of every race and nationality, while Hoover had little interest in and less knowledge of blacks and immigrants. But like Hoover, Smith managed to combine a basic conservatism with humanitarian concern for the underprivileged.

Unwilling to challenge the public's complacent view of Coolidge prosperity, the Democrats adopted a conservative platform. Smith appointed John J. Raskob, a wealthy automobile executive, to manage his campaign. Franklin D. Roosevelt, who ran for governor of New York at Smith's urging in 1928, charged that Hoover's expansion of the functions of the Department of Commerce had been at least mildly socialistic. This strategy failed miserably. Nothing Smith could do or say was capable of convincing many businessmen that he was a better choice than Hoover. Catholicism, his brashness, his criticism of prohibition, his machine connections, and his urban background hurt him in rural areas, especially in the normally Democratic South. In the election Hoover won a smashing triumph, 444 to 87 in the electoral college, 21.4 million to 15 million in the popular vote.

After this defeat the Democratic party appeared on the verge of extinction. Nothing could have been further from the truth. The religious question and his big-city roots had hurt Smith, but the chief reason he lost was the prosperity—and the good times were soon to end. Hoover's overwhelming victory also concealed a political realignment that was taking place. Working-class voters in the cities, largely Catholic and unimpressed by Coolidge prosperity, had swung heavily to the Democrats. In 1924 the 12 largest cities had been solidly Republican; in 1928 all went Democratic. In agricultural states like Iowa, Smith ran far better than Davis had in 1924, for Coolidge's vetoes of the bills designed to raise farm prices had caused considerable resentment. A new coalition of urban workers and dissatisfied farmers was in the making.

Economic Problems

The American economic system of the 1920s had grave flaws. Certain industries—coal, for example, and textiles—did not share in the good times. The movement toward consolidation in industry, somewhat checked during the latter part of the Progressive Era, resumed. By 1929 a mere 200 corporations controlled nearly half the nation's corporate assets. General Motors, Ford, and Chrysler turned out nearly 90 percent of all American cars and trucks. Four tobacco companies produced over 90 percent of the cigarettes. Even retail merchandising, traditionally the domain of the small shopkeeper, reflected the trend. The A&P food chain expanded from 400 stores in 1912 to 17,500 in 1928. The Woolworth chain of five-and-ten-cent stores experienced similar growth.

Consolidation did not necessarily lead to monopoly. "Regulated" competition was the order of the day, oligopoly the typical situation. The trade association movement flourished; producers formed voluntary organizations to exchange information, discuss policies toward government and the public, and "administer" prices in their industry. Usually the largest corporation, such as U.S. Steel in the iron and steel business, became the "price leader," its competitors, some themselves giants, following slavishly.

The success of the trade associations depended in part on the attitude of the federal government, for such organizations might well have been attacked under the antitrust laws. Their defenders argued that the associations made business more efficient and prevented violent gyrations of prices and production. President Harding accepted this line of reasoning. Secretary of Commerce Hoover put the facilities of his department at the disposal of the associations. After Coolidge became president, the Antitrust Division of the Justice Department itself encouraged policies that had previously been considered violations of the Sherman Act.

Even more important to the trade associations were the good times. With profits high and markets expanding, the most powerful producers could afford to share the bounty with smaller, less efficient competitors.

The weakest element in the economy was agriculture. In addition to the slump in farm prices, farmers' costs mounted. Besides having to purchase expensive machinery in order to compete, farmers were confronted by high foreign tariffs and in some cases quotas on the importation of foodstuffs.

Despite the efforts of the farm bloc, the government did little to improve the situation. President Harding opposed direct aid to agriculture as a matter of principle. "Every farmer is a captain of industry," he declared. "The elimination of competition among them would be impossible without sacrificing that fine individualism that still keeps the farm the real reservoir from which the nation draws so many of the finest elements of its citizenship." During his administration Congress strengthened the laws regulating railroad rates and grain exchanges and made it easier for farmers to borrow money, but it did nothing to increase agricultural income. Nor did the high tariffs on agricultural produce have much effect. Being forced to sell their surpluses abroad, farmers found that world prices depressed domestic prices despite the tariff wall.

In 1921 George N. Peek, a plow manufacturer, advanced a scheme to "make the tariff effective for agriculture." The federal government, Peek suggested in "Equality for Agriculture," should buy up the surplus American production of wheat.* This additional demand would cause domestic prices to rise. Then the government could sell the wheat abroad at the lower world price. It could recover its losses by assessing an "equalization fee" on the wheat farmers.

Peek's plan had flaws. If the price of staples rose, farmers would tend to increase output. Yet this problem might have been solved by imposing production controls. It was certainly a promising idea; hundreds of organizations in the Farm Belt endorsed it. Farm bloc congressmen took it up and in 1927 the McNary-Haugen bill was passed, only to be vetoed by President Coolidge. Congress passed a similar bill in 1928, and again Coolidge rejected it.

Thus while most economic indicators reflected an unprecedented prosperity, the boom rested on unstable foundations. The problem was mainly maldistribution of resources. Productive capacity raced ahead of buying power. Too large a share of the profits went into too few pockets. The 27,000 families with the highest annual incomes in 1929 received as much money as the 11 million with annual incomes of under $1,500, the minimum sum required at that time to maintain a family decently. High earnings and low taxes permitted huge sums to pile up in the hands of individuals who did not invest the money productively. A good deal of it went into stock market speculation, which led to the "big bull market" and eventually to the Great Depression.

*He soon extended his plan to cover cotton and other staples.

The Crash of 1929

In the spring of 1928, prices on the New York Stock Exchange, already at a historic high, began to surge ahead. As the presidential campaign gathered momentum, the market increased its upward pace. Through the first half of 1929, the market climbed still higher. A mania for speculation swept the country, thousands of small investors pouring their savings into common stocks.

In September the market wavered. Amid volatile fluctuations, stock averages eased downward. Most analysts contended that the Exchange was "digesting" previous gains. A Harvard economist expressed the prevailing view when he said that stock prices would soon resume their advance. On October 24 a wave of selling sent prices spinning. Nearly 13 million shares changed hands—a record. Bankers and politicians rallied to check the decline, as they had during the Panic of 1907. President Hoover assured the people that "the business of the country . . . is on a sound and prosperous basis." But on Tuesday, October 29, the bottom seemed to drop out. More than 16 million shares were sold, prices plummeting. The boom was over.

James N. Rosenberg, an attorney and amateur artist, sketched this grim view of the Wall Street financial district, October 29, 1929 ("Black Tuesday"), as a Day of Judgment.

Hoover and the Depression

The collapse of the stock market did not cause the depression; stocks rallied late in the year, and business activity did not begin to decline significantly until the spring of 1930. The Great Depression was a worldwide phenomenon caused chiefly by economic imbalances resulting from the chaos of the World War. In the United States too much wealth had fallen into too few hands, with the result that consumers were unable to buy all the goods produced. The trouble came to a head mainly because of the easy-credit policies of the Federal Reserve Board and the Mellon tax structure, which favored the rich. Its effects were so profound and prolonged because the politicians did not fully understand what was happening or what to do about it.

The chronic problem of underconsumption operated to speed the downward spiral. Unable to rid themselves of mounting inventories, manufacturers closed plants and laid off workers, thereby causing demand to shrink further. Automobile output fell from 4.5 million units in 1929 to 1.1 million in 1932. When Henry Ford closed his Detroit plants in 1931, some 75,000 workers lost their jobs, and the decline in auto production affected a host of suppliers and intermediaries as well.

The financial system cracked under the strain. More than 1,300 banks closed their doors in 1930, another 3,700 during the next two years. Each failure deprived thousands of persons of funds that might have been used to buy goods. And of course the industrial depression exacerbated the depression in agriculture by further reducing the demand for American foodstuffs. Every economic indicator reflected the collapse. New investments declined, and national income fell. Unemployment, under 1 million at the height of the boom, rose to at least 13 million.

President Hoover was an intelligent man, experienced in business matters and knowledgeable in economics. Secretary of the Treasury Mellon believed that the economy should be allowed to slide unchecked until the cycle had found its bottom. Hoover realized that such a policy would cause unbearable hardship for millions.

Hoover's program for ending the depression evolved gradually. At first he called on business to maintain prices and wages. The government should cut taxes in order to increase consumers' spendable income, institute public works programs to stimulate production and create jobs for the unemployed, lower interest rates to make it easier for businesses to borrow in order to expand, and make loans to banks and industrial corporations threatened with collapse and to homeowners unable to meet mortgage payments. The president also proposed measures making it easier for farmers to borrow money, and he suggested that cooperative farm marketing schemes designed to solve the problem of overproduction be supported by the government. He also suggested expanding state and local relief programs, and he urged all who could afford it to give more to charity. Above all, he tried to restore public confidence. The economy was basically healthy. The Depression was only a minor downturn. Prosperity was "just around the corner."

In other words, Hoover rejected classical economics. Indeed, many laissez-faire theorists attacked his handling of the depression. Numbers of "liberal" economists, on the other hand, praised the Hoover program.

Though Hoover's plans were theoretically sound, they failed to check the economic slide, in part because he placed far too much reliance on his powers of persuasion and the willingness of citizens to act in the public interest without legal compulsion. He urged manufacturers to maintain wages and keep their factories in operation, but the manufacturers, under the harsh pressure of economic realities, soon slashed wages and curtailed output sharply. He permitted the Federal Farm Board (created under the Agricultural Marketing Act of 1929) to establish semipublic stabilization corporations with authority to buy surplus wheat and cotton, but he refused to countenance crop or acreage controls. The stabilization corporations poured out hundreds of millions of dollars without checking falling agricultural prices because farmers increased production faster than the corporations could buy up the excess for disposal abroad.

Hoover resisted proposals to shift responsibility from state and local agencies to the federal government, despite the fact—soon obvious—that they lacked the resources to cope with the emergency. More serious was his refusal, on constitutional grounds, to allow federal funds to be used for the relief of individuals. State and municipal agencies and private charities must take care of the needy.

Unfortunately, the depression was drying up the sources of funds of private charities just as the demands on these organizations were expanding. State and municipal agencies were swamped at a time when their capacities to tax and borrow were shrinking. By 1932 more than 40,600 Boston families were on relief (compared with 7,400 families in 1929); in Chicago 700,000 persons—40 percent of the work force—were unemployed. Only the national government possessed the power and the credit to deal adequately with the crisis. Yet Hoover would not act. For the federal government to take over relief would "lead to the super-state where every man becomes the servant of the state and real liberty is lost."

Federal loans to business were constitutional, he believed, because the money could be put to productive use and eventually repaid. When drought destroyed the crops of farmers in the South and Southwest in 1930, the government lent them money to buy seed and even food for their livestock, but Hoover would permit no direct relief for the farmers themselves. In 1932 he approved the creation of the Reconstruction Finance Corporation to lend money to banks, railroads, and insurance companies. Its loans were commercial transactions, not gifts; the agency did almost nothing for individuals in need of relief. The same could be said of the Glass-Steagall Banking Act of 1932, which eased the tight credit situation by permitting Federal Reserve banks to accept a wider variety of commercial paper as security for loans. The public grew increasingly resentful of the president's doctrinaire adherence to principle while breadlines lengthened and millions of willing workers searched fruitlessly for jobs.

As the depression grew worse, Hoover put more stress on balancing the federal budget, reasoning that since citizens had to live within their limited means in hard times, the government should set a good example. This policy was counterproductive; by reducing its expenditures, the government made things worse. The policy was also impossible to carry out because the government's income fell precipitously. By June 1931 the budget was nearly $500 million in the red.

Hoover understood the importance of pumping money into the economy. The difficulty lay in the fact that nearly all "informed" opinion believed that a balanced budget was essential to recovery. When Hoover said, "Prosperity cannot be restored by raids on the public Treasury," he was mistaken; but it is equally wrong to criticize him for failing to understand what almost no one understood in the 1930s.

Hoover can, however, be faulted for allowing his anti-European prejudices to interfere with the implementation of his program. In 1930 Congress passed the Hawley-Smoot Tariff Act, which raised duties on most manufactured products to prohibitive levels. This measure made it impossible for European nations to earn the dollars they needed to continue making payments on their World War I debts to the United States, and it helped bring on a financial collapse in Europe in 1931. When that happened, Hoover wisely proposed a one-year moratorium on all international obligations. But the efforts of Great Britain and many other countries to save their own skins by devaluing their currencies in order to encourage foreigners to buy their goods led him to blame them for the depression itself.

Much of the contemporary criticism of Hoover and a good deal of that heaped on him by later historians was unfair. Yet his record as president shows that he was too rigidly wedded to a particular theory of government to cope effectively with the problems of the day. He was his own worst enemy, too uncompromising to get on well with the politicians and too aloof to win the confidence and affection of ordinary people. As the historian Joan Hoff Wilson has written, he refused "to backslap, fraternize with local supporters, kiss babies." When he failed to achieve the results he anticipated, he attracted, despite his devotion to duty and his concern for the welfare of the country, not sympathy but scorn.

Hitting Bottom

During the spring of 1932, as the economy sounded the depths, thousands of Americans faced starvation. In Philadelphia during an 11-day period when no relief funds were available, hundreds of families existed on stale bread, thin soup, and garbage. In the nation as a whole, only about one-quarter of the unemployed were receiving any public aid. Many people who had been evicted from their homes gathered in ramshackle communities constructed of packing boxes, rusty sheet metal, and similar refuse on swamps, dumps, and other wasteland. People began to call these places "Hoovervilles."

Thousands of unemployed, homeless people roamed the countryside begging for food. At the same time, food prices fell so low that farmers burned corn for fuel. The world seemed to have been turned upside down. Professor Felix Frankfurter of the Harvard Law School remarked only half humorously that henceforth the terms B.C. and A.D. would mean "Before Crash" and "After Depression."

The national mood ranged from apathy to resentment. In 1931 federal immigration agents and local groups in the Southwest began rounding up Mexican-Americans and deporting them. Unemployed Mexicans were ejected because they might become public charges, those with jobs because presumably they were taking bread from the mouths of citizens.

In June and July 1932 some 20,000 World War I veterans marched on Washington to demand immediate payment of their "adjusted compensation" bonuses. When Congress rejected their appeal, 2,000 of them refused to leave, settling in a jerry-built camp of shacks and tents at Anacostia Flats, a swamp bordering the Potomac. President Hoover, alarmed, charged incorrectly that the "Bonus Army" was largely composed of criminals and radicals and sent troops into the Flats to disperse it with bayonets, tear gas, and tanks. The task was accomplished amid much confusion; fortunately, no one was killed. The protest had been aimless and not entirely justified, yet the spectacle of the United States government chasing unarmed veterans with tanks appalled the nation.

The unprecedented severity of the depression led some persons to favor radical economic and political changes. The disparity between the lots of the rich and the poor, always a challenge to democracy, became more striking and engendered considerable bitterness. The Communist party gained few converts among farmers and industrial workers, but a considerable number of intellectuals, alienated by the trends of the 1920s, responded positively to the communists' emphasis on economic planning and the total mobilization of the state to achieve social goals. Even the cracker-barrel humorist Will Rogers was impressed by reports of the absence of serious unemployment in Russia. "All roads in our day lead to Moscow," the former muckraker Lincoln Steffens wrote.

Victims of the Depression

Depression is a word used by economists but also by psychologists, and the depression of the 1930s had profound psychological effects on its victims. Almost without exception, people who lost their jobs at first searched energetically for new ones, but when they remained unemployed for more than a few months, they sank gradually into apathy. E. Wight Bakke, a Yale sociologist who interviewed hundreds of unemployed men in the United States and England during the depression, described the final stage of decline as "permanent readjustment," by which he meant that the long-term jobless simply gave up.

People who had worked all their adult lives often became ashamed of themselves when they could not find a job. A purely physiological factor was often involved as well. When money ran low, people had to cut down on relatively expensive foods like fruit, meat, and dairy products. In New York City, for example, milk consumption fell by a million quarts a day. In nutritional terms they consumed more carbohydrates and less food rich in energy-building vitamins and proteins. Listlessness (another word for apathy) often resulted.

This psychological depression helps explain why the unemployed were not, in general, very radical. There were meetings and protest marches and also strikes, but the former were usually organized by people who were not themselves unemployed, and strikers, almost by definition, are people who are refusing to work, not those who have no job to quit.

The depression caused a dramatic drop in the birthrate, from 27.7 per thousand population in 1920 to 18.4 per thousand in the early 1930s, the lowest in American history. The economic crunch also sometimes strengthened family ties. Some unemployed men spent more time with their children and helped their wives with cooking and housework. Others, however, refused to help around the house, sulked, or took to drink.

The influence of wives in families struck by

A breadline in Chicago. The Great Depression, an English observer said, "outraged and baffled" the nation that took it as "an article of faith . . . that America, somehow, was different from the rest of the world."

unemployment tended to increase, and in this respect women suffered less psychologically from the depression. They were usually too busy trying to make ends meet to become apathetic. Some were sympathetic, others scornful when the "breadwinner" came home with empty hands.

Children often caused strains. Parental authority declined when there was less money available to supply children's needs. Some youngsters became angry when denied something they particularly wanted. Some adolescents found part-time jobs to help out. Others refused to go to school. In general, where relationships were close and loving, they became stronger; where they were not, the results could be disastrous.

The Election of 1932

As the end of his term approached, President Hoover seemed to grow daily more petulant and pessimistic. The depression, coming after 12 years of Republican rule, probably ensured a Democratic victory in any case, but his attitude as the election neared alienated many voters and turned defeat into rout.

Confident of victory, the Democrats chose Governor Franklin Delano Roosevelt of New York as their presidential candidate. Roosevelt owed his nomination chiefly to his success as governor. Under his administration, New York had led the nation in providing relief for the needy and had enacted an impressive program of old-age pensions, unemployment insurance, and conservation and public power projects. The governor also had the advantage of the Roosevelt name (he was a distant cousin of T.R.), and his sunny, magnetic personality contrasted favorably with that of the glum and colorless Hoover.

Roosevelt was hardly a radical. During the 1920s he had not seriously challenged the basic tenets of Coolidge prosperity. He never had much difficulty adjusting his views to prevailing attitudes. For a time he even served as head of the American Construction Council, a trade association. Indeed, his life before the depression gave little indication that he understood the aspirations of ordinary people or had any special commitment to social reform.

Roosevelt was born to wealth and social status. He was educated at the exclusive Groton School and then at Harvard, where he proceeded, as his biographer Frank Freidel has written, "from one extracurricular triumph to another." Ambition as much as the desire to render public service motivated his career in politics; even after an attack of polio in 1921 crippled both his legs, he refused to abandon his hopes for high office.

To some observers Roosevelt seemed rather a lightweight intellectually. Many critics judged him too irresolute, too amiable, too eager to please all factions to be a forceful leader. Herbert Hoover thought he was "ignorant but well-meaning," and the political analyst Walter Lippmann, in a now-famous observation, called him "a pleasant man who, without any important qualifications for the job, would very much like to be President."

Despite his physical handicap, Roosevelt was a marvelous campaigner. He traveled back and forth across the country, radiating confidence and good humor even when directing his sharpest barbs at the Republicans. He soaked up information and ideas from a thousand sources—from professors like Raymond Moley and Rexford Tugwell of Columbia, from politicians like the Texan vice-presidential candidate John N. Garner, from social workers, businessmen, and lawyers.

To those seeking specific answers to the questions of the day, Roosevelt was seldom satisfying. On such vital matters as farm policy, the tariff, and government spending, he equivocated, contradicted himself, or remained silent. Aided by hindsight, historians have discovered portents of much of his later program in his campaign speeches. These pronouncements, buried among dozens of conflicting generalities, often passed unnoticed at the time. He said, for example:

> *If starvation and dire need on the part of any of our citizens make necessary the appropriation of additional funds which would keep the budget out of balance, I shall not hesitate to . . . ask the people to authorize the expenditure of that additional amount.*

In the same speech, however, he called for steep cuts in federal spending and a balanced budget, and he castigated Hoover for presiding over "the greatest spending administration in peace time in our history."

Nevertheless, Roosevelt's basic position was unmistakable. There must be a "re-appraisal of values," a "New Deal." Instead of adhering to conventional limits on the extent of federal power, the government should do whatever was necessary to protect the unfortunate and advance the public good. Lacking concrete answers, Roosevelt advocated a point of view rather than a plan: "The country needs bold, persistent experimentation. It is common sense to take a method and try it. If it fails, admit it frankly and try another. But above all, try something."

The popularity of this approach was demonstrated in November. Hoover, who had lost only eight states in 1928, won only six, all in the Northeast, in 1932. Roosevelt amassed 22.8 million votes to Hoover's 15.8 million and carried the electoral college, 472 to 59.

During the interval between the election and Roosevelt's inauguration in March 1933, the Great Depression reached its nadir. The holdover "lame duck" Congress, last of its kind, proved incapable of effective action.*

*The Twentieth Amendment (1933) provided for convening new Congresses in January instead of the following December. It also advanced the date of the president's inauguration from March 4 to January 20. The nation, curiously apathetic in the face of so much suffering, drifted aimlessly, like a sailboat in a flat calm.

Milestones

1921 Washington disarmament conference

1922 Fordney-McCumber Tariff protecting "infant industries"

1923 President Harding dies; Coolidge becomes president

Teapot Dome and other "Harding scandals" exposed

1924 Dawes Plan restructures German reparations payments

National Origins Act establishes immigration quotas

1927 McNary-Haugen farm relief bill vetoed by President Coolidge

1928 Kellogg-Briand Treaty outlaws war as "an instrument of national policy"

1929 New York Stock Exchange crash ends "big bull market"

Young Plan further reduces German reparations

1930 Clark Memorandum renounces the Roosevelt Corollary to the Monroe Doctrine

Hawley-Smoot Tariff raises duties on foreign manufactures

1931 Japanese invade Manchuria

Hoover Moratorium on war debts

1932 Bonus Marchers in Washington dispersed by troops

Reconstruction Finance Corporation created

Franklin D. Roosevelt elected president

Supplementary Reading

The political history of the 1920s is surveyed in J. D. Hicks, **Republican Ascendancy** (1960), R. K. Murray, **The Politics of Normalcy** (1973), and E. W. Hawley, **The Great War and the Search for a Modern Order** (1979). Labor history is discussed in R. H. Zieger, **Republicans and Labor** (1969).

The best brief biography of Harding is Andrew Sinclair, **The Available Man** (1965); and D. R. McCoy, **Calvin Coolidge: The Quiet President** (1967), is the best life of Coolidge. R. F. Himmelberg, **The Origins of the National Recovery Act** (1976), is good on the trade associations.

Diplomatic developments are summarized in Selig Adler, **The Uncertain Giant** (1965). See also Akira Iriye, **After Imperialism** (1965), and **Across the Pacific** (1967), and T. H. Buckley, **The United States and the Washington Conference** (1970). J. H. Wilson, **American Business and Foreign Policy** (1971), is an important study of American interest in foreign markets in the 1920s.

On isolationism see R. A. Divine, **The Reluctant Belligerent** (1965) and **The Illusion of Neutrality** (1962), and Manfred Jonas, **Isolationism in America** (1966). On Latin American relations see I. F. Gellman, **Good Neighbor Diplomacy** (1979).

For details on the stock market crash, see Robert Sobel, **The Great Bull Market** (1968), and J. K. Galbraith, **The Great Crash** (1961). Hoover's role is analyzed in M. L. Fausold, **The Presidency of Herbert Hoover** (1985), and Joan Hoff Wilson, **Herbert Hoover: Forgotten Progressive** (1975). L. V. Chandler, **America's Greatest Depression** (1970), is a good introduction to the economic problems, but see also M. A. Bernstein, **The Great Depression** (1987), and J. A. Garraty, **The Great Depression** (1986), which puts American developments in world perspective.

CHAPTER 28

The New Deal, 1933–1941

■ ■ ■ ■ ■ AS THE DATE OF FRANKLIN ROOSEVELT'S inauguration approached, the banking system disintegrated. Starting in the rural West and spreading to major cities like Detroit and Baltimore, a financial panic swept the land. Hundreds of banks collapsed. By inauguration day, four-fifths of the states had suspended all banking operations.

The Hundred Days

Something drastic had to be done. The most conservative business leaders were as ready for government intervention as the most advanced radicals. Partisanship, though not disappearing, was for once subordinated to broad national needs. Even before Roosevelt took office, Congress submitted to the states the Twenty-first Amendment, putting an end to prohibition. By the end of the year it had been ratified by the necessary three-fourths of the states, and the prohibition era was over.

But there is no denying that Franklin D. Roosevelt provided the spark that reenergized the American people. His inaugural address reassured the country and at the same time stirred it to action: "The only thing we have to fear is fear itself." "Our true destiny is not to be ministered unto but to minister to ourselves and to our fellow men." "This Nation asks for action, and action now." "I assume unhesitatingly the leadership of this great army of our people." Many such lines punctuated the brief address, which concluded with a stern pledge:

> *In the event that Congress shall fail . . . I shall not evade the clear course of duty that will then confront me. I shall ask the Congress for the one remaining instrument to meet the crisis—broad Executive power to wage a war against the emergency.*

The inaugural captured the heart of the country. When Roosevelt summoned Congress into special session on March 9, the legislators outdid one another to enact his proposals into law. "I had as soon start a mutiny in the face of a foreign foe as . . . against the program of the President," one repre-

Chapter-opening illustration:
The National Recovery Administration logo featured a blue eagle holding a cogwheel, representing industry, and a lightning rod, symbolizing energy.

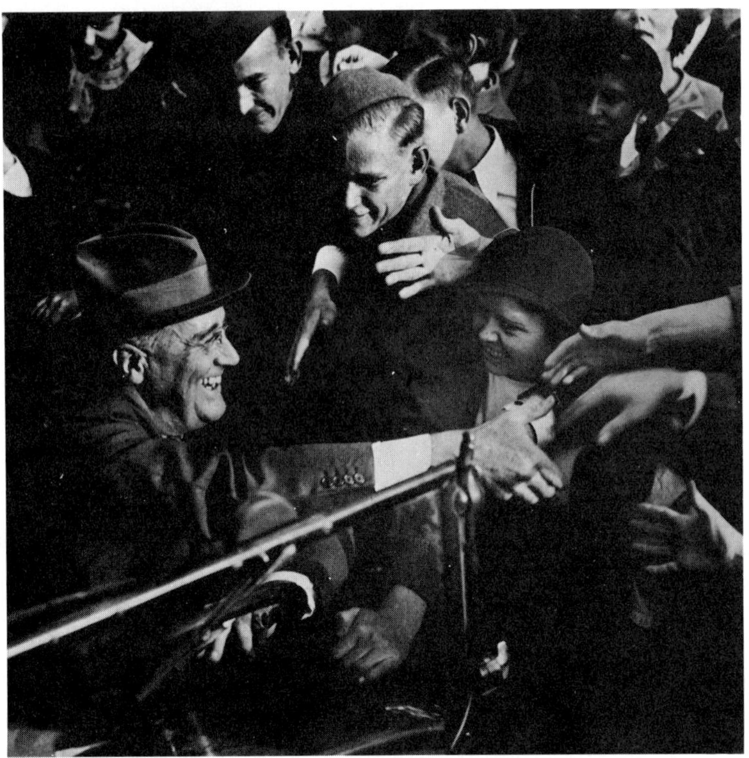

Well-wishers greet the president at Warm Springs, Georgia, in 1933. The Roosevelt "magic," unfeigned and inexhaustible, amazed his associates. "I have never had contact with a man who was loved as he is," reported Secretary of the Interior Harold L. Ickes.

sentative declared. In the next "Hundred Days," serious opposition, in the sense of an organized group committed to resisting the administration, simply did not exist.

Roosevelt had the power and the will to act but no comprehensive plan of action. He and his eager congressional collaborators proceeded in a dozen directions at once, sometimes wisely, sometimes not, often at cross-purposes. As a result, one of the first administration measures was the Economy Act, which reduced the salaries of federal employees and cut veterans' benefits. Such belt-tightening measures could only make the depression worse. But most New Deal programs were designed to stimulate the economy. All in all, an impressive body of new legislation was placed on the statute books.

On March 5, Roosevelt declared a nationwide bank holiday and placed an embargo on the exportation of gold. To explain the complexities of the banking problem to the public, Roosevelt delivered the first of his "fireside chats" over a national radio network. "I want to talk for a few minutes with the people of the United States about banking," he explained. His warmth and steadiness reassured millions of listeners. A plan for reopening the banks under Treasury Department licenses was devised, and soon most of them were functioning again, public confidence in their solvency restored. This solved the problem, but it also determined that the banks would remain private institutions. Reform, not radical change, had been decided on at the very start of Roosevelt's presidency.

April, Roosevelt took the country off the gold standard, hoping thereby to cause prices to rise. Before the session ended, Congress established the Federal Deposit Insurance Corporation (FDIC) to guarantee bank deposits. It also forced the separation of investment banking and commercial banking concerns while extending the power of the Federal Reserve Board over both types of institutions, and it created the Home Owners Loan Corporation (HOLC) to refinance mortgages and prevent foreclosures. It passed the Federal Securities Act requiring promoters to make public full financial information about new stock issues and giving the

Federal Trade Commission the right to regulate such transactions.*

The National Recovery Administration

Problems of unemployment and industrial stagnation had high priority during the Hundred Days. Congress appropriated $500 million for relief of the needy and created the Civilian Conservation Corps to provide jobs for men between the ages of 18 and 25 in reforestation and other conservation projects. To stimulate industry, Congress passed one of its most controversial measures, the National Industrial Recovery Act (NIRA). Besides establishing the Public Works Administration, with authority to spend $3.3 billion, this law permitted manufacturers to draw up industrywide codes of "fair business practices." Under the law, producers could agree to raise prices and limit production without violating the antitrust laws. The law gave workers the protection of minimum wage and maximum hours regulations and guaranteed them the right "to organize and bargain collectively through representatives of their own choosing," an immense stimulus to the union movement.

The act created a government agency, the National Recovery Administration (NRA), to supervise the drafting and operation of the business codes. Drafting posed difficult problems, first because each industry insisted on tailoring the agreements to its special needs and second because most manufacturers were unwilling to accept all the provisions of Section 7a of the law dealing with the rights of labor. While thousands of employers agreed to the pledge "We Do Our Part" in order to receive the Blue Eagle symbol of the NRA, many were more interested in the monopolistic aspects of the act than in boosting wages and encouraging unionization. In practice, the codes were drawn up by the largest manufacturers in each industry.

The effects of the NIRA were both more and less than the designers of the system had intended. It did not end the depression. There was a brief upturn in the spring of 1933, but the expected revival of industry did not take place; in nearly every case the dominant producers in each industry used their power to raise prices and limit production rather than to hire more workers and increase output.

Beginning with the cotton textile code, the agreements succeeded in doing away with the centuries-old problem of child labor in industry. They established the principle of federal regulation of wages and hours and led to the organization of thousands of workers, even in industries where unions had seldom been significant. Within a year John L. Lewis's United Mine Workers expanded from 150,000 members to half a million. About 100,000 automobile workers joined unions, as did a comparable number of steelworkers.

Labor leaders cleverly used the NIRA to persuade workers that the popular President Roosevelt wanted them to join unions—which was something of an overstatement. In 1935, because the conservative and craft-oriented AFL had displayed little enthusiasm for enrolling unskilled workers on an industrywide basis, Lewis, together with officials of the garment trade unions, formed the Committee for Industrial Organization (CIO) and set out to rally workers in each of the mass-production industries into one union without regard for craft lines, a far more effective method of organization. The AFL expelled these unions, however, and in 1938 the CIO became the Congress of Industrial Organizations. Soon it rivaled the AFL in size and importance.

The Agricultural Adjustment Administration

Roosevelt was more concerned about the plight of the farmers than that of any other group because he believed that the nation was overcommitted to industry. The New Deal farm program, incorporated in the Agricultural Adjustment Act of May 1933, combined compulsory restrictions on production with government subsidies to growers of wheat, cotton, tobacco, pork, and a few other crops. The money for these payments was raised by levying processing taxes on middlemen such as flour millers. The object was to lift agricultural prices to "parity" with industrial prices. In return for withdrawing part of their land from cultivation, farmers received "rental" pay-

*In 1934 this task was transferred to the new Securities and Exchange Commission, which was given broad authority over the activities of stock exchanges.

ments from the Agricultural Adjustment Administration (AAA).

Since the 1933 crops were growing when the law was passed, Secretary of Agriculture Henry A. Wallace decided to pay farmers to destroy the crops in the field. Cotton planters plowed up 10 million acres of growing crops, receiving $100 million in return. Six million baby pigs and 200,000 pregnant sows were slaughtered. Such ruthlessness appalled observers, particularly when they thought of the millions of hungry Americans who could have eaten all that pork.

Thereafter, limitation of acreage proved sufficient to raise some agricultural prices considerably. Tobacco growers benefited, and so did farmers who raised corn and hogs. The price of wheat also rose, though more because of bad harvests than the AAA program. But dairy farmers and cattlemen were hurt, as were the railroads (which had less freight to haul) and, of course, consumers. A far more serious weakness of the program was its failure to assist tenant farmers and sharecroppers, many of whom lost their livelihoods completely when owners took land out of production to obtain AAA payments. Yet in 1933 even farmers with large holdings were in desperate trouble, and they at least were helped. Acreage restrictions and mortgage relief saved thousands.

The Tennessee Valley Authority

Another striking achievement of the Hundred Days was the creation of the Tennessee Valley Authority (TVA). During World War I the government had constructed a hydroelectric plant at Muscle Shoals, Alabama, to provide power for factories manufacturing synthetic nitrate explosives. After 1920, farm groups and public power enthusiasts had blocked administration plans to turn these facilities over to private capitalists. Their efforts to have the site operated by the government had been defeated by presidential vetoes.

Roosevelt wanted to have the entire Tennessee Valley area incorporated into a broad experiment in social planning. Besides expanding the hydroelectric plants and developing nitrate manufacturing in order to produce cheap fertilizers, he envisioned a coordinated program of soil conservation, reforestation, and industrialization.

Over the objections of private power companies, led by Wendell L. Willkie of the Commonwealth and Southern Corporation, Congress passed the TVA Act in May 1933. This law created a board authorized to build dams, power plants, and transmission lines and sell fertilizers and electricity to individuals and local communities. The board could undertake flood control, soil conservation, and reforestation projects. The TVA greatly improved the standard of living of millions of inhabitants of the valley. In addition to producing electricity and fertilizers and providing a "yardstick" whereby the efficiency, and thus the rates, of private power companies could be tested, it took on other functions, ranging from the eradication of malaria to the development of recreational facilities.

The New Deal Spirit

By the end of the Hundred Days the country had made up its mind about Roosevelt's New Deal and for a decade never really changed it. A large majority considered the New Deal a solid success. Considerable recovery had taken place, but more basic was the fact that Roosevelt, recruiting an army of forceful officials to staff the new government agencies, had infused his administration with a spirit of bustle and optimism.

Although Roosevelt was not much of an intellectual, he was eager to draw on the ideas and energies of experts. New Deal agencies soon teemed with college professors and young lawyers without political experience. However, the New Deal lacked a consistent ideological base. It drew on the old populist tradition, as seen in its antipathy toward bankers and its willingness to adopt schemes for inflating the currency; on the New Nationalism of Theodore Roosevelt in its dislike of competition and its deemphasis of the antitrust laws; and on the ideas of social workers trained in the Progressive Era. Techniques developed by the Wilsonians also found a place in the system: Louis D. Brandeis had considerable influence on Roosevelt's financial reforms, and New Deal labor policy grew directly out of the experience of the War Labor Board of 1917–1918.

Within the administrative maze that Roosevelt

created, rival bureaucrats battled to enforce their views. The "spenders," led by Columbia economist Rexford G. Tugwell, clashed with advocates of strict economy, who gathered around Lewis Douglas, director of the budget. Blithely disregarding logically irreconcilable differences, Roosevelt mediated between the factions. Washington became a battleground for dozens of special interest groups: the Farm Bureau Federation, the unions, the trade associations, the silver miners. William E. Leuchtenburg has described New Deal policy as "interest-group democracy"; though superior to that of Roosevelt's predecessors—who had allowed one interest, big business, to predominate—it slighted the unorganized majority. The NRA aimed frankly at raising the prices paid by consumers of manufactured goods; the AAA processing tax came ultimately from the pocketbooks of ordinary citizens.

The Unemployed

At least 9 million persons were still without work in 1934, and hundreds of thousands of them were in real need. Malcolm Little (later famous as Malcolm X) remembered growing up in the depression this way:

> *This [1934] was about the worst depression year, and no one we knew had enough to eat. . . . There were times when there wasn't even a nickel and we would be so hungry we were dizzy. My mother would boil a big pot of dandelion greens and we would eat that.*

Yet the Democrats confounded the political experts, by increasing their already large majorities in both houses of Congress in the 1934 elections. All the evidence indicates that most of the jobless continued to support the administration. Their loyalty can best be explained by Roosevelt's unemployment policies.

In May 1933, Congress had established the Federal Emergency Relief Administration (FERA) and given it $500 million to be dispensed through state relief organizations. Roosevelt appointed Harry L. Hopkins, a social worker, to direct the FERA. Hopkins insisted that the unemployed needed jobs, not handouts. In November he persuaded Roosevelt to create the Civil Works Administration (CWA), and within a month he put more than 4 million persons to work building and repairing roads and public buildings, teaching, decorating the walls of post offices with murals, and applying their special skills in dozens of other ways.

The cost of this program frightened Roosevelt—Hopkins spent about $1 billion in less than five months—and he soon abolished the CWA. But an extensive public works program was continued throughout 1934 under the FERA.

In May 1935, Roosevelt put Hopkins in charge of a new agency, the Works Progress Administration (WPA). By the time this agency was disbanded in 1943, it had spent $11 billion and found employment for 8.5 million persons. Besides building public works, the WPA made important cultural contributions. It developed the Federal Theater Project, which put thousands of actors, directors, and stagehands to work; the Federal Writers' Project, which turned out valuable guidebooks, collected local lore, and published about a thousand books and pamphlets; and the Federal Art Project, which employed needy painters and sculptors. In addition, the National Youth Administration created part-time jobs for more than 2 million high school and college students and a larger number of other youths.

The WPA did not reach all the unemployed. At no time in the 1930s did unemployment fall below 10 percent of the work force. Like so many New Deal programs, the WPA did not go far enough, chiefly because Roosevelt could not escape his fear of unbalancing the federal budget drastically. Halfway measures did not provide the massive stimulus the economy needed. The president also hesitated to pay adequate wages to WPA workers and to undertake projects that might compete with private enterprises for fear of offending business. Yet his caution did him no good politically; the business interests he sought to placate were becoming increasingly hostile to the New Deal.

Literature in the Depression

Some American novelists found Soviet communism attractive and wrote "proletarian" novels in which ordinary workers were the heroes. Most of these books were of little artistic merit. The best of the

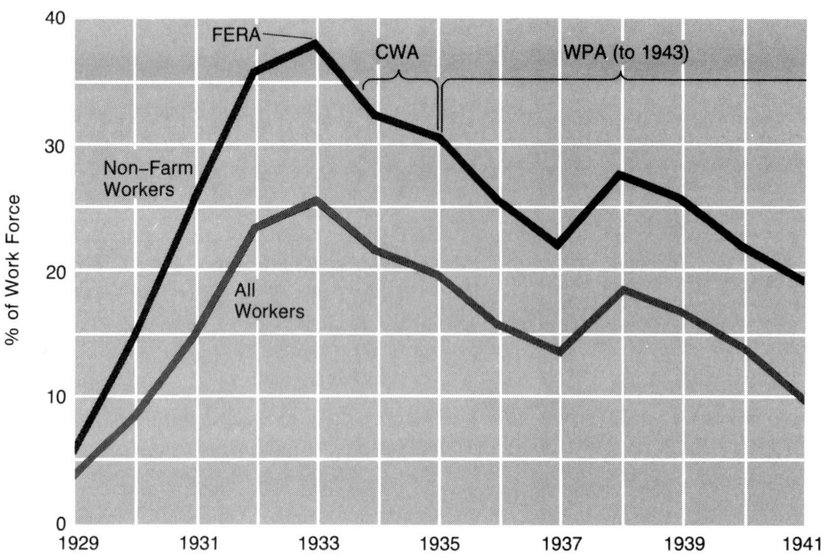

UNEMPLOYMENT AND FEDERAL ACTION, 1929–1941

Unemployment of nonfarm workers reached nearly 40 percent by early 1933. The Federal Employment Relief Act (FERA) of May 1933 was followed by the Civil Works Administration (CWA) later that year and the Works Progress Administration (WPA) in April 1935.

depression writers avoided the party line, though they were critical of many aspects of American life. One was John Dos Passos, author of the trilogy *U.S.A.* (1930–1936). This massive work, rich in detail and intricately constructed, advanced a fundamentally anticapitalist and deeply pessimistic point of view. It portrayed American society between 1900 and 1930 in broad perspective, interweaving the stories of five major characters and a galaxy of lesser figures. Throughout the narrative Dos Passos scattered capsule sketches of famous people, ranging from Andrew Carnegie and William Jennings Bryan to the movie idol Rudolph Valentino and the architect Frank Lloyd Wright. He included "newsreel" sections recounting events of the period and "camera eye" sections in which he revealed his personal reactions to the passing parade. Dos Passos's method was relentless, cold, methodical—utterly realistic. He displayed immense craftsmanship but no sympathy for his characters or their world.

The novel that best portrayed the desperate plight of the millions impoverished by the depression was John Steinbeck's *Grapes of Wrath* (1939), which described the fate of the Joads, an Oklahoma farm family driven by drought and bad times to abandon the land and become migratory laborers in California. Steinbeck captured the patient bewilderment of the downtrodden, the callous brutality bred of fear that characterized their exploiters, and the ultimate indignation of a people repeatedly degraded. "In the eyes of the hungry there is a growing wrath. In the souls of the people the grapes of wrath are filling and growing heavy, growing heavy for the vintage."

Like many other writers of the 1930s, Steinbeck was an angry man. "There is a crime here that goes beyond denunciation," he wrote. He had the compassion that Dos Passos lacked, and this quality raised *The Grapes of Wrath* to the level of great tragedy. In other works Steinbeck described the life of California cannery workers and ranchers with moving warmth but without excessive sentiment.

William Faulkner, perhaps the finest modern American novelist, responded to the era in still another way. Born in 1897, within a year of Fitzgerald and Hemingway, he attained literary maturity only in the 1930s. Between 1929 and 1932 he burst into prominence with four major novels: *The Sound and the Fury, As I Lay Dying, Sanctuary,* and *Light in August.*

Faulkner created a local world, Yoknapatawpha County, and peopled it with some of the most remarkable characters in American fiction—the Sartoris family, typical of the old southern aristocracy worn down at the heels; the Snopes clan, shrewd, unscrupulous, boorish representatives of the new day; and many others. Vividly he pictured the South's poverty and its pride, its dreadful racial problem, the guilt and obscure passions plaguing white and black alike. No contemporary excelled him as a commentator on the multiple dilemmas of modern life. His characters are possessed, driven to pursue high ideals yet weighted down with their awareness of their inadequacies and their sinfulness. They are imprisoned in their surroundings, however they may strive to escape them. As the French novelist Simone de Beauvoir once wrote, Faulkner "offered us a glimpse of . . . those secret, shameful fires that rage in the bellies of men and women alike."

The Extremists

Roosevelt's moderation irked extremists both on the left and on the right. The most formidable was Louisiana's Senator Huey Long, the "Kingfish." Long was controversial in his day, and so he has remained. He was certainly a demagogue. Yet the plight of all poor people concerned him deeply. More important, he tried to do something about it.

Long did not question segregation or white supremacy. He used the word *nigger* without self-consciousness, even when addressing northern black leaders. But he treated black-baiters with scathing contempt. When Hiram W. Evans, Imperial Wizard of the Ku Klux Klan, announced that he intended to campaign against him in Louisiana, Long told reporters: "Quote me as saying that that Imperial bastard will never set foot in Louisiana, and that when I call him a sonofabitch I am not using profanity, but am referring to the circumstances of his birth."

As a reformer, Long stood in the populist tradition; he hated bankers and "the interests." He believed that poor people, regardless of color, should have a chance to earn a decent living and get an education. His arguments were simplistic, patronizing, possibly insincere, but effective. "Don't say I'm working for niggers," he told a northern black journalist. "I'm for the poor man—all poor men. Black and white, they all gotta have a chance. . . . 'Every Man a King'—that's my slogan."

Raffish, unrestrained, yet shrewd, Long had supported the New Deal at the start, but partly because he thought Roosevelt too conservative and partly because of his own ambition, he soon broke with the administration. By 1935 his Share Our Wealth movement had a membership of over 4.6 million. His program called for the confiscation of family fortunes of more than $5 million and a tax of 100 percent on incomes of over $1 million a year. The money collected would be enough to buy every family a "homestead" (a house, a car, and other necessities) and provide an annual family income of $2,000 to $3,000 plus old-age pensions, educational benefits, and veterans' pensions. Long planned to organize a third party to split the liberal vote in the 1936 election. He assumed that the Republicans would win the election and so botch the job of fighting the depression that he could sweep the country in 1940.

Less powerful than Long but more widely influential was Father Charles E. Coughlin, the "Radio Priest." Coughlin began his public career in 1926, broadcasting a weekly religious message over station WJR in Detroit. His mellifluous voice and orotund rhetoric won him a huge national audience, and the depression gave him a secular cause. In 1933 he had been an eager New Dealer, but his need for ever more sensational ideas to hold his radio audience from week to week led him to turn away. By 1935 he was calling Roosevelt a "great betrayer and liar."

Although Coughlin's National Union for Social Justice was especially appealing to Catholics, it attracted people of every faith, particularly in the lower-middle-class districts of the big cities. Coughlin attacked bankers, New Deal planners, Roosevelt's farm program, and the alleged sympathy of the administration for communists and Jews, both groups that Coughlin detested. His program resembled fascism more than any leftist philosophy, but he posed a threat, especially in combination with Long, to the continuation of Democratic rule.

Another rapidly growing movement alarmed the Democrats in 1934 and 1935: Dr. Francis E. Townsend's campaign for "old-age revolving pensions." Townsend was colorless and low-key, but he had an oversimplified and thus appealing "solution" to the nation's troubles: paying every person 60 and over a pension of $200 a month, the only conditions being that the pensioners must not hold jobs and must spend the entire sum within 30 days. A stiff transaction tax, collected whenever any commodity changed hands, would pay for the program.

Economists quickly pointed out that with about 10 million persons eligible for the Townsend pensions, the cost would amount to $24 billion a year, roughly half the national income. But among the elderly the scheme proved extremely popular. Although most Townsendites were anything but radical politically, their plan, like Long's Share Our Wealth scheme, would have revolutionized the distribution of wealth in the country. The movement reflected, on the one hand, a reactionary spirit like that of religious fundamentalists and, on the other, the emergence of a new force in American society: With medical advances lengthening the average life span, the percentage of old people in the population was rising.

With the possible exception of Long, the extremists had little understanding of practical affairs. (It could be said that Townsend knew what to do with money but not how to get it, and Coughlin knew how to get money but not what to do with it.) Collectively, they represented a threat to Roosevelt; their success helped him see that he must move boldly to restore good times or face serious political trouble in 1936.

Political imperatives had much to do with his decision, and the influence of Justice Brandeis and his disciples, notably Felix Frankfurter, was great. They urged Roosevelt to abandon his pro-business programs, especially the NRA, and stress restoring competition and taxing corporations more heavily. The fact that most businessmen were turning from him encouraged the president to accept this advice; so did the Supreme Court's decision in *Schechter* v. *United States* in May 1935, which declared the National Industrial Recovery Act unconstitutional.

The Second New Deal

Existing laws had failed to end the depression; extremists were luring away some of Roosevelt's supporters, and conservatives had failed to appreciate his moderation. Thousands of ordinary people were clamoring for further reforms. At the same time, the Supreme Court was declaring many New Deal laws unconstitutional. For these many reasons, Roosevelt, in June 1935, launched the Second New Deal.

The Second Hundred Days was one of the most productive periods in the history of American legislation. The National Labor Relations Act—commonly known as the Wagner Act—restored the labor guarantees wiped out by the Schechter decision. It gave workers the right to bargain collectively and prohibited employers from interfering with union organizational activities in their factories. The National Labor Relations Board (NLRB) was established to supervise plant elections and designate successful unions as official bargaining agents when a majority of the workers approved. The NLRB forced antiunion corporations to bargain "in good faith" as the law required and to rehire workers discharged for union activities.

The Social Security Act of August 1935 set up a system of old-age insurance, financed partly by a tax on wages (paid by workers) and partly by a tax on payrolls (paid by employers). It created a state-federal system of unemployment insurance, similarly financed. Liberal critics considered this social security system inadequate because it did not cover agricultural workers, domestics, self-employed persons, and some other groups particularly in need of its benefits. Health insurance was not included, and because the size of pensions depended on the amount earned, the lowest-paid workers could not count on much support after reaching age 65. Over the years the pension payments were increased, and the classes of workers covered were expanded.

Among other important laws enacted at this time was the Public Utility Holding Company Act, which outlawed the pyramiding of control of gas and electricity companies through the use of holding companies and gave various federal commissions the power to regulate the rates and financial practices of these companies. The Rural Electrification Administration (REA), created by executive order, also began to function during this remarkable period. The REA lent money at low interest rates to utility companies and to farmer cooperatives interested in supplying electricity to rural areas. When the REA went into operation, only one farm in ten had electricity; by 1950 only one in ten did not.

Another important measure was the Wealth Tax Act of August 1935, which, while not the "soak the rich" measure both its supporters and its opponents claimed, raised taxes on large incomes considerably. Estate and gift taxes were also increased.

Herbert Hoover epitomized the attitude of conservatives when he called the New Deal "the most stupendous invasion of the whole spirit of Liberty that the nation has witnessed." Undoubtedly, many opponents of the New Deal sincerely believed that it was undermining the foundations of American freedom. The cost of the New Deal also alarmed them. By 1936 some members of the administration had fallen under the influence of the British economist John Maynard Keynes, who argued that the world depression could be conquered if governments would unbalance their budgets by reducing interest rates and taxes and increasing expenditures in order to stimulate consumption and investment.

Roosevelt never accepted Keynes's theories, but the imperatives of the depression forced him to spend more than the government was collecting in taxes. Conservative businessmen considered him financially irresponsible, and the fact that deficit spending seemed to be good politics made them seethe with rage.

The Election of 1936

The election of 1936 loomed as a showdown. "America is in peril," the Republican platform declared. The GOP candidate, Governor Alfred M. Landon of Kansas, was reasonably liberal, but he was handicapped by the reactionary views of many of his backers. Against Roosevelt's charm and political astuteness, Landon's arguments—chiefly that he could administer the government more efficiently than the president—made little impression.

The radical fringe put a third candidate in the field, Congressman William Lemke of North Dakota, who ran on the Union party ticket. Father Coughlin rallied his National Union for Social Justice behind Lemke; Dr. Townsend also supported him. However, the extremists were losing ground by 1936. Huey Long had fallen victim to an assassin in September 1935, and his organization was taken over by a blatantly demagogic rightist, Gerald L. K. Smith. The Townsendites fell under a cloud because of rumors that some of their leaders had their fingers in the organization's treasury. Father Coughlin's slanderous assaults on Roosevelt caused a backlash; a number of American Catholic prelates denounced him, and the Vatican issued an unofficial but influential rebuke. Lemke got only 892,000 votes.

Roosevelt did not win in 1936 because of the inadequacies of his foes. Having abandoned his efforts to hold the businessmen, whom he now denounced as "economic royalists," he appealed for the votes of workers and the underprivileged. The new labor unions gratefully poured thousands of dollars into the campaign to reelect him. Black voters switched to the Democrats in record numbers. Farmers liked Roosevelt because of his evident concern for their welfare: When the Supreme Court declared the Agricultural Adjustment Act unconstitutional (*United States* v. *Butler,* 1936), he immediately rushed through a new law, the Soil Conservation and Domestic Allotment Act, which accomplished the same objective by paying farmers to divert land from commercial crops to soil-building plants like clover and soybeans. Countless elderly persons backed him out of gratitude for the Social Security Act. Homeowners were grateful for his program guaranteeing mortgages. A modest upturn in industrial output to the levels of 1930 played into Roosevelt's hands. For the first time since 1931, U.S. Steel was showing a profit.

On election day the country gave the president a tremendous vote of confidence. He carried every state but Maine and Vermont. Both Roosevelt's personality and his program had captivated the land. He seemed irresistible, the most powerfully entrenched president in the history of the United States.

Roosevelt and the "Nine Old Men"

On January 20, in his second inaugural, Roosevelt spoke feelingly of the plight of millions of citizens. A third of the nation, he said without exaggeration, was "ill-housed, ill-clad, ill-nourished." He interpreted his landslide victory as a mandate for further reforms, and with his prestige and his immense congressional majorities, nothing appeared to stand in his way—nothing, that is, except the Supreme Court.

Throughout Roosevelt's first term, the Court had stood almost immovable against increasing the scope of federal authority and broadening the general power of government, state as well as national, to cope with the exigencies of the depression. Four of the nine justices—James C. McReynolds, Willis Van Devanter, Pierce Butler, and George Sutherland—were intransigent reactionaries. Chief Justice Charles Evans Hughes and Justice Owen J. Roberts, while more open-minded, tended to side with the reactionaries on many questions.

Much of the early New Deal legislation had been drafted without proper regard for the Constitution. Even the liberal justices considered the National Industrial Recovery Act unconstitutional (the Schechter decision had been unanimous). The Court had also voided the federal Guffey-Snyder Act, establishing minimum wages in the coal industry, and a New York minimum wage law, thereby creating, as Roosevelt remarked, a "no man's land" where neither national nor state government could act. Worse, the reactionaries on the Court seemed governed by no consistent constitutional philosophy; they tended to limit the police power of the states when wages-and-hours laws came before them and to interpret it broadly when state laws restricting civil liberties were under consideration. In 1937 all the major measures of the Second Hundred Days appeared doomed.

Roosevelt decided to ask Congress to shift the balance on the Court by increasing the number of justices, thinly disguising the purpose of his plan by making it part of a general reorganization of the judiciary. A member of the Court reaching the age of 70 would have the option of retiring at full pay. Should such a justice choose not to retire, the president was to appoint an additional justice, up to a maximum of six, to ease the burden of work for the aged jurists who remained on the bench.

Roosevelt knew that this measure would run into resistance, but he expected Congress to pass it. No astute politician had erred so badly in estimating the effects of an action since Stephen A. Douglas introduced the Kansas-Nebraska bill in 1854. To the expected denunciations of conservatives were added the complaints of liberals fearful that the principle of court packing might in the future be used to subvert civil liberties. Opposition in Congress was immediate and intense; many representatives and senators who had cheerfully supported every New Deal bill came out against the plan. The press denounced it, and so did most local bar associations. Chief Justice Hughes released a devastating critique; even the liberal Brandeis—the oldest judge on the court—rejected the bill out of hand.

For months Roosevelt stubbornly refused to concede defeat, but in July 1937 he had to yield. Minor administrative reforms of the judiciary were enacted, but the size of the Court remained unchanged.

The struggle did save the legislation of the Second New Deal. Alarmed by the threat to the Court, Justices Hughes and Roberts, never entirely committed to the conservative position, beat a strategic retreat on a series of specific issues. While the debate was raging in Congress, they sided with the liberals in upholding first a minimum wage law of the state of Washington that was little different from the New York act the Court had recently rejected, then the Wagner Act, then the Social Security Act. In May, Justice Van Devanter retired, and Roosevelt replaced him with Senator Hugo Black of Alabama, a New Dealer. The conservative justices thereupon gave up the fight, and soon Roosevelt was able to appoint enough new judges to give the Court a large pro–New Deal majority. No further measure of significance was declared unconstitutional during his presidency.

The Court fight hurt Roosevelt severely. His prestige never fully recovered. Conservative Democrats who had feared to oppose him because of his supposedly invulnerable popularity took heart and began to join with the Republicans on key issues. When the president summoned a special session of Congress in November 1937 and submitted a program of "must" legislation, not one of his bills was passed.

The New Deal Winds Down

The Court fight marked the beginning of the end of the New Deal. Social and economic developments contributed to its decline, and the final blow originated in the area of foreign affairs. With unemployment high, wages low, and workers relatively powerless against their employers, most Americans had liked New Deal labor legislation and sympathized with the industrial unions whose growth it stimulated. The NRA, the Wagner Act, and the CIO's organizing of such industries as steel and automobiles changed the power structure within the economy. Aside from higher wages, shorter hours, and similar benefits, unionization had provided both fair methods of settling labor-management disputes and job security based on seniority for thousands of workers. The CIO had also increased the influence of labor in politics and brought many blacks and other minorities into the labor movement.

In 1937 a series of "sit-down strikes" broke out, beginning at the General Motors plant in Flint, Michigan. Striking workers barricaded themselves inside the factories; when police and strikebreakers tried to dislodge them, they fought with barrages of soda bottles, tools, spare parts, and crockery. The tolerant attitude of the Roosevelt administration assured the strikers the government would not intervene. Fearful that all-out efforts to clear their plants would result in the destruction of expensive machinery, most employers capitulated to the workers' demands.

A group of sit-down strikers inside the Chevrolet plant in Flint, Michigan, looking out. They are hanging a "GM stoolpigeon" in effigy. The sign directly above the dummy reminds fellow workers: "Don't Scab."

The major steel companies, led by U.S. Steel, recognized the CIO and granted higher wages and a 40-hour workweek. The auto and steel unions alone boasted more than 725,000 members by late 1937; other CIO units conquered numerous industries, including rubber and textiles. These gains gave many members of the middle class second thoughts about the fairness of labor's demands. The enthusiasm of such people for reform cooled rapidly.

While the sit-down strikes and the Court fight were going on, the New Deal suffered another heavy blow. Business conditions had been gradually improving since 1933. Heartened by the trend, Roosevelt, who had never fully grasped the importance of government spending in stimulating recovery, cut back sharply on the relief program in June 1937, with disastrous results. Between August and October the economy slipped downward like sand through a chute. Stock prices plummeted; unemployment rose by 2 million; industrial production slumped. This "Roosevelt recession" further damaged the president's reputation.

In April 1938, Roosevelt finally committed himself to heavy deficit spending. At his urging Congress passed a \$3.75 billion public works bill. Two major pieces of legislation were also enacted at about this time. A new AAA program in February 1938 set marketing quotas and acreage limitations for growers of staples like wheat, cotton, and tobacco and authorized the Commodity Credit Corporation to lend money to farmers on their surplus crops. The surpluses were to be stored by the government. When prices rose, farmers could repay the loans, reclaim their produce, and sell it on the open market, thereby maintaining an "ever-normal granary."

The second measure, the Fair Labor Standards Act, abolished child labor and established a national minimum wage of 40 cents an hour and a maximum workweek of 40 hours, with time and a half for overtime. Although the law failed to cover many of the poorest-paid types of labor, its passage meant wage increases for 750,000 workers. In later years many more workers were brought within its protection, and the minimum wage was repeatedly increased.

These measures further alienated conservatives without dramatically improving economic conditions. The resistance of many Democratic congressmen to additional economic and social "experiments" hardened. As the 1938 elections approached, Roosevelt decided to go to the voters in an effort to strengthen party discipline and reenergize the New Deal. He singled out a number of conservative Democratic senators and tried to "purge" them by backing other Democrats in the primaries. The purge failed. Voters liked Roosevelt but resented his interference in local politics. The senators were easily renominated and then reelected in November. In the nation at large, the Republicans made important gains for the first time since Roosevelt had taken office.

Significance of the New Deal

After World War II broke out in 1939, the Great Depression was swept away on a wave of orders from the beleaguered European democracies. For this prosperity Roosevelt received much undeserved credit. His New Deal had not returned the country to full employment. Despite the aid given the jobless, the generation of workers born between 1900 and 1910 who entered the 1930s as unskilled laborers had their careers permanently stunted by the depression. Roosevelt's willingness to experiment with different means of combating the depression made sense because no one really knew what to do; however, his uncertainty about the ultimate objectives of the New Deal was counterproductive. He vacillated between seeking to stimulate the economy through deficit spending and trying to balance the budget, between a narrow "America first" economic nationalism and a broad-gauged international approach, between regulating monopolies and trust-busting; between helping the underprivileged and bolstering those already strong. He could never make up his mind whether to try to rally liberals to his cause without regard for party or to run the government as a partisan leader, conciliating the conservative Democrats.

Roosevelt's fondness for establishing new agencies to deal with specific problems vastly increased the federal bureaucracy. His cavalier attitude toward constitutional limitations on executive power, which he justified as being necessary in a national emergency, set in motion trends that so increased the prestige and authority of the presidency that the balance among the executive, legislative, and judicial branches was threatened.

Yet these criticisms ignore what one historian has called the "sense of urgency and haste" that made the New Deal "a mixture of accomplishment, frustration, and misdirected effort." On balance, the New Deal had an immense constructive impact. By 1939 the country was committed to the idea that the federal government should accept responsibility for the national welfare and act to meet specific problems in every necessary way. What was most significant was not the proliferation of new agencies or the expansion of federal power. The importance of the "Roosevelt revolution" was that it removed the issue from politics. "Never again," a presidential candidate was to say in 1952, "shall we allow a depression in the United States."

Because of New Deal decisions, many formerly unregulated areas of American life became subject to federal authority: the stock exchange, agricultural prices and production, labor relations, old-age pensions, relief of the needy. If the New Deal failed to end the depression, it effected changes that have prevented later economic declines from becoming catastrophes. By encouraging the growth of unions, the New Deal probably helped workers obtain a larger share of the profits of industry. By putting a floor under the income of many farmers, it checked the decline of agricultural living standards, though not that of the agricultural population. The social security program, with all its inadequacies, lessened the impact of bad times on an increasingly large proportion of the population and provided immense psychological benefits to all.

Among other important social changes, the TVA and the New Deal rural electrification program made farm life literally more civilized. Urban public housing, though never undertaken on a massive scale, helped rehabilitate some of the nation's worst slums. Exploitation of the natural resources of the West was checked. The NIRA and later labor legislation forced business leaders to reexamine their role in American life and to become more socially conscious. The WPA art and theater programs widened the horizons of millions. All in all, the spirit of the New Deal heightened the people's sense of community, revitalized national energies, and stimulated the imagination and creative instincts of countless citizens.

Women New Dealers: The Network

Largely because of First Lady Eleanor Roosevelt and Molly Dewson, head of the Women's Division of the Democratic National Committee, the Roosevelt administration employed far more women in positions of importance than any earlier one. Secretary of Labor Frances Perkins, the first woman appointed to a Cabinet post, had been active in labor relations for more than 20 years as secretary of the Consumers' League, as a factory inspector, and as chair of the New York State Industrial Commission. As secretary of labor she helped draft New Deal labor legislation and kept Roosevelt informed on various labor problems outside the government.

In addition to Perkins, there were dozens of other women New Dealers; Molly Dewson and Eleanor Roosevelt headed an informal but effective "network"—women in key posts who were always seeking to place reform-minded women in government jobs. (According to the historian William Chafe, "Washington seemed like a perpetual convention of social workers as women . . . [took] on government assignments.")

As for Eleanor Roosevelt, through her newspaper column, "My Day," and as a speaker on public issues, she became a major political force—in the words of the historian Tamara Hareven, "an ombudsman with the increasingly bureaucratized and impersonal [federal] government." Her influence was large, especially in the area of civil rights, where the administration needed constant prodding.

She was particularly identified with efforts to obtain better treatment for blacks, in and out of government. Her best-known action occurred in 1939 after the Daughters of the American Revolution refused to permit the use of their Washington auditorium for a concert by the black contralto Marian Anderson. Eleanor Roosevelt resigned from the D.A.R. in protest, and after the president arranged for Anderson to sing at the Lincoln Memorial, she persuaded a small army of dignitaries to sponsor the concert. An interracial crowd of 75,000 people attended the performance. The Chicago *Defender,* noted that the First Lady "stood like the Rock of Gibraltar against pernicious encroachments on the rights of minorities." (A disgruntled southerner made the same point differently: "She goes around telling the Negroes they are as good as anyone else.")

Blacks During the New Deal

The shift of black voters from the Republican to the Democratic party during the New Deal years was one of the most significant political turnarounds in American history. In 1932, when things were at their worst, fewer blacks defected from the Republican party than the members of any other traditionally Republican group. Four years later, however, blacks voted for Roosevelt in overwhelming numbers.

Blacks supported the New Deal for the same reasons that whites did, but how the New Deal affected blacks in general and racial attitudes specifically are more complicated questions. Many of the early New Deal programs treated blacks as second-class citizens. They were often paid at lower rates than whites under NRA codes (and so joked that NRA stood for "Negro Run Around" and "Negroes Ruined Again"). The early farm programs shortchanged black tenants and sharecroppers. Blacks in the Civilian Conservation Corps were assigned to all-black camps. TVA developments were rigidly segregated too. New Deal urban housing projects effectively increased the concentration of blacks in particular neighborhoods. The Social Security Act excluded agricultural laborers and domestic servants from coverage. In 1939 unemployment was twice as high among blacks as among whites, and whites' wages were double the level of blacks' wages.

The fact that members of racial minorities got less than they deserved did not keep most of them from becoming New Dealers. Secretary of the Interior Harold L. Ickes appointed Charles Forman as a special assistant assigned "to keep the government honest when it came to race." Mary McLeod Bethune, founder of Bethune-Cookman College, was appointed head of the Division of Negro Affairs in the National Youth Administration (NYA). She developed training programs for disadvantaged black youngsters and lobbied throughout the Washington bureaucracy on behalf of better opportunities for blacks.

In the labor movement the new CIO unions

recruited black members, and this was particularly significant because these unions were organizing industries—steel, automobiles, and mining, among others—that employed large numbers of blacks. Thus while black Americans suffered horribly during the depression, New Deal efforts to counteract its effects brought them some relief and a measure of hope.

A New Deal for Indians

As in many other matters, New Deal policy toward American Indians built on early trends but carried them further. During the Harding and Coolidge administrations, more Indian land had passed into the hands of whites, and agents of the Bureau of Indian Affairs had tried to suppress any element of Indian culture that they considered "pagan" or "lascivious." In 1924 Congress finally granted citizenship to all Indians, but whites still generally agreed that Indians should be treated as wards of the state. Assimilation had failed; indeed, tribal cultures had proved remarkably enduring. Indian languages and religious practices, patterns of family life, arts and crafts—all had resisted generations of efforts to "civilize" the tribes.

Government policy took a new direction in 1933 when President Roosevelt named John Collier commissioner of Indian affairs. In the 1920s Collier had studied the Indians of the Southwest and was appalled by what he learned. He became executive secretary of the American Indian Defense Association and in 1925 editor of a reform-oriented magazine, *American Indian Life.* By the time he was appointed commissioner, the depression had reduced to penury perhaps one-third of the 320,000 Indians living on reservations.

Collier was convinced that something should be done to revive the spirits of these people. He favored a pluralistic approach, seeking to help the Indians preserve their ancient cultures but also, somewhat contradictorily, to help them earn more money and make use of modern medical advances and modern techniques of soil conservation. He was particularly eager to encourage the revival of tribal governments that could represent the Indians in dealings with the U.S. government and function as community service centers.

In part because of Collier's urging, Congress passed the Indian Reorganization Act of 1934. This law did away with the Dawes Act allotment system and enabled Indians to establish tribal governments with powers like those of cities, and it encouraged, but did not require, Indians to return individually owned lands to tribal control. In various ways about 4 million of the 90 million acres of Indian land lost under the allotment system were returned to the tribes. In addition, Harry Hopkins made special efforts to see that needy Indians who were not living on reservations got relief aid. There was also a special Indian division of the Civilian Conservation Corps that organized work for Indians right on their reservations.

New Deal Indian policy was controversial among Indians as well as other groups. Some critics charged Collier with trying to turn back the clock. Others attacked him as a segregationist and claimed that he was trying to restore "pagan" religious practices and convert the Indians to communism. Still others objected to his employing numerous professional anthropologists with supposedly "advanced" ideas.

In truth the problem was more complicated than Collier had imagined. Indians who owned profitable allotments, such as those in Oklahoma who held valuable oil and mineral rights, did not relish turning their land over to tribal control. In New Mexico, the Navajos, whose lands had relatively little commercial value, nonetheless voted decisively against going back to the communal system. All told, 77 of 269 tribes voted against communal holdings. Nevertheless, like so many of its programs, the New Deal's Indian policy marked an important and necessary shift of perspective, a bold effort to deal constructively with a long-standing national problem.

The Role of Roosevelt

How much of the credit for New Deal policies belongs personally to Franklin D. Roosevelt is debatable. He had little to do with many of the details and some of the broad principles behind the New Deal. His knowledge of economics was skimpy, his understanding of many social problems superficial, his political philosophy distressingly vague. The British leader Anthony Eden described him as "a conjurer, skillfully juggling with balls of dynamite, whose nature he failed to understand," and the historian David Brody writes shrewdly of Roosevelt's "unreflective acceptance" of the basic structure of American society.

Nevertheless, every aspect of the New Deal bears the brand of Roosevelt's remarkable personality. Rexford Tugwell made one of the best-balanced judgments of the president. "Roosevelt was not really very much at home with ideas," Tugwell explained. He preferred to stick with what he already knew. But he was always open to new facts, and something within him "forbade inaction when there was something to be done." Roosevelt's political genius constructed the coalition that made the program possible; his humanitarianism made it a reform movement of major significance. Although considered by many a terrible administrator because he encouraged rivalry among his subordinates, assigned different agencies overlapping responsibilities, failed to discharge many incompetents, and frequently put off making difficult decisions, he was in fact one of the most effective chief executives in the nation's history. His seemingly haphazard practice of dividing authority among competing administrators unleashed the energies and sparked the imaginations of his aides, which gave the ponderous federal bureaucracy remarkable flexibility and élan.

Like Andrew Jackson, Roosevelt maximized his role as leader of all the people. His informal biweekly press conferences kept the public in touch with developments and himself in tune with popular thinking. He made the radio an instrument for communicating with the masses in the most direct way imaginable: His fireside chats convinced millions that he was personally interested in each citizen's life and welfare, as in a way he was. At a time when the size and complexity of the government made it impossible for any one person to direct the nation's destiny, Roosevelt managed the minor miracle of personifying that government to 130 million people. Under Hoover, a single clerk was able to handle the routine mail that flowed into the office of the president from ordinary citizens; under Roosevelt, the task required a staff of 50.

While the New Deal was still evolving, contemporaries recognized Roosevelt's right to a place beside Washington, Jefferson, and Lincoln among the great presidents. The years have not altered their judgment. Yet as his second term drew toward its close, some of his most important work still lay in the future.

The Triumph of Isolationism

Franklin Roosevelt was at heart an internationalist, but his highest priority was to end the depression, and like most world leaders in the 1930s, he placed the revival of his own country's limping economy ahead of general world recovery. In April 1933 he took the United States off the gold standard, hoping that devaluing the dollar would make it easier to sell American goods abroad. His decision increased international ill feeling.

Against this background, vital changes in American foreign policy took place. Unable to persuade the country to take positive action against aggressors, internationalists like Secretary of State Stimson had begun in 1931 to work for a discretionary arms embargo law, to be applied by the president in time of war against whichever side had broken the peace. By early 1933 Stimson had obtained President Hoover's backing for an embargo bill, as well as the support of President-elect Roosevelt. First the munitions manufacturers and then the isolationists pounced on it, and in the resulting debate it was amended to make the embargo apply impartially to *all* belligerents. Stimson's policy would have permitted arms shipments to China but not to Japan. As amended, the embargo would have automatically applied to both sides, thus removing the United States as an influence in the conflict. Though Roosevelt accepted the change, the internationalists in Congress did not, and when they withdrew their support, the measure died.

The attitude of the munitions makers, who opposed both forms of the embargo, led to a series of studies of the industry. The most important was a Senate investigation (1934–1936) headed by Gerald P. Nye of North Dakota. Nye was convinced that "the interests" had conspired to drag America into World War I; his investigation was more an inquisition than an honest effort to discover what American bankers and munitions makers had been doing between 1914 and 1918. The committee's staff, ferreting into subpoenaed records, uncovered sensational facts about the lobbying activities and profits of various concerns. The Du Pont company's earnings, for example, had soared from $5 million in 1914 to $82 million in 1916. The Nye report convinced millions of citizens that the bankers who had lent the Allies money and the "merchants of death" who had sold them arms had tricked the country into war and that the "mistake" of 1917 must never be repeated.

These developments led in 1935 to what the historian Robert A. Divine has called the "triumph of isolation." The danger of another world war mounted steadily as Germany, Italy, and Japan repeatedly resorted to force to achieve their expansionist aims. In March 1935, Hitler instituted universal military training. In May, Mussolini massed troops in Italian Somaliland, using a trivial border clash as pretext for threatening the ancient kingdom of Ethiopia.

Congress responded by passing the Neutrality Act of 1935, which forbade the sale of munitions to all belligerents whenever the president should proclaim that a state of war existed. Americans who took passage on belligerent ships after such a proclamation had been issued would do so at their own risk. Roosevelt would have preferred a discretionary embargo or no new legislation at all, but he dared not arouse the ire of the isolationists by vetoing the bill.

The next summer, civil war broke out in Spain. The rebels, led by General Francisco Franco and strongly backed by Italy and Germany, sought to overthrow the somewhat leftist Spanish Republic. Here, clearly, was a clash between democracy and fascism, and the neutrality laws did not apply to civil wars. However, Roosevelt now became more fearful of involvement than some isolationists. He was afraid that American interference might cause the conflict in Spain to become a global war, and he was wary of antagonizing the substantial number of American Catholics who were sympathetic to the Franco regime. At his urging Congress passed another neutrality act broadening the arms embargo to cover civil wars.

Isolationism now reached its peak. A public opinion poll revealed in March 1937 that 94 percent of the people thought American policy should be directed at keeping out of all foreign wars rather than trying to prevent wars from breaking out. In April, Congress passed still another neutrality law. It continued the embargo on munitions and loans, forbade Americans to travel on belligerent ships, and gave the president discretionary authority to place the sale of other goods to belligerents on a cash-and-carry basis. In theory this would preserve the nation's profitable foreign trade without the risk of war; in fact it played into the hands of the aggressors. While German planes and cannons were turning the tide in Spain, the United States was denying the hard-pressed Spanish loyalists even a case of cartridges. The *New York Herald Tribune* pointed out that the neutrality legislation was literally reactionary—designed to keep the United States out of the war 1914–1918, not the conflict looming on the horizon. The American people, like wild creatures before a forest fire, were rushing in blind panic from the conflagration.

War Again in Europe

There were limits beyond which Americans would not go. In July 1937, Japan again attacked China, pressing ahead on a broad front. Roosevelt believed that invoking the neutrality law would only help the well-armed Japanese. Taking advantage of the fact that neither side had formally declared war, he allowed the shipment of arms and supplies to both sides.

Then, in October, he proposed a "quarantine" of nations that were "creating a state of international anarchy." But his speech provoked a windy burst of isolationist rhetoric that forced him to back down. "It's a terrible thing," he said, "to look over your shoulder when you are trying to lead—and to find no one there."

Roosevelt came gradually to the conclusion that resisting aggression was more important than keeping out of war, but when he did, his fear of the isolationists led him at times to be less than candid in his public statements. Hitler's annexation of Austria in March 1938 caused him deep concern. The Nazis' vicious anti-Semitism had caused many of Germany's 500,000 Jewish citizens to seek refuge abroad. Now 190,000 Austrian Jews were under Nazi control. When Roosevelt learned that the Germans were burning synagogues, expelling Jewish children from schools, and otherwise mistreating innocent people, he said that he "could scarcely believe that such things could occur." But public opinion opposed changing the immigration law so that more refugees could be admitted, and the president did nothing.

In September 1938, Hitler forced Czechoslovakia to cede the German-speaking Sudetenland region to the Reich. Roosevelt failed again to speak out, but when the Nazis seized the rest of Czechoslovakia in March 1939, Roosevelt called for "methods short of war" to demonstrate America's determination to check the fascists.

In August 1939, Germany and the Soviet Union signed a nonaggression pact, prelude to their joint assault on Poland, which began on September 1. This at last provoked Great Britain and France to declare war on Germany. Roosevelt immediately summoned Congress into special session and again asked for repeal of the arms embargo. In November, in a vote that followed party lines closely, the Democratic majority pushed through a law permitting the sale of arms and other contraband on a cash-and-carry basis. American vessels were forbidden to carry any products to the belligerents. Since the Allies controlled the seas, cash-and-carry gave them a tremendous advantage.

The German attack on Poland effected a basic change in American public opinion. Keeping out of the war remained an almost universal hope, but preventing a Nazi victory became the ultimate, if not always conscious, objective. In Roosevelt's case it was perfectly conscious. But he moved slowly, responding to rather than directing the course of events.

Cash-and-carry did not stop the Nazis. Poland fell in less than a month; then, after a winter lull that cynics called the "phony war," between April 9 and June 22, 1940, the Germans taught the world the awful meaning of *Blitzkrieg:* "lightning war." Denmark, Norway, the Netherlands, Belgium, and France were successively overwhelmed. The British army, pinned against the sea at Dunkirk, saved itself from annihilation only by fleeing across the English Channel. After the French submitted to his harsh terms on June 22, Hitler controlled nearly all of western Europe.

Roosevelt responded to these disasters in a number of ways. In the fall of 1939, reacting to warnings from Albert Einstein and other scientists that the Germans were trying to develop atomic weapons, he committed federal funds to a top secret program to build an atomic bomb. Without legal authority, he authorized the sale of surplus government arms to Britain and France. When Italy entered the war and invaded France, Roosevelt called the attack a stab in the back. To strengthen national unity, he name Henry L. Stimson secretary of war* and another Republican, Frank Knox, secretary of the navy.

After the fall of France, Hitler attempted to bomb and starve the British into submission. The epic air battles over England during the summer of 1940 ended in a decisive defeat for the Nazis, but the Royal Navy, which had only about 100 destroyers, could not control German submarine attacks on shipping. Far more destroyers were needed. In this desperate hour, Prime Minister Winston Churchill, who had replaced Chamberlain in May 1940, asked Roosevelt for 50 old American destroyers to fill the gap.

The navy had 240 destroyers in commission and more than 50 under construction. But direct loan or sale of the vessels would have violated both international and American laws. Roosevelt therefore arranged to "trade" the destroyers for six British naval bases in the Caribbean. In addition, Great Britain leased bases in Bermuda and Newfoundland to the United States.

The destroyers-for-bases deal was one of Roosevelt's most masterful achievements. It helped Great Britain, and at the same time it circumvented isolationist prejudices, since the president could present it as a shrewd bargain that bolstered America's defenses. A string of island bastions in the Atlantic was more valuable than 50 old destroyers.

Lines were hardening throughout the world. In September 1940, Congress enacted the first peacetime draft in American history. Some 1.2 million draftees were summoned for one year of service, and 800,000 reservists were called to active duty. That same month Japan signed a mutual-assistance pact with Germany and Italy, thus turning the struggle into a global war.

A Third Term for FDR

In the midst of these events, the 1940 presidential election took place. Why Roosevelt decided to run for a third term is much-debated question. Partisanship had something to do with it, for no other Demo-

*Stimson had held this post from 1911 to 1913 in the Taft Cabinet.

crat seemed so likely to carry the country. Nor would the president have been human had he not been tempted to hold on to power, especially in such critical times. His conviction that no one else could keep a rein on the isolationists was probably decisive. Vice-president Garner, who had become disenchanted with Roosevelt and the New Deal, did not seek a third term; at Roosevelt's urging, the Democratic convention nominated Secretary of Agriculture Henry A. Wallace to replace him.

The leading Republican candidates were Senator Robert A. Taft of Ohio, son of the former president, and District Attorney Thomas E. Dewey of New York, who had won fame as a "racket buster." But Taft was extremely conservative and lacking in political glamour, and Dewey, barely 38, seemed too young and inexperienced. Instead the Republicans nominated the darkest of dark horses, Wendell L. Willkie of Indiana, the utility magnate who had led the fight against the TVA in 1933.

Despite his political inexperience, Willkie made an appealing candidate. An energetic and openhearted man with a rough-hewn rural manner (one Democrat called him "a simple, barefoot Wall Street lawyer"), he won wide support in farm districts. Willkie had difficulty, however, finding issues on which to oppose Roosevelt. Good times were at last returning. The New Deal reforms were too popular and too much in line with his own thinking to invite attack. He believed as strongly as the president that America could no longer ignore the Nazi threat.

While rejecting the isolationist position, Willkie charged that Roosevelt intended to get the United States into the war. Roosevelt retorted (disingenuously, since he knew he was not a free agent in the situation), "I have said this before, but I shall say it again and again and again: Your boys are not going to be sent into any foreign wars." In November, Roosevelt carried the country handily. The popular vote was 27 million to 22 million, the electoral count 449 to 82.

The Undeclared War

The election encouraged Roosevelt to act more boldly. When Prime Minister Churchill informed him that Great Britain was rapidly exhausting its financial resources, he decided at once to provide the British with whatever they needed. Since lending them money was certain to evoke memories of the vexatious war debt controversies, Roosevelt devised the lend-lease program, one of his most ingenious and imaginative creations.

First he delivered a fireside chat that stressed the dangers that a German victory would create for America. Aiding Britain should be looked at as a form of self-defense. "As planes and ships and guns and shells are produced," he said, American defense experts would decide "how much shall be sent abroad and how much shall remain at home." In January 1941 he asked Congress for $7 billion for war materials that the president could sell, lend, lease, exchange, or transfer to any country whose defense he deemed vital to that of the United States. After two months of debate, Congress gave him what he had asked for.

Roosevelt did not minimize the dangers involved. Yet his mastery of practical politics was never more in evidence. To counter Irish-American prejudices against the English, he pointed out that Ireland would surely fall under Nazi domination if Hitler won the war. He coupled his demand for heavy military expenditures with his enunciation of the idealistic "Four Freedoms"—freedom of speech, freedom of religion, freedom from want, and freedom from fear—for which, he said, the war was being fought.

After the enactment of lend-lease, the American navy began to patrol the North Atlantic, shadowing German submarines and radioing their locations to British warships and planes. In May the president declared a state of unlimited national emergency. After Hitler invaded the Soviet Union in June, Roosevelt moved slowly, for anti-Soviet feeling in the United States was intense, but in November $1 billion in lend-lease aid was put at the disposal of the Soviets.

Meanwhile, the draft law was extended in August—by the margin of a single vote in the House of Representatives. In September the German submarine *U-652* fired a torpedo at the U.S. destroyer *Greer* in the North Atlantic. The *Greer*, which had provoked the attack by tracking *U-652* and flashing its position to a British plane, avoided the torpedo and dropped 19 depth charges in an effort to sink the submarine.

Roosevelt (nothing he ever did provided more ammunition for his critics) announced that the *Greer* had been innocently "carrying mail to Iceland." He called the U-boats "the rattlesnakes of the Atlantic" and ordered the navy to "shoot on sight" any German craft in the waters south and west of Iceland. After the Germans sank the U.S. destroyer *Reuben James* on October 30, Congress voted to allow the arming of American merchant ships and to permit them to carry cargoes to Allied ports. For all practical purposes, though not yet officially, the United States had gone to war.

Milestones

New Deal Agencies

1933 Civilian Conservation Corps (CCC)
Federal Emergency Relief Administration (FERA)
Agricultural Adjustment Administration (AAA)
Tennessee Valley Authority (TVA)
Home Owners Loan Corporation (HOLC)
National Recovery Administration (NRA)
Federal Deposit Insurance Corporation (FDIC)
Public Works Administration (PWA)
Civil Works Administration (CWA)

1934 Securities and Exchange Commission (SEC)

1935 Works Progress Administration (WPA)
Rural Electrification Administration (REA)
National Youth Administration (NYA)
National Labor Relations Board (NLRB)

Supplementary Reading

Of the many biographies of Roosevelt, see especially Frank Freidel, **Franklin Roosevelt** (1990), and J. M. Burns, **Roosevelt: The Lion and the Fox** (1956). On Eleanor Roosevelt see Lois Sharf, **Eleanor Roosevelt: First Lady of American Liberalism** (1987).

Useful special studies of the New Deal include Theodore Saloutos, **American Farmers and the New Deal** (1982), D. E. Conrad, **The Forgotten Farmers: The Story of Sharecroppers in the New Deal** (1965), Richard Lowitt, **The New Deal in the West** (1984), E. W. Hawley, **The New Deal and the Problem of Monopoly** (1966), Barbara Blumberg, **The New Deal and the Unemployed** (1979), Harvard Sitkoff, **A New Deal for Blacks** (1978), N. J. Weiss, **Farewell to the Party of Lincoln** (1983), C. H. Trout, **Boston, the Great Depression, and the New Deal** (1977), B. F. Schwartz, **The Civil Works Administration** (1984), J. S. Olson, **Saving Capitalism** (1988), W. L. Creese, **TVA's Public Planning** (1990), and M. H. Leff, **The Limits of Symbolic Reform** (1984). On the impact of the New Deal on women, see W. H. Chafe, **The American Woman** (1972), and Susan Ware, **Beyond Suffrage** (1981) and **Partner and I** (1987). On the Indian New Deal consult, K. R. Philip, **John Collier's Crusade for Indian Reform** (1977).

On the activities of the "radical fringe," consult D. H. Bennett, **Demagogues in the Depression** (1969), Alan Brinkley, **Voices of Protest** (1982), and T. H. Williams, **Huey Long** (1969). On the events leading to American entry in World War II, see Waldo Heinrichs, **Threshold of War** (1988), W. S. Cole, **Roosevelt and the Isolationists** (1983), and, on lend-lease, W. F. Kimball, **The Most Unsordid Act** (1969).

CHAPTER 29

War and Peace

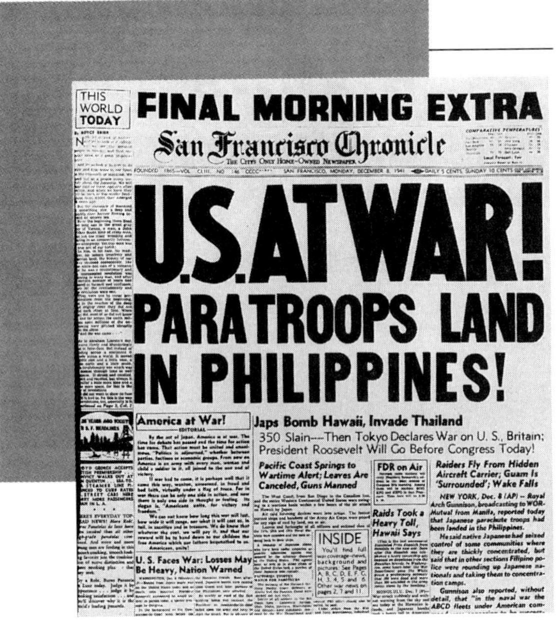

THIS WORLD TODAY

FINAL MORNING EXTRA

San Francisco Chronicle

U.S. AT WAR!

PARATROOPS LAND IN PHILIPPINES!

America at War!

Japs Bomb Hawaii, Invade Thailand

350 Slain—Then Tokyo Declares War on U. S., Britain; President Roosevelt Will Go Before Congress Today!

Pacific Coast Springs to Wartime Alert; Leaves Are Canceled, Guns Manned

FDR on Air

Raiders Fly From Hidden Aircraft Carrier; Guam Is 'Surrounded'; Wake Falls

NEW YORK, Dec. 8 (AP) — Royal Arch Gunnison, broadcasting to WOR-Mutual from Manila, reported today that Japanese parachute troops had been landed in the Philippines.

He said native Japanese had seized control of some communities where they are thickly concentrated, but said that in other sections Filipino police were rounding up Japanese nationals and taking them to concentration camps.

Gunnison also reported, without detail, that "in the naval war the ABCD fleets under American com-

Raids Took a Heavy Toll, Hawaii Says

INSIDE

You'll find full war coverage—news, background and pictures. See Pages A, B, C, D, E, F, G, H, 3, 4, 5 and 6. Other war news on pages 2, 7 and 11.

U. S. Faces War; Losses May Be Heavy, Nation Warned

BY DECEMBER 1941 THE UNITED States was in fact at war, but it is hard to see how a formal declaration could have come about had it not been for Japan. Japanese-American relations had worsened steadily after Japan resumed its war on China in 1937. In July 1940, with Japanese troops threatening French Indochina, Congress placed exports of aviation gasoline and certain types of scrap iron to Japan under a licensing system; in September all sales of scrap were banned. After the Japanese signed a treaty of alliance with Germany and Italy in September 1940, Roosevelt extended the embargo to include machine tools and other items. The Japanese, pushed ahead relentlessly despite the economic pressures.

The Road to Pearl Harbor

Neither the United States nor Japan wanted war. In the spring of 1941 Secretary of State Hull conferred in Washington with the Japanese ambassador, Kichisaburo Nomura, in an effort to resolve their differences. Hull demanded that Japan withdraw from China and promise not to attack the Dutch and French colonies in Southeast Asia. How he expected to get Japan to give up its conquests without either making concessions or going to war is not clear.

Japan might well have accepted limited annexations in the area in return for the removal of American trade restrictions, but Hull seemed bent on converting the Japanese to pacifism by exhortation. He insisted on total withdrawal, to which even the moderates in Japan would not agree. When Hitler invaded the USSR, thereby removing the threat of Soviet intervention in the Far East, Japan decided to occupy Indochina even at the risk of war with the United States. Roosevelt retaliated in July 1941 by freezing Japanese assets in the United States and clamping an embargo on oil.

Now the war party in Japan assumed control. Nomura was instructed to tell Hull that his country would refrain from further expansion if the United States and Great Britain would cut off all aid to China and lift the economic blockade. When the United States rejected these demands, the Japanese pre-

Chapter-opening illustration:
The day after the bombing at Pearl Harbor, Congress declared war on Japan. The *San Francisco Chronicle* for December 8, 1941, heralds the news.

pared to assault the Dutch East Indies, British Malaya, and the Philippines. To immobilize the U.S. Pacific Fleet, they planned a surprise aerial raid on the Hawaiian naval base at Pearl Harbor.

An American cryptanalyst, Colonel William F. Friedman, had cracked the Japanese diplomatic code and the government had good reason to believe that war was imminent. But in the hectic rush of events, both military and civilian authorities failed to make effective use of the information collected. They expected the blow to fall somewhere in Southeast Asia, possibly in the Philippines.

The garrison at Pearl Harbor was alerted against "a surprise aggressive move in any direction." The commanders there, Admiral Husband E. Kimmel and General Walter C. Short, believing an attack impossible, took precautions only against Japanese sabotage. Thus when planes from Japanese aircraft carriers swooped down on Pearl Harbor on the morning of December 7, they found easy targets. In less than two hours they reduced the Pacific Fleet to a smoking ruin.

Never had American arms suffered a more devastating or shameful defeat. On December 8, Congress declared war on Japan. Formal war with Germany and Italy was still not inevitable—isolationists were far more ready to resist the "yellow peril" in Asia than to fight in Europe. The Axis powers, however, honored their treaty obligations to Japan and on December 11 declared war on the United States. America was now fully engaged in the great world conflict.

Mobilizing the Home Front

War placed immense strains on the American economy and produced immense results. About 15 million men and women entered the armed services; they, and in part the millions more in Allied uniforms, had to be fed, clothed, housed, and supplied with equipment ranging from typewriters and paper clips to rifles and grenades, tanks and airplanes. Congress granted wide emergency powers to the president. It refrained from excessive meddling in administrative problems and in military strategy.

Roosevelt was an inspiring war leader but not a very good administrator. Any honest account of the war on the home front must reveal glaring examples of confusion, inefficiency, and pointless bickering. The squabbling and waste characteristic of the early New Deal period made relatively little difference—what mattered then was raising the nation's spirits and keeping people occupied; efficiency was less than essential, however desirable. In wartime the nation's fate, perhaps that of the entire free world, depended on delivering weapons and supplies to the battlefronts.

The confusion attending economic mobilization can easily be overstressed. Nearly all Roosevelt's basic decisions were sensible and humane: to pay a large part of the cost of the war by collecting taxes rather than by borrowing and to base taxation on ability to pay; to ration scarce raw materials and consumer goods; to regulate prices and wages. If these decisions were not always translated into action with perfect effectiveness, they always operated in the direction of efficiency and the public good.

Roosevelt's greatest accomplishment was his inspiring of business leaders, workers, and farmers with a sense of national purpose. In this respect his function duplicated his earlier role in fighting the depression, and he performed it with even greater success.

A sense of the tremendous economic expansion caused by the demands of war can most easily be captured by reference to official statistics of production. In 1939 the United States was still mired in the Great Depression. The gross national product amounted to about $91.3 billion. In 1945, after allowing for changes in the price level, it was $166.6 billion. Manufacturing output nearly doubled, and agricultural output rose 22 percent. In 1939 the United States turned out fewer than 6,000 airplanes; in 1944, more than 96,000.

Wartime experience proved that the Keynesian economists were correct in predicting that government spending would spark economic growth. About 8 million persons were unemployed in June 1940. After Pearl Harbor, unemployment practically disappeared, and by 1945 the civilian work force had increased by nearly 7 million. Military mobilization had begun well before December 1941, by which time 1.6 million men were already under arms. Economic mobilization proceeded much more slowly, mainly because the president refused to centralize authority. For months after Pearl Harbor various civilian agencies squabbled with the military over everything from the allocation of scarce raw materials to the technical specifications of weapons. Roosevelt refused to settle these interagency conflicts as only he could have.

The War Economy

Yet by early 1943 the nation's economic machinery had been converted to a wartime footing and was functioning smoothly. Supreme Court Justice James F. Byrnes resigned from the Court to become a sort of "economic czar." His Office of War Mobilization had complete control over the issuance of priorities and over prices. Rents, food prices, and wages were strictly regulated, and items in short supply were rationed to consumers. Wages and prices had soared during 1942, but after April 1943 they leveled off. Thereafter, the cost of living scarcely changed until controls were lifted after the war.

Expanded industrial production together with conscription caused a labor shortage that increased the bargaining power of workers. At the same time, the national emergency required some limitation on the workers' right to take advantage of this power. After Pearl Harbor, Roosevelt created the National War Labor Board to arbitrate disputes and stabilize wage rates. All changes in wages had to have the board's approval.

Prosperity and stiffer government controls added significantly to the strength of organized labor; indeed, the war had more to do with institutionalizing industrywide collective bargaining than the New Deal period. As workers recognized the benefits of union membership, they flocked into the organizations. Generally speaking, wages and prices remained in fair balance. Overtime work fattened paychecks, and a new stress in labor contracts on paid vacations, premium pay for night work, and various forms of employer-subsidized health insurance were added benefits. The war effort had almost no adverse effect on the standard of living of the average citizen, a vivid demonstration of the productivity of the American economy. The manufacture of automobiles ceased and pleasure driving became next to impossible because of gasoline rationing, but most civilian activities went on much as they had before Pearl Harbor. Plastics replaced metals in toys, containers, and other products. Although items such as meat, sugar, and shoes were rationed, they were doled out in amounts adequate for the needs of most persons. Americans had both guns and butter; belt-tightening of the type experienced by the other belligerents was unnecessary.

The federal government spent twice as much money between 1941 and 1945 as in its entire previous history. This made heavy borrowing necessary. The national debt, which stood at less than $49 billion in 1941, increased by more than that amount each year between 1942 and 1945. However, more than 40 percent of the total was met by taxation, a far larger proportion than in any earlier war.

This policy helped check inflation by siphoning off money that would otherwise have competed for scarce consumer goods. High taxes on incomes (up to 94 percent) and on excess profits (95 percent), together with a limit of $25,000 a year after taxes on salaries, convinced the people that no one was profiting inordinately from the war effort.

The income tax, which had never before touched the mass of white-collar and industrial workers, was extended downward until nearly everyone had to pay it. To ensure efficient collection of the relatively small sums paid by most persons, Congress adopted the payroll-deduction system proposed by Beardsley Ruml, chairman of the Federal Reserve Bank of New York. Employers withheld the taxes owed by workers from their paychecks and turned the money over to the government.

The steeply graduated tax rates, combined with a general increase in the income of workers and farmers, effected a substantial shift in the distribution of wealth in the United States. The poor became richer, while the rich, if not actually poorer, collected a smaller proportion of the national income. The wealthiest 1 percent of the population had received 13.4 percent of the national income in 1935 and 11.5 percent in 1941. In 1944 this group received 6.7 percent.

War and Social Change

Enormous social effects stemmed from this shift, but World War II altered the patterns of American life in so many ways that it would be wrong to ascribe the transformations to any single source. Never was the population more fluid. The millions who put on uniforms found themselves transported first to training camps in every section of the country and then to battlefields scattered from Europe and Africa to the far reaches of the Pacific. Burgeoning new defense plants drew other millions to places like Hanford, Washington, and Oak Ridge, Tennessee, where great atomic energy installations were constructed, and to the aircraft factories of California and other states. The population of California increased by more than 50 percent in the 1940s, that of other far western states almost as much.

During the war, marriage and birth rates rose steeply because many people had been forced to put off marrying and having children for financial reasons during the Great Depression. Now wartime prosperity put an end to that problem at the same time that young couples were feeling the need to put down roots when the husbands were going off to risk death in distant lands. The population of the United States had increased by only 3 million during the depression decade of the 1930s; during the next *five* years it rose by 6.5 million.

Minorities in Time of War: Blacks, Hispanics, and Indians

Several factors operated to improve the lot of black Americans. One was their own growing tendency to demand fair treatment. Another was the reaction of Americans to Hitler's barbaric treatment of millions of Jews, which compelled millions of white citizens to reexamine their views about race. If the nation expected blacks to risk their lives for the common good, how could it continue to treat them as second-class citizens? Black leaders pointed out the inconsistency between fighting for democracy abroad and ignoring it at home. "We want democracy in Alabama," the NAACP announced, and this argument too had some effect on white thinking.

Blacks in the armed forces were treated more fairly than they had been in World War I. They were enlisted for the first time in the air force and the marines, and they were given more responsible positions in the army and navy. The army commissioned its first black general. Some 600 black pilots won their wings. Altogether about a million served, about half of them overseas.

However, segregation in the armed services was maintained, and black soldiers were mistreated in and around army camps, especially those in the South. In 1943 William Hastie, a former New Dealer who was serving as an adviser on racial matters, resigned in protest because of the "reactionary policies and discriminatory practices of the Army and Air Force in matters affecting Negroes."

Economic realities operated significantly to the advantage of black civilians. More of them had been unemployed in proportion to their numbers than any other group; now the labor shortage brought employment for all. More than 5 million blacks moved from rural areas to cities between 1940 and 1945 in search of work. At least a million found defense jobs in the North and on the West Coast. The black population of a dozen important cities more than doubled in that brief period. The migrants were mostly forced to live in dreadful urban ghettos, but their very concentration made them important politically.

These gains failed to satisfy black leaders. The NAACP, which increased its membership tenfold during the war, adopted a more militant stance than in World War I. Discrimination in defense plants seemed far less tolerable than it had in 1917. A. Philip Randolph, president of the Brotherhood of Sleeping Car Porters, organized a march of blacks on Washington in 1941 to demand equal opportunity for black workers. Fearing possible violence and the wrath of southern members of Congress, Roosevelt tried to persuade Randolph to call off the march. "It would make the country look bad," he claimed. But Randolph persisted, and Roosevelt finally agreed to issue an order prohibiting discrimination in plants with defense contracts. He also set up the Fair Employment Practices Committee to see that the order was carried out. Executive Order 8802 was poorly enforced, but it opened up better jobs to some workers.

Prejudice and mistreatment did not cease. In areas around defense plants, white resentment of the black "invasion" mounted. By 1943 some 50,000 new blacks residents had crowded into Detroit. A wave of strikes disrupted production at plants where white workers were protesting the hiring of blacks. In June a race riot marked by looting and bloody fighting went on for three days. By the time federal troops restored order, 25 blacks and 9 whites had been killed. Rioting also erupted in New York and many other cities.

In Los Angeles the attacks were on Mexican-born "zoot suiters," gangs whose uniforms were broad-brimmed fedoras, long coats, and pegged trousers. Wartime employment needs resulted in a reversal of the depression policy of forcing Mexicans out of the Southwest, and many thousands flocked north. Most had to accept menial jobs, but work was plentiful and well paid compared to Mexican rates.

Some of the young Hispanics formed gangs. They had money in their pockets and their behavior was not always as circumspect as local residents would have preferred. A grand jury undertook an investigation and the Los Angeles City Council even debated banning the wearing of zoot suits. In 1943 rioting broke out when sailors on shore leave began roaming the area attacking anyone they could find wearing a zoot suit.

There were understandable reasons why white city dwellers resented the black and Hispanic newcomers, but the willingness of white leaders to tolerate discriminatory behavior at a time when national unity was so necessary was particularly frustrating. For example, blood plasma from blacks and whites was kept separately even though the two "varieties" were indistinguishable and the process of storing plasma had been devised by a black doctor, Charles Drew.

Blacks became increasingly bitter. Roy Wilkins, head of the NAACP, put it this way in 1942: "No Negro leader with a constituency can face his members today and ask full support for the war in the light of the atmosphere the government has created." Many black newspaper editors were so critical of the administration that conservatives demanded they be indicted for sedition.

Roosevelt would have none of that, but he thought the militants should hold their demands in abeyance until the war had been won. Apparently he failed to realize the depth of black anger, and in this he was no different from the majority of whites. A revolution was in the making, yet in 1942 a poll revealed that a solid majority of whites still believed that black Americans were satisfied with their place in society.

Concern about national unity did lead to a reaction against the New Deal policy of encouraging Indians to develop self-governing communities. There was even talk of trying to "assimilate" Indians into the larger society. John Collier resigned as commissioner of Indian affairs in disgust in 1945.

The war encouraged assimilation in several ways. More than 24,000 Indians served in the armed forces, an experience that brought them in contact with new people, new places, and new ideas. Many thousands more left the reservations to work in defense industries in cities all over the country.

The Treatment of German-, Italian-, and Japanese-Americans

However, although World War II affected the American people far more drastically than World War I had, it produced much less intolerance and fewer examples of the repression of individual freedom of opinion. People seemed able to distinguish between Italian fascism and Italian-Americans and between the government of Nazi Germany and Americans of German descent in a way that had escaped their parents. The fact that few Italian-Americans admired Mussolini and that nearly all German-Americans were anti-Nazi helps explain this. So does the fact that both groups were prepared to use their considerable political power to protect themselves against abuse.

But the underlying public attitude was more important. Americans went to war in 1941 without illusions and without enthusiasm, determined to win but expecting only to preserve what they had. They therefore found it easier to tolerate dissent and to concentrate on the real foreign enemy without venting their feelings on domestic scapegoats.

The one flagrant example of intolerance was the relocation of the West Coast Japanese in internment camps in Wyoming, Arizona, and other interior states. About 110,000 Americans of Japanese ancestry, the majority of them native-born citizens, were rounded up and sent off against their will. Not one was accused of sabotage or spying.

The Japanese were properly indignant but also baffled, in some cases hurt more than angry. "We didn't feel Japanese. We felt American," one woman, the mother of three small children, recalled many years later. A fisherman remembered that besides his nets and all his other equipment, he had to leave behind a "brand-new 1941 Plymouth." "We hadn't done anything wrong. We obeyed the laws," he told an interviewer. "I lost everything." Then he added, almost plaintively, "But I don't blame anyone. It was a war."

The government's excuse was fear that some of

the Japanese *might* be disloyal. (It must not be forgotten that the Japanese had attacked Pearl Harbor without warning, something that even the Nazis had not done.) Nevertheless, racial prejudice (the "yellow peril") and frustration at not being able to strike a quick blow at Japan in retaliation had much to do with the callous decision to force people into camps. The Supreme Court upheld the relocation order in *Korematsu* v. *United States* (1944), but in *Ex parte Endo* it forbade the internment of loyal Japanese-American citizens. Unfortunately, the latter decision was not handed down until December 1944.

Women's Contribution to the War Effort

With economic activity on the rise and millions of men going off to war, a sudden need for women workers developed. By 1944 fully 6.5 million additional women had entered the work force, and at the peak of war production in 1945 more than 19 million women were employed. Further thousands were serving in the armed forces.

At first there was considerable resistance to what was happening. About one husband in three objected in principle to his wife's taking a job. Many employers in fields traditionally dominated by men doubted that women could handle their tasks. Unions frequently made the same point. A Seattle official of the International Brotherhood of Boilermakers and Iron Shipbuilders said of women job applicants: "If one of these girls pressed the trigger on the yard rivet guns, she'd be going one way and the rivet the other." This was perhaps reasonable, though many women were soon doing "men's work" in the shipyards. But the Seattle taxicab union objected to women drivers on the ground that "drivers are forced to do things and go places that would be embarrassing for a woman to do."

These male attitudes lost force in the face of the escalating demand for labor. That employers usually did not have to pay women as much as men made them attractive, as did the fact that they were not subject to the draft. Soon women were working not

Women welders beveling armor plate on tank bodies, photographed in 1943 by Margaret Bourke-White of *Life*.

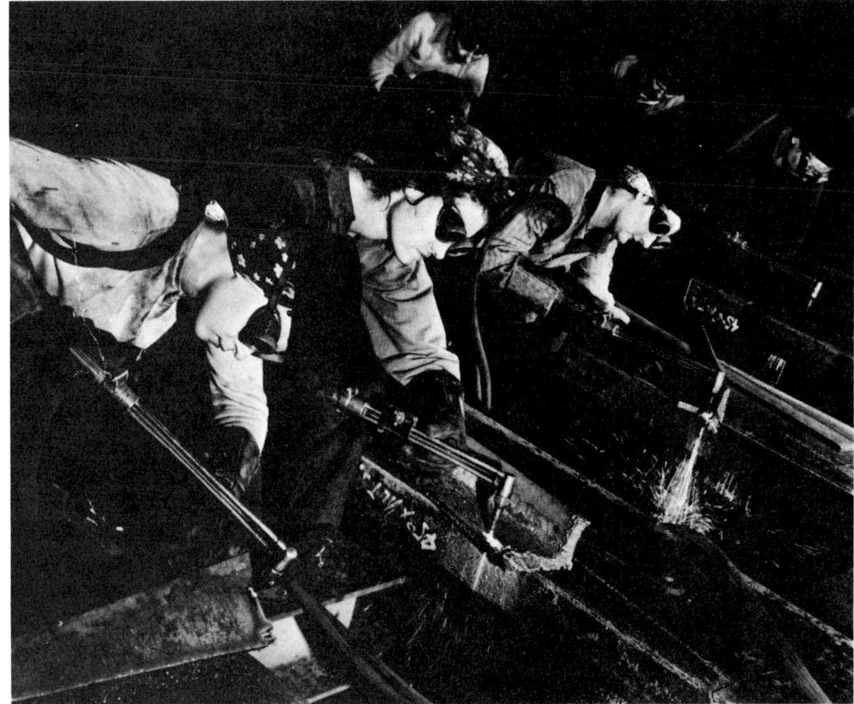

only as riveters and cab drivers but also as welders, machine tool operators, and in dozens of other occupations formerly the exclusive domain of men.

Women took wartime jobs for many reasons other than the obvious economic ones. Patriotism was important, but so were the desire for independence and even loneliness. "It's thrilling work, and exciting, and something women have never done before," one women reported. She was talking about driving a taxi.

Black women workers had a particularly difficult time, employers often hesitating to hire them because they were black, black men looking down on them because they were women. But the need for willing hands was vast. Sybil Lewis of Sapula, Oklahoma, went to Los Angeles and found a job as a waitress. Then she entered a training program at Lockheed Aircraft and became a riveter making airplane gas tanks. When an unfriendly foreman gave her a less attractive assignment, she moved on to Douglas Aircraft. By 1943 she was working as a welder in a shipyard.

Few wartime jobs were easy, and for women there were special burdens, not the least of which was the prejudice of many of the men they worked with. For married women there was housework to do after a long day. One War Manpower Commission bureaucrat figured out that Detroit defense plants were losing 100,000 woman-hours a month because of employees' taking a day off to do the family laundry. Although the government made some effort to provide day-care facilities, there were never enough; this was one reason why relatively few women with small children entered the labor market during the war.

The war also affected the lives of women who did not take jobs. Families by the tens and hundreds of thousands pulled up stakes and moved to the centers of war production, such as Detroit and southern California. Housing was always in short supply, and while the men went off to the familiar surroundings of yard and factory, their wives had to cope with cramped quarters, ration books, the absence of friends and relatives, and the problems encountered by their children in strange schools and playgrounds.

Newlywed wives of soldiers and sailors (known generally as "war brides") often followed their husbands to training camps, where life was often as difficult as it was around defense plants. Whatever their own behavior, war brides quickly learned that society applied a double standard to infidelity, especially when it involved a man presumably risking his life in some far-off land. There was a general relaxation of sexual inhibitions, part of a decades-long trend accelerated by the war. So many hasty marriages, followed by long periods of separation, also brought a rise in divorces.

Of course, "ordinary" housewives also had to deal with shortages, ration books, and other inconveniences during the war. In addition, most took on other duties and bore other burdens, such as tending "victory gardens" and preserving their harvests, using crowded public transportation when there was no gas for the family car, mending and patching old clothes, participating in salvage drives, and doing volunteer work for hospitals, the Red Cross, or various civil defense and servicemen's centers.

Allied Strategy: Europe First

Only days after Pearl Harbor, Prime Minister Churchill and his military chiefs met in Washington with Roosevelt and his advisers. In every quarter of the globe, disaster threatened. The Japanese were gobbling up the Far East. Hitler's armies were preparing for a massive attack in the direction of Stalingrad, on the Volga River. German divisions under General Erwin Rommel were beginning a drive across North Africa toward the Suez Canal. U-boats were taking a heavy toll in the North Atlantic.

The decision of the strategists was to concentrate first against the Germans. Japan's conquests were in remote and, from the Allied point of view, relatively unimportant regions. If Russia surrendered, Hitler might well be able to invade Great Britain, thus making his position in Europe impregnable.

During the summer of 1942, Allied planes began to bomb German cities. Though air attacks did not destroy the German armies' capacity to fight, they hampered war production, tangled communications, and brought the war home to the German people in awesome fashion.

In November 1942 an Allied army commanded by General Dwight D. Eisenhower struck at French North Africa. After the fall of France, the Nazis had set up a puppet regime in the parts of France not occupied by their troops, with headquarters at Vichy in central France. This collaborationist Vichy government controlled French North Africa. But the North African commandant, Admiral Jean Darlan, promptly switched sides when Eisenhower's forces landed. After a brief show of resistance, the French surrendered.

Eisenhower then pressed forward quickly against the Germans. In February 1943 at Kasserine Pass in the desert south of Tunis, American tanks met Rommel's Afrika Korps. The battle ended in a standoff, but with British troops closing in from Egyptian bases to the east, the Germans were soon trapped and crushed. In May, after Rommel had been recalled to Germany, his army surrendered.

WORLD WAR II, EUROPEAN THEATER

In July 1943, while air attacks on Germany continued and the Russians slowly pushed the Germans back from the gates of Stalingrad, the Allies invaded Sicily from Africa. In September they advanced to the Italian mainland. Mussolini had already fallen from power, and his successor, Marshal Pietro Badoglio, surrendered. However, the German troops in Italy threw up an almost impregnable defense across the rugged Italian peninsula. The Anglo-American army inched forward, paying heavily for every advance. Rome did not fall until June 1944, and months of hard fighting remained before the country was cleared of Germans.

Germany Overwhelmed

By the time the Allies had taken Rome, the mighty army needed to invade France had been collected in England under Eisenhower's command. On D day, June 6, 1944, the assault forces stormed ashore along the coast of Normandy, supported by a great armada and thousands of planes and paratroops. Against fierce but ill-coordinated German resistance, they established a beachhead; within a few weeks a million troops were on French soil.

Thereafter victory was assured, though nearly a year of fighting still lay ahead. In August the American Third Army under General George S. Patton erupted southward into Brittany and then veered east toward Paris. Another Allied army invaded France from the Mediterranean in mid-August and advanced rapidly north. Free French troops were given the honor of liberating Paris on August 25, and by mid-September the Allies were fighting on the edge of Germany itself.

While Eisenhower was regrouping, the Germans on December 16 launched a counterattack, planned by Hitler himself, against the Allied center in the Ardennes Forest. The Germans hoped to break through to the Belgian port of Antwerp, thereby splitting the Allied armies in two. The plan was foolhardy and therefore unexpected, and it almost succeeded. But once the element of surprise had been overcome, their chance of breaking through to the sea was lost. Eisenhower concentrated first on preventing them from broadening the break in his lines and then on blunting the point of their advance. By late January 1945 the old line had been reestablished. The so-called Battle of the Bulge cost the United States 77,000 casualties and delayed Eisenhower's offensive, but it exhausted the Germans' last reserves.

The Allies then pressed forward to the Rhine, winning a bridgehead on the far bank of the river on March 7. Thereafter, another German city fell almost daily. With the Russians racing westward against crumbling resistance, the end could not be long delayed.

As the Americans drove swiftly forward, they began to overrun Nazi concentration camps where millions of Jews had been murdered. Word of this holocaust in which no less than 6 million people were slaughtered had reached the United States much earlier. At first the news had been dismissed as propaganda. Hitler was known to hate Jews and to have persecuted them, but that he could order the murder of millions of innocent people, even children, seemed beyond belief. By 1943, however, the truth could not be denied.

Little could be done about people already in the camps, but there were thousands of refugees in occupied Europe who might have been spirited to safety. President Roosevelt declined to make the effort; he even refused to bomb the death camps on the grounds that the destruction of German soldiers and military equipment took precedence over any other objective. Thus when American journalists entered the camps with the advancing troops, saw the heaps of still unburied corpses, and talked with the emaciated survivors, their reports caused a storm of protest.

Why Roosevelt acted as he did has never been satisfactorily explained. In any case, in April, American and Russian forces made contact at the Elbe River. A few days later, with Russian shells reducing his capital to rubble, Hitler, by then probably insane, took his own life in his Berlin air raid shelter. On May 8, Germany surrendered.

The Naval War in the Pacific

While armies were being trained and matériel accumulated for the attack on Germany, much of the available American strength was diverted to the task of preventing further Japanese expansion. The navy's aircraft carriers had escaped destruction at Pearl Harbor, a stroke of immense good fortune because the airplane had revolutionized naval warfare. Commanders discovered that carrier-based planes were far more effective against warships than the heaviest naval artillery thanks to their greater range and more concentrated firepower.

This truth was demonstrated in May 1942 in the Battle of the Coral Sea, which lies northeast of Australia and south of New Guinea and the Solomon Islands. Mastery of these waters would cut Australia off from Hawaii and thus from American aid. Japanese Admiral Isoroku Yamamoto had dispatched a large fleet of troop ships, screened by many warships to attack Port Moresby, on the southern New Guinea coast. On May 7 and 8, planes from the American carriers *Lexington* and *Yorktown* struck the convoy's screen, sinking a small carrier and damaging a large one. Superficially, the battle seemed a victory for the Japanese, for their planes mortally wounded the *Lexington* and sank two other ships, but the troop transports had been forced to turn back, and Port Moresby was saved. Although large numbers of cruisers and destroyers took part in the action, all the destruction was wrought by carrier aircraft.

Encouraged by the Coral Sea "victory," Yamamoto decided to attack Midway Island, west of Hawaii. Between June 4 and 7, control of the Central Pacific was decided entirely by air power. American dive bombers sent four large carriers to the bottom. About 300 Japanese planes were destroyed. The United States lost only the *Yorktown* and a destroyer. The initiative in the Pacific war shifted to the Americans.

American land forces were under the command of Douglas MacArthur, a brilliant but egocentric general whose judgment was sometimes distorted by his intense concern for his own reputation. MacArthur was in command of American troops in the Philippine Islands when the Japanese struck in December 1941. President Roosevelt had him evacuated by PT boat to escape capture.

Thereafter, MacArthur was obsessed with the idea of personally leading an American army back to the Philippines, and he convinced the Joint Chiefs of Staff, who determined strategy. They organized two separate drives, one from New Guinea toward the Philippines under MacArthur, the other through the

WORLD WAR II, PACIFIC THEATER

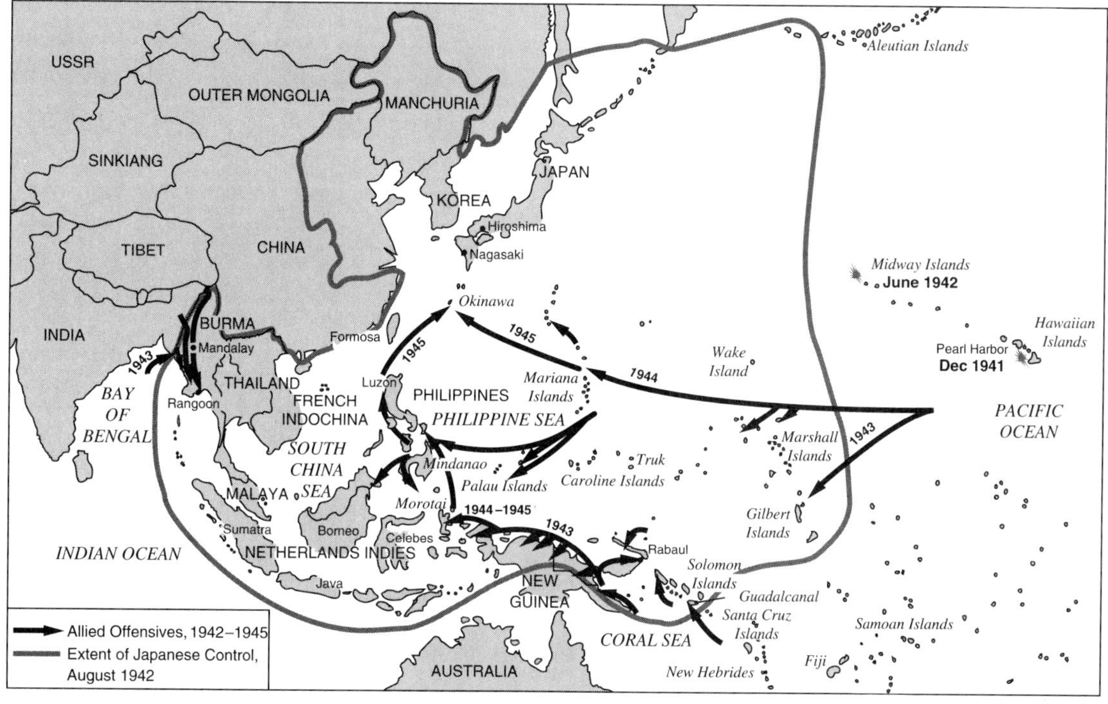

central Pacific toward Tokyo under Admiral Chester W. Nimitz.

Island Hopping

Before commencing this two-pronged advance, the Americans had to eject the Japanese from the Solomon Islands. Beginning in August 1942, a series of land, sea, and air battles raged around Guadalcanal Island in this archipelago. Once again American air power was decisive, and by February 1943, Guadalcanal had been secured.

In the autumn of 1943 the American drives toward Japan and the Philippines got under way at last. In the central Pacific campaign the Guadalcanal action was repeated on a smaller scale from Tarawa in the Gilbert Islands to Kwajalein and Eniwetok in the Marshalls. The Japanese soldiers on these islands fought like the Spartans at Thermopylae for every foot of ground. They had to be blasted and burned from tunnels and concrete pillboxes with hand grenades, flamethrowers, and dynamite. They almost never surrendered. But Admiral Nimitz's forces were in every case victorious. By midsummer of 1944 this arm of the American advance had taken Saipan and Guam in the Marianas. Now land-based bombers were within range of Tokyo.

Meanwhile, MacArthur was leapfrogging along the New Guinea coast toward the Philippines. In October 1944 he made good his promise to return to the islands, landing on Leyte, south of Luzon. Two great naval clashes in Philippine waters, the Battle of the Philippine Sea (June 1944) and the Battle for Leyte Gulf (October 1944), completed the destruction of Japan's sea power and reduced its air force to a band of fanatical suicide pilots called *kamikazes,* who tried to crash bomb-laden planes against American warships and airstrips. The *kamikazes* caused much damage but could not turn the tide. In February 1945, MacArthur liberated Manila.

The end was now inevitable. B-29 Superfortress bombers from the Marianas rained high explosives and firebombs on Japan. The islands of Iwo Jima and Okinawa, only a few hundred miles from Tokyo, fell to the Americans in March and June 1945. But it seemed possible that it would take another year of fighting and a million more American casualties to subdue the main Japanese islands.

"The Shatterer of Worlds"

At this point came the most controversial decision of the entire war, and it was made by a newcomer on the world scene. In November 1944, Roosevelt had been elected to a fourth term, easily defeating Thomas E. Dewey. Instead of renominating Henry A. Wallace for vice-president, the Democrats had picked Senator Harry S Truman of Missouri. In April 1945, President Roosevelt suddenly died of a cerebral hemorrhage. Thus it was Truman who had to decide what to do when a mere three months later American scientists placed in his hands a new and awful weapon, the atomic bomb.

After Roosevelt had responded to Albert Einstein's warning in 1939, government-sponsored atomic research had proceeded rapidly. The manufacture of the artificial element plutonium at Hanford, Washington, and uranium 235 at Oak Ridge, Tennessee, continued along with the design and construction of a transportable atomic bomb at Los Alamos, New Mexico. A successful bomb was exploded in the New Mexican desert on July 16, 1945.

Should a bomb with the destructive force of 20,000 tons of TNT be employed against Japan? By striking a major city, its dreadful power could be demonstrated convincingly, yet doing so would bring death to tens of thousands of Japanese civilians. Truman was torn between his awareness that the bomb was "the most terrible thing ever discovered" and his hope that using it "would bring the war to an end" and thus save lives, Japanese as well as Allied. On a less humane level, Truman was influenced by a desire to end the war before the Soviet Union could intervene effectively and thus claim a role in the peacemaking. For these and perhaps other reasons, the president chose to go ahead.

The moral soundness of Truman's decision has been debated ever since. Hatred of the Japanese must have had something to do with the decision. But it is also likely that more Japanese civilians would have died, far more than the American soldiers who would have perished, if Japan had had to be invaded.

In any case, on August 6 the Superfortress *Enola Gay* dropped an atomic bomb on Hiroshima, killing about 78,000 persons and injuring nearly 100,000 more out of a population of 344,000. Three days later, while the stunned Japanese still hesitated, a second bomb, the only other one so far assembled, hit Nagasaki. This second drop was far less defensible morally, but it had the desired result. On August 15, Japan surrendered.

Thus ended the greatest war in history. Its cost was beyond calculation. No accurate count could be made even of the dead; we know only that it was in the neighborhood of 20 million. No one could call the war a benefit to mankind, but in the late summer of 1945 the future looked bright. Fascism was dead. Many believed that the Soviet communists were ready to cooperate in rebuilding Europe. In the United States isolationism had disappeared.

Out of the death and destruction had come new technology that seemed to herald a better and more peaceful world. Advances in airplane design and the development of radar were about to revolutionize travel and the transportation of goods. Improvements in surgery and other medical advances held the promise of saving millions of lives, and the development of penicillin and other antibiotics, which had greatly reduced the death rate among troops, would perhaps banish infectious disease. Above all, there was the power of the atom, which could be harnessed to serve peaceful ends.

The period of reconstruction would be prolonged, but with all the great powers adhering to the new United Nations charter, drafted at San Francisco in June 1945, international cooperation could be counted on to ease the burdens of the victims of war and help the poor and underdeveloped parts of the world toward economic and political independence. Such at least was the hope of millions in the victorious summer of 1945.

Wartime Diplomacy

That hope was not realized, chiefly because of a conflict that developed between the Soviet Union and the western allies. During the course of World War II every instrument of mass persuasion in the country had been directed at convincing the people that the Russians were fighting America's battle as well as their own. Even before Pearl Harbor, former Ambassador Joseph E. Davies wrote in his best-selling *Mission to Moscow* (1941) that the communist leaders were "a group of able, strong men" with "honest convictions and integrity of purpose" who were "devoted to the cause of peace for both ideological and practical reasons." Communism was based "on the same principle of the 'brotherhood of man' which Jesus preached."

During the war Americans with as different points of view as General Douglas MacArthur and Vice-President Henry A. Wallace took strongly pro-Soviet positions. In 1943 *Time* named Stalin its "Man of the Year." A number of motion pictures also contributed to revising the attitude of the average American toward the USSR. In *One World* (1943), Wendell Willkie wrote glowingly of the Russian people, their "effective society," and their simple, warmhearted leader. When he suggested jokingly to Stalin that if he continued to make progress in improving the education of his people he might educate himself out of a job, the dictator "threw his head back and laughed and laughed," Willkie recorded. "Mr. Willkie, you know I grew up a Georgian peasant. I am unschooled in pretty talk. All I can say is I like you very much."

These views were naive, to say the least, but the identity of interests of the United States and the Soviet Union was very real during the war. Russian military leaders conferred regularly with their British and American counterparts and fulfilled their obligations scrupulously.

The Soviets repeatedly expressed a willingness to cooperate with the Allies in dealing with postwar problems. The USSR was in January 1942 one of the 26 signers of the Declaration of the United Nations, in which the Allies promised to eschew territorial aggrandizement after the war, to respect the right of all peoples to determine their own form of government, to work for freer trade and international economic cooperation, and to force the disarmament of the aggressor nations.

In October 1943, during a conference in Moscow with U.S. Secretary of State Cordell Hull and British Foreign Minister Anthony Eden, Soviet Foreign Minister V. M. Molotov joined in setting up the European Advisory Commission to divide Germany into occupation zones after the war. That December, at a conference in Teheran, Iran, Roosevelt, Churchill, and Stalin discussed plans for a new league of nations. When Roosevelt described the kind of world organization he envisaged, the Soviet dictator offered a number of constructive suggestions.

At another meeting at Yalta, Ukraine, in February 1945, the three leaders joined in a call for a conference to be held in San Francisco to draft a charter for the United Nations. At the San Francisco gathering it was decided that each member of the UN should have a seat in the General Assembly. The locus of authority, however, was placed in the Security Council, which was to consist of five permanent members (the United States, the Soviet Union, Great Britain, France, and China) and six others elected for two-year terms. Thus any great power could veto any UN action it did not like. The charter paid lip service to the Wilsonian ideal of an international police force, but it limited that force by incorporating the limitations Henry Cabot Lodge had proposed in his 1919 reservations to the League of Nations covenant.

The Cold War Under Way

Long before the war in Europe ended, however, the Allies had clashed over important policy matters. Since later world tensions developed from decisions made at this time, an understanding of the disagreements is essential for evaluating several decades of history. Unfortunately, complete understanding is not yet possible, which explains why the subject remains controversial.

Much depends on one's view of the postwar Soviet system. If the Soviet government under Stalin was bent on world domination, events of the so-called Cold War fall readily into one pattern of interpretation. If the USSR, having bravely and at enormous cost endured an unprovoked assault by the Nazis, was seeking only to protect itself against the possibility of another invasion, these events are best explained differently.

Because the United States has opened nearly all its diplomatic records, we know a great deal about how American foreign policy was formulated and about the mixed motives and mistaken judgments of American leaders. This helps explain why many scholars have been critical of American policy and the "cold warriors" who made and directed it. The Soviet Union, in stark contrast, excluded historians from its archives, and consequently we know little about the motivations and inner workings of Soviet policy. Was Russia "committed to overturning the international system and to endless expansion in pursuit of world dominance?" Daniel Yergin asks in *Shattered Peace.* Only access to Soviet records can make possible an answer to this vitally important question.

The Soviets resented the British-American delay in opening up a second front. They were fighting for survival against the full power of the German armies; any invasion, even an unsuccessful one, would relieve some of the pressure. Roosevelt

Churchill, Roosevelt, and Stalin photographed at the week-long Yalta conference in February 1945. By April 1945, Roosevelt was dead.

and Churchill would not move until they were ready, and Stalin had to accept their decision. At the same time, Stalin never concealed his determination to protect his country against future attack by extending its western boundary after the war. He warned the Allies repeatedly that he would not tolerate any anti-Soviet government along Russia's western boundary.

Most Allied leaders, including Roosevelt, admitted privately during the war that the Soviet Union would annex territory and possess preponderant power in eastern Europe after the defeat of Germany, but they never said this publicly. They believed that free governments could somehow be created in countries like Poland and Bulgaria and that the Soviets would trust them enough to leave them to their own devices.

The Polish question was a terribly difficult one. The war, after all, had been triggered by the German attack on Poland; the British in particular felt a moral obligation to restore that nation to its prewar independence. Public opinion in Poland (and indeed in all the states along the USSR's western frontier) was strongly anti-Soviet. Yet the Soviets' legitimate interests (to say nothing of their power in the area) could not be ignored.

Yalta and Potsdam

At the Yalta conference, Roosevelt and Churchill agreed to Soviet annexation of part of Poland. In return they demanded that free elections be held in Poland itself. Stalin apparently could not understand why his allies were so concerned about the fate of a small country so remote from their strategic spheres; he could see no difference between the Soviet Union's dominating Poland and maintaining a government there that did not reflect the wishes of a majority of the Polish people and the United States' dominating many Latin American nations and supporting unpopular regimes within them. Roosevelt, however,feared that Polish-Americans of eastern European extraction would be furious if the Soviets took over their homeland.

In July 1945, following the surrender of Germany, the new president, Truman, met with Stalin and Churchill at Potsdam, outside Berlin.* They agreed to try the Nazi leaders as war criminals, made plans for exacting reparations from Germany, and confirmed the division of the country into four zones to be occupied separately by American, Russian, British, and French troops. Berlin, deep in the Soviet zone, had been split into four sectors too. Stalin rejected all arguments that he loosen his hold on eastern Europe, and Truman (who received news of the successful testing of the atomic bomb while at Potsdam) made no concessions. On both sides suspicions were mounting, positions hardening.

Yet all the advantages seemed to be with the United States. Besides its army, navy, and air force and its immense industrial potential, alone among the nations it possessed the atomic bomb. When Stalin's actions made it clear that he intended to control eastern Europe and to exert influence elsewhere in the world, most Americans first reacted somewhat in the manner of a mastiff being worried by a yapping terrier: with resentment tempered by amazement. The war had caused a fundamental change in international politics. The United States might be the strongest country in the world, but the western European nations, victor and vanquished alike, were reduced to the status of second-class powers. The Soviet Union, by contrast, had regained the influence it had held under the czars and had lost as a result of World War I and the Communist Revolution.

*Clement R. Attlee replaced Churchill during the conference after his Labour party won the British elections.

Milestones

1941 Roosevelt creates Fair Employment Practices Committee (FEPC)
Japanese attack Pearl Harbor

1942 West Coast Japanese ordered to relocation camps
Fall of the Philippines
Battle of the Coral Sea
Battle of Midway
American troops invade North Africa

1943 Race riots in Detroit and Los Angeles
Invasion of Italy
Teheran Conference

1944 Allied invasion of Normandy, France
Liberation of Paris
Battle of the Bulge

1945 Yalta Conference
San Francisco Conference to draft UN Charter
Germany surrenders (V-E Day)
Capture of Okinawa
Atomic bomb tested at Alamogordo, New Mexico
Potsdam Conference
Atomic bombs dropped on Hiroshima and Nagasaki, Japan
Japan surrenders (V-J Day)

Supplementary Reading

On prewar American-Japanese relations see Akira Iriye, **After Imperialism** (1965), and on Pearl Harbor, G. W. Prange, **At Dawn We Slept** (1981), and M. S. Slackman, **Target: Pearl Harbor** (1990). L. C. Gardner, **Economic Aspects of New Deal Diplomacy** (1971), is a critical scholarly analysis. Akira Iriye, **Power and Culture: The Japanese-American War** (1981), looks at the war in the Pacific from both sides.

The home front is discussed in Richard Polenberg, **War and Society** (1972), and A. M. Winkler, **Home Front U.S.A.** (1988). H. M. Harris, et al., eds., **The Homefront** (1984), contains a sampling of reminiscences by people in all walks of life. Social trends are covered in Steven Mintz and Susan Kellogg, **Domestic Revolutions** (1988).

The effect of the war on blacks is discussed in N. A. Wynn, **The Afro-American and the Second World War** (1976), D. J. Capeci, Jr., **Race Relations in Wartime Detroit** (1984), and A. R. Buchanan, **Black Americans in World War II** (1977). On the relocation of the Japanese, see Roger Daniels, **Concentration Camps USA** (1971), and Peter Irons, **Justice at War** (1984). The effects of the war on women are described in Karen Anderson, **Wartime Women** (1981), and S. M. Hartmann, **The Home Front and Beyond** (1982).

A. R. Buchanan, **The United States in World War II** (1964), provides an excellent overall survey of the military side of the conflict. See also David Eisenhower, **Eisenhower: At War** (1986), Stephen Ambrose, **Eisenhower** (1983), Ed Cray, **General of the Army: George C. Marshall** (1990), and D. S. Wyman, **The Abandonment of the Jews** (1984).

Wartime diplomacy is discussed in J. L. Gaddis, **The United States and the Origins of the Cold War** (1972), Gar Alperovitz, **Atomic Diplomacy** (1965), Martin Sherwin, **A World Destroyed** (1975), and Gaddis Smith, **American Diplomacy during the Second World War** (1965).

CHAPTER 30

■ ■ ■ ■ ■ ■ ■

The American Century

■ ■ ■ ■ ■ IN LATE 1945 MOST AMERICANS WERE probably more concerned with what was happening at home than with foreign developments, and no one was more aware of this than Harry Truman. When he received the news of Roosevelt's death, he claimed that he felt as though "the moon, the stars, and all the planets" had suddenly fallen on him. Although he could not have been quite as surprised as he indicated (Roosevelt was known to be in extremely poor health), he was acutely conscious of his own limitations.

Truman was born in Missouri in 1884. After service with a World War I artillery unit, he became a minor cog in the Missouri political machine of boss Tom Pendergast. In 1934 he was elected to the United States Senate, where he proved to be a loyal but obscure New Dealer. The 1944 vice-presidential nomination marked for him the height of achievement.

As president, Truman sought to carry on in the Roosevelt tradition. Curiously, he was both humble and cocky, idealistic and cold-bloodedly political. He adopted liberal objectives only to pursue them sometimes by rash, even repressive means. Too often he insulted opponents instead of convincing or conciliating them. Complications tended to confuse him, in which case he either dug in his heels or struck out blindly, usually with unfortunate results. On balance, however, he was a strong chief executive and in many ways a successful one.

The Postwar Economy

Nearly all the world leaders were worried by the possibility of a serious postwar depression, and nearly all accepted the necessity of employing government authority to stabilize the economy and speed national development. The Great Depression and the successful application of the theories of John Maynard Keynes during the war had convinced most Americans, Democrats and Republicans alike, that it was possible to prevent sharp swings in the business cycle and therefore to do away with serious unemployment by monetary and fiscal manipulation. "The agents of government must . . . put a brake at certain points where boom forces develop . . . and support

---

Chapter-opening illustration:
Dwight D. Eisenhower's victories in the 1952 and 1956 presidential elections testified that a majority of American voters did, indeed, "like Ike."

purchasing power when it becomes unduly depressed," the newly created Council of Economic Advisers reported.

When World War II ended, nearly everyone wanted to demobilize the armed forces, remove wartime controls, and reduce taxes. Yet everyone also hoped to prevent any sudden economic dislocation, check inflation, and make sure that goods in short supply were distributed fairly. Neither the politicians nor the public was able to reconcile these conflicting objectives. Labor wanted price controls retained but wage controls lifted; industrialists wished to raise prices and keep the lid on wages; farmers wanted subsidies but opposed price controls and the extension of social security benefits to agricultural workers.

President Truman failed to win either the confidence of the people or the support of Congress. On the one hand, he proposed a comprehensive program of new legislation that included a public housing scheme, aid to education, medical insurance, civil rights guarantees, a higher minimum wage, broader social security coverage, additional conservation and public power projects patterned after the TVA, increased aid to agriculture, and the retention of anti-inflationary controls. On the other hand, he ended rationing and other controls and signed a bill cutting taxes by some $6 billion. Whenever opposition to his plans developed, he vacillated between compromise and inflexibility.

Yet the country weathered the reconversion period with remarkable ease. The pent-up demand for homes, automobiles, clothing, washing machines, and countless other products, backed by the war-enforced savings of millions of people, kept factories operating at capacity. Economists had feared that the flood of veterans into the job market would cause serious unemployment. But when the veterans returned, few were unoccupied for long. The demand for labor was large and growing. In addition, the government made an unprecedented educational opportunity available to veterans. Instead of a general bonus, in 1944 Congress passed the GI Bill of Rights, which subsidized veterans who wished to continue their education, learn a new trade, or start a small business. About 8 million veterans took advantage of these grants.

Cutting taxes and removing price controls did cause a period of rapid inflation. Food prices rose more than 25 percent between 1945 and 1947, which led to demands for higher wages and a wave of strikes—nearly 5,000 in 1946 alone. Inflation and labor unrest helped the Republicans win control of both houses of Congress in 1946 for the first time in two decades.

High on the Republican agenda was the passage of a new labor relations act. Labor leaders tended to support the Democrats, for they remembered gratefully the Wagner Act and other help given them by the Roosevelt administration during the labor-management struggles of the 1930s. In 1943 the CIO had created a political action committee to mobilize the labor vote. But the strikes of 1946 had alienated many citizens because they delayed satisfaction of the demand for consumer goods. They even led President Truman, normally sympathetic to organized labor, to seize the coal mines, threaten to draft railroad workers, and ask Congress for other special powers to prevent national tie-ups.

This was the climate when in June 1947 the new Congress passed the Taft-Hartley Act over the president's veto. The measure outlawed the closed shop (a provision written into many labor contracts requiring new workers to join the union before they could be employed) and declared illegal secondary boycotts and strikes called as a result of disputes between unions over the right to represent workers. Most important, it authorized the president to seek court injunctions to prevent strikes that in his opinion endangered the national interest. The injunctions would hold for 80 days—a "cooling-off" period during which a presidential fact-finding board could investigate and make recommendations.

The Taft-Hartley Act made the task of unionizing unorganized industries more difficult, but it did not seriously hamper existing unions. Though it outlawed the closed shop, it permitted union shop contracts, which forced new workers to join the union after accepting employment.

Postwar Society: The Baby Boomers

The trend toward early marriage and larger families begun during the war accelerated when the conflict ended. In one year, 1946, more than 10 percent of all the single American females over the age of 14 got married. The birthrate soared.

Most servicemen had idealized the joys of domesticity while abroad, and they and their wives and sweethearts were eager to concentrate on "making a home and raising a family" now that the war had ended. People faced the future hopefully, encouraged by the booming economy and the sudden profusion of consumer goods. At the same time, perhaps because of the confusion produced by rapid change, people tended to be conformists, looking over their shoulders, so to speak, rather than tackling life head on.

The period was marked by "a reaffirmation of domesticity," Elaine Tyler May writes in *Homeward Bound: American Families in the Cold War Era.* "Nearly everyone believed that family togetherness, focused on children, was the mark of a successful and wholesome personal life." In 1955 a University of Michigan psychologist completed a study of 300 middle-class couples conducted over two decades. Many of the women queried were college graduates who had gone to college primarily to find a mate with a good future, but others had cheerfully sacrificed plans for a professional career because "the right man" had come along. Encouraged by magazines like the *Ladies' Home Journal* and *Women's Home Companion* and by films that described the trials and triumphs of family life, many college-educated women made a career of home management and child development.

The men of this generation also professed to have found fulfillment in family life. They stressed such things as the satisfactions gained by taking on the responsibilities that marriage and fatherhood entailed and "the incentive to succeed" produced by such responsibilities. For many men, however, these responsibilities provided a refuge from the competitive corporate world where they earned their livings. The need to subordinate one's personal interests to the requirements of "the organization," described in William Whyte's *Organization Man* (1956) and in novels like Sloan Wilson's *Man in the Gray Flannel Suit* (1955), caused strains that could best be relieved in the warmth and security of one's family. Blue-collar workers and clerical employees were not subjected to these pressures to the same extent, but most held similar attitudes toward marriage and child rearing.

Government policies buttressed the inclinations of the people. Income tax deductions encouraged taxpayers to have children and to borrow money to purchase houses and furniture. Having a large family became a kind of national objective. Life was family-centered, and family life was child-centered. Doctor Benjamin Spock's *Baby and Child Care* (1946), which sold well over 20 million copies in 20-odd years, was not as "permissive" as has often been suggested. But Spock certainly emphasized the importance of loving care. "Children raised in loving families want to learn, want to conform, want to grow up," he explained.

Containment and the Marshall Plan

While ordinary people concentrated almost compulsively on their personal affairs, foreign policy issues continued to vex the Truman presidency. Stalin seemed intent on extending his power deep into war-devastated central Europe. The Soviet Union also controlled Outer Mongolia, parts of Manchuria, and northern Korea, and it was fomenting trouble in Iran. By January 1946, Truman had decided to stop "babying" the Soviets. "Only one language do they understand," he noted in a memorandum. "How many divisions have you?"

American and Soviet attitudes stood in sharp confrontation when the control of atomic energy came up for discussion in the UN. Everyone recognized the threat to human survival posed by the atomic bomb. In November 1945 the United States suggested allowing the UN to supervise all nuclear energy production, and the General Assembly promptly created the Atomic Energy Commission to study the question. In June 1946, Commissioner Bernard Baruch offered a plan for the eventual outlawing of atomic weapons. A system would be set up under which UN inspectors could operate without restriction anywhere in the world to make sure that no country was making bombs clandestinely. When, at an unspecified date, the system had been established, the United States would destroy its stockpile of bombs.

Most Americans thought the Baruch plan magnanimous, and some considered it positively foolhardy, but the Soviets rejected it. They would neither permit UN inspectors in the Soviet Union nor surrender their veto power over Security Council actions dealing with atomic energy. They demanded that the United States destroy its bombs at once.

"What struck most observers," the historian John Lewis Gaddis wrote, "was the utter imperviousness of Stalin's regime to the gestures of restraint and goodwill that emanated from the West." Unwilling under the circumstances either to trust the Soviets or to surrender what they considered their "winning weapon," the American leaders refused to agree. The resulting stalemate increased international tension.

Postwar cooperation had failed. By early 1946 a new policy was emerging. Many minds contributed to its development, but the key ideas were provided by George F. Kennan, a scholarly Foreign Service officer. Kennan, a student of Soviet history, believed that the Soviet leaders saw the world as divided into socialist and capitalist camps separated by irreconcilable differences. Nothing the United States might do would reduce Soviet hostility, Kennan claimed. Therefore, the nation should accept this hostility as a fact of life and wait for time to bring about some change in Soviet policy. A policy of "long-term, patient but firm and vigilant containment" based on the "application of counter-force" was the best means of dealing with Soviet pressures. The Cold War could be won if America maintained its own strength and convinced the communists that it would resist aggression firmly in any quarter of the globe. This proved correct.

Kennan's second alternative seemed both irresponsible and dangerous, whereas "getting tough" would find wide popular support. According to polls, a majority considered American policy "too soft." During 1946 the Truman administration gradually adopted a tougher stance. The decisive policy shift came early in 1947 as a result of a crisis in Greece, where communists were receiving aid from communist Yugoslavia and Bulgaria. Great Britain was assisting the monarchists but could no longer afford this drain on its resources. In February 1947 the British informed President Truman that they would have to cut off further aid to Greece.

The news shocked American policymakers because it made them realize that their European allies had not been able to rebuild their war-weakened economies. The Soviet "Iron Curtain" (a phrase coined by Winston Churchill) seemed about to ring down on another nation.

Truman therefore asked Congress to approve what became known as the Truman Doctrine. If Greece or Turkey fell to the communists, he said, all the Middle East might be lost. To prevent this "unspeakable tragedy," he asked for $400 million for military and economic aid for Greece and Turkey. "It must be the policy of the United States to support free peoples who are resisting attempted subjugation by armed minorities or by outside pressures," he said.

By exaggerating the consequences of inaction, Truman attained his objective. But once official sanction was given to the communism-versus-democracy approach to foreign relations, foreign policy began to dominate domestic policy and to become more rigid.

The communist threat loomed large. With western Europe, in Churchill's words, "a rubble-heap, a charnel house, a breeding-ground of pestilence and hate," the entire continent seemed in danger of falling into communist hands. For humane reasons as well as for political advantage, the United States felt obliged to help these nations regain some measure of economic stability.

How might this be done? George Kennan provided an answer. He proposed a broad program to finance European economic recovery. The Europeans themselves should work out the details, America providing the money, materials, and technical advice.

George C. Marshall, army chief of staff during World War II and now secretary of state, formally suggested this program, which became known as the Marshall Plan, in a commencement speech at Harvard in June 1947. The objective, he said, was to restore "the confidence of the European people in the economic future of their own countries. . . . The program should be a joint one, agreed to by a number [of] if not all European nations."

The European powers seized eagerly on Marshall's suggestion. Within six weeks 16 nations set up the Committee for European Economic Cooperation, which soon submitted plans calling for up to $22.4 billion in American aid. After protracted debate, much influenced by a communist coup in Czechoslovakia in February 1948, which drew still another country behind the Iron Curtain, Congress appropriated over $13 billion for the program. Results exceeded all expectations. By 1951 western Europe was booming.

Containment and the Marshall Plan were America's response to the power vacuum created in Europe by the debilitating effects of the war. Just as the Soviet Union extended its influence over the eastern half of the continent, the United States extended its influence in the western. Both powers were driven by worry that the other was seeking world domination.

The Marshall Plan formed the basis for western European economic recovery and political cooperation. In March 1948, Great Britain, France, Belgium, the Netherlands, and Luxembourg signed an alliance aimed at social, cultural, and economic collaboration. The western nations abandoned their understandable but self-defeating policy of crushing Germany economically. They instituted currency reforms in their zones and announced plans for creating a single West German republic with a large degree of autonomy.

These decisions further alarmed the Soviets. In June 1948 they retaliated by closing off surface access to Berlin from the west. For a time it seemed that the Allies must either fight their way into the city or abandon it to the communists. Unwilling to adopt either alternative, Truman decided to fly supplies through the air corridors leading to the capital from Frankfurt, Hanover, and Hamburg. American C-47 and C-54 transports shuttled back and forth in weather fair and foul, carrying enough food, fuel, and other goods necessary to maintain more than 2 million West Berliners. The Berlin Airlift put the Soviets in an uncomfortable position: If they were really determined to keep supplies from West Berlin, they would have to begin the fighting. They were not prepared to do so. In May 1949 they lifted the blockade.

Containment, some of its advocates argued, required the development of a powerful military force. In May 1948, Republican Senator Arthur H. Vandenberg of Michigan, a prewar leader of the isolationists who had been converted to internationalism largely by President Roosevelt's solicitous attention to his views, introduced a resolution stating the "determination" of the United States "to exercise the right of individual or collective self-defense . . . should any armed attack occur affecting its national security." The Senate approved this resolution by a vote of 64 to 4, proof that isolationism had ceased to be an important force in American politics.

Dealing with Japan and China

Containment worked well in Europe, at least in the short run; in the Far East, where the United States lacked powerful allies, it was both more expensive and less effective. V-J Day found the Far East a shambles. Much of Japan was a smoking ruin. In China chaos reigned: Nationalists under Chiang Kai-shek dominated the south, communists under Mao Tse-tung controlled the northern countryside, and Japanese troops still held most northern cities.

President Truman acted decisively and effectively with regard to Japan, unsurely and with unfortunate results where China was concerned. Even before the Japanese surrendered, he had decided not to allow the Soviet Union any significant role in the occupation of Japan. The four-power Allied Control Council was established, but American troops commanded by General MacArthur governed the country.

The Japanese, revealing the same remarkable adaptability that had made possible their swift westernization in the latter half of the 19th century, accepted political and social changes that involved universal suffrage and parliamentary government, the encouragement of labor unions, the breakup of large estates and big industrial combines, and the deemphasis of the importance of the emperor. Japan lost its far-flung island empire and all claim to Korea and the Chinese mainland. It emerged economically strong, politically stable, and firmly allied with the United States.

The difficulties in China were probably insurmountable. Few Americans appreciated the latent power of the Chinese communists. When the war ended, Truman tried to bring Chiang's nationalists and Mao's communists together. He sent General Marshall to China to seek a settlement, but neither Chiang nor Mao would make significant concessions. Mao was convinced—correctly, as time soon proved—that he could win all of China by force, while Chiang, presiding over a corrupt and incompetent regime, grossly exaggerated his popularity among the Chinese people. In January 1947, Truman recalled Marshall and named him secretary of state. Soon thereafter, civil war erupted in China.

The Election of 1948

In the spring of 1948 President Truman's fortunes were at low ebb. Public opinion polls suggested that a majority of the people considered him incompetent or worse. The Republicans seemed sure to win the 1948 presidential election, especially if Truman was the Democratic candidate. Governor Dewey, who again won the Republican nomination, ran confidently, even complacently, certain that he would carry the election with ease.

Truman's position seemed hopeless because he had alienated both southern conservatives and northern liberals. The southerners were particularly distressed because in 1946 the president had established the Committee on Civil Rights, which had recommended antilynching and anti-poll-tax legislation and the creation of a permanent Fair Employment Practices Commission. When the Democratic convention adopted a strong civil rights plank, the southern delegates walked out. Southern conservatives then founded the States' Rights ("Dixiecrat") party and nominated J. Strom Thurmond of South Carolina for president.

As for the liberals, in 1947 a group of them had founded Americans for Democratic Action (ADA) and sought an alternative candidate for the 1948 election. A faction led by former Vice-President Henry A. Wallace, which believed Truman's containment policy a threat to world peace, organized a new Progressive party and nominated Wallace. Most members of ADA, however, thought Wallace too pro-Soviet; in the end the organization supported Truman. Yet with two minor candidates sure to cut into the Democratic vote, the president's chances seemed minuscule.

Truman launched an aggressive campaign, making hundreds of informal but hard-hitting speeches. He excoriated the "do-nothing" Republican Congress, which had rejected his program and passed the Taft-Hartley Act, and he warned labor, farmers, and consumers that if Dewey won, Republican "gluttons of privilege" would do away with all the gains of the New Deal years.

Millions were moved by his arguments and by his courageous fight against great odds. The success of the Berlin Airlift during the presidential campaign helped him considerably. The Progressive party fell increasingly into the hands of communist sympathizers, driving away many liberals who might otherwise have supported Wallace. Dewey's smug, lackluster campaign failed to attract independents. The president was therefore able to reinvigorate the New Deal coalition, and he won an amazing upset victory on election day. He collected

In 1948 the strongly Republican *Chicago Daily Tribune* guessed wrong in headlines written for its postelection editions before all the returns were in. For Truman, it was the perfect climax to his hard-won victory.

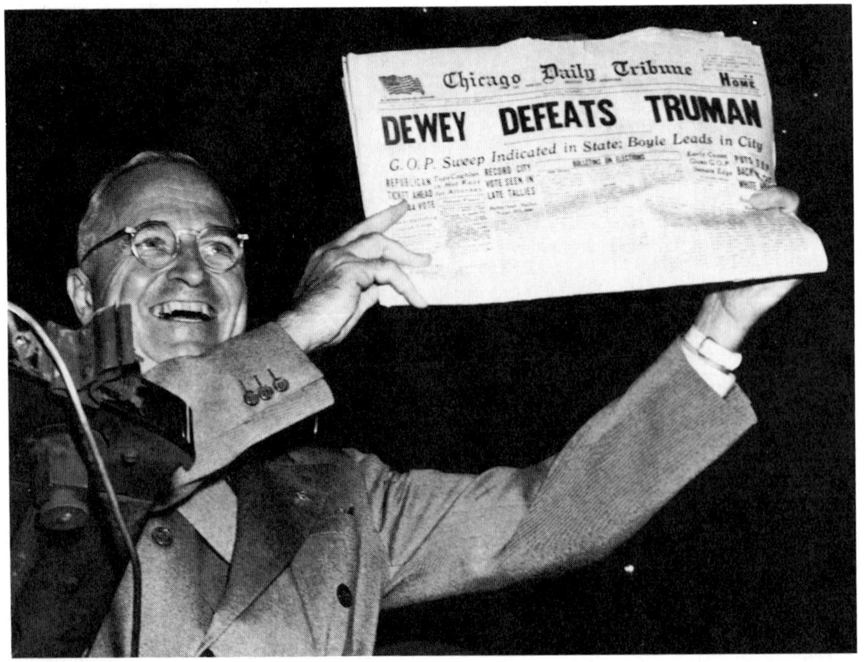

24.1 million votes to Dewey's 21.9 million, the two minor candidates being held to about 2.3 million. In the electoral college his margin was a thumping 303 to 189.

Truman's victory gave ADA considerable influence over what the president called his Fair Deal program. ADA leaders took a middle-of-the-road approach, well described in a book by Arthur M. Schlesinger, Jr.'s *The Vital Center* (1949), that left room for individualism and social welfare, government regulation of the economy, and the encouragement of private enterprise. The approach fitted well with Cold War conditions, which favored both massive military output and continued expansion of the supply of civilian goods. Economic growth would solve all problems, social as well as material. Through growth, the poor could be helped without taking from the rich. The way to check inflation, for example, was not by freezing prices, profits, or wages but by expanding production.

However, relatively little of Truman's Fair Deal was enacted into law. Congress approved a federal housing program and measures increasing the minimum wage and social security benefits, but these were merely extensions of New Deal legislation.

Containing Communism Abroad

During Truman's second term the confrontation between the United States and the Soviet Union, and more broadly between what was seen as "democracy" and "communism," dominated the headlines and occupied a major part of the attention of the president and most other government officials. To strengthen ties with the European democracies, in April 1949 the North Atlantic Treaty was signed in Washington, establishing the North Atlantic Treaty Organization (NATO). Further disturbed by the news, released in September 1949, that the Soviet Union had produced an atomic bomb, Congress appropriated $1.5 billion to arm NATO, and in 1951 General Eisenhower was recalled to active duty and placed in command of all NATO forces.

The success of containment was heartening but not without price; every move evoked a Soviet response. The Marshall Plan led to the seizure of Czechoslovakia, the buildup of Germany to the Berlin blockade, the creation of NATO to the multilateral military alliance known as the Warsaw Pact. George Kennan, the "father" of containment, now downplayed the Soviet military threat. He called the rearmament of Europe a "regrettable diversion" from the task of economic reconstruction. In any case, both sides contributed by their actions and their continuing suspicions to the heightening of Cold War tensions.

In Asia the effort to contain communism exploded into war. By the end of 1949 Mao's communist armies had administered a crushing defeat to the nationalists. The remnants of Chiang's forces fled to the island of Formosa, now called Taiwan. The "loss" of China to communism strengthened right-wing opponents of internationalism in the Republican party. They and other critics charged that Truman had not backed the nationalists strongly enough and that he had stupidly underestimated Mao's dedication to the cause of world revolution. Despite a superficial plausibility, neither charge made much sense. American opinion would not have supported military intervention, nor could any American action have changed the outcome in China.

The attacks of his American critics aroused Truman's combativeness and led him into serious miscalculations elsewhere in Asia. After the war, the province of Korea was taken from Japan and divided at 38° north latitude into the Democratic People's Republic (North Korea), backed by the Soviet Union, and the Republic of Korea (South Korea), backed by the United States and the UN. Both powers withdrew their troops from the peninsula, the Soviets leaving behind a well-armed local force in the north, whereas the army in the south was weak and ill-trained.

American strategists seeking to "contain" communism in the Far East decided that the Asiatic mainland was too difficult to defend. In January 1950, Dean Acheson, Marshall's successor as secretary of state, deliberately excluded Korea from the "defensive perimeter" of the United States in Asia. It was up to the South Koreans, backed by the UN, to protect themselves. This they were unable to do when a North Korean army struck suddenly across the 38th parallel in June 1950.

At this point President Truman exhibited his finest qualities: decisiveness and courage. With the backing of the UN Security Council (but without asking Congress to declare war), he sent American planes into battle.* Ground troops soon followed.

Nominally, the Korean War was a struggle between the invaders and the United Nations. General MacArthur, placed in command, flew the blue UN flag over his headquarters, and no less than 16 nations supplied troops for his army. However, more than 90 percent of the forces employed were American. At first the North Koreans pushed them back rapidly to the southern tip of Korea. Then MacArthur executed a brilliant amphibious flanking maneuver, striking at the west coast city of Inchon, about 50 miles south of the 38th parallel. Outflanked, the North Koreans retreated in disorder. By October the battlefront had moved north of the 1945 boundary.

General MacArthur now proposed the conquest of North Korea, the bombing of "privileged sanctuaries" on the Chinese side of the Korean border, and the redeployment of Chinese nationalist troops on the mainland. Most of Truman's civilian advisers, led by George Kennan, opposed any advance beyond the 38th parallel, fearing intervention not only by the Red Chinese but also by the Soviets.

Faced with conflicting advice, Truman authorized MacArthur to advance as far as the Yalu River, the boundary between North Korea and China, but to avoid war with China or the Soviet Union at all cost. It was a momentous and unfortunate decision, an example of how power, once unleashed, gets out of hand. As the advance progressed, ominous rumblings came from the Chinese that they would not "supinely tolerate seeing their neighbors being savagely invaded by imperialists." Chinese "volunteers" began to turn up among the captives taken by UN units. Alarmed, Truman flew to Wake Island in the Pacific to confer with MacArthur, but the general assured him that the Chinese would not dare to intervene. If they did, MacArthur added, his army would crush them easily; the war would be over by Christmas.

Seldom has a general miscalculated so badly. On November 26 a total of 33 Chinese divisions suddenly smashed through the center of MacArthur's line. Overnight a triumphant advance became a disorganized retreat. MacArthur now justified his earlier confidence by claiming, not without reason, that he was fighting "an entirely new war."

The UN army rallied south of the 38th parallel, and by the spring of 1951 the front had been stabilized. MacArthur then urged that he be permitted to bomb Chinese installations north of the Yalu. He also suggested a naval blockade of the coast of China and the use of Chinese nationalist troops in Korea. When Truman rejected these proposals on the grounds that they would lead to a third world war, MacArthur attempted to rally Congress and the public against the president by criticizing administration policy openly. Truman ordered him to be silent, and when the general persisted, the president removed him from command.

At first the Korean "police action" had been popular in the United States, but as the months

THE KOREAN WAR, 1950–1953

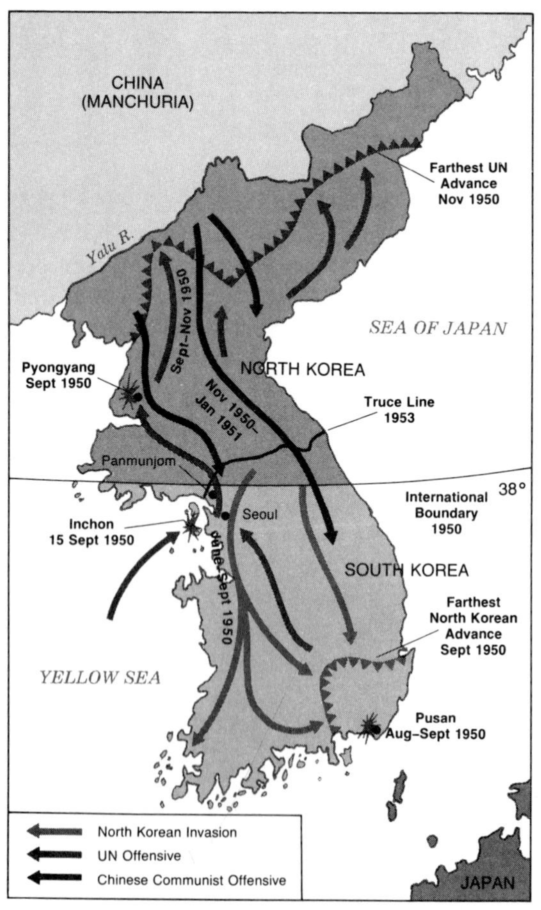

*The USSR, which could have vetoed this action, was at the moment boycotting the Security Council because the UN had refused to give the Mao regime China's seat on that body.

passed and the casualties mounted, many citizens became disillusioned and angry. To Americans accustomed to triumph and fond of oversimplifying complex questions, containment seemed, as its costs in blood and dollars mounted, a monumentally frustrating policy.

But in time the fundamental correctness of Truman's policy and his decision to remove MacArthur became apparent. Military men backed the president almost unanimously. General Omar N. Bradley, chairman of the Joint Chiefs of Staff, declared that a showdown with the Chinese "would involve us in the wrong war, at the wrong place, at the wrong time and with the wrong enemy." In June 1951 the communists agreed to discuss an armistice in Korea, and though the negotiations dragged on, with interruptions, for two years while thousands more died along the static battlefront, both MacArthur and talk of bombing China subsided.

The Communist Issue at Home

The frustrating Korean War highlighted the paradox that at the pinnacle of its power, the influence of the United States in world affairs was declining. Its monopoly of nuclear weapons had been lost. China had passed into the communist orbit. Elsewhere in Asia and throughout Africa, new nations, formerly colonial possessions of the western powers, were adopting a "neutralist" position in the Cold War. Despite the billions poured into armaments and foreign aid, the safety and even the survival of the country seemed far from assured.

Internal as well as external dangers loomed. Alarming examples of communist espionage in Canada, Great Britain, and in the United States itself convinced many citizens that clever conspirators were everywhere at work undermining American security. Both the Republicans and Democratic critics were charging that Truman was "soft" on communists.

There were relatively few communists in the United States, and party membership plummeted after the start of the Cold War. However, the possibility that a handful of spies could do enormous damage fueled a kind of panic that could be used for partisan purposes. In 1947, hoping to defuse the communists-in-government issue by being more zealous in pursuit of spies than his critics, Truman established the Loyalty Review Board. Even sympathy for a long list of vaguely defined "totalitarian" or "subversive" organizations was made grounds for dismissal. During the following ten years about 2,700 government workers were discharged, hardly any for legitimate reasons. A much larger number resigned.

In 1948 Whittaker Chambers, an editor of *Time* who had formerly been a communist, charged that Alger Hiss, president of the Carnegie Endowment for International Peace and a former State Department official, had been a communist in the 1930s. Hiss denied the charge and sued Chambers for libel. Chambers then produced microfilms purporting to show that Hiss had copied classified documents for dispatch to Moscow. Hiss could not be indicted for espionage because of the statute of limitations; instead he was charged with perjury. His first trial resulted in a hung jury; his second, ending in January 1950, in conviction and a five-year jail term.

The Hiss case fed the fears of people who believed in the existence of a powerful communist underground in the United States. The disclosure in February 1950 that a respected British scientist, Klaus Fuchs, had betrayed atomic secrets to the Soviets heightened these fears, as did the arrest and conviction of his American associate, Harry Gold, and two other American traitors, Julius and Ethel Rosenberg, on the same charge.

Although the information the Rosenbergs revealed was not very important, they were executed for treason, to the consternation of many liberals. However, information gathered by other spies had speeded the Soviet development of nuclear weapons. This fact encouraged some Republicans to press the communists-in-government issue hard.

McCarthyism

In February 1950, Senator of Joseph R. McCarthy of Wisconsin casually introduced this theme in a speech before the Women's Republican Club of Wheeling, West Virginia. The State Department, he said, was "infested" with communists. He had no shred of evidence to back up this statement, as a Senate committee headed by the conservative Democrat Millard Tydings of Maryland soon demonstrated. He never exposed a single spy or even a secret American communist. One reporter quipped that McCarthy could not tell Karl Marx from Groucho Marx. But thousands of people were too eager to believe him to listen to reason. Within a few weeks he was the most talked-about person in Congress. Inhibited neither by scruples nor by logic, he lashed out in every direction, attacking international experts like Professor Owen Lattimore of Johns Hopkins and diplomats such as John S. Service and John Carter Vincent, who were already under attack for having pointed out the deficiencies of the Chiang regime during the Chinese civil war.

When McCarthy's victims indignantly denied his charges, he distracted the public by striking out with still more sensational accusations directed at other innocents. The "big lie" was McCarthy's most effective weapon; the enormity of his charges and the status of his targets convinced thousands that there must be *some* truth to what he was saying. Fainthearted members of Congress dared not incur his wrath, and large numbers of Republicans found it hard to resist the temptation to take advantage of his voter appeal.

Dwight D. Eisenhower

As the 1952 presidential election approached, Truman's popularity was again at a low ebb. Senator McCarthy attacked him relentlessly for his handling of the Korean conflict and his "mistreatment" of General MacArthur. In choosing their candidate, the Republicans passed over the twice-defeated Dewey and their most prominent leader, Senator Robert A. Taft of Ohio, an outspoken conservative, and nominated General Dwight D. Eisenhower.

Eisenhower's popularity did not grow merely out of his achievements in World War II. After the bristly, combative Truman, his genial tolerance and evident desire to avoid controversy proved widely appealing. His reluctance to seek political office reminded the country of Washington, and his seeming ignorance of current political issues was no more a handicap to his campaign than the similar ignorance of Jackson and Grant in their times. People liked "Ike" for his personality—he radiated warmth and sincerity—and because his management of the Allied armies reassured them that he would be competent as head of the complex federal government. His promise to go to Korea if elected to try to bring the war to an end was a political masterstroke.

The Democrats nominated Governor Adlai E. Stevenson of Illinois, whose grandfather had been vice-president under Cleveland. Stevenson's unpretentiousness and his witty, urbane speeches captivated intellectuals. In retrospect, however, it is clear that he had not the remotest chance of defeating the popular Eisenhower. Disillusionment with the Korean War and a widespread belief that the Democrats had been too long in power were added handicaps. His foes turned his strongest assets against him, denouncing his humor as frivolity, characterizing his appreciation of the complexities of life as self-doubt, and tagging his intellectual followers "eggheads," an appellation that effectively caricatured the balding, slope-shouldered, somewhat endomorphic candidate. "The eggheads are for Stevenson," one Republican pointed out, "but how many eggheads are there?" There were far too few to carry the country, as the election revealed. The result was a Republican landslide: Eisenhower received almost 34 million votes to Stevenson's 27 million, and in the electoral college his margin was 442 to 89.

On the surface, Eisenhower seemed the antithesis of Truman. The Republicans had charged the Democratic administration with being wasteful and extravagant. Eisenhower planned to run his administration on sound business principles and to eschew increases in the activities of the federal government. He spoke scornfully of "creeping socialism," called for more local control of government affairs, and promised to reduce federal spending in order to balance the budget and cut taxes. He believed that by battling with Congress and pressure groups over the details of legislation, his immediate predecessors had sacrificed part of their status as chief representative of the American people. Like Washington, he tried to avoid being caught up in narrow partisan conflicts. Like Washington, he was not always able to do so.

Having successfully managed the complexities of military administration, Eisenhower used the same kind of staff system as president. He gave his Cabinet officers more responsibility than many other presidents because he did not like to devote time and energy to administrative routine. This did not mean that he was lazy or politically naive. He knew that if he left too many small decisions to others, they would soon be controlling, if not actually making, the large decisions as well.

Some economists claimed that he reacted too slowly in dealing with business recessions and that he showed insufficient concern for speeding the rate of national economic growth. Yet he adopted an almost Keynesian approach to economic problems; that is, he tried to check downturns in the business cycle by stimulating the economy. In his memoir *Mandate for Change* (1963), he wrote of resorting to "preventative action to arrest the downturn [of 1954] before it might become severe" and of being ready to use "any and all weapons in the federal arsenal, including changes in monetary and credit policy, modification of the tax structure, and a speed-up in the construction of . . . public works" to accomplish this end. He approved the extension of social security to an additional 10 million persons; created the Department of Health, Education, and Welfare; and in 1955 came out for federal support of school and highway construction.

Eisenhower's somewhat doctrinaire belief in decentralization and private enterprise reduced the effectiveness of his social welfare measures, but on balance, he proved to be a first-rate politician. He knew how to be flexible without compromising his basic values. His "conservatism" became first "dynamic conservatism" and then "progressive moderation." He summarized his attitude by saying that he was liberal in dealing with individuals but conservative "when talking about . . . the individual's pocketbook."

The Eisenhower-Dulles Foreign Policy

After the 1952 election Eisenhower kept his pledge to go to Korea. His trip produced no immediate result, but the truce talks, suspended before the election, were resumed. In July 1953, perhaps influenced by a hint that the United States might use small "tactical" atomic bombs in Korea, the communists agreed to an armistice. Korea remained divided, its people far worse off than when the fighting began. The United States had suffered more than 135,000 casualties, including 33,000 dead. Yet aggression had been confronted and fought to a standstill.

The American people, troubled and uncertain, were counting on Eisenhower to find a way to employ the nation's immense strength constructively. The new president shared the general feeling that a drastic change of tactics in foreign affairs was needed. He counted on Congress and his secretary of state to solve the practical problems.

Given this attitude, his choice of John Foster Dulles as secretary of state seemed inspired. Dulles's experience in diplomacy dated to 1907, when he had served as secretary to the Chinese delegation at the Second Hague Conference, and he was later an adviser to Wilson at Versailles. More recently he had been a representative of the United States in the UN General Assembly.

Dulles combined strong moral convictions with amazing energy. Only "the force of Christianity," he said, could solve "the great perplexing international problems" of the day. His objectives were magnificent, his strategy grandiose. Instead of waiting for the communist powers to make a move and then "containing" them, the United States should put more emphasis on nuclear bombs and less on conventional weapons. Such a "New Look" would prevent the United States from becoming involved in "local" conflicts like the Korean War and save money too. Potential enemies would know that "massive retaliation" would be the fate of any aggressor. With the communists immobilized by this threat, positive measures aimed at "liberating" eastern Europe and "unleashing" Chiang against the Chinese mainland would follow. Dulles professed great faith in NATO, but he believed that if America's allies lacked the courage to follow its lead, the nation would have to undertake an "agonizing reappraisal" of its commitments to them.

Despite his determination, energy, and high ideals, Dulles failed to make the United States a more effective force in world affairs. Massive retaliation made little sense when the Soviet Union possessed nuclear weapons as powerful as those of the United States. In November 1952, America had won the race to make a hydrogen bomb, but the Soviets duplicated this feat in less than a year. Thereafter, the only threat behind massive retaliation was the threat of human extinction.

Actually, the awesome force of hydrogen bombs, the smallest of which dwarfed the bomb dropped on Hiroshima, provided both powers with a true deterrent. Willy-nilly, nuclear power had established itself as a formidable force for world peace.

McCarthy Self-Destructs

Dulles's saber-rattling tactics were badly timed. While he was planning to avert future Koreas, the Soviet Union was shifting its approach. Stalin died in March 1953, and after a period of internal conflict within the Kremlin, Nikita Khrushchev emerged as the new Soviet master. Khrushchev set out to obtain his objectives by indirection. He appealed to the antiwestern prejudices of countries just emerging from the yoke of colonialism, offering them economic aid and pointing to Soviet achievements in science and technology, such as the launching of *Sputnik,* the first artificial satellite (1957), as proof that communism would soon "bury" the capitalist system without troubling to destroy it by force. The Soviet Union was the friend of all peace-loving nations, he insisted.

Khrushchev was a master hypocrite, yet he was a realist too. While Dulles, product of a system that made a virtue of compromise and tolerance, insisted that the world must choose between American good and Soviet evil, Khrushchev, trained to believe in the incompatibility of communism and capitalism, began to talk of "peaceful coexistence."

Dulles failed to win the confidence of America's allies or even that of the State Department. Senator McCarthy moderated his attacks on the department not a jot when it came under the control of his own party. In 1953 its overseas information program received his special attention. He denounced Voice of America broadcasters for quoting the works of "controversial" authors and sent Roy M. Cohn, youthful special counsel of his Committee on Governmental Operations, on a mission to Europe to ferret out subversives in the United States Information Service.

Dulles did not come to the defense of his people. Instead he seemed determined to out-McCarthy McCarthy in his zeal to get rid of "undesirables" of all sorts. He sanctioned the discharge of nearly 500 State Department employees, not one of whom was proved to have engaged in subversive activities. By making "concessions" to McCarthy, Dulles hoped to end attacks on the administration's foreign policy. The tactic failed; its only result was to undermine the morale of Foreign Service officers.

But McCarthy finally overreached himself. Early in 1954 he turned his guns on the army. After a series of charges and countercharges, he accused army officials of trying to blackmail his committee and announced a broad investigation. The resulting Army-McCarthy hearings, televised across the country, proved the senator's undoing. For weeks his dark scowl, his blind combativeness, and his disregard for every human value stood exposed for millions to see. After the hearings ended, the Senate, with President Eisenhower quietly applying pressure behind the scenes, at last moved to censure him in December 1954. This reproof completed the destruction of his influence. Although he continued to issue statements and wild charges, the country no longer listened. In 1957 he died of cirrhosis.

Asian Policy After Korea

While the final truce talks were taking place in Korea, new trouble was erupting far to the south in

Senator Joseph McCarthy conferring with his aide, Roy M. Cohn, during the 1954 televised hearings into alleged communist infiltration of the army. McCarthy's bullying tactics and evidence that he had tried to secure preferred treatment from the army for another aide cost him most of the popular support and political clout his outspoken anticommunism had earlier won him.

French Indochina. Since December 1946 nationalist rebels led by the communist Ho Chi Minh had been harassing the French in Vietnam. When Communist China recognized the rebels and supplied them with arms, Truman, applying the containment policy, countered with economic and military assistance to the French. When Eisenhower succeeded to the presidency, he continued and expanded this assistance.

Early in 1954 Ho Chi Minh's troops trapped and besieged a French army in the remote stronghold of Dien Bien Phu. Faced with the loss of 20,000 soldiers, France asked the United States to commit its air force to the battle. Eisenhower, after long deliberation, refused. Since the communists were "secreted all around in the jungle," he said, "how are we, in a few air strikes, to defeat them?"

In May the garrison at Dien Bien Phu surrendered, and in July, while the United States watched from the sidelines, France, Great Britain, the USSR, and China signed an agreement at Geneva dividing Vietnam along the 17th parallel. France withdrew from the area. The northern sector became the Democratic Republic of Vietnam, controlled by Ho Chi Minh; the southern remained in the hands of the emperor, Bao Dai. An election to settle the future of all Vietnam was scheduled for 1956.

When it seemed likely that the communists would win that election, Bao Dai was overthrown by a conservative anticommunist, Ngo Dinh Diem. The United States supplied the new South Vietnamese government liberally with aid. The planned election was never held. Vietnam remained divided. Dulles responded to this diplomatic setback by establishing the Southeast Asia Treaty Organization (SEATO) in September 1954, but only three Asian nations—the Philippine Republic, Thailand, and Pakistan—joined this alliance.*

The Middle East Cauldron

Dulles also faced trouble in the Middle East. American policy in that region, aside from the ubiquitous problem of restraining Soviet expansion, was influenced by the huge oil resources—about 60 percent of the world's known reserves—and by the conflict between the new Jewish state of Israel (formerly the British mandate of Palestine) and its Arab neighbors. Although he tried to woo the Arabs, President Truman had consistently placed support for Israel before other considerations in the Middle East.

Angered by the creation of Israel, the surrounding Arab nations tried to destroy the country, but the Israelis drove them off with relative ease. With them departed nearly a million Palestinian Arabs, thereby creating a desperate refugee problem in nearby countries. Truman's support of Israel and the millions of dollars contributed to the new state by American Jews provoked much Arab resentment of the United States.

Dulles and Eisenhower tried to redress the balance by deemphasizing American support of Israel. In 1952 a revolution in Egypt had overthrown the dissolute King Farouk. Colonel Gamal Abdel Nasser emerged as the strongman of Egypt. The United States promptly offered Nasser economic aid and tried to entice him into a broad Middle East security pact. But it would not sell Egypt arms; the communists would. For this reason Nasser drifted steadily toward the communist orbit.

When Eisenhower withdrew his offer of American financial support for the giant Aswan Dam project, the key element in an Egyptian irrigation and electric power program designed to expand and modernize the country, Nasser responded by nationalizing the Suez Canal. This move galvanized the British and French; without consulting the United States, they decided to take back the canal by force. The Israelis, alarmed by repeated Arab hit-and-run raids along their borders, also decided to attack Egypt.

Events moved swiftly. Israeli armored columns crushed the Egyptian army in the Sinai peninsula in a matter of days. France and Britain occupied Port Said, at the northern end of the canal. Nasser blocked the canal by sinking ships in the channel. In the UN the Soviet Union and the United States introduced resolutions calling for a cease-fire. Both were vetoed by Britain and France.

Then Khrushchev threatened to send "volunteers" to Egypt and launch atomic missiles against France and Great Britain if they did not withdraw. President Eisenhower also demanded that the invaders pull out of Egypt. On November 6, only nine days

*The other signatories were Great Britain, France, the United States, Australia, and New Zealand.

after the first attack, British Prime Minister Eden announced a cease-fire. Israel withdrew its troops. The crisis subsided as rapidly as it had arisen.

The United States had won a measure of respect in the Arab countries, but at what cost! Its major allies had been humiliated. The ill-timed attack had enabled the Soviets to recover much of the prestige lost as a result of their brutal suppression of a Hungarian revolt that had broken out a week before the Suez fiasco. Britain and France believed that Dulles's futile attempt to win Arab friendship without abandoning Israel had placed them in a dilemma and that the secretary had behaved dishonorably or at least disingenuously in handling the Egyptian problem.

The bad feeling within the western alliance soon passed. When the Soviet Union seemed likely to profit from its "defense" of Egypt in the crisis, the president in January 1957 announced the Eisenhower Doctrine, which stated that the United States was "prepared to use armed force" anywhere in the Middle East against "aggression from any country controlled by international communism."

Eisenhower and the Soviets

In Europe the Eisenhower and Dulles policies differed little from those of Truman. When Eisenhower announced his plan to rely more heavily on nuclear deterrents, the Europeans drew back in alarm, believing that in any atomic showdown they were sure to be destroyed. Khrushchev's talk of peaceful coexistence found many receptive ears, especially in France.

The president therefore yielded to European pressures for a diplomatic summit conference with the Soviets to discuss disarmament and the reunification of West and East Germany. The meeting, held in Geneva in July 1955, produced no specific agreement, but with the Soviets talking of peaceful coexistence and with Eisenhower pouring martinis and projecting his famous charm, observers noted a softening of tensions that was dubbed the "spirit of Geneva." In 1956 Eisenhower was reelected, defeating Adlai Stevenson even more decisively than he had in 1952. Despite their evident satisfaction with their leader, however, the mood of the American people was sober. Hopes of pushing back the Soviet Union with clever stratagems and moral fervor were fading. America's first successful earth satellite, launched in January 1958, brought cold comfort, for it was much smaller than the earth-circling Soviet *Sputniks.*

In 1957 Dulles underwent surgery for an abdominal cancer, and in April 1959 he had to resign; a month later he was dead. Eisenhower then took over much of the task of conducting foreign relations himself. Amid the tension that followed the Suez crisis, the belief persisted in many quarters that the spirit of Geneva could be revived if only a new summit meeting could be arranged. World opinion was insistent that the great powers stop making and testing nuclear weapons, for every test explosion was contaminating the atmosphere with radioactive debris that threatened the future of all life. Unresolved controversies, especially the argument over the divided Germany, might erupt at any moment into a globe-shattering war.

Neither the United States nor the Soviet Union dared ignore these dangers; each, therefore, adopted a more accommodating attitude. In the summer of 1959 Vice-President Richard M. Nixon visited the Soviet Union and in September Khrushchev came to America. At the end of his stay, he and President Eisenhower agreed to convene a new four-power summit conference.

The meeting never took place. On May 1, 1960, high over Sverdlovsk, an industrial center deep in the Soviet Union, an American U-2 reconnaissance plane was shot down by antiaircraft fire. The pilot of the plane survived the crash and confessed to being a spy. When Eisenhower assumed full responsibility for the mission, Khrushchev accused the United States of "piratical" and "cowardly" acts of aggression. The summit was canceled.

Latin America Aroused

Events in Latin America compounded Eisenhower's difficulties. During World War II the United States, needing Latin American raw materials, had supplied its southern neighbors liberally with economic aid. In the period following victory, an era of amity and prosperity seemed assured. A hemispheric mutual-defense pact was signed at Rio de Janeiro in September 1947, and the following year the Organization of

American States (OAS) came into being. In the OAS, decisions were reached by a two-thirds vote; the United States had neither a veto nor any special position.

The United States tended to neglect Latin America during the Cold War years. Economic problems plagued the region, and in most nations reactionary governments reigned. Radical Latin Americans accused the United States of supporting cliques of wealthy tyrants, and indeed, checking communism continued to receive first priority. Eisenhower, eager to improve relations, stepped up economic assistance. Nevertheless, he continued to support conservative regimes kept in power by bayonets.

That there was no easy solution to Latin American problems was demonstrated by events in Cuba. In 1959 a revolutionary movement headed by Fidel Castro overthrew Fulgencio Batista, one of the most noxious of the Latin American dictators. Eisenhower recognized the Castro government, but the Cuban leader soon began to criticize the United States in highly colored speeches and to seize American property in Cuba without adequate compensation. Castro entered into close relations with the Soviet Union. After he negotiated a trade agreement with the USSR in February 1960 that enabled the Soviets to obtain Cuban sugar at bargain rates, the United States retaliated by prohibiting the importation of Cuban sugar into America.

Khrushchev then announced that if the United States intervened in Cuba, he would defend the country with atomic weapons. "The Monroe Doctrine has outlived its time," he warned. Shortly before he left office, Eisenhower broke off diplomatic relations with Cuba.

The Politics of Civil Rights

During Eisenhower's presidency a major change occurred in the legal status of American blacks. Eisenhower had relatively little to do with this change, which was part of a broad shift in attitudes toward the rights of minorities in democracies. After 1945 the question of racial equality took on special importance because of the ideological competition with communism. Evidence of color prejudice in the United States damaged the nation's image, particularly in Asia and Africa, where the United States and the Soviet Union were competing for influence. An

Vice-President Richard M. Nixon and Soviet leader Nikita Khrushchev engaged in their "kitchen debate" over the future of capitalism at a Moscow trade fair in 1959. Though this encounter did little to advance U.S.-Soviet relations, it established Nixon's credentials as a tough negotiator.

awareness of foreign criticism of American racial attitudes, along with resentment that almost a century after the Emancipation Proclamation they were still second-class citizens, produced a growing militancy among American blacks. At the same time, fears of communist subversion in the United States led to the repression of the rights of many whites, culminating in the excesses of McCarthyism. Both these aspects of the civil rights question divided Americans along liberal and conservative lines.

As we have seen, the World War II record of the federal government on civil rights was mixed. As early as 1940, in the Smith Act, Congress made it illegal to advocate or teach the overthrow of the government by force or to belong to an organization with this objective. The law was used in the Truman era to jail the leaders of the American Communist party.

In 1950 Congress passed the McCarran Internal Security Act, which made it unlawful "to combine, conspire or agree with any other person to perform any act that would substantially contribute to the establishment . . . of a totalitarian dictatorship." The law required every "Communist-front organization" to register with the attorney general. Members of such organizations were barred from defense work and from traveling abroad. Aliens who had ever been members of any "totalitarian party" were denied admission to the United States, a foolish provision that prevented many anticommunists behind the Iron Curtain from fleeing to America; even a person who had belonged to a communist youth organization was kept out by this provision.

As for blacks, besides setting up the Committee on Civil Rights and beginning to desegregate the armed forces, Truman sought to establish a permanent Fair Employment Practices Commission. Congress, however, did not pass the necessary legislation.

Under Eisenhower, while the McCarthy hysteria reached its peak and declined, the government compiled a spotty record on civil rights. The search for subversive federal employees continued. Eisenhower did complete the formal integration of blacks in the armed forces and appointed a Civil Rights Commission, but he was temperamentally incapable of a frontal assault on the racial problem. This was done by the Supreme Court, which interjected itself into the civil rights controversy in dramatic fashion in 1954.

For some years the Court had been gradually undermining the "separate but equal" principle laid down in *Plessy* v. *Ferguson* in 1896. First it ruled that in graduate education, segregated facilities must be truly equal. In 1938 it ordered a black student admitted to the University of Missouri law school because no law school for blacks existed in the state. This decision gradually forced some southern states to admit blacks to advanced programs. In 1950, when Texas actually attempted to fit out a separate law school for a single black applicant, the Court ruled that truly equal education could not be provided under such circumstances.

In 1953 President Eisenhower appointed California's Governor Earl Warren Chief Justice of the United States. Convinced that the Court must take the offensive in the cause of civil rights, Warren succeeded in welding his associates into a unit on the question. In 1954 an NAACP-sponsored case, *Brown* v. *Board of Education of Topeka,* came up for decision. This case challenged the "separate but equal" doctrine at the elementary school level. Speaking for a unanimous Court, Warren reversed the Plessy decision. "In the field of public education, the doctrine of 'separate but equal' has no place," he declared. "Separate educational facilities are inherently unequal." The next year the Court ordered the states to proceed "with all deliberate speed" in integrating their schools.

Despite these decisions, few districts in the southern and border states tried to integrate their schools. White citizens' councils dedicated to all-out opposition sprang up throughout the South. In Virginia the governor announced a plan for "massive resistance" to integration that denied state aid to local school systems that wished to desegregate. When the University of Alabama admitted a single black woman in 1956, riots broke out. University officials forced the student to withdraw and then expelled her when she complained more forcefully than they deemed proper.

President Eisenhower thought equality for blacks could not be obtained by government edict. "The fellow who tries to tell me you can do these things by force is just plain nuts," he said. But in 1957 events compelled him to act. When the school board of Little Rock, Arkansas, opened Central High School to a handful of black children, the governor called out the National Guard to prevent them from attending. Unruly crowds taunted the children and their parents.

Eisenhower could not ignore the direct flouting

of federal authority. After the mayor of Little Rock informed him that his police could not control the situation, the president dispatched 1,000 paratroopers to Little Rock and summoned 10,000 National Guardsmen to federal duty. The black children then began to attend classes. A token force of soldiers was stationed at Central High for the entire school year to protect them.

Extremist resistance strengthened the determination of blacks and many northern whites to make the South comply with the desegregation decision. Besides pressing cases in the federal courts, leaders of the movement organized a voter registration drive among southern blacks. As a result, the administration introduced what became the Civil Rights Act of 1957. It authorized the attorney general to obtain injunctions to stop election officials from interfering with blacks seeking to register and vote. The law also established the Civil Rights Commission with broad investigatory powers and a civil rights division in the Department of Justice. Enforcing the Civil Rights Act was another matter. A later study of a typical county in Alabama revealed that between 1957 and 1960 more than 700 blacks with

Angry jeers from whites rain down on Elizabeth Eckford, one of the first black students to arrive for registration at Little Rock's Central High School in 1957. State troops turned black students away from the school until President Eisenhower called in the National Guard to enforce integration.

high school diplomas were rejected as unqualified by white election officials when they sought to register.

The Supreme Court under Chief Justice Warren did not limit itself to protecting the rights of black people. It reinstated the "clear and present danger" principle that had been undermined in a case upholding the Smith Act ban on merely "advocating" the overthrow of the government by force. The rights of persons accused of crimes were enlarged in cases providing free legal counsel for indigent defendants, requiring the police to inform accused persons of their right to remain silent, and giving accused persons the right to have a lawyer present while being questioned by the authorities.

In *Baker* v. *Carr* (1962), *Lucas* v. *Colorado* (1964), and other decisions, the Court declared that unequal representation in state and local legislative bodies was unconstitutional, thus establishing the principle known as "one man, one vote." In a different area, the Court in *Griswold* v. *Connecticut* (1965) struck down a Connecticut statute banning the use of contraceptives on the ground that it violated individuals' right of privacy.

The Election of 1960

As the end of his second term approached, Eisenhower somewhat reluctantly endorsed Vice-President Nixon as the Republican candidate to succeed him. Richard Nixon had skyrocketed to national prominence by exploiting the public fear of communist subversion. "Traitors in the high councils of our government," he charged in 1950, "have made sure that the deck is stacked on the Soviet side of the diplomatic tables." In 1947 he was an obscure young congressman from California; in 1950 he won a seat in the Senate; two years later Eisenhower chose him as his running mate.

Whether Nixon believed what he was saying at this period of his career is not easily discovered; with his "instinct for omnidirectional placation," he seemed wedded to the theory that politicians should slavishly represent their constituents' opinions rather than hold to their own views. Frequently he appeared to count noses before deciding what he thought. He projected an image of almost frantic earnestness, yet he pursued a flexible course more suggestive of calculation than sincerity.

Reporters generally had a low opinion of Nixon, and relatively few independent voters found him attractive. He was always controversial, distrusted by liberals even when he supported liberal measures. But his defense of traditional American values made him popular with conservatives.

The Democrats nominated Senator John F. Kennedy of Massachusetts, with his chief rival at the convention, Lyndon B. Johnson of Texas, the Senate majority leader, as his running mate. Kennedy was the son of a wealthy businessman and promoter who had served as ambassador to Great Britain under Franklin Roosevelt. As a PT boat commander in World War II, he was severely injured in action. In 1946 he was elected to Congress. Besides wealth, intelligence, good looks, and charm, Kennedy had the advantage of his war record and his Irish-Catholic ancestry, the latter a particularly valuable asset in heavily Catholic Massachusetts. After three terms in the House, he moved on to the Senate in 1952 by defeating Henry Cabot Lodge, Jr.

After his landslide reelection in 1958, only Kennedy's religion seemed to limit his political future. No Catholic had ever been elected president, and the defeat of Alfred E. Smith in 1928 had convinced most students of politics that none ever would be elected. Nevertheless, influenced by his victories in the Wisconsin and West Virginia primaries—the latter establishing him as an effective campaigner in a predominantly Protestant region—the Democratic convention nominated him.

Kennedy had not been a particularly liberal congressman. He was friendly with Richard Nixon and admitted frankly that he liked Senator Joseph McCarthy and thought that "he may have something" in his campaign against supposed communists in government. However, as a presidential candidate, he sought to appear more forward-looking. He promised to open a "New Frontier" and accused the Republicans of neglecting national defense and losing the Cold War. Nixon ran on the Eisenhower record, which he promised to extend in liberal directions.

A series of television debates between the candidates, observed by some 70 million viewers, helped Kennedy by enabling him to demonstrate his warmth, maturity, and mastery of the issues. Where Nixon appeared to lecture the unseen audience like an ill-at-ease schoolmaster, Kennedy seemed relaxed, thoughtful, and confident of his powers. Although both candidates laudably avoided it, the religious issue was important. His Catholicism helped Kennedy in eastern urban areas but injured him in many farm districts and throughout the West. On balance, it probably hurt him more than it helped. Nevertheless, he won. His margin of victory, 303 to 219 in the electoral college, was paper-thin in the popular vote, 34,227,000 to 34,109,000. Kennedy carried Illinois by fewer than 9,000 votes out of nearly 4.8 million, and it is possible that the Democratic machine of Mayor Richard J. Daley of Chicago supplied that margin by unlawful means.

Although Kennedy was rich, white, and a member of the upper crust by any definition, his was a victory of minority groups (Jews, blacks, and blue-collar "ethnics" as well as Catholics gave him overwhelming support) over the "traditional" white Protestant majority, which went as heavily for Nixon as it had four years earlier for Eisenhower.

Kennedy's New Frontier

Kennedy made a striking and popular president. He projected an image of originality and imaginativeness combined with moderation and good sense. He flouted convention by making his younger brother Robert F. Kennedy attorney general. (When critics objected to this appointment, the president responded with a quip, saying that he had "always thought it was a good thing for a young attorney to get some government experience before going out into private practice.")

Kennedy had a genuinely inquiring mind. He kept up with dozens of magazines and newspapers and consumed books of all sorts voraciously. He invited leading scientists, artists, writers, and musicians to the White House. Jefferson had sought to teach Americans to value the individual regardless of status. Kennedy seemed intent on teaching the country to respect its most talented minds.

Kennedy seemed determined to change the direction in which the nation was moving. He hoped to revitalize the economy and extend the influence of the United States abroad. His inaugural address was a call for commitment: "Ask not what your country can do for you," he said. "Ask what you can do for your country." But he was neither a Woodrow Wilson nor a Franklin Roosevelt when it came to bending Congress to his will. Perhaps he was too amiable, too diffident and conciliatory in his approach. A coalition of Republicans and conservative southern Democrats resisted his plans for federal aid to education, for urban renewal, for a higher minimum wage, for medical care for the aged.

The president reacted mildly, almost ruefully, when opponents in Congress blocked proposals that in his view were reasonable and moderate. He seemed to doubt at times that the cumbersome machinery of the federal government could be made to work. Even to some of his warmest supporters he sometimes appeared strangely paralyzed, unwilling either to exert strong pressure on Congress or to appeal to public opinion. Pundits talked of a "deadlock of democracy" in which party discipline had crumbled and positive legislative action had become next to impossible.

During the presidential campaign Kennedy had promised to "get the country moving again." The relatively slow growth of the economy in the Eisenhower years had troubled some economists. Three recessions occurred between 1953 and 1961, each marked by increases in unemployment. In the latter years of Eisenhower's presidency the rate of inflation began to rise.

During the recessions the Eisenhower administration reacted in the orthodox Keynesian manner, cutting taxes, easing credit, and expanding public works programs. However, liberal economists argued that it was not employing the Keynesian medicine in large enough doses.

At first Kennedy rejected proposals for increasing government spending. But in January 1963 the economist Walter Heller persuaded him to try a different approach. If personal and corporate income taxes were lowered, Heller argued, the public would have more money to spend on consumer goods and corporations could invest in new facilities for producing these goods. Federal expenditures need not be cut because the increase in economic activity would raise private and corporate incomes so much that tax revenues would rise even as the tax rate was falling.

Although the prospect of lower taxes was tempting, Kennedy's call for reductions of $13.5 billion ran into strong opposition. Republicans and conservative Democrats thought the reasoning behind the scheme too complex and theoretical to be practicable. It went nowhere.

Two of President Kennedy's chief advisors on the Vietnam War, General Maxwell Taylor and Secretary of Defense Robert McNamara, meet with the president in the Oval Office, October 2, 1963.

The Cuban Crises

Kennedy's curious lack of determined leadership also marred his management of foreign affairs, particularly during his first year in office. He hoped to reverse the Truman-Eisenhower policy of backing reactionary regimes merely because they were anticommunist. Recognizing that American economic aid could accomplish little in Latin America unless accompanied by internal reforms, he organized the Alliance for Progress, which committed the Latin Americans to land reform and economic development projects with the assistance of the United States. At the first sign of pro-Soviet activity in any Latin American country, however, he tended to overreact.

His most serious mistake involved Cuba. Anti-Castro exiles were eager to organize an invasion of their homeland, reasoning that the Cuban masses would rise up against Castro as soon as "democratic" forces provided a standard they could rally to. Under Eisenhower the Central Intelligence Agency had begun training some 2,000 of these men in Central America.

Kennedy was of two minds about this plan, and his advisers were split on the question. But after much soul-searching, he authorized the attack. The exiles were given American weapons, but no planes or warships were committed to the operation.

The invaders struck on April 17, 1961, landing at the Bay of Pigs, on Cuba's southern coast. But the Cuban people failed to flock to their lines, and they were soon pinned down and forced to surrender. Since America's involvement could not be disguised, the affair exposed the country to all the criticisms that a straightforward assault would have produced without accomplishing the overthrow of Castro. Worse, it made Kennedy appear impulsive as well as unprincipled. Castro soon acknowledged that he was a Marxist and tightened his connections with the Soviet Union. For his part, Kennedy imposed an economic blockade on Cuba, and he appears to have gone along with a CIA attempt to assassinate Castro.

In June, Kennedy met with Premier Khrushchev in Vienna. During their discussions he evidently failed to convince the Russian that he would resist pressure with determination. In August, Khrushchev abruptly closed the border between East and West Berlin and erected an ugly wall of concrete blocks and barbed wire across the city to check the exodus of dissident East Germans. Resuming the testing of nuclear weapons, Khrushchev exploded a series of gigantic hydrogen bombs, one with a power 3,000 times that of the bomb that had devastated Hiroshima.

When the Soviets resumed nuclear testing, Kennedy followed suit. He expanded the American space program,* vowing that an American would land on the moon by the end of the 1960s, and called on Congress for a large increase in military spending. At the same time he pressed forward along more constructive lines by establishing the Agency for International Development to administer American economic aid throughout the world and the Peace Corps, an organization that mobilized American idealism and technical skills to help developing nations.

These actions had no observable effect on the Soviets. In 1962 Khrushchev devised the boldest and most reckless challenge of the Cold War—he moved military equipment and thousands of Soviet technicians into Cuba. U-2 reconnaissance planes photographed these sites, and by mid-October, Kennedy had proof that they were approaching completion. The president faced a dreadful decision. When he confronted Soviet Foreign Minister Andrei Gromyko, the Russian insisted that only "defensive" (antiaircraft) missiles were being installed.

Kennedy decided that he must take strong action. On October 22 he went before the nation on television. The Soviet buildup was "a deliberately provocative and unjustified change in the status quo," he said. The navy would stop and search all vessels headed for Cuba and turn back any containing "offensive" weapons. Kennedy called on Khrushchev to dismantle the missile bases and remove from the island all weapons capable of striking the United States. Any Cuban-based nuclear attack would result, he warned, in "a full retaliatory response upon the Soviet Union."

For days, while the world held its breath, work on the missile bases continued. Then Khrushchev backed down. He withdrew the missiles and cut back his military establishment in Cuba to modest proportions. Kennedy then lifted the blockade.

Critics have argued that Kennedy overreacted to the missiles. There was no evidence that the Soviets were planning an attack, and they already had missiles in Siberia capable of striking American targets. The Cuban missiles might be seen as a deterrent against a possible attack on the Soviet Union by United States missiles in Europe, and by demanding their withdrawal Kennedy risked triggering a nuclear holocaust as much as Khrushchev did. Yet he probably had no choice once the existence of the sites was known to the public. (In some respects this is the most frightening aspect of the crisis.)

For better or worse, Kennedy's firmness in the missile crisis repaired the damage done to his reputation by the Bay of Pigs affair. It also led to a lessening of Soviet-American tensions. Khrushchev agreed to the installation of a telephone "hot line" between the White House and the Kremlin so that in any future crisis the leaders of the two nations could be in instant communication. The arms race continued, but in July 1963 all the powers except France and China signed a treaty banning the testing of nuclear weapons in the atmosphere.

Tragedy in Dallas

Although his domestic policies were making little progress, Kennedy retained his hold on public opinion. Most observers believed he would easily win a second term. Then, while visiting Dallas, Texas, on November 22, 1963, he was shot in the head by an assassin, Lee Harvey Oswald, and died almost instantly.

This senseless murder precipitated an extraordinary series of events. Oswald had fired on the president with a rifle from an upper story of a warehouse. No one saw him pull the trigger, but a mass of evidence connected him with the crime. Before he could be brought to trial, however, he was himself murdered by the owner of a Dallas nightclub while being transferred, in the full view of television cameras, from one place of detention to another.

This amazing incident, together with the fact that Oswald had defected to the Soviet Union in 1959 and then returned to the United States, convinced many people that some nefarious conspiracy lay at the root of the tragedy. Oswald, the argument ran, was a pawn, his murder designed to keep him from exposing the masterminds who had engineered the assassination. An investigation by a special commis-

*Russian superiority in space was gradually reduced. In April 1961 the cosmonaut Yuri Gagarin orbited the earth; in August another Russian circled the globe 17 times. The first American to orbit the earth, John Glenn, made his voyage in February 1962. In 1965 the United States kept a two-man Gemini craft in orbit two weeks, effecting a rendezvous between it and a second Gemini.

sion headed by Chief Justice Earl Warren came to the conclusion that Oswald acted alone, yet doubts persisted in many minds.

Kennedy's election had seemed the start of a new era in American history. Instead, his assassination marked the end of an old one. The three postwar presidents had achieved, at minimum, the respect of nearly everyone. There were critics who felt that the job was too big for Truman, others who considered Eisenhower a political amateur and Kennedy a compulsive, even reckless womanizer and too much a showman. But their honesty and patriotism were beyond question. This was not to be said of their immediate successors.

Milestones

1944 GI Bill of Rights
1945 Roosevelt dies; Truman becomes president
1946 Benjamin Spock, *Baby and Child Care*
Baruch Plan for control of atomic energy
1947 Taft-Hartley Act
Truman Doctrine
Marshall Plan proposed
Loyalty Review Board
1948–1949 Berlin Airlift
1949 North Atlantic Treaty Organization (NATO) established
1950 North Korea invades South Korea
Alger Hiss convicted of perjury
Senator McCarthy charges that the State Department is riddled with communists
UN counterattack in Korea driven back by Red Chinese army
1953 New Look foreign policy
Korean War armistice
1954 Army-McCarthy hearings
Siege of Dien Bien Phu; French withdraw from Vietnam
Supreme Court orders school desegregation *(Brown* v. *Board of Education of Topeka)*
1956 Suez crisis
1957 National Guard used to desegregate Little Rock high school
Civil Rights Commission established
1960 U-2 affair
United States breaks diplomatic relations with Cuba
1961 Bay of Pigs affair
1962 Cuban Missile Crisis
1963 President Kennedy assassinated

Supplementary Reading

A good summary of the Cold War is T. G. Paterson, **On Every Front: The Making of the Cold War** (1979), which makes an effort to explain Soviet motives and tactics objectively. See also two books by J. L. Gaddis, **Strategies of Containment** (1982) and **The Long Peace** (1987). Daniel Yergin, **Shattered Peace** (1977), is more critical of American policy.

Postwar domestic politics is treated in W. L. O'Neill, **Riding High** (1986), and A. L. Hamby, **The Imperial Years** (1976) and **Beyond the New Deal: Harry S Truman and American Liberalism** (1973).

For the postwar presidents, see D. R. McCoy, **The Presidency of Harry S Truman** (1984), R. J. Donovan, **Conflict and Crisis** (1977), W. E. Pemberton, **Harry S. Truman** (1989), S. E. Ambrose's two-volume biography, **Eisenhower** (1983, 1984), Herbert Parmet, **Eisenhower and the American Crusades** (1972), and Charles Alexander, **Holding the Line** (1975).

Among many analyses and evaluations of American foreign policy, G. F. Kennan's writings stand out, both as primary sources and as interpretations. See his **Memoirs** (1969, 1972), **Realities of American Foreign Policy** (1954), and **Russia and the West under Lenin and Stalin** (1961).

On Truman's foreign policy, see Donovan's **Conflict and Crisis**, M. J. Hogan, **The Marshall Plan** (1987), and W. P. Davison, **The Berlin Blockade** (1958). On Eisenhower's policies, see R. A. Divine, **Eisenhower and the Cold War** (1981). For the Korean War, the fullest account is Clay Blair, **Forgotten War: America in Korea** (1988).

McCarthyism and the Hiss case are covered in David Caute, **The Great Fear** (1978), and Allen Weinstein, **Purgery: The Hiss-Chambers Case** (1978).

Economic trends are considered in Herbert Stein, **The Fiscal Revolution in America** (1969). On labor, consult Philip Taft, **Organized Labor in American History** (1964), John Barnard, **Walter Reuther** (1983), and R. H. Zieger, **John L. Lewis** (1988). On agriculture, see A. J. Matusow, **Farm Policies & Politics in the Truman Years** (1970). For postwar constitutional issues, see P. L. Murphy, **The Constitution in Crisis Times** (1972). Richard Kluger, **Simple Justice** (1976), is an excellent account of the Brown case.

On Kennedy, David Burner's, **John F. Kennedy** is a good brief biography. H. S. Parmet, **Jack: The Struggles of John F. Kennedy** (1980), and **JKF: The Presidency of John F. Kennedy** (1983), provide a fuller account. A. M. Schlesinger, Jr., **A Thousand Days** (1965), and Theodore Sorensen, **Kennedy** (1965), are rich in eyewitness detail but extremely pro-Kennedy.

CHAPTER 31

■ ■ ■ ■ ■ ■ ■

The Best of Times, the Worst of Times

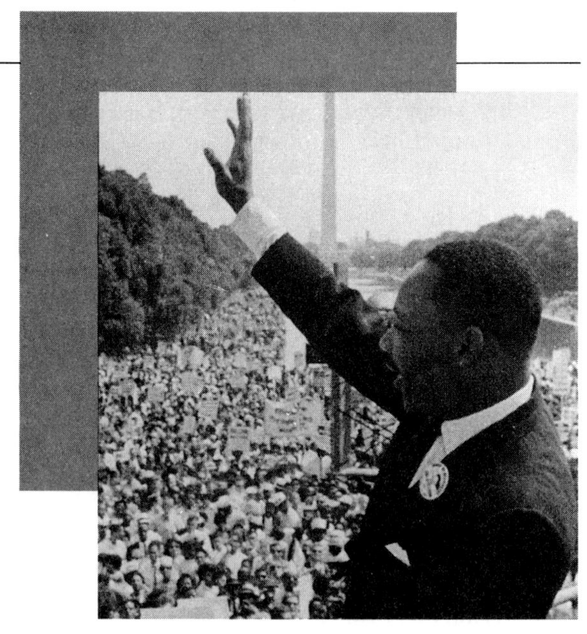

■ ■ ■ ■ ■ JOHN F. KENNEDY'S DEATH MADE LYNDON B. Johnson president. The two had never been close. When Kennedy offered Johnson the vice-presidency at the 1960 Democratic convention, he had expected him to refuse. From 1949 until his election as vice-president Johnson had been a senator and, for most of that time, Senate Democratic leader. Early on he had displayed what one adviser called an extraordinary "capacity for manipulation and seduction." He could be both heavy-handed and subtle, and also devious, domineering, persistent, and obliging. Above all, he knew what to do with political power. "Some men," he said, "want power so they can strut around to 'Hail to the Chief.' . . . I wanted it to use it." Johnson benefited from the sympathy of the world and from the shame felt by many who had opposed Kennedy's proposals for political or selfish reasons. Sensing the public mood, he pushed Kennedy's programs forward with great skill and energy. Bills that had long been buried in committee sailed through Congress. Early in 1964 Kennedy's tax cut was passed, and the resulting economic stimulus caused a boom of major dimensions. A few months later an expanded version of another Kennedy measure became law, the Civil Rights Act of 1964.

"We Shall Overcome"

Kennedy's original approach to the race question had been exceedingly cautious. He did not integrate the National Guard, for example, because he was afraid that if he did, southern Guard units would withdraw. His lack of full commitment dismayed many who were concerned about the persistence of racial discrimination in the country. But seemingly without plan, a grass-roots drive for equal treatment had sprung up among southern blacks themselves.

It began during the Eisenhower administration in the tightly segregated city of Montgomery, Alabama. On the evening of Friday, December 1, 1955, Rosa Parks boarded a bus on her way home from her job as a seamstress at a department store. She dutifully took a seat toward the rear as law and custom required. After white workers and shoppers had

Chapter-opening illustration:
On August 28, 1963, Dr. Martin Luther King, Jr., told the crowd of demonstrators gathered in front of the Lincoln Memorial in Washington, D.C., of his dream of an end to racial discrimination and inequality.

filled the forward section, the driver ordered her to give up her place. Parks, who was also secretary of the Montgomery NAACP chapter, refused. She had decided, she later recalled, "that I would have to know once and for all what rights I had."

Rosa Parks was arrested. The blacks of Montgomery organized a boycott of the bus lines. The boycott was a success. The black people of Montgomery, writes Taylor Branch in his stirring account, *Parting the Waters,* "were turning the City Bus Lines into a ghost fleet."

Most Montgomery blacks could not afford to miss even one day's wages, and getting to work was difficult. Black-owned taxis reduced their rates, and when the city declared this illegal, car pools were organized. But few blacks owned cars; there were never more than 350 available to carry about 10,000 people back and forth to their jobs. Nevertheless, the boycott went on.

A young clergyman, Martin Luther King, Jr., a gifted speaker who was emerging as a leader of the boycott, became a national celebrity; money poured in from all over the country. Finally, after more than a year, the Supreme Court ruled that the Montgomery segregation law was unconstitutional. Montgomery had to desegregate its transportation system.

This success had encouraged blacks elsewhere in the South to band together against the caste system. A new organization, the Southern Christian Leadership Conference, headed by King, moved to the forefront of the civil rights movement. Other organizations joined the struggle, notably the Congress of Racial Equality (CORE), which had been founded in 1942.

In February 1960 four black students in Greensboro, North Carolina, sat down at a lunch counter in a five-and-ten-cent store and refused to leave when they were denied service. Their "sit-in" sparked a national movement; students in dozens of other southern towns and cities copied the Greensboro blacks' example.

In May 1961, black and white foes of segregation organized a "freedom ride" to test the effectiveness of federal regulations prohibiting discrimination in interstate transportation. Boarding buses in Washington, they traveled across the South, heading for New Orleans. In Alabama they ran into bad trouble: At Anniston racists set fire to their bus; in Birmingham they were assaulted by a mob. But violence could not stop the freedom riders. Other groups descended on the South, many deliberately seeking arrest in order to test local segregation ordinances in the courts. Repeatedly these actions resulted in the breaking down of racial barriers.

Integrationists like King attracted an enormous following, but some blacks, proud of their race and contemptuous of white prejudices, were urging their fellows to reject "American" society and all it stood for. Black nationalism became a potent force. The followers of Elijah Muhammad, leader of the Black Muslim movement, disliked whites so intensely that they advocated racial separation. They demanded that a part of the United States be set aside for the exclusive use of blacks. The Muslims called Christianity "a white man's religion." They urged their followers to be industrious, thrifty, and abstemious—and to view all whites with suspicion and hatred. "This white government has ruled us and given us plenty of hell," Elijah Muhammad said. Another important Black Muslim, Malcolm X, put it this way: "For the white man to ask the black man if he hates him is just like the rapist asking the raped, or the wolf asking the sheep, 'Do you hate me?' "

Pushed by all these developments, President Kennedy reluctantly began to change his policy. But while the administration gave lip service to desegregation when confrontations arose, the president hesitated, arguing that it was up to state officials to enforce the law. Ordinary black southerners (even schoolchildren) became increasingly impatient. In the face of brutal repression by local police, many adopted King's tactic of nonviolent protest. After leading a series of demonstrations in Birmingham, Alabama, in 1963, King was thrown in jail. When local white clergymen urged an end to the "untimely" protests, which, they claimed, "incite hatred and violence," King wrote his now-famous "Letter from Birmingham Jail":

> *When you have seen hate-filled policemen curse, kick, brutalize and even kill your black brothers and sisters with impunity; . . . when you take a cross-country drive and find it necessary to sleep night after night in the uncomfortable corners of your automobile because no motel will accept you; when you are humiliated day in and day out by nagging signs reading "white" and "colored";*

. . . then you will understand why we find it so difficult to wait.

The brutal repression of the Birmingham demonstrations brought a flood of recruits and money to the protesters' cause. Finally Kennedy gave his support to a comprehensive new civil rights bill that made racial discrimination in hotels, restaurants, and other places of public accommodation illegal.

When this bill ran into stiff opposition in Congress, blacks organized a demonstration in Washington, attended by 200,000 people. At this gathering King delivered his "I Have a Dream" address, looking forward to a time when racial prejudice no longer existed and people of all religions and colors could join hands and say, "Free at last! Free at last!"

Kennedy had sympathized with the purpose of the Washington gathering, but he feared it would make passage of the civil rights bill more difficult rather than easier. As in other areas, he was not a forceful advocate of his own proposals.

The Great Society

As finally passed, the new civil rights act outlawed discrimination against blacks and also against women. It broke down the last legal barriers to black voting in the southern states and banned formal racial segregation of all sorts. Johnson's success in steering this and other Kennedy measures through Congress convinced him that he could be a reformer in the tradition of Franklin Roosevelt. He declared war on poverty and set out to create a "great society" in which poverty no longer existed.

During the New Deal, Franklin Roosevelt was accused of exaggeration when he said that one-third of the nation was "ill-housed, ill-clad, ill-nourished." In fact Roosevelt had underestimated the extent of poverty when he made that statement in 1937. Wartime economic growth reduced the percentage of poor people in the country substantially, but in 1960 between 20 and 25 percent of all American families—about 40 million persons—were living below the so-called poverty line (a government standard of minimum subsistence based on income and family size).

That so many millions could be poor in a reputedly affluent society was deplorable but not difficult to explain. Entire regions in the United States, the best known being the Appalachian area, had been bypassed by economic development. And technological advances that raised living standards also raised job requirements. A strong back and a willingness to work no longer guaranteed that the possessor could earn a decent living. Educated workers with special skills could easily find well-paid jobs. Persons who had no special skills or who were poorly educated could often find nothing.

Certain less obvious influences were at work too. Poverty tends to be more prevalent among the old and the young than among those in the prime of life; in the postwar decades these two groups were growing more rapidly than those in between. Social security payments amounted to less than the elderly needed to maintain themselves decently, and some of the poorest workers, such as agricultural laborers, were not covered by the system at all. Unemployment was twice as high among youths in their late teens as in the nation as a whole and far higher among young blacks than young whites.

Poverty exacted a heavy price, both from its victims and from society. Statistics reflected the relationship between low income and bad health. Only about 4 percent of people from middle-income families were chronically ill, whereas more than 16 percent of poor families were so afflicted. Mental illness varied inversely with income, as did alcoholism, drug addiction, and crime.

Johnson's war on poverty had two objectives: to give poor people a chance to improve themselves and to provide them with direct assistance. The first took the form of the Economic Opportunity Act of 1964. This law created a mélange of programs, among them the Job Corps, similar to the New Deal's Civilian Conservation Corps; a community action program to finance local efforts; an educational program for small children; a work-study program for college students; and a system for training the unskilled unemployed and for lending money to small businesses in poor areas. The Economic Opportunity Act combined the progressive concept of the welfare state with the conservative idea of individual responsibility. The government would support the weak and disadvantaged by giving them a fair chance to make it on their own.

Buttressed by this and other legislative triumphs, Johnson sought election as president in his own right in 1964. He achieved this ambition in unparalleled fashion. His championing of civil rights won him the almost unanimous support of blacks; his economy drive attracted the well-to-do and the business interests; his war on poverty held the allegiance of labor and other elements traditionally Democratic. His southern antecedents counterbalanced his liberalism on the race question in the eyes of many white southerners.

The Republicans played into his hands by nominating a conservative, Senator Barry M. Goldwater of Arizona. A large majority of the voters found Goldwater out of date on economic questions and dangerously aggressive on foreign affairs. During the campaign Democrats told a joke that went something like this:

(Goldwater is president. An aide rushes into his office.)

AIDE: Mr. President, the Russians have just launched an all-out nuclear attack on us. Their missiles will strike in 15 minutes. What shall we do?

GOLDWATER: Have all the wagons form a circle.

In November, Johnson won a sweeping victory, collecting over 61 percent of the popular vote and carrying all the country except Goldwater's Arizona and five states in the Deep South. Quickly he pressed ahead with his Great Society program. In January 1965 he proposed a compulsory hospital insurance system for persons over the age of 65. As amended by Congress, this system, known as Medicare, combined hospital insurance for retired people (funded by social security taxes) with a voluntary plan to cover doctors' bills (paid for in part by the government). The law also provided for grants to the states to help pay the medical expenses of poor people below the retirement age of 65. This part of the system was called Medicaid.

Next Congress passed the Elementary and Secondary Education Act. This measure supplied funds to improve the education of poor children, the theory being that children from city slums and impoverished rural areas tended to be "educationally deprived" and thus in need of extra help. Related to the Education Act was a program for poor preschool children, known as Head Start. Besides preparing young children for elementary school, this program contributed incidentally to improving their health by providing medical examinations and good meals.

Other laws passed at Johnson's urging in 1965 and 1966 dealt with support for the arts and for scientific research, highway safety, crime control, slum clearance, clean air, and the preservation of historic sites. Of special significance was the Immigration Act of 1965, which did away with the national-origin system of admitting newcomers. Instead, priorities were based on such things as skill and the need for political asylum.

A shot of President Johnson using his hands to emphasize a point while speaking to reporters conveys the talkative, intense, persuasive nature of the man.

The Great Society program was one of the most remarkable outpourings of important legislation in American history. The results, however, were mixed. Head Start and a related program to help students in secondary schools prepare for college were unqualified successes. But the 1965 Education Act proved a disappointment, and although Medicare and Medicaid provided good medical treatment for millions of people, since the patients no longer paid most of the bills, doctors, hospitals, and drug companies were able to raise fees and prices without fear of losing business. The Job Corps, which was designed to help poor people get better-paying jobs by providing them with vocational training, had no measurable effect on the unemployment rate. On balance, the achievements of the Great Society fell far short of what President Johnson had promised.

The War in Vietnam

In the fall of 1967 President Johnson seemed to have every intention of running for a second full term. Whether he would be reelected was not clear, but that any Democrat could prevent this shrewd and powerful politician from being nominated seemed out of the question. Nevertheless, within a few months opposition to him had become so bitter that he withdrew as a candidate for renomination. The cause of this opposition was his handling of a conflict on the other side of the world—the war in Vietnam.

When Vietnam was divided following the defeat of the French in 1954, a handful of American military "advisers" were sent there to train a South Vietnamese army. As time passed, more American aid and "advice" were dispatched in a futile effort to establish a stable government. Pro-communist forces, now called the Vietcong, soon controlled large sections of the country, some almost within sight of the capital city, Saigon.

Gradually the Vietcong, drawing supplies from North Vietnam and indirectly from China and the Soviet Union, increased in strength. In response, more American money and more military advisers were sent to bolster Ngo Dinh Diem's regime in the south. By the end of 1961 there were 3,200 American military men and women in the country; by late 1963 the numbers had risen to more than 16,000, and 120 American soldiers had been killed. Shortly before Kennedy was assassinated, a group of South Vietnamese generals overthrew Diem and killed him. The following summer, after announcing that North Vietnamese gunboats had fired on American destroyers in the Gulf of Tonkin, President Johnson demanded, and in an air of crisis obtained, an authorization from Congress to "repel any armed attack against the forces of the United States and to prevent further aggression."

With this blank check, and buttressed by his sweeping defeat of Goldwater in the 1964 presidential election, Johnson sent combat troops to South Vietnam and directed air attacks against targets in both South and North Vietnam.

At first the American ground troops were supposed to be merely teachers and advisers of the South Vietnamese army. Then they were said to be there to defend air bases, with the understanding that they would return fire if they were attacked. Next came word that the troops were being used to assist South Vietnamese units when they came under enemy fire. In fact the Americans were soon attacking the enemy directly, mounting search-and-destroy missions aimed at clearing the foe from villages and entire sections of the country.

At the end of 1965 some 184,000 Americans were in the field; a year later, 385,000; after another year, 485,000. By the middle of 1968 the number exceeded 538,000. Each increase was met by corresponding increases from the other side. The United States was engaged in a full-scale war, one that Congress never declared.

Hawks and Doves

From the beginning, the war divided the American people sharply. Defenders of the president's policy, called *hawks,* emphasized the nation's moral responsibility to resist aggression and what President Eisenhower had called the domino theory, which predicted that if the communists were allowed to take over one country, they would soon take its neighbors, then their neighbors, and so on until the entire world had been conquered. The United States was not an aggressor in Vietnam, the hawks insisted.

American opponents of the war, called *doves,* argued that the struggle between the South Vietnamese government and the Vietcong was a civil war in which Americans should not meddle. They stressed the repressive, undemocratic character of the Diem regime and of those that followed as proof that the war was not a contest between democracy and communism. They objected to the massive aerial bombings (more explosives were dropped on Vietnam between 1964 and 1968 than on Germany and Japan combined in World War II); to the use of napalm and other chemical weapons such as the defoliants that were sprayed on forests and crops, which wreaked havoc among noncombatants; and to the killing of civilians by American troops. And they deplored the heavy loss of American life—over 40,000 dead by 1970—and the enormous cost in money. Because so many people objected to the war, Johnson refused to ask Congress to raise taxes to pay for it. The deficit forced the government to borrow huge

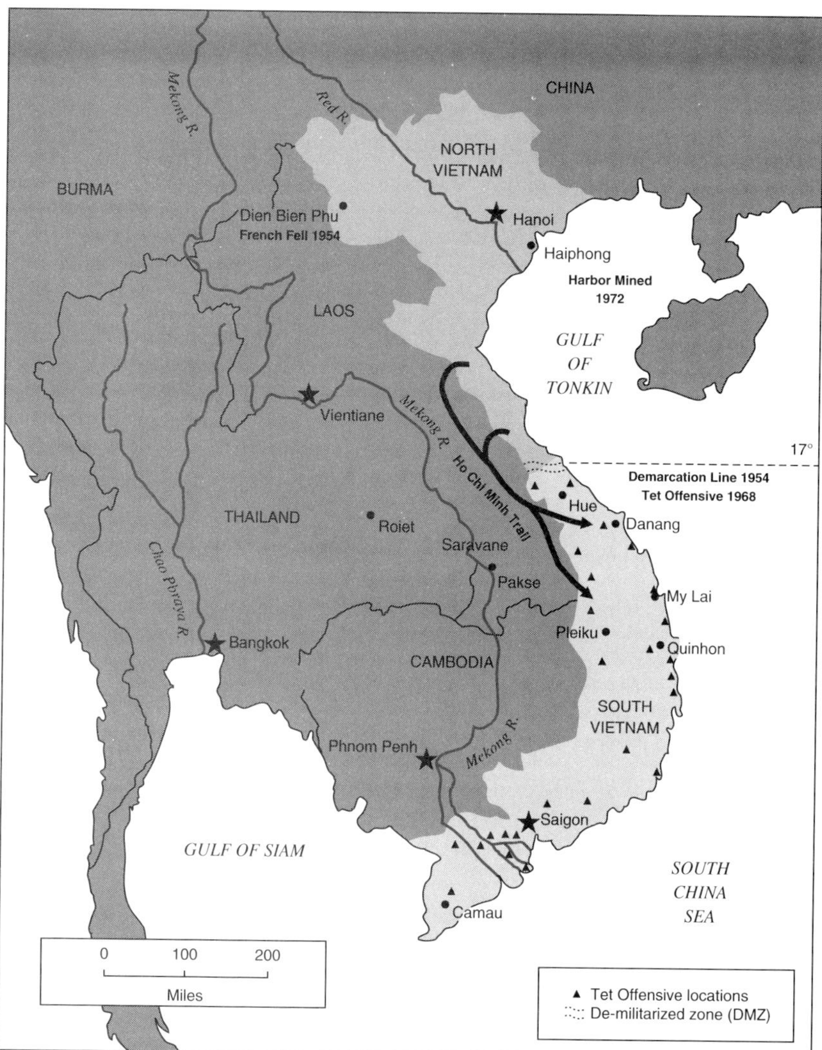

SOUTHEAST ASIA, 1954–1975

sums, which caused interest rates to soar, adding to the upward pressure on prices.

Although Johnson's financial policies were shortsighted if not outright irresponsible, and although his statements about the war were often lacking in candor, he and his advisers believed they were defending freedom and democracy. "If I got out of Vietnam," the President said, "I'd be giving a big fat reward for aggression."

What became increasingly clear as time passed was that military victory was impossible. Yet American leaders were extraordinarily slow to grasp this fact. Repeatedly they advised the president that one more escalation would break the enemy's will to resist. The smug arrogance bred by America's brief postwar monopoly of nuclear weapons persisted in some quarters long after the monopoly had been lost.

Kennedy's authorization of the Bay of Pigs fiasco was an example of this, but as late as 1965 McGeorge Bundy, President Johnson's special assistant for national security affairs, apparently told an interviewer that "the United States was the locomotive at the head of mankind, and the rest of the world the caboose." And like the proverbial donkey plodding after the carrot on the stick, Johnson repeatedly followed the advice of hawks like Bundy.

The Election of 1968

Gradually the doves increased in number. Then, in November 1967, Senator Eugene McCarthy of Minnesota announced that he was a candidate for the 1968 Democratic presidential nomination. Opposition to the war was his issue.

Preventing Johnson from getting the Democratic nomination in 1968 seemed on the surface impossible. Aside from the difficulty of defeating a "reigning" president, there were the solid domestic achievements of Johnson's Great Society program. McCarthy took his chances of being nominated so lightly that he did not trouble to set up a real organization. He entered the campaign only because he believed that someone must step forward to put the Vietnam question before the voters.

Suddenly, early in 1968, North Vietnam and Vietcong forces launched a general offensive to correspond with their Lunar New Year (Tet). Striking 39 of the 44 provincial capitals, many other towns and cities, and every American base, they caused chaos throughout South Vietnam. They held Hue, the old capital of the country, for weeks. To root them out of Saigon, the Americans had to level large sections of the city. Elsewhere the destruction was total, an irony highlighted by the remark of an American officer after the recapture of the village of Ben Tre: "It became necessary to destroy the town to save it."

Tet cost North Vietnam and the Vietcong heavily, but the psychological impact of the offensive in South Vietnam and in the United States made it a clear victory for the communists. When General William C. Westmoreland described Tet as a communist defeat and when it came out that the administration was considering sending an additional 206,000 troops to South Vietnam, McCarthy, campaigning before the first presidential primary in New Hampshire, became a formidable figure. Thousands of students and other volunteers flocked to the state to ring doorbells in his behalf. On election day he polled 42 percent of the Democratic vote.

The political situation was monumentally confused. Many New Hampshire voters had supported McCarthy because they believed that Johnson was not prosecuting the war vigorously enough and saw voting for another person as a way to rebuke him. After the primary, former attorney general Robert F. Kennedy, brother of the slain president, entered the race. Had Kennedy done so earlier, McCarthy might have withdrawn. After New Hampshire, McCarthy understandably decided to remain in the contest.

Compounding this confusion, President Johnson withdrew from the race. Vice-President Hubert H. Humphrey then announced his candidacy, though not until it was too late for him to run in the primaries. Kennedy carried the primaries in Indiana and Nebraska. McCarthy won in Wisconsin and Oregon. In the climactic contest in California, Kennedy won by a small margin. However, immediately after his victory speech in a Los Angeles hotel, he was assassinated by Sirhan Sirhan, a young Arab nationalist who had been incensed by Kennedy's support of Israel. In effect, Kennedy's death ensured the nomination of Humphrey; most professional politicians distrusted McCarthy, who was rather diffident and aloof politician.

The contest for the Republican nomination was far less dramatic, though its outcome, the nomination of Richard M. Nixon, would have been hard to predict a few years earlier. After his defeat in the California gubernatorial election of 1962, Nixon joined a prominent New York law firm. He remained active in Republican affairs, making countless speeches and attending political meetings throughout the country. He announced his candidacy in February 1968, swept the primaries, and won an easy first-ballot victory at the Republican convention.

Nixon then astounded the country and dismayed liberals by choosing Governor Spiro T. Agnew of Maryland as his running mate. Agnew was a political unknown outside Maryland, but he had spoken harshly about black radicalism. Nixon chose him primarily to attract southern votes.

Placating the South seemed necessary because Governor George C. Wallace of Alabama was making a determined bid to win enough electoral votes for his American Independent party to prevent any candidate's obtaining a majority. Wallace was flagrantly antiblack and sure to attract substantial southern and conservative support.

This Republican strategy disturbed liberals and heightened the tension surrounding the Democratic convention, held in Chicago in late August. Humphrey delegates controlled the convention. The vice-president had a solid liberal record on domestic issues, but he had supported Johnson's Vietnam policy with equal solidity. Voters who could not stomach the Nixon-Agnew ticket and who opposed the war faced a difficult choice. Hundreds of radicals and young activists descended on Chicago to put pressure on the delegates to repudiate the Johnson Vietnam policy.

In the tense atmosphere that resulted, the party hierarchy overreacted. The mayor of Chicago, Richard J. Daley, an old-fashioned political boss, ringed the convention with barricades and policemen to protect it from disruption. Inside the building the delegates nominated Humphrey and adopted a war plank satisfactory to Johnson. Outside, however, provoked by the abusive language and violent behavior of radical demonstrators, the police tore into the protesters, brutally beating dozens while millions watched on television in fascinated horror.

At first the mayhem at Chicago seemed to benefit Nixon. He campaigned at a deliberate, dignified pace, making relatively few public appearances, relying instead on carefully arranged television interviews and taped commercials prepared by an advertising agency. He stressed firm enforcement of the law, and his desire "to bring us together." Agnew, however, assaulted Humphrey and left-wing dissident groups in a series of blunt, coarse speeches. Critics, remembering Nixon's political style in the heyday of Joseph McCarthy, called Agnew "Nixon's Nixon."

The Democratic campaign was badly organized. Humphrey seemed far behind in the early stages. Shortly before election day, President Johnson helped him by suspending air attacks on North Vietnam, and in the long run the Republican strategy helped too. Black voters and the urban poor had no practical choice but to vote Democratic. Gradually Humphrey gained ground, and on election day the popular vote was close: Nixon slightly less than 31.8 million votes, Humphrey nearly 31.3 million. Nixon's electoral college margin, however, was substantial—301 to 191. The remaining 46 electoral votes went to Wallace, whose 9.9 million votes came to 13.5 percent of the total. Despite Nixon's triumph, the Democrats retained control of both houses of Congress.

Nixon as President

When he took office in January 1969, Richard Nixon projected an image of calm and deliberate statesmanship; he introduced no startling changes, proposed no important new legislation. The major economic problem facing him, inflation, was primarily a result of the heavy military expenditures and easy-money policies of the Johnson administration. Nixon cut federal spending and balanced the 1969 budget, while the Federal Reserve Board forced up interest rates in order to slow the expansion of the money supply. Even its supporters admitted that this policy would check inflation only slowly, and when prices continued to rise, uneasiness mounted. Labor unions demanded large wage increases. The problem was complicated by rising deficits in the United States' balance of trade with foreign nations, the result of an overvaluation of the dollar that encouraged Americans to buy foreign goods.

In 1970 Congress passed a law giving the president power to regulate prices and wages. Nixon had opposed this legislation, but in the summer of 1971 he decided to use it. First he announced a 90-day price and wage freeze (Phase I) and placed a 10 percent surcharge on imports. Then he set up a pay board and a price commission with authority to limit wage and price increases when the freeze ended (Phase II). These controls did not check inflation completely—and they angered union leaders, who felt that labor was being shortchanged—but they did slow the upward spiral. A devaluation of the dollar in December 1971 helped the economy by making American products more competitive in foreign markets.

In handling other domestic issues, the president was less decisive. He advocated shifting the burden of welfare payments to the federal government and equalizing such payments in all the states, and he came out for a minimum income for poor families. These measures got nowhere in Congress, despite his "southern strategy" of seeking the support of conservative southern Democrats by appointing "strict constructionist" judges to the federal courts.

"Vietnamizing" the War

Whatever his difficulties on the domestic front, Nixon considered the solution of the Vietnam problem his chief task. During the 1968 campaign, he suggested no policy very different from what Johnson was doing, though he insisted he would end the war on "honorable" terms if elected.

In office, Nixon proposed a phased withdrawal of all non–South Vietnamese troops, to be followed by an internationally supervised election in South Vietnam. The North Vietnamese rejected this scheme and insisted that the United States withdraw its forces unconditionally. Their intransigence left the president in a difficult position. He could not compel the foe to negotiate meaningfully, yet every passing day added to the strength of antiwar sentiment, which, as it expressed itself in ever more emphatic terms, in turn led to deeper divisions in the country.

The president responded to the dilemma by trying to build up the South Vietnamese armed forces so that American troops could pull out without the communists overrunning South Vietnam. Soon South Vietnam had the fourth largest air force in the world. The trouble with this strategy of "Vietnamization" was that for 15 years the United States had been employing it without success. The South Vietnamese troops had seldom displayed much enthusiasm for the kind of tough jungle fighting at which the North Vietnamese and the Vietcong excelled. Nevertheless, efforts at Vietnamization were stepped up, and in June 1969, Nixon announced that he would soon reduce the number of American soldiers in Vietnam by 25,000. In September he promised that an additional 35,000 men would be withdrawn by mid-December.

These steps did not quiet American protesters. On October 15 a nationwide antiwar demonstration, Vietnam Moratorium Day, organized by students, attracted an unprecedented turnout all over the country. This massive display evoked one of Vice-President Agnew's most notorious blasts of adjectival invective: He said that the moratorium was an example of "national masochism" led by "an effete corps of impudent snobs who characterize themselves as intellectuals."

A second Moratorium Day brought a crowd estimated at 250,000 to Washington, but the president remained unmoved. On November 3 he defended his policy in a televised speech and announced that he planned to remove all American ground forces from Vietnam. The next day, reporting a flood of telegrams and calls supporting his position, he declared that the "silent majority" of the American people approved his course.

For a season, events appeared to vindicate Nixon's position. Troop withdrawals continued in an orderly fashion. A new lottery system for drafting men for military duty eliminated some of the inequities in the selective service law. But the war continued. Early in 1970 the revelation that an American unit two years earlier had massacred civilians, including dozens of women and children, in a Vietnamese hamlet known as My Lai, revived the controversy over the purposes of the war and its corrosive effects on those who were fighting it. The American people, it seemed, were being torn apart by the war: one from another according to each one's interpretation of events, many within themselves as they tried to balance the war's horrors against their pride, their dislike of communism, and their unwillingness to turn their backs on their elected leader.

Not even Nixon's most implacable enemy could find reason to think that he wished the war to go on. Its human, economic, and social costs could only vex his days and threaten his future reputation. When he reduced the level of the fighting, the communists merely waited for further reductions. When he raised it, many of his own people denounced him. If he pulled out of Vietnam entirely, other Americans would be outraged.

The Cambodian "Incursion"

Late in April 1970, Nixon announced that Vietnamization was proceeding more rapidly than he had hoped, that communist power was weakening, that within a year another 150,000 American soldiers would be extracted from Vietnam. A week later he announced that military intelligence had indicated that the enemy was consolidating its "sanctuaries" in neutral Cambodia and that he was therefore dispatching thousands of American troops to destroy these bases.* He was in fact escalating the war. He even resumed the bombing of targets in North Vietnam. "Let's go blow the hell out of them," he told the Joint Chiefs of Staff.

To foes of the war, Nixon's decision seemed appallingly unwise. The contradictions between his confident statements about Vietnamization and his alarmist description of powerful enemy forces poised like a dagger 30-odd miles from Saigon did not seem the product of a reasoning mind. His failure

*American planes had been bombing Cambodia for some time, but this fact was not known to the public (or to Congress) until 1973.

to consult congressional leaders or many of his personal advisers before drastically altering his policy, the critics claimed, was unconstitutional and irresponsible. His insensitive response to the avalanche of criticism that descended on him further disturbed observers.

Students took the lead in opposing the invasion of Cambodia. Young people had been prominent in the opposition to the war from early in the conflict. Some objected to war in principle. Many more believed that this particular war was wrong because it was being fought against a small country on the other side of the globe where America's vital interests did not seem to be threatened. As the war dragged on and casualties mounted, student opposition to the draft became intense.

Nixon's shocking announcement triggered many campus demonstrations. One college where feeling ran high was Kent State University in Ohio. For several days students there clashed with local police; they broke windows and caused other damage to property. When the governor of Ohio called out the National Guard, angry students showered the soldiers with stones. During a noontime protest on May 4, the Guardsmen, who were poorly trained in crowd control, suddenly opened fire. Four students were killed, two of them women passing by on their way to class. While the nation reeled from this shock, two black students at Jackson State University were killed by Mississippi state policemen. A wave of student strikes followed, closing down hundreds of colleges, including many that had seen no previous unrest.

Nixon pulled American ground troops out of Cambodia quickly, but he did not change his Vietnam policy, and in fact Cambodia stiffened his determination. The balance of forces remained in uneasy equilibrium through 1971. Late in March 1972 the North Vietnamese again mounted a series of assaults throughout South Vietnam. The U.S. president responded with heavier bombing, and he ordered the approaches to Haiphong and other northern ports sown with mines to cut off the communists' supplies.

Détente

In the midst of these aggressive actions, Nixon and his principal foreign policy adviser, Henry Kissinger, devised a bold and ingenious diplomatic offensive. Abandoning a lifetime of treating communism as a single worldwide conspiracy aimed at destroying capitalism, Nixon sent Kissinger to China and the Soviet Union to arrange summit meetings with the communist leaders. In February 1972, Nixon and Kissinger flew to Beijing to consult with Chinese officials. They agreed to support the admission of China to the United Nations and to develop economic and cultural exchanges with the Chinese. Although these results appeared small, Nixon's visit, ending more than 20 years of adamant refusal by the American government to accept the reality of the Chinese Revolution, marked a dramatic reversal of policy; as such it was hailed in the United States and elsewhere in the world.

In May, Nixon and Kissinger flew to Moscow. This trip also produced striking results. The first Strategic Arms Limitation Treaty (SALT) was the main concrete gain. Nixon also agreed to permit large sales of American grain to the Soviets.

Nixon and Kissinger called the new policy *détente,* a French term meaning "relaxation of tensions. Détente lowered the cost of containment for the United States. SALT did not end the production of atomic weapons, but the fact that it did check American and Soviet arms production was encouraging. That both China and the Soviet Union had been willing to work for improved relations with the United States before America withdrew from Vietnam was also significant. This fact, plus the failure of their offensive to overwhelm South Vietnam, led the North Vietnamese to make diplomatic concessions in the interest of getting the United States out of the war. By October the draft of a settlement that provided for a cease-fire, the return of American prisoners of war, and the withdrawal of United States forces from Vietnam had been hammered out. Shortly before the presidential election, Kissinger announced that peace was "at hand."

Nixon Triumphant

A few days later President Nixon was reelected, defeating the Democratic candidate, Senator George McGovern of South Dakota, in a landslide—521 electoral votes to 17. McGovern's campaign had been hampered by divisions within the Democratic party and by his tendency to advance poorly thought-out proposals. McGovern also lost support over his han-

President and Mrs. Nixon dining with Chinese officials in Beijing in February 1972. Even Nixon's harshest critics conceded that his initiative in reopening U.S.-China relations was a diplomatic masterstroke.

dling of the revelation, shortly after the nominating convention, that his running mate, Senator Thomas Eagleton of Missouri, had in the past undergone electroshock treatments following serious psychological difficulties. After some backing and filling, which left many voters with the impression that he was indecisive, McGovern forced Eagleton to withdraw. Sargent Shriver, former head of the Peace Corps, took Eagleton's place on the ticket.

Nixon interpreted his triumph as an indication that the people approved of everything he stood for. He had won over hundreds of thousands of normally Democratic voters. The "solid South" was now solidly Republican. Nixon's southern strategy of reducing the pressure for school desegregation also appealed to northern blue-collar workers. Many people smarting from the repeated setbacks the country had experienced in Vietnam and resentful of what they considered the unpatriotic tactics of the doves also approved of Nixon's refusal to pull out of Vietnam.

Suddenly Nixon loomed as one of the most powerful and successful presidents in American history. His bold attack on inflation, even his harsh Vietnamese policy suggested decisiveness and self-confidence, qualities he had often seemed to lack. His willingness to negotiate with the communist nations to lessen world tensions indicated a new flexibility and reasonableness. His landslide victory appeared to demonstrate that the people approved of his way of tackling the major problems of the times.

His first reaction was to try to extract more favorable terms from the Vietnamese communists. Announcing that they were not bargaining in good faith over the remaining details of the peace treaty, he resumed the bombing of North Vietnam in December 1972, this time sending the mighty B-52s directly over Hanoi and other cities. The attacks caused much destruction, but their effectiveness as a means of forcing concessions from the North Vietnamese was at best debatable, and they led for the first time to the loss of large numbers of the big strategic bombers.

Nevertheless, both sides had much to gain from ending the war. In January 1973 an agreement was finally reached. The North Vietnamese retained control of large sections of the South, and they agreed to release American prisoners of war within 60 days. When this was accomplished, the last American troops were pulled out of Vietnam. More than 57,000 Americans had died in the long war, and over 300,000 more had been wounded. The cost had reached $150 billion.

Whatever the price, the war was over for the United States, and Nixon took the credit for having ended it. He immediately turned to domestic issues, determined, he made clear, to strengthen the power of the presidency vis-à-vis Congress and to decentralize administration by encouraging state and local management of government programs. He announced that he intended to reduce the interference of the federal government in the affairs of individuals. People should be more self-reliant, he said, and he denounced what he called "permissiveness." Overconcern for the interests of blacks and other minorities must end. Criminals should be punished "without pity."

These aims brought Nixon into conflict with liberal legislators of both parties, with the leaders of minority groups, and with persons concerned about the increasing power of the executive. The conflict came to a head over the president's anti-inflation policy. After his second inauguration he ended Phase II price and wage controls and substituted Phase III, which depended on voluntary "restraints" (except in the areas of food, health care, and construction). This approach did not work. Prices soared; it was the most rapid inflation since the Korean War. In an effort to check the rise, Nixon set a rigid limit on federal expenditures, cutting or abolishing many social welfare programs, and reducing federal grants in support of science and education. He even impounded (refused to spend) funds already appropriated by Congress for purposes he disapproved of.

When the Democratic Congress failed to override vetoes of bills challenging his policy, it appeared that Nixon was in total command. The White House staff, headed by H. R. Haldeman and John Ehrlichman, dominated the Washington bureaucracy like oriental viziers and dealt with legislators as though they were dealing with lackeys or eunuchs. When asked to account for their actions, they took refuge behind the shield of "executive privilege," the doctrine, never before applied so broadly, that discussions and communications within the executive branch were confidential and therefore immune from congressional scrutiny.

The Watergate Break-in

On March 19, 1973, James McCord, a former FBI agent accused of burglary, wrote a letter to the judge presiding at his trial. His act precipitated a series of disclosures that destroyed the Nixon administration.

McCord had been employed during the 1972 presidential campaign as a security officer of the Committee to Re-elect the President (CREEP). At about 1 A.M. on June 17, 1972, he and four other men had broken into Democratic headquarters at the Watergate, an apartment house and office building complex in Washington. The burglars had been caught rifling files and installing electronic eavesdropping devices. Two other Republican campaign officials were soon implicated. Nixon denied responsibility for their actions. "No one on the White House staff, no one in this Administration presently employed, was involved in this very bizarre incident," he announced. Most persons took the president at his word, and the affair did not materially affect the election. When brought to trial early in 1973, most of the defendants pleaded guilty.

Before Judge John J. Sirica imposed sentences on the culprits, however, McCord wrote his letter. High Republican officials had known about the burglary in advance and had persuaded most of the defendants to keep their connection secret, McCord claimed. Perjury had been committed during the trial.

The truth of McCord's charges swiftly became apparent. The head of CREEP, Jeb Stuart Magruder, and President Nixon's lawyer, John W. Dean III, admitted their involvement. Among the disclosures that emerged over the following months were these:

That the acting director of the FBI, L. Patrick Gray, had destroyed documents related to the case.

The burglars had been paid large sums of money at the instigation of the White House to ensure their silence.

The CIA had, perhaps unwittingly, supplied equipment used in this burglary.

CREEP officials had attempted to disrupt the campaigns of leading Democratic candidates during the 1972 primaries in illegal ways.

A number of corporations had made large contributions to the Nixon reelection campaign in violation of federal law.

The Nixon administration had placed illegal wiretaps on the telephones of some of its own officials as well as on those of reporters critical of its policies.

These revelations led to the discharge of Dean and the resignations of most of Nixon's closest advisers, including Haldeman, Ehrlichman, and Attorney General Richard Kleindienst. They also raised the question of the president's personal connection with the scandals. This he steadfastly denied. He insisted that he would investigate the Watergate affair thoroughly and see that the guilty were punished. He refused, however, to allow investigators to examine White House documents, again on grounds of executive privilege.

In the face of Nixon's denials, John Dean, testifying under oath before a special Senate Watergate investigation committee headed by Sam Ervin, Jr., of North Carolina, stated flatly and in circumstantial detail that the president had been closely involved in the Watergate cover-up. Dean had been a persuasive witness, but many people were reluctant to believe that a president could lie so cold-bloodedly to the entire country. Therefore, when it came out during later hearings of the Ervin committee that the president had systematically made secret tape recordings of White House conversations and telephone calls, it

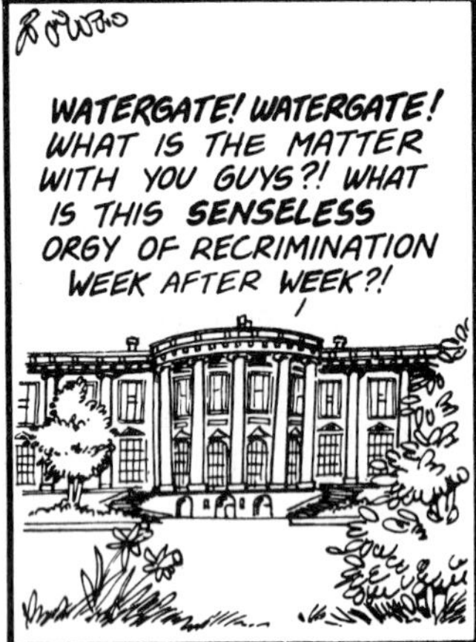

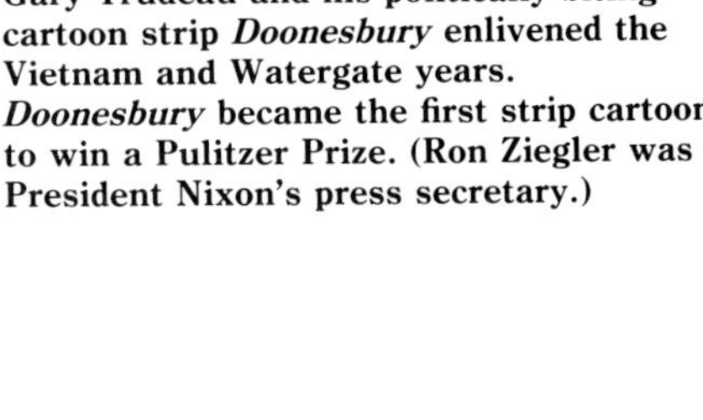
Gary Trudeau and his politically biting cartoon strip *Doonesbury* enlivened the Vietnam and Watergate years. *Doonesbury* became the first strip cartoon to win a Pulitzer Prize. (Ron Ziegler was President Nixon's press secretary.)

seemed obvious that these tapes would settle the question of Nixon's involvement once and for all.

When the president refused to release the tapes, calls for his resignation, even for impeachment, began to be heard. Yielding to pressure, he agreed to the appointment of an "independent" special prosecutor to investigate the Watergate affair, and he promised the appointee, Archibald Cox of the Harvard Law School, full cooperation. Cox, however, swiftly aroused the president's ire by demanding White House records, including the tapes. When Nixon refused, Cox obtained a subpoena from Judge Sirica ordering him to do so. The administration appealed and lost in the appellate court. Then, while the case was headed for the Supreme Court, Nixon ordered the new attorney general, Elliot Richardson, to dismiss Cox. Both Richardson and his chief assistant, William Ruckelshaus, resigned rather than do so. Solicitor General Robert Bork, third-ranking officer of the Justice Department, carried out Nixon's order.

These events, which occurred on Saturday, October 20, were promptly dubbed the Saturday Night Massacre. They caused an outburst of public indignation. Congress was bombarded by thousands of letters and telegrams demanding the president's impeachment. The House Judiciary Committee, headed by Peter W. Rodino, Jr., of New Jersey, began an investigation to see if enough evidence for impeachment existed.

Once again Nixon backed down. He agreed to turn over the tapes to Judge Sirica with the understanding that relevant materials could be presented to the grand jury investigating the Watergate affair, but nothing would be revealed to the public. He then named a new special prosecutor, Leon Jaworski, and promised him access to whatever White House documents he needed. However, it soon came out that some of the tapes were missing and that an important section of another had been deliberately erased.

More Troubles

The nation had never before experienced such a series of morale- shattering crises. While the seemingly unending complications of Watergate were unfolding during 1973, a number of unrelated disasters struck. First, pushed by a shortage of grains resulting from massive Russian purchases authorized by the administration as part of its détente with the Soviet Union, food prices shot up—wheat from $1.45 a bushel to over $5.00. Nixon imposed another price freeze, which led to shortages, and when the freeze was lifted, prices resumed their steep ascent.

Then Vice-President Agnew was accused of income tax fraud and of having accepted bribes while county executive of Baltimore and governor of Maryland. After vehemently denying all the charges for two months, Agnew, to escape a jail term, admitted in October that he had been guilty of tax evasion and resigned as vice-president.

Under the new Twenty-fifth Amendment, President Nixon nominated Gerald R. Ford of Michigan as vice-president, and the nomination was confirmed by Congress. Ford had served continuously in the House since 1949, as minority leader since 1964. His positions on public issues were close to Nixon's.

Not long after the Agnew fiasco, Nixon, responding to charges that he had paid almost no income taxes during his presidency, published his 1969–1972 returns. They showed that he had indeed paid very little—only about $1,600 in two years during which his income had exceeded half a million dollars. Although Nixon claimed that his tax returns had been perfectly legal—he had taken huge deductions for the gift of some of his vice-presidential papers to the National Archives—the legality and the propriety of his deductions were so questionable that he felt obliged, during a televised press conference, to assure the audience: "I am not a crook."

The Oil Crisis

Still another disaster followed as a result of the war that broke out in October 1973 between Israel and the Arab states. The fighting, though bloody, was brief and inconclusive; a truce was soon arranged under the auspices of the United States and the Soviet Union. But in an effort to force western nations to compel Israel to withdraw from lands held since the Six-Day War of 1967, the Arabs cut off oil shipments to the United States, Japan, and most of western Europe. A worldwide energy crisis ensued.

The immediate shortage resulting from the Arab oil boycott was ended by the patient diplomacy of Henry Kissinger, whom Nixon had made secretary of state at the beginning of his second administration. After weeks of negotiating in the spring of

1974, Kissinger obtained a tentative agreement that involved the withdrawal of Israel from some of the territory it had occupied in 1967. The Arab nations then lifted the boycott.

A revolution had taken place. From the middle of the 19th century until after World War II, the United States had produced far more oil than it could use. However, the phenomenal expansion of oil consumption that occurred after the war soon absorbed the surplus. By the late 1960s American car owners were driving more than a trillion miles a year. Petroleum was being used to manufacture nylon and other synthetic fibers as well as paints, insecticides, fertilizers, and many plastic products. Oil and natural gas became the principal fuels for home heating. Natural gas in particular was used increasingly in factories and electric utility plants because it was less polluting than coal and most other fuels. The Clean Air Act of 1965 speeded the process of conversion from coal to gas by countless industrial consumers. Because of these developments, at the outbreak of the 1973 Arab-Israeli war the United States was importing one-third of its oil.

In 1960 the principal oil exporters, Venezuela, Saudi Arabia, Kuwait, Iraq, and Iran, had formed a cartel, the Organization of Petroleum Exporting Countries (OPEC). For many years OPEC had been unable to control the world price of oil, which, on the eve of the 1973 war, was about $3.00 a barrel. The success of the Arab oil boycott served to unite the members of OPEC, and when the boycott was lifted, they boldly announced that the price was going up to $11.65 a barrel.

The announcement caused consternation throughout the industrial world. Soaring prices for oil meant soaring prices for everything made from petroleum or with petroleum-powered machinery. In the United States gasoline prices doubled overnight, and all prices rose at a rate of more than 10 percent a year. This double-digit inflation, which afflicted nearly all the countries of the world, added considerably to President Nixon's woes.

The Judgment: "Expletive Deleted"

Meanwhile, special prosecutor Jaworski continued his investigation of the Watergate scandals, and the House Judiciary Committee pursued its study of the impeachment question. In March 1974 a grand jury indicted Haldeman, Ehrlichman, former attorney general John Mitchell, who had been head of CREEP at the time of the break-in, and four other White House aides for conspiring to block the Watergate investigation. The jurors also named Nixon an "unindicted co-conspirator," Jaworski having informed them that their power to indict a president was constitutionally questionable. Judge Sirica thereupon turned over the jury's evidence against Nixon to the Judiciary Committee. Then both the Internal Revenue Service and a joint congressional committee, having separately audited the president's income tax returns, announced that most of his deductions had been unjustified. The IRS assessed him nearly half a million dollars in taxes and interest, which he agreed to pay.

In an effort to check the mounting criticism, Nixon late in April released edited transcripts of the tapes he had turned over to the court the previous November. If he had expected the material to convince the public that he had been ignorant of the attempt to cover up the administration's connection with Watergate, he was sadly mistaken. In addition to much incriminating evidence, the transcripts provided a fascinating view of how he conducted himself in private. His repeated use of foul language, so out of keeping with his public image, offended millions. The phrase "expletive deleted," inserted in place of words considered too vulgar for publication in family newspapers, became a catchword. His remarks came across as unfocused and lacking in any concern for the public interest or the law. The publication of the transcripts led some of his strongest supporters to demand that he resign. And once the Judiciary Committee obtained the actual tapes, it came out that much material prejudicial to the president's case had been suppressed.

Yet impeaching a president seemed so drastic a step that many people felt that more direct proof of Nixon's involvement in the cover-up was necessary. Nixon insisted that all the relevant information was contained in these tapes; he adamantly refused to turn over others to the special prosecutor or the Judiciary Committee. Nevertheless, prosecutor Jaworski subpoenaed 64 additional tapes. Nixon, through his lawyer, James St. Clair, refused to obey the subpoena. Swiftly, the case of *United States* v. *Richard M. Nixon* went to the Supreme Court.

In the summer of 1974 the Watergate drama

reached its climax. The Judiciary Committee, following months of study of the evidence behind closed doors, decided to conduct its deliberations in open session. While millions watched on television, 38 members of the House of Representatives debated the charges. The discussions revealed both the thoroughness of the investigation and the soul-searching efforts of the representatives to render an impartial judgment. Three articles of impeachment were adopted. They charged the president with obstructing justice, misusing the powers of his office, and failing to obey the committee's subpoenas. On the first two, many of the Republicans on the committee joined with the Democrats in voting aye, a clear indication that the full House would vote to impeach.

On the eve of the debates, the Supreme Court had ruled unanimously that the president must turn over the 64 subpoenaed tapes to the special prosecutor. Executive privilege had its place, the Court stated, but no person, not even a president, could "withhold evidence that is demonstrably relevant in a criminal trial." For reasons that soon became obvious, Nixon seriously considered defying the Court. Only when convinced that to do so would make his impeachment and conviction certain did he agree to comply.

He would not, however, resign. Even if the House impeached him, he was counting on his ability to hold the support of 34 senators (one-third plus one of the full Senate) to escape conviction. But events were passing beyond his control. When the 64 subpoenaed tapes were transcribed and analyzed, Nixon's fate was sealed. Three recorded conversations between the president and H. R. Haldeman on June 23, 1972—less than a week after the break-in and only one day after Nixon had assured the nation that no one in the White House had been involved in the affair—proved conclusively that Nixon had tried to get the CIA to persuade the FBI not to follow up leads in the case on the spurious claim that national security was involved.

The president's defenders had insisted not so much that he was innocent as that solid proof of his guilt had not been demonstrated. Where, they asked, in the metaphor of the moment, was the "smoking gun"? That weapon had now been found, and it bore the fingerprints of Richard M. Nixon.

Exactly what happened in the White House is not yet known. The president's chief advisers pressed him to release the material at once and to admit that he had erred in holding it back. This he did on August 5. After reading the new transcripts, all the Republican members of the Judiciary Committee who had voted against the impeachment articles reversed themselves. Republican congressional leaders told Nixon that the House would impeach him and that no more than a handful of the senators would vote to acquit him.

The Meaning of Watergate

On August 8, Nixon announced his resignation, and at noon on August 9, Gerald Ford was sworn in as president. The meaning of Watergate became immediately the subject of much speculation. Whether Nixon's crude efforts to dominate Congress, to crush or inhibit dissent, and to subvert the electoral process would have permanently altered the American political system had they succeeded is probably beyond knowing. However, the orderly way in which these efforts were checked suggests that the system would have survived in any case.

Nixon's own drama is and must remain one of the most fascinating and enigmatic episodes in American history. Despite his fall from the heights because of personal flaws, his was not a tragedy in the Greek sense. Even when he finally yielded power, he seemed without remorse or even awareness of his transgressions. He was devoid of the classic hero's pride. Did he really intend to smash all opposition and rule like a tyrant, or was he driven by lack of confidence in himself? His stubborn aggressiveness and his overblown view of executive privilege may have reflected a need for constant reassurance that he was a mighty leader. One element in his downfall, preserved for posterity in videotapes of his television appearances, was that even while he was assuring the country of his innocence most vehemently, he did not look like a victim of the machinations of overzealous supporters. Perhaps at some profound level he did not want to be believed.

Milestones

1942 Congress of Racial Equality (CORE) founded

1955–1956 Montgomery, Alabama, bus boycott

1956 Southern Christian Leadership Conference founded

1961 Freedom Riders "invade" the South

1963 President Ngo Dinh Diem of South Vietnam assassinated
Martin Luther King, Jr., "Letter from Birmingham Jail"

1964 Gulf of Tonkin Resolution leads to escalation of Vietnam War
Civil Rights Act
Economic Opportunity Act

1965 Immigration Act ends national-origin system
Medicare Act
Elementary and Secondary Education Act
Clean Air Act

1968 Communist Tet offensive in South Vietnam
American troop strength in Vietnam reaches 538,000
Lyndon Johnson withdraws as presidential candidate

1969 Nixon announces "Vietnamization" of the war

1970 Nixon announces "incursion" in Cambodia
Demonstrating antiwar students killed at Kent State and Jackson State universities

1971 Nixon freezes prices

1972 Break-in at Democratic headquarters in Washington, D.C.
Nixon and Kissinger visit China and the Soviet Union
Strategic Arms Limitation Treaty (SALT)

1973 House Judiciary Committee begins impeachment hearings
Vice-President Spiro Agnew resigns
Last American troops withdraw from South Vietnam
Nixon fires special prosecutor Archibald Cox (Saturday Night Massacre)

1973–1974 Arab oil boycott

1974 Supreme Court orders release of Nixon's White House tapes
Nixon resigns; Gerald R. Ford becomes president

Supplementary Reading

On Lyndon Johnson, major biographies by Robert Caro and Robert Dallek, the former bitterly critical, have not yet reached the presidential years. See J. F. Heath, **Decade of Disillusionment** (1980), and A. J. Matusow, **The Unraveling of America** (1984). W. M. O'Neill, **Coming Apart: An Informal History of the 1960s** (1971), and Geoffrey Hodgson, **America in Our Time** (1976), deal more broadly with the period.

For civil rights developments, consult Taylor Branch, **Parting the Waters** (1988), and David Garrow, **Bearing the Cross** (1981). On the election of 1968, T. H. White, **The Making of the President, 1968** (1969), is lively and entertaining. The best biography of Nixon is Stephen Ambrose, **Nixon** (1987–1991), but see also William Safire, **Before the Fall** (1975).

The literature on the war in Vietnam is enormous. George Herring, **America's Longest War** (1986), is an excellent survey. Stanley Karnow, **Vietnam: A History** (1983), is a straightforward narrative account. See also Melvin Small, **Johnson, Nixon, and the Doves** (1988), Neil Sheehan, **A Bright and Shining Lie** (1988), and David Halberstam, **The Best and the Brightest** (1972), which contains a mass of detail on the evolution of American policy, based on extensive interviews. William Shawcross, **Side-Show: Kissinger, Nixon, and the Destruction of Cambodia** (1979), is extremely critical.

R. S. Litwak, **Détente and the Nixon Doctrine** (1984), is a useful study of U.S.-Soviet relations in the Nixon era, and Henry Kissinger's memoirs, **White House Years** (1979) and **Years of Upheaval** (1982), are important though, like most such works, self-serving. The best analysis of the Watergate affair is S. I. Kutler, **The Wars of Watergate** (1990), but see also Carl Bernstein and Robert Woodward, **All the President's Men** (1974) and **Final Days** (1976).

CHAPTER 32

Society in Flux, 1945–1980

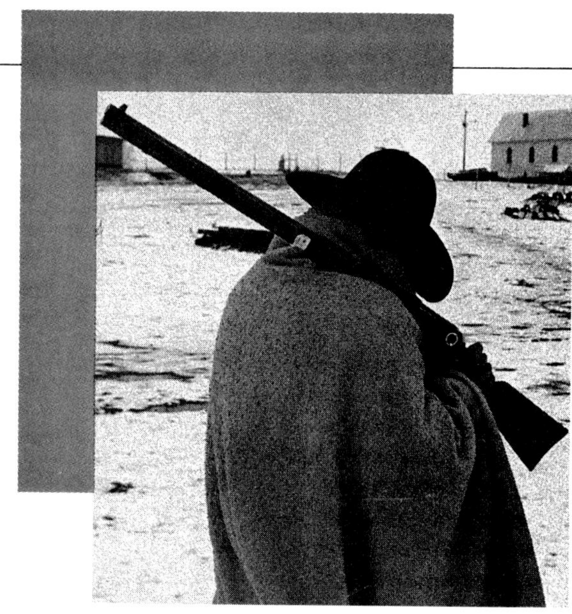

DESPITE LYNDON JOHNSON'S EXTRAVAGANT style and his landslide defeat of Barry Goldwater in the 1964 presidential election, the tone of his inaugural address in January 1965 was uncharacteristically restrained. The nation was "prosperous, great, and mighty," he said, but "we have no promise from God that our greatness will endure." He was obviously thinking of the enormous changes that were occurring in the country. He spoke of "this fragile existence," and he warned the people that they lived "in a world where change and growth seem to tower beyond the control, and even the judgment of men."

A Dynamic Society

The population was expanding rapidly. During the depressed 1930s it had increased by 9 million; in the 1950s it rose by more than 28 million, by 24 million more in both the 1960s and 1970s. Population experts observed startling shifts within this expanding mass. The westward movement had by no means ended with the closing of the frontier in the 1890s. One indication of this was the admission of Hawaii and Alaska to the Union in 1959. More significant was the growth of the Sun Belt—Florida and the states of the Southwest. California added more than 5 million to its population between 1950 and 1960, and in 1963 it passed New York to become the most populous state in the Union. Nevada and Arizona were expanding at an even more rapid rate.

The climate of the Southwest was particularly attractive to older people, and the population growth reflected the prosperity that enabled pensioners and other retired persons to settle there. At the same time the area attracted millions of young workers, for it became the center of the aircraft and electronics industries and the government's atomic energy and space programs. These industries displayed the best side of modern capitalism: high wages, comfortable working conditions, complex and efficient machinery, and the marriage of scientific technology and commercial utility.

Advances in transportation and communication

Chapter-opening illustration:
Huddled against the cold, an Indian sentry patrols the trading post at Wounded Knee, South Dakota, during the 1973 occupation of the site.

added to geographic mobility. In the postwar decades the automobile entered its golden age. In the booming 1920s, when the car became an instrument of mass transportation, about 31 million autos were produced by American factories. During the 1960s fully 77 million rolled off the assembly lines.

Gasoline use increased accordingly. The more mobile population drove farther in more reliable and more comfortable vehicles over smoother and less congested highways. And the new cars were heavier and more powerful than their predecessors. Gasoline consumption first reached 15 billion gallons in 1931; it soared to 92 billion in 1970. A new business, the motel industry (the word, typically American, was a blend of *motor* and *hotel*), developed to service the millions of tourists and business travelers who burned all this fuel.

The development of the interstate highway system, begun under Eisenhower in 1956, was a major stimulus to increased mobility. The new roads did far more than facilitate long-distance travel; they accelerated the shift of population to the suburbs and the consequent decline of inner-city districts.

Despite the speeds that cars maintained on them, the new highways were much safer than the old roads. The traffic death rate per mile driven fell steadily, almost entirely because of the interstates. However, the environmental impact of the system was frequently severe. Elevated roads cut ugly swaths through cities, and the cars they carried released tons of noxious exhaust fumes into urban air. Hillsides were gashed, marshes filled in, forests felled, all in the name of speed and efficiency.

Although commercial air travel had existed in the 1930s, it truly came of age when the first jetliner, the Boeing 707, went into service in 1958. Almost immediately jets came to dominate long-distance travel, to the detriment of railroad and steamship passenger service.

Television

Another important postwar change was the advent of television as a means of mass communication. Throughout the 1950s the public bought sets at a rate of 6 to 7 million annually; by 1961 there were 55 million in operation, receiving the transmissions of 530 stations. During the 1960s the National Aeronautics and Space Agency (NASA) began launching satellites capable of transmitting television pictures to earth, and the American Telephone and Telegraph Company (AT&T) orbited private commercial satellites that could relay television programs from one continent to another.

Television combined the immediacy of radio with the visual impact of films, and it displayed most of the strengths and weaknesses of both in exaggerated form. It swiftly became indispensable to the political system, both for its coverage of public events and as a vehicle for political advertising.

Some excellent drama was presented, especially on the National Educational Television network, along with many filmed documentaries. "Sesame Street," a children's program presented on the educational network, won international recognition for its entertainment value and for its success in motivating underprivileged children. Commercial television indirectly improved the level of radio broadcasting by siphoning off much of the mass audience; more radio time was devoted to serious discussion programs and to classical music, especially after the introduction of frequency modulation (FM) transmissions.

The lion's share of television time was devoted to uninspired and vulgar serials, routine variety shows, giveaway and quiz programs designed to reveal and revel in the ignorance of the average citizen, and reruns of old movies cut to fit rigid time periods and repeatedly interrupted at climactic points by commercials.

Another dubious virtue of television was its capacity for influencing the opinions and feelings of viewers. The insistent and strident claims of advertisers punctuated every program with monotonous regularity. Politicians discovered that no other device or method approached television as a means of reaching large numbers of voters with an illusion of intimacy. Since television time was expensive, only candidates who had access to huge sums could afford to use the medium—a dangerous state of affairs in a democracy. In time Congress clamped a lid on campaign expenditures, but this action did not necessarily reduce the amounts spent on television.*

*The government now provides substantial public funds to candidates in presidential elections.

"A Nation of Sheep"

Another postwar change was the marked broadening of the middle class. In 1947 only 5.7 million American families had what might be considered middle-class incomes—enough to provide something for leisure, entertainment, and cultural activities as well as for life's necessities. By the early 1960s more than 12 million families, about a third of the population, had such incomes. As they prospered, middle-class Americans became more culturally homogeneous, their interests widened.

The percentage of immigrants in the population declined steadily; by the mid-1960s over 95 percent of all Americans were native-born. This trend contributed to social and cultural uniformity. So did the rising incomes of industrial workers and the changing character of their labor. Blue-collar workers invaded the middle class by the tens of thousands. They moved to suburbs previously reserved for junior executives, shopkeepers, and the like. They shed their work clothes for business suits. They took up golf. In sum, they adopted values and attitudes commensurate with their new status—which helps explain the growing conservatism of labor unions.

Religion in Changing Times

Sociologists and other commentators found in the expansion of the middle class another explanation of the tendency of the country to glorify the conformist. They attributed to this expansion the national obsession with moderation and consensus, the complacency of so many Americans, and their tendency, for example, to be more interested in the social aspects of churchgoing than with the philosophical aspects of religion.

Organized religion traditionally deals with eternal values, but it is always influenced by social, cultural, and economic developments. After World War II, all the major faiths, despite their differences, were affected. The prosperity and buoyant optimism of the period led to an expansion of religious activity. The Catholic church alone built over a thousand new schools and more than a hundred hospitals along with countless new churches. By 1950 the Southern Baptists had enrolled nearly 300,000 new members and built some 500 churches for them to worship in, and between 1945 and 1965 American Jews spent at least $1 billion building synagogues.

Most faiths prospered materially, tending to accept the world as it was. In *Catholic, Protestant, Jew* (1955), Will Herberg argued that in America, religious toleration had become routine. According to a Gallup poll, nearly everyone in America believed in God. However, another poll revealed that large numbers of Christians were unable to tell pollsters the name of any of the four Gospels.

Church and state were by law and the Constitution separate institutions, yet acts of Congress and state legislatures frequently had indirect effects on organized religion. New Deal welfare legislation took on a large part of a burden previously borne by church groups. The expansion of higher education appeared to make people somewhat more tolerant of the beliefs of others, religious beliefs included. However, studies showed that better-educated people tended to be less involved in the formal aspects of organized religion. An "education gap" separated religious liberals from religious conservatives.

Unlike prewar critics who had attacked "rugged individualism," many post–New Deal social critics, alarmed by the conformity of the 1950s, urged people to be more individualistic. In *The Lonely Crowd* (1950), David Riesman drew a distinction between old-fashioned "inner-directed" people and new "other-directed" conformists who were group-centered, materialistic, and accommodating.

The civil rights movement and the Vietnam War also had important religious implications. Many militant blacks (Malcolm X was an early example) were attracted to Islam by its lack of racial bias. Among those in the public eye who became Muslims were the heavyweight champion boxer Cassius Clay, who changed his name to Muhammad Ali, and Lew Alcindor, the basketball star, who became Kareem Abdul Jabbar.

Nearly all religious denominations played significant roles in the fight for racial justice that erupted after the Supreme Court outlawed segregation. Priests, ministers, and rabbis joined in antiwar demonstrations, too. Shocking photographs of police dogs being used to "subdue" demonstrating Catholic nuns in the Deep South converted uncounted thousands to the campaign for racial justice.

All the social changes of the period had religious ramifications. Feminists objected to male domination of most Christian churches and called for the ordination of female ministers and priests. Every aspect of new sexual mores (the "sexual revolution"), from the practice of couples living together openly outside marriage to the tolerance of homosexuality and pornography to the legalization of contraception and abortion, caused shock waves in the religious community.

Scientific and technological developments also affected both religious values and the way people worshiped. The social effects of Darwin's theory of evolution were to some extent still unresolved. Many religious groups still believed in the biblical explanation of Creation and sought to have "Creation theory" taught in the schools.

On another level, the prestige of secular science gave it a kind of religious aspect disturbing to some church leaders. Medical advances that some people marveled at, such as in vitro fertilization of human eggs, organ transplants, and the development of machines capable of keeping terminally ill people alive indefinitely, seemed to others "against nature" and indeed sacrilegious. Controversies over the use of atomic energy in peace and war and over the conservation of natural resources often had religious roots.

Radio and television had more direct effects on organized religion. The airwaves enabled rhetorically skilled preachers to reach millions with emotionally charged messages on religious topics and also on political and social questions. The most successful were the leaders of evangelical Protestant sects. These TV preachers tended to found churches and educational institutions of their own and to use radio and television to raise money to support them.

However, in the mid-1980s a number of scandals caused disillusionment and widespread defections among their followers, and by 1990 the national television congregation had shrunk drastically.

Literature and Art

For a time after World War II the nation seemed on the verge of a literary outburst comparable to the one that followed World War I. A number of excellent novels based on the military experiences of young writers appeared, the most notable being *The Naked and the Dead* (1948) by Norman Mailer and *From Here to Eternity* (1951) by James Jones. Ralph Ellison's *Invisible Man* (1952) was a vived portrayal of the black experience. Unfortunately, a new renaissance did not develop. The most talented younger writers preferred to bewail their fate rather than rebel against it. Jack Kerouac, founder of the "beat" (for *beatific*) school, reveled in the chaotic description of violence, perversion, and madness. At the other extreme, J. D. Salinger, the particular favorite of college students—*The Catcher in the Rye* (1951) sold nearly 2 million copies—was an impeccable stylist, witty, contemptuous of all pretense; but he too wrote about people entirely wrapped up in themselves.

In *Catch-22* (1955), the book that replaced *Catcher in the Rye* in the hearts of college students, Joseph Heller produced a farcical war novel that was an indignant denunciation of the stupidity and waste of warfare. In *The Victim* (1947), *The Adventures of Augie March* (1953), *Herzog* (1964), and many other novels, Saul Bellow described characters possessed of their full share of eccentricities and weaknesses without losing sight of the positive side of modern life. Bellow won many literary awards, including a Nobel Prize.

All these novelists and a number of others were widely read. Year after year sales of books increased, despite much talk about how television and other diversions were undermining the public's interest in reading. Sales of paperbacks, first introduced in the United States in 1939 by Pocket Books, reached enormous proportions. By 1965 about 25,000 titles were in print, and sales were approaching 1 million copies a day.

Cheapness and portability accounted only partly for the popularity of paperbacks. Readers could purchase them in drugstores, bus terminals, and supermarkets as well as in bookstores. Teachers, delighted to find out-of-print volumes easily available, assigned hundreds of them in their classes. And there was a psychological factor at work: The paperback became fashionable. People who rarely bought hardcover books purchased weighty volumes of literary criticism, translations of the works of obscure foreign novelists, specialized historical monographs, and difficult philosophical treatises now that they were available in paper covers.

The expansion of the book market, like so many other changes, was not an unalloyed benefit even for writers. It remained difficult for unknown authors to earn a decent living. Publishers tended to concentrate on authors already popular and on books aimed at a mass audience. Even among successful writers of unquestioned ability, the temptations involved in large advances and in book club contracts and movie rights diverted many from making the best use of their talents.

American painters were affected by the same forces that influenced writers. In the past the greatest American artists had been shaped by European influences. This situation changed dramatically after World War II with the emergence of abstract expressionism, or action painting. This "New York school" was led by Jackson Pollock (1912–1956), who composed huge abstract designs by laying his canvas on the floor of his studio and drizzling paint on it directly from tube or pot in a wild tangle of color. The abstract expressionists were utterly subjective in their approach to art. "The source of my painting is the Unconscious," Pollock explained. "I am not much aware of what is taking place; it is only after that I see what I have done." Pollock tried to produce not the representation of a landscape but, as the critic Harold Rosenberg put it, "an inner landscape that is part of himself."

Untutored observers found the abstract expressionists crude, chaotic, devoid of interest. The swirling, dripping chaos of the imitators of Pollock, the vaguely defined planes of color favored by Mark Rothko and his disciples, and the sharp spatial confrontations composed by the painters Franz Kline, Robert Motherwell, and Adolph Gottlieb required too much verbal explanation to communicate their meaning to the average observer. Viewed in its social context, however, abstract expressionism, like much of modern literature, reflected the estrangement of the artist from the world of the atomic bomb and the computer, a revolt against contemporary mass culture with its unthinking acceptance of novelty for its own sake.

The experimental spirit released by the abstract expressionists led to "op" (for *optical*) art, which employed the physical impact of pure complementary colors to produce dynamic optical effects. Even within the rigid limitations of severely formal designs composed of concentric circles, stripes, squares, and rectangles, such paintings appeared to be constantly in motion, almost alive.

Op was devoid of social connotations; another variant, "pop" (for *popular*) art, playfully yet often with acid incisiveness satirized many aspects of American culture: its vapidity, its crudeness, its violence. The painters Jasper Johns, Roy Lichtenstein, and Andy Warhol created portraits of mundane objects such as flags, comic strips, soup cans, and packing cases. Op and pop art reflected the mechanized aspects of life; the painters made use of technology in their work—for example, they enhanced the shock of vibrating complementary colors by using fluorescent paints. Some artists imitated newspaper photograph techniques by fashioning their images of sharply defined dots of color. Others borrowed from contemporary commercial art, employing spray guns, stencils, and masking tape to produce flat, hard-edged effects. The line between op and pop was frequently crossed, as in Robert Indiana's *Love,* which was reproduced and imitated on posters, Christmas cards, book jackets, buttons, rings, and even a postage stamp.

The pace of change in artistic fashion was dizzying—far more rapid than changes in literature. Aware that their generation was leading European artists instead of following them gave both artists and art lovers a sense of participating in events of historic importance.

As with literature, the effects of such success were not all healthy. Successful artists became nationally known personalities, a few of them enormously rich. For these, each new work was exposed to the glare of publicity, sometimes with unfortunate results. Too much attention, like too much money, could be distracting, even corrupting, especially for young artists who needed time and obscurity to develop their talents.

Two Dilemmas

The many changes of the era help explain why President Johnson expressed so much uncertainty in his inaugural address. Looking at American society more broadly, two dilemmas confronted people in the 1960s. One was that progress was often self-defeating. Reforms and innovations instituted with the best of motives often made things worse rather than better. For example, DDT, a powerful chemical developed to kill insects that were spreading disease and destroying valuable food crops, proved to have lethal effects on birds and fish—and perhaps indirectly on human beings. Goods manufactured to make life fuller and happier (automobiles, detergents, electric power) produced waste products that disfigured the land and polluted air and water. Cities built to bring culture and comfort to millions became pestholes of crime, poverty, and depravity.

Change occurred so fast that experience—the recollection of how things had been—tended to become less useful and sometimes even counterproductive as a guide for dealing with current problems. Foreign policies designed to prevent wars, based on the causes of past wars, led in different circumstances to new wars. Parents who sought to transmit to their children the accumulated wisdom of their years found their advice rejected, often with good reason, because it had little application to the problems the children had to face.

The second dilemma was that modern industrial society placed an enormous premium on social cooperation, at the same time undermining the individual citizen's sense of being part of a functioning society. The economy was as complicated as a fine watch; a breakdown in any one sector had ramifications that spread swiftly to other sectors. Yet specialization had progressed so far that individual workers had little sense of the importance of their personal contributions and thus felt little responsibility for the smooth functioning of the whole. Effective democratic government required that all voters be knowledgeable and concerned, but few could feel that their individual voices had any effect on elections or public policies.

People tried to deal with this dilemma by joining organizations dedicated to achieving particular goals, such as the American Association of Retired People (AARP), the conservationist Sierra Club, and the National Association for the Advancement of Colored People (NAACP). But such groups became so large that members felt almost as incapable of influencing them as they did of influencing the larger society. The groups were so numerous and had so many conflicting objectives that instead of making citizens more socially minded, they often made them more self-centered.

These dilemmas produced a paradox. The United States was the most powerful nation in the world, its people the best educated, richest, and probably the most energetic. American society was technologically advanced and dynamic; American traditional values were idealistic, humane, democratic. Yet the nation seemed incapable of mobilizing its resources to confront the most obvious challenges, its citizens unable to achieve much personal happiness or identification with their fellows, the society helpless in trying to live up to its most universally accepted ideals.

In part the paradox was a product of the strengths of the society and the individuals who made it up. The populace as a whole was more sophisticated. People were more aware of their immediate interests, less willing to suspend judgment and follow leaders or to look on others as better qualified to decide what they should do. They belonged to the "me generation"; they knew that they lived in a society and that their lives were profoundly affected by that society, but they had trouble feeling that they were part of a society.

President Johnson recognized the problem. He hoped to solve it by establishing a "consensus" and building his Great Society. No real consensus emerged; American society remained fragmented, its members divided against themselves and often within themselves.

The Costs of Prosperity

The vexing character of modern conditions could be seen in every aspect of life. The economy, after decades of hectic expansion, accelerated still more rapidly. The gross national product approached $1 trillion, but inflation was becoming increasingly serious. Workers were under constant pressure to demand raises—which only served to drive prices still higher. Socially the effect was devastating; it became impossible to expect workers to see inflation as a national problem and to restrain their personal demands. Putting their individual interests before those of the whole, they were prepared to disrupt the economy whatever the social cost. Even public employees traditionally committed to a no-strike policy because they worked for the entire community—teachers, garbage collectors, firefighters, the police—succumbed to this selfish, if understandable, way of looking at life.

Economic expansion resulted in large measure from technological advances, and these too proved to be mixed blessings. As we have seen, the needs of World War II stimulated the development of materials such as plastics, nylon, and synthetic rubber and such electronic devices as radar and television.

In 1951 scientists began to manufacture electricity from nuclear fuels; in 1954 the first atomic-powered ship, the submarine *Nautilus,* was launched. Although the peaceful use of atomic energy remained small compared to other sources of power, its implications were immense. Equally significant was the perfection of the electronic computer, which revolutionized the collection and storage of records, solved mathematical problems beyond the scope of the most brilliant human minds, and speeded the work of bank tellers, librarians, billing clerks, statisticians—and income tax collectors.

Computers lay at the heart of industrial automation, for they could control the integration and adjustment of the most complex machines. In automobile factories they made it possible to produce entire engine blocks automatically. In steel mills molten metal could be poured into molds, cooled, rolled, and cut into slabs without the intervention of a human hand, the computers locating defects and adjusting the machinery to correct them far more accurately than the most skilled steelworker, all in a matter of seconds. Taken in conjunction with a new oxygen smelting process six or eight times faster than the open-hearth method, computer-controlled continuous casting promised to have an impact on steelmaking as great as that of the Bessemer process in the 1870s.

The material benefits of technology commonly had what the microbiologist René Dubos described as "disastrous secondary effects, many of which are probably unpredictable." The consumption of petroleum necessary to produce power soared and began to outstrip supplies, threatening shortages that would disrupt the entire economy. The burning of this fuel released immeasurable tons of smoke and other polluting gases into the atmosphere, endangering the health of millions. "Life is enriched by one million automobiles," Dubos noted, "but can be made into a nightmare by one hundred million."

The vast outpouring of flimsy plastic products and the increased use of paper, metal foil, and other disposable packaging materials seemed about to bury the country beneath mountains of trash. The commercial use of nuclear energy also caused problems. Scientists insisted that the danger from radiation was nonexistent, but the possibility of accidents could not be eliminated entirely, and the safe disposal of radioactive wastes became increasingly difficult.

Even an apparently ideal form of scientific advance, the use of commercial fertilizers to boost food output, had unfortunate side effects: Phosphates washed from farmlands into streams sometimes upset the ecological balance and turned the streams into malodorous death traps for aquatic life. Above all, technology increased the capacity of the earth to support people. As population increased, production and consumption increased, exhausting supplies of raw materials and speeding the pollution of air and water resources. Where would the process end? Viewed from a world perspective, it was obvious that the population explosion must be checked or it would check itself by pestilence, war, starvation, or some combination of these scourges. Yet how to check it?

New Racial Turmoil

President Johnson and most supporters of his policies expected that the 1964 Civil Rights Act, the Economic Opportunity Act, Medicare and Medicaid, and the other elements in the War on Poverty would produce an era of racial peace and genuine social harmony—the Great Society that everyone wanted. In fact, official recognition of past injustices made blacks more insistent that all discrimination be ended. The very process of righting some past wrongs gave them the strength to fight more vigorously. Black militancy burst forth so powerfully that even the most smug and obtuse white citizens had to accept its existence.

The Student Nonviolent Coordinating Committee (SNCC), which had been born out of the struggle for racial integration, had become by 1964 a radical organization openly scornful of interracial cooperation. Many students had been radicalized by the violence they had experienced while trying to register rural blacks and organize schools for black children in the South. The slogan of the radicals was "Black Power," an expression that was given national currency by Stokely Carmichael, chairman of SNCC. Carmichael was adamantly opposed to cooperating with whites. "The time for white involvement in the fight for equality is ended," he said in 1966. The movement "should be black-staffed, black-controlled, and black-financed." On another occasion he said, "Integration is a subterfuge for . . . white supremacy." Black Power caught on swiftly among militants. This troubled white liberals because they feared that Black Power would antagonize white conservatives.

Meanwhile, black anger erupted in a series of destructive urban riots. The most important occurred in Watts, a ghetto of Los Angeles, in August 1965. A trivial incident—police officers halted a motorist who seemed to be drunk and attempted to give him a sobriety test—brought thousands into the streets. The neighborhood almost literally exploded: For six days Watts was swept by fire, looting, and bloody fighting. The following summer saw similar outbursts in New York, Chicago, and other cities. In 1967 further riots broke out, the most serious in Newark, where 25 were killed, and Detroit, where the death toll came to 43. Then, in April 1968, the revered Martin Luther King, Jr., was murdered in Memphis, Tennessee, by a white man, James Earl Ray. Blacks in more than 100 cities swiftly unleashed their anger in paroxysms of burning and looting. White opinion was shocked and profoundly depressed: King's death seemed to destroy the hope that his doctrine of pacific appeal to reason and right could solve the racial problem.

The rioters were expressing frustration and despair; their resentment was directed more at the social system than at individuals. The basic cause was an attitude of mind, the "white racism" that deprived blacks of access to good jobs, crowded them into slums, and, for the young in particular, eroded all hope of escape from such misery. Ghettos bred crime and depravity, as slums always have, and the complacent refusal of whites adequately to invest money and energy in helping ghetto residents, or even to acknowledge that the black poor deserved help, made the modern slum unbearable. While the ghettos expanded, middle-class whites tended more and more to flee to the suburbs or to call on the police to "maintain law and order," a euphemism for cracking down hard on deviant black behavior.

The victims of racism employed violence not so much to force change as to obtain psychic release; it was a way of getting rid of what they could not stomach, a kind of vomiting. When fires broke out in black districts, the firefighters who tried to extinguish them were often showered with bottles and bricks and sometimes shot at, while above the roar of the flames and the hiss of steam rose the apocalyptic chant, "Burn, baby, burn!"

The most frightening aspect of the riots was their tendency to polarize society along racial lines. Advocates of Black Power became more determined to separate themselves from white influence. They exasperated white supporters of school desegregation by demanding schools of their own. Extremists formed the Black Panther party and collected weapons to resist the police.

Middle-class city residents often resented what seemed the favoritism of the federal government and of state and local administrations, which sought through so-called affirmative action to provide blacks with new economic opportunities and social benefits. Efforts to desegregate ghetto schools by busing children out of their local neighborhoods was a particularly bitter cause of conflict. Persons already subjected to the pressures caused by inflation, specialization, and rapid change that were undermining social solidarity and worried by the sharp rise in urban crime rates and welfare costs found black radicalism infuriating. In the face of the greatest national effort in history to aid them, blacks, they said, were displaying not merely ingratitude but contempt.

The Unmeltable Ethnics

Mexican-Americans responded to discrimination in much the same manner as the blacks. After World War I, thousands of Mexicans flocked into the Southwest. When the Great Depression struck, about half a million were either deported or persuaded to return to Mexico. But during World War II and again between 1948 and 1965, federal legislation encouraged the importation of temporary farm workers called *braceros,* and many other Mexicans entered the country illegally. Many of these Mexicans, and other Spanish-speaking people from Puerto Rico who could immigrate to the mainland legally, settled in the great cities, where low-paying but usually steady work was available. They lived in slums called *barrios,* as segregated, crowded, and crime-ridden as the black ghettos.

Spanish-speaking newcomers were for a time largely apolitical; they tended to mind their own business and to make little trouble. But in the early

1960s a new spirit of resistance arose. Leaders of the new movement called themselves Chicanos. They demanded better education for their children and urged their fellows to take pride in their traditions, demand their rights, and organize politically.

One Chicano nationalist group, the Crusade for Justice, focused on achieving social reforms and setting up political action groups. Its slogan, *"Venceremos,"* was Spanish for Martin Luther King's pledge: We shall overcome.

The Chicano leader with the widest influence was César Chávez, who concentrated on what was superficially a more limited goal: organizing migrant farm workers into unions. After serving in the navy during World War II, Chávez became general director of the Community Service Organization (CSO), a group seeking to raise the political consciousness of the poor and develop self-help programs among them. But he resigned in 1962 because he believed it was not devoting enough attention to the plight of migrant workers. He then founded the National Farm Workers Association, later known as the United Farm Workers Organizing Committee.

In 1965 Chávez turned a strike of grape pickers in Delano, California, into a nationwide crusade against the migrant labor system. Avoiding violence, he enlisted the support of church leaders and organized sit-ins, a march on the state capital, and then a national consumer boycott of grapes. He proved that migrant workers could be unionized and that the militant demands of minorities for equal treatment did not necessarily lead to separatism and class or racial antagonism.

The struggles of blacks radicalized many American Indians, who used the term "Red Power" as blacks spoke of Black Power and referred to more conservative colleagues as "Uncle Tomahawks." The National Indian Youth Council and later the American Indian Movement (AIM) demanded the return of lands taken illegally from their ancestors. They called for a concerted effort to revive tribal cultures, even the use of peyote, a hallucinogenic controlled substance, in religious ceremonies.*

Some AIM leaders sought total separation from the United States; they envisaged setting up states within states such as the Cherokees had established in Georgia in Jacksonian days. In 1973 radicals occupied the town of Wounded Knee, South Dakota (site of one of the most disgraceful massacres of Indians in the 19th century), and held it at gunpoint for weeks.

While traditionalists resisted the militants, liberal white opinion proved to be generally sympathetic. In 1975 Congress passed the Indian Self-determination Act, which gave individual tribes much greater control over such matters as education, welfare programs, and law enforcement.

Militant ethnic pride characterized the behavior of many Americans. Blacks donned African garments and wore their hair in natural "Afro" styles. Italian-Americans, Polish-Americans, and descendants of other "new immigrant" groups eagerly studied their histories in order to preserve their culture. The American melting pot, some historians now argued, had not amalgamated the immigrant strains as completely as had been thought.

The concern for origins was in part nostalgic and romantic. As the number of, say, Greek-Americans who had ever seen Greece declined, the appeal of Greek culture increased. But for blacks, whose particular origins were obscured by the catastrophe of slavery, awareness of their distinctiveness was more important. Racial pride was a reflection of the achievements that blacks had made in the postwar period. There was a black on the Supreme Court (Thurgood Marshall, tactician of the fight for school desegregation). President Johnson had named the first black to a Cabinet post (Robert Weaver, secretary of housing and urban development). The first black since Reconstruction (Edward W. Brooke of Massachusetts) was elected to the United States Senate in 1966. A number of large cities elected black mayors.

The color line was broken in major league baseball in 1947, and soon all professional sports were open to black athletes. Whereas the reign of black heavyweight boxing champion Jack Johnson (1908–1915) had inspired an open search for a "white hope" to depose him, and whereas the next black champion, Joe Louis (1937–1949), was accepted by whites because he "knew his place" and was "well behaved," it was possible for champion Muhammad Ali to be a hero to both white and black boxing fans despite his boastfulness ("I am the greatest"), his militant advocacy of racial equality, and adoption of the Muslim religion.

*The California Supreme Court upheld the right to use peyote in this way in *People* v. *Woody* (1964).

Black Americans had found real self-awareness. The attitude of mind that ran from the lonely Denmark Vesey to Frederick Douglass to W. E. B. Du Bois had become the black consensus.

Rethinking Public Education

Young people were in the forefront in both the fight for the rights of blacks and the women's liberation movement. In a time of uncertainty and discontent, full of conflict and dilemma, youth was affected more strongly than the older generations, and it reacted more forcefully. No established institution escaped its criticisms, not even the vaunted educational system, which, youth discovered, poorly suited its needs. This was still another paradox of modern life, for American public education was probably the best (it was certainly the most comprehensive) in the world.

After World War I, under the impact of Freudian psychology, the emphasis in elementary education shifted from using the schools as instruments of social change, as John Dewey had recommended, to using them to promote the emotional development of the students. "Child-centered" educators played down academic achievement in favor of "adjustment." It probably stimulated the students' imaginations and may possibly have improved their psychological well-being, but observers soon noted that the system produced poor work habits, fuzzy thinking, and plain ignorance.

The demands of society for rigorous intellectual achievement made this distortion of progressive education increasingly unsatisfactory. Following World War II, critics began a concerted assault on the system. The leader of the attack was James B. Conant, former president of Harvard. His book *The American High School Today* (1959) sold nearly half a million copies. Conant flayed the schools for their failure to teach English grammar and composition effectively, for neglecting foreign languages, and for ignoring the needs of both the brightest and the slowest of their students.

The success of the USSR in launching *Sputnik* in 1957 increased the influence of critics like Conant. To match the Soviets' achievement, the United States needed thousands of engineers and scientists, and the schools were not turning out enough graduates prepared to study science and engineering at the college level. Suddenly the schools were under enormous pressure, for with more and more young people wanting to go to college, the colleges were raising their admission standards. The traditionalists thus gained the initiative, academic subjects enjoyed revived prestige. The National Defense Education Act of 1958 supplied a powerful stimulus by allocating funds for upgrading work in the sciences, foreign languages, and other subjects and for expanding guidance services and experimenting with television and other new teaching devices.

Concern for improving the training of the children of disadvantaged minority groups (Mexican-Americans, Puerto Ricans, Indians, blacks) pulled the system in a different direction. Many of these children lived in horrible slums, often in broken homes. They lacked the incentives and training that middle-class children received in the family. Many did poorly in school, in part because they were poorly motivated, in part because the system was poorly adapted to their needs. But catering to the needs of such children threatened to undermine the standards being set for other children. Added to the strains imposed by racial conflicts, the effect was to create the most serious crisis American public education had ever faced.

The post-*Sputnik* stress on academic achievement profoundly affected education, too. Critics demanded that secondary schools and colleges raise their standards and place more stress on the sciences. Prestige institutions such as Harvard, Yale, Columbia, Stanford, and dozens of other colleges and universities raised their entrance requirements. By the mid-1960s, the children of the baby boom generation were flocking into the nation's high schools and colleges. Population growth and the demands of society for specialized intellectual skills were causing educational institutions to burst at the seams. Enrollments had risen rapidly after World War II, mostly because of the G.I. Bill; by 1950 there were 2.6 million students in American colleges and universities. Twenty years later the total had risen to 8.6 million, a decade after that to about 12 million. To bridge the gap between high school and college, two-year junior colleges proliferated. Almost unknown before 1920, there were more than 1,300 junior colleges in the late 1980s.

The federal and state government, together with private philanthropic institutions such as the

Carnegie Corporation and the Ford Foundation, poured millions of dollars into education at every level—from preschool programs like Head Start, into classroom and dormitory construction, into teacher training, into scholarship funds. At the graduate level, the federal government's research and development program provided billions for laboratories, equipment, professors' salaries, and student fellowships.

Students in Revolt

For a time after the war, the expansion of higher education took place with remarkable smoothness. Veterans, eager to make up for lost time, concentrated on their studies, and most younger students followed their lead. But in the 1960s the mood changed. This college generation had grown up during the postwar prosperity and had been trained by teachers who were, by and large, New Deal liberals. The youngsters had been told that the government was supposed to regulate the economy and help the weak against the strong. But many did not think it was performing these functions adequately. Modern industrial society with its "soulless" corporations, its computers, and its almost equally unfeeling human bureaucracies made them feel insignificant and powerless. Their advantages also made them feel guilty when they thought about the millions of Americans who did not have them. The existence of poverty in a country as rich as the United States seemed intolerable, race prejudice both stupid and evil. The response of their elders to McCarthyism appeared craven cowardice of the worst sort.

All these influences were encapsulated in a manifesto put forth at a meeting of Students for a Democratic Society (SDS) held at Port Huron, Michigan, in 1962. "We are the people of this generation . . . looking uncomfortably to the world we inherit," their Port Huron Statement began. How to reconcile the contradictions between the idea that "all men are created equal" with "the facts of Negro life"? The government says it is for peace yet makes huge "economic and military investments in the Cold War." "We would replace power rooted in possession, privilege, or circumstance," the SDS manifesto ran, by power "rooted in love."

SDS grew rapidly, powered by the war in Vietnam and a seemingly unending list of local campus issues. Radical students generally had little tolerance for injustice, and their dissatisfaction often found expression in public protests. The first great outburst convulsed the University of California at Berkeley in the fall of 1964. Angry students staged sit-down strikes to protest the prohibition of political canvassing on the campus. Hundreds were arrested; the state legislature threatened reprisals; the faculty became involved in the controversy.

On campus after campus in the late 1960s, students organized sit-ins and employed other disruptive tactics. Frequently professors and administrators played into the radicals' hands, being so offended by their methods and manners that they refused to recognize the legitimacy of some of their demands. At Columbia in 1968, SDS and black students occupied university buildings and issued "nonnegotiable" demands concerning the university's involvement in secret military research and its relations with neighborhood minority groups. When, after long delays, the police were called in to clear the buildings, dozens of students, some of them innocent bystanders, were clubbed and beaten.

Equally significant in altering the student mood was the frustration that so many of them felt with traditional aspects of college life. Dissidents denounced rules that restricted their personal lives, such as prohibitions on the use of alcohol and the banning of members of the opposite sex from dormitories. They complained that required courses inhibited their intellectual development. They demanded a share in the government of their institutions, long the private preserve of administrators and professors.

Beyond their specific complaints, the radicals refused to put up with anything they considered wrong. The knotty social problems that made their elders gravitate toward moderation led these students to become intransigent absolutists. Racial prejudice was evil: It must be eradicated. War in a nuclear age was insane: Armies must be disbanded. Poverty amid plenty was an abomination: End poverty now. To the counsel that evil can be eliminated only gradually, they responded with scorn. Extremists adopted a nihilistic position: The only way to deal with a "rotten" society was to destroy it; reform was impossible, constructive compromise corrupting.

Critics found the radical students infantile because they refused to tolerate frustration or delay, old-fashioned because their absolutist ideas had been exploded by several generations of philosophers and scientists, authoritarian because they rejected majority rule. As time passed SDS was plagued by factional disputes. Radical women claimed that it was run by male chauvinists; women who sought some say in policy matters, one of them has written, were met with "indifference, ridicule, and anger."

By the end of the 1960s SDS had lost much of its influence with the general student body. Nevertheless, it had succeeded in focusing attention on genuine social and political weaknesses both on the campuses and in the larger world.

Black students influenced the academic world in a variety of ways. Most colleges tried to increase black enrollments by their use of scholarship funds and by lowering academic entrance requirements when necessary to compensate for the poor preparation many black students had received. But most black students were dissatisfied with college life. They tended to keep to themselves and usually had little to do with the somewhat elitist SDS. But they demanded more control over all aspects of their education than whites typically did. They wanted black studies programs taught and administered by blacks. Achievement of these goals was difficult because of the shortage of black teachers and because professors—including most black professors—considered student control of appointments and curricula unwise and in violation of the principles of academic freedom.

Unlike white radical students, blacks tended to confine their demands to matters directly related to local conditions. Although generalization is difficult, probably the majority of academics drew a distinction between black radicals, whose actions they found understandable, and white radicals, many of whom the academics considered self-indulgent or emotionally disturbed.

The Counterculture

Some young people, generally known as hippies, were so repelled by the modern world that they retreated from it, finding refuge in communes, drugs, and mystical religions. Groups could be found in every big city in the United States and Europe. Some hippies, like the poet Allen Ginsberg and the novelist Ken Kesey, were genuinely creative people. Ginsberg's dark, desperate masterpiece, *Howl,* written in 1955, is perhaps the most widely read poem of the postwar era, certainly a work of major literary significance. *Howl* begins: "I saw the best minds of my generation destroyed by madness, starving hysterical naked," and goes on to describe the wanderings and searchings of these "angelheaded hipsters . . . seeking jazz or sex or soup" in Houston, "whoring in Colorado," and "investigating the F.B.I. in beards and shorts" in California, all the while denouncing "the narcotic tobacco haze of Capitalism." Others, however, such as the "Yippies" Abbie Hoffman and Jerry Rubin, are best described as professional iconoclasts. (In 1968 Yippies went through the motions of nominating a pig named Pigassus for president.)

The hippies developed a "counterculture" so directly opposite to the way of life of their parents' generation as to suggest to critics that they were still dominated by the culture they rejected. They wore old blue jeans and (it seemed) any nondescript garments they happened to find at hand. Male hippies wore their hair long and grew beards. Females avoided makeup, bras, and other devices more conventional women used to make themselves attractive to men. Both sexes rejected the old Protestant ethic; being part of the hippie world meant not caring about money, material goods, or power over other people. Love was more important than money or influence, feelings more significant than thought, natural things superior to anything manufactured.

Most hippies resembled the radicals in their political and social opinions, but they rejected activism. Theirs was a world of folk songs and blaring "acid rock" music, of "be-ins," casual sex, and drugs. Their slogan, "Make love, not war," was a general pacifist pronouncement, not necessarily a specific criticism of events in Vietnam. Indeed, passivity was with them a philosophy, almost a principle. At rock concerts they listened where earlier generations had danced. Hallucinogenic drugs heightened users' "experiences" while they were in fact in a stupor. Another hippie motto, "Do your own thing," can work only in social situations where no one does anything. Hippie communes were a far cry from the busy centers of social experimentation of the pre–Civil War Age of Reform.

Charles A. Reich, a professor at Yale, praised the hippie view of the world in *The Greening of America* (1970), calling it "Consciousness III." Reich's Consciousness I was the do-it-yourself, laissez-faire approach to life—having "more faith in winning than in love"; Consciousness II was the psychology of "liberal intellectuals," marked by faith in institutional solutions to problems. Reich taught a course called "Individualism in America." One semester he had over 500 students, not one of whom failed. According to the *Yale Course Guide,* published by students, Professor Reich "thinks kids are neat and what can be bad about someone telling you how the system and the older generation have warped and destroyed things for us?"

The Sexual Revolution

Young people made the most striking contribution to the revolution that took place in the late 1960s in public attitudes toward sexual relationships. Almost overnight, it seemed, conventional ideas about premarital sex, contraception and abortion, homosexuality, pornography, and a host of related matters were openly challenged. Probably the behavior of the majority of Americans did not alter radically. But the majority's beliefs and practices were no longer automatically acknowledged to be the only valid ones. It became possible for individuals to espouse different values and to behave differently with at least relative impunity.

The causes of this revolution were complex and interrelated; one change led to others. More efficient methods of birth control and antibiotics that cured venereal diseases removed the two principal practical arguments against sex outside marriage; with these barriers down, many people found their moral attitudes changing. Almost concurrently, Alfred C. Kinsey's *Sexual Behavior in the Human Male* (1948), which was based on thousands of confidential interviews, revealed that where sex was concerned, large numbers of Americans did not practice what they preached. Premarital sex, marital infidelity, homosexuality, and various forms of perversion were, Kinsey's figures showed, far more common than most persons had suspected.

Sexual Behavior in the Human Male shocked many people and when Kinsey published *Sexual Behavior in the Human Female* in 1958, which demonstrated that the sexual practices of women were as varied as those of men, he was subjected to a storm of abuse and deprived of the foundation support that had financed his research.

Kinsey has been called "the Marx of the sexual revolution." Once it became possible to accept the idea that one's own urges might not be as uncommon as one had been led to believe, it became much more difficult to object to any sexual activity practiced in private by consenting adults. Homosexuals, for example, demanded that the heterosexual society cease harassing and discriminating against them.

The sexual revolution in its many aspects served useful functions. Reducing inhibitions was liberating for many persons of both sexes, and this tended to help young people form permanent associations on the basis of deeper feelings than their sexual drives. Women surely profited from the new freedom, just as a greater sharing of family duties by husbands and fathers opened men's lives to many new satisfactions.

But like other changes, the revolution produced new problems. For young people, sexual freedom could be very unsettling; sometimes it generated social pressures that propelled them into relationships they were not yet prepared to handle. Equally perplexing was the rise in the number of illegitimate births. Easy cures did not eliminate venereal disease; on the contrary, the relaxation of sexual taboos produced an epidemic of gonorrhea, a frightening increase in the incidence of syphilis, and the emergence of a deadly new disease, acquired immune deficiency syndrome (AIDS).

Exercising the right to advocate and practice previously forbidden activities involved subjecting people who found those activities offensive—still a large proportion of the population—to embarrassment and even acute emotional distress. Some people believed pornography to be ethically wrong, and most feminists considered it degrading to women. Abortion raised difficult legal and moral questions that exacerbated already serious social conflicts.

Women's Liberation

Sexual freedom also contributed to the revival of the women's rights movement. For one thing, freedom involved a more drastic revolution for women than for men. Effective methods of contraception obviously affected women more directly than men, and the new attitudes heightened women's awareness how the old sexual standards had restricted their entire existence. In fact the two movements interacted. Concern for better job opportunities and for equal pay for equal work, for example, fed the demand for day-care centers for children.

Still another cause of the new drive for women's rights was concern for improving the treatment of minorities. Participation in the civil rights movement encouraged women to speak out more forcefully for their own rights. Feminists argued that they were being demeaned and dominated by a male-dominated society and must fight back.

When World War II ended, women who had taken jobs because of the labor shortage were expected to surrender them to veterans and return to their traditional roles as housewives and mothers. Some did; in 1940 about 15 percent of American women in their early thirties were unmarried, in 1965 only 5 percent. Many, however, did not meekly return to the home, and many of those who did continued to hold down jobs. Other women went to work to counterbalance the onslaught of inflation, still others simply because they enjoyed the money and the independence that jobs provided. Between 1940 and 1960 the proportion of women workers doubled. The rise was particularly swift among married women, and the difficulties faced by anyone trying to work while having to perform household duties increased the resentment of these workers.

Women workers still faced job discrimination of many kinds. In nearly every occupation they were paid less than men. Many interesting jobs were either closed to them entirely or doled out on the basis of some illogical and often unwritten quota system. Many women objected to this state of affairs even in the 1950s; in the 1960s their protest erupted into an organized and vociferous demand for change.

Betty Friedan, author of *The Feminine Mystique,* spearheaded women's rights demonstrations like the National Women's Strike in August 1970. The strike called on women to boycott four consumer products whose advertising the protesters considered insulting to women.

One of the leaders of the new women's movement was Betty Friedan. In *The Feminine Mystique* (1963), Friedan argued that advertisers, popular magazines, and other opinion-shaping forces were undermining the capacity of women to use their intelligence and their talents creatively by a pervasive and not very subtle form of brainwashing designed to convince them of the virtues of domesticity. She argued that without understanding why, thousands of women living supposedly happy lives were experiencing vague but persistent feelings of anger and discomfort. "The only way for a woman . . . to know herself as a person is by creative work of her own," she wrote. A "problem that had no name" was stifling women's potential.

The Feminine Mystique "raised the consciousness" of women and men—over a million copies were quickly sold. Friedan was deluged by letters from women who had thought that their feelings of unease and depression despite their "happy" family life were both unique to themselves and unreasonable.

Friedan had assumed that if able women acted with determination, employers would stop discriminating against them. This did not happen. In 1966 she and other feminists founded the National Organization for Women (NOW). Copying the tactics of black activists, NOW called for equal employment opportunities and equal pay as civil rights. "The time has come for a new movement toward true equality for all women in America and toward a fully equal partnership of the sexes," the leaders

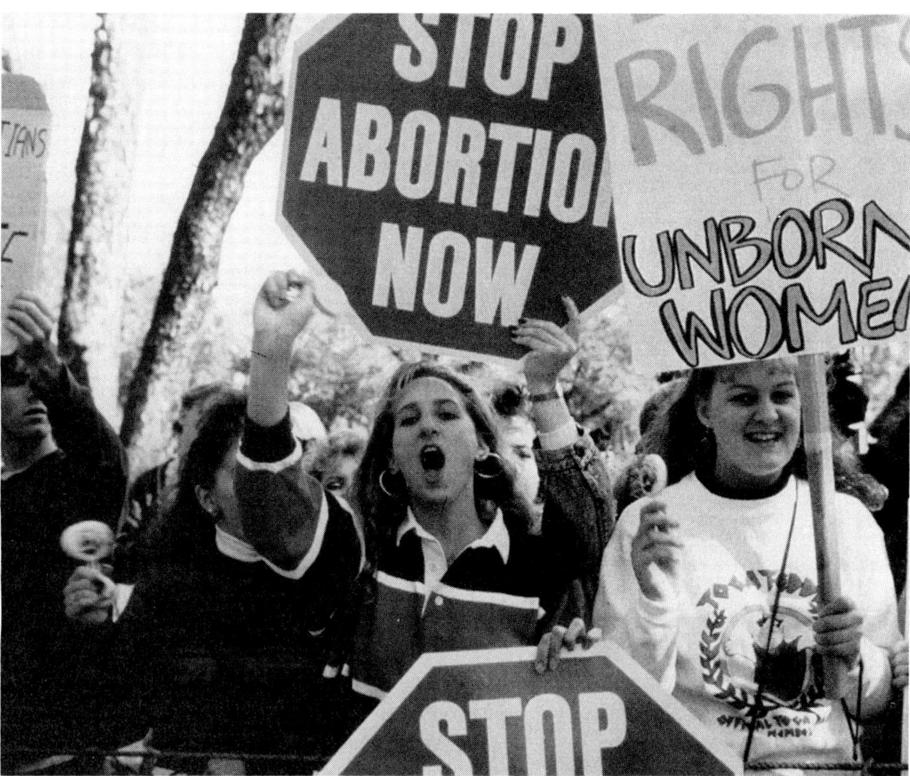

An antiabortion or, as its adherents preferred, a right-to-life rally opposing the 1973 Supreme Court ruling upholding the right of a woman to terminate a pregnancy. Defenders of abortion, or of freedom of choice, have been no less willing to take to the barricades when they sense a possible change in federal policy on this highly charged issue.

announced. In 1967 NOW came out for an equal rights amendment to the Constitution, for changes in the divorce laws, and for the legalization of abortion, the right of "control of one's body."

By 1967 some feminists were arguing that NOW was not radical enough. They deplored its hierarchical structure and its imitation of conventional pressure-group tactics. Equality of the two sexes smacked of "separate but equal" to these women.

Typical was Kate Millett, whose *Sexual Politics* (1970) called for a "sexual revolution" to do away with "traditional inhibitions and taboos." Millett denounced male supremacy and drew a distinction between the immutable biological differences between men and women and gender, how men and women relate to one another socially and culturally, which are learned ways of behaving and thus capable of change. For example, people must stop thinking of words like *violent* and *efficiency* as male and *passive* and *tenderness* as female.

The radicals gathered in small consciousness-raising groups to discuss questions as varied as the need for government child-care centers, how best to denounce the annual Miss America contests, and lesbianism. They held conferences and seminars and published magazines, the most widely known being *Ms.,* edited by Gloria Steinem. Academics among them organized women's studies programs at dozens of colleges.

Some radical feminists advocated raising children in communal centers and doing away with marriage as a legal institution. "The family unit is a decadent, energy-absorbing, destructive, wasteful institution," one prominent feminist declared. Others described marriage as "legalized rape."

The militants attacked the standard image of the female sex. Avoiding the error of the Progressive

Era reformers who had fought for the vote by stressing differences between the sexes, they insisted on total equality. Clichés such as "the weaker sex" made them see red. They insisted that the separation of "Help Wanted—Male" and "Help Wanted—Female" classified ads in newspapers violated the Civil Rights Act of 1964, and they demanded that men bear more of the burden of caring for their children, cooking, and housework. They took courses in self-defense in order to be able to protect themselves from muggers, rapists, and casual mashers. They denounced the use of masculine words like *chairman* (favoring *chairperson*) and of such terms as *mankind* and *men* to designate people in general.* They substituted *Ms.* for both *Miss* and *Mrs.* on the grounds that the language drew no such distinction between unmarried and married men.

The most radical of the feminists went still further. As Todd Gitlin put it in *The Sixties: Years of Hope, Days of Rage,* they attacked "not just capitalism, but men."

At the other extreme, many women rejected the position even of moderate feminists like Betty Friedan. Conservatives campaigned against the equal rights amendment. After the Supreme Court declared in *Roe* v. *Wade* (1973) that women had a constitutional right to have an abortion during the early stages of pregnancy, a right-to-life movement dedicated to the overturn of the decision sprang up. But few people escaped being affected by the women's movement. Even the most unregenerate male seemed to recognize that the balance of power and influence between the sexes had been altered. Clearly, the sexual revolution was not about to end, the direction of change in relationships not to be turned back.

*The difficulty here was that this form of discrimination was built into the structure of the language. Even the word *woman* derives from the Anglo-Saxon *wif-mann,* "wife of a man." Efforts to avoid the use of masculine words in general references led to such awkward expressions as *his/her* and *(s)he.*

Milestones

1948 Alfred C. Kinsey, *Sexual Behavior in the Human Male*
1950 David Riesman, *The Lonely Crowd*
1954 Launching of U.S.S. *Nautilus,* first atomic-powered ship
1955 Allen Ginsberg, *Howl*
1957 Russians launch first *Sputnik*
1958 National Defense Education Act
1962 Students for a Democratic Society's Port Huron Statement
1963 Betty Friedan, *The Feminine Mystique*
1964 Free speech movement at University of California at Berkeley
1965 César Chávez organizes boycott to support grape pickers
1965–1967 Riots in ghettos
1966 National Organization for Women (NOW) founded
1968 Student strike at Columbia University broken by police
Martin Luther King, Jr., assassinated
1970 Kate Millett, *Sexual Politics*
1973 Supreme Court guarantees right to abortion in early stages of pregnancy *(Roe* v. *Wade)*
1975 Indian Self-determination Act

Supplementary Reading

J. F. Heath, **Decade of Disillusionment: The Kennedy-Johnson Years** (1980), and A. J. Matusow, **The Unraveling of America** (1984), contain material related to this chapter as do W. M. O'Neill, **Coming Apart: An Informal History of the 1960s** (1971), and Godfrey Hodgson, **America in Our Time** (1976). Todd Gitlin, **The Sixties** (1987), is an "insider's" account. K. T. Jackson, **Crabgrass Frontier** (1985), analyzes the movement to the suburbs.

For television, see David Marc, **Demographic Vistas: Television in American Culture** (1984), and Barbara Matusow, **The Evening Stars** (1988). Morris Dickstein, **Gates of Eden: American Culture in the Sixties** (1977), is part history, part literary criticism, part memoir. Modern art is discussed in Barbara Rose, **American Art Since 1900** (1967).

For the causes and character of the poverty and urban problems that led Johnson to devise his Great Society program, see Michael Harrington, **The Other America** (1962).

On the black radicals see Malcolm X, **Autobiography** (1966), Stokely Carmichael and C. V. Hamilton, **Black Power** (1967), and Eldridge Cleaver, **Soul on Ice** (1967). Other important books on race relations include Taylor Branch, **Parting the Waters** (1988), on the career of Martin Luther King, Jr., Clayborne Carson, **In Struggle: SNCC and the Black Awakening of the 1960s** (1981), and August Meier and Elliott Rudwick, **CORE: A Study in the Civil Rights Movement** (1973). On the integration of baseball see Jules Tygiel, **The Great Experiment** (1983). M. S. Meier and Feliciano Rivera, **The Chicanos** (1972), provides a sympathetic discussion of the problems and aspirations of Mexican-Americans. See also A. F. Corwin, **Immigrants—and Immigrants** (1978), and J. R. Garcia, **Operation Wetback** (1980).

Educational trends are discussed in Martin Mayer, **The Schools** (1961), and Robert Coles, **Children of Crisis** (1967). On militancy among college students, see Kenneth Kenniston, **Young Radicals** (1968), Roger Kahn, **The Battle of Morningside Heights** (1970), and Kirkpatrick Sale, **SDS** (1973). See also Irwin Unger, **The Movement: A History of the American New Left** (1974).

The literature on the women's movement is voluminous and difficult to evaluate. In addition to W. H. Chafe, **The American Woman** (1972) and **Women and Equality** (1977), see Betty Friedan, **The Feminine Mystique** (1963), S. M. Rothman, **Woman's Proper Place** (1978), and Sara Evans and H. C. Boyte, **Free Spaces** (1986).

For postwar religious trends, see Robert Wuthnow, **The Restructuring of American Religion** (1988), and Will Herberg, **Catholic, Protestant, Jew** (1955).

CHAPTER 33

Our Times

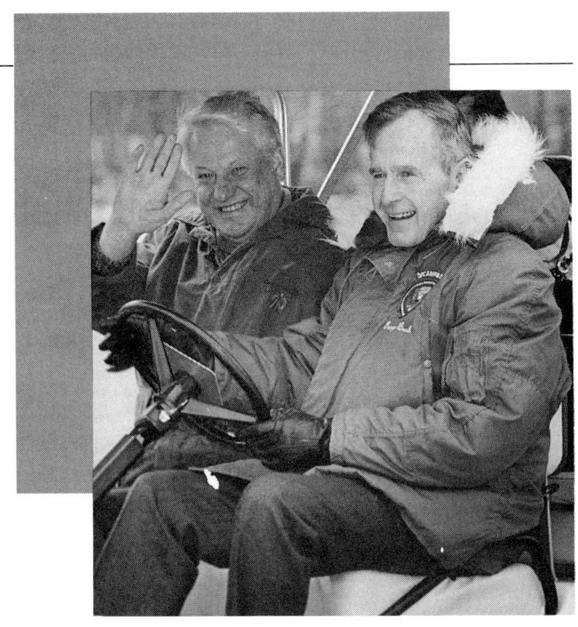

THE COUNTRY GREETED THE ACCESSION of Gerald Ford to the presidency with a collective sigh of relief. Most observers considered Ford unimaginative, but his record was untouched by scandal. He was Nixon's opposite as a person, being gregarious and open, and he stated repeatedly that he took a dim view of Nixon's high-handed way of dealing with Congress. The president and Congress must work together in the nation's interest, he insisted.

Ford as President

Ford obviously desired to live up to public expectations, yet he was soon embroiled in controversy. At the outset he aroused widespread resentment by pardoning Nixon for whatever crimes, known or unknown, he had committed in office. Not many Americans wanted to see the ex-president lodged in jail, but pardoning him seemed incomprehensible when he had admitted no guilt and had not yet been officially charged with any crime. Ugly rumors of a deal worked out before Nixon resigned were soon circulating, for the pardon seemed grossly unfair. Why should Nixon go scot-free when his chief underlings, Mitchell, Haldeman, and Ehrlichman, were being brought to trial for their part in the Watergate scandal? (All three were eventually convicted and jailed.)

Ford displayed inconsistency and apparent incompetence in managing the economy. He announced that inflation was the major problem and called on patriotic citizens to signify their willingness to fight it by wearing buttons inscribed "Whip Inflation Now." Almost immediately the economy entered a precipitous slump. Production fell and the unemployment rate rose above 9 percent. The president was forced to ask for tax cuts and other measures aimed at stimulating business activity. While pressing for them, he continued to fulminate against spending money on social programs designed to help the urban poor.

That Ford would never act rashly proved to be an incorrect assumption. Ford had always taken a hawkish position on the Vietnam War. As the military situation deteriorated in the spring of 1975, he

Chapter-opening illustration:
U.S. President George Bush and Russian President Boris Yeltsin met in February 1992 at Camp David to discuss development of a global antimissile shield.

tried to persuade Congress to pour more arms into the South to stem the North Vietnamese advance. The legislators flatly refused to do so, and late in April, Saigon fell. The long Vietnam War was finally over.

Two weeks earlier local communists of a particularly radical persuasion had overturned the pro-American regime in Cambodia. On May 12, Cambodian naval forces seized the American merchant ship *Mayaguez* in the Gulf of Siam. Without allowing the new regime time to respond to his perfectly proper demand that the *Mayaguez* and its crew be freed, Ford ordered Marine units to attack Tang Island, where the captured vessel had been taken. The assault succeeded in that the Cambodians released the *Mayaguez* and its crew of 39, but 38 Marines died in the operation. Since the Cambodians had released the ship before the Marines struck, Ford's reflexive response was probably unnecessary.

After some hesitation Ford decided to seek the Republican presidential nomination in 1976. He was opposed by Ronald Reagan, ex-governor of California, a movie actor turned politician who was the darling of the Republican right wing. Reagan's campaign was well organized and well financed. He was an excellent speaker, where Ford proved somewhat bumbling on the stump. The contest was close, both candidates winning important primaries and gathering substantial blocs of delegates in nonprimary states. At the convention in August, Ford obtained a slim majority.

The Democrats chose James Earl Carter, a former governor of Georgia, as their candidate. Carter had been a naval officer and a substantial peanut farmer and warehouse owner before entering politics. He was elected governor of Georgia in 1970. While governor he won something of a reputation as a southern public official who treated black citizens fairly. (He hung a portrait of Martin Luther King, Jr., in his office.)

Carter's political style was informal—he insisted on being called Jimmy. During the campaign he turned his inexperience in national politics to his advantage, emphasizing his lack of connection with the Washington establishment rather than apologizing for it. He repeatedly called attention to his integrity and his deep religious faith. "I'll never lie to you," he promised voters, a pledge that no candidate would have bothered to make before Nixon's disgrace.

In the election campaign Ford stressed controlling inflation, Carter high unemployment. After a close but uninspiring contest, Carter was elected, 297 electoral votes to 241, having carried most of the South and a few large industrial states. A key element in his victory was the fact that he got an overwhelming majority of the black vote (partly on his record in Georgia, partly because Ford had been unsympathetic toward the demands of the urban poor). He also ran well in districts where labor unions were influential.

The Carter Presidency

Carter shone brightly in comparison with Nixon, and he seemed more forward-looking and imaginative than Ford. He tried to give a tone of democratic simplicity and moral fervor to his administration. He enrolled his daughter Amy, a fourth grader, in a largely black Washington public school. Soon after taking office he held a "call-in," for two hours answering questions phoned in by people from all over the country.

As an administrator, Carter fared poorly. He submitted many complicated proposals to Congress but failed in most instances to follow them up. This tendency led to frequent changes in policy. After campaigning on the need to restrain inflation, he came out for a $50 income tax rebate that would surely have caused prices to rise if Congress had passed it. He also tended to blame others when his plans went awry. In an important television address, he described a national malaise that was sapping people's energies and undermining civic pride. Although there was some truth to this observation, it made the president seem ineffective and petulant.

Cold War or Détente?

In foreign affairs Carter announced that he would put defense of "basic human rights" before all other concerns. He cut off aid to Chile and Argentina because of human rights violations and negotiated treaties gradually transferring control of the Panama Canal to Panama. He also sought to continue the Nixon-Kissinger policy of détente.

In 1979 he agreed to exchange ambassadors

Egypt's President Anwar Sadat, Jimmy Carter, and Israeli Prime Minister Menachem Begin clasp hands after the signing of the Camp David Agreement in 1978. Carter's active role in the peace negotiations showed his hands-on approach to the presidency.

with the People's Republic of China. However, maintaining good relations with the Soviet Union was more difficult. He did negotiate another Strategic Arms Limitation Treaty (SALT II) with the Soviet Union in the summer of 1979, but when the Soviets sent troops into Afghanistan to overthrow a government they disapproved of, Carter denounced the invasion and threatened to use force if they invaded any country bordering on the Persian Gulf. Carter also stopped shipments of grain and technologically advanced products to the Soviet Union and withdrew the new SALT treaty.

Carter's one striking diplomatic achievement was the so-called Camp David Agreement between Israel and Egypt. Avoiding war in the Middle East was crucial because war in that part of the world was likely to result in a cutoff of oil supplies from the Arab nations. In September 1978 the president of Egypt, Anwar Sadat, and Prime Minister Menachem Begin of Israel came to the United States at Carter's invitation to negotiate a peace treaty ending the state of war that had existed between their countries for many years. For two weeks they conferred at Camp David, the presidential retreat outside the capital, and Carter's mediation had much to do with their successful negotiations. In the treaty Israel promised to withdraw from territory captured from Egypt during the Six-Day War of 1967. Egypt in turn recognized Israel as a nation, the first Arab country to do so.

A Time of Troubles

Carter had promised to fight inflation by reducing government spending and balancing the budget and to stimulate the economy by cutting taxes. He advanced an admirable, if complicated, plan for conserving energy and reducing the dependence of the United States on OPEC oil. It involved raising the tax on gasoline and imposing a new tax on "gas guzzlers," cars that got relatively few miles per gallon. But in typical fashion he did not press for these measures.

For reasons that were not entirely Carter's fault, national self-confidence was at a low ebb. The United States had lost considerable international prestige. To a degree this was unavoidable. The very success of American policies after World War II had something to do with the decline of American influence in the world. The Marshall Plan, for example, enabled the nations of western Europe to rebuild their economies; thereafter they were less dependent on outside aid, and in the course of pursuing their own interests they sometimes adopted policies that did not seem to be in the best interests of the United States. Under American occupation, Japan rebuilt its shattered economy. By the 1960s and 1970s it had become one of the world's leading manufacturing nations, its exporters providing fierce competition in markets previously dominated by Americans.

At home the decay of the inner sections of many cities was a continuing cause of concern. The older cities seemed almost beyond repair. Crime rates were high, public transportation was dilapidated and expensive, other city services were understaffed and inefficient, the schools were crowded, and student performance was poor. Blacks, Hispanics, and other minorities made up a large percentage of the population in decaying urban areas. That they had to live in such surroundings made a mockery of the commitment made by the civil rights legislation of the 1960s and Lyndon Johnson's Great Society program to treat all people equally and improve the lives of the poor.

Double-Digit Inflation

The most vexing problem in the Carter years was soaring inflation. Prices had been rising for an unusually long period and in recent years at an unprecedentedly rapid pace. In 1971 an inflation rate of 5 percent had so alarmed President Nixon that he had imposed a price freeze. In 1979 a 5 percent rate would have seemed almost deflationary—the actual rate was nearly 13 percent.

Double-digit inflation had a devastating effect on the poor, the retired, and others who were living on fixed incomes. However, the squeeze that price increases put on these unfortunates was only part of the damage done. People began to anticipate inflation. They bought goods they did not really need, on the assumption that whatever today's price, tomorrow's would be higher still. This behavior increased demand and pushed prices up still more. At another level, a kind of "flight from money" began. Well-to-do individuals transferred their assets from cash to durable goods such as land and houses, gold, works of art, jewelry, rare postage stamps, and other "collectibles." Interest rates rose rapidly as lenders demanded higher returns to compensate for expected future inflation.

Congress raised the minimum wage to help low-paid workers cope with inflation. It pegged social security payments to the cost-of-living index in an effort to protect retirees. The poor and the pensioners got some immediate relief because of these laws, but their increased spending power caused further upward pressure on prices. Inflation was feeding on itself, and the price spiral seemed unstoppable.

The federal government made matters worse in several ways. People's wages and salaries rose in response to inflation, but their taxes went up more because higher dollar incomes put them in higher tax brackets. This "bracket creep" caused resentment and frustration among middle-class families. There were "taxpayer revolts" as many people turned against government programs for aiding the poor. Inflation also increased the government's need for money. Year after year it spent more than it received in taxes. By thus unbalancing the budget it pumped billions of dollars into the economy, and by borrowing to meet the deficits it pushed up interest rates, increasing costs to businesses that had to borrow.

The Carter Recession

Carter had little to suggest that was different from the policies of Nixon and Ford. In 1978 he named a conservative banker, Paul A. Volcker, as chairman of the Federal Reserve Board. Volcker believed that the way to check inflation was to limit the growth of the money supply. Under his direction the board adopted a tight-money policy, which caused already high interest rates to soar. High interest rates hurt all borrowers, but they were especially damaging to the automobile and housing industries, because car and home buyers tend to borrow a large portion of the purchase price. High interest charges caused tens of thousands of automobile workers, carpenters, bricklayers, and other skilled workers to lose their jobs. Savings and loan institutions were especially hard hit because they were saddled with mortgages made when rates were as low as 4 and 5 percent. Now they had to pay much more than that to hold deposits and offer even higher rates to attract new money.

The Iranian Crisis: Origins

By the autumn of 1979 Carter's standing in public opinion polls was extremely low and his chances of being elected to a second term seemed dim. But at this point a dramatic upheaval in the Middle East revived his prospects. On November 4, 1979, about 400 armed Muslim militants broke into the American Embassy compound in Teheran, Iran, and took everyone within the walls captive.

The seizure had roots that ran far back in Iranian history. During World War II, Great Britain, the Soviet Union, and later the United States occupied Iran and forced its pro-German shah into exile, replacing him with his 22-year-old son, Muhammad Reza Pahlavi. In the early 1950s, when liberal and nationalist elements in Iran, led by premier Muhammad Mossadegh, sought to reduce the power of the Anglo-Iranian Oil Company, American mediators engineered a compromise that increased the price Iran received for its petroleum. Mossadegh was a liberal by Iranian standards but by western standards somewhat eccentric. He went about in pink pajamas and broke into tears at the slightest provocation. In 1953 a CIA coup presumably designed to prevent the nationalization of Iranian petroleum resources and the abolition of the monarchy resulted in his overthrow. His fall helped the international oil industry to export billions of barrels of cheap oil, but it turned most Iranians against the United States and Shah Reza Pahlavi. His unpopularity led the shah to purchase enormous amounts of American arms. President Nixon authorized the shah to buy any nonnuclear weapon in the American arsenal, so the shah, whose oil-based wealth was vast, proceeded to load up on sophisticated F-14 and F-15 fighters and other weapons. Over the years Iran became the most powerful military force in the region. While running for president, Carter had criticized Nixon's arms sales to Iran, but in office, in typical fashion, he reversed himself, even selling the shah state-of-the-art F-16 fighters and several expensive AWACs, observation planes equipped with ultrasophisticated radar.

Although Iran was an enthusiastic member of the OPEC cartel, the shah was for obvious reasons a firm friend of the United States. Iran seemed, as President Carter said in 1977, "an island of stability" in the troubled Middle East.

The appearance of stability was deceptive because of the shah's unpopularity. He suppressed liberal opponents brutally, and his attempts to introduce western ideas and technology angered conservatives. Muslim religious leaders were particularly offended by such "radical" policies as the shah's tentative efforts to improve the position of women in Iranian society. Because of his American-supplied army and his American-trained secret police, his opponents hated the United States almost as much as they hated their ruler.

Throughout 1977, riots and demonstrations convulsed Iran. When soldiers fired on protesters, the bloodshed caused more unrest. The whole country seemed to rise against the shah. In January 1979, he was forced to flee. A revolutionary government headed by a revered religious leader, the Ayatollah Ruhollah Khomeini, assumed power.

Khomeini denounced the United States, the "Great Satan" whose support of the shah, he said, had caused the Iranian people untold suffering. When President Carter allowed the shah to come to the United States for medical treatment, the seizure of the Teheran embassy resulted.

The Iranian Crisis: Carter's Dilemma

The militants announced that the captive Americans would be held as hostages until the United States returned the shah to Iran for trial as a traitor. They also demanded that the shah's vast wealth be confiscated and surrendered to the Iranian government. President Carter naturally rejected these demands. Deporting the shah, who had entered the United States legally, and confiscating his property were not possible under American law. Instead, Carter froze Iranian assets in the United States and banned trade with Iran until the hostages were freed.

A stalemate developed. Months passed. Even after the shah, who was terminally ill with cancer, left the United States for Panama, the Iranians remained adamant. The crisis provoked a remarkable emotional response in the United States. For once the entire country agreed on something. One result of this was a revival of Carter's political fortunes. Before the attack, Senator Edward M. Kennedy of Massachusetts, youngest brother of John F. Kennedy, had decided to seek the Democratic presidential nomination. He seemed a likely winner until the seizure of the hostages, which caused the public to rally around the president.

Nevertheless, the hostages languished in Iran, and an intense debate raged within the administration about whether or not to attempt to rescue them. In April 1980, Carter finally ordered a team of marine commandos flown into Iran in helicopters in a desperate attempt to free them. The raid was a fiasco. Several helicopters broke down. While the others were gathered at a desert rendezvous south of Teheran, Carter called off the attempt, and the Iranians made political capital of the incident, gleefully displaying on television the wrecked aircraft and captured American equipment. The stalemate continued. And when the shah died in July 1980, it made no difference to the Iranians.

The Election of 1980

Despite the failure of the raid, Carter had more than enough delegates at the Democratic convention to

THE MIDDLE EAST

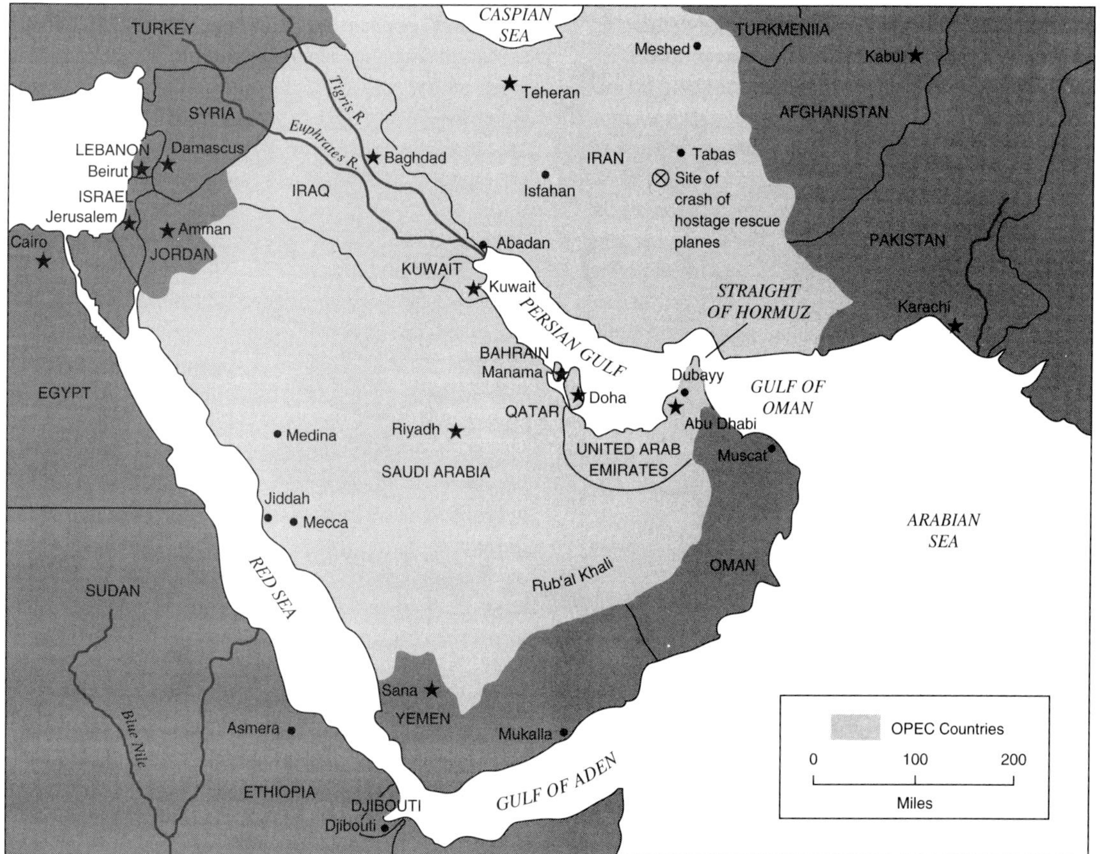

win nomination on the first ballot. His Republican opponent in the campaign that followed was Ronald Reagan, the candidate who had almost defeated Gerald Ford for the nomination in 1976. Reagan had been a New Deal Democrat, but after World War II he became disillusioned with liberalism. He denounced government inefficiency and high taxation. When his movie career ended, he did publicity for General Electric and worked for various conservative causes. In 1966 he was elected governor of California.

The 1980 presidential campaign ranks among the most curious in American history. One of Reagan's opponents at the Republican convention, Congressman John Anderson of Illinois, ran for president as an independent. Both Carter and Reagan spent much time explaining why the other was unsuited to be president. Carter defended his record, though without much conviction. Reagan denounced criminals, drug addicts, and all varieties of immorality and spoke favorably of patriotism, religion, and family life. He also promised to reduce spending and cut taxes, at the same time insisting that the budget could be balanced and inflation sharply reduced.

Reagan's tendency to depend on popular magazine articles, half-remembered conversations, and other informal sources for his economic "facts" reflected a mental imprecision that alarmed his critics. But his sunny disposition and his reassuring, relaxed style compared favorably with Carter's personality. The president seemed tight-lipped and tense even when flashing his habitual toothy smile. A television debate between Carter and Reagan pointed up their personal differences, but Reagan's question to the audience—"Are you better off now than you were four years ago?"—had more effect on the election than any statement on policy.

In November, voter turnout was light but lopsided, Reagan garnering over 43 million votes to Carter's 35 million and Anderson's 5.6 million. Dissatisfaction with the Carter administration seems to have accounted for the result. The Republicans also won control of the Senate and cut deeply into the Democratic majority in the House of Representatives.

Carter devoted his last weeks in office to the continuing hostage crisis. War had broken out between Iran and Iraq. The additional strain on an Iranian economy already shattered by revolution raised hopes that the Ayatollah Khomeini would release the captive Americans. With Algeria acting as intermediary, American and Iranian diplomats worked out an agreement. Perhaps for fear that the new president might take some drastic action, Iran at last agreed to release the hostages in return for its assets in the United States. After 444 days in captivity, the 52 hostages were set free on January 20, the day Reagan was inaugurated.

Reagan as President

Despite his amiable, unaggressive style, Reagan acted rapidly and with determination once in office. He hoped to change the direction in which the country was moving by turning many functions of the federal government over to the states and relying more on individual initiative. The marketplace, not bureaucratic regulations, should govern most economic decisions. Yet he also set out to increase military spending and defend American interests more vigorously in order to check what he saw as a steadily increasing gap between the strength and influence of the United States and that of the Soviet Union.

In August 1981, Reagan displayed his determination in convincing fashion when the nation's air traffic controllers went on strike. The law forbade them to do so, and Reagan ordered them to return to work. When more than 11,000 controllers refused to obey this order, Reagan discharged them and began a crash program to train replacements. Even after the strike collapsed, Reagan refused to rehire the strikers. The air controllers' union was destroyed.

Reagan made cutting taxes his first priority. He persuaded Congress to lower income taxes by 25 percent over three years and to check the growth of federal spending on social services such as welfare payments and food stamps. He insisted that in the long run poor people and everyone else would benefit more from his program than from these "handouts."

His reasoning was based on what was known as "supply-side economics." He claimed that people would have more money to invest because of the tax cut, that they would invest the money in productive ways rather than spend it on consumer goods (because they would be able to keep a larger share of their profits), and that the investments would lead to increased production, more jobs, prosperity, and therefore more tax income for the government despite the lower tax rates.

"Reaganomics," as administration policy was called, was not a new theory. Carter had advocated tax cuts, reduced federal spending, and tight money, and during his term the airlines were freed from control by the Civil Aeronautics Board. But supply-side economics was old-fashioned to the point of being antique. It differed little from the policy Herbert Hoover had favored in the Great Depression, which his critics had derided as the "trickle-down" theory.

Most economists did not think that Reaganomics would work. By December 1982 the economy was in a full-scale recession. More than 10 percent of the work force was unemployed. Lower tax rates and a slumping economy were further unbalancing the budget. In 1983 the budget deficit topped $195 billion, up from $59 billion only three years earlier. The treasury was forced to borrow billions, which kept interest rates high. Only the fact that inflation was slowing brightened the gloomy picture.

Then, however, the economy began to pick up. With inflation down from more than 12 percent to less than 4 percent, the Federal Reserve Board relaxed its tight-money policy. Interest rates then declined, making it easier for people to finance the purchase of homes and automobiles. Unemployment, while still high, fell below 8 percent in 1984.

But the recovery did not lead to much new business investment. People seemed to be spending their additional income on consumer goods. Together with the federal deficits caused by the large increase in military expenditures, this spending prevented interest rates from going down as far as economists had hoped.

Many of Reagan's advisers urged him to reduce the military budget and seek some kind of tax increase in order to bring the government's income more nearly in line with its outlays. However, the president insisted that the military buildup was necessary because of the threat posed by the Soviet Union, which he called an "evil empire," and pursued a hard-line anticommunist foreign policy. Claiming that the communists were sending arms and supplies to the leftist government of Nicaragua and encouraging communist rebels in El Salvador, Reagan sought to undermine the Nicaraguan regime and bolster the conservative government of El Salvador. He used American troops to overthrow a Cuban-backed regime on the Caribbean island of Grenada. With the reluctant support of the western democracies, he installed new nuclear missiles in Europe.

Four More Years

Although some Americans considered both his domestic and foreign policies wrongheaded, Reagan's standing in public opinion polls remained high. At the 1984 Republican convention he was nominated for a second term without opposition.

The Democrats' choice was not made so easily. The leading candidate was Walter Mondale of Minnesota, who had been vice-president under Carter. He was opposed in the primaries by half a dozen others, including Senator John Glenn of Ohio, the former astronaut; Senator Gary Hart of Colorado; and the Reverend Jesse Jackson, a prominent civil rights activist. But by time of the Democratic convention, Mondale had a majority of the delegates and was nominated on the first ballot. He then electrified the country by choosing a woman, Representative Geraldine Ferraro of New York, as his running mate. His choice was widely praised. The Democrats expected that she would win the votes of many Republican women and that her selection would counter the claims of Mondale's critics that he was unimaginative and overly cautious. On the stump she drew large crowds and proved to be an excellent campaign orator.

Reagan began the campaign with several important advantages. He was especially popular among religious fundamentalists and other social conservatives. Many fundamentalist TV preachers campaigned in his behalf. "Americans are sick and tired of . . . amoral liberals," the Reverend Jerry Falwell, founder of the Moral Majority movement, declared. Falwell was against drugs, the "coddling" of criminals, homosexuality, communism, and abortion—views that Reagan shared. Though not openly anti-black, Falwell disapproved of forced busing and a number of other government policies designed to help blacks and other minorities. Of course, Walter Mondale was also against many of the things that Falwell and his followers denounced, but Reagan was against them all.

But Moral Majority, despite its name, was far from an actual majority. Reagan's support was much more broadly based. Thousands of working people and an enormous percentage of white southerners, types that had been solidly Democratic during the New Deal and beyond, now voted Republican.

The president's personality was another important plus. Voters continued to admire his informal yet firm style and his stress on patriotism and other old-fashioned virtues. He was a confirmed optimist, telling the voters over and over that things were getting better and that four more years of Republican leadership would make them better still.

Mondale emphasized the difficulties that he saw ahead for the nation. He blamed Reagan for the huge increase in the federal deficit and accused him of misleading the public by saying that he would not raise taxes if reelected. He stated frankly that he *would* raise taxes if elected. This admission, most unusual for a person running for office, was another attempt to counter his reputation for political caution.

All the president's economic policies, Mondale insisted, hurt the poor, women, and minorities. He pointed out, correctly, that the number of people living below the poverty line had grown in the Reagan years to over 35 million, 15.2 percent of the population.

Most polls showed Reagan far in the lead when the campaign began, and this remained true throughout the contest. Optimism and opportunity were his catchwords. Mondale argued his case forcefully, but the nature of that case sometimes made him seem gloomy, complaining, and mean-spirited. Reagan avoided specifics, promising only that if he was elected, prosperity would continue and the future would be bright. Reagan's advanced age (73) was a legitimate issue, but when asked by a reporter whether he thought "the age question" important, he responded with a quip—he would not make an issue of his opponent's youth. On election day the president swept the nation, gathering nearly 60 percent of the popular vote and losing only in Mondale's Minnesota and the District of Columbia. His margin in the electoral college was 525 to 13.

Of all the elements in the New Deal coalition, only the blacks, who voted Democratic overwhelmingly, remained loyal, and their very unity may have accounted for the shift of so many white Democrats to Reagan. The Democratic strategy of nominating a woman for vice-president failed. Far more women voted for Reagan than for the Mondale-Ferraro ticket. Reagan's victory, like the Eisenhower landslides of the 1950s, was a personal one. The Republicans made only minor gains in the House of Representatives and actually lost two seats in the Senate.

The "Reagan Revolution"

Reagan's agenda for his second term closely resembled that of his first. In foreign affairs his anti-Soviet policies, and particularly his belligerent rhetoric, attracted no better than lukewarm support among all but the most fervent American anticommunists. This was particularly true after Mikhail S. Gorbachev became the Soviet premier in March 1985. Gorbachev was far more moderate and flexible than his predecessors and much more concerned about public opinion in the western democracies. He encouraged political debate and criticism in the Soviet Union—the policy known as *glasnost*—and sought to stimulate the stagnant Soviet economy by decentralizing administration and rewarding individual enterprise *(perestroika).*

Gorbachev also announced that he would continue to honor the unratified SALT II agreement, whereas Reagan seemed bent on pushing ahead with the expansion of America's nuclear arsenal. He wished to develop a computer-controlled Strategic Defense Initiative (SDI) that would supposedly be capable of destroying enemy missiles in outer space where they could do no damage. Despite his insistence that SDI would be a defensive system, the Soviets objected to it vociferously.

But when he realized that the Soviets were eager to limit nuclear weapons, Reagan met with Gorbachev in October 1986 in Iceland to negotiate an arms control agreement. This summit got nowhere, partly because Reagan was determined to push SDI and partly because he apparently did not understand the implications of nuclear disarmament for western Europe. The Europeans, fearing Soviet superiority in conventional weapons, were horrified by the thought of total nuclear disarmament. The Iceland setback, however, proved temporary, and in 1988, at a second summit, Reagan and Gorbachev signed a treaty eliminating medium-range nuclear missiles.

Reagan nevertheless persisted in pressing his SDI scheme. After the spectacular Apollo program, which sent six expeditions to the moon between 1969 and 1972, NASA's prestige was beyond measurement. Its Skylab orbiting space station program (1973–1974) was equally successful. Early in 1981 the manned space shuttle *Columbia,* after orbiting for several days, returned to earth intact, gliding on its stubby, swept-back wings to an appointed landing strip. *Columbia* and other shuttles were soon transporting satellites into space for the government and private companies, and its astronauts were conducting military and scientific experiments of great importance.

Congress, however, boggled both at the enormous estimated cost of SDI and the idea of relying for national defense on the complex technology involved. The entire space program suffered a further setback in 1986, when the space shuttle *Challenger* exploded shortly after takeoff, killing its seven-member crew. This disaster put a stop to the program while complex engineering changes were made. Finally, however, in 1989 the shuttles began flying again.

The president was more successful in winning public support for his get-tough-with-terrorists policy. In October 1985, four Arabs seized control of a cruise ship in the Mediterranean. After killing an elderly American tourist, they surrendered to Egyptian authorities on condition that they be provided with safe passage to Libya on an Egyptian airliner.

The terrorists chose Libya because its president, Muammar al-Qaddafi, was a bitter enemy of Israel and the United States. On Reagan's orders Navy F-14 jets forced the Egyptian pilot to land in Italy instead of Libya, and the terrorists were taken into custody.

Then, after a Libyan-planned bombing of a West German club frequented by American servicemen, Reagan launched an air strike against Libyan bases from airfields in Great Britain. This attack greatly alarmed Europeans, but in America the president's popularity reached an all-time high.

Reagan's basic domestic objectives—to reduce the scope of federal activity, particularly in the social welfare area; to lower income taxes; and to increase the strength of the armed forces—did not

The arms cuts made at the 1988 Moscow summit showed how Ronald Reagan's ideas about the "evil empire" had changed. Yet Reagan was surprised to find that Mikhail Gorbachev believed "the communist propaganda he's grown up hearing about our country"—above all, that business dominates the government.

change either. Despite the tax cuts already made, congressional leaders agreed to the Income Tax Act of 1986, which reduced the top levy on personal incomes from 50 percent to 28 percent and the tax on corporate profits from 46 percent to 34 percent. "When I think of coming here with the tax rate at 70 percent and ending my first term under 30 percent, it's amazing," one delighted Republican senator told reporters.

Liberal members of Congress had found it politically difficult to oppose the measure. The old tax system was full of "loopholes" benefiting particular interests and the new law did away with most tax shelters that had enabled high-income citizens to reduce their tax bills sharply. The law also relieved 6 million low-income people from paying any federal income tax at all. The objective of the law was to require people with similar incomes to pay roughly equal taxes.

But the law undermined the principle of progressive taxation—the practice, dating back to the first income tax enacted after the adoption of the Sixteenth Amendment in 1913, of requiring high-income people to pay a larger *percentage* of their income than those with smaller incomes. The new law set only two rates: 15 percent on taxable incomes below $29,750 for families, and 28 percent on incomes above this limit. A family with a taxable income of $30,000 would pay at the same rate as one with $30 million, should any such exist.

Reagan advanced another of his objectives by appointing conservatives to federal judgeships. In 1981 he named Sandra Day O'Connor to the Supreme Court. Justice O'Connor was the first woman to be appointed to the Court, but she was nevertheless conservative on most constitutional questions. When Chief Justice Warren C. Burger resigned in 1986, Reagan replaced him with Associate Justice William H. Rehnquist, probably the most conservative member of the Court, and he filled the vacancy with Antonin Scalia, an even more conservative judge. After the resignation of Associate Justice Lewis F. Powell in 1987, the president nominated the extremely conservative Robert Bork, the man who, while Nixon's solicitor general, had discharged the Watergate special prosecutor, Archibald Cox. But the Senate refused to confirm Bork, and eventually the appointment went to a less controversial but by no means liberal judge, Anthony M. Kennedy. By 1988 Reagan had appointed well over half of all the members of the federal bench.

Change and Uncertainty

But if the Reagan Revolution seemed to have triumphed, powerful forces were at work that no individual or party could effectively control. For one thing, the makeup of the American people, always in a state of flux, was changing at a rate approaching that of the early 1900s when the "new immigration" was at its peak. In the 1970s, after the Immigration Act of 1965 had put an end to the national-origin system, more than 4 million immigrants entered the country, the vast majority from Asia and Latin America. This trend continued; of the 601,000 who arrived in 1986, nearly 500,000 were from these regions. In addition, uncounted thousands entered the country illegally, most crossing the long, sparsely settled border with Mexico.

Some of the immigrants were refugees fleeing from repressive regimes in Vietnam, Cuba, Haiti, and Central America, and nearly all were poor. Most tended, like their predecessors, to crowd together in ethnic neighborhoods. Spanish could be heard more often that English in sections of Los Angeles, New York, Miami, and many other cities.

But no strong demand for immigration restriction developed, perhaps because so many Americans were themselves the children of immigrants. However, conservatives found it appalling that so many people could enter the country illegally, and even Americans sympathetic to the undocumented aliens agreed that control was desirable. Finally, in 1986, Congress passed a law offering amnesty to illegal immigrants long resident in the country but penalizing employers who hired illegal immigrants in the future. Many persons legalized their status under the new law, but the influx of illegal immigrants continued.

There were other disturbing trends. The postwar population explosion and the subsequent decline in the birthrate made pressure on the social security system inevitable when the baby boomers reached retirement age in the early 21st century. More immediately, the traditional family, consisting of a husband and wife and their children, the man the breadwinner and the woman the housewife, seemed in danger of ceasing to be the norm. An ever-larger number of families were headed by single parents, in most cases by women, often black and nearly always poor.

Year after year more than a million marriages

ended in divorce. The tendency of couples to live together without getting married continued, helping to explain why the number of illegitimate births rose steadily. So did the number of abortions—from 763,000 in 1974 after abortion was legalized to an annual average of 1.3 million in the 1980s.

The Reagan administration devoted much effort to fighting crime, but despite the fact that the number of prison inmates reached an all-time high, little progress was made. A campaign against illegal drugs resulted in many arrests, but the drugs remained widely available. Cocaine became, in a cheap, smokable, and especially addictive form called "crack," a problem of epidemic proportion.

The drug problem was part of a larger and still more threatening one, the spread of the deadly new disease, AIDS. AIDS was caused by a virus that destroyed the body's immune system, exposing the victim to a host of deadly diseases. It was inevitably fatal. Since it is transmitted by the exchange of bodily fluids, intravenous drug users (who frequently shared needles) and homosexuals were its chief victims in the United States. But since it is a venereal disease, the possibility of its spreading through the general population is a constant danger.

Other social and economic changes that were difficult to control included the continuing shift of employment opportunities from the production of goods to the production of services—from raising wheat and manufacturing steel to advertising, banking, and record keeping. This meant a shift from blue- to white-collar work, which called for more better-educated workers than were currently available and increasing joblessness for the unskilled. Union membership had been falling since long before Reagan became president, but by 1985 it was down to about 19 percent of the work force, in large part because white-collar workers were difficult to organize.

The Merger Movement

Another worrisome trend was the merger movement, which saw often unrelated companies swallowing up one another in unprecedented fashion. By using borrowed funds, corporations could even buy businesses far larger than themselves, though the result left the new combination burdened with heavy debts. The movement began while Carter was president, and Reagan's abandonment of strict enforcement of the antitrust laws encouraged it. So did the federal tax structure; corporations pay taxes on stock dividends but can take the interest they pay to bondholders as tax deductions.

Piratical corporate "raiders" raised cash by issuing high-interest bonds secured by the assets of the company purchased. The system made it possible for a single entrepreneur to buy a giant corporation. In 1985 Ronald Perelman, who had recently obtained control of a supermarket chain with a net worth of about $145 million, managed to take over the cosmetics and health care firm Revlon, the net worth of which exceeded $1 billion. One deal often led to another. In 1985 the R. J. Reynolds Tobacco Company purchased the food conglomerate Nabisco for $4.9 billion. Three years later this new giant, RJR Nabisco, was itself taken over at a cost of $24.9 billion.

Still another economic trend that defied national control was the falling world price of petroleum. This eased inflationary pressures and helped speed recovery in the United States, but cheaper oil dealt a devastating blow to the economy of the Southwest, a region where support of Reagan's policies was particularly strong. Lower oil prices also forced oil-producing countries in and out of OPEC to cut back on their imports of manufactured goods. Mexico was hit so hard that it could not even pay the interest on its debts without obtaining further loans. Many American banks suffered heavy losses when domestic and foreign oil-related loans went sour.

But by that time inflation had slowed to a crawl because of the tight money policy, and world agricultural prices were falling. Between 1982 and 1986 the value of American wheat exports fell from $8 billion to less than half that amount. For many debt-ridden farmers, this meant bankruptcy. More generally, the popularity of the Reagan tax reductions and the president's refusal to consider any change in course on this subject meant that the federal government continued to run at a huge deficit; the shortfall rose from $179 billion in 1985 to more than $220 billion in 1986.

The Iran-Contra Arms Deals

All these matters were partly beyond human control, or at least beyond what seemed practicable under the American political system. Overall, they diminished the effectiveness of the Reagan administration. But the administration suffered most from two self-inflicted wounds involving American policy in Central America and the Middle East.

The Central American problem resulted from a revolution in Nicaragua, where in 1979 leftist rebels had overthrown the dictatorial regime of Anastasio Somoza. Because the victorious Sandinista government turned out to be Marxist-oriented (and supported by both Cuba and the Soviet Union), President Reagan was determined to force it from power. He backed anti-Sandinista elements in Nicaragua known as the Contras and in 1981 persuaded Congress to provide these "freedom fighters" with arms.

But the Contras made little progress, and many Americans feared that aiding them would lead, as it had in Vietnam, to the use of American troops in the fighting. In October 1984, in the Boland Amendment, Congress banned further military aid to the rebels. The president then sought to persuade other countries and private American groups to help the Contras (as he put it) to keep "body and soul together."

In the Middle East, war had been raging between Iran and Iraq since 1980. The chief interest of the United States in the conflict was to make sure that it did not cause the flow of Middle Eastern oil to the West to be cut off. But public opinion in the country was particularly incensed against the Iranians. Memories of the hostage crisis of the Carter years did not fade, and Iran was widely believed to be responsible for the fact that a number of Americans were being held hostage by terrorists in Lebanon. Reagan was known to oppose any bargaining with terrorists. Nevertheless, he was eager to find some way to free the captive Americans. During 1985 he made the fateful decision to allow the indirect shipment of arms to Iran by way of Israel, his hope being that this would result in the hostages' release. When it had no effect, he went further. In January 1986 he authorized the secret sale of American weapons directly to the Iranians.

The arms sale was arranged by Marine Colonel Oliver North, an aide of Reagan's national security adviser, Admiral John Poindexter. North was already in charge of the administration's effort to supply the Nicaraguan Contras indirectly. With Poindexter's knowledge, he used $12 million of the profit from the Iranian sales to provide weapons for the Contras, in plain violation of the congressional ban on such aid. North prepared a memorandum describing the transaction for Poindexter to show Reagan, but Poindexter testified under oath that he did not do so, in order, he claimed, to spare the president possible embarrassment.

News of the sales to Iran and of the use of the profits to supply the Contras came to light in November 1986 and of course caused a sensation. Poindexter resigned; Colonel North was fired from his job with the security council; a special prosecutor, Lawrence E. Walsh, was appointed to investigate the affair; and both a presidential committee and a joint congressional committee began investigations. Reagan insisted that he knew nothing about the aid to the Contras, but according to polls, a majority of the people did not believe him, and critics pointed out that if he was telling the truth it was almost as bad, since that meant that he had not been in control of his own administration. Although he remained personally popular, his influence with Congress and his reputation as a political leader plummeted.

The Election of 1988

The decline of Reagan's influence was also related to his status as a lame-duck president entering the last year of his tenure. In both the major political parties, attention turned to the choice of presidential candidates.

After a shaky start, Reagan's vice-president, George Bush, ran away with the Republican primaries and won the nomination easily. The Democratic race was more complicated by far. So many candidates entered the field that the average citizen found it hard to tell them apart. Wits began to call the Democratic hopefuls the "seven dwarfs," suggesting both their lack of distinguishing qualities and their lack of distinction.

Gradually, however, the field shrank and the race settled down to a contest between Governor Michael S. Dukakis of Massachusetts and the black leader Jesse Jackson. Jackson proposed to reduce military spending sharply and invest the savings in improving education, health care, and other social services. As in the 1980 campaign, he had the support of most blacks, but he also attracted a larger percentage of white Democrats than in 1984.

Dukakis stressed his record as an efficient manager—the Massachusetts economy was booming. His campaign was well organized and well financed. By the end of the primary season he had a solid majority of convention delegates. He selected a conservative senator, Lloyd Bentsen of Texas, as his running mate.

In his capacity as vice-president, Bush had been accused by critics of being a "wimp"—a weak, bloodless person who fawningly accepted every Reagan policy. As candidate for president, he set out to destroy this impression without rejecting the conservative Reagan philosophy. He attacked Dukakis savagely, charging him with coddling criminals because of a Massachusetts law granting furloughs to prisoners serving life sentences for murder.

Dukakis conducted a curiously lifeless campaign. He stressed his supposed leadership qualities and his administrative abilities, but he avoided speaking out strongly for the liberal social policies that every Democratic presidential candidate since Franklin Roosevelt had supported. Consequently, he found himself more often than not on the defensive against Bush's emotion-charged attacks.

Bush's choice of Senator Dan Quayle of Indiana as his running mate proved politically damaging to the Republicans. Although Quayle was an ardent supporter of military preparedness, it came out that he had avoided the Vietnam draft by enrolling in the Indiana National Guard. More seriously, he proved rather slow-witted in political debate, and Bush had difficulty even explaining why he had selected Quayle.

As the campaign progressed, neither presidential candidate aroused much enthusiasm among voters, but most polls indicated that Bush was gradually pulling away from his Democratic opponent. On election day he won handily, garnering 54 percent of the popular vote and carrying the electoral college, 426 to 112.

President and Mrs. Bush and Vice-President and Mrs. Quayle greet the crowd at inaugural festivities, January 1989.

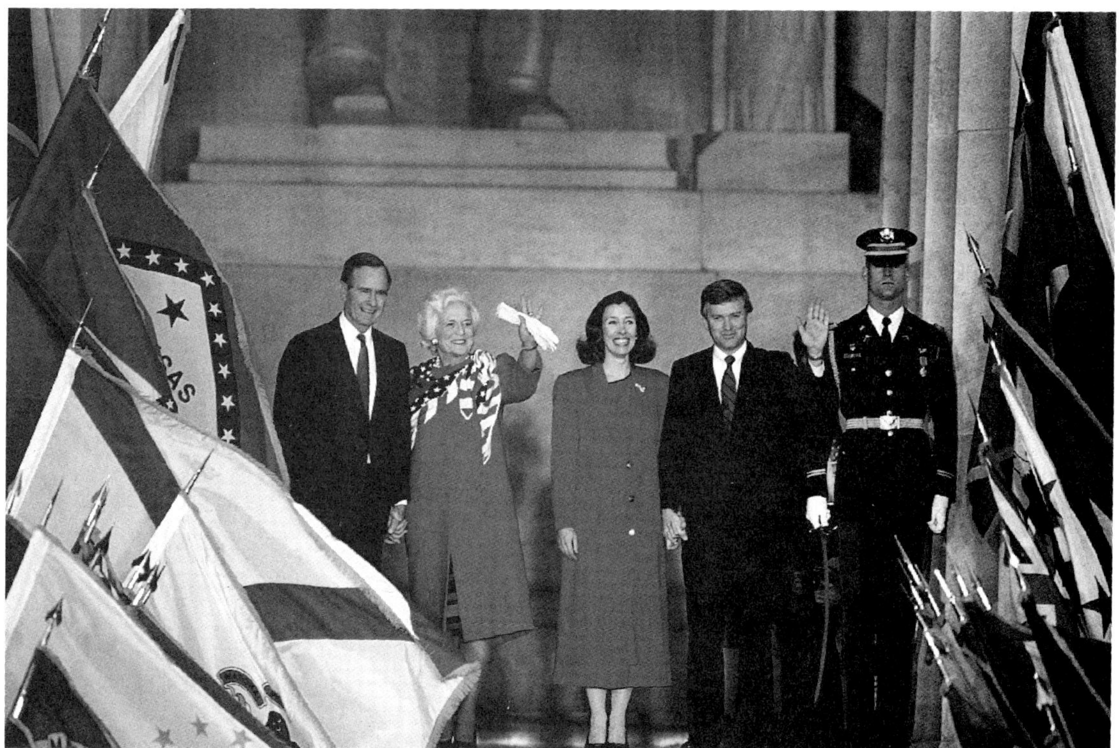

The End of the Cold War

Once in office, President Bush softened his tough tone, saying that he hoped to "make kinder the face of the nation and gentler the face of the world." He also displayed a more traditional command of the workings of government than his predecessor, which was reassuring to persons put off by Reagan's lack of interest in the details of government. He pleased "Reagan loyalists" by his opposition to abortion and gun control and by calling for a constitutional amendment prohibiting the burning of the American flag. His standing in the polls soared.

One important reason for this was the flood of good news from abroad. In Moscow, President Mikhail Gorbachev announced that the Soviet Union would not use force to keep communist governments in power in the satellite nations of eastern Europe. Swiftly the people of Poland, Hungary, Czechoslovakia, Bulgaria, Romania, and East Germany did away with the repressive regimes that had ruled them throughout the postwar era and moved toward more democratic forms of government. Except in Romania, where the dictator Nicolae Ceausescu was executed by revolutionary leaders, all these fundamental changes were carried out in an orderly manner.

Almost overnight the international political climate changed. Soviet-style communism had been discredited. The Warsaw Pact was no longer a significant force in European international politics. The Cold War was over at last. With pro-democratic forces in power in East Germany, demand for union with West Germany quickly emerged. The infamous Berlin Wall was torn down, and talks were begun that led quickly to unification.

The United States had nothing to do with the eastern European upheavals, but President Bush profited from them immensely. He expressed moral support for the new governments (and provided some with modest amounts of financial assistance) but refrained from trying to embarrass the Soviets. His policy won the support of both Republican and Democratic leaders. At a summit meeting in Washington in June 1990, Bush and Gorbachev signed agreements reducing American and Russian stockpiles of long-range nuclear missiles by 30 percent and eliminating chemical weapons. They also announced plans for still further cuts in weaponry, and President Bush agreed to the relaxation of barriers on trade with the Soviet Union.

More controversial was the president's decision to send troops into Panama to overthrow General Manuel Noriega, who had refused to yield power even when his figurehead presidential candidate was defeated in a national election. Noriega was under indictment in the United States for drug trafficking, and after temporarily seeking refuge in the Vatican Embassy in Panama, he surrendered to the American forces and was taken to the United States to stand trial. Bush thus accomplished the objective of the invasion. But Latin Americans were alarmed at the United States' use of force in the region. The president's popularity, however, was not seriously affected.

The president also benefited from the ending of the conflict between the Sandinistas and the Contras in Nicaragua, although as in eastern Europe, he did not contribute much to its solution. For the first time in that small nation's history, a free presidential election was held. The result was a victory for middle-of-the-road democratic forces.

Domestic Problems and Possibilities

Bush's approach to domestic issues aroused a great deal of criticism even among Republicans. In general, like Reagan, he urged voluntarism rather than new legislation for dealing with problems. During the presidential campaign he made a politically popular promise not to raise taxes if elected, prefacing his statement with a phrase made famous by the actor Clint Eastwood: "Read my lips." In office he recommitted himself to that objective; in fact, he proposed reducing the tax on capital gains, a measure that would increase revenues briefly but cost the government billions in the long run. No one enjoys paying taxes; however, the national debt was huge and rapidly increasing. Dealing with it by reducing nonmilitary expenditures was extremely difficult.

Moreover, unforeseen needs for *more* expenditures were constantly arising. Nearly everyone favored extending aid to Poland and other eastern European countries struggling to revive their stagnant economies. The invasion of Panama had been expensive, and the cost of repairing the damage and helping the new government get on its feet was also substantial.

Larger still were the sums needed to bail out the invalid savings and loan industry. The combination of Reagan-inspired bank deregulation, inflation, and rising interest rates had led many savings and loan institutions to lend money recklessly. A large number invested huge sums in risky junk bonds that paid high interest rates and in questionable real estate ventures. In booming states like Texas, Florida, and California such policies led to disaster when the economy cooled. In some cases the bankers had been no better than thieves, but their depositors were innocent victims, and in any case their deposits were insured. The government (meaning the general public) had to make good, and the price was enormous. Shortly after his inauguration, Bush estimated the cost as $50 billion. Within months estimates had risen to $500 million. Some economists feared it would mount still higher.

Logic would suggest that if the tax burden had been roughly proportional to the needs of society when President Bush was elected, these unplanned but legitimate new expenses justified and indeed required a tax increase. But Bush refused to be influenced by such logic, and the Democrats were unwilling to press for new revenues unless he would agree. One indirect result of the no-new-taxes policy was to strain the resources of state governments, which had to assume burdens previously borne by Washington.

Another result was the tendency of the Bush administration to settle for half measures even when considering matters the president considered important. Bush professed to be concerned about Japanese domination of the electronics industry, yet he cut back support of research on high-definition television, semiconductors, and similar projects. He called himself the "education president," and he recognized the government's obligation to tackle the drug problem, to protect the environment, and to support efforts to discover a cure for AIDS. In all these areas, however, the sums budgeted by the administration were relatively small.

When the economy slowed in 1990, the resulting increase in the federal budget deficit finally forced the president to capitulate to reality and agree to the raising of the top income tax rate from 28 percent to 31 percent and to higher taxes on gasoline, liquor, and certain expensive luxuries. This angered conservative Republicans. By midsummer the nation was heading into a serious recession, and Bush's standing in the polls suffered a substantial decline.

The War in the Persian Gulf

Early in August 1990, President Saddam Hussein of Iraq suddenly launched an all-out attack on Iraq's tiny neighbor, the oil-rich sheikdom of Kuwait. His pretext was Kuwait's supposed draining off of oil from the Rumalia oil field, much of which lay on the Iraqi side of their border. Saddam hoped to conquer Kuwait, thus increasing his nation's already large oil reserves to about 25 percent of the world total, and then to force up the world price of petroleum in order to replenish his treasury, badly depleted during his long, bloody war with Iran. His soldiers overran Kuwait swiftly, then began systematically to carry off anything of value they could transport back to Iraq. Within a week Saddam formally annexed Kuwait and he also massed troops along the border of neighboring Saudi Arabia. His army greatly outnumbered Saudi forces, and if he got control of Saudi Arabia's vast oil fields he would be able to dictate world oil prices.

The Saudis and the Kuwaitis turned at once to the United States and other nations for help, and it was quickly given. In a matter of days the UN had applied trade sanctions against Iraq, and at the invitation of Saudi Arabia, the United States (along with Great Britain, France, Italy, Egypt, and Syria) began to move troops to bases in the area. Saddam then seized 6,500 foreigners in the land under his control, for use, he announced, as hostages in case of an attack on his territory.

The anti-Iraq build-up took time, for aside from troops, planes, tanks, ammunition, and all sorts of other military equipment had to be transported by sea and air nearly half way across the globe. But from the start the build-up deterred the Iraqis from invading Saudi Arabia. Instead, they concentrated their forces in strong defensive positions in Kuwait and southern Iraq. This led President Bush to increase the American force in the area from 180,000 to more than 500,000, an army deemed capable of driving the Iraqis from their defenses and liberating Kuwait. In late November the UN took the fateful

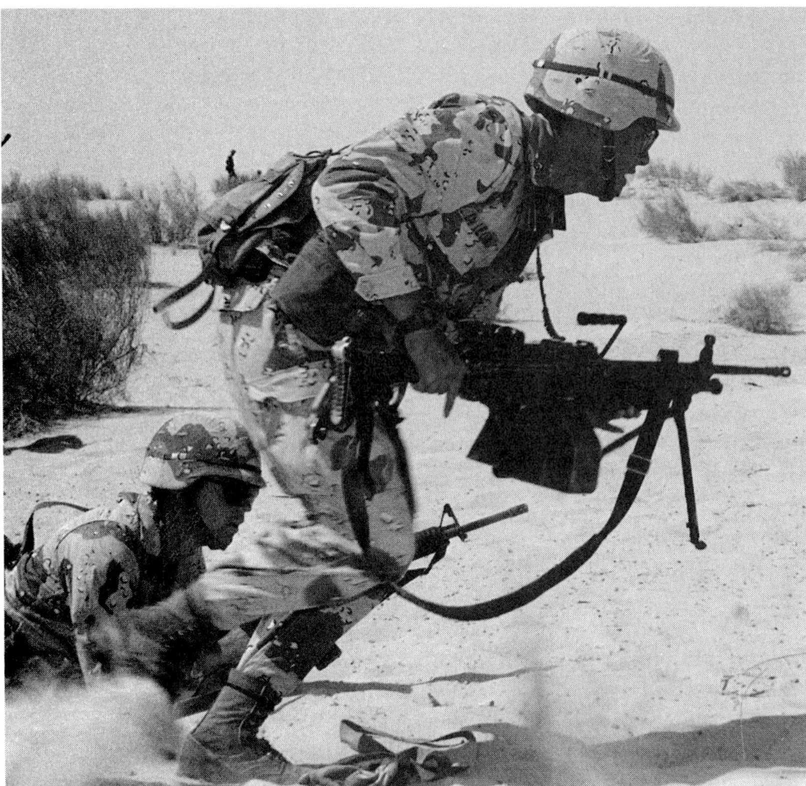

In preparation for the air and ground attack on Iraq, troops from the 82nd Airborne Division conduct a live fire exercise in the Saudi desert, October 1990.

step of authorizing the use of this force if Saddam Hussein did not withdraw from Kuwait by January 15, 1991. Saddam flatly refused to do so, though in mid-December he released the foreign hostages.

American opinion was divided between those who favored starving Saddam into submission by means of the blockade and those who favored the use of force. A solid majority of Congress finally voted for the latter course as the UN deadline approached, and on January 17, the Americans unleashed an enormous air attack, directed by General Norman Schwartzkopf.

This air assault went on for nearly a month and it reduced a good deal of Iraq to rubble. The Iraqi forces, aside from firing a number of Scud missiles on Israel and Saudi Arabia, and setting fire to hundreds of Kuwaiti oil wells, simply endured the rain of destruction that fell on them daily.

On February 23 Bush issued an ultimatum to Saddam: Pull out of Kuwait or face an invasion. When Saddam ignored the deadline, UN troops, more than 200,000 strong, struck with overwhelming force. Between February 24 and February 27 they retook Kuwait, killing tens of thousands of Iraqis in the process and capturing still larger numbers. Some 4000 tanks and enormous quantities of other military equipment were destroyed.

President Bush then ordered an end to the attack and Saddam agreed to UN terms that included paying reparations to Kuwait. Polls indicated that about 90 percent of the American people approved both the president's management of the war and his overall performance as chief executive. These were the highest presidential approval ratings ever recorded.

Things Go Wrong

President Bush and indeed most observers expected Saddam to be driven from power in disgrace by his own people. Indeed, Bush publicly urged the Iraqis to do so. The Kurds in northern Iraq and pro-Iranian Shiite Moslems in the south then took up arms, but Saddam used the remnants of his army to crush them. He also refused repeatedly to carry out the terms of the peace agreement, which included destruction of his capacity for manufacturing missiles and developing atomic weapons. This led critics to argue that Bush should not have stopped the fighting until Baghdad, the Iraqi capital, had been captured and Saddam's army totally crushed.

To make matters worse, the American economy, which had suffered a setback because of the Gulf crisis and which was expected to revive after the war ended, continued to be sluggish. Production lagged and unemployment rose to 7 percent in June 1991. Output and employment picked up slightly during the summer, but then fell back again. Automobile sales slumped to new lows despite steep cuts in interest rates. Hard times made people feel insecure and thus reluctant to spend, further dampening economic activity. All these developments caused President Bush's popularity to fall steeply from its heady level at the end of the Gulf War.

Meanwhile, political and economic conditions in eastern Europe and the Soviet Union continued to deteriorate. The Warsaw Pact binding the former Soviet satellites ceased to exist. In the summer of 1991, civil war broke out in Yugoslavia as Croatia and Slovenia sought independence from the Serbian dominated central government. Throughout the Soviet Union, nationalist and anticommunist groups demanded more local control of their affairs. President Gorbachev, who opposed the breakup of the Union, sought compromise, backing a draft treaty that would increase local autonomy and further "privatize" the Soviet economy.

In August, however, before this treaty could be ratified, hard-line communists attempted a coup. They arrested Gorbachev, who was vacationing in the Crimea, and attempted to cow resistance by pouring tanks into Moscow. But Boris Yeltsin, the anticommunist president of the Russian Republic, defied the rebels and roused the people of Moscow. The coup then swiftly collapsed. Its leaders were arrested, the Communist Party was officially disbanded, and the Soviet Union itself was replaced by a federation of states, of which Russia, led by Yeltsin, was the most important. Gorbachev, who had begun the process of liberation, thus found himself without a job.

These events further shook the world economy and did little to check the decline in public support for President Bush, who seemed indecisive, unable to make up his mind on how to deal with the new situation.

The Election of 1992

The overwhelming American victory in the Persian Gulf War of January–February 1991 increased President Bush's already high standing in public opinion polls. His reelection seemed almost certain, and that discouraged many prominent Democrats from seeking their party's presidential nomination. The best organized of the Democrats who did enter the primaries was Governor Bill Clinton of Arkansas. Despite the fact that he was charged with having misrepresented what he had done to avoid being drafted during the Vietnam War, he won most of the primaries and was nominated at the convention on the first ballot. Senator Al Gore of Tennessee was his choice for vice president.

Although many conservative Republicans resented President Bush's having broken his promise not to raise taxes, he won solid victories in the Republican primaries. For a time H. Ross Perot, a billionaire Texan, entered the race as an independent. Perot was ready, he said, to spend $100 million of his own money on his campaign. He proposed a mixture of liberal and conservative policies, but his main argument was that both the Democrats and the Republicans were out of touch with "the people."

Perot was strong in Texas and the Southwest, a traditionally Republican region, so he seemed a greater threat to Bush than to Clinton. However, when subject to close and critical questioning, he lost his taste for campaigning and in mid-July, he withdrew from the race, disappointing thousands of admirers. A month later, at the Republican convention, Bush and Vice President Dan Quayle were nominated without opposition.

In the campaign Clinton accused Bush of failing to deal effectively with domestic problems, especially the lingering economic recession, which had caused unemployment to increase considerably. He promised to create jobs by undertaking public works projects and encouraging private investment, and to improve the nation's education and health insurance systems. He also called for raising taxes on persons with incomes of more than $200,000. Bush played down the seriousness of the recession and emphasized the need to reduce the national deficit and balance the budget. He also accused Clinton of "waffling" (refusing to take clear stands on controversial issues) and of having avoided the draft by dishonorable means.

Most polls showed Clinton well ahead as the fall campaign progressed. But then Ross Perot dramatically announced that he was reentering the race. This was possible because his name was on the ballot in every state. In October the candidates faced one another in three televised debates. This enabled Perot, who specialized in simplifying complex issues, to reattract many of those who had supported him before he withdrew.

Worried by his standing in the polls, President Bush launched a tremendous attack on Clinton's character, arguing that he was devious and unreliable. All to no avail. On election day more than 100 million citizens voted, a record. About 44 million voted for Clinton, 38 million for Bush, and 20 million for Perot. This translated into a 370 to 168 electoral college victory for Clinton. Despite his obtaining nearly 20 percent of the popular vote, Perot did not win any electoral college votes.

The Imponderable Future

If historians can locate suitable records and other sources about a past event, they are able to explain, or at least make plausible guesses about, what it was and why it happened at that time, no matter how remote. Historians are also probably better than most other people at explaining how things got to be the way they are at any present moment. This is because events have causes and results, and these are things that historians are trained to study and understand. But historians are no better than anyone else at predicting the future. Results, quite obviously, come after the events that cause them; it takes time for them to unfold, which means that "at present," even the most hardworking and intelligent historians do not know anything important about what the future will bring.

Another way of putting this is to point out that in the modern world just about everything that happens is in some way related to everything else that is going on. There are far too many things happening (all producing results of some kind) for anyone to sort out which of them is going to have what effect on events that will happen tomorrow, let alone next year or in the 21st century. "Then" (whether tomorrow or next year or the 21st century) historians will be able to study those particular events that interest them and puzzle out their chief causes—but not "now."

Yet "now" is where we happen to be, and thus this book, so full of events and their causes and results, must end inconclusively. No one knows what will happen next. But of course not knowing what will happen next is one of the main reasons life is so interesting.

Milestones

1974 President Ford pardons Richard Nixon
1975 Vietnam War ends
1978 Camp David Agreement between Israel and Egypt
Paul A. Volcker named chairman of Federal Reserve Board
1979 Sandinistas overthrow Somoza government in Nicaragua
The Reverend Jerry Falwell founds Moral Majority
American interest rates exceed 10 percent
United States recognizes People's Republic of China
Shah forced to flee Iran; Ayatollah Khomeini rules nation
Radical students seize U.S. Embassy in Iran and hold occupants as hostages
1980 Commando raid designed to free hostages in Iran aborted
1981 American hostages in Iran released
Reagan appoints Sandra Day O'Connor to U.S. Supreme Court
Tax Reform Act lowers rates and eliminates loopholes
1984 Boland Amendment bans military aid to Nicaraguan Contras
1985 Mikhail Gorbachev becomes premier of Soviet Union
President Reagan proposes Strategic Defense Initiative
1986 American retaliatory air raid on Libya
Reagan-Gorbachev summit meeting in Iceland
Immigration Act grants amnesty to long-term illegal aliens
Secret Iran-Contra arms deal exposed
1987 Senate rejects nomination of Robert Bork to U.S. Supreme Court
1988 American-Soviet treaty bans medium-range missiles
1989 Gorbachev allows eastern European nations to establish independent democratic governments
1990 Iraq invades and conquers Kuwait
UN applies sanctions and authorizes use of force if Iraq does not evacuate Kuwait by January 15, 1991
1991 Bombardment of Iraq begins on January 17
UN land attack drives Iraq from Kuwait, February 24–27
Failure of conservative coup against reform government in Soviet Union
1992 Bill Clinton elected president

Supplementary Reading

Authoritative works on recent history are hard to find. On Gerald Ford, see Clark Mollenhoff, **The Man Who Pardoned Nixon** (1976), Richard Reeves, **A Ford, Not a Lincoln** (1975), and Ford's autobiography, **A Time to Heal** (1979). Betty Ford's frank **The Times of My Life** (1978) is a cut above most such memoirs.

For the Carter years, see Betty Glad, **Jimmy Carter in Search of the Great White House** (1980), which is critical of Carter's style and actions. Zbigniew Brzezinski, **Power and Principle** (1983), discusses the foreign policy of the administration, while James A. Bill, **The Eagle and the Lion** (1988), and Michael Ledeen and William Lewis, **Debacle** (1981), cover the Iranian hostage crisis.

Books dealing with Reagan and his administration include Hedrick Smith, **Reagan, the Man, the President** (1980), Robert Dallek, **Ronald Reagan; the Politics of Symbolism** (1984), and Rowland Evans and Robert Novak, **The Reagan Revolution** (1981). D. A. Stockman, **The Triumph of Politics** (1986), contains a frank discussion of administration fiscal policies. Of the memoirs by insiders, Martin Anderson, **Revolution** (1988), is favorable to Reagan, D. T. Regan, **For the Record** (1988), is critical. Peggy Noonan, **What I Saw at the Revolution** (1990), is both insightful and amusing. For the Reagan foreign policy, see J. J. Girkpatrick, **Dictatorships and Double Standards** (1982), and Strobe Talbott, **The Russians and Reagan** (1984). W. S. Cohen and G. J. Mitchell, **Men of Zeal** (1988), describe the congressional Iran-Contra headings.

Contrasting views of recent conservative trends are provided by Alan Crawford, **Thunder on the Right** (1980), and Richard Viguerie, **The New Right** (1981). See also John Kater, **Christians on the Right** (1982).

THE DECLARATION OF INDEPENDENCE

When in the Course of human events, it becomes necessary for one people to dissolve the political bands which have connected them with another, and to assume among the Powers of the earth, the separate and equal station to which the Laws of Nature and of Nature's God entitle them, a decent respect to the opinions of mankind requires that they should declare the causes which impel them to the separation.

We hold these truths to be self-evident, that all men are created equal, that they are endowed by their Creator with certain unalienable Rights, that among these are Life, Liberty and the pursuit of Happiness. That to secure these rights, Governments are instituted among Men, deriving their just powers from the consent of the governed, That whenever any Form of Government becomes destructive of these ends, it is the Right of the People to alter or to abolish it, and to institute new Government, laying its foundation on such principles and organizing its powers in such form, as to them shall seem most likely to effect their Safety and Happiness. Prudence, indeed, will dictate that Governments long established should not be changed for light and transient causes; and accordingly all experience hath shown, that mankind are more disposed to suffer, while evils are sufferable, than to right themselves by abolishing the forms to which they are accustomed. But when a long train of abuses and usurpations, pursuing invariably the same Object evinces a design to reduce them under absolute Despotism, it is their right, it is their duty, to throw off such Government, and to provide new Guards for their future security.—Such has been the patient sufferance of these Colonies; and such is now the necessity which constrains them to alter their former Systems of Government. The history of the present King of Great Britain is a history of repeated injuries and usurpations, all having in direct object the establishment of an absolute Tyranny over these States. To prove this, let Facts be submitted to a candid world.

He has refused his Assent to Laws, the most wholesome and necessary for the public good.

He has forbidden his Governors to pass Laws of immediate and pressing importance, unless suspended in their operation till his Assent should be obtained; and when so suspended, he has utterly neglected to attend to them.

He has refused to pass other Laws for the accommodation of large districts of people, unless those people would relinquish the right of Representation in the Legislature, a right inestimable to them and formidable to tyrants only.

He has called together legislative bodies at places unusual, uncomfortable, and distant from the depository of their Public Records, for the sole purpose of fatiguing them into compliance with his measures.

He has dissolved Representative Houses repeatedly, for opposing with manly firmness his invasions on the rights of the people.

He has refused for a long time, after such dissolutions, to cause others to be elected; whereby the Legislative Powers, incapable of Annihilation, have returned to the People at large for their exercise; the State remaining in the mean time exposed to all the dangers of invasion from without, and convulsions within.

He has endeavoured to prevent the population of these States; for that purpose obstructing the Laws of Naturalization of Foreigners; refusing to pass others to encourage their migration hither, and raising the conditions of new Appropriations of Lands.

He has obstructed the Administration of Justice, by refusing his Assent to Laws for establishing Judiciary Powers.

He has made Judges dependent on his Will alone, for the tenure of their offices, and the amount and payment of their salaries.

He has erected a multitude of New Offices, and sent hither swarms of Officers to harass our People, and eat out their substance.

He has kept among us, in times of peace, Standing Armies without the Consent of our legislature.

He has affected to render the Military independent of and superior to the Civil Power.

He has combined with others to subject us to a

jurisdiction foreign to our constitution, and unacknowledged by our laws; giving his Assent to their acts of pretended legislation:

For quartering large bodies of armed troops among us:

For protecting them, by a mock Trial, from Punishment for any Murders which they should commit on the Inhabitants of these States:

For cutting off our Trade with all parts of the world:

For imposing taxes on us without our Consent:

For depriving us in many cases, of the benefits of Trial by Jury:

For transporting us beyond Seas to be tried for pretended offences:

For abolishing the free System of English Laws in a neighbouring Province, establishing therein an Arbitrary government, and enlarging its Boundaries so as to render it at once an example and fit instrument for introducing the same absolute rule into these Colonies:

For taking away our Charters, abolishing our most valuable Laws, and altering fundamentally the Forms of our Governments:

For suspending our own Legislature, and declaring themselves invested with Power to legislate for us in all cases whatsoever.

He has abdicated Government here, by declaring us out of his Protection and waging War against us.

He has plundered our seas, ravaged our Coasts, burnt our towns, and destroyed the lives of our people.

He is at this time transporting large armies of foreign mercenaries to compleat the works of death, desolation and tyranny, already begun with circumstances of Cruelty & perfidy scarcely paralleled in the most barbarous ages, and totally unworthy the Head of a civilized nation.

He has constrained our fellow Citizens taken Captive on the high Seas to bear Arms against their Country, to become the executioners of their friends and Brethren, or to fall themselves by their Hands.

He has excited domestic insurrections amongst us, and has endeavoured to bring on the inhabitants of our frontiers, the merciless Indian Savages, whose known rule of warfare, is an undistinguished destruction of all ages, sexes and conditions.

In every stage of these Oppressions We have Petitioned for Redress in the most humble terms: Our repeated Petitions have been answered only by repeated injury. A Prince, whose character is thus marked by every act which may define a Tyrant, is unfit to be the ruler of a free People.

Nor have We been wanting in attention to our British brethren. We have warned them from time to time of attempts by their legislature to extend an unwarrantable jurisdiction over us. We have reminded them of the circumstances of our emigration and settlement here. We have appealed to their native justice and magnanimity, and we have conjured them by the ties of our common kindred to disavow these usurpations, which, would inevitably interrupt our connections and correspondence. They too have been deaf to the voice of justice and of consanguinity. We must, therefore, acquiesce in the necessity, which denounces our Separation, and hold them, as we hold the rest of mankind, Enemies in War, in Peace Friends.

We, therefore, the Representatives of the United States of America, in General Congress, Assembled, appealing to the Supreme Judge of the world for the rectitude of our intentions, do, in the Name, and by Authority of the good People of these Colonies, solemnly publish and declare, That these United Colonies are, and of Right ought to be Free and Independent States; that they are Absolved from all Allegiance to the British Crown, and that all political connection between them and the State of Great Britain, is and ought to be totally dissolved; and that as Free and Independent States, they have full Power to levy War, conclude Peace, contract Alliances, establish Commerce, and to do all other Acts and Things which Independent States may of right do. And for the support of this Declaration, with a firm reliance on the Protection of Divine Providence, we mutually pledge to each other our Lives, our Fortunes and our sacred Honor.

John Hancock,

Josiah Bartlett, Wm Whipple, Saml Adams, John Adams, Robt Treat Paine, Elbridge Gerry, Steph. Hopkins, William Ellery, Roger Sherman, Samel Huntington, Wm Williams, Oliver Wolcott, Matthew Thornton, Wm Floyd, Phil Livingston, Frans Lewis, Lewis Morris, Richd Stockton, Jno Witherspoon, Fras Hopkinson, John Hart, Abra Clark, Robt Morris, Benjamin Rush, Benja Franklin, John Morton, Geo Clymer, Jas Smith, Geo. Taylor, James Wilson, Geo. Ross, Caesar Rodney, Geo Read, Thos M:Kean, Samuel Chase, Wm Paca, Thos Stone, Charles Carroll of Carrollton, George Wythe, Richard Henry Lee, Th. Jefferson, Benja Harrison, Thos Nelson, Jr., Francis Lightfoot Lee, Carter Braxton, Wm Hooper, Joseph Hewes, John Penn, Edward Rutledge, Thos Heyward, Junr., Thomas Lynch, Junor., Arthur Middleton, Button Gwinnett, Lyman Hall, Geo Walton.

THE CONSTITUTION OF THE UNITED STATES

We the People of the United States, in Order to form a more perfect Union, establish Justice, insure domestic Tranquility, provide for the common defence, promote the general Welfare, and secure the Blessings of Liberty to ourselves and our Posterity, do ordain and establish this CONSTITUTION for the United States of America.

Article I

Section 1. All legislative Powers herein granted shall be vested in a Congress of the United States, which shall consist of a Senate and House of Representatives.

Section 2. The House of Representatives shall be composed of Members chosen every second Year by the People of the several States, and the Electors in each State shall have the Qualifications requisite for Electors of the most numerous Branch of the State Legislature.

No Person shall be a Representative who shall not have attained to the Age of twenty-five Years, and been seven Years a Citizen of the United States, and who shall not, when elected, be an Inhabitant of that State in which he shall be chosen.

Representatives and direct Taxes shall be apportioned among the several States which may be included within this Union, according to their respective Numbers, which shall be determined by adding to the whole Number of free Persons, including those bound to Service for a Term of Years, and excluding Indians not taxed, three fifths of all other Persons. The actual Enumeration shall be made within three Years after the first Meeting of the Congress of the United States, and within every subsequent Term of ten Years, in such Manner as they shall by Law direct. The Number of Representatives shall not exceed one for every thirty Thousand, but each State shall have at Least one Representative; and until such enumeration shall be made, the State of New Hampshire shall be entitled to chuse three, Massachusetts eight, Rhode-Island and Providence Plantations one, Connecticut five, New-York six, New Jersey four, Pennsylvania eight, Delaware one, Maryland six, Virginia ten, North Carolina five, South Carolina five, and Georgia three.

When vacancies happen in the Representation from any State, the Executive Authority thereof shall issue Writs of Election to fill such Vacancies.

The House of Representatives shall chuse their Speaker and other Officers; and shall have the sole Power of Impeachment.

Section 3. The Senate of the United States shall be composed of two Senators from each State, chosen by the Legislature thereof, for six Years; and each Senator shall have one Vote.

Immediately after they shall be assembled in Consequence of the first Election, they shall be divided as equally as may be into three Classes. The Seats of the Senators of the first Class shall be vacated at the Expiration of the second Year, of the second Class at the Expiration of the fourth Year, and of the third Class at the Expiration of the sixth Year, so that one-third may be chosen every second Year; and if Vacancies happen by Resignation, or otherwise, during the Recess of the Legislature of any State, the Executive thereof may make temporary Appointments until the next Meeting of the Legislature, which shall then fill such Vacancies.

No Person shall be a Senator who shall not have attained to the Age of thirty Years, and been nine Years a Citizen of the United States, and who shall not, when elected, be an Inhabitant of that State in which he shall be chosen.

The Vice President of the United States shall be President of the Senate, but shall have no vote, unless they be equally divided.

The Senate shall chuse their other Officers, and also a President pro tempore, in the absence of the Vice President, or when he shall exercise the Office of the President of the United States.

The Senate shall have the sole Power to try all Impeachments. When sitting for that purpose, they shall be on Oath or Affirmation. When the President of the United States is tried, the Chief Justice shall preside: And no person shall be convicted without the Concurrence of two thirds of the Members present.

Judgment in Cases of Impeachment shall not extend further than to removal from Office, and disqualification to hold and enjoy any Office of honor, Trust, or Profit under the United States: but the Party convicted shall nevertheless be liable and subject to Indictment, Trial, Judgment, and Punishment, according to Law.

Section 4. The Times, Places and Manner of holding Elections for Senators and Representatives, shall be prescribed in each state by the Legislature thereof; but the Congress may at any time by Law make or alter such Regulations, except as to the Places of Chusing Senators.

The Congress shall assemble at least once in every Year, and such Meeting shall be on the first Monday in December, unless they shall by Law appoint a different Day.

Section 5. Each House shall be the Judge of the Elections, Returns and Qualifications of its own Members, and a Majority of each shall constitute a Quorum to do Business; but a smaller number may adjourn from day to day, and may be authorized to compel the Attendance of absent Members, in such Manner, and under such Penalties, as each House may provide.

Each House may determine the Rules of its Proceedings, punish its Members for disorderly Behavior, and, with the Concurrence of two thirds, expel a Member.

Each House shall keep a Journal of its Proceedings, and from time to time publish the same, excepting such Parts as may in their Judgment require Secrecy; and the Yeas and Nays of the Members of either House on any question shall, at the Desire of one fifth of those Present, be entered on the Journal.

Neither House, during the Session of Congress, shall, without the Consent of the other, adjourn for more than three days, nor to any other Place than that in which the two Houses shall be sitting.

Section 6. The Senators and Representatives shall receive a Compensation for their Services, to be ascertained by Law, and paid out of the Treasury of the United States. They shall in all Cases, except Treason, Felony, and Breach of the Peace, be privileged from arrest during their Attendance at the Session of their respective Houses, and in going to and returning from the same; and for any Speech or Debate in either House, they shall not be questioned in any other Place.

No Senator or Representative shall, during the Time for which he was elected, be appointed to any civil Office under the Authority of the United States, which shall have been created, or the Emoluments whereof shall have been increased, during such time; and no Person holding any Office under the United States shall be a Member of either House during his continuance in Office.

Section 7. All Bills for raising Revenue shall originate in the House of Representatives; but the Senate may propose or concur with Amendments as on other bills.

Every Bill which shall have passed the House of Representatives and the Senate, shall, before it become a Law, be presented to the President of the United States; If he approve he shall sign it, but if not he shall return it, with his Objections, to that House in which it shall have originated, who shall enter the Objections at large on their Journal, and proceed to reconsider it. If after such Reconsideration two thirds of that House shall agree to pass the bill, it shall be sent, together with the objections, to the other House, by which it shall likewise be reconsidered, and if approved by two thirds of that House, it shall become a Law. But in all such Cases the Votes of both Houses shall be determined by Yeas and Nays, and the Names of the Persons voting for and against the Bill shall be entered on the Journal of each House respectively. If any Bill shall not be returned by the President within ten Days (Sundays excepted) after it shall have been presented to him, the Same shall be a Law, in like Manner as if he had signed it, unless the Congress by their Adjournment prevent its Return, in which Case it shall not be a Law.

Every Order, Resolution, or Vote to which the Concurrence of the Senate and House of Representatives may be necessary (except on a question of Adjournment) shall be presented to the President of the United States; and before the Same shall take Effect, shall be approved by him, or being disapproved by him, shall be repassed by two thirds of the Senate and House of Representatives, according to the Rules and Limitations prescribed in the Case of a Bill.

Section 8. The Congress shall have Power To lay and collect Taxes, Duties, Imposts and Excises, to pay the Debts and provide for the common Defence and general Welfare of the United States; but all Duties, Imposts and Excises shall be uniform throughout the United States;

To borrow money on the credit of the United States;

To regulate Commerce with foreign Nations, and among the several States, and with the Indian Tribes;

To establish an uniform Rule of Naturalization, and uniform Laws on the subject of Bankruptcies throughout the United States;

To coin Money, regulate the Value thereof, and of foreign Coin, and fix the Standard of Weights and Measures;

To provide for the Punishment of counterfeiting the Securities and current Coin of the United States;

To establish Post Offices and post Roads;

To promote the Progress of Science and useful Arts, by securing for limited Times to Authors and Inventors the exclusive Right to their respective Writings and Discoveries;

To constitute Tribunals inferior to the Supreme Court;

To define and punish Piracies and Felonies committed on the high Seas, and Offences against the Law of Nations;

To declare War, grant Letters of Marque and Reprisal, and make Rules concerning Captures on Land and Water;

To raise and support Armies, but no Appropriation of Money to that Use shall be for a longer Term than two Years;

To provide and maintain a Navy;

To make Rules for the Government and Regulation of the land and naval forces;

To provide for calling forth the Militia to execute the Laws of the Union, suppress Insurrections and repel Invasions;

To provide for organizing, arming, and disciplining the Militia, and for governing such Part of them as may be employed in the Service of the United States, reserving to the States respectively, the Appointment of the Officers, and the Authority of training the Militia according to the discipline prescribed by Congress;

To exercise exclusive Legislation in all Cases whatsoever, over such District (not exceeding ten Miles square) as may, by Cession of particular States, and the acceptance of Congress, become the Seat of Government of the United States, and to exercise like Authority over all Places purchased by the Consent of the Legislature of the State in which the Same shall be, for the Erection of Forts, Magazines, Arsenals, dock-Yards, and other needful Buildings;—And

To make all Laws which shall be necessary and proper for carrying into Execution the foregoing Powers, and all other Powers vested by this Constitution in the government of the United States, or in any Department or Officer thereof.

Section 9. The Migration or Importation of such Persons as any of the States now existing shall think proper to admit, shall not be prohibited by the Congress prior to the Year one thousand eight hundred and eight, but a tax or duty may be imposed on such Importation, not exceeding ten dollars for each Person.

The privilege of the Writ of Habeas Corpus shall not be suspended, unless when in Cases of Rebellion or Invasion the public Safety may require it.

No Bill of Attainder or ex post facto Law shall be passed.

No capitation, or other direct, Tax shall be laid unless in Proportion to the Census or Enumeration herein before directed to be taken.

No Tax or Duty shall be laid on Articles exported from any State.

No Preference shall be given by any Regulation of Revenue to the Ports of one State over those of another: nor shall Vessels bound to, or from, one State, be obliged to enter, clear, or pay Duties in another.

No Money shall be drawn from the Treasury, but in Consequence of Appropriations made by Law; and a regular Statement and Account of the Receipts and Expenditures of all public Money shall be published from time to time.

No Title of Nobility shall be granted by the United States: And no Person holding any Office of Profit or Trust under them, shall, without the Consent of the Congress, accept of any present, Emolument, Office, or Title, of any kind whatever, from any King, Prince, or foreign State.

Section 10. No State shall enter into any Treaty, Alliance, or Confederation; grant Letters of Marque and Reprisal; coin Money; emit Bills of Credit; make any Thing but gold and silver Coin a Tender in Payment of Debts; pass any Bill of Attainder, ex post facto Law, or Law impairing the Obligation of Contracts, or grant any Title of Nobility.

No State shall, without the Consent of the Congress, lay any Imposts or Duties on Imports or Exports, except what may be absolutely necessary for executing its inspection Laws: and the net Produce of all Duties and Imposts, laid by any State on Imports or Exports, shall be for the Use of the Treasury of the United States; and all such Laws shall be subject to the Revision and Control of the Congress.

No State shall, without the Consent of Congress, lay any duty of Tonnage, keep Troops, or Ships of War in time of Peace, enter into any Agreement or Compact with another State, or with a foreign Power, or engage in War, unless actually invaded, or in such imminent Danger as will not admit of delay.

Article II

Section 1. The executive Power shall be vested in a President of the United States of America. He shall hold his Office during the Term of four years, and, together with the Vice President, chosen for the same Term, be elected, as follows:

Each State shall appoint, in such Manner as the Legislature thereof may direct, a Number of Electors, equal to the whole Number of Senators and Representatives to which the State may be entitled in the Congress; but no Senator or Representative, or Person holding an Office of Trust or Profit under the United States, shall be appointed an Elector.

The Electors shall meet in their respective States, and vote by Ballot for two persons, of whom one at least shall not be an Inhabitant of the same State with themselves. And they shall make a List of all the Persons voted for, and of the Number of Votes for each; which List they shall sign and certify, and transmit sealed to the Seat of the Government of the United States, directed to the President of the Senate. The President of the Senate shall, in the Presence of the Senate and House of Representatives, open all the Certificates, and the Votes shall then be counted. The Person having the greatest Number of Votes shall be the President, if such Number be a Majority of the whole Number of Electors appointed; and if there be more than one who have such Majority, and have an equal Number of Votes, then the House of Representatives shall immediately chuse by Ballot one of them for President; and if no Person have a Majority, then from the five highest on the List the said House shall in like Manner chuse the President. But in chusing the President, the votes shall be taken by States, the Representation from each State having one Vote; a quorum for this Purpose shall consist of a Member or Members from two-thirds of the States, and a Majority of all the States shall be necessary to a Choice. In every Case, after the Choice of the President, the Person having the greatest Number of Votes of the Electors shall be the Vice President. But if there should remain two or more who have equal votes, the Senate shall chuse from them by Ballot the Vice President.

The Congress may determine the time of chusing the Electors, and the Day on which they shall give their Votes; which Day shall be the same throughout the United States.

No person except a natural-born Citizen, or a Citizen of the United States, at the time of the Adoption of this Constitution, shall be eligible to the Office of President; neither shall any Person be eligible to that Office who shall not have attained to the Age of thirty-five years, and been fourteen Years a Resident within the United States.

In Case of the Removal of the President from Office, or of his Death, Resignation, or Inability to discharge the Powers and Duties of the said Office, the same shall devolve on the Vice President, and the Congress may by Law provide for the Case of Removal, Death, Resignation, or Inability, both of the President and Vice President, declaring what Officer shall then act as President, and such Officer shall act accordingly, until the disability be removed, or a President shall be elected.

The President shall, at stated Times, receive for his Services a Compensation, which shall neither be increased nor diminished during the Period for which he shall have been elected, and he shall not receive within that Period any other Emolument from the United States, or any of them.

Before he enter on the execution of his Office, he shall take the following Oath or Affirmation:—"I do solemnly swear (or affirm) that I will faithfully execute the Office of President of the United States, and will, to the best of my Ability, preserve, protect, and defend the Constitution of the United States."

Section 2. The President shall be Commander in Chief of the Army and Navy of the United States, and of the Militia of the several States, when called into the actual Service of the United States; he may require the Opinion, in writing, of the principal Officer in each of the executive Departments, upon any subject relating to the Duties of their respective Offices, and he shall have Power to Grant Reprieves and Pardons for Offences against the United States, except in Cases of Impeachment.

He shall have Power, by and with the Advice and Consent of the Senate, to make Treaties, provided two thirds of the Senators present concur; and he shall nominate, and by and with the Advice and Consent of the Senate, shall appoint Ambassadors, other public Ministers and Consuls, Judges of the supreme Court, and all other Officers of the United States, whose Appointments are not herein otherwise provided for, and which shall be established by Law: but the Congress may by Law vest the Appointment of such inferior Officers, as they think proper, in the President alone, in the Courts of Law, or in the Heads of Departments.

The President shall have Power to fill up all Vacancies that may happen during the Recess of the Senate, by granting Commissions which shall expire at the End of their next Session.

Section 3. He shall from time to time give to the Congress Information of the State of the Union, and recommend to their Consideration such Measures as he shall judge necessary and expedient; he may, on extraordinary occasions, convene both Houses, or either of them, and in Case of Disagreement between them, with respect to the Time of Adjournment, he may adjourn them to such Time as he shall think proper; he shall receive Ambassadors and other public Ministers; he shall take Care that the Laws be faithfully executed, and shall Commission all the Officers of the United States.

Section 4. The President, Vice President and all civil Officers of the United States, shall be removed from Office on Impeachment for, and Conviction of, Treason, Bribery, or other high Crimes and Misdemeanors.

Article III

Section 1. The judicial Power of the United States shall be vested in one supreme Court, and in such inferior Courts as the Congress may from time to time ordain and establish. The Judges, both of the supreme and inferior Courts, shall hold their Offices during good Behaviour, and shall, at stated Times, receive for their Services, a Compensation, which shall not be diminished during their Continuance in Office.

Section 2. The judicial Power shall extend to all Cases, in Law and Equity, arising under this Constitution, the Laws of the United States, and treaties made, or which shall be made, under their Authority;—to all Cases affecting ambassadors, other public ministers and consuls;—to all cases of admiralty and maritime

Jurisdiction;—to Controversies to which the United States shall be a Party;—to Controversies between two or more States;—between a State and Citizens of another State;—between Citizens of different States,—between Citizens of the same State claiming Lands under Grants of different States, and between a State, or the Citizens thereof, and foreign States, Citizens or Subjects.

In all Cases affecting Ambassadors, other public Ministers and Consuls, and those in which a State shall be Party, the supreme Court shall have original Jurisdiction. In all the other Cases before mentioned, the supreme Court shall have appellate Jurisdiction, both as to Law and Fact, with such Exceptions, and under such Regulations as the Congress shall make.

The trial of all Crimes, except in Cases of Impeachment, shall be by Jury; and such Trial shall be held in the State where the said Crimes shall have been committed; but when not committed within any State, the Trial shall be at such Place or Places as the Congress may by Law have directed.

Section 3. Treason against the United States, shall consist only in levying War against them, or in adhering to their Enemies, giving them Aid and Comfort. No Person shall be convicted of Treason unless on the testimony of two Witnesses to the same overt Act, or on Confession in open Court.

The Congress shall have power to declare the Punishment of Treason, but no Attainder of Treason shall work Corruption of Blood, or Forfeiture except during the Life of the Person attained.

Article IV

Section 1. Full Faith and Credit shall be given in each State to the public Acts, Records, and judicial Proceedings of every other State. And the Congress may by general Laws prescribe the Manner in which such Acts, Records and Proceedings shall be proved, and the Effect thereof.

Section 2. The Citizens of each State shall be entitled to all Privileges and Immunities of Citizens in the several States.

A Person charged in any State with Treason, Felony, or other Crime, who shall flee from Justice, and be found in another State, shall on demand of the executive Authority of the State from which he fled, be delivered up, to be removed to the State having Jurisdiction of the crime.

No Person held to Service or Labour in one State, under the Laws thereof, escaping into another, shall, in Consequence of any Law or Regulation therein, be discharged from such Service or Labour, but shall be delivered up on Claim of the Party to whom such Service or Labour may be due.

Section 3. New States may be admitted by the Congress into this Union; but no new State shall be formed or erected within the Jurisdiction of any other State; nor any State be formed by the Junction of two or more States, or parts of States, without the Consent of the Legislatures of the States concerned as well as of the Congress.

The Congress shall have Power to dispose of and make all needful Rules and Regulations respecting the Territory or other Property belonging to the United States; and nothing in this Constitution shall be so construed as to Prejudice any Claims of the United States, or of any particular State.

Section 4. The United States shall guarantee to every State in this Union a Republican Form of Government, and shall protect each of them against Invasion; and on Application of the Legislature, or the Executive (when the Legislature cannot be convened) against domestic Violence.

Article V

The Congress, whenever two-thirds of both Houses shall deem it necessary, shall propose Amendments to this Constitution, or, on the Application of the Legislatures of two-thirds of the several States, shall call a Convention for proposing Amendments, which, in either Case, shall be valid to all Intents and Purposes, as part of this Constitution, when ratified by the Legislatures of three-fourths of the several States, or by Conventions in three-fourths thereof, as the one or the other Mode of Ratification may be proposed by the Congress; Provided that no Amendment which may be made prior to the Year One thousand eight hundred and eight shall in any Manner affect the first and fourth Clauses in the Ninth Section of the first Article; and that no State, without its Consent, shall be deprived of its equal Suffrage in the Senate.

Article VI

All Debts contracted and Engagements entered into, before the Adoption of this Constitution, shall be as valid against the United States under this Constitution, as under the Confederation.

This Constitution, and the Laws of the United States which shall be made in Pursuance thereof; and all Treaties made, or which shall be made, under the Authority of the United States, shall be the supreme Law of the Land; and the Judges in every State shall be bound thereby, any Thing in the Constitution or Laws of any State to the Contrary notwithstanding.

The Senators and Representatives before mentioned, and the Members of the several State Legislatures, and all executive and judicial Officers, both of the United States and of the several States, shall be bound by Oath or Affirmation to support this Constitution; but no religious Test shall ever be required as a qualification to any Office or public Trust under the United States.

Article VII

The Ratification of the Conventions of nine States shall be sufficient for the Establishment of this Constitution between the States so ratifying the same.

Done in Convention by the Unanimous Consent of the States present the Seventeenth Day of September in the Year of our Lord one thousand seven hundred and Eighty seven, and of the Independence of the United States of America the Twelfth. In Witness whereof We have hereunto subscribed our Names.

Go. Washington, *President and deputy from Virginia; Attest* William Jackson, *Secretary; Delaware:* Geo. Read,* Gunning Bedford, Jr., John Dickinson, Richard Bassett, Jaco. Broom; *Maryland:* James McHenry, Daniel of St. Thomas' Jenifer, Danl. Carroll; *Virginia:* John Blair, James Madison, Jr.; *North Carolina:* Wm. Blount, Richd. Dobbs Spaight, Hu Williamson; *South Carolina:* J. Rutledge, Charles Cotesworth Pinckney, Charles Pinckney, Pierce Butler; *Georgia:* William Few, Abr. Baldwin; *New Hampshire:* John Langdon, Nicholas Gilman; *Massachusetts:* Nathaniel Gorham, Rufus King; *Connecticut:* Wm. Saml. Johnson, Roger Sherman;* *New York:* Alexander Hamilton; *New Jersey:* Wil. Livingston, David Brearley, Wm. Paterson, Jona. Dayton; *Pennsylvania:* B. Franklin,* Thomas Mifflin, Robt. Morris,* Geo. Clymer,* Thos. FitzSimons, Jared Ingersoll, James Wilson, Gouv. Morris.

Articles in Addition to, and Amendment of, the Constitution of the United States of America, Proposed by Congress, and Ratified by the Legislatures of the Several States, Pursuant to the Fifth Article of the Original Constitution.

Amendment I [1791]

Congress shall make no law respecting an establishment of religion, or prohibiting the free exercise thereof; or abridging the freedom of speech, or of the press; or the right of the people peaceably to assemble, and to petition the Government for a redress of grievances.

*Also signed the Declaration of Independence

Amendment II [1791]

A well regulated Militia, being necessary to the security of a free State, the right of the people to keep and bear Arms shall not be infringed.

Amendment III [1791]

No Soldier shall, in time of peace, be quartered in any house, without the consent of the Owner, nor in time of war, but in a manner to be prescribed by law.

Amendment IV [1791]

The right of the people to be secure in their persons, houses, papers, and effects, against unreasonable searches and seizures, shall not be violated, and no Warrants shall issue, but upon probable cause, supported by Oath or affirmation, and particularly describing the place to be searched, and the persons or things to be seized.

Amendment V [1791]

No person shall be held to answer for a capital or otherwise infamous crime, unless on a presentment or indictment of a Grand Jury, except in cases arising in the land or naval forces, or in the Militia, when in actual service in time of War or public danger; nor shall any person be subject for the same offence to be twice put in jeopardy of life or limb; nor shall be compelled in any criminal case to be a witness against himself, nor be deprived of life, liberty, or property, without due process of law; nor shall private property be taken for public use, without just compensation.

Amendment VI [1791]

In all criminal prosecutions, the accused shall enjoy the right to a speedy and public trial, by an impartial jury of the State and district wherein the crime shall have been committed, which district shall have been previously ascertained by law, and to be informed of the nature and cause of the accusation; to be confronted with the witnesses against him; to have compulsory process for obtaining witnesses in his favor, and to have the Assistance of Counsel for his defence.

Amendment VII [1791]

In suits at common law, where the value in controversy shall exceed twenty dollars, the right of trial by jury shall be preserved, and no fact tried by a jury, shall be otherwise reexamined in any Court of the United States, than according to the rules of the common law.

Amendment VIII [1791]

Excessive bail shall not be required, nor excessive fines imposed, nor cruel and unusual punishments inflicted.

Amendment IX [1791]

The enumeration in the Constitution, of certain rights, shall not be construed to deny or disparage others retained by the people.

Amendment X [1791]

The powers not delegated to the United States by the Constitution, nor prohibited by it to the States, are reserved to the States respectively, or to the people.

Amendment XI [1798]

The Judicial power of the United States shall not be construed to extend to any suit in law or equity, commenced or prosecuted against one of the United States by Citizens of another State, or by Citizens or Subjects of any Foreign State.

Amendment XII [1804]

The Electors shall meet in their respective States and vote by ballot for President and Vice-President, one of whom, at least, shall not be an inhabitant of the same State with themselves; they shall name in their ballots the person voted for as President, and in distinct ballots the person voted for as Vice-President, and they shall make distinct lists of all persons voted for as President, and of all persons voted for as Vice-President, and of the number of votes for each, which lists they shall sign and certify, and transmit sealed to the seat of the government of the United States, directed to the President of the Senate;—The President of the Senate shall, in the presence of the Senate and House of Representatives, open all the certificates and the votes shall then be counted;—The person having the greatest number of votes for President, shall be the President, if such number be a majority of the whole number of Electors appointed; and if no person have such majority, then from the persons having the highest numbers not exceeding three on the list of those voted for as President, the House of Representatives shall choose immediately, by ballot, the President. But in choosing the President, the votes shall be taken by states, the representation from each state having one vote; a quorum for this purpose shall consist of a member or members from two-thirds of the states, and a majority of all the states shall be necessary to a choice. And if the House of Representatives shall not choose a President whenever the right of choice shall devolve upon them, before the fourth day of March next following, then the Vice-President shall act as President, as in the case of the death or other constitutional disability of the President.—The person having the greatest number of votes as Vice-President, shall be the Vice-President, if such number be a majority of the whole number of Electors appointed, and if no person have a majority, then from the two highest numbers on the list, the Senate shall choose the Vice-President; a quorum for the purpose shall consist of two-thirds of the whole number of Senators, and a majority of the whole number shall be necessary to a choice. But no person constitutionally ineligible to the office of President shall be eligible to that of Vice-President of the United States.

Amendment XIII [1865]

Section 1. Neither slavery nor involuntary servitude, except as a punishment for crime whereof the party shall have been duly convicted, shall exist within the United States, or any place subject to their jurisdiction.
Section 2. Congress shall have power to enforce this article by appropriate legislation.

Amendment XIV [1868]

Section 1. All persons born or naturalized in the United States, and subject to the jurisdiction thereof, are citizens of the United States and of the State wherein they reside. No State shall make or enforce any law which shall abridge the privileges or immunities of citizens of the United States; nor shall any State deprive any person of life, liberty, or property, without due process of law; nor deny to any person within its jurisdiction the equal protection of the laws.

Section 2. Representatives shall be apportioned among the several States according to their respective numbers, counting the whole number of persons in each State, excluding Indians not taxed. But when the right to vote at any election for the choice of electors for President and Vice-President of the United States, Representatives in Congress, the Executive and Judicial officers of a State, or the members of the Legislature thereof, is denied to any of the male inhabitants of such State, being twenty-one years of age, and citizens of the United States, or in any way abridged, except for participation in rebellion, or other crime, the basis of representation therein shall be reduced in the proportion which the number of such male citizens shall bear to the whole number of male citizens twenty-one years of age in such State.

Section 3. No person shall be a Senator or Representative in Congress, or elector of President and Vice-President, or hold any office, civil or military, under the United States, or under any State, who, having previously taken an oath, as a member of Congress, or as an officer of the United States, or as a member of any State legislature, or as an executive or judicial officer of any State, to support the Constitution of the United States, shall have engaged in insurrection or rebellion against the same, or given aid or comfort to the enemies thereof. But Congress may by a vote of two-thirds of each House, remove such disability.

Section 4. The validity of the public debt of the United States, authorized by law, including debts incurred for payment of pensions and bounties for services in suppressing insurrection or rebellion, shall not be questioned. But neither the United States nor any State shall assume or pay any debt or obligation incurred in aid of insurrection or rebellion against the United States, or any claim for the loss or emancipation of any slave; but all such debts, obligations, and claims shall be held illegal and void.

Section 5. The Congress shall have the power to enforce, by appropriate legislation, the provisions of this article.

Amendment XV [1870]

Section 1. The right of citizens of the United States to vote shall not be denied or abridged by the United States or by any State on account of race, color, or previous condition of servitude—

Section 2. The Congress shall have power to enforce this article by appropriate legislation.

Amendment XVI [1913]

The Congress shall have power to lay and collect taxes on incomes, from whatever source derived, without apportionment among the several States, and without regard to any census or enumeration.

Amendment XVII [1913]

The Senate of the United States shall be composed of two Senators from each State, elected by the people thereof, for six years; and each Senator shall have one vote. The electors in each State shall have the qualifications requisite for electors of the most numerous branch of the State legislatures.

When vacancies happen in the representation of any State in the Senate, the executive authority of such State shall issue writs of election to fill such vacancies: *Provided,* That the legislature of any State may empower the executive thereof to make temporary appointments until the people fill the vacancies by election as the legislature may direct.

This amendment shall not be so construed as to affect the election or term of any Senator chosen before it becomes valid as part of the Constitution.

Amendment XVIII [1919]

Section 1. After one year from the ratification of this article the manufacture, sale, or transportation of intoxicating liquors within, the importation thereof into, or the exportation thereof from the United States and all territory subject to the jurisdiction thereof for beverage purposes is hereby prohibited.

Section 2. The Congress and the several States shall have concurrent power to enforce this article by appropriate legislation.

Section 3. This article shall be inoperative unless it shall have been ratified as an amendment to the Constitution by the legislatures of the several States, as provided in the Constitution, within seven years from the date of the submission hereof to the States by the Congress.

Amendment XIX [1920]

The right of citizens of the United States to vote shall not be denied or abridged by the United States or by any State on account of sex.

Congress shall have power to enforce this article by appropriate legislation.

Amendment XX [1933]

Section 1. The terms of the President and Vice-President shall end at noon on the 20th day of January, and the terms of Senators and Representatives at noon on the 3d day of January, of the years in which such terms would have ended if this article had not been ratified; and the terms of their successors shall then begin.
Section 2. The Congress shall assemble at least once in every year, and such meeting shall begin at noon on the 3d day of January, unless they shall by law appoint a different day.
Section 3. If, at the time fixed for the beginning of the term of the President, the President elect shall have died, the Vice-President elect shall become President. If a President shall not have been chosen before the time fixed for the beginning of his term, or if the President elect shall have failed to qualify, then the Vice-President elect shall act as President until a President shall have qualified; and the Congress may by law provide for the case wherein neither a President elect nor a Vice-President elect shall have qualified, declaring who shall then act as President, or the manner in which one who is to act shall be selected, and such person shall act accordingly until a President or Vice-President shall have qualified.
Section 4. The Congress may by law provide for the case of the death of any of the persons from whom the House of Representatives may choose a President whenever the right of choice shall have devolved upon them, and for the case of the death of any of the persons from whom the Senate may choose a Vice-President whenever the right of choice shall have devolved upon them.
Section 5. Sections 1 and 2 shall take effect on the 15th day of October following the ratification of this article.
Section 6. This article shall be inoperative unless it shall have been ratified as an amendment to the Constitution by the legislatures of three-fourths of the several States within seven years from the date of its submission.

Amendment XXI [1933]

Section 1. The eighteenth article of amendment to the Constitution of the United States is hereby repealed.
Section 2. The transportation or importation into any State, Territory, or possession of the United States for delivery or use therein of intoxicating liquors, in violation of the laws thereof, is hereby prohibited.
Section 3. This article shall be inoperative unless it shall have been ratified as an amendment to the Constitution by conventions in the several States, as provided in the Constitution, within seven years from the date of the submission hereof to the States by the Congress.

Amendment XXII [1951]

No person shall be elected to the office of the President more than twice, and no person who has held the office of President, or acted as President, for more than two years of a term to which some other person was elected President shall be elected to the office of the President more than once.

But this Article shall not apply to any person holding the office of President when this Article was proposed by the Congress, and shall not prevent any person who may be holding the office of President, or acting as President, during the term within which this Article becomes operative from holding the office of President or acting as President during the remainder of such term.

Amendment XXIII [1961]

Section 1. The District constituting the seat of Government of the United States shall appoint in such manner as the Congress may direct:

A number of electors of President and Vice President equal to the whole number of Senators and Representatives in Congress to which the District would be entitled if it were a State, but in no event more than the least populous State; they shall be in addition to those appointed by the States, but they shall be considered, for the purposes of the election of President and Vice President, to be electors appointed by a State; and they shall meet in the District and perform such duties as provided by the twelfth article of amendment.
Section 2. The Congress shall have power to enforce this article by appropriate legislation.

Amendment XXIV [1964]

Section 1. The right of citizens of the United States to vote in any primary or other election for President or Vice President, for electors for President or Vice President, or for Senator or Representative in Congress, shall not be denied or abridged by the United

States or any State by reason of failure to pay any poll tax or other tax.

Section 2. The Congress shall have the power to enforce this article by appropriate legislation.

Amendment XXV [1967]

Section 1. In case of the removal of the President from office or his death or resignation, the Vice President shall become President.

Section 2. Whenever there is a vacancy in the office of the Vice President, the President shall nominate a Vice President who shall take the office upon confirmation by a majority vote of both houses of Congress.

Section 3. Whenever the President transmits to the President pro tempore of the Senate and the Speaker of the House of Representatives his written declaration that he is unable to discharge the powers and duties of his office, and until he transmits to them a written declaration to the contrary, such powers and duties shall be discharged by the Vice President as Acting President.

Section 4. Whenever the Vice President and a majority of either the principal officers of the executive departments, or of such other body as Congress may by law provide, transmit to the President pro tempore of the Senate and the Speaker of the House of Representatives their written declaration that the President is unable to discharge the powers and duties of his office, the Vice President shall immediately assume the powers and duties of the office as Acting President.

Thereafter, when the President transmits to the President pro tempore of the Senate and the Speaker of the House of Representatives his written declaration that no inability exists, he shall resume the powers and duties of his office unless the Vice President and a majority of either the principal officers of the executive departments, or of such other body as Congress may by law provide, transmit within four days to the President pro tempore of the Senate and the Speaker of the House of Representatives their written declaration that the President is unable to discharge the powers and duties of his office. Thereupon Congress shall decide the issue, assembling within 48 hours for that purpose if not in session. If the Congress, within 21 days after receipt of the latter written declaration, or, if Congress is not in session, within 21 days after Congress is required to assemble, determines by two-thirds vote of both houses that the President is unable to discharge the powers and duties of his office, the Vice President shall continue to discharge the same as Acting President; otherwise, the President shall resume the powers and duties of his office.

Amendment XXVI [1971]

Section 1. The right of citizens of the United States, who are 18 years of age or older, to vote shall not be denied or abridged by the United States or any state on account of age.

Section 2. The Congress shall have the power to enforce this article by appropriate legislation.

PICTURE CREDITS

Unless otherwise acknowledged, all photographs are the property of Scott, Foresman and Company. Page abbreviations are as follows: (T) top, (B) bottom, (L) left, and (R) right. Page numbers and abbreviations are in italics preceding each credit.

1 Tozzer Library/Harvard University Libraries *6* Courtesy of the Trustees of the British Museum *19* Mary Evans Picture Library *22* New York State Historical Association, Cooperstown *28* Library of Congress *33* Gift of Mr. and Mrs. John D. Rockefeller III/ The Fine Arts Museum of San Francisco *47* Library Company of Philadelphia *61* The Essex Institute, Salem, Mass. *68* Chicago Historical Society *70* Copyright Yale University Art Gallery *80* Anne S. K. Brown Military Collection, Brown University *84* Courtesy The Brooklyn Museum *86* Stokes Collection/New York Public Library, Astor, Lenox and Tilden Foundations *87* Mrs. Warren N. Saris Collection *95* National Portrait Gallery/Smithsonian Institution/Art Resource, NY *105* Smithsonian Institution *106* Worcester Art Museum, Worcester, Massachusetts *112* Missouri Historical Society *119* The Historic New Orleans Collection *120* Library Company of Philadelphia *126* Courtesy The Henry Francis du Pont Winterthur Museum *130* Collection of Davenport West, Jr./The Picture Collection, The New York Public Library *133* The Rhode Island Historical Society *136* Hood Museum of Art, Dartmouth College *137* National Portrait Gallery, Smithsonian Institution/Art Resource, NY *143* Culver Pictures *145* The New-York Historical Society, New York City *150* Collection of Arthur Ziern, Jr./St. Louis Art Museum *156* Stokes Collection/New York Public Library, Astor, Lenox and Tilden Foundations *158* The Granger Collection, New York *161* The Museum of the City of New York *163* Musée d'Histoire Naturelle, Le Havre, France *169* Library of Congress *173* Stokes Collection/New York Public Library *174* Yale University Library/Beinecke Rare Books Library *181* Brown Brothers *185* The New-York Historical Society, New York City *186* Library of Congress *189* M. and M. Karolik Collection/Courtesy, Museum of Fine Arts, Boston *192* The New-York Historical Society, New York City *193* The National Archives *195* Gift of Franklin Murphy, Jr., 1926/Collection of The Newark Museum, New Jersey *196* Courtesy, Museum of Fine Arts, Boston *202* Courtesy of Glenbow Museum, Calgary, Alberta, Canada *204* Library of Congress *209* Yale University Library/Beinecke Rare Books Library *218* Library of Congress *219* The Granger Collection, New York *225* *L'Illustration,* Paris *230* Library of Congress *234* *Frank Leslie's Illustrated Newspaper,* June 27, 1857 *235* The Granger Collection, New York *239* Library Company of Philadelphia *242L* Chicago Historical Society *242R* Library of Congress *244* Gift of Mr. and Mrs. Carl Stoeckel/The Metropolitan Museum of Art *249* Brown Brothers *251* Courtesy The Museum of the Confederacy, Richmond, Va. *256* Library of Congress *258* Library of Congress *261* GAF Historic Photo Collection *263* Library of Congress *268* *Harper's Weekly,* November 16, 1867 *269* Library of Congress *274* *Harper's Weekly,* June 23, 1866 *276* Culver Pictures *283* The Granger Collection, New York *287* Tuskegee Institute/U.S. Department of the Interior, National Park Service *290* The National Archives *293* The Bettmann Archive *298* Solomon D. Butcher Collection/Nebraska State Historical Society *300* Library of Congress *302* Minnesota Historical Society *306* *Puck,* March 6, 1901 *316* *Harper's Weekly,* 1886 *318* Library of Congress *323* Jacob Riis Collection, Museum of the City of New York *325* The New-York Historical Society, New York City *332* The Granger Collection, New York *333* Joseph Pulitzer Jr. Collection *339* The Bettmann Archive *341* The Bettmann Archive

344 Missouri Historical Society *351* The Kansas State Historical Society, Topeka *354* The Granger Collection, New York *358* The Granger Collection, New York *362* Library of Congress *373* Chicago Historical Society *376* New York Public Library, Astor, Lenox and Tilden Foundations *380* Culver Pictures *382* Brown Brothers *392* The National Archives *396* UPI/Bettmann *400* The National Archives *406* Reproduced by permission of *Punch* *411* From the Collection of Duncan P. Schiedt *420T* Brown Brothers *420B* Courtesy Ernest Hemingway Foundation *423* Courtesy Ford Motor Company *424* Culver Pictures *427* UPI/Bettmann *433* Library of Congress *436* UPI/Bettmann *439* The National Archives *444* UPI/Bettmann *453* AP/Wide World *462* *San Francisco Chronicle,* December 8, 1941 *467* © 1943/Life Magazine Time Warner Inc. *474* UPI/Bettmann *477* Wayne Miller/Magnum Photos *482* UPI/Bettmann *488* UPI/Bettmann *491* Elliott Erwitt/Magnum Photos *493* UPI/Bettmann *496* F. W. Owen/Black Star *500* AP/Wide World *503* UPI/Bettmann *510* Magnum Photos *512* © 1973, G. B. Trudeau/UNIVERSAL PRESS SYNDICATE. Reprinted w/permission. All Rights Reserved *517* UPI/Bettmann *530* UPI/Bettmann *531*` P. F. Gero/ Sygma *534* AP/Wide World *536* Dennis Brack/Black Star *543* Larry Downing/Woodfin Camp & Associates *547* Tom Sobolik/Black Star *550* AP/Wide World

INDEX